If you're wondering why you need this new edition of *Understanding the Presidency*, here are 8 good reasons!

1. A new essay by Peter Francia, Gregory Fortelny, and Clyde Wilcox analyzes the extraordinary fundraising efforts of the Obama campaign.

2. James Ceasar and Daniel DiSalvo recap the 2008 election in their essay, "The Magnitude of the 2008 Democratic Victory: By the Numbers."

3. In a new essay, Richard Waterman argues that the "unitary executive" theory developed by the Bush administration would leave Congress out of major public policy areas traditionally shared by Congress and the president.

4. A new essay by John Burke examines President Obama's first six months in office, and analyzes how successfully a new president can "hit the ground running."

5. Mark Rozell and Mitchel Sollegberger analyze the confrontation between President Bush and the Democratic 110th Congress over the firing of U.S. attorneys, and stress the importance of maintaining a balance in the separation of powers system.

6. A new essay by Louis Fisher questions the constitutionality of modern presidents' claims to executive authority in foreign affairs in "Presidential Power in National Security."

7. Roger H. Davidson explores the linkage between campaigns and governance in his essay focusing on the 2004 through 2008 elections and their aftermath.

8. A new essay by James Pfiffner evaluates the quality of the decision-making process in the George W. Bush White House.

PEARSON

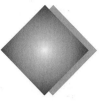

Understanding the Presidency

SIXTH EDITION

EDITED BY

James P. Pfiffner
George Mason University

Roger H. Davidson
University of California, Santa Barbara

Pearson

Boston   Columbus   Indianapolis   New York   San Francisco   Upper Saddle River
Amsterdam   Cape Town   Dubai   London   Madrid   Milan   Munich   Paris   Montreal   Toronto
Delhi   Mexico City   São Paulo   Sydney   Hong Kong   Seoul   Singapore   Taipei   Tokyo

Editor-in-Chief: Eric Stano
Editorial Assistant: Elizabeth Alimena
Senior Marketing Manager: Lindsey Prudhomme
Production Manager: Ellen MacElree
Project Coordination, Text Design, and Electronic Page Makeup: S4Carlisle
   Publishing Services
Cover Design Manager: Wendy Ann Fredericks
Cover Designer: Nancy Sacks
Cover Photo: Copyright © Wally McNamee/Terra/Corbis
Senior Manufacturing Buyer: Dennis J. Para
Printer and Binder: R. R. Donnelley & Sons, Crawfordsville
Cover Printer: R. R. Donnelley & Sons, Crawfordsville

Library of Congress Cataloging-in-Publication Data
   Understanding the presidency / edited by James P. Pfiffner, Roger H.
Davidson.—6th ed.
      p. cm.
   ISBN 978-0-205-79158-3 (alk. paper)
   1.   Presidents—United States. 2.   Presidents—United States—Election.
3.   United States—Politics and government. I.   Pfiffner, James P.
II.   Davidson, Roger H.

JK516.U53 2011
352.230973—dc22
                                                                    2010001074

1 2 4 5 6 7 8 9 10—DOC—13 12 11 10 09
      Longman
      is an imprint of

www.pearsonhighered.com

ISBN-10: 0-205-79158-1
ISBN-13: 978-0-205-79158-3

Contents

Preface

The genesis of this book lies in our classroom experience. We both have been teaching courses on the presidency for a number of years at the graduate and undergraduate levels. Each semester, we have sought the right combination of texts to give our students the optimum mix of basic principles, readings, and source materials on the presidency. Unable to find the right mix and balance of these materials in a single collection, we began to put together a book ourselves. We decided that an effective edited volume on the presidency ought to be comprehensive, to include both historical and current perspectives, to contain both "classic" articles and original essays, and to be accessible to undergraduates.

We both have had experience assigning comprehensive texts in our presidency courses. Although the best of these texts ensure good coverage of all important aspects of the presidency, supplementary readings can provide more in-depth coverage of specific issues in the distinctive voices of scholars in their areas of expertise. We have also taught the presidency course using short supplementary texts. What is often missing, or at least difficult to achieve with this approach, is comprehensive coverage of all the important topics. Thus, we envisioned a presidency reader that would include selections on the most important dimensions of the subject. We designed the coverage of our text with this in mind.

From our experience in the classroom, we are aware that our students need a greater appreciation of the history of the United States. Thus, we have included essays on the creation of the presidency and the development of the office over two centuries. Among these are several seminal statements by the Framers as well as important interpretations by Abraham Lincoln, Theodore Roosevelt, Woodrow Wilson, and William Howard Taft. Because we also appreciate that student interest is often piqued by contemporary events and issues, we have included selections on current issues.

We wanted to include a number of articles we consider the classics of presidency studies from 20th-century scholarship: ideas and authors to whom our students ought to be exposed. Thus, we have included selections by Richard Neustadt, Hugh Heclo, and Stephen Skowronek. But we also wanted to offer students original analyses of some of the best presidency scholars of the day. We sought out articles by Lara Brown, John Burke, James Campbell, Louis Fisher, George Edwards, Michael Genovese, John Anthony Maltese, Richard Pious, Mark Rozell, Mitch Sollenberger, and Clyde Wilcox. We asked these authors to take up the issues of their scholarly specialties but to aim their analyses at a general and accessible level; we are grateful that each of them has written an original article for our volume. In addition, the volume includes several articles by each of the editors and new articles by each of us for the sixth edition.

New to the Sixth Edition

Since the last edition, the George W. Bush presidency has ended, and several new selections describe some of the constitutional highlights of his presidency. Richard Waterman analyzes the unitary executive theory; Mark Rozell and Mitchel Sollenberger examine the use of executive privilege; Louis Fisher provides an analysis of how national security policymaking is divided between the president and Congress; and James Pfiffner looks at decision making in the Bush White House.

Regardless of how Barack Obama handles his challenges and opportunities as president, his election in 2008 was historic in that, for the first time, an African American was elected to the presidency. Analyses of the electoral landscape at the 2008 elections are provided by Lara Brown and James Campbell. Peter Francia, Gregory Fortelny, and Clyde Wiscox – experts on campaign finance – analyze the record breaking 2008 campaign expenditures, and James Ceaser and Daniel DiSalvo put the 2008 election in historical perspective. We wanted an analysis of President Obama's first months in office, and John Burke has provided his analysis of the Obama transition and first six months in office. Roger Davidson has provided a new analysis of the presidential and congressional elections from 2004 through 2008 and their impact on governance as well as a completely updated account of congressional-presidential relations. John Maltese has updated his analysis of Supreme Court Appointments through President Obama's successful nomination of Sonia Sotamayor in 2009.

Our goal has been to make available for our own classes and other college courses a broad presidency reader that covers the important topics that ought to be covered in college courses. The selections in this volume, we believe, represent some of the best presidential scholarship available and yet remain compelling and engaging for undergraduates.

James P. Pfiffner
Roger H. Davidson

SECTION

CONSTITUTIONAL ORIGINS OF THE PRESIDENCY

In creating the presidency, the Constitution's drafters had to improvise. As advocates of parliamentary power, they had no intention of installing an all-important executive. No form of monarchy—not even a constitutionally limited one—was acceptable. Strong, legitimate legislative assemblies were deeply implanted in New World soil through the colonial (and later state) legislatures, the Continental Congresses, and finally, the Articles of Confederation's Congress.

The very tradition of strong legislatures and weak executives, however, caused trouble. The Articles of Confederation failed to promote political or economic stability; under the Articles, Congress proved to be unequal to the tasks of providing for the common defense, conducting relations with foreign powers, and regulating commerce and coinage. James Madison declared that executives in the new nation had become "ciphers," while legislatures were "omnipotent." He complained that constitutional limits were "readily overleaped by the legislature on the spur of an occasion."

The question of governmental powers had been addressed by a remarkable body of political writing from such British and Continental thinkers as James Harrington (1611–1677), John Locke (1632–1704), Baron de Montesquieu (1689–1755), and William Blackstone (1723–1780). These philosophers favored parliamentary power as the most authentic expression of the will of the community. But this power was not unlimited. National emergencies, for example, might require executives to take action beyond existing legislative statutes or even against them (Locke's "prerogative power"). In addition, according to Locke, Blackstone, and especially Montesquieu, liberty is best preserved by dividing governmental powers among several separate entities that can check and balance each other.

Another set of influences emanated from the North American side of the Atlantic Ocean. No one should ignore the fact that 180 years elapsed between the first English settlements at Jamestown, Virginia, and the Constitutional Convention of 1787. These New World experiences were at least as vivid in the Founders' thinking as the Old World parliamentary struggles and philosophical writings. Citizens' experiences, first as colonists under British rule and then as citizens of the new nation, shaped their approach to government and, in particular, to executive authority. Although the Founders naturally favored legislative institutions, some of their most articulate leaders sought a strong, independent executive to counterbalance any legislative supremacy. They saw that Congress under the Articles of Confederation (which lacked a separate executive or judicial branch)—not to mention the all-powerful legislatures of the new states—were unable to act decisively to resolve common problems and ensure order in the widely spread new nation. They found their model, as historian Charles C. Thach, Jr., has shown, in the newly strengthened governorships of New York and Massachusetts, which were created when those states revised their original constitutions to achieve a more balanced government.

Another model for the presidential office must not be overlooked: the dignified yet modest presence of George Washington, who presided over the Philadelphia convention. There is scant evidence that Washington voiced any important substantive suggestions concerning the document's content. Yet his calm demeanor was of incalculable value to the whole enterprise. Indeed, the very term "president" comes from the Latin verb *praesidere*, "to preside."

So even if no precise historical precedent existed, the delegates could see before them the kind of individual they desired. "*Entre nous*," Pierce Butler wrote to an English friend, "I do [not] believe they [the executive powers] would have been so great, had not many of the members cast their eyes toward General Washington as President, and shaped their Ideas of the Powers to be given a President, by their opinions of his Virtue." Benjamin Franklin sagely remarked that "The first man put at the helm will be a good one. Nobody knows . . . what sort may come afterwards."

Advocates of an independent and potentially strong executive—Madison of Virginia, James Wilson and Gouverneur Morris of Pennsylvania, and Alexander Hamilton of New York—were among the liveliest minds at the Constitutional Convention. Often called the father of the presidency, Wilson wanted an executive with "energy, dispatch, and responsibility." A champion of strong government, Hamilton wrote that "energetic government" was the most prized goal of the Convention. A leader of the Convention's drafting committee, Morris favored a strong, independent—and popularly elected—executive.

Led by these individuals, the Convention reached a series of fateful decisions that outlined the features of the modern presidency. The most prominent provisions were:

1. The president is an individual (not a council).
2. The president is selected independently of Congress, at least under normal conditions (The House makes the selection when no candidate has a majority in the Electoral College).
3. The president's mandate is vaguely stated but potentially broad—for example, the "vesting" and "take care" clauses.
4. The president is head of the executive branch.
5. The president shares policymaking powers with Congress: He may recommend legislation and veto acts of Congress (but vetoes can be overturned by a two-thirds vote in both chambers).
6. The president is chief diplomat, but foreign policy is shared with Congress: The president makes treaties only with the advice and consent of the Senate.
7. The so-called "war powers" also are split. The president is commander-in-chief; but Congress has power to declare war as well as to raise and support armies, provide and maintain a navy, and make rules governing the military forces, including those governing "captures on land and water."
8. The president has the power to appoint "officers of the United States," subject to the Senate's advice and consent.
9. The president is eligible for reelection (later limited to two terms by the 22nd Amendment) and can be removed from office only by impeachment and conviction for "treason, bribery, or other high crimes and misdemeanors."

Shortly after the Philadelphia Convention, James Madison—unquestionably the Convention's most influential member—wrote to his colleague Thomas Jefferson (who was in France and not involved in drafting the Constitution) to report on the Convention's work. His letter, reprinted in this text, reviews the main objectives of the Convention; debate over the definition of the executive (whether a single person or a plurality); method of selecting the president (whether by Congress, the executives of the states, or the people at large); duration of executive tenure; eligibility for reelection; and appointment power of the president.

The Federalists—those who supported the new Constitution and, especially, the notion of an independent executive—eloquently made their case in a series of articles that appeared between October 1787 and July 1788 in a New York newspaper, the *Independent Journal*. The authors were Madison, Hamilton, and John Jay, writing under the pseudonym "Publius." These 85 *Federalist Papers* are considered to be the most important work of political theory ever written in the United States. At the very least, they offer clear evidence of what the most influential architects of the Constitution thought they had achieved and how they justified ratification of their handiwork. Hamilton was the most passionate advocate of a strong executive; *Federalist* Nos. 69 and 70 are the most eloquent of his 11 essays (numbers 67 through 77) on this subject. In the first of these two essays, Hamilton reviews the president's constitutional powers, at the same time taking pains to calm citizens' fears by enumerating the limits and checks upon these powers (compared to, say, British sovereigns). In the second, by contrast, he extols the necessity of an "energetic executive" and explains its ingredients.

The Constitution's opponents—the anti-Federalists—argued that the new Constitution granted excessive power to the executive and restored much of the same royal authority they had sought to overthrow. For example, New York Governor George Clinton (1777–1795; 1800–1803) opposed ratifying the Constitution because the document seemed to condone indefinite reelection of the president, which could result in presidents establishing themselves in office for life. Clinton also worried about the absence of a council to advise and assist the president, as well as the enormous grants of power: over appointments, receiving ambassadors, vetoing legislation, and granting pardons. In addition, he was troubled because, unlike the governor of New York, the president was not elected directly by the people.

Although the Federalists narrowly won ratification of their design for what Hamilton termed "energetic government," battles still rage between advocates of strong central authority and those who favor rolling back federal power and returning it to states, localities, and private entities. Even after more than two centuries, Americans are of two minds about national government: on the one hand, they insist on the benefits that it provides, but on the other, they distrust its ability to solve problems and resent its inevitable intrusions on their individual pursuits.

One seemingly innocuous provision dealt with qualifications for the office of president. The delegates dismissed most proposed limitations—in particular, religion or property ownership. In the end, only three qualifications were named for federal elected officers: in the case of the presidency, age (at least 35 years), residency (at least 14 years), and citizenship (an aspirant today must be "a natural born citizen"—that is, born in this country or, if born abroad, a child of a U.S. citizen). The citizenship requirement undoubtedly flowed from understandable 18th-century fears of foreign intervention in the affairs of a newly created nation. This requirement seems outdated for a strong and stable world power with a diverse population, and it may deprive us of the potential leadership talent of individuals who do not happen to be "natural born" citizens.

The most peculiar constitutional provision, however, is the Founders' arcane device for selecting presidents: the Electoral College. The presidency, contrary to popular belief, is *not* a popularly elected office. The Framers in Philadelphia—divided over the role that Congress, the states, and the citizenry should play in choosing the president—came up with a scheme that embraced all of those elements. Skeptical of popular democracy—doubting, for example, that average citizens would know enough about the contenders to make an informed choice—the drafting committee devised a scheme that allowed both the states and the two houses of Congress to play a role. Presidents are selected by electors, who in turn are chosen by their respective states. In case no candidate attained a majority of all the electors (the Electoral College), the House would choose the president—and the Senate the vice president—with each state delegation casting a single vote.

Who could have predicted that, within a few decades, the states would turn over selection of electors to a general vote? Who would have thought that advances in communication and transportation could blanket the entire country with information about candidates and their political parties? Who would have known that the president and vice president would run together on a slate put up by their political party? And who would have guessed that members of the Electoral College themselves would be chosen from party slates and that they would be required (in many states) to vote for their party's nominee? All of these eventualities came to pass, profoundly changing the nature and conduct of presidential elections.

Yet the Electoral College survives, along with the possibility that the candidate with the popular-vote majority could lose the electoral vote. Such a result occurred most recently in 2000, when a bitterly contested Florida victory gave George W. Bush a narrow Electoral College margin, even though he trailed his rival, Democrat Al Gore, by some half-million popular votes. James P. Pfiffner reviews the Electoral College's historical quirks, and explains the proposals to simplify or scrap the existing system (none of which, alas, have much chance of adoption).

Arguments over executive power are similarly recurrent, although these battle lines often are rather different from those waged over the proper scope of the federal government itself. The problem arises in large part from the Constitution itself, which separates policymaking responsibilities, describing presidential powers and duties far less precisely than it does those given to Congress. The famous dictum of constitutional scholar Edward S. Corwin—that the document is "an invitation to struggle" between the two branches—referred to foreign policy, but it is even more true in domestic affairs. Thus, the powers of the modern presidency in large part are the outcome of initiatives and precedents that have accumulated over more than two centuries of history, including crises, wars, depressions, political realignments, and institutional adjustments both large and small.

The ultimate paradox of the presidency, as political scientist Thomas E. Cronin wrote, is that "it is always too powerful and yet it is always inadequate." By some accounts, the office is weak and confined; by others, it is dangerously out of control. Citizens, too, are ambivalent about presidential power. Seemingly, they enjoy seeing their presidents humbled or cut down to size. At the same time, people continue to yearn for heroic presidents—extraordinary leaders who can somehow rise above the clamor of "mere politicians" and set the country on the right course.

Selected Bibliography

Corwin, Edward S., *The President: Office and Powers 1787–1957,* 4th rev. ed. (New York: New York University Press, 1957).

Cronin, Thomas E., and Michael A. Genovese, *The Paradoxes of the American Presidency* (New York: Oxford University Press, 2004).

Edwards, George C., III, *Why the Electoral College Is Bad for America* (New Haven: Yale University Press, 2004).

Hamilton, Alexander, James Madison, and John Jay, *The Federalist Papers,* ed. Clinton Rossiter (New York: Penguin Books, 1961).

Mansfield, Harvey C., Jr., *Taming the Prince: The Ambivalence of Modern Executive Power* (Baltimore, MD: The Johns Hopkins University Press, 1989).

Milkis, Sidney M., and Michael Nelson, *The American Presidency: Origins and Development, 1776-2007* (Washington, DC: CQ Press, 2008).

Thach, Charles C., Jr., *The Creation of the Presidency 1775–1789* (Baltimore, MD: The Johns Hopkins University Press, 1989).

James Madison

James Madison to Thomas Jefferson

New York October 24, 1787

You will herewith receive the result of the Convention, which continued its session till the 17th of September. I take the liberty of making some observations on the subject, which will help to make up a letter, if they should answer no other purpose.

This ground-work being laid, the great objects which presented themselves were (1) to unite a proper energy in the Executive, and a proper stability in the Legislative departments, with the essential characters of Republican Government (2) to draw a line of demarkation which would give to the Central Government every power requisite for general purposes, and leave to the States every power which might be most

Source: From Max Farrand, "James Madison to Thomas Jefferson" in *The Records of the Federal Convention of 1787,* vol. 3, 1966. Copyright © 1966 Yale University, © 1911, 1937 by Yale University Press. Reprinted by permission.

beneficially administered by them (3) to provide for the different interests of different parts of the Union (4) to adjust the clashing pretensions of the large and small States. Each of these objects was pregnant with difficulties. The whole of them together formed a task more difficult than can be well conceived by those who were not concerned in the execution of it. Adding to these considerations the natural diversity of human opinions on all new and complicated subjects, it is impossible to consider the degree of concord which ultimately prevailed as less than a miracle.

The first of these objects, as respects the Executive, was peculiarly embarrassing. On the question whether it should consist of a single person, or a plurality of co-ordinate members, on the mode of appointment, on the duration in office, on the degree of power, on the re-eligibility, tedious and reiterated discussions took place. The plurality of co-ordinate members had finally but few advocates. Governour Randolph was at the head of them. The modes of appointment proposed were various, as by the people at large—by electors chosen by the people—by the Executives of the States—by the Congress, some preferring a joint ballot of the two Houses—some a separate concurrent ballot, allowing to each a negative on the other house—some, a nomination of several candidates by one House, out of whom a choice should be made by the other. Several other modifications were stated. The expedient at length adopted seemed to give pretty general satisfaction to the members. As to the duration in office, a few would have preferred a tenure during good behaviour—a considerable number would have done so in case an easy & effectual removal by impeachment could be settled. It was much agitated whether a long term, seven years for example, with a subsequent & perpetual ineligibility, or a short term with a capacity to be re-elected, should be fixed. In favor of the first opinion were urged the danger of a gradual degeneracy of re-elections from time to time, into first a life and then a hereditary tenure, and the favorable effect of an incapacity to be reappointed on the independent exercise of the Executive authority. On the other side it was contended that the prospect of necessary degradation would discourage the most dignified characters from aspiring to the office, would take away the principal motive to the faithful discharge of its duties—the hope of being rewarded with a reappointment would stimulate ambition to violent efforts for holding over the Constitutional term—and instead of producing an independent administration, and a firmer defence of the constitutional rights of the department, would render the officer more indifferent to the importance of a place which he would soon be obliged to quit forever, and more ready to yield to the encroachments. of the Legislature of which he might again be a member. The questions concerning the degree of power turned chiefly on the appointment to offices, and the control on the Legislature. An *absolute* appointment to all offices—to some offices—to no offices, formed the scale of opinions on the first point. On the second, some contended for an absolute negative, as the only possible means of reducing to practice the theory of a free Government which forbids a mixture of the Legislative & Executive powers. Others would be content with a revisionary power, to be overruled by three fourths of both Houses. It was warmly urged that the judiciary department should be associated in the revision. The idea of some was that a separate revision should be given to the two departments—that if either objected two thirds, if both, three fourths, should be necessary to overrule.

Alexander Hamilton

Federalist No. 69

Proceed now to trace the real characters of the proposed Executive, as they are marked out in the plan of the convention. This will serve to place in a strong light the unfairness of the representations which have been made in regard to it.

The first thing which strikes our attention is that the executive authority, with few exceptions, is to be vested in a single magistrate. This will scarcely, however, be considered as a point upon which any comparison can be grounded; for if, in this particular, there be a resemblance to the king of Great Britain, there is not less a resemblance to the Grand Seignior, to the khan of Tartary, to the Man of the Seven Mountains or to the governor of New York.

That magistrate is to be elected for *four* years; and is to be re-eligible as often as the people of the United States shall think him worthy of their confidence. In these circumstances there is a total dissimilitude between *him* and a king of Great Britain, who is an *hereditary* monarch, possessing the crown as a patrimony descendible to his heirs forever; but there is a close analogy between *him* and a governor of New York, who is elected for *three* years, and is re-eligible without limitation or intermission. . . .

The President of the United States would be liable to be impeached, tried, and, upon conviction of treason, bribery, or other high crimes or misdemeanours, removed from office; and would afterwards be liable to prosecution and punishment in the ordinary course of law. The person of the king of Great Britain is sacred and inviolable; there is no constitutional tribunal to which he is amenable; no punishment to which he can be subjected without involving the crisis of a national revolution. In this delicate and important circumstance of personal responsibility, the President of Confederated America would stand upon no better ground than a governor of New York, and upon worse ground than the governors of Maryland and Delaware.

The President of the United States is to have power to return a bill which shall have passed the two branches of the legislature for reconsideration; and the bill so returned is to become a law if, upon that reconsideration, it be approved by two thirds of both houses. The king of Great Britain, on his part, has an absolute negative upon

Source: This essay by "Publius" was originally published in the *New York Packet*, March 14, 1788.

the acts of the two houses of Parliament. The disuse of that power for a considerable time past does not affect the reality of its existence; and is to be ascribed wholly to the crown's having found the means of substituting influence to authority, or the art of gaining a majority in one or the other of the two houses, to the necessity of exerting a prerogative which could seldom be exerted without hazarding some degree of national agitation. The qualified negative of the President differs widely from this absolute negative of the British sovereign; and tallies exactly with the revisionary authority of the council of revision of this State, of which the governor is a constituent part. . . .

The President is to be the "commander-in-chief of the army and navy of the United States, and of the militia of the several States, when called into the actual service of the United States. He is to have power to grant reprieves and pardons for offences against the United States, *except in cases of impeachment;* to recommend to the consideration of Congress such measures as he shall judge necessary and expedient; to convene, on extraordinary occasions, both houses of the legislature, or either of them, and, in case of disagreement between them *with respect to the time of adjournment,* to adjourn them to such time as he shall think proper; to take care that the laws be faithfully executed; and to commission all officers of the United States." In most of these particulars the power of the President will resemble equally that of the king of Great Britain and of the governor of New York. The most material points of difference are these:—*First.* The President will have only the occasional command of such part of the militia of the nation as by legislative provision may be called into the actual service of the Union. The king of Great Britain and the governor of New York have at all times the entire command of all the militia within their several jurisdictions. In this article, therefore, the power of the President would be inferior to that of either the monarch or the governor. *Secondly.* The President is to be commander-in-chief of the army and navy of the United States. In this respect his authority would be nominally the same with that of the king of Great Britain, but in substance much inferior to it. It would amount to nothing more than the supreme command and direction of the military and naval forces, as first general and admiral of the Confederacy; while that of the British king extends to the *declaring* of war and to the *raising* and *regulating* of fleets and armies—all which, by the Constitution under consideration, would appertain to the legislature. . . . *Thirdly.* The power of the President, in respect to pardons, would extend to all cases, *except those of impeachment.* The governor of New York may pardon in all cases, even in those of impeachment, except for treason and murder. Is not the power of the governor, in this article, on a calculation of political consequences, greater than that of the President? . . .

Fourthly. The President can only adjourn the national legislature in the single case of disagreement about the time of adjournment. The British monarch may prorogue [discontinue] or even dissolve the Parliament. The governor of New York may also prorogue the legislature of this State for a limited time; a power which, in certain situations, may be employed to very important purposes.

The President is to have power, with the advice and consent of the Senate, to make treaties, provided two thirds of the senators present concur. The king of Great Britain is the sole and absolute representative of the nation in all foreign transactions. He can of his own accord make treaties of peace, commerce, alliance, and of every other description.

. . . It must be admitted that, in this instance, the power of the federal Executive would exceed that of any State Executive. But this arises naturally from the sovereign power which relates to treaties. If the Confederacy were to be dissolved it would become a question whether the Executives of the several States were not solely invested with that delicate and important prerogative.

The President is also to be authorised to receive ambassadors and other public ministers. This, though it has been a rich theme of declamation, is more a matter of dignity than of authority. It is a circumstance which will be without consequence in the administration of the government; and it was far more convenient that it should be arranged in this manner than that there should be a necessity of convening the legislature, or one of its branches, upon every arrival of a foreign minister, though it were merely to take the place of a departed predecessor.

The President is to nominate and, *with the advice and consent of the Senate*, to appoint ambassadors and other public ministers, judges of the Supreme Court, and in general all officers of the United States established by law, and whose appointments are not otherwise provided for by the Constitution. The king of Great Britain is emphatically and truly styled the fountain of honour. He not only appoints to all offices, but can create offices. He can confer titles of nobility at pleasure; and has the disposal of an immense number of church preferments. There is evidently a great inferiority in the power of the President, in this particular, to that of the British king; nor is it equal to that of the governor of New York, if we are to interpret the meaning of the constitution of the State by the practice which has obtained under it. . . .

Hence it appears that, except as to the concurrent authority of the President in the article of treaties, it would be difficult to determine whether that magistrate would, in the aggregate, possess more or less power than the Governor of New York. And it appears yet more unequivocally that there is no pretence for the parallel which has been attempted between him and the king of Great Britain. But to render the contrast in this respect still more striking, it may be of use to throw the principal circumstances of dissimilitude into a closer group.

The President of the United States would be an officer elected by the people for *four* years; the king of Great Britain is a perpetual and *hereditary* prince. The one would be amenable to personal punishment and disgrace; the person of the other is sacred and inviolable. The one would have a *qualified* negative upon the acts of the legislative body; the other has an *absolute* negative. The one would have a right to command the military and naval forces of the nation; the other, in addition to this right, possesses that of *declaring* war, and of *raising* and *regulating* fleets and armies by his own authority. The one would have a concurrent power with a branch of the legislature in the formation of treaties; the other is the *sole possessor* of the power of making treaties. The one would have a like concurrent authority in appointing to offices; the other is the sole author of all appointments. The one can confer no privileges whatever; the other can make denizens of aliens, noblemen of commoners; can erect corporations with all the rights incident to corporate bodies. The one can prescribe no rules concerning the commerce or currency of the nation; the other is in several respects the arbiter of commerce, and in this capacity can establish markets and fairs, can regulate weights and measures, can lay embargoes for a limited time, can coin money, can authorise or prohibit the circulation of foreign coin. The one has no particle of spiritual jurisdiction; the other is the supreme head and governor of the national church! What answer shall we give to those who would persuade us that things so unlike resemble each other? The same that ought to be given to those who tell us that a government, the whole power of which would be in the hands of the elective and periodical servants of the people, is an aristocracy, a monarchy, and a despotism.

Publius

Alexander Hamilton

Federalist No. 70

There is an idea, which is not without its advocates, that a vigorous Executive is inconsistent with the genius of republican government. . . . Energy in the Executive is a leading character in the definition of good government. It is essential to the protection of the community against foreign attacks; it is not less essential to the steady administration of the laws; to the protection of property against those irregular and high-handed combinations which sometimes interrupt the ordinary course of justice; to the security of liberty against the enterprises and assaults of ambition, of faction, and of anarchy.

There can be no need, however, to multiply arguments or examples on this head. A feeble Executive implies a feeble execution of the government. A feeble execution is but another phrase for a bad execution; and a government ill executed, whatever it may be in theory, must be, in practice, a bad government. . . .

The ingredients which constitute energy in the Executive are, first, unity; secondly, duration; thirdly, an adequate provision for its support; fourthly, competent powers.

The ingredients which constitute safety in the republican sense are first, a due dependence on the people; secondly, a due responsibility.

Source: This essay by "Publius" was originally published in the *New York Packet,* March 14, 1788.

Those politicians and statesmen who have been the most celebrated for the soundness of their principles and for the justice of their views, have declared in favor of a single Executive and a numerous legislature. They have, with great propriety, considered energy as the most necessary qualification of the former, and have regarded this as most applicable to power in a single hand; while they have, with equal propriety, considered the latter as best adapted to deliberation and wisdom, and best calculated to conciliate the confidence of the people and to secure their privileges and interests.

That unity is conducive to energy will not be disputed. Decision, activity, secrecy, and despatch will generally characterize the proceedings of one man in a much more eminent degree than the proceedings of any greater number; and in proportion as the number is increased, these qualities will be diminished.

This unity may be destroyed in two ways: either by vesting the power in two or more magistrates of equal dignity and authority; or by vesting it ostensibly in one man, subject, in whole or in part, to the control and cooperation of others, in the capacity of counsellors to him. Of the first, the two Consuls of Rome may serve as an example; of the last, we shall find examples in the constitutions of several of the States. New York and New Jersey, if I recollect right, are the only States which have intrusted the executive authority wholly to single men. Both these methods of destroying the unity of the Executive have their partisans; but the votaries of an executive council are the most numerous. They are both liable, if not to equal, to similar objections, and may in most lights be examined in conjunction. . . .

Wherever two or more persons are engaged in any common enterprise or pursuit, there is always danger of difference of opinion. If it be a public trust or office, in which they are clothed with equal dignity and authority, there is peculiar danger of personal emulation and even animosity. From either, and especially from all these causes, the most bitter dissentions are apt to spring. Whenever these happen, they lessen the respectability, weaken the authority, and distract the plans and operations of those whom they divide. If they should unfortunately assail the supreme executive magistracy of a country, consisting of a plurality of persons, they might impede or frustrate the most important measures of the government, in the most critical emergencies of the state. And what is still worse, they might split the community into the most violent and irreconcilable factions, adhering differently to the different individuals who composed the magistracy.

Men often oppose a thing, merely because they have had no agency in planning it, or because it may have been planned by those whom they dislike. But if they have been consulted, and have happened to disapprove, opposition then becomes, in their estimation, an indispensable duty of self-love. They seem to think themselves bound in honor, and by all the motives of personal infallibility, to defeat the success of what has been resolved upon contrary to their sentiments. . . .

In the legislature, promptitude of decision is oftener an evil than a benefit. The differences of opinion, and the jarrings of parties in that department of the government, though they may sometimes obstruct salutary plans, yet often promote deliberation and circumspection, and serve to check excesses in the majority. When a resolution too is once taken, the opposition must be at an end. That resolution is a law, and resistance to it punishable. But no favorable circumstances palliate or atone for the disadvantages of dissension in the executive department. Here, they are pure and unmixed. There is no point at which they cease to operate. They serve to embarrass and weaken the execution of the plan or measure to which they relate, from the first step to the final conclusion of it. They constantly counteract those qualities in the Executive which are the most necessary ingredients in its composition,—vigor and expedition, and this without any counter-balancing good. In the conduct of war, in which the energy of the Executive is the bulwark of the national security, every thing would be apprehended from its plurality. . . .

> But one of the weightiest objections to a plurality in the Executive, and which lies as much against the last as the first plan, is that it tends to conceal faults and destroy responsibility. Responsibility is of two kinds—to censure and to punishment. The first is the more important of the two, especially in an elective office. Man, in public trust, will much oftener act in such a manner as to render him unworthy of being any longer trusted than in such a manner as to make him obnoxious to legal punishment. But the multiplication of the Executive adds to the difficulty of detection in either case. It often becomes impossible, amidst mutual accusations to determine on whom the blame the punishment of a pernicious measure or series of pernicious measures, ought really to fall. . . .

It is evident from these considerations, that the plurality of the Executive tends to deprive the people of the two greatest securities they can have for the faithful exercise of any delegated power, *first*, the restraints of public opinion, which lose their efficacy, as well on account of the division of the censure attendant on bad measures among a number, as on account of the uncertainty on whom it ought to fall: and, *secondly*, the opportunity of discovering with facility and clearness the misconduct of the persons they trust, in order either to their removal from office, or to their actual punishment in cases which admit of it.

In England, the king is a perpetual magistrate; and it is a maxim which has obtained for the sake of the public peace, that he is unaccountable for his administration, and his person sacred. Nothing, therefore, can be wiser in that kingdom, than to annex to the king a constitutional council, who may be responsible to the nation for the advice they give. Without this, there would be no responsibility whatever in the executive department—an idea inadmissible in a free government. But even there the king is not bound by the resolutions of his council, though they are answerable for the advice they give. He is the absolute master of his own conduct in the exercise of his office, and may observe or disregard the counsel given to him at his sole discretion.

But in a republic, where every magistrate ought to be personally responsible for his behavior in office, the reason which in the British Constitution dictates the propriety of a council, not only ceases to apply, but turns against the institution. In the monarchy of Great Britain, it furnishes a substitute for the prohibited responsibility of the chief magistrate, which serves in some degree as a hostage to the national justice for his good behavior. In the American republic, it would serve to destroy, or would greatly diminish, the intended and necessary responsibility of the Chief Magistrate himself.

The idea of a council to the Executive, which has so generally obtained in the State constitutions, has been derived from that maxim of republican jealousy which considers power as safer in the hands of a number of men than of a single man. If the maxim should be admitted to be applicable to the case, I should contend that the advantage on that side would not counterbalance the numerous disadvantages on the opposite side.

But I do not think the rule at all applicable to the executive power. I clearly concur in opinion, in this particular, with a writer whom the celebrated Junius pronounces to be "deep, solid, and ingenious," that "the executive power is more easily confined when it is ONE"; that it is far more safe there should be a single object for the jealousy and watchfulness of the people; and, in a word, that all multiplication of the Executive is rather dangerous than friendly to liberty. . . .

I will only add that, prior to the appearance of the Constitution, I rarely met with an intelligent man from any of the States, who did not admit, as the result of experience, that the UNITY of the executive of this State was one of the best of the distinguishing features of our constitution.

Publius

George Clinton

To the Citizens of the State of New York

November 8, 1787

Admitting, however, that the vast extent of America, together with the various other reasons which I offered you in my last number, against the practicability of the just exercise of the new government are insufficient to convince; still it is an undesirable truth, that its several parts are either possessed of principles, which you have heretofore considered as ruinous and that others are omitted which you have established as fundamental to your political security, and must in their operation, I will venture to assert, fetter your tongues and minds, enchain your bodies, and ultimately extinguish all that is great and noble in man.

In pursuance of my plan I shall begin with observations on the executive branch of this new system; and though it is not the first in order, as arranged therein, yet being the *chief*, is perhaps entitled by the rules of rank to the first consideration. The executive power as described in the 2d article, consists of a president and vice-president, who are to hold their offices during the term of four years; the same article has marked the manner and time of their election, and established the qualifications of the president; it also

---

Source: "The Letters of Cato," *New York Journal* (November 8 and 22, 1787).

provides against the removal, death, or inability of the president and vice-president—regulates the salary of the president, delineates his duties and powers; and, lastly, declares the causes for which the president and vice-president shall be removed from office.

Notwithstanding the great learning and abilities of the gentlemen who composed the convention, it may be here remarked with deference, that the construction of the first paragraph of the first section of the second article is vague and inexplicit, and leaves the mind in doubt as to the election of a president and vice-president, after the expiration of the election for the first term of four years: in every other case, the election of these great officers is expressly provided for; but there is no explicit provision for their election in case of expiration of their offices, subsequent to the election which is to set this political machine in motion; no certain and express terms as in your state constitution, that *statedly* once in every four years, and as often as these offices shall become vacant, by expiration or otherwise, as is therein expressed, an election shall be held as follows, &c., this inexplicitness perhaps may lead to an establishment for life.

It is remarked by Montesquieu, in treating of republics, that *in all magistracies, the greatness of the power must be compensated by the brevity of the duration, and that a longer time than a year would be dangerous*. It is, therefore, obvious to the least intelligent mind to account why great power in the hands of a magistrate, and that power connected with considerable duration, may be dangerous to the liberties of a republic, the deposit of vast trusts in the hands of a single magistrate, enables him in their exercise to create a numerous train of dependents: this tempts his *ambition,* which in a republican magistrate is also remarked, *to be pernicious,* and the duration of his office for any considerable time favors his views, gives him the means and time to perfect and execute his designs, *he therefore fancies that he may be great and glorious by oppressing his fellow-citizens, and raising himself to permanent grandeur on the ruins of his country*. And here it may be necessary to compare the vast and important powers of the president, together with his continuance in office, with the foregoing doctrine—his eminent magisterial situation will attach many adherents to him, and he will be surrounded by expectants and courtiers, his power of nomination and influence on all appointments, the strong posts in each state comprised within his superintendence, and garrisoned by troops under his direction, his control over the army, militia, and navy, the unrestrained power of granting pardons for treason, which may be used to screen from punishment those whom he had secretly instigated to commit the crime, and thereby prevent a discovery of his own guilt, his duration in office for four years: these, and various other principles evidently prove the truth of the position, that if the president is possessed of ambition, he has power and time sufficient to ruin his country.

Though the president, during the sitting of the legislature, is assisted by the senate, yet he is without a constitutional council in their recess; he will therefore be unsupported by proper information and advice, and will generally be directed by minions and favorites, or a council of state will grow out of the principal officers of the great departments, the most dangerous council in a free country.

The ten miles square, which is to become the seat of government, will of course be the place of residence for the president and the great officers of state; the same observations of a great man will apply to the court of a president possessing the powers of a monarch, that is observed of that of a monarch—*ambition with idleness—baseness* with pride—the thirst of riches without labor—aversion to truth—flattery—treason—perfidy—violation of engagements—contempt of civil duties—hope from the magistrate's weakness; but above all, the perpetual ridicule of virtue—these, he remarks, are the characteristics by which the courts in all ages have been distinguished.

The language and the manners of this court will be what distinguishes them from the rest of the community, not what assimilates them to it; and in being remarked for a behavior that shows they are not *meanly born*, and in adulation to people of fortune and power.

The establishment of a vice-president is as unnecessary as it is dangerous. This officer, for want of other employment, is made president of the senate, thereby blending the executive and legislative powers, besides always giving to some one state, from which he is to come, an unjust pre-eminence.

It is a maxim in republics that the representative of the people should be of their immediate choice; but by the manner in which the president is chosen, he arrives to this office at the fourth or fifth hand, nor does the highest vote, in the way he is elected, determine the choice, for it is only necessary that he should be taken from the highest of five, who may have a plurality of votes.

Compare your past opinions and sentiments with the present proposed establishment, and you will find, that if you adopt it, that it will lead you into a system which you heretofore reprobated as odious. Every American Whig, not long since, bore his emphatic testimony against a monarchical government, though limited, because of the dangerous inequality that it created among citizens as relative to their rights and property; and wherein does this president, invested with his powers and prerogatives, essentially differ from the king of Great Britain (save as to name, the creation of nobility, and some immaterial incidents, the offspring of absurdity and locality). The direct prerogatives of the president, as springing from his political character, are among the following: It is necessary, in order to distinguish him from the rest of the community, and enable him to keep, and maintain his court, that the compensation for his services, or in other words, his revenue, should be such as to enable him to appear with the splendor of a prince; he has the power of receiving ambassadors from, and a great influence on their appointments to foreign courts; as also to make treaties, leagues, and alliances with foreign states, assisted by the Senate, which when made become the supreme law of land: he is a constituent part of the legislative power, for every bill which shall pass the House of Representatives and Senate is to be presented to him for approbation; if he approves of it he is to sign it, if he disapproves he is to return it with objections, which in many cases will amount to a complete negative; and in this view he will have a great share in the power of making peace, coining money, etc., and all the various objects of legislation, expressed or implied in this Constitution: for though it may be asserted that the king of Great Britain has the express power of making peace or war, yet he never thinks it prudent to do so without the advice of his Parliament, from whom he is to derive his support, and therefore these powers, in both president and king, are substantially the same: he is the generalissimo of the nation, and of course has the command and control of the army, navy and militia; he is the general conservator of the peace of the union—he may pardon all offences, except in cases of impeachment, and the principal fountain of all offices and employments. Will not the exercise of these powers therefore tend either to the establishment of a vile and arbitrary aristocracy or monarchy? The safety of the people in a republic depends on the share or proportion they have in the government; but experience ought to teach you, that when a man is at the head of an elective government invested with great powers, and interested in his reelection, in what circle appointments will be made; by which means an *imperfect aristocracy* bordering on monarchy may be established.

You must, however, my countrymen, beware that the advocates of this new system do not deceive you by a fallacious resemblance between it and your own state government which you so much prize; and, if you examine, you will perceive that the chief magistrate of this state is your immediate choice, controlled and checked by a just and full representation of the people, divested of the prerogative of influencing war and peace, making treaties, receiving and sending embassies, and commanding standing armies and navies, which belong to the power of the confederation, and will be convinced that this government is no more like a true picture of your own than an Angel of Darkness resembles an Angel of Light.

November 22, 1787

In my last number I endeavored to prove that the language of the article relative to the establishment of the executive of this new government was vague and inexplicit; that the great powers of the president, connected with his duration in office, would lead to oppression and ruin; that he would be governed by favorites and flatterers, or that a dangerous council would be collected from the great officers of state; that the ten miles square, if the remarks of one of the wisest men, drawn from the experience of mankind, may be credited, would be the asylum of the base, idle, avaricious and ambitious, and that the court would possess a language and manners different from yours; that a vice-president is as unnecessary as he is dangerous in his influence; that the president cannot represent you because he is not of your own immediate choice; that if you adopt this government you will incline to an arbitrary and odious aristocracy or monarchy; that the president, possessed of the power given him by this frame of government, differs but very immaterially from the establishment of monarchy in Great Britain; and I warned you to beware of the fallacious resemblance that is held out to you by the advocates of this new system between it and your own state governments.

And here I cannot help remarking that inexplicitness seems to pervade this whole political fabric; certainly in political compacts, which Mr. Coke calls *the mother and nurse of repose and quietness* the want of which induced men to engage in political society, has ever been held by a wise and free people as essential to their security; as on the one hand it fixes barriers which the ambitious and tyrannically disposed magistrate dare not over-leap, and on the other, becomes a wall of safety to the community—otherwise stipulations between the governors and governed are nugatory; and you might as well deposit the important powers of legislation and execution in one or a few and permit them to govern according to their disposition and will; but the world is too full of examples, which prove that to *live by one man's will became the cause of all men's misery*. Before the existence of express political compacts it was reasonably implied that the magistrate should govern with wisdom and justice; but mere implication was too feeble to restrain the unbridled ambition of a bad man, or afford security against negligence, cruelty or any other defect of mind. It is alleged that the opinions and manners of the people of America are capable to resist and prevent an extension of prerogative or oppression, but you must recollect that opinion and manners are mutable, and may not always be a permanent obstruction against the encroachments of government; that the progress of a commercial society begets luxury, the parent of inequality, the foe to virtue, and the enemy to restraint; and that ambition and voluptuousness, aided by flattery, will teach magistrates where limits are not explicitly fixed to have separate and distinct interests from the people; besides, it will not be denied that government assimilates the manners and opinions of the community to it. Therefore, a general presumption that rulers will govern well is not a sufficient security. You are then under a sacred obligation to provide for the safety of your posterity, and would you now basely desert their interests, when by a small share of prudence you may transmit to them a beautiful political patrimony, which will prevent the necessity of their travelling through seas of blood to obtain that which your wisdom might have secured? It is a duty you owe likewise to your own reputation, for you have a great name to lose; you are characterized as cautious, prudent and jealous in politics; whence is it therefore that you are about to precipitate yourselves into a sea of uncertainty, and adopt a system so vague, and which has discarded so many of your valuable rights? Is it because you do not believe that an American can be a tyrant? If this be the case, you rest on a weak basis: Americans are like other men in similar situations, when the manners and opinions of the community are changed by the causes I mentioned before; and your political compact inexplicit, your posterity will find that great power connected with ambition, luxury and flattery, will as readily produce a Caesar, Caligula, Nero and Domitian in America, as the same causes did in the Roman Empire.

James P. Pfiffner

Reevaluating the Electoral College

Alexander Hamilton concluded in Federalist No. 68 that the electoral method of choosing the chief executive of the new republic was one of the few parts of the proposed constitution that raised few objections, even by opponents of ratification. "The mode of appointment of the Chief Magistrate of the United States is almost

Source: ORIGINALLY PREPARED FOR THIS VOLUME.

the only part of the system, of any consequence, which has escaped without severe censure, or which has received the slightest mark of approbation from its opponents." He concluded that if the manner of choice "be not perfect, it is at least excellent."

Yet experience soon provided evidence of problems in the design of the constitutional electoral mechanism. In the election of 1796, the presidential candidate of the losing faction, Thomas Jefferson (a Republican), became the vice president when Federalist John Adams was elected President.[1] In 1800, Jefferson and his vice presidential running mate Aaron Burr tied in the electoral vote, and it took 36 ballots in the House before Jefferson was elected president. The next century brought other electoral problems, and the Electoral College has been the subject of more than 700 proposals in Congress to reform the system.[2] In 1967, the American Bar Association declared in a report: "The electoral college method of electing a President of the United States is archaic, undemocratic, complex, ambiguous, indirect, and dangerous."[3]

This essay will first briefly examine problematic elections involving the Electoral College and the purposes of the Framers in designing the electoral mechanism. It will then examine arguments for changing the electoral provisions of the Constitution based on the democratic premise that the candidate with the most popular votes should not lose the election. Objections in principle and practicality to proposals for change will then be examined. The essay will conclude that the constitutional issues raised by the 2000 election are sufficient to reexamine the electoral mechanism for selecting the president of the United States.

Problematic Elections: 1800, 1825, 1876, 1888

In the election of 1800, both Thomas Jefferson and Aaron Burr received the same number of electoral votes for president, even though it was well known that Jefferson was the intended nominee for president and Burr for vice president. With no majority of electoral votes, the lame-duck Federalist House of Representatives had to choose the president, and it took them 36 ballots to do so. In light of the 1800 experience, the Twelfth Amendment to the Constitution, providing for separate ballots for president and vice president, was passed and ratified.[4]

Several other presidential elections turned out to be problematic in other ways. In the election of 1824, states had begun to give their voters the right to choose the state electors, and Andrew Jackson received the most popular votes (about 38 percent); he also received the most electoral votes (99 of 261), but not a majority. Thus, the House of Representatives again had to make the choice, and it chose John Quincy Adams who had received about 32 percent of the popular vote and 84 electoral votes. Because the Twelfth Amendment reduced the number of candidates from whom the House had to choose from five to three, Speaker of the House Henry Clay—with 14 percent of the popular vote and 37 electoral votes—threw his support behind Adams, who was elected. When Clay was appointed Secretary of State in Adams's administration, Jackson charged that a corrupt deal had been made.

After the 1876 election, the nation did not know who would be president until March 2, 1877, because two separate slates of electors were sent to Congress from Florida, Louisiana, and South Carolina. When both houses of Congress failed to agree on which slates to accept as the legitimate ones, a special commission was created to make the decision. The commission consisted of five representatives, five senators, and five members of the Supreme Court. The partisan split was seven Democrats and seven Republicans, with the independent Chief Justice David Davis intended to chair the commission. When the Illinois legislature appointed Davis to be senator from Illinois, he was replaced by Republican Justice Joseph Philo Bradley who voted with the other Republicans to award all of the 20 disputed electoral votes to the Republican candidate. This decision gave Rutherford Hayes the 185 to 184 victory in the electoral vote count and the majority he needed to win the presidency. Democrat Samuel Tilden won 4,300,590 popular votes to 4,036,298 cast for Hayes. Thus the runner-up in the popular vote won 264,292 more votes than the winner of the presidency.

The election of 1888 was the only election in which the uncontested winner of the popular vote came in second in the electoral vote count and lost the presidency. Democrat Grover Cleveland won 5,537,857 votes compared to 5,447,129 votes of Indiana's Republican Benjamin Harrison. Yet Harrison won 233 of the 401 electoral votes and became president.[5] Thus, there were three elections in the 19th century in which the runner-up in the popular vote became president because of the electoral vote provisions of the Constitution and its contingency provisions. There have been a number of close calls in the 20th century (e.g. 1948, 1960, 1968, and 1976), though the odds are against the runner-up in the popular election becoming president.[6]

But the unexpected happened in the presidential election of 2000. The race between Democrat Al Gore and Republican George W. Bush was extremely close, with the winner being determined by Florida's 25 electoral votes, which were won by Bush by a margin of 537 popular votes. Gore won the national popular vote 50,996,116 to Bush's 50,456,169, a margin of 539,947 (51.6 percent).[7] Bush won 271 electoral votes, one more than a majority; and Gore won 266 (one District of Columbia elector cast a blank ballot). Another case of the runner-up in the popular votes being elected president raises again the question of the Electoral College mechanism for selecting the president.[8]

The Design of the Framers

Deciding how to select the chief executive was one of the most complex challenges faced by the Framers in the summer of 1787. The method was deliberated at the Constitutional Convention on 22 different days and was the subject of 30 separate votes.[9] The result was not a coherent design based on clear political principles, but rather a complex compromise that reflected the interests of different states. The main variables that the Framers had to consider in the selection of the executive were: who would select the person, how long the term of office would be, and whether the person would be eligible for more than one term.

For most of the convention, the assumption was that the chief executive would be chosen by the legislature, as was contemplated in the Virginia Plan drafted by James Madison. When the convention adjourned on July 25, 1787, the chief executive was to be chosen by the legislature, but the term of office was not set nor was the question of reeligibility.[10] The Committee of Detail reported on August 6 this formula:

> The Executive Power of the United States shall be vested in a single Person. His Stile shall be, "The President of the United States of America;" and his Title shall be, "His Excellency". He shall be elected by ballot by the Legislature. He shall hold his office during the term of seven years; but shall not be elected a second time."[11]

But there were still objections that a president chosen by the legislature would be too beholden to it and thus not independent enough. For this reason, James Wilson and Gouverneur Morris both argued for election by the people.[12]

The problem with selection by the people was not the Framers' distrust of this method's democratic nature (though the Framers were not trying to create a democracy). From their perspective, there were two problems with direct popular election of the president. The first was the probability that most citizens would not be personally familiar with all of the most qualified potential candidates. This was George Mason's concern; Mason thought that popular election of the president would be impractical.[13] "He conceived it would be as unnatural to refer the choice of a proper character for chief Magistrate to the people, as it would, to refer a trail of colours to a blind man. The extent of the Country renders it impossible that the people can have the requisite capacity to judge of the respective pretensions of the Candidates."[14]

But the more important problem was the disadvantage some states would face if the vote were based only on population. The ratio of population of the largest state, Virginia, to the smallest in population, Delaware, was about ten to one.[15] In addition to the overall problem of the small states, most of the slave states had smaller populations; with a direct election, they would not be able to count their slave population as they could in calculating their representation in the House of Representatives (counting three-fifths of the slave population).

Thus the proposal to base the election of the president on the ratio of votes that was established in the Connecticut Compromise for representation in Congress was attractive. It reassured the small states, because the ratio of influence in the vote would not be the ten to one between largest and smallest, but rather a four to one ratio. In addition, the slave states' representation would reflect three-fifths of their slave populations. Madison put it this way: "The people at large was in his opinion the fittest in itself," for choosing the president, but:

> There was one difficulty, however, of a serious nature attending an immediate choice by the people. The right of suffrage was much more diffusive in the Northern than the Southern States; and the latter could have no influence in the election on the score of the Negroes. The Substitution of electors obviated this difficulty and seemed on the whole to be liable to the fewest objections.[16]

Thus the Brearley Committee on Unfinished Parts worked for four days and reported back to the Convention on September 4 with a plan for the Electoral College. Under its plan, the selection of president would be removed from the legislature and given, in effect, to an independent "ad hoc Congress" convened solely for the purpose of selecting the president.[17] Electors would be chosen by state legislatures, but they could not be members of the national government and would not meet together because of the danger of plots and cabals. The ratio of the states to the membership of the college was exactly the same as their representation in the legislature, with the number of electors equaling the number of representatives and senators to which each state was entitled. Any changes in population among the states would be reflected in changes in their congressional representation.

Each elector could vote for two persons for president, one of whom could not be an inhabitant of the same state as the elector, and the winner had to receive a majority of all electors appointed. In the event that no candidate received a majority, the choice would devolve on the House of Representatives (changed from the Senate in the original Brearley Committee plan), which would choose the president from among the top five persons receiving electoral votes. In a concession to the small states, the state delegations in the House would cast only one vote per state.

Thus, the Framers did not come up with their formulation because of a distrust of direct election by the citizens. Shlomo Slonim argues that "Only a few delegates—most notably Mason, Gerry, and Butler—were opposed in principle to direct election of the executive. . . . anti-majoritarianism was by no means the primary motivation behind the creation of the Electoral College." Rather, according to Slonim:

> The delegates were confronted with a practical problem arising from the constellation of clashing forces at Philadelphia, and they devised a practical solution—an ad hoc congress that would faithfully reflect the pattern of weighted voting that was an integral part of the operation of the real Congress.[18]

Lucius Wilmerding, citing a number of statements by the Framers when they were explaining and defending the Constitution after the convention, also argued that their intent was for presidential selection to be based on the wishes of the citizenry. "It is clear," he argues, "that the Framers wanted and expected the popular principle to operate in the election of the President."[19]

If this reasoning is sound, recent proposals to change the method of selecting the president to more closely reflect the popular vote cannot be dismissed as undermining the Framers' intentions. The Framers came up with the Electoral College device because of the peculiar constellation of political forces facing them at the founding, not because of fundamental political principles. Insofar as some of those important forces, most importantly the differences between large and small states and slave and non-slave states, have dissipated over two centuries, proposals for change can be made without worry of violating the fundamental principles of the Framers.

The defense of the Electoral College system against change, then, must rest on arguments about how its current operation protects other fundamental values, such as federalism or the two-party system. Or the argument can be made that any alternative proposed to the Electoral College will have serious defects that outweigh the claimed advantages of change.

The Argument for Reforming the Electoral College System

The Electoral College system is "flawed" from the perspective of those who think that the candidate who wins the most popular votes should be elected president, or at least that the runner-up in the popular election should not become president. According to Arthur Schlesinger, Jr., "It is intolerable because it is undemocratic. And it is intolerable because it imposes a fatal burden on the minority president."[20] This perspective, it can be argued, is consistent with evolving democratic values in the United States over the past two centuries.

But first it must be recognized that the United States is not, nor was it meant to be, a pure democracy, even insofar as that might even be possible in a large nation state of 308 million citizens. Nor was it contemplated that the United States government would operate under a general principle of majority rule; though majority rule is often used in decision making within governmental institutions. The governmental system was designed by the Framers to be a republic, with representatives of the people chosen to govern. In fact, under the original Constitution, members of the House of Representatives were the only government officials to be chosen directly by the citizens of the United States. Other government officials were to be chosen by indirect means, with Senators selected by state legislatures, president and vice president by electors, and judges appointed by the president with consent of the Senate.

In addition to governmental structure, there were other important ways in which the government was not intended to be a simple democracy of majority rule. The separation of powers system with checks and balances was designed to filter popular moods and fads and slow any impulse to sudden change. The Bill of Rights was intended to ensure that the simple will of the majority could not easily infringe on the rights of citizens. The federal nature of the government was ensured by representation of the states and citizens in the Senate and House of Representatives and the independence of state governments. Thus, the United States is a federal democratic republic in its fundamental structure.

Nevertheless, since the founding of the republic the nature of our polity has changed in important ways, the Constitution has been amended to reflect some of those changes. With respect to the selection of the president, the original expectations of the Framers have been modified a number of times. The states individually have made the most important decisions by deciding to place the right to select presidential electors in the citizens of the states. For the first quarter-century of the republic, half of the states chose electors through election by the state legislature. Half of the remainder gave the selection to the citizens by district and half by a general ticket mode in which the plurality winner received all of the votes of the state. After 1820, the general ticket method began to predominate, and by 1832, all of the states except South Carolina selected electors by popular vote.[21] States also decided that using the winner-take-all rule rather than a district plan maximized their influence. In the modern era, only Maine and Nebraska use a district method of selecting electors (with a bonus of two for whichever candidate receives the plurality of votes in the state).

In addition to the states' separate decisions to base the selection of electors in the voters of each state, the scope of the franchise has been broadened by the passage of six constitutional amendments:

1. The Fifteenth Amendment (1870) extended the franchise to African Americans.
2. The Seventeenth Amendment (1913) provided for direct election of Senators.
3. The Nineteenth Amendment (1920) gave the right to vote to women.
4. The Twenty-third Amendment (1961) gave the vote to citizens of the District of Columbia.
5. The Twenty-fourth Amendment (1964) outlawed the poll tax.
6. The Twenty-sixth Amendment (1971) gave the vote to citizens 18 years of age.

Perhaps the most compelling argument that the president should be elected by direct popular vote is based on the premise that the president and vice president are the only national officials who represent the people as a whole and that the choice of the people is best approximated by the candidate who wins the most votes. This argument is buttressed by the declaration in the Preamble to the Constitution: "We the people. . . ." The Framers intentionally required that the Constitution be ratified by special conventions called in the separate states and not by the legislatures of the states. The import of their decision is that "the people" created the Constitution. It is not too far a stretch to argue that the choice of the people ought to determine the only national elective offices in the government.

Arguing that the president should be popularly elected in no way implies that all elements of the government ought to be chosen by majority vote. Clearly we have a mixed form of government in terms of geographic representation (the Senate) and appointed officials (federal judges). Accepting the popular election of the president in principle does not imply that all other officials ought to be popularly elected any more than accepting the appointment of judges implies that all other officials should be appointed.[22]

The legitimacy of the popular election of the president among the populace is buttressed by the probability that many, if not most, citizens who go to the polls to vote for president think that they are voting for president rather than a slate of electors. Some state ballots specify that the presidential vote is for a slate of electors, and some even list the individual electors, but many do not. At least this perception of many voters held until November 8, 2000.

Proposals for Reforming the Electoral College

One of the effects of the Electoral College system is that the ballots cast by all of the voters do not carry the same weight. That is, the ratio of electoral votes to population varies from state to state, benefitting the smallest states. For example, the ratio of electoral votes to population in Wyoming (with 453,588 people and three electoral votes) is one to 151,196 and in California (with 29,760,021 people and 54 electoral votes) is one to 551,112. Thus a vote in Wyoming is several times more influential in selecting electors than a vote in California.[23]

But small states are not necessarily the largest winners in the Electoral College scheme. Because most states have chosen to award all of their electors to the winner of the plurality of the votes in the state (called the unit rule or winner-take-all), the largest prizes in electoral votes are in the most populous states. Thus, inhabitants of the large states benefit from candidates' courting their votes. But in any given election whether any large state will be courted depends on whether it is "in play" in the sense that either candidate might win the plurality of its votes. For instance, in the 2000 election, George W. Bush did not spend much time campaigning in New York, because he had conceded that a majority of New York voters would probably vote for Al Gore in any case. For the same reason, Gore did not have a large incentive to spend much time in New York, except to shore up the party faithful. After his nomination, Al Gore did not even campaign in California, visiting the state only once, because he calculated that a majority of its votes were his anyway.[24] Similarly, Gore did not campaign much in Texas, because Bush had the state sewn up.

But the abstract inequalities of voter weight in the Electoral College system do not constitute the major problem with the system. As long as the winner of the popular vote also wins the electoral vote, there is little objection to the differently weighted votes. But this is not always the case, and the most important objection to the Electoral College design is that the runner-up in the popular vote can end up being elected president. There are three circumstances in which this can happen:

1. If several "faithless electors" do not vote as they pledged to vote, the runner-up may win the presidency.
2. If no candidate wins a majority in the Electoral College, the House of Representatives selects the president from among the top three electoral vote winners and does not have to consider the popular vote.
3. A candidate can win the majority of electoral votes without winning most of the popular votes.

The probability that electors will not vote for the candidate for whom they are pledged is not high. Electors are chosen for faithful service to their party and are firmly committed to the candidate of their party. There is little incentive for them to vote for someone else. Historically, there were only nine faithless electors out of a total of 19,744 electoral votes cast from 1789 to 1988.[25] Most recently, in 1988, a Democratic elector from West Virginia cast a vote for Lloyd Bentsen (the vice presidential nominee) for president rather than for Michael Dukakis, and in 1976 a Washington Republican elector voted for Ronald Reagan for president rather than the Republican nominee Gerald Ford. In the 2000 election, a 10th faithless elector was added to the list when an elector from the District of Columbia cast a blank ballot rather than voting for Al Gore, for whom she was pledged. She said that her vote was intended to protest the lack of voting representation of the District of Columbia in Congress.

In addition to the low probability of an elector's not voting for the expected nominee, the likelihood that a few faithless electors could change the outcome of an election is remote. The Electoral College usually exaggerates the margin of victory of the winner of the popular vote. Nevertheless, it is possible that a close electoral vote could be changed by the defection of just a few electors. The 2000 election is a case in point. Although Al Gore won the popular vote by a margin of more than 500,000 votes, the electoral vote was 271 to 266. In such a situation, the defection of just a few of Bush's electors could have denied a majority to either candidate, or a switch of several could have given the election to Gore. (The exact number depends on whether the blank ballot would have been counted as a vote or not.)

Although such a switch was unlikely, electors had switched before, and the temptation to go down in the history books might have tempted a few electors, as it did the elector from the District of Columbia. States, of course, have an incentive to prevent electors from defecting, and 26 states plus the District of Columbia have laws binding electors to vote for the candidate for whom they are pledged.[26] The constitutionality of such laws, however, would be in some doubt, because the Constitution provides that the electors will cast their ballots for president and vice president and does not bind them in any way.

The second situation has happened twice in our history. In the election of 1800, Jefferson and Burr were tied, requiring the House to choose between them. And in 1824, the House chose John Quincy Adams over Andrew Jackson, who came in first in both the popular and the electoral vote. The third scenario happened three times in our history. In 1888, the winner of the popular vote was clearly the loser in the Electoral College, and there was no dispute. In 1876, Hayes, the runner-up in the popular vote, was granted the 20 votes he needed to win a majority by the special commission created by Congress to decide how to allocate the slates of electors from the three disputed states. In general, a candidate could win the popular vote yet lose the electoral vote by losing by narrow margins in the large states and winning by large majorities in the small states. This is what happened in 2000 when George W. Bush lost the popular vote by more than 500,000 but won the electoral vote 271 to 266.

In addition to the previously mentioned elections, there have been a number of close calls in the 20th century—when the switch of a relatively small number of votes in key states could have put the election in the House or have changed the outcome of the election: 1948, 1960, 1968, and 1976.[27]

Proposals to Change the Electoral College System

Over the years, there have been many proposals to reform the Electoral College system, some proposing relatively minor changes, some proposing a constitutional amendment to provide for the direct popular election of the president. The "automatic plan" would eliminate the problem of the faithless elector by automatically casting each state's electoral votes in favor of the candidate who won the plurality of popular votes in the state. There would be no individual electors to cast ballots and thus no opportunity for a vote to be cast in an unexpected direction. It would take a constitutional amendment to make such a change.[28]

The "district plan" would give one electoral vote to the candidate who won a plurality of votes in each congressional district within a state. The extra two electoral votes would be granted to the candidate who won the most popular votes in the state as a whole. Because state legislatures now can decide how electoral votes are to be determined, this change could be made by individual states. In fact, Maine (with four electoral votes) and Nebraska (with five electoral votes) have adopted the district approach. Most states, however, have judged that their own influence is maximized by casting their electoral ballots in a block and follow the "unit rule" (winner-take-all) approach. Thus, it is improbable that most states would adopt the district approach on a voluntary basis. The district plan would make the outcome of the Electoral College vote more closely mirror the popular vote, but it would not entirely eliminate the possibility of the runner-up becoming president.

The "national bonus" plan would grant a bonus of 102 electoral votes (two for each state plus the District of Columbia) to the candidate who wins the most popular votes, providing the winner has at least 40 percent of the vote. This approach would virtually eliminate the possibility that the runner-up in the popular vote would become president while at the same time, preserving the distribution of electoral votes by states (though in a diluted form).[29] Arthur Schlesinger, Jr. endorsed the national bonus plan and was a member of a Twentieth Century Fund Task Force that proposed its adoption in 1978. According to Schlesinger, the plan "would preserve both the constitutional and the practical role of the states in the presidential election process."[30]

But by far the most basic and important proposal to change the Electoral College system is the proposal to amend the Constitution to provide for the direct popular election of the president. A version of this plan that was considered by Congress from 1966 to 1979 provided that "The people . . . shall elect the President." The person "having the greatest number of votes shall be elected President. . . ." If neither slate of president and vice presidential candidates wins 40 percent of the vote, a runoff election would be held between the top two vote-getting teams of candidates.[31] After hearings in Congress, the proposed Constitutional amendment was passed by the House in 1969 by 339 to 70. Hearings in the Senate were held over the next 10 years, and in 1979, the Senate voted 51 to 48 in favor of sending the proposal to the states for ratification, well short of the two-thirds majority necessary to pass a constitutional amendment.[32]

Defense of the Electoral College and Objections to Change

The defense of the Electoral College system of electing the president is not based on the intent of the Framers. Their intention was to devise a compromise that would satisfy a number of different constituencies needed to ratify the Constitution, primarily the small states and the slave states. One of the most vigorous defenders of the Electoral College system, Judith Best, admits that "the Electoral College has not worked as the framers anticipated. . . ." And she even favors putting the unit rule (winner-take-all) in the Constitution, because it protects federalism.[33]

The strongest defense of the Electoral College system lies in the effect of the system on the constitutional structure in practice over two centuries. The Constitutional defense of the Electoral College system emphasizes how federalism might be affected by any change. The political defense of the system stresses the importance of the two-party system to political stability and the ways the direct popular vote might imperil the two-party system. Opponents of change also predict that in addition to splintering the party system, a direct popular vote approach would lead to disruptive recounts and challenged elections.

Federalism

The strongest constitutional argument against direct popular election is that it would undermine the federal nature of our government. Judith Best argues that direct popular election would "deform our Constitution" and would constitute a serious "implicit attack on the federal principle."[34] William C. Kimberling argues that national popular election "would strike at the very heart of the federal structure laid out in our Constitution and would lead to the nationalization of our central government—to the detriment of the States."[35]

By guaranteeing a specific number of electoral votes to each state, the Electoral College system ensures that presidential candidates must appeal to coalitions of voters that are widely distributed throughout the country. If the federal requirement were not there, candidates might appeal to regional clusters of voters whose votes could be aggregated across states and regions. This could potentially be divisive and lead to discord. This argument for the Electoral College depends in great part on the fact that states have individually adopted the unit rule of counting all of their electoral votes as a block. That is why Best would put the unit rule in the Constitution and why Wilmerding was against it.[36]

Proponents of direct popular vote argue that federalism is indeed an important component of the constitutional system, but that the Electoral College system is not crucial to its maintenance. Certainly the electoral votes of small states do not attract active campaigning by major party candidates, who tend to go where there are large blocks of electoral votes. More importantly, larger states will be contested only if there is a reasonable chance of their blocks of votes going either way. With direct popular election, all votes would count for candidates, and they would be less likely to write off many states merely because they could not win the plurality in that state. They also argue that federalism is well protected by members of the House and Senate as well as by the legislatures and governors of the states. In the words of constitutional historian Jack Rakove, "States have no interest, as states, in the election of a president, only citizens do, and the vote of a citizen in Coeur d'Alene should count equally with one in Detroit."[37]

The Two-Party System

Defenders of the Electoral College system also argue that it is one of the key bulwarks of the two-party system in the United States and that direct popular voting for president would lead to the splintering of the two-party system and a proliferation of minor parties. They argue that minor political factions will have an incentive to run candidates for president with the hope that they will be able to force a runoff election and extract concessions in return for their support. Judith Best argues that "It is the very existence of a popular vote runoff, a second chance provision, that tempts more candidates to enter and voters to cast what they would otherwise consider to be a protest vote—a 'send them a message' vote."[38]

The hope of these minor parties would be to attract enough votes, along with other splinter parties, to prevent either of the two-party candidates from winning 40 percent of the vote and thus force a runoff. Best argues, for example, that if the 40 percent runoff rule had been in effect in 1992, Ross Perot would not have temporarily withdrawn from the race and could have offered his support in a runoff to one of the candidates for policy concessions.[39] Arthur Schlesinger, Jr. argued that direct popular election "would hasten the disintegration of the party system. Direct election with a runoff would give single-issue movements, major-party dissidents and freelance media adventurers an unprecedented incentive to jump into presidential contests." These parties would ". . . extract concessions from the runoff candidates in exchange for promises of support."[40]

Proponents of direct popular vote argue that, in addition to our political culture, the real structural basis for our two-party system is the use of single- member districts (plurality wins or first-past-the-post) for representation in Congress. It is difficult to build a viable political party if there is little chance of electing government officials. Proportional representation systems for parliamentary elections encourage smaller parties to form because they can realistically win public office. In a presidential election, the probability of winning enough popular votes to force a runoff, even in conjunction with other minor parties, is low. The present system does not prevent many minor party candidates from qualifying for inclusion on ballots in many states. Nor does it prevent significant candidates from running, such as Theodore Roosevelt or Ross Perot.

In a popular election system, even if one minor party were able to win a significant portion of the vote, and there were a runoff election, how could the leaders of that party force their voters to vote for the person with whom the candidate made a deal? In the present system, however, electors are chosen by the party (or candidate) on the basis of loyalty. With the Electoral College, if a candidate, for example, Ross Perot, were able to win sufficient electoral votes to produce a majority for another candidate in the Electoral College, the candidate would have much more leverage in convincing his few loyalists on his slates of electors to vote for whom he chose in the Electoral College vote than a candidate would have in convincing millions of voters to vote one way or another in a runoff election. Thus, a third party forcing concessions on one of the major parties is more likely in the Electoral College system than in a popular election with a runoff provision.

Contested Elections

Another argument critics of the direct popular vote plan make is that it would lead to endless recounts and challenges. Best argues that it would remove "the quarantine on fraud and recounts."[41] The reasoning is that if the election were close or the 40-percent threshold was in doubt, challenges and contests would not be limited to one or a few states but would be undertaken throughout the country: ". . . a recount of every ballot box in the country could be necessary. . . ."[42] In the election of 2000, some commentators raised the specter that *if you think that what is happening during the recounts in Florida is complicated, if we had direct popular elections, this would be happening throughout the whole country.*

But one of the attractions of direct popular election is that recounts would be less likely. In order to undertake a recount, there has to be the reasonable possibility that enough incorrect or fraudulent votes can be found to change the election outcome. It is intuitively evident that the fewer the total votes involved, the more likely it is that a close contest may result in a small number of votes deciding the election. Thus, in the present system, a few votes in one state may be able to make the difference in swinging a large block of electoral votes and possibly decide the election. This is what happened in Florida in the 2000 presidential election; the election was so close that the swing of a few hundred votes might realistically have changed the election outcome. Thus, a recount had a plausible possibility of changing the election outcome.

In Florida, Al Gore had to find several hundred votes in order to change the outcome. If the election had been by popular vote, George Bush would have had to find more than 500,000 votes, a daunting task. Even in 1960, when Richard Nixon's supporters were pondering challenges in Illinois, they would have had to find about 9,000 votes to change the outcome. And if they had finally won Illinois, they would have had to find about 40,000 votes in Texas. Because winning both of these states through recounts was unlikely, Nixon's supporters gave up. It would have been even harder to find more than 100,000 votes throughout the country, if the popular vote determined the outcome. Thus, the argument of those supporting direct popular voting for president is that recounts and challenges would be less likely, not more likely, because the number of votes needed to change a national outcome would be much larger than the number needed to change the outcome in one state that controlled a large or deciding block of electoral votes.

Conclusion

The question of how we elect our president is a fundamental one in the constitutional system, and it has been debated many times over the past two centuries. It has not been fully settled, just as the important constitutional issues of the right balance between the president and Congress or the balance between the states and the national government have not been finally settled. The presidential election of 2000, with the runner-up becoming president, has raised the issue again. Without prejudging the outcome, it is appropriate to begin a national dialogue and to deliberate about the best mode for electing the president.

Acknowledgments

The author would like to thank Robert Dudley for comments on an earlier version of this essay.

Endnotes

1. Richard J. Ellis, *Founding the American Presidency* (Lanham, MD: Rowman and Littlefield, 1999), p. 114. The Federalists had arranged to withhold several votes from Adams's vice presidential candidate, Thomas Pinckney, so that there would be no tie between Adams and Pinckney. But they miscalculated and withheld too many, giving Thomas Jefferson the second most number of electoral votes and the vice presidency.
2. See Shlomo Slonim, "Designing the Electoral College," in Thomas E. Cronin, ed. *Inventing the American Presidency* (Lawrence, KS: University Press of Kansas, 1989), p. 33. First published as "The Electoral College at Philadelphia: The Evolution of an Ad Hoc Congress for Selection of a President," *Journal of American History*, Vol. 73 (June 1986).
3. American Bar Association, *Electing the President: A Report of the Commission on Electoral College Reform* (Chicago: American Bar Association, 1967), p. 3.
4. The forthcoming election of 1804 was also on the minds of those who supported the Twelfth Amendment. See Lucius Wilmerding, Jr. *The Electoral College* (Boston: Beacon Press, 1958), p. 38.
5. The voting data in these elections are from Joseph Nathan Kane, *Presidential Fact Book* (NY: Random House, 1999).
6. For data on these close elections see Neal R. Peirce and Lawrence D. Longley, *The People's President* (New Haven, CT: Yale University Press, 1981), pp. 257–258.
7. The voting results were reported in *The New York Times*, December 30, 2000, p. A11. Other candidates: Ralph Nader, 2,864,810 (2.72%); Pat Buchanan, 448,750 (.43%); Harry Brown, 386,024 (.37%); *The Washington Post* (December 21, 2000), p. A9.
8. It is a historical oddity that every time the son or grandson of a president has been nominated for president, he has been elected with fewer popular votes than his opponent. In 1824, John Quincy Adams, the son of John Adams, was elected by the House. In 1888, Benjamin Harrison, grandson of William Henry Harrison, won the electoral vote, but came in second to Grover Cleveland in the popular count. George Bush is the third son or grandson of a president to be elected, again with fewer popular votes than his opponent.
9. See Shlomo Slonim, "Designing the Electoral College," in Thomas E. Cronin, ed. *Inventing the American Presidency* (Lawrence, KS: University Press of Kansas, 1989), pp. 33–60. First published as "The Electoral College at Philadelphia: The Evolution of an Ad Hoc Congress for Selection of a President, *Journal of American History*, Vol. 73 (June 1986).
10. Slonim, "Designing the Electoral College," p. 45.
11. Max Farrand, ed., *The Records of the Federal Convention of 1787* (New Haven, CT: Yale University Press, 1966), Vol. 2, p. 171.
12. Slonim, "Designing the Electoral College," pp. 48–49.
13. Max Farrand, *The Records of the Federal Convention of 1787* (New Haven, CT: Yale University Press, 1966), Vol. I, p. 69 (June 1, 1787).
14. Max Farrand, *The Records of the Federal Convention of 1787* (New Haven, CT: Yale University Press, 1966), Vol. II, p. 31 (July 17, 1787).
15. Richard J. Ellis, ed. *Founding the American Presidency* (Lanham, MD: Rowman and Littlefield, 1999), p. 113.
16. Farrand, *Records of the Federal Convention of 1787*, Vol. 2, pp. 56–57.
17. Slonim, "Designing the Electoral College," p. 50.
18. Slonim, "Designing the Electoral College," p. 55.
19. Wilmerding, *The Electoral College*, p. 21.
20. Arthur Schlesinger, Jr., "Fixing the Electoral College," *The Washington Post* (December 19, 2000), p. A39. In his first annual address, President Andrew Jackson argued: "that in proportion as agents to execute the will of the people are multiplied there is danger of their wishes being frustrated. . . . It is safer for them to express their own will. . . . A President elected by a minority can not enjoy the confidence necessary to the successful discharge of his duties." Quoted in Arthur Schlesinger, Jr., *The Cycles of American History* (Boston: Houghton Mifflin, 1986), p. 318.

21. Richard J. Ellis, ed. *Founding the American Presidency* (Lanham, MD: Rowman and Littlefield, 1999), pp. 118–119.

22. William C. Kimberling in "The Electoral College," argues that "Indeed, if we become obsessed with government by popular majority as the only consideration, should we not abolish the Senate which represents states regardless of population? . . . If there are any reasons to maintain State representation in the Senate and House as they exist today, then surely these same reasons apply to the choice of president. Why, then, apply a sentimental attachment to popular majorities only to the Electoral College?" The reason for state representation in the House and Senate is that each body is intended to represent citizens in local or state areas. The basis for electing the president by national vote is that the president is supposed to represent the nation rather than only one part of it. Kimberling's article is found on the National Archives and Records Administration Web site (www.nara.gov).

23. Another way to calculate differential influence of voters on the Electoral College vote is to divide the number of electoral votes by all of those who voted for the winner in each state (because the votes of those voting for the loser in a state do not count for that candidate at all). See Adam Clymer, "Now What? This Time, Cries For 'Blood' Seem Unthinkable," *The New York Times* (November 12, 2000), p. wk 5. See also the analysis of Lawrence D. Longley and Neal R. Peirce in *The Electoral College Primer* (New Haven, CT: Yale University Press, 1996), pp. 143–144.

24. George F. Will, "A Brief Moment," *The Washington Post* (December 17, 2000), p. B7. If questions about how a possible change in the Electoral College system might change campaign patterns are of concern, some empirical evidence can be brought to bear. Patterns of campaign activity in recent elections can be measured. For example, in the 2000 election, eight mountain states received no visits by candidates; all of them had few electoral votes and all were solidly Republican. The number of presidential campaign ads in Green Bay (WI) and Grand Rapids (MI) far outnumbered (by more than 5,000) the ads in the New York City or Los Angeles media markets. To win candidates' attention, states must be "in play" and have a significant number of electoral votes. For data on candidate state visits and media market ads, see Alexis Simendinger, James A. Barnes, and Carl M. Cannon, "Pending a Popular Vote," *National Journal* (November 18, 2000), p. 3653.

25. Joseph Nathan Kane, *Presidential Fact Book* (NY: Random House, 1999), p. 374.

26. National Archives and Record Administration, Web site: www.nara.gov.

27. For details and specific numbers of votes that would have to change in order to change the outcome in these elections, see Lawrence D. Longley and Neal R. Peirce, *The Electoral College Primer* (New Haven, CT: Yale University Press, 1996), pp. 35–36.

28. The Center for the Study of the Presidency sponsored a panel that issued a report in 1992 that recommended a version of the automatic plan that would have eliminated the office of elector. The panel also recommended that if there were no majority in the electoral vote that there be a runoff election rather than letting the House of Representatives decide. See Elizabeth P. McCaughey, "Electing the President: Report of the Panel on Presidential Selection," Center for the Study of the Presidency, 1992. Ronald Reagan, in a talk on April 13, 1977, also proposed casting votes automatically rather than giving any discretion to electors. See William Safire, "Reagan Writes," *The New York Times Magazine* (December 31, 2000), p. 38.

29. See Thomas E. Cronin, "The Electoral College Controversy," in Judith A. Best, *The Choice of the People? Debating the Electoral College* (Lanham, MD: Rowman and Littlefield, 1996), pp. xxi–xxiv.

30. See "Winner Take All: Report of the Twentieth Century Fund Task Force on Reform of the Presidential Election Process," (NY, 1978). See Schlesinger's analysis of the national bonus plan in *The Cycles of American History* (Boston: Houghton Mifflin, 1986), pp. 320–321.

31. The proposed Amendment is reprinted in Judith A. Best, *The Choice of the People? Debating the Electoral College* (Lanham, MD: Rowman and Littlefield, 1996), pp. 115–117. The legitimacy of a president who wins the election with less than 50 percent of the vote is not a problem. Seventeen presidential elections have resulted in such a "minority president"

(Grover Cleveland and Bill Clinton two times each). Only Lincoln polled slightly less than 40 percent. The lack of a majority of the popular votes did not prevent some of these minority presidents being reelected, including Lincoln, Cleveland, Wilson, Nixon, and Clinton.

32. Judith A. Best, *The Choice of the People? Debating the Electoral College* (Lanham, MD: Rowman and Littlefield, 1996), p. 83.

33. Judith A. Best, *The Choice of the People? Debating the Electoral College* (Lanham, MD: Rowman and Littlefield, 1996), pp. 84 and 14.

34. Judith A. Best, *The Choice of the People? Debating the Electoral College* (Lanham, MD: Rowman and Littlefield, 1996), p. 55.

35. William C. Kimberling, "The Electoral College," on the National Archives and Records Administration Web site (www.nara.gov). Kimberling was Deputy Director of the Federal Election Commission Office of Election Administration in 2000.

36. Best, *The Choice of the People?* p. 14. Wilmerding, *The Electoral College*: "In committing the appointment of the Electors to the people, the state legislatures have fulfilled the intention of the Constitution; but in requiring the Electors to be appointed by a mode which gives to a single party the whole of a state's representation in the Electoral College, they have defeated that intention. They have put the presidency on a federative rather than a national basis. They have taken the choice of the President from the people of the nation at large and given it, in effect, to the people of the large states." (p. xi).

37. Jack Rakove, "The Accidental Electors," *The New York Times* (December 19, 2000), p. A31.

38. Judith A. Best, *The Choice of the People? Debating the Electoral College* (Lanham, MD: Rowman and Littlefield, 1996), p. 56. This objection also applies to proposals for an "instant runoff" in which voters would vote for several candidates in order of preference. If no candidate receives 40 percent of the votes on the first round, the candidate with the least votes would be dropped from the calculations in an iterative fashion until one candidate received the 40 percent requirement.

39. Judith A. Best, *The Choice of the People? Debating the Electoral College* (Lanham, MD: Rowman and Littlefield, 1996), p. 56.

40. Schlesinger, *The Cycles of American History*, pp. 319–320.

41. Judith A. Best, *The Choice of the People? Debating the Electoral College* (Lanham, MD: Rowman and Littlefield, 1996), p. 57.

42. Judith A. Best, *The Choice of the People? Debating the Electoral College* (Lanham, MD: Rowman and Littlefield, 1996), p. 58.

SECTION

2

HISTORICAL PERSPECTIVES
ON THE PRESIDENCY

· · · · · · · · · · · · ▬▬▬▬▬▬▬▬▬▬▬▬▬▬▬

Because Article II of the Constitution left many blank spaces to be filled in by the workings of history, the views of successive presidents naturally comprise important extensions, and even emendations, of the constitutional text. The contributions of the first president, George Washington, cannot be understated. As noted in the previous section, his character and fame were essential to the success of the Constitutional Convention, and his talents framed a model for the document's list of presidential powers.

Despite the fact that he was twice the unanimous choice of the Electoral College, Washington served out of a sense of duty rather than a desire for greater fame. Washington "never ran for the presidency," writes Joel Achenbach. "He ran *from* it. The job stalked him from the moment the Framers conceived it."[1] Yet he gave the job a much-needed dignity, and he remained in office long enough to establish certain precedents—in conducting foreign affairs and in dealing with cabinet members and Congress. At the end of two terms, moreover, he gratefully retired to his beloved Mount Vernon estate—setting an example of an orderly transfer of power.

As he left office, Washington prepared a farewell address, which contained thoughts about his nation's condition and advice to his countrymen. Although still read dutifully in the chambers of Congress every year on Washington's birthday, the document is very much the work of a literate 18th-century gentleman—alas, lacking some of the directness of expression that graces the writings of, say, Thomas Jefferson or the authors of *The Federalist Papers*. After thanking citizens for the honors bestowed on him, he extols the virtues of liberty and union: "[Y]our union ought to be considered as a main prop to your liberty, and . . . love of the one ought to endear to you the preservation of the other.[2] (He observes in this context that citizens should avoid "overgrown Military establishments, which under any form of government are inauspicious to liberty, and which are . . . particularly hostile to Republican Liberty.")[3] He further commends the constitutional machinery:

> . . .[R]emember, especially, that for the efficient management of your common interests, in a country so extensive as ours, a Government of as much vigor as is consistent with the perfect security of Liberty is indispensable. Liberty itself will find in such a Government, with powers properly distributed and adjusted, its surest Guardian.[4]

Finally, Washington takes pains to warn his countrymen of two dangers that had bedeviled his presidency: the "common and continual mischiefs of the spirit of Party" and "the insidious wiles of foreign influence." Despite his fame, Washington was assaulted by vicious attacks from anti-Federalists, who came to rally around Thomas Jefferson. Partisan spirit may be useful in monarchies; but it should be discouraged in popular, elective governments:

> From their natural tendency, it is certain there will always be enough of that [partisan] spirit for every salutary purpose. And there being constant danger of excess, the effort ought to be, by force of public opinion, to mitigate and assuage it. A first not to be quenched, it demands a uniform vigilance to prevent its bursting into a flame, lest instead of warming it should consume.[5]

As for foreign influence, Washington declares that

> The Great rule of conduct for us, in regard to foreign Nations is in extending our commercial relations to have with them as little political connection as possible. So far as we have already formed engagements let them be fulfilled, with perfect good faith. Here let us stop. . . .
> 'Tis our true policy to steer clear of permanent Alliances, with any portion of the foreign world. . . . Taking care always to keep ourselves, by suitable establishments, on a respectably defense posture, we may safely trust to temporary alliances for extraordinary emergencies.[6]

This section offers several notable presidential statements about the powers of the office—in logical progression rather than chronological order. The section closes with a distinguished scholar's historical classification of presidencies in terms of the strength or weakness of their political coalitions.

Historically, many presidents have taken a restrictive view of their duties. "I shall have no policy of my own to interfere with the people," declared Ulysses S. Grant upon accepting the Republican nomination for president in 1868. In other words, Grant would defer to the GOP-controlled Congress. This view was perhaps best expressed by an early 20th-century president, William Howard Taft, who served from 1909 to 1913. Taft's true ambition was fulfilled in 1921, however, when President Warren Harding appointed him Chief Justice of the Supreme Court, where Taft served until his death in 1930—the only person to have served in both posts. Three years after being defeated for reelection, Taft reflected on the presidency in a series of lectures that he entitled "Our Chief Magistrate and His

Powers." He held a narrowly literal, or Whig, view of the office; that is, he counseled strict deference to the text of the Constitution and specific laws passed by Congress. "The true view of the executive functions," he declared, is that "the president can exercise no power which cannot be fairly and reasonably traced to some specific grant of power or justly implied and included within such express grant as proper and necessary to its exercise." He dismissed more expansive claims, such as Theodore Roosevelt's "stewardship theory," as "unsafe." Taft concluded that "there is no undefined residuum of power which [the president] can exercise because it seems to be in the public interest."

A more ambitious view of the presidency—that of a servant or steward directly responsible to the people—often has been used to explain or justify presidential actions. Andrew Jackson (1829–1837), touted as a "man of the people," tailored many of his crucial actions to cultivate mass support. It was, however, Theodore Roosevelt (1901–1909), who best articulated what he called the "stewardship theory" in explaining his actions as president. A student of history, Roosevelt wanted to be a great president and had a clear vision of how a great president should behave. He tried to model himself on presidents such as Washington and, especially, Lincoln; he had nothing but scorn for "honorable and well-meaning" predecessors (and, as it turned out, his successor, William Howard Taft) who took the "narrowly legalistic view that the president is the servant of Congress rather than of the people."

As president, Roosevelt acted with vigor, boldness, and a shrewd understanding of public sentiment and media influence. In domestic policy, he is best remembered for his attacks against the giant business trusts ("malefactors of great wealth," he called them) and support for conserving public and private lands. He bargained incessantly with congressional leaders, but when he encountered fierce opposition, he appealed to public opinion and often won his way. In foreign affairs, he pushed executive power toward its limits, although he consulted Congress when legally obliged to do so. Roosevelt took advantage of political instability in Central America to gain access to the Isthmus of Panama and build the Panama Canal; he settled the Alaskan boundary dispute on his own terms, sent the battle fleet around the world to impress other naval powers, and intervened vigorously in the Russo-Japanese War (for which he received the Nobel Peace Prize).

In his autobiography published in 1913, Roosevelt explained that he "acted for the common well-being of all our people, whenever and in whatever manner was necessary, unless prevented by direct constitutional or legislative prohibition." His activism was matched by the vigor and directness of his writing:

> I did and caused to be done many things not previously done by the President and the heads of the departments. I did not usurp power, but I did greatly broaden the use of executive power. In other words, I acted for the public welfare. . . . I did not care a rap for the mere form and show of power; I cared immensely for the use that could be made of the substance.

Another activist view of presidential powers was provided by Woodrow Wilson (1913–1921). Trained in both law and politics/history/economics, Wilson received his Ph.D. from Johns Hopkins University in 1885 and became one of the founders of the modern scholarly discipline of political science. His dissertation, published as *Congressional Government* (1885), critically described the gilded age of congressional dominance and presidential weakness. "Congress [is] the dominant, nay, the irresistible, power of the federal system," whereas "the president [is] the first official of a carefully graded and impartially regulated civil service system . . . and his duties call rather for training than for constructive genius."

More than 20 years later, Wilson, by this time the president of Princeton University and about to become governor of New Jersey, delivered a series of lectures in which he articulated a radically different view of the presidency. Wilson's newfound fascination with the office no doubt reflected his assessment of the administrations of William McKinley and Theodore Roosevelt. Wilson's ideal president, however, was an inspired, even heroic leader of public opinion, not simply Roosevelt's steward, who embodies or interprets popular sentiment. His now-famous phrases are a manifesto for the modern public, or "rhetorical," presidency. "He is the only national voice in affairs . . . . His office is anything he has the sagacity and force to make it." Six years after writing these words, Wilson himself was elected president—the only political scientist, and the only person with an earned doctorate, to reach that post. One inevitably compares Wilson's ringing phrases with his subsequent performance in the Oval Office— the triumphs of his New Freedom domestic agenda and victory in the Great War, followed by the final, tragic defeat of his cherished League of Nations plan.

The most expansive view of presidential powers—that it embraces a prerogative to act to preserve the Constitution itself, even if that means bending or breaking specific written laws—was expressed by Abraham Lincoln (1861–1865). Lincoln's invocation of the prerogative power came in response to the most profound crisis in the nation's history: the secession of the Confederacy, with its prospect of dissolving the Union.

Such a broad reading of executive power, to be sure, had been claimed even by thinkers normally suspicious of executive authority. Most advocates of parliamentary supremacy, for example, conceded the existence of a realm of royal prerogative, usually associated with diplomacy and military command. Readers of John Locke's *Second Treatise on Government* may well be startled when they reach Chapter 14, on "prerogative power," which he defines as "the power to act according to discretion for the public good, without the prescription of the law and sometimes even against it."[7] Why should people have such discretion in executing the law? Legislators simply cannot foresee every possible eventuality, Locke explains; thus, written laws often fail to give adequate guidance. Presumably, Locke was thinking about crises or emergencies that imperil the safety of the entire community. "[T]he laws themselves should in some cases give way to the executive power—or rather, to the fundamental law of nature [that] all the members of the society are to be preserved."[8] Not that such power is unchecked. Ultimately, it is subject to the people's will, and it may be protested in the usual ways. It remains significant, however, that Locke—the great champion of legislative power and a "balanced constitution"—condones such a broad reading of executive power.

An orthodox Whig during his early career (serving in the 30th Congress, 1847–1849), Lincoln had denounced Andrew Jackson's vigorous use of presidential power. "Were I president," Lincoln said, "I should desire the legislation of the country to rest with Congress, uninfluenced by the executive . . . and undisturbed by the veto unless in very special and clear cases." Confronting the extraordinary circumstances of civil strife in the spring of 1861, however, Lincoln took bold, unprecedented actions. Among other things, he augmented the armed forces, both regulars and volunteers; he spent unappropriated funds; he proclaimed a blockade of southern ports; he proclaimed martial law and suspended the writ of habeas corpus in selected places; and he imposed a wide variety of wartime restrictions. Many of his actions invaded subjects that previously were considered to be the domain of Congress. Even so, Lincoln was in no hurry to seek legislative ratification of his actions (although Congress eventually approved most of them). "Whether strictly legal or not," he explained, "[my actions] were ventured upon under what appeared to be a popular demand and a public necessity; trusting then as now that Congress would readily ratify them."

Lincoln justified his actions in terms that Locke might well have understood: ultimately, they were needed to preserve the nation itself. His was a unique reading of the Constitution's injunction that presidents shall "take care that the laws be faithfully executed," yet here, "the laws" are nothing less than the supreme law of the land: the Constitution and the "more perfect Union" it had created. As Lincoln later asked, "Was it possible to lose the nation and yet preserve the Constitution?" And again: "Was it possible for all the laws *except one* to be preserved?" In his letter to Albert G. Hodges, dated April 4, 1864, Lincoln defended his use of presidential power in the simple eloquence that seemingly flowed naturally from his pen.

Lincoln nonetheless drew a bright line between his personal moral sentiments and his public duties. His career had been built upon his opposition to slavery ("If slavery is not wrong, nothing is wrong"). But his oath of office bound him to a public morality: preservation of the union, with or without slavery. ". . . I have never understood that the presidency conferred upon me an unrestricted right to act officially upon [my] judgment and feeling," he writes. Thus, he temporized about the issue of abolishing slavery: having already alienated the slave-holding states, he now he now angered the Civil War's most fervent supporters, especially the abolitionists. His Emancipation Proclamation—a limited grant of freedom to slaves residing outside the rebellious states—came only after battlefield victories made his words credible. Lincoln's subtle but powerful argument speaks to today's elected officials, who are often challenged to choose between their personal ethical views and their responsibilities in public office— which may call for a distinct loyalty to what might be called a public morality.

The final essay in this section, Stephen Skowronek's "The Presidency in the Political Order," is a bold attempt to classify presidential roles in their historical contexts. Skowronek plants himself right in the middle of the Oval Office: Political history, he argues, is defined in terms of "presidentially driven sequences of change encompassing the generation and degeneration of coalitional systems or partisan regimes." He describes how presidents "make politics" by tirelessly building constituencies for change and striving to remove obstacles that stand in the way of their high-priority projects.

Presidents' varying roles—what Skowronek calls the "emergent structures" of presidential policy making—depend on whether a president challenges or adheres to the prevailing political order. When presidents oppose an established but discredited political order, they are free to strike out in new directions (Skowronek's "politics of reconstruction"). "Presidents stand preeminent in American politics when government has been most thoroughly discredited, and when political resistance to the presidency is weakest, presidents tend to remake the government wholesale." Jackson, Lincoln, and Franklin Roosevelt are among the great reconstructive presidents. In contrast, those presidents who cling to a mode of politics that has lost its usefulness and credibility (the "politics of disjunction") are doomed, and often singled out as political failures. Examples are the two Adamses (John and John Quincy), James Buchanan, Herbert Hoover, and Jimmy Carter.

Presidents who inherit an established, robust political tradition are fortunate: their task is to articulate the basic themes of the prevailing ideology—acting as "regime boosters"—and innovate within that consensus (the "politics of articulation"). Presidents such as James K. Polk, Theodore Roosevelt, and Lyndon Johnson "came to power in the wake of a strong reaffirmation of majority party government, and no extraordinary crises distracted them from the business of completing the agenda." But such presidents are at risk when they face unexpected events (the Vietnam War, in Johnson's case) that shake the partisan consensus that swept them into office.

Finally, there are presidents who attain their office despite the fact that they oppose the political consensus of their era ("politics of preemption"). They are political "flukes." Their election defies the prevailing partisan divisions, and often they must deal with Congresses controlled by the opposition party. Examples include Andrew Johnson, Woodrow Wilson, and Richard Nixon. Despite their activities (even their successes), these presidents failed to alter the underlying political allegiances, and many times were brought to their knees by Congresses controlled by their enemies.

Skowronek's analysis reminds us once again that the presidential job description is expansive and variable. It is a blend of the president's own political commitments and the tenor of the times. Out of this mix emerge some presidents who are deemed great and others who are judged as failures.

Selected Bibliography

Agar, Herbert, *The Price of Union* (Boston, MA: Houghton Mifflin, 1950).

Ford, Henry Jones, *The Rise and Growth of American Politics* (New York: Da Capo Press, 1967). Originally published by Macmillan in 1898.

Greenstein, Fred I., ed., *Leadership in the Modern Presidency* (Cambridge, MA: Harvard University Press, 1988).

Landy, Marc, ed., *Modern Presidents and the Presidency* (Lexington, MA: Lexington Books, 1995).

Pyle, Christopher H., and Richard M. Pious, eds., *The President, Congress, and the Constitution* (New York: Free Press, 1984).

Skowronek, Stephen, *The Politics Presidents Make: Leadership from John Adams to George Bush* (Cambridge, MA: Harvard University Press, 1993).

Wilson, Woodrow, *Congressional Government* (Baltimore, MD: Johns Hopkins University Press, 1981). Originally published in 1885.

Wilson, Woodrow, *Constitutional Government in the United States* (New York: Columbia University Press, 1961). Originally published in 1908.

Endnotes

1. Joel Achenbach, *The Grand Idea: George Washington's Potomac and the Race to the West* (New York: Simon & Schuster, 2004), 157.
2. Washington*: Writings,* ed. John Rhodehamel, The Library of America (New York: Penguin Books, 1997), 966. All quotations from the farewell address are drawn from this volume, 962–977.
3. Ibid.
4. Ibid., 969.
5. Ibid., 970.
6. Ibid., 974–975.
7. John Locke, *The Second Treatise of Government,* ed. Thomas Peardon (Indianapolis: The Library of Liberal Arts/Bobbs-Merrill, 1952), 93.
8. Locke, 91.

William Howard Taft

The Strict Constructionist Presidency

While it is important to mark out the exclusive field of jurisdiction of each branch of the government, Legislative, Executive and Judicial, it should be said that in the proper working of the government there must be cooperation of all branches, and without a willingness of each branch to perform its function, there will follow a hopeless obstruction to the progress of the whole government. Neither branch

---

Source: William Howard Taft, *Our Chief Magistrate and His Powers* (New York: Columbia University Press, 1916), pp. 138–145.

can compel the other to affirmative action, and each branch can greatly hinder the other in the attainment of the object of its activities and the exercise of its discretion.

The true view of the Executive functions is, as I conceive it, that the President can exercise no power which cannot be fairly and reasonably traced to some specific grant of power or justly implied and included within such express grant as proper and necessary to its exercise. Such specific grant must be either in the Federal Constitution or in an act of Congress passed in pursuance thereof. There is no undefined residuum of power which he can exercise because it seems to him to be in the public interest, and there is nothing in the Neagle case and its definition of a law of the United States, or in other precedents, warranting such an inference. The grants of Executive power are necessarily in general terms in order not to embarrass the Executive within the field of action plainly marked for him, but his jurisdiction must be justified and vindicated by affirmative constitutional or statutory provision, or it does not exist. There have not been wanting, however, eminent men in high public office holding a different view and who have insisted upon the necessity for an undefined residuum of Executive power in the public interest. They have not been confined to the present generation. We may learn this from the complaint of a Virginia statesman, Abel P. Upshur, a strict constructionist of the old school, who succeeded Daniel Webster as Secretary of State under President Tyler. He was aroused by Story's commentaries on the Constitution to write a monograph answering and criticizing them, and in the course of this he comments as follows on the Executive power under the Constitution:

> The most defective part of the Constitution beyond all question, is that which is related to the Executive Department. It is impossible to read that instrument, without being struck with the loose and unguarded terms in which the powers and duties of the President are pointed out. So far as the legislature is concerned, the limitations of the Constitution, are, perhaps, as precise and strict as they could safely have been made; but in regard to the Executive, the Convention appears to have studiously selected such loose and general expressions, as would enable the President, by implication and construction either to neglect his duties or to enlarge his powers. *We have heard it gravely asserted in Congress that whatever power is neither legislative nor judiciary, is of course executive, and, as such, belongs to the President under the Constitution.* How far a majority of that body would have sustained a doctrine so monstrous, and so utterly at war with the whole genius of our government, it is impossible to say, but this, at least, we know, that it met with no rebuke from those who supported the particular act of Executive power, in defense of which it was urged. Be this as it may, it is a reproach to the Constitution that the Executive trust is so ill-defined, as to leave any plausible pretense even to the insane zeal of party devotion, for attributing to the President of the United States the powers of a despot; powers which are wholly unknown in any limited monarchy in the world.

The view that he takes as a result of the loose language defining the Executive powers seems exaggerated. But one must agree with him in his condemnation of the view of the Executive power which he says was advanced in Congress. In recent years there has been put forward a similar view by executive officials and to some extent acted on. Men who are not such strict constructionists of the Constitution as Mr. Upshur may well feel real concern if such views are to receive the general acquiescence. Mr. Garfield, when Secretary of the Interior, under Mr. Roosevelt, in his final report to Congress in reference to the power of the Executive over the public domain, said:

> Full power under the Constitution was vested in the Executive Branch of the Government and the extent to which that power may be exercised is governed wholly by the discretion of the Executive unless any specific act has been prohibited either by the Constitution or by legislation.

In pursuance of this principle, Mr. Garfield, under an act for the reclamation of arid land by irrigation, which authorized him to make contracts for irrigation works and incur liability equal to the amount on deposit in the Reclamation Fund, made contracts with associations of settlers by which it was agreed that if these settlers would advance money and work, they might receive certificates from the government engineers of the labor and money furnished by them, and that such certificates might be received in the future in the discharge of their legal obligations to the government for water rent and other things under the statute. It became necessary for the succeeding administration to pass on the validity of these government certificates. They were held by Attorney-General Wickersham to be illegal, on the ground that no authority existed for their issuance. He relied on the Floyd acceptances in 7th Wallace, in which recovery was sought in the Court of Claims on commercial paper in the form of acceptances signed by Mr. Floyd when Secretary of War and delivered to certain contractors. The Court held that they were void because the Secretary of War had no statutory authority to issue them. Mr. Justice Miller, in deciding the case, said:

> The answer which at once suggests itself to one familiar with the structure of our government, in which all power is delegated, and is defined by law, constitutional or statutory, is, that to one or both of these sources we must resort in every instance. We have no officers in this government, from the President down to the most subordinate agent, who does not hold office under the law, with prescribed duties and limited authority. And while some of these, as the President, the Legislature, and the Judiciary, exercise powers in some sense left to the more general definitions necessarily incident to fundamental law found in the Constitution, the larger portion of them are the creation of statutory law, with duties and powers prescribed and limited by that law.

My judgment is that the view of Mr. Garfield and Mr. Roosevelt, ascribing an undefined residuum of power to the President is an unsafe doctrine and that it might lead under emergencies to results of an arbitrary character, doing irremediable injustice to private right. The mainspring of such a view is that the Executive is charged with responsibility for the welfare of all the people in a general way, that he is to play the part of a Universal Providence and set all things right, and that anything that in his judgment will help the people he ought to do, unless he is expressly forbidden not to do it. The wide field of action that this would give to the Executive one can hardly limit.

Theodore Roosevelt

The Stewardship Presidency

My view was that every executive officer, and above all every executive officer in high position, was a steward of the people bound actively and affirmatively to do all he could for the people, and not to content himself with the negative merit of keeping his talents undamaged in a napkin. I declined to adopt the view that what was imperatively necessary for the nation could not be done by the President unless he could find some specific authorization to do it. My belief was that it was not only his right but his duty to do anything that the needs of the nation demanded unless such action was forbidden by the Constitution or by the laws. Under this interpretation of executive power I did and caused to be done many things not previously done by the President and the heads of the departments. I did not usurp power, but I did greatly broaden the use of executive power. In other words, I acted for the public welfare, I acted for the common well-being of all our people, whenever and in whatever manner was necessary, unless prevented by direct constitutional or legislative prohibition. . . .

The course I followed, of regarding the Executive as subject only to the people, and, under the Constitution, bound to serve the people affirmatively in cases where the Constitution does not explicitly forbid him to render the service, was substantially the course followed by both Andrew Jackson and Abraham Lincoln. Other honorable and well-meaning Presidents, such as James Buchanan, took the opposite and, as it seems to me, narrowly legalistic view that the President is the servant of Congress rather than of the people, and can do nothing, no matter how necessary it be to act, unless the Constitution explicitly commands the action. Most able lawyers who are past middle age take this view, and so do large numbers of well-meaning, respectable citizens. My successor in office took this, the Buchanan, view of the President's powers and duties.

For example, under my administration we found that one of the favorite methods adopted by the men desirous of stealing the public domain was to carry the decision of the secretary of the interior into court. By vigorously opposing such action, and only by so doing, we were able to carry out the policy of properly

Source: Theodore Roosevelt, *The Autobiography of Theodore Roosevelt,* Centennial ed. (New York: Charles Scribner's Sons, 1913), pp. 197–200.

protecting the public domain. My successor not only took the opposite view, but recommended to Congress the passage of a bill which would have given the courts direct appellate power over the secretary of the interior in these land matters. . . . Fortunately, Congress declined to pass the bill. Its passage would have been a veritable calamity.

I acted on the theory that the President could at any time in his discretion withdraw from entry any of the public lands of the United States and reserve the same for forestry, for water-power sites, for irrigation, and other public purposes. Without such action it would have been impossible to stop the activity of the land-thieves. No one ventured to test its legality by lawsuit. My successor, however, himself questioned it, and referred the matter to Congress. Again Congress showed its wisdom by passing a law which gave the President the power which he had long exercised, and of which my successor had shorn himself.

Perhaps the sharp difference between what may be called the Lincoln-Jackson and the Buchanan-Taft schools, in their views of the power and duties of the President, may be best illustrated by comparing the attitude of my successor toward his Secretary of the Interior, Mr. Ballinger, when the latter was accused of gross misconduct in office, with my attitude toward my chiefs of department and other subordinate officers. More than once while I was President my officials were attacked by Congress, generally because these officials did their duty well and fearlessly. In every such case I stood by the official and refused to recognize the right of Congress to interfere with me excepting by impeachment or in other constitutional manner. On the other hand, wherever I found the officer unfit for his position, I promptly removed him, even although the most influential men in Congress fought for his retention. The Jackson-Lincoln view is that a President who is fit to do good work should be able to form his own judgment as to his own subordinates, and above all, of the subordinates standing highest and in closest and most intimate touch with him. My secretaries and their subordinates were responsible to me, and I accepted the responsibility for all their deeds. As long as they were satisfactory to me I stood by them against every critic or assailant, within or without Congress; and as for getting Congress to make up my mind for me about them, the thought would have been inconceivable to me. My successor took the opposite, or Buchanan, view when he permitted and requested Congress to pass judgment on the charges made against Mr. Ballinger as an executive officer. These charges were made to the President; the President had the facts before him and could get at them at any time, and he alone had power to act if the charges were true. However, he permitted and requested Congress to investigate Mr. Ballinger. The party minority of the committee that investigated him, and one member of the majority, declared that the charges were well-founded and that Mr. Ballinger should be removed. The other members of the majority declared the charges ill-founded. The President abode by the view of the majority. Of course believers in the Jackson-Lincoln theory of the presidency would not be content with this town meeting majority and minority method of determining by another branch of the government what it seems the especial duty of the President himself to determine for himself in dealing with his own subordinate in his own department. . . .

Woodrow Wilson

The Public Presidency

The makers of our federal Constitution followed the scheme as they found it expounded in Montesquieu, followed it with genuine scientific enthusiasm. The admirable expositions of the *Federalist* read like thoughtful applications of Montesquieu to the political needs and circumstances of America. They are full of the theory of checks and balances. The President is balanced off against Congress, Congress against the President, and each against the courts. . . .

. . . The presidency has been one thing at one time, another at another, varying with the man who occupied the office and with the circumstances that surrounded him. One account must be given of the office during the period 1789 to 1825, when the government was getting its footing both at home and abroad, struggling for its place among the nations and its full credit among its own people; when English precedents and traditions were strongest; and when the men chosen for the office were men bred to leadership in a way that attracted to them the attention and confidence of the whole country. Another account must be given of it during Jackson's time, when an imperious man, bred not in deliberative assemblies or quiet councils, but in the field and upon a rough frontier, worked his own will upon affairs, with or without formal sanction of law, sustained by a clear undoubting conscience and the love of a people who had grown deeply impatient of the regime he had supplanted. Still another account must be given of it during the years 1836 to 1861, when domestic affairs of many debatable kinds absorbed the country, when Congress necessarily exercised the chief choices of policy, and when the Presidents who followed one another in office lacked the personal force and initiative to make for themselves a leading place in counsel. After that came the Civil War and Mr. Lincoln's unique task and achievement, when the executive seemed for a little while to become by sheer stress of circumstances the whole government, Congress merely voting supplies and assenting to necessary laws, as Parliament did in the time of the Tudors. From 1865 to 1898 domestic questions, legislative matters in respect of which Congress had naturally to make the initial choice, legislative leaders the chief decisions of policy, came once more to the front, and no President except Mr. Cleveland played a leading and decisive part in the quiet drama of our national life. Even Mr. Cleveland may be said to have owned his great role in affairs rather to his own native force and the

Source: Woodrow Wilson, *Constitutional Government in the United States* (New York: Columbia University Press, 1908), pp. 56–81.

confused politics of the time, than to any opportunity of leadership naturally afforded him by a system which had subordinated so many Presidents before him to Congress. The war with Spain again changed the balance of parts. Foreign questions became leading questions again, as they had been in the first days of the government, and in them the President was of necessity leader. Our new place in the affairs of the world has since that year of transformation kept him at the front of our government, where our own thoughts and the attention of men everywhere is centered upon him. . . .

The makers of the Constitution seem to have thought of the President as what the stricter Whig theorists wished the king to be: only the legal executive, the presiding and guiding authority in the application of law and the execution of policy. His veto upon legislation was only his 'check' on Congress,—was a power of restraint, not of guidance. He was empowered to prevent bad laws, but he was not to be given an opportunity to make good ones. As a matter of fact he has become very much more. He has become the leader of his party and the guide of the nation in political purpose, and therefore in legal action. The constitutional structure of the government has hampered and limited his action in these significant rôles, but it has not prevented it. . . . Greatly as the practice and influence of Presidents has varied, there can be no mistaking the fact that we have grown more and more inclined from generation to generation to look to the President as the unifying force in our complex system, the leader both of his party and of the nation.

As legal executive, his constitutional aspect, the President cannot be thought of alone. He cannot execute laws. Their actual daily execution must be taken care of by the several executive departments and by the now innumerable body of federal officials throughout the country. In respect of the strictly executive duties of his office the President may be said to administer the presidency in conjunction with the members of his cabinet, like the chairman of a commission. He is even of necessity much less active in the actual carrying out of the law than are his colleagues and advisers. It is therefore becoming more and more true, as the business of the government becomes more complex and extended, that the President is becoming more and more a political and less and less an executive officer. His executive powers are in commission, while his political powers more and more center and accumulate upon him and are in their very nature personal and inalienable. . . .

He cannot escape being the leader of his party except by incapacity and lack of personal force, because he is at once the choice of the party and of the nation. He is the party nominee, and the only party nominee for whom the whole nation votes. Members of the House and Senate are representatives of localities, are voted for only by sections of voters, or by local bodies of electors like the members of the state legislatures. There is no national party choice except that of President. No one else represents the people as a whole, exercising a national choice; and inasmuch as his strictly executive duties are in fact subordinated, so far at any rate as all detail is concerned, the President represents not so much the party's governing efficiency as its controlling ideals and principles. He is not so much part of its organization as its vital link of connection with the thinking nation. He can dominate his party by being spokesman for the real sentiment and purpose of the country, by giving direction to opinion, by giving the country at once the information and the statement of policy which will enable it to form its judgments alike of parties and of men.

For he is also the political leader of the nation, or has it in his choice to be. The nation as a whole has chosen him, and is conscious that it has no other political spokesman. His is the only national voice in affairs. Let him once win the admiration and confidence of the country, and no other single force can withstand him, no combination of forces will easily overpower him. His position takes the imagination of the country. He is the representative of no constituency, but of the whole people. When he speaks in his true character, he speaks for no special interest. If he rightly interpret the national thought and boldly insist upon it, he is irresistible; and the country never feels the zest of action so much as when its President is of such insight and calibre. Its instinct is for unified action, and it craves a single leader. It is for this reason that it will often prefer to choose a man rather than a party. A President whom it trusts can not only lead it, but form it to his own views.

. . . If he lead the nation, his party can hardly resist him. His office is anything he has the sagacity and force to make it.

. . . [We] can safely predict that as the multitude of the President's duties increases, as it must with the growth and widening activities of the nation itself, the incumbents of the great office will more and more come to feel that they are administering it in its truest purpose and with greatest effect by regarding themselves as less and less executive officers and more and more directors of affairs and leaders of the nation,—men of counsel and of the sort of action that makes for enlightenment.

Abraham Lincoln

The Prerogative Presidency

Letter to A. G. Hodges (April 4, 1864)

My *dear Sir:* You ask me to put in writing the substance of what I verbally said the other day in your presence, to Governor Bramlette and Senator Dixon. It was about as follows:

"I am naturally antislavery. If slavery is not wrong, nothing is wrong. I cannot remember when I did not so think and feel, and yet I have never understood that

Source: John Nicolay and John Hay, eds., *The Complete Works of Abraham Lincoln*, Vol. 10 (New York: Francis D. Tandy Co., 1894), pp. 65–68. (Albert G. Hodges was editor of the Frankfort, KY, *Commonwealth*; this letter was used as a campaign document in the 1864 election.)

the presidency conferred upon me an unrestricted right to act officially upon this judgment and feeling. It was in the oath I took that I would, to the best of my ability, preserve, protect, and defend the Constitution of the United States. I could not take the
office without taking the oath. Nor was it my view that I might take an oath to get
power, and break the oath in using the power. I understood, too, that in ordinary civil
administration this oath even forbade me to practically indulge my primary abstract
judgment on the moral question of slavery. I had publicly declared this many times,
and in many ways. And I aver that, to this day, I have done no official act in mere deference to my abstract judgment and feeling on slavery. I did understand, however, that
my oath to preserve the Constitution to the best of my ability imposed upon me the
duty of preserving, by every indispensable means, that government—that nation, of
which that Constitution was the organic law. Was it possible to lose the nation and
yet preserve the Constitution? By general law, life and limb must be protected, yet
often a limb must be amputated to save a life; but a life is never wisely given to save
a limb. I felt that measures otherwise unconstitutional might become lawful by
becoming indispensable to the preservation of the Constitution through the preservation of the nation. Right or wrong, I assume this ground, and now avow it. I could
not feel that, to the best of my ability, I had even tried to preserve the Constitution,
if, to save slavery or any minor matter, I should permit the wreck of government,
country, and Constitution all together. When, early in the war, General Frémont
attempted military emancipation, I forbade it, because I did not then think it an
indispensable necessity. When, a little later, General Cameron, then Secretary of
War, suggested the arming of the blacks, I objected because I did not yet think it an
indispensable necessity. When, still later, General Hunter attempted military emancipation, I again forbade it, because I did not yet think the indispensable necessity had
come. When in March and May and July, 1862, I made earnest and successive appeals
to the border States to favor compensated emancipation, I believed the indispensable
necessity for military emancipation and arming the blacks would come unless averted
by that measure. They declined the proposition, and I was, in my best judgment,
driven to the alternative of either surrendering the Union, and with it the Constitution, or of laying strong hand upon the colored element. I chose the latter. In choosing it, I hoped for greater gain than loss; but of this, I was not entirely confident. More
than a year of trial now shows no loss by it in our foreign relations, none in our home
popular sentiment, none in our white military force—no loss by it anyhow or anywhere. On the contrary it shows a gain of quite a hundred and thirty thousand
soldiers, seamen, and laborers. These are palpable facts, about which, as facts, there
can be no caviling. We have the men; and we could not have had them without the
measure."

"And now let any Union man who complains of the measure test himself by
writing down in one line that he is for subduing the rebellion by force of arms; and
in the next, that he is for taking these hundred and thirty thousand men from the
Union side, and placing them where they would be but for the measure he condemns.
If he cannot face his case so stated, it is only because he cannot face the truth."

I add a word which was not in the verbal conversation. In telling this tale I
attempt no compliment to my own sagacity. I claim not to have controlled events,
but confess plainly that events have controlled me. Now, at the end of three years'

struggle, the nation's condition is not what either party, or any man, devised or expected. God alone can claim it. Whither it is tending seems plain. If God now wills
the removal of a great wrong, and wills also that we of the North, as well as you of
the South, shall pay fairly for our complicity in that wrong, impartial history will find
therein new cause to attest and revere the justice and goodness of God. *Yours truly,*
    A. Lincoln

Stephen Skowronek

The Presidency In The Political Order

Order and Time in Presidential Studies

The American presidency reflects nothing so clearly as the idiosyncrasies of personality and circumstance. The discrete dynamics of the men and *their* times are naturally
pronounced; the general dynamics that define the institution *in* time, correspondingly
obscured. This makes thematic analysis of the presidency peculiarly dependent on
uncovering broad-ranging patterns in institutional history. By isolating different
historical regularities we can locate different dimensions of the problem and significance of presidential action.

Sorting out these various dimensions of order in presidential history is one of
those basic conceptual exercises that tends to get lost in the divisions of contemporary scholarly discourse. . . . Still, it is possible to identify two broad-ranging
historical constructs at work in the current literature, and by distinguishing the
conceptions of institutional order and time that they bring to presidential studies,
we can begin to think in terms of other possibilities for organizing research.

Without question, the key organizing concept in the current literature is the
"modern presidency." As an analytic tool, the modern presidency construct relates
changes in international relationships, social relationships, and technological

Source: Stephen Skowronek, "Notes on the Presidency in the Political Orders" in
Studies in American Political Development, Vol. 1, pp. 286–302, 1986. Copyright © 1986 Yale
University Press, New Haven, CT. Reprinted by permission.

capacities to changes in the governing responsibilities, institutional resources, and political position of recent incumbents. The concept tracks the emergence of a new kind of presidential politics in recent years, and in so doing, it draws a fairly sharp distinction between what is past and what is still significant in presidential history. . . . The establishment of the Executive Office of the President in 1939 seems to have offered scholars the clearest benchmark of the modern order in presidential politics, for this event signaled a permanent alternation in the governmental purview and institutional operations of the office. As [Fred Greenstein] put it: "The transformation of the office has been so profound that the modern presidencies have more in common with one another in the opportunities they provide and the demands they place on their incumbents than they have with the entire sweep of traditional presidencies from Washington's to Hoover's."

The significance of the changes illuminated by the modern presidency construct is clear enough. But the modern/traditional dichotomy that it brings to presidential research remains a matter of analytic perspective, and like any other perspectives, its basic assumptions and limitations need always to be kept in view. Most obviously, the modern presidency construct consigns almost three-quarters of an already small universe of incumbents to virtual irrelevance. Moreover, by detaching incumbents after FDR from their predecessors and treating them as a coherent group, the modern presidency construct naturally attends to what the members of the group share; their differences, on the other hand, tend to get relegated back to the impenetrable idiosyncrasies of personality and circumstance. Finally, as the modern presidency construct defines the significance of the institution in terms of relationships that are emergent in American politics, it naturally submerges the significance of those that have been constant or recurrent.

In this regard, the more traditional "constitutional presidency" construct takes on special significance. Instead of a great historical disjunction, this construct carries a strong ascription of continuity and integrity in the institution over the entire course of its operation. In the constitutional construction of order and time, the presidency is situated as one institution operating in a fixed and enduring structure of separated institutions that share powers. Presidents are engaged in a perpetual and unresolvable struggle over the scope of their institutional prerogatives. The constitutional balance has tilted this way and that, and the constitutional order as a whole has adapted to new governing demands, but in its most fundamental aspects, the American Constitution has not "developed." The basic constitutional dynamics are timeless . . . This approach takes the imperial implications out of the emergence of the modern presidency and identifies in their place important linkages among institutional origins, institutional capacities, and contemporary institutional crises.

. . . When considered side by side the "modern presidency" and the "constitutional presidency" appear as two heuristic devices delineating distinct analytic positions and offering complementary insights into the subject at hand. Furthermore, by bringing two dimensions of presidential history to the center of attention, this juxtaposition immediately prompts consideration of others and, thus, opens the door to a range of complementary historical/structural investigations.

Political Order and Political Time

From this vantage point, we can begin to distinguish a specifically political dimension in presidential history. The president stands at the critical intersection between order and change in American politics. His office is vital to the security of interests in power, his action always a potential threat to previously established power arrangements. This perspective brings into view a somewhat different presidency, an "order-shattering," "order-affirming," "order-creating" institution that holds a pivotal place in the dynamics of systemic political change.[1]

A study of the presidency in these terms requires careful consideration at the outset of the analytic construction of order and time most appropriate to the task at hand. When we think thematically about the politics of presidential leadership, we are likely to think in terms of the demands and resources of the modern presidency and their relationship to the basic constitutional structure. But neither the modern nor the constitutional construction of presidential history directly addresses the presidency as an institution operating in a political order or the president as an actor in political time. . . .

I will begin with a conventional, albeit not uncontroversial, construction of political history. This scheme, often grounded in the dynamics of electoral alignments and party systems, divides American history into a succession of distinctive political regimes—the Jeffersonian (1800-28), the Jacksonian (1828-60), the Republican (1860-1932), and the New Deal (1932-80). In elaborating upon the ideas, interests, and institutions that have distinguished each of these regimes in the organization of our political life, scholars have pointed to the significance of the presidency in the ongoing process of regime construction and disintegration. In taking up this cue, we naturally focus on political relationships that have periodically recurred in American presidential history. There are, after all, several beginnings and several endings in this construction of order and time. . . .

What I am suggesting, then, is that . . . we approach the presidency as an institution that is mediated by the generation and degeneration of political orders, and that we approach presidents as leaders who actively intervene at various stages in this process. In this way, the modern period can be dissected as a sequence of political change, and the various political problems of presidential action presented in the modern period can be understood with reference to past sequences. Unlike the "constitutional presidency" construction of order and time, this perspective does not address presidential history as a piece; rather, it divides presidential history into distinct periods and distinguishes the different political opportunity structures for presidential action within each. Unlike the "modern presidency" construction of order and time, this perspective does not detach the modern incumbents from the rest and approach them as a coherent group; rather, it brings to the fore problems of political action that distinguish the modern presidents from one another and link them individually across historical periods to their counterparts in political time. When presidential history is broken into regime segments, and presidents are grouped together for an analysis informed by the similar positions they hold in political time, the past becomes something more than an extended prelude to the present and the modern presidents something more than a group apart.

The Dynamics of Political Development and the Structures of Presidential Leadership

Each regime begins with the rise to power of a new political coalition that is able to construct and legitimize a particular set of governing arrangements and, in so doing, to define relations between state and society in ways advantageous to its members. The dominant coalition then attempts to perpetuate its position by responding to changes in the nation at large through modifications and elaborations of its basic agenda. Once established, however, coalition interests can have an enervating effect on the governing capacities of these regimes. An immediate and constant problem is posed by conflicts of interest within the dominant coalition. The danger here, of course, is that attempts to elaborate the coalition's political agenda will focus a sectarian struggle, weaken regime support through factional disaffection, and open new avenues to power for the political opposition. A longer-range and ultimately more devastating problem is posed to changes in the nation at large that throw into question the dominant coalition's most basic commitments of ideology and interest. The danger here, of course, is that the entire political regime will be called into question as an inadequate governing instrument and then repudiated wholesale in a nation-wide crisis of political legitimacy.

Considering the history of the presidency in this light, two relationships stand out as especially significant for an analysis of the politics of leadership. First is the president's affiliation with the political complex of interests, institutions, and ideas that dominated state/society relations prior to his coming to office. Second is the current standing of these governmental arrangements in the nation at large. These relationships are, of course, always highly nuanced, but certain basic variations can be discerned. To get at them we might conceptualize the leadership problem with reference to those institutions with which political regimes are invariable identified in America, namely, the political parties. Using this shorthand, we can approach presidential history with two questions in mind: Is the president affiliated with the previously dominant political party, and how vulnerable are the governmental commitments of that party to direct repudiation as failed and irrelevant responses to the problems of the day?

From the answers to these questions, it is possible to specify four typical opportunity structures for the exercise of political leadership by a president. In the first, the basic governmental commitments of the previously dominant political party are vulnerable to direct repudiation, and the president is associated with the opposition to them. In the second, basic governmental commitments of the previously dominant political party are again on the line, but this time the president is politically affiliated with them. In the third, the governmental commitments of the previously dominant political party still appear timely and politically resilient, but the president is linked with the political opposition to them. In the fourth, the governmental commitments of the previously dominant political party again appear timely and politically resilient, and the president is affiliated with them. These four opportunity structures are represented in Table 10.1, with the "previously dominant political party" designated as the "regime party" for easy reference.

Table 10.1 The Political Structure of Presidential Leadership

Standing of the Regime Party's Commitments in the Nation at Large	Regime Party opposed	President's Relationship to the affiliated
vulnerable	politics of reconstruction	politics of disjunction
resilient	politics of preemption	politics of articulation

Each of these structured situations defines a different institutional relationship between the presidency and the political order, each engages the president in a different type of politics, and each defines a different kind of leadership challenge. In the discussion that follows, the presidents that best fit each type are grouped together. The object is to highlight the distinctive problems and dynamics of political action that seem to adhere to the institution in these situations, and not, of course, to deny differences in the ways incumbents actually approached these problems or grappled with these dynamics. Cross currents among the types will also be noted. The second point is that this typology does not offer an independent explanation of the historical patterns on which it draws. There is no accounting here for whether a regime affiliate or a regime opponent will actually be elected (or otherwise come into office), nor for when in the course of the nation's development a regime's basic governmental commitments will be called into question. . . . My purpose is to suggest the ways in which political structure has delimited the political capacities of the presidency and informed the significance of presidential action.

The *politics of reconstruction* has been most closely approximated in the administrations of Thomas Jefferson, Andrew Jackson, Abraham Lincoln, and Franklin Roosevelt. . . . They shared the most promising of all situations for the exercise of creative political leadership. Each came to power on the heels of an upheaval in electoral politics. More specifically, their victories were driven by widespread discontent with the established order of things and were potent enough to displace a long-established majority party from its dominant position in both Congress and the presidency. With political obligations to the past thus severed, these presidents were thrust beyond the old regime into a political interregnum where they were directly engaged in a system recasting of the government's basic commitments of ideology and interest. (It might be noted in passing that other elections that have also been classified as "critical" in terms of their effects on old political alignments were quite different in their political impact on the presidency. The election of 1896, reaffirming and extending as it did the Republican party's hold over the national government, is perhaps the most obvious case in point. William McKinley was not engaged in a political reconstruction but in the consolidation of the Republican regime.)

The political preeminence of the presidency appears to be most naturally pronounced, then, when the old regime has been discredited, when old alliances have been thrown into disarray, and when new interests have been thrust afresh upon governmental institutions. More important, however, is what the performance of leaders in this situation can tell us about the structured capacities of the presidency as a political institution. Order-shattering elections do not themselves shape the future, but they vastly expand the president's capacities to break the governmental commitments of the immediate past and to orchestrate a political reordering of the rules and conditions of state/society relations. It is significant in this regard that none of the presidents who have been engaged in this politics of reconstruction had much success in actually resolving the tangible problems that gave rise to the nationwide crisis of political legitimacy in the first place. Jefferson's attempt to deal with the problems at issue in the international crisis of 1798 proved a total failure; Jackson's attempt to deal with the long-festering problem of national banking precipitated an economic panic and ultimately exacerbated a devastating depression; Lincoln's proposed solution to the sectional conflict of the 1850s plunged the nation into a civil war; and Roosevelt's New Deal failed to pull the nation out of the Depression. But what these presidents could do that their predecessors could not was to redefine thoroughly the significance of the events they oversaw and the solutions they proposed. Released from the burden of upholding the integrity of the old regime, these presidents were not restricted in their leadership to mere problem solving. Situated just beyond the old regime, they reformulated the nation's political agenda as a direct response to the manifest failures of the immediate past and galvanized political support for the release of governmental power on entirely new terms.

The leadership opportunities afforded by this kind of political breakthrough are duly matched by certain characteristic political challenges. In penetrating to the core of the political system and orchestrating a political reordering of state/society relations, these presidents ultimately found it imperative to try to secure a governmental infrastructure capable of perpetuating the new order. The shape of the new regime will hinge on the way party lines are recast and on how institutional relationships within the government are reorganized, and it may be observed that the natural dovetailing of party-building efforts with efforts at institutional reconstruction is a distinctive mark of this leadership situation. The assertion of presidential control over these fundamentals of political reordering is problematic, of course, because the distillation of new power arrangements inherent in a "Court Battle," a "Bank War," or a military occupation crystallizes opposition as well as support. The point, however, is that in examining the politics of reconstruction we can look beyond the great deeds of great men. We can examine the expansive capacities of the presidency in a political interregnum where prior governmental commitments are most vulnerable.

The *politics of disjunction* has been most closely approximated in the administrations of John Quincy Adams, Franklin Pierce, James Buchanan, Herbert Hoover, and Jimmy Carter. . . . They share what might well be taken as the very definition of the impossible leadership situation. Rather than orchestrating a political breakthrough in state/society relations, these presidents were compelled to cope with the breakdown of those relations. Their affiliation with the old regime at a time when its basic commitments of ideology and interest were being called into question turned their office into the focal point of a nationwide crisis of political legitimacy. This situation imparted to them a consuming preoccupation with a political challenge that is really a prerequisite of leadership, that of simply establishing their own political credibility.

Each of the major historical episodes in the politics of disjunction has been fore-shadowed by a long-festering identity crisis within the old majority parties them-selves. The candidacies of Adams, Pierce, Hoover, and Carter were propelled to success more by default than by the enthusiasm of the traditional centers of party power. The exhaustion of the political orthodoxy of each regime is strongly suggested by the failure of stalwart party leaders to command authority and control the nomi-nating process. Also clearly in evidence is the cumulative toll that sectarian contro-versies within the dominant coalition can take on the credibility of the candidate in just assuming the role of party leader. But the distinctiveness of this juncture in political time . . . lies in changes within the nation that obscure the regime's rele-vance as an instrument of governance and cloud its legitimacy as caretaker of the national interest. Adams, Hoover, and Carter are, after all, presidents as notable for their personal determination to pull their respective regimes into a new era as they are for the weakness of their political connections to the party establishment. The fact that they each came to epitomize the bankruptcy of the old regime brings us face to face with the most perplexing and paralyzing of all leadership dilemmas.

In this situation, a Hobson's choice is presented between upholding the integrity of the old order and repudiating its basic commitments. On the one side, the presi-dent is all too easily stigmatized as a symptom of the nation's problems and a symbol of the failure of the entire regime; on the other, he is all too easily isolated from his most natural allies and rendered politically impotent. The stakes of innovation thus pit regime integrity directly against regime effectiveness, and the president shatters both by trying to respond to radically new governmental conditions within the re-ceived terms and conditions of political discourse. Herein lies an explanation for the striking propensity of presidents in this situation to grapple with great national issues as technical, nonpolitical problems, even when the political implications of the in-novations they propose necessarily involve significant departures from the govern-mental commitments of the past. Unable to address directly the most basic political question he faces—the regime's legitimacy—the president finds his capacity to pen-etrate national politics and mobilize support severely attenuated, and leadership is reduced to mere problem solving. In examining the politics of disjunction, then, we can look beyond the failures of individuals. We can come to terms with the con-stricted capacities of the presidency during the collapse of old political definitions and with the particular challenges faced by the president as leader of an enervated regime.

The *politics of preemption* has engaged a large number of presidents, some of the more aggressive leaders among them being John Tyler, Andrew Johnson, Woodrow Wilson, and Richard Nixon. The men in this grouping stand out as wild cards in American political history. As their experiences indicate, the politics of leadership in this situation are especially volatile, and perhaps least susceptible to generaliza-tion. Tyler was purged from the ranks of the party that elected him; Wilson took a disastrous plunge from the commanding heights of world leadership into the politi-cal abyss; Johnson and Nixon were crippled by impeachment proceedings. Of all the presidents that might be grouped in this situation, only Dwight Eisenhower finished a second term without suffering a precipitous reversal of political fortune, but this exception is itself suggestive, for Eisenhower alone kept whatever intentions he might have had for altering the shape of national politics well hidden.

As the leader of the opposition to a previously dominant party that can still muster formidable political, ideological, and institutional support, the president interrupts the working agenda of national politics and intrudes into the establishment as an alien power. The exercise of creative political leadership hinges on expanding and altering the base of opposition support, and here the leader is naturally drawn toward latent interest cleavages and factional discontent within the ranks of the regime's traditional supporters. These leadership opportunities are not hard to find, but the political terrain to be negotiated in exploiting them is treacherous. To preempt the political discourse of an established regime, the president will simultaneously have to maintain the support of the stalwart opposition, avoid a direct attack on regime orthodoxy, and offer disaffected interests normally affiliated with the dominant coalition a modification of the regime's agenda that they will find more attractive. Testing both the tolerance of the opposition and the resilience of the establishment, the leader openly tempts a massive political repudiation from both.

Compared to a president engaged in a politics of disjunction, the leader here has a much greater opportunity to establish and exploit a posture of political independence. Compared to a president engaged in a politics of reconstruction, however, he faces a much greater risk of political isolation. Probing alternative lines of political cleavage, the president may well anticipate new party building possibilities, but, short of a systemic electoral break with the immediate past, opposition leadership mainly has the effect of wreaking havoc on the established political regime. The example of Woodrow Wilson stands out for special attention in this regard, for the fortuitous rupture within the Republican party that brought him to power carried the strongest overtones of a reconstructive breakthrough. Wilson ably exploited the opportunities opened by Republican divisions and discontent among progressives to realize a monumental legislative program, but this achievement, worked as it was through the regular Democratic party, only held the Republican resurgence at bay. Even before the end of Wilson's first term, it was apparent that a reconstruction of the Democratic party along progressive lines was not in the cards and that his innovations would not have any transformative effect on the shape of national politics. Wilson explored new lines of independent political action with the public, and his program broached the possibility of recasting the political identity of the Democratic party; but the resilience of the old political divisions, and Wilson's own appreciation of their primacy, delimited and personalized both his political achievements and his ultimate collapse. . . .

The *politics of articulation* has engaged the largest number of presidents. . . . Here the presidency is the font of political orthodoxy and the president, the minister to the faithful. The opportunity for the exercise of political leadership lies in moving forward on the outstanding political commitments on the regime's agenda and in prodding the establishment to adjust to changing times. The corresponding challenge is to mitigate and manage the factional ruptures within the ranks of the regime's traditional supporters that inevitably accompany any new specification of regime purposes.

In each of America's major political regimes, there has been one particular episode of the politics of articulation that stands out, not only as typical of the problems and prospects this situation holds for presidential leadership but also as pivotal in the course of each regime's development. In the Jeffersonian era, it came in the first term of James Monroe; in the Jacksonian era, in the administration of James Polk; in the Republican era, in the administration of Theodore Roosevelt; in the New Deal era, in the administration of Lyndon Johnson. These men exercised power in especially propitious circumstances. At the outset of each of these administrations we find a long-established majority party reaffirmed in its control of the entire national government, and a national posture so strong at home and abroad that it left no excuses for not finally delivering on long-heralded regime promises. Each president thus set full sail at a time when it was possible to think about completing the unfinished business of national politics and realizing the regime's highest moral vision for the nation. But if a leadership project of culmination and completion suggests a great leap forward, it also implies the maintenance of certain fundamental political commitments. In these presidencies, a regime at the apex of its projection of national power and purpose became mired in the dilemmas of reconciling commitments with the expansive political possibilities at hand, and assiduous efforts by the president to serve all interests in the pursuit of new initiatives set off an explosion of conflicting expectations. Paradoxically, then, as these leaders pushed ahead with the received business of national politics, they formented deep schisms within the ranks and instigated real political changes that they could not openly address without aggravating the situation. On the verge of its fullest political articulation as a governing instrument, each regime was pulled into an accelerated sectarian struggle over the true meaning of orthodoxy.

. . . Whereas in the politics of reconstruction, the president stands opposed to the old regime and orchestrates the breakthrough to a new one, here the leader is pulled by the competing impulses to maintain the political regime and to fulfill its potential through innovation and change. Finally, just as every episode in the politics of preemption entices the leader to probe for reconstructive possibilities, every episode in the politics of articulation challenges the leader to hold at bay the specter of a political disjunction.

In this context, one cannot help but observe that James Polk, Theodore Roosevelt, and Lyndon Johnson each prematurely disavowed the further pursuit of political power. The balance between the creative and destructive capacities of leadership is so precariously poised in the politics of articulation that those most thoroughly possessed by the impulses to lead seem compelled to try to escape the consequences of their own actions. Political self-sacrifice appears in this light as a kind of personal absolution for the real political changes instigated by executive innovation. By voluntarily stepping out of political contention the president can assert the integrity of his faith in the pursuit of policies that will lead his natural allies to question it. The example of Theodore Roosevelt as he wrestled with the relationship between executive innovation and regime maintenance is perhaps most suggestive here. As president, Roosevelt launched his most vigorous reform efforts on the heels of an announcement that he would not run for reelection. He sought to secure his effort to turn the Republican party toward reform by handpicking his own successor, but this only passed to Taft

Roosevelt's own political problems with reconciling orthodoxy and innovation in the Republican regime. When Taft faltered, Roosevelt reentered national politics in the incongruous guise of an insurgent party-builder bent on displacing the old regime altogether. But despite his enormous popularity, he had even less success attacking established power broadside than he did trying to recast it from within. Roosevelt's insurgency proved both self-defeating and politically disastrous. . . .

Presidential Leadership as Creative Repudiation

A typology of the political structures of presidential leadership is useful to the extent that it illuminates a significant and relatively unattended historical dimension in which this most idiosyncratic of institutions has operated. Complementing our conceptions of the presidency as an institution operating in a constitutional order of separated institutions sharing powers, and an institution operating in a modern order of world power, expanded administrative capacities, and high technology, there is here at least a working conception of the presidency as an institution operating in a political order of changing party alignments, coalition agendas, and public discourse. Presidents, by their very nature as historical actors, seek to articulate and effect timely alterations in the previously established political order; but the politics of leadership emerges here as a contingency that hinges in large measure on the structure of relations among the incumbent, the old regime, and the nation at large.

If there is one overarching theme running through this framework, it is that the creative political capacities of the presidency are inextricably linked to the contingent political authority of the incumbent to challenge the governmental commitments of the immediate past. The underlying question in all presidential efforts to respond to the present and shape the future is always how much of the past (ideas, institutions, interests, and precedents) can be and must be called into question. Consider again in this light the extremes of failure and success in creative political leadership that get juxtaposed periodically in presidential history. John Quincy Adams and Andrew Jackson, James Buchanan and Abraham Lincoln, Herbert Hoover and Franklin Roosevelt, Jimmy Carter and Ronald Reagan—each of these pairs had to grapple with an especially stark confrontation between past and present in American national development, and each pair divides on the structured political authority of the president to repudiate the past.

The creative and destructive sides of presidential leadership seem to be most effectively and openly joined in a politics of reconstruction. But they are by no means absent in the other situations. By more closely attending to the double-edged character of executive innovation and the political determinants of executive authority, we may begin to formulate a clearer view of the presidency as a driving force of political change in its own right. The themes of the typology might ultimately be turned around to address directly the question of how the political dynamics of presidential leadership reflect back upon the broader political system. Here the various dispositions of the presidency in the political order would be marked as an essential counterpoint to the changing shape of electoral politics and party systems.

Endnotes

1. I have drawn these terms from Edward Shils's discussion of the "charisma of office" in traditional and legal rational societies. See Edward Shils, *The Constitution of Society* (Chicago, IL: University of Chicago Press, 1982), 119-42. My usage of "political order" deserves some clarification at this point for there are two closely related ideas implied by the term that need to be distinguished. First, we may speak of the historical political orders or political regimes that have dominated state/society relations in America for relatively long periods of time as durable arrangements of political interests, ideas, and institutions. In this way, scholars have traditionally spoken of the Jeffersonian era and the Jacksonian era as coherent and distinctive orders, and contemporary scholars have spoken of the New Deal political order extending over the modern period. I will so far as practical use the term *regime* to refer to these historical orders. At a more abstract level, it is possible to speak of the political order in terms of the regularities that have underscored the sequential generation and degeneration of these historical regimes. In this sense, the historical regimes are the materials out of which an overarching conception of political order as an analytic construct can be derived. Thus, to modify Shils's terms a bit, it might be more accurate to speak of the presidency in the political order as a "regime"-shattering, "regime"-affirming, "regime"-creating institution. The order is found in the recurrent patterns of regime change. It is this historically abstracted and analytic usage of the term *political order* that parallels the "modern" order and "constitutional order" as heuristic constructs drawn from presidential history.

S E C T I O N

SELECTING PRESIDENTS:
CAMPAIGNS, ELECTIONS,
AND MANDATES

Presidents are not born, they are made. They are survivors of a long, drawn-out, exhausting, and often humiliating process of presidential selection. With but one exception, all of the occupants of the Oval Office have been elected in their own right, either as president or as vice president. (The exception was Gerald R. Ford, who in 1973 was nominated by President Richard Nixon to replace Vice President Spiro Agnew, who had resigned; he was confirmed by Congress and became president the following year when Nixon himself resigned.)

The tortuous nomination and election process demands individuals of stamina, resilience, and an infinite capacity for constant exposure and even public embarrassment. Only the most driven and thick-skinned individuals will survive.

Such hurdles overwhelm many potential candidates. Indeed, most of the nation's most talented figures, even those already holding public office, decline to try for the presidency. Some decline to run for tactical reasons. In some recent selection cycles, very few of the individuals who would have been on an impartial handicapper's short list of qualified presidential aspirants actually made the race.

Other potential candidates may falter because they carry personal baggage of a controversial nature. In the 1960s, New York Governor Nelson Rockefeller was shunned by Republican kingmakers and primary voters, in part because he had divorced his wife in favor of a younger woman. Divorce apparently no longer disqualifies one (Ronald Reagan and John Kerry, among other contenders, were divorced). Nor do "youthful indiscretions" bar a candidacy; voters tended to overlook such matters concerning Presidents Bill Clinton and George W. Bush (though Clinton's were hardly "youthful"). In 2008, the talented former Florida Governor Jeb Bush sat out the race: his older brother's unpopularity in the White House had snuffed out the Bush family legacy, at least for the time being.

Still other potential candidates are disqualified because, despite their talents, they are simply unelectable. When in 1888, the British scholar and diplomat James Bryce wrote his famous work, *The American Commonwealth*, he entitled his third chapter, "Why Great Men Are Not Chosen Presidents." His proposition is at least as true today, more than a century later. In every generation, there are men and women of singular talent, skill, or vision who are simply unsuited to the rigors of electoral campaigns, or who disdain the indignities of modern presidential contests, or who for one reason or another prove unattractive to a large segment of voters.

The selection process has two distinct though closely related phases: *nomination* and *election*. The Constitution embraces a convoluted scheme—much modified by historical practice—for electing presidents; but no mechanism was contemplated for choosing candidates for the office.

Almost from the beginning, presidential candidates have been nominated by political groups: congressional factions at first, and then modern mass political parties through national conventions—whose delegates are chosen in various ways, but now mainly by statewide primary elections. It is fair to say that nominees are chosen by an interplay of forces: preferences of party leaders and core constituents that are mitigated by evidence of an individual's electability—as determined by opinion surveys, organizational and fundraising success, and primary election outcomes—all aimed a winning delegates to the parties' quadrennial conventions. Insofar as parties tend to be dominated by hard-core leaders or loyal groups, their candidate choices may not always square with what the general public might prefer. This is true even when candidates (or rather, delegates pledged to support them) are chosen by open primary elections, because participation levels at the nominating stage are often quite low.

The complicated rules of the nominating game are the product of several forces. Federal laws govern certain aspects of the process, especially with regard to nondiscrimination and campaign finance. By enacting rules, the parties themselves set standards for the selection process—for example, acceptable methods of selecting delegates, their fairness and representativeness, and so forth. But it is the states—influenced by state party organizations—that enact the laws specifying the details for selecting delegates. The states also control the timetable for selection—by primaries, conventions, or caucuses—during the presidential election year. Although the national parties have specified "windows" during which delegates are supposed to be selected, many states have been reluctant to comply.

These contests stretch over nearly six months, from January through June. The few early contests—most notably, the Iowa caucuses and the New Hampshire primary—command media attention, because they are first "real" tests of candidate strength. Formerly the state contests were scattered throughout the six-month period. Now, however, they tend to be bunched toward the beginning of the season, as politicians in the various states strive to maximize their influence over the selection. Students describe the process as "front-loaded": that is, winners are expected to emerge quickly. The 2008 nominating season was supposed to be dominated by "super Tuesday" (February 5), when contests occurred in 23 states (including California, Georgia, Illinois, and New York). Only 11 states scheduled contests after the end of March.[1]

The quick-result scenario worked in 2008 for the Republicans, whose delegates tend to be awarded in a winner-take-all fashion—that is, candidates who win majorities or even pluralities of popular votes tend to win all the state's delegates. The Democrats, however, labor under a proportional-representation system, in which candidates with at least 15 percent of the popular vote are entitled to their share of the state's delegates. In 2008, the leading candidates—Hillary Clinton and Barack Obama—rivaled in popular victories and delegate counts, so that the contest remained close to the end.

Candidates not only vie to win in these critical states, but also to solidify their support among their party's most loyal supporters—for example, feminists, Blacks, and Latinos for the Democrats, small businesspeople and religious conservatives for the Republicans (to name just a few such groups). Endorsements from well-known party or interest group leaders are one way of demonstrating such support. Finally, candidates strive to establish and maintain credibility through favorable poll results and successful fundraising. Each aspect of nominating politics is monitored, publicized, and interpreted by the press, who seem to have usurped the party leaders' traditional role in winnowing out candidates.

The nominating process is deeply flawed. It is long, chaotic, costly, and demeaning. It is influenced too much by early contests that, at least in the past, have occurred in unrepresentative states like Iowa and New Hampshire. Participation, even in primary elections, is unimpressive; the most likely participants tend to be those who are the most militant partisans or who are followers of organized interest groups. Many, perhaps most, of the nation's ablest leaders are unwilling to make the personal and financial sacrifices required to run the race.

In laying out the politics of nominations, James E. Campbell explains how they influence the conduct and outcomes of the general election contests. Historically, the easier the candidates' paths to party nomination, the more likely they are to prevail in the election that follows. Divisive nomination battles complicate the eventual winner's campaign strategy and financing. A unified party, on the other hand, bestows many blessings: enthusiastic party loyalists who decide early to support the nominee; an ability to direct funds toward the inter-party contest; and an absence of lingering criticisms supplied by former intra-party rivals.

In her essay, Lara M. Brown recounts the history of presidential nominations and how they developed. The Constitution made no explicit provision for how parties should determine their nominees for the presidency, so the process has changed over the decades depending on the political development of political parties. Primary elections were introduced in the early 20th century, but they did not come to dominate the process until the 1970s when reforms made them the main path for aspirants to win delegates to national party conventions and thus their party's nomination. Brown analyzes the many advantages enjoyed by "frontrunners," especially in today's front-loaded nomination schedule, and argues that frontrunners tend to win nomination.

The general election—pitting the parties' chosen candidates against one another—is a period of intense press scrutiny and frantic fundraising. Coverage of the game (or "horse race"), although especially prevalent at the nomination stage, outpaces substantive coverage throughout the campaign. Another problem is that press reports are increasingly dominated by reporters themselves, who allow the candidates less and less time to speak for themselves. In 1968, the average "sound bite"—a block of uninterrupted speech by a candidate—was all of 42 seconds. By 1992, according to one study, candidates were given only 7.3 seconds of uninterrupted time to speak.[2] Candidates and their handlers are not blameless: they strive for brief attention-getting phrases that have little relevance to real issues or achievable policies. Politics is a great game, to be sure, but to treat it or report it as merely a game has the inevitable effect of reducing voters to mere spectators and heightening their sense of alienation from the campaign and election.

National campaigns require huge amounts of money to finance all aspects of the candidates' and the parties' endeavors. The flow of money has not been stemmed by federal campaign finance rules. Spurred by scandals involving campaign money, Congress enacted the Federal Election Campaign Act (FECA) of 1974 (revised in 1976). The act provided for public funding (financed through taxpayers' check-off on their annual tax returns) and limited the spending of presidential candidates. In presidential primaries, matching public funds are available to each candidate who meets the eligibility requirement and agrees to overall spending limits. In the general election, candidates may opt for full campaign funding through the fund. Minor-party or independent candidates may receive a portion of full funding. The formula for them is based on past or current votes received. The law also provides funds for pre-convention campaigning and for national party conventions.

FECA's intent was thwarted by the Supreme Court (*Buckley v. Valeo*, 1976), which upheld the act's spending limits but struck down contribution limits as an abridgement of the First Amendment's guarantee of free speech. These rules were frequently violated by candidates of both parties. And unlimited giving to party committees for "party-building" purposes—"soft money"—could easily be re-channeled into candidates' campaigns.

Further campaign funding scandals led in 2002 to the Bipartisan Campaign Reform Act (BCRA). The law—essentially ratified by a closely divided Supreme Court (*McConnell v. Federal Election Commission*, 2003)—banned soft money contributions but raised contribution limits and also encouraged independent groups' participation in campaigns.

Most of the major candidates—including those in 2008—shunned public general election campaign funds in favor of exploiting huge networks of private contributors. Separate but parallel campaigns staged by independent groups supplied added funds, media appeals, and even personnel for get-out-the-vote (GOTV) drives. The result was campaigning funding that blew away all previous fundraising records. As Peter Francia, Gregory Fortelny, and Clyde Wilcox and Peter Francia explain, by December 2007, Hillary Clinton had raised more money than any candidate in history and had the commitment of most of the Democratic party's major fundraisers. But Barack Obama put together an unorthodox Internet fundraising campaign to supplement other techniques, and raised more money from small donors during the spring of 2008 than any candidate in history.

The 2008 election also marked the probable death of the public financing system. When Barack Obama refused federal funds in order to be able to spend unlimited amounts, he was able to outspend John McCain by a very sizable margin. It will be difficult for any leading candidate to accept the public grant in future campaigns, knowing that their opponent might raise several times that amount.

James Ceaser and Daniel DiSalvo analyze the victory of the Democratic Party in the 2008 elections and put the presidential election into historical perspective. They maintain that, although Obama's personal electoral victory was significant, it was not massive or unusual by historical standards. The congressional elections, coming after the Democratic congressional gains in the 2006 elections, reinforced a trend toward the Democrats. Nevertheless, 2008 was by no means a "realigning" election, and the durability of the Democratic advantage would depend on the outcomes of the 2010 congressional elections and the 2012 presidential contest.

Given the prevailing image—that campaigns are run by opportunists and reported by cynics—it might be hard to determine what meaning to attach to a candidate's victory or defeat. Yet candidates do attempt to interpret the results, giving them the most favorable "spin." Winning candidates—especially those who win big—view their victory as a public mandate endorsing certain policies and rejecting others. "The Myth of Presidential Mandate" is exploded by the distinguished Yale political scientist Robert A. Dahl. After recounting the history of presidents' claimed mandates, Dahl asks whether electoral results can accurately be construed as a reflection of the voters' policy views. The question is especially hard to answer for presidencies before about 1940—that is, before public opinion surveys became common. Since 1940, however, Dahl finds little support for the existence of presidential mandates regarding specific issues. More modestly, elections confer on presidents the right to establish their agendas and try to gain their adoption.

The linkage between campaigns and governing is further explored in Roger H. Davidson's essay, which focuses on the 2004 through 2008 elections and their aftermath. The strategic dilemma for campaigning—and governing—is whether to focus upon the core supporters (typically, ideologues of the left or the right) or appeal to the moderate center of the populace, the swing voters.

Core supporters are active and loyal, whereas centrists tend to be fickle and un-reliable at the polls. Most recent candidates—especially George W. Bush in 2004—have therefore chosen to appeal to their core voters in order to raise their enthusiasm and ensure their turnout. Centrist voters in 2004 were attracted to Bush's perceived leadership qualities and his vows to protect the U.S. from terrorist attacks—even though many of those same people opposed his policies.

Within a year of the 2004 balloting, Bush's strategy of catering to his core supporters—so successful over the first five years of his presidency— turned against him. Although he had initially promised to be a "uniter" of the people, he became a "divider."[3] The Iraq war—originally portrayed as an extension of the war on terror—dragged on and gradually lost public support. In 2006 and 2008, the Democrats took advantage of the political climate, which was favorable to them and unfavorable to Republicans. The Democrats took back control of Congress in 2006 and increased their margins in 2008. Barack Obama was swept into office with promises of "change we can believe in." Although he won some early, significant policy victories, his very ambitious agenda was opposed by most Republicans in Congress. If he were to win further policy victories in Congress, he had to keep together a fractious Democratic majority.

Selected Bibliography

Abramson, Paul R., John H. Aldrich, and David W. Rohde, *Change and Continuity in the 2004 Elections* (Washington, DC: CQ Press, 2006).

Ceaser, James W., *Red over Blue: The 2004 Elections and American Politics* (Lanham, MD: Rowman & Littlefield, 2005).

Fiorina, Morris P., with Samuel J. Abrams and Jeremy C. Pope, *Culture War? The Myth of a Polarized America* (New York: Longman, 2005).

Johnson, Haynes, and Dan Balz, *The Battle for America 2008* (New York: Viking, 2009).

Mayer, William G., ed., *The Making of the Presidential Candidates 2004* (Lanham, MD: Rowman & Littlefield, 2003).

Mayer, William G., and Andrew E. Busch, *The Front-Loading Problem in Presidential Nominations* (Washington, DC: Brookings Institution Press, 2003).

Nelson, Michael, ed., *The Elections of 2004* (Washington, DC: CQ Press, 2005).

Patterson, Thomas E., *The Vanishing Voter: Public Involvement in an Age of Uncertainty* (New York: Vintage Books, 2003).

Sabato, Larry J., *Divided States of America: The Slash and Burn Politics of the 2004 Election* (New York: Longman, 2005).

Wattenberg, Martin P., *The Rise of Candidate-Centered Politics* (Cambridge, MA: Harvard University Press, 1991).

Wayne, Stephen J., *The Road to the White House 2008* (Boston, MA: Wadsworth, 2008).

Endnotes

1. Democrats and Republicans vote on separate dates in some states.
2. Robert Lichter and Richard Noyes, *Good Intentions Make Bad News* (Lanham, MD: Rowman & Littlefield, 1996).
3. See Gary C. Jacobson, *A Divider, Not a Uniter* (New York: Pearson Longman, 2007).

James E. Campbell

Nomination Politics, Party Unity, and Presidential Elections

"In every American election there are two acts of choice, two periods of contest. The first is the selection of the candidate from within the party by the party; the other is the struggle between the parties for the place."

—James Bryce, *from The American Commonwealth,* 1891[1]

Many changes occurred in the nomination process and campaigning in the century before Lord Bryce made this observation and certainly many more in the century since. The presidential nomination process, first controlled by a caucus of the parties in Congress, later evolved into a system in which delegates chosen by the state parties effectively decided the nomination in national nominating conventions. Efforts in the late 1960s to reform the nominating process into a more open and democratic system led to a proliferation of primaries, and decentralized caucuses spread out over several months. In the 1980s, states moved their primaries and caucuses to earlier in the year, creating the compressed or front-loaded primary-dominated, postreform system that exists today. The basic sequence—a party nomination process followed by the general election—remained through all of these changes.

It also remained the case that the political parties' presidential nomination process is important in two respects. First, in our two-party system, among the many who might serve as president, the choice of who will serve is narrowed to the two candidates nominated by the major parties. Whoever is elected president in 2008 will be either a Democrat or a Republican, as it has been in every election since 1852.

Second, the nomination process is important because the way candidates are nominated affects their prospects of victory in the general election campaign that follows. This consequence of nominations is less fully appreciated. Whether a party quickly and enthusiastically unites behind its nominee or engages in a rancorous internal struggle over who should be the party's standard-bearer substantially affects the

---

Source: Original essay written for this volume.

nominee's chances in the general election campaign. The presidential nomination process is important in its own right for what it says about the political party, who controls the party, and what the party stands for. But it is also important as part of the larger electoral process, as the prelude to the general election campaign. Whether a candidate gets a head start or starts from behind makes a big difference to who wins the race.

The Post-Reform Nomination Process

There is no definite starting date for campaigns to win a political party's presidential nomination. Years before the nomination is formally made at a party's national nominating convention, potential candidates for the nomination explore their possibilities. They consult with advisors. They size up their likely competitors, both in their own party and the candidate from the opposing party who they might face in the general election. They talk with supporters and those who might contribute financially to their campaigns. They weigh their options: the likely costs and benefits, politically and personally, for the immediate election and down the road. Then they make their decision either to throw their hat in the ring, as Theodore Roosevelt colorfully described it, or to sit it out. Out of these individual deliberations, typically made more than a year in advance of the election, comes the field of candidates for the nomination contest.[2]

Once a candidate has decided to seek a party's nomination, the race is on, at least for that candidate. He or she must then recruit a campaign staff, clarify the campaign's message (the reason why voters in the party should choose him or her rather than someone else), raise millions of dollars to fund the campaign so that the message can get out to potential voters, develop a strategy to use the campaign's resources most effectively within the rules of the nomination process, and assemble a network of supporters and campaign workers across the nation and particularly in those states thought to be most important to winning the nomination. In order to win a party's nomination, a candidate must devise a strategy for winning a majority of delegates selected in the states through party caucuses and primary elections. In 2004, Democrats selected 4,353 delegates to their national nominating convention and Republicans selected 2,509 to theirs.[3] For most candidates, the nomination strategy means devising a way to win, or at least to exceed expectations, in the early nomination contests so that they can gain additional contributions, receive more media attention for their campaigns, attract more supporters, and drive opponents out of the race.

Even before a vote is cast in a caucus or primary, candidates try to develop positive expectations about their candidacies among the media and activists. They must cultivate an image as a viable candidate; someone that primary voters should seriously consider supporting. This is particularly important in a crowded field of contenders. This phase of the campaign has been called "the invisible primary" and the winner of the invisible primary (as seen in the pre-primary polls) is the candidate to beat for the nomination.[4]

The official process of selecting delegates begins with the Iowa caucuses in late January of the election year and a week later with the New Hampshire presidential primary. The process of delegate selection across the individual states (mostly by primary elections) extends for several months. In 2004, the official delegate selection process ended with a set of primaries in early June, about five and a half months after the Iowa caucuses. The nomination process officially ends when the delegates nominate the party's presidential candidate at the parties' national nominating conventions, traditionally held in July and August.

In reality, the nomination process is not this long. Although a few states still select delegates late in the spring and into the early summer months, most have moved their delegate selection processes earlier in the year to gain greater influence. This compression or front-loading of the delegate selection calendar is the result of many individual state and state party decisions. States that select their delegates later in the year (in April, May, or June) found that the eventual nominee had usually accumulated enough delegate votes to win the nomination before the state even held its primary or caucus. The incentive has been clear: If people want their state to matter in determining the parties' presidential nominees, they must select the state's delegates early in the year before the nominations are effectively settled. In 2004, 24 of the 36 states holding Democratic Party presidential primaries held them by the middle of March. Three-quarters of the delegates were selected in the seven weeks following the New Hampshire primary.[5]

This front-loading of the primary and caucus schedule has been a huge boon to front-running candidates. The compressed schedule now requires candidates to run in a large number of states at once, a feat only a candidate with a large national organization and lots of money can do well. The front-loading of the primaries and caucuses prevents long-shot candidates from exploiting early victories and gaining momentum. A frontrunner has the resources to recover from a setback; a lesser-known candidate does not have the time to gain significantly greater recognition, organizational strength, and resources before the next set of primaries and caucuses are conducted. As William Mayer has observed, "Not since Jimmy Carter's campaign in 1976 has a momentum-driven candidacy been successful"; and Carter's emergence from the pack of Democratic hopefuls in 1976 was before the front-loading of primaries began.[6]

The campaign financing system also provides a considerable advantage to front-running candidates, especially if they are able to raise enough money that they can afford to forgo federal matching monies (as George W. Bush, Howard Dean, and John Kerry did in 2004) and the regulatory strings that go with those funds. Long-shot candidates who accept federal matching funds for their contributions must observe numerous restrictions on how much they can spend in different states. As a result, these candidates are forced by the campaign financing system to pursue a suboptimal campaign strategy. That is, they must comply with restrictions on how much they can spend in different states as opposed to what might be the best strategy of spending to increase their chances of winning the nomination. Combining the front-loaded nomination calendar and the campaign financing system, the current nomination system is one that looks open to many candidates (lured into the process by the apparent openness of the primary dominated system) but is in reality a system strongly inclined toward frontrunners (when there is a frontrunner) and one that settles on a nominee several months before the summer conventions. The conventions, aside from establishing the party's platform on the issues and ratifying the choice of a vice-presidential candidate for the ticket, have evolved into more of a kickoff for the general election campaign than the close of the nomination process.

All Nominations Are Not Equal

As Lord Bryce observed, the nominating process in choosing the parties' presidential candidates is an important "act of choice." This is true as far as it goes, but it does not go far enough in reflecting the relation of the nominating system and the electoral process. The nomination system should be understood as part of the electoral process, rather than a distinct process providing the candidates for the general election. For a presidential candidate, the issue is not just *whether* you win your party's nomination, but *how* you win it. A presidential candidate's prospects in the general election hinge to a great extent on the amount of internal party unity coming out of the nomination. This is as true today—when nominations are effectively decided in the first few weeks in a flurry of presidential primaries and caucuses—as it was in the old days, when nominations were actually decided at the parties' national conventions.

A candidate who emerges from the nomination process with a unified party has five substantial advantages over a candidate who lacks a unified party at the outset of the general election campaign: votes in the bank, strategy, turnout, resources, and ammunition.

First, a substantial majority of voters decide how they will vote before the general election campaign gets underway. In the typical election between 1952 and 2004, about 43 percent of voters reported that they decided how they would vote before the conventions, and another 21 percent said they decided during the conventions.[7] In 2004, more than 70 percent of voters indicated that they had decided before or during the party conventions. A candidate with a unified party providing a significant base of committed voters to work from has a shorter distance to go in assembling an electoral majority than a candidate with smaller group of committed followers at the start of the campaign.

A unified party in the nomination phase of the campaign also provides a candidate with a strategic advantage. Elections cannot be won with the party's most loyal voters alone (its base) but cannot be won without them. Candidates must shore up support from those most likely to support them but then must reach out to win the votes of those undecided and swing voters. A candidate who already has a secure base has a head start in trying to win over uncommitted and wavering voters. Without a unified party, the candidate must build some enthusiasm in his or her base of support while simultaneously reaching out to swing voters. This is no easy task, particularly when appeals to the party's loyalists are generally more ideological than those that might appeal to more centrist voters.

A party unified at the outset also suggests greater enthusiasm for the candidate, and this may lead to higher partisan turnout on Election Day. On the other hand, a candidate whose partisans indicate more tepid support at the start of the campaign may have a more difficult time mobilizing these partisans to vote. Although most partisans will vote (if sometimes grudgingly), some of those who have mixed feelings about their party's nominee at the outset may not muster the effort to vote. Previous research indicates that the turnout rates of party identifiers of the winning presidential party are higher than otherwise expected, and the turnout rates of party identifiers of the losing presidential party are lower than otherwise expected.[8]

A candidate who is not seriously challenged for the party's nomination has the advantage also of directing campaign finances toward the cause of the general election campaign. A candidate fighting for the nomination does not have this luxury. Without a secured nomination, campaign money must be directed at fending off challengers within the party. The clearest recent example of this difference was the 1996 campaign. Whereas President Clinton was essentially unopposed for the Democratic Party's nomination, Senator Bob Dole had to battle a significant group of opponents for the GOP nomination. While Clinton used $30.4 million (not to mention substantial "soft money") essentially to get a head start to the general election campaign, Dole was forced to use his campaign's resources ($34.5 million) on battling his Republican opponents for the nomination.[9]

A candidate having a unified party at the outset also has an ammunition advantage of sorts. In a hotly contested nomination battle, fellow partisans make charges against each other that can be used by the opposing party's candidate during the general election campaign. One of the clearest examples of ammunition for the opposition coming out of a divided nomination contest is from the 1980 campaign. In the general election that year, Democrats frequently reminded voters that George Bush, Reagan's running mate and former competitor for the Republican nomination, had called Reagan's economic proposals "voodoo economics." Four years later, President Reagan used ammunition supplied in the Democratic nomination battle against his opponent, former Vice President Walter Mondale. While campaigning in Ohio in 1984, Reagan attacked Mondale's record by using charges leveled against him in the nomination campaign by nomination foe Senator Gary Hart. Reagan told the crowd: "My opponent has done a very good job of slipping, sliding, and ducking away from his record. But here in Ohio during the primaries, Senator Gary Hart got his message through by reminding you, the Ohio voters, of the true record. And I quote—he said, 'Walter Mondale may pledge stable prices, but Carter-Mondale could not cure 12 percent inflation. 'Walter Mondale,' he added, 'has come to Ohio to talk about jobs, but Carter-Mondale watched helpless as 180,000 Ohio jobs disappeared in the period between 1976 and 1980.' Now I didn't say that. Those are Gary Hart's words."[10]

Nominations Affect Elections

While these are plausible advantages for a candidate coming out of a more unified nomination process, do they really make a difference? What is the evidence that divided nomination campaigns and party disunity before the general election actually harms the nominee's chances of attracting votes in the general election? A number of studies have examined divisive primaries at the state level and have generally found that they hurt a candidate's vote in the general election, though there is some disagreement as to whether party disunity existing before the primary or disunity caused by the primary make the difference.[11] Martin Wattenberg has also examined the impact of party disunity with an interesting (but somewhat ad hoc) index of "nomination fighting" and concluded that "the candidate with the most united party won every election from 1964 to 1988."[12] In this section, we will examine the impact of party unity in presidential nominations on general election results over 136 years of electoral history using two different national measures of party satisfaction with its presidential candidate at the time of the nomination.

Unified or Divided Conventions

One measure of party unity in the nomination process is whether a majority of the party's convention delegates voted for the eventual nominee on the convention's first ballot. Although every convention since 1956 has produced a first ballot nomination, multiple ballots were common in earlier conventions. In the 22 presidential elections from 1868 to 1952, the major parties held 44 national conventions. The nomination was settled on the first ballot in 26 of these conventions, but at least a second balloting of the delegates was required in 18 conventions.[13] Of these 18 cases, we set aside elections in which a first ballot nomination was denied a candidate with a majority of delegate votes (because of the Democratic Party's two-thirds rule), elections in which multiple ballots were required in both parties' nominations, and the 1912 election in which the Republican Party was so divided that it split before the renomination of President William Howard Taft. This leaves nine presidential candidates in these 22 elections (41 percent of the elections) who were nominated by a divided convention (no first ballot majority) while their opponent was nominated on the first ballot of the opposing party's convention. Table 11.1 lists these nine, the lack of party unity about their nominations as reflected in the convention voting, and their fates in the general election. These are the candidates who might have been disadvantaged in the general election by party divisions over the nomination.

As the table indicates, the parties were more divided over some of these nominations than over others.[14] Probably the least divided of these divided conventions was the Republican convention of 1948. New York Governor Thomas E. Dewey, having won the Republican nomination four years earlier, went into the 1948 convention with 40 percent of the delegates supporting him on the first ballot.[15] His closest competitor for the nomination, Senator Robert A. Taft of Ohio, however, was a distant second with 20 percent of first ballot votes, and when Dewey picked up another 7 percent of the delegates on the second ballot, the momentum to a third ballot nomination was unstoppable.

At the other end of the spectrum were far more divided nominations. In 1868, Democratic Party delegates cast 22 ballots before turning in desperation to New York Governor Horatio Seymour who had received no delegate votes on the first ballot and only 7 percent of votes on the 22nd ballot before delegates switched their votes to make him the nominee. But perhaps the most divided nomination was the Democratic nomination of John W. Davis of New York in 1924 after 17 days and 103 ballots. The convention turned to Davis only after it became apparent that the northern urban wing of the party and the southern rural wing of the party could not abide each other's nominees.[16]

Despite differences in the extent of internal party divisions in the nomination period, candidates emerging from a divided nomination process (whether badly or horribly divided) clearly do not do well in the general election that follows.[17] Of the nine candidates who lacked a majority of delegate votes going into their party's nominating

Table 11.1 Elections with One Divided Major-Party Presidential Nominating Convention, 1868–1952

Year	Presidential Nominee	Political Party	Number of Ballots to Nomination	Nominee's Delegate Percent on 1st Ballot	Percentage of the Two-Party Popular Vote	General Election Outcome
1868	Horatio Seymour	Democratic	22	0 –	47.3	Lost
1876	Rutherford B. Hayes	Republican	7	8 (5th)	48.5	Won
1888	Benjamin Harrison	Republican	8	10 (4th)	49.6	Won
1896	William Jennings Bryan	Democratic	5	15 (2nd)	47.8	Lost
1916	Charles Evans Hughes	Republican	3	26 (1st)	48.4	Lost
1924	John W. Davis	Democratic	103	3 (15th)	34.8	Lost
1940	Wendell L. Willkie	Republican	6	11 (3rd)	45.0	Lost
1948	Thomas E. Dewey	Republican	3	40 (1st)	47.7	Lost
1952	Adlai Stevenson	Democratic	3	22 (2nd)	44.6	Lost

Note: A divided nominating convention is one in which multiple ballots were required to select the nominee, and the nominee did not have a majority of delegates on the first ballot. In two Democratic Party conventions (1876 and 1932) the nominee had a first-ballot majority, but multiple ballots were required because of the party's two-thirds rule. Both major parties had divided conventions in 1880, 1884, and 1920. Also, because of the Republican progressive bolt to Teddy Roosevelt's campaign in 1912, both parties are considered as having divided nomination contests in that year. The number beside the nominee's delegate percentage on the first convention ballot is the ranking of the eventual nominee on that first ballot.

conventions, only two were elected president: Hayes in 1876 and Harrison in 1888. In terms of the national popular vote, none of the nine presidential candidates received a popular vote plurality. Both Hayes and Harrison became presidents by virtue of their electoral vote majorities, but their opponents (Tilden and Cleveland) received more popular votes nationwide. The record could hardly be clearer: Parties divided over their nominations are in big trouble in the general election.

The Loyalty of Early Deciding Partisans

Although party divisions over its presidential nomination are less evident in national nominating conventions since 1952 (with the notable exception of the 1968 Democratic convention and possibly the 1964 Republican and 1972 Democratic conventions), the degree of party unity before the general election campaigns can be gauged more directly and accurately for recent campaigns through survey data. In every election since 1952, the American National Election Study (NES) has asked a national sample of voting age Americans about their party identification, if and how they voted for president, and when they decided how they would vote. Using these data, we can determine the percentage of party identifiers in both parties who decided how they would vote at or before the parties' nominating conventions and decided to vote for their party's candidate. This provides the basis for a relative measure of party unity at the time of the nominations. In many respects, this is the best measure of whether a party was truly divided in its nomination or otherwise failed to select a candidate who could generate enthusiasm within the party.[18] The relative index is computed as the percentage of early deciding Democrats who reported that they voted for the Democratic presidential candidate minus the percentage of early deciding Republicans who reported that they voted for the Republican presidential candidate.[19] A positive value indicates that Democrats were more unified around their nominee than Republicans were around theirs, and a negative value indicates that the Republicans exhibited more early party unity. Normally at least 85 percent of those who decide how they will vote before or during the conventions end up voting for their party's candidate, with early loyalty rates being a bit higher among Republicans.[20] Nevertheless, despite high rates of loyalty by early deciders within both parties, varying degrees of enthusiasm for their party's nominee cause differences in how uniformly loyal these early deciding partisans are from year to year.

The extent of party unity at the time of the nomination reflects several conditions. It reflects both the absolute enthusiasm for the party's nominee and the relative enthusiasm for the nominee compared to other candidates who competed or might have sought the party's nomination as well as reactions to candidates in the opposing party. It also reflects the roughness of the nomination campaign and any lingering ill will from it. Finally, it reflects the effectiveness of the nomination end game and the convention in reunifying the party behind its standard bearer. Conventions typically provide their nominees with a convention bump in the polls, especially for the party that was less unified and trailed in the polls.[21] A candidate who appeals to the party faithful more than the alternatives in or outside the party, has won the nomination without political bloodshed, and has energized the party with a positive nominating convention should have his or her party's early deciding voters firmly behind him or her and be well positioned to make a strong race in the general election.

Figure 11.1 plots the index of relative Democratic Party early unity against the Democratic candidate's actual national popular vote. It is clear that the relative extent of unity within the party at convention time is related to how well the party's candidate does in the November election. Going into the fall campaign, the more unified a party is relative to the opposing party, the greater the expected vote for its candidate. Historically, a party's presidential candidate can expect about 4 percentage points more of the two-party vote in November for every 10 percentage points of greater party loyalty than the opposition at the end of the nomination process. Moreover, the election's outcome hinges more on the relative party unity of those who decided how they would vote at the time of the nomination than the extent of party loyalty of those who decide how they will vote after the parties' nominating conventions.[22]

Each party benefitted by a large difference in party nomination unity in one election in this era. For the Democrats that election was 1964. That year, 95 percent of

Figure 11.1 Party Unity of Early-Deciding Party Identifiers and the General Election Vote, 1952–2000

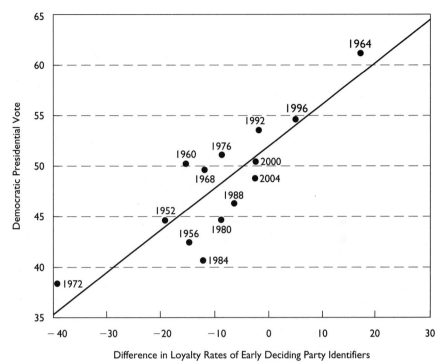

Difference in Loyalty Rates of Early-Deciding Party Identifiers

Note: The Democratic presidential candidate's vote is the percentage of the two-party national popular vote. The difference in loyalty rates of the early-deciding party identifies is computed as the percentage of early-deciding Democrats who reported voting for their party's candidate minus the percentage of early-deciding Republicans who reported voting for their party's candidate. Early deciders are those who indicated that they decided how they would vote at the time of or before the national conventions and who did not change their reported vote from their earlier stated vote intention. The data are from the National Election Studies and have been adjusted to the known national vote division. See Campbell, 2000, Appendix B and p. 98 entries for the 2000 election computed by the author. The regression of early loyalty difference and the general election vote has a constant of 52.15, a slope of .42 (P<.001), and an adjusted R-square of .73 (N=13).

Source: Original essay written for the volume.

Democratic Party identifiers who said that they decided how they would vote at the time or before the national conventions voted for their party's candidate Lyndon Johnson. Republicans that year faced a revolution from the right in the candidacy of Senator Barry Goldwater from Arizona. Goldwater's unabashed conservatism conveyed in his convention speech proclaiming "extremism in the defense of liberty is no vice," and his campaign slogan that "in your heart, you know he's right" threatened the party's moderates. Only 78 percent of the Republicans who decided how they would vote before the fall campaign began (about half of all Republicans) voted for Goldwater—compared to normal GOP loyalty rates in the middle to upper 90 percent range among early deciders. The relative disunity doomed the Goldwater candidacy.

At the other end of the early loyalty difference spectrum, Republicans enjoyed a large party unity advantage going into the 1972 campaign. Although Nixon had nominal opposition en route to his renomination, his support among early deciding Republicans was almost perfect (about 98.7 percent). The Democratic Party, in contrast, was in disarray. Much as Goldwater's candidacy had represented the conservative wing of the Republican Party, the candidacy of Senator George McGovern of South Dakota in 1972 represented the liberal wing taking control of the Democratic Party, alienating the party's moderates. Only 59 percent of early deciding Democrats voted for McGovern in 1972. Even when the extreme cases of 1964 and 1972 are set aside, the relative degree of party unity at the end of the nomination process is clearly important to the general election results.[23]

As noted previously, Republicans have generally benefitted from greater early party unity than Democrats over this period, though this appears to be changing. Of the 14 elections, Democrats were more united at the outset than Republicans in only two cases—the 1964 election and the 1996 Clinton-Dole race, both involving White House incumbents. In three other elections, the 1992 Clinton-Bush-Perot election, the 2000 Bush-Gore election, and the 2004 Bush-Kerry election, loyalty rates at the outset only mildly favored the Republicans. Overall, Democratic presidential candidates won popular vote pluralities in four elections in which they started the campaign with a party unity deficit. In 1992, with the help of the Perot candidacy and with just a slim Republican unity advantage (owing perhaps to the Buchanan nomination candidacy as well as Perot), Clinton defeated Bush (the elder). The other three Democratic vote pluralities without an early loyalty edge (1960, 1976, and 2000) were all very narrow.

The most raucous nomination battle of this period (and perhaps any other) was the 1968 Democratic nomination of Vice President Hubert Humphrey during the height of the Vietnam War protests. Protesters and the police in the convention city of Chicago battled in the streets, and bad tempers raged in the convention hall itself. While moderate liberals and more radical liberals fought for the nomination, the southern conservative wing of the party deserted to support Alabama Governor George Wallace as a third-party presidential candidate. While this divisive nomination battle undoubtedly hurt the party with its base and with potential swing voters, loyalty rates of early deciding Democrats were not as low as they had been in the 1950s when Dwight Eisenhower attracted Democratic voters away from Adlai Stevenson or as they would be four years later when George McGovern appeared too liberal to many party moderates. Nevertheless, early deciding Democrats were about 12 percentage points less committed to Humphrey than early deciding Republicans were to Nixon. The impact of the 1968 nomination battle was also evident elsewhere. The nomination conflict kept many Democrats from making an early decision. A smaller percentage of Democrats in 1968 had decided their votes at the time of the nomination than in any other election from 1952 to 2004; and of those Democrats who held off deciding, a smaller percentage ended up voting for the Democratic presidential candidate (54 percent) than in any other year. The end result was that Humphrey was unable to pull the badly damaged Democratic majority coalition together in time for the November vote and Republican Richard Nixon narrowly won the election.

In general, the differences in the degree of pre-campaign party harmony are not as great as they once were. In each of the six elections from 1952 to 1972, there were double-digit differences between the early loyalty rates of Democrats and Republicans for their respective standard-bearers. In the eight elections since 1972, only the Republicans in their support of President Reagan in 1984 had more than a 10-point advantage over their opponent in early party unity. Whether the result of the polarization between the parties causing disagreements within the parties to be set in perspective, or parties becoming more adept at handling internal divisions, or the partisan realignment making each party more ideologically homogeneous, the unity differences between the parties in recent elections have not been as pronounced as they had been.[24]

The Usual Beneficiary of Early Party Unity

If early party unity (whether exhibited by first-ballot nominations or by higher loyalty rates among early deciding partisans) is important for later electoral success, what candidates tend to enjoy an easy nomination, and what candidates tend to have a tougher time pulling their party together? Although situations within the parties change from year to year and with the ambitions and opportunities afforded various candidates under changing nomination methods and rules, incumbent presidents usually have an easier route to the nomination and a more united party as the fall campaign gets underway.

The incumbency advantage in having a unified party in the nomination stage of the election is evident in both the divided convention and the party loyalty of early deciding partisans. None of the nine presidential candidates in Table 11.1 who lacked a delegate vote majority on the first ballot of their nominating conventions were incumbents. In fact, none of the 17 presidential candidates who were nominated at multiple-ballot conventions from 1868 to 1952 were incumbent presidents.[25] In this span of history, there were only two exceptions to incumbents having a unified party. The first exception was the Republican Party in 1912 in which former president Theodore Roosevelt split from the Republican Party, leaving incumbent President William Howard Taft with only part of the Republican Party and a humiliating third-place finish in the general election (winning only the eight electoral votes of Utah and Vermont). The other exception was the Democratic Party in 1948, in which Democrats on both the left—under former Vice President Henry Wallace—and on the right—under South Carolina Governor Strom Thurmond—split from the party. President Harry Truman was left with the colossal task of pulling the party's coalition back together over the course of the campaign—a feat that he was able to accomplish. Nevertheless, Taft and Truman are the exceptions. Most incumbents have unified parties in their renomination and reelection campaigns.

Party unity behind incumbents is also generally evident in the voting loyalty of early deciding partisans in Figure 11.1. In elections since 1952, the relative early party unity for incumbents was about nine points higher than it was for their challengers.[26] Eight of the nine incumbents in this period entered the fall campaign season with a more unified party than their challengers.[27] This early unity advantage for incumbents translates into about a three-point advantage in the November vote. This is not to say that incumbents can take for granted a united party at the nomination stage. Incumbents have not always had an easy path to nomination. President Jimmy Carter in 1980 faced a serious challenge from Senator Edward M. Kennedy of Massachusetts. Republicans that year had an eight-point unity advantage among early deciding partisans, even though they had a crowded and contentious battle for their nomination. Reagan was opposed by George H. W. Bush, Howard Baker, and John Anderson, among others.

President Bush (the elder) in 1992 did not have an easy time of it either. Although Republicans who decided their votes early overwhelmingly supported his re-election (about 95 percent), many were unsure enough about their support that they held off making their decision. While typically more than 60 percent of Republicans have decided how they will vote at or before conventions, fewer than half of voting Republicans in 1992 felt comfortable enough about their candidate to reach an early decision. The only other modern election in which so few Republicans made an early decision was in 1964 when Lyndon Johnson defeated Republican Barry Goldwater in a landslide.

The Carter and Bush cases aside, incumbents since 1952 have had strong and early party backing from their party and this has helped their general election runs.[28] Eisenhower in 1956, Johnson in 1964, Nixon in 1972, Reagan in 1984, Clinton in 1996, and G. W. Bush in 2004 all had their parties firmly behind them as they embarked on their reelection runs.

Looking Back at 2004 and Ahead to 2008

Outcomes of general elections depend a great deal on the unity of the parties coming out of the nomination stage of the campaign. The candidate with the more unified party is better positioned to attract votes in the general election and incumbents normally have the more united party going into the election. This proved to be the case, albeit only slightly, in 2004. Both parties had grown polarized and were solidly unified behind their standard bearers before the campaign began, but Republicans were a bit more enthusiastic and united front in their support of President Bush than Democrats were for Senator Kerry.

On the Republican side, conditions favored party unity. President Bush was unopposed for renomination. Despite concerns about the conduct of the war in Iraq and about job creation at home, conditions tilted in favor of his re-election, and the case was felt particularly strongly within his party. Objective economic conditions were not much different from what they had been in 1996 when President Clinton was re-elected; a substantial majority of Americans favored Bush over Kerry when it came to conducting the war against terrorism.[29] Although President Bush's pre-campaign approval ratings with the general public were unimpressive (high 40s to low 50s), his standing with Republicans was rock solid. Among Republicans, the President's approval rating averaged an stratospheric 90 percent in Gallup polls from January through May, never dipping below 88 percent. Still mindful of the Clinton years and the razor-thin victory of 2000, Republicans rallied to Bush. Three-quarters of Republican partisans decided how they were going to vote before or at the time of the conventions, and 97 percent of them voted for President Bush, almost two points higher than in 2000. Republican unity and enthusiasm was also reflected in the number of Republicans reaching early vote decisions. Three-quarters of all Republican voters in 2004 decided how they would vote before the campaign began, a 16-percentage-point increase over 2000. Finally, Republicans' enthusiasm was evidenced in their turnout. For the first time since the NES began conducting their election year surveys in 1952, strong Republicans outnumbered strong Democrats among voters (though not among all respondents), and Bush carried the nine states in which turnout increased the most over 2000.

Nomination politics for the Democrats in 2004 were more complicated, but the party was also united as it entered the fall campaign. Unlike the Republicans, Democrats in 2004 had a wide field of candidates contesting for their party's nomination. Ten candidates sought the party's presidential nomination, with former Vermont Governor Howard Dean emerging as "the candidate to beat." This changed dramatically, however, in the week before Iowa. Democrats turned away from Dean and toward Senator John Kerry of Massachusetts. Kerry's more reserved and temperate demeanor convinced many Democrats that he had a better chance of defeating President Bush. Kerry finished first in both Iowa and New Hampshire. His support snowballed in the states that followed. Even with the front-loading of the nomination system, Kerry's momentum set him squarely on a course for the Democratic Party's presidential nomination.

Although the crowded field of candidates and their changing fortunes might suggest disarray among the Democrats, it was quite to the contrary. The party was uncertain about its leadership but not divided over it. The great concern among Democrats was for their candidate's electability. This spurred the overnight exodus from Dean to Kerry. Democratic Party unity was grounded in three factors. First, Democrats were unified ideologically. Both Democratic candidates and voters easily pledged their support for the party's standard bearer without reservation. Second, Democrats and Republicans were polarized, standing poles apart ideologically. With Democrats clearly the liberal party and Republicans clearly the conservative party, partisans saw a greater threat from the election of the opposition. This difference also had a personal dimension. Many Democrats had demonized President Bush from the time of his election and desperately wanted to avenge their loss in 2000. Finally, Bush was considered beatable, but not easily so. This made party unity of added importance to Democrats. Although there were some reservations about Kerry being too liberal, 70 percent of Democrats decided their vote before or at the time of the conventions (5 percent fewer than Republicans), and 92 percent of them (again, about 5 percent less than Republicans) supported their party's candidate. Democrats were slightly more united than they were in 2000 behind Al Gore but still not quite as united as the Republicans. With the number of partisans on each side now near parity, this slight early unity difference was important to President Bush's re-election.

As we look to the 2008 presidential election, there are be a number of differences from 2004. Most notably, with President Bush completing his second term, there is no incumbent in the race. Unlike 2004, the Republican field is wide open with no clear favorite, at least not several years away from the election. Circumstances are a bit different on the Democratic side. Though there are a number of candidates likely to seek the Democratic Party's nomination, many observers consider Senator Hillary Clinton to be the early frontrunner for the Democratic nod. Will Republicans divide over their nomination while Democrats unite behind the former first lady? If recent elections serve as a guide, both parties will fall squarely in line behind their candidates and the nomination of Senator Clinton may do as much to unite the Republicans as to unite the Democrats. American politics is now so polarized that upward of 70 percent of both Democrats and Republicans will decide which party they will vote for by the time of the conventions (if they have not already done so) and upward of 90 percent of them will stay with their party—whoever its nominee is. The only real question is how far "upward" both of these numbers are for each party, because in another close election that can spell the difference.

Acknowledgments

The author thanks Roger Davidson and Bill Mayer for their comments on an earlier version of this chapter.

Endnotes

1. James Bryce, *The American Commonwealth,* 2 Vols. (New York: Macmillan, 1891) v. 2: 170.
2. Michael G. Hagen and William G. Mayer, "The Modern Politics of Presidential Selection: How Changing the Rules Really Did Change the Game," in William G. Mayer, ed., *In Pursuit of the White House 2000: How We Choose Our Presidential Nominees* (New York: Chatham House, 2000), p. 25.
3. According to Wikipedia at http://en.wikipedia.org/wiki/U.S._presidential_nominating_convention (accessed October 1, 2005), there were 4,353 delegates and 611 alternates attending the 2004 Democratic National Convention in Boston between July 26 and 29 of 2004 and 2,509 delegates and 2,344 alternates attending the 2004 Republican National Convention in New York City between August 30 and September 2.
4. Arthur T. Hadley, *The Invisible Primary: The Inside Story of the Other Presidential Race: The Making of the Candidate* (Englewood Cliffs, NJ: Prentice-Hall, 1976). William Mayer also notes that "in seven of the last 10 contested nomination races, the eventual nominee was leading in the polls for at least a year before the Iowa caucuses." See William G. Mayer, "Forecasting Presidential Nominations or, My Model Worked Just Fine, Thank You," *PS: Political Science and Politics,* 36 (April 2003): 155.
5. Michael L. Goldstein, *Guide to the 2004 Presidential Election* (Washington, DC: CQ Press), p. 35–6.
6. Mayer, "Forecasting Presidential Nominations or, My Model Worked Just Fine, Thank You," p. 155. See also, Thomas E. Patterson, *The Vanishing Voter: Public Involvement in an Age of Uncertainty* (New York, Alfred A. Knopf, 2002): 114–15. John Kerry's wresting of the Democratic Party's frontrunner mantle from Howard Dean in 2004 indicates that

frontrunners are not invincible, at least before they have established their bona fides in an actual caucus or primary.

7. James E. Campbell, *The American Campaign: U.S. Presidential Campaigns and the National Vote* (College Station, TX: Texas A&M University Press, 2000): 8. The data are originally from the American National Election Studies from 1952 to 2004. The 2000 and 2004 time of decision for voters was calculated by the author.

8. James E. Campbell, *The Presidential Pulse of Congressional Elections,* second edition. (Lexington, KY: University Press of Kentucky, 1997): 183.

9. Stephen J. Wayne, *The Road to the White House 2000: The Politics of Presidential Elections* (Boston, MA: Bedford/St. Martin's, 2000): 54.

10. Ronald Reagan, *Public Papers of the Presidents of the United States.* (Washington, D.C.: U.S. Government Printing Office, 1987): 1511.

11. See, Richard Born, "The Influence of House Primary Election Divisiveness on General Election Margins, 1962–76," *The Journal of Politics,* 43 (August 1981): 640–55; Patrick J. Kenney and Tom W. Rice, "The Relationship between Divisive Primaries and General Election Outcomes," *American Journal of Political Science,* 31 (February 1987): 31–44; and James I. Lengle, Diana Owen, and Molly W. Sonner, "Divisive Nominating Mechanisms and Democratic Party Electoral Prospects," *The Journal of Politics,* 57 (May 1995): 370–83. See also, Lonna Rae Atkeson, "Divisive Primaries and General Election Outcomes: Another Look at Presidential Campaigns," *American Journal of Political Science,* 42 (January 1998): 256–71. Atkeson examines the national effects of divisive primaries and finds no significant effect once economic and presidential evaluations are taken into account. Her study ranges from 1936 to 1996. The problem with these findings is that primary divisiveness probably said very little about nomination divisiveness when primaries were a minor component in the nomination process, as they were before 1972. For example, Lyndon Johnson in 1964 had highly unified party behind him, but ran in very few primaries and received less than 18 percent of the primary total vote (see, Moore, Preimesberger, and Tarr, *Congressional Quarterly's Guide to U.S. Elections, fourth edition,* v. 1: 350). Several others have claimed that the same factors hurting a candidate's nomination success or primary vote also hurt the candidate's general election vote and that the divisiveness of the nomination is a reflection of party disunity rather than a cause of it. See Andrew Hacker, "Does a 'Divisive' Primary Harm a Candidate's Election Chances?" *American Political Science Review,* 59 (March 1965): 105–10; James E. Piereson and Terry B. Smith, "Primary Divisiveness and General Election Success: A Re-Examination," *The Journal of Politics,* 37 (May 1975): 555–62; and William G. Mayer, *The Divided Democrats: Ideological Unity, Party Reform, and Presidential Elections* (Boulder CO: Westview, 1996), pp. 43–71. Although these studies indicate that the expression of party disunity (by the divided primary vote) is not the major cause of party disunity in the nomination phase, the analyses do not rule out nomination divisiveness as contributing to or reinforcing disunity. The main point here, in any case, is that party disunity, however caused, at the time of the nomination is extremely damaging to the general election prospects of the nominee.

12. Martin P. Wattenberg, "The Republican Presidential Advantage in the Age of Party Disunity," In Gary W. Cox and Samuel Kernell, *The Politics of Divided Government* (Boulder, CO: Westview Press, 1991), pp. 39–55. Wattenberg creates a five point index of nomination fighting from four dummy variables based on a rough coding of whether there were early primary contests, late primary contests, a convention battle, and a healing vice presidential choice. The index was coded for the 14 candidates in the seven elections from 1964 to 1988. I examined the difference in Wattenberg's index for candidates running in the same year and compared it to the early loyalty difference index. The two were surprisingly highly correlated (r 5 .85), adding a degree of confidence in both measures.

13. The data on the conventions and delegate vote counts come from Moore, Preimesberger, and Tarr, *Congressional Quarterly's Guide to U.S. Elections,* v. 2: 441–641.

14. These divided nominations were about as likely to be in the Democratic Party (4) as Republican Party (5) and were about as likely to involve running against an incumbent (5) as running for a open seat (4).

15. Like the 1912 election, the 1948 case might also be set aside because the Democratic Party splintered before its first ballot nomination of Harry Truman. The southern conservative wing bolted and ran Strom Thurmond as a Dixiecrat candidate and the progressive wing bolted and ran former Vice President Henry Wallace as a presidential candidate. Even without the 1948 case, the record of divided conventions of one party is eight major party candidacies without a single popular vote plurality.

16. For a colorful history of the 1924 Democratic convention see Robert K. Murray, *The 103rd Ballot: Democrats and the Disaster in Madison Square Garden* (New York: Harper and Row, 1976).

17. For an alternative assessment of the impact of divided conventions see Paul T. David, Ralph M. Goldman, and Richard C. Bain, *The Politics of National Party Conventions* (Washington, DC: The Brookings Institution, 1960), pp. 221–39.

18. The ideas of a divisive nomination and the lack of party unity at the nomination stage are conceptually distinct. That is, a party may not be unified behind its nominee because of a divisive nomination process or some other reason. It is quite possible that the nomination process failed to generate enthusiasm for a candidate because of the candidate, the candidate's positions on the issues, or the candidate's poor prospects for election. The point here is that whatever causes a lack of party unity at the time of the nomination, that disunity is very harmful to the candidate's chances in the general election.

19. The NES data have been corrected for their differences from the actual reported presidential popular vote. Leaning independents are counted as party identifiers with the party they lean toward. The adjustments and the adjusted data used to compute the loyalty rates are in Campbell, *The American Campaign: U.S. Presidential Campaigns and the National Vote*, pp. 62–3, 98, appendix B. Because third-party support can draw votes from a party's candidate, loyalty rates were based on votes for all candidates. The 2000 and 2004 data were calculated by the author from the NES studies. The 2000 early loyalty rate for Democrats was 92.4 percent and the early loyalty rate for Republicans was 95.3, for a difference of 22.9 percentage points. The 2004 early loyalty rate for Democrats was 94.1 percent and the early loyalty rate for Republicans was 96.9, for a difference of 22.9 percentage points.

20. Wattenberg in "The Republican Presidential Advantage in the Age of Party Disunity" using a very different measure also finds that Republicans throughout much of this period exhibited greater unity in support of their presidential candidate than did Democrats.

21. James E. Campbell, Lynna L. Cherry, and Kenneth A. Wink, "The Convention Bump," *American Politics Quarterly* 20 (July 1992): 287–307; and Campbell, *The American Campaign: U.S. Presidential Campaigns and the National Vote*, pp. 145–51. The updated analysis of the later study indicates that frontrunners (those with more unified parties) typically have received about a 4 percentage point boost in the polls after their conventions, while trailing candidates (those with less unified parties) typically get a 7 percentage point bump. The analysis finds that about a third of the net bump carries through to the November vote and two-thirds is dissipated in the weeks following the conventions.

22. A regression accounting for variance in the Democratic candidate's two-party popular vote was estimated using the relative loyalty differences among early deciding party identifiers and the relative loyalty differences among late deciding party identifiers (those deciding their votes after the conventions or changing their vote from their pre-election vote intention). The coefficients for the loyalty differentials were .34 for the early deciders and 20 for the late deciders (with standardized coefficients of .73 for the loyalty of early deciding partisans and .35 for the loyalty of late deciding partisans). Both were statistically significant at p, .02, one-tailed and the adjusted R^2 was .81 (N 5 14). Adding the difference of the percentage of Democratic and Republican identifiers voting increases the adjusted R^2 to .98. The difference in early party loyalty was again the most important variable, more important that the difference of the percentage of Democratic and Republican party identifiers in the electorate. The standardized coefficients were .74 for the early loyalty difference, .51 for the later loyalty difference, and .41 for the difference of the percentages of Democratic and Republican identifiers among all voters.

23. Excluding both the 1964 and 1972 landslides, an equation with both the early and late party loyalty differences and the difference of the percentage of Democratic and Republican party identifiers in the electorate still accounts for 98 percent of the vote variance. The standardized coefficients were .47 for the early loyalty difference, .80 for the later loyalty difference, and .52 for the difference of the party identifiers among voters.
24. I discuss the staggered realignment toward competitive balance in "Party Systems and Realignments in the United States, 1868–2004," *Social Science History*, forthcoming.
25. These include the nine candidates in Table 11.1 plus the seven of the eight candidates nominated by multiple-ballot conventions in elections in which both parties had divided conventions (1880, 1884, 1912, and 1920) and the two candidates nominated by multiple-ballot conventions even though they had a first-ballot majority (Tilden in 1876 and Franklin Roosevelt in 1932).
26. The 8.9 percentage point advantage in early party unity for incumbents is the median value of the early party loyalty difference between each of the nine incumbent-candidates and their challengers between 1952 to 2004.
27. President Carter in 1980 was the exception who had a less unified Democratic Party than the his opponent Ronald Reagan.
28. Two other cases in recent times also may qualify for incumbent trouble. President Lyndon Johnson in 1968 undoubtedly would have faced a seriously divided party had he sought renomination. Also, President Gerald Ford in 1976 faced a serious challenge from Ronald Reagan. Despite this challenge however, Republicans were more united at the close of the nomination process in 1976 than were Democrats. Jimmy Carter's emergence from a crowded field of Democrats that year left many Democrats still skeptical at the time of the nomination.
29. I evaluate the evidence of the pre-campaign conditions more thoroughly in "Why Bush Won the Presidential Election of 2004: Incumbency, Ideology, Terrorism, and Turnout," *Political Science Quarterly* 120 (Summer 2005): 219–41.

12

Lara M. Brown

A High-Speed Chase: Presidential Aspirants and the Nomination Process[1]

The modern presidential nomination process tends to be both chaotic *and* fairly predictable. Like watching the police pursue a car at high speeds on television, the anticipation derives from knowing what could happen (a fiery crash or a shootout) rather than from what usually does (an arrest). Mesmerized by the chase, viewers often wonder

Source: Original essay written for this volume.

whether the lead car will escape, hit another vehicle, or drive off the road. Similarly, though election observers know that few frontrunners lose their party's nomination, most continue to entertain such questions as: who has the momentum; who has the most money; who holds the lead in the polls; what states will matter most; and will the frontrunner will stumble, an underdog will attack, or a dark horse will emerge?

This contradictory state of affairs grew out of the reform efforts that began with the McGovern-Fraser Commission in 1968 and led to the proliferation of state primaries and party caucuses,[2] but is largely attributable to one consequent trend: front-loading (the propensity of more and more states to schedule their nomination contests early in the electoral cycle), which shows no signs of abating in the near future.[3] Prior to describing the effects of front-loading and the campaigns of George W. Bush in 2000 and John F. Kerry in 2004, this essay considers the history of the nomination process and the reforms undertaken to include rank-and-file partisans in the quadrennial national party conventions from the perspective of the presidential aspirants.[4] Looking at the 2008 nominating calendar, it appears that the political parties have lost control of the process and that they are on the verge of adopting reforms that would establish a single national primary day for the 2012 presidential cycle and beyond. Thus, the high-speed chase, which began in earnest in 1980, has not only sped up, but shows no signs of slowing down.

The History of Nomination Process and the Reforms since 1968

The Constitution provides no mechanism for nominating presidential candidates.[5] Instead, it describes a selection process whereby temporary electors from each state (chosen in a method devised by their state legislature) meet in their respective states, vote for president (and later vice president as well) and send their sealed ballots to Washington.[6] If no candidate receives a majority of the electoral votes cast, then the House of Representatives (voting by state delegations, rather than by individual member) selects the president, choosing from the five (later this number was reduced to three) candidates who earned the most electoral votes.[7]

Reflecting on these procedures, it appears that the Framers thought that future candidates worthy of the position would be honorable men of national standing (similar to George Washington), who would wait for the Congress to inform them of the electors' (or if need be the House's) choice for president.[8] It seems they also believed that the Electoral College, as the procedures came to be known, would deter unsavory cabals[9] and deny unworthy candidates of the office.[10] This federal structure of temporary electors, however, ended up making presidential aspirants, who proved ambitious and creative, more political than reticent. Looking to secure an electoral vote majority, presidential aspirants expanded and exploited the two nascent political parties (Federalists and Republicans).[11] Further, once the political parties were developed, then only partisans could credibly vie for the presidency. As John H. Aldrich explains: "The standard line that anyone can grow up to be president may be true, but it is true only if one grows up to be a major party nominee."[12] Thus, since at least 1796 (if not since 1792), presidential aspirants have had to first capture their party's nomination (win the confidence of enough of their fellow partisans to become the nominee), if they desired to win the presidency (use the party apparatus to gain the majority of electoral votes in the states).

Although the current process for securing the nomination from one of the major political parties is quite complex (governed by federal laws, state laws, and party rules, which often change between election cycles), it began rather informally. A small network of notables who shared a similar governing philosophy and were active in national politics, coalesced around one candidate they felt was worthy of the presidency.[13] After the 1796 election, however, when a lack of party coordination among the Federalists resulted in Thomas Jefferson, the Republican nominee, becoming the vice president under John Adams, the Federalist nominee, the political parties began to formalize their nominating processes.[14]

In 1800, members of Congress began meeting in partisan caucuses to recommend party nominees for president. This method, known as the "King Caucus," continued for several presidential cycles, eventually failing in 1824. It had likely worked early on because the country was relatively small and the national political elite—mostly members of the "founding generation"—were held in high esteem. The Federalists last nominated a candidate for president, Rufus King, in the 1816 election. In 1820, the Republican, James Monroe, had no organized opposition (he earned all but one of the electoral votes cast). By 1824, factions had emerged within the Republican Party, and few partisans remained in favor of members of Congress making the nomination decision.[15] Later that year, Andrew Jackson earned a plurality of electoral votes, but he lost the presidential election to John Quincy Adams, who was chosen by the House of Representatives. Adams's presidential selection provided the final blow to the legitimacy of the congressional caucus—which had chosen Treasury Secretary William Crawford over the other, better known contenders: Adams, Jackson, and Henry Clay.

With no formal process in place, Andrew Jackson secured nominations from several state legislatures before the 1828 election. Although these state legislative endorsements likely served as a precedent for state-based delegations nominating candidates at national conventions, the Anti-Mason Party provided the model for a national party convention in 1831.[16] The following year, the Democratic Party (formerly the Democratic-Republicans) held its first national convention. The Whigs (formerly the National-Republicans) followed suit in 1836, and when the Republicans formed in the 1850s, they joined in the tradition in 1856. Quadrennial national party conventions have been held ever since. Even though these national conventions opened up the political parties to state-based elites, participation by rank-and-file partisans was rare. National delegates were chosen at state party conventions and state delegates were chosen at local party conventions. Further, most of the decisions, including whom should receive the presidential nomination were made in the "smoke-filled backrooms" by state or local party bosses, who served as delegates and traded votes for favors, such as federal pork and patronage.

In 1896, Republican presidential aspirant William McKinley – aware of the growing Populist movement in the country and looking for a way around the machines – decided to run on a slogan of "the People against the Bosses." He won the Republican Party's nomination by garnering the delegate votes of southern Republicans, who had mostly been neglected by the party's elite.[17] He then went on to win the presidency. While McKinley altered the power bases within the Republican Party, the Progressive Party led the nation in opening up the presidential nomination process to more voters. In 1901, Florida's legislature enacted a law, allowing rank-and-file partisans to vote for national convention delegates. Fifteen years later, in 1916, presidential primary elections were held in 26 states.[18] Even though the national conventions in these years became more representative of rank-and-file partisans, party elites continued to determine their outcomes. Not only were these delegates chosen in primaries not bound to vote for any specific candidate, but the primary elections themselves had not attracted as much support as the reformers had thought they would (turnout was often low). During the 1930s, many states repealed their statutes. In addition, Franklin Roosevelt – as both an aspirant and a president – pushed for several reforms in the Democratic Party, encouraging a more "professional" approach to politics and campaigning.[19] While his approach undermined many of the party bosses, it also entrenched a new group of party elites who were active and involved between elections, meaning that rank-and-file partisans were once again excluded. Primary elections came to be regarded as vehicles by which presidential aspirants could demonstrate their electoral viability to party elites. In 1960, for example, John F. Kennedy, a Catholic, showed he was electable with his strong performance in primaries (especially in Protestant West Virginia).

In 1968, Vice President Hubert Humphrey won his party's nomination after a raucous national convention in Chicago that included protestors, riots, and police brutality. The turmoil erupted in part because Humphrey had not entered any primary elections. Although he had the support of President Lyndon Johnson and the convention delegates, he did not have the support of the rank-and-file activists or the anti-war (Vietnam War) wing of the party who were not represented inside the convention hall in large numbers.[20] The convention delegates attempted to resolve the party's split by forming a commission to consider and propose new nomination rules. George McGovern, a senator from South Dakota and a presidential aspirant who had challenged Humphrey for the nomination after Senator Robert F. Kennedy had been assassinated, was named the chair.

The McGovern-Fraser Commission (Donald Fraser, a representative from Minnesota, took over for McGovern when the latter decided to run for the 1972 presidential election) came forward with recommendations in 1970 that required states to: ensure that delegates were chosen in the same year as the convention; give "adequate public notice" about delegate selection; include individuals as delegates who had traditionally been discriminated against (affirmative action); and use proportional representation in the awarding of pledged delegates to candidates in primaries and caucuses. In the years following the commission's report, many states adopted presidential primaries because they ensured that the composition of the state's delegation would not be challenged by the national party as violating the "fair reflection rule."[21] By 1976, more than 70 percent of delegates were awarded in these types of contests.[22] The Democratic rules were modified again after the 1980 election to formalize the "window" for holding nominating contests, establish a threshold percentage of the vote for earning delegates, and create a new group of delegates who could change their votes at any time, called "super delegates" or PLEOs – party leaders and elected officials. These latter reforms came about because the national party felt that some of the reforms used in 1972 and 1976 had not worked as they had hoped.[23]

The changes made to the state laws governing the Democratic Party's nomination process more often than not ended up affecting the Republican Party's nomination process because throughout most of the 1970s and 1980s, Democrats controlled the majority of the state legislatures and passed these electoral laws. As a result, by the 2000 presidential election, both political parties selected over 85 percent of their respective national convention delegates through primary elections in over forty states.[24] Though the Republicans maintain some differences in their procedures (no affirmative action requirement, no PLEOs, most states award delegates by winner-take-all and not proportional representation), both parties appear to be struggling with front-loading: the major consequence of all of these reforms.

A Wild Course: The Front-loaded Nomination Process

As was mentioned at the outset, front-loading has both predictable and chaotic effects. On the predictable side, front-loading tends to increase the cost of elections; stretch the length of the electoral cycle; compress the decisive time-frame; and depress turnout in states that come later in the process. Taken together, these trends have led to a less deliberative nomination process, because the voting is over nearly as quickly as it begins.[25] Front-loading also helps lock-in aspirants who lead in the early public opinion polls, amass large numbers of elite endorsements, receive ample media coverage, and raise substantial sums during the "invisible primary"[26] time frame.[27] These aspirants become known as front-runners, and as Andrew E. Busch and William G. Mayer note: "Of all the candidates who have been nominated since 1980, *every one* of them can plausibly be regarded as, if not *the* front-runner, at least one of the top-tier candidates."[28] This list of frontrunners includes not only incumbent presidents who have run for re-election (Reagan in 1984, G. H. W. Bush in 1992, Clinton in 1996, and G. W. Bush in 2004), but also partisans who have been thought to be the heir apparent (G. H. W. Bush in 1988, Dole in 1996, Gore in 2000, and G. W. Bush in 2000). That said, there have been cycles in which frontrunners lose (Humphrey in 1972 and 1976); outsiders capture momentum (Reagan in 1976, Kennedy in 1980, McCain in 2000, and Dean in 2004); and dark horses catch the light late and win (Dukakis in 1988, Clinton in 1992, and Kerry in 2004).[29] It is just that typically these events occur before the majority of voters have either cast a ballot or have even noticed that there is a nomination race underway, which undermines the intended purpose of the reforms.[30]

Still, a front-loaded nomination process that relies on aspirants earning delegates by winning pluralities in primary elections (or caucuses) in nearly every state is not a staid production. State parties (and state legislatures) tend to do battle with each other and the national parties as part of their attempts to secure an early spot on the nominating calendar, which provides them with the opportunity to disproportionately influence the process and garner tangible benefits, like increased media coverage, economic gains, and specific policy concessions from the aspirants.[31] With the exception of the Iowa caucus and the New Hampshire primary – contests that have traditionally been held first[32] – each election cycle produces a different ordering, as well as clustering of the states, which tends to confuse not only elected officials, party leaders, and journalists, but also the candidates and the voters. The confusion is multiplied by the fact that each state determines the electoral rules and timelines for its nomination contest (whether they will hold a primary or a caucus, the number of signatures required to be on the ballot, amount of the filing fee, filing deadline, absentee, and early vote procedures, etc.). This situation requires each presidential aspirant to have a flexible and competent campaign staff that can stay on top of the varying rules and processes of each state.

Providing an example, Table 12.1 compares the 2000 nomination calendar with the 2008 calendar. In 2000, Iowa was in January, New Hampshire was in February, and 15 contests were held on March 7, designated "Super Tuesday."[33] By the end of February, 12 states had voted. In 2008, five contests were held in January, including Iowa and New Hampshire on the third and the eighth of the month, and 24 contests were held on February 5 or "Tsunami Tuesday." By the end of February, 43 contests had taken place. Contrasting these cycles with 1976 provides a stark contrast: Iowa held their caucus in late January and New Hampshire held their primary in late February, and then only five states held contests in March. Thus, a large majority of states held their contests between April and July.

Because a front-loaded system tends to advantage the front-runner, presidential aspirants frequently find themselves in a position in which they cannot afford to wait – for fear that the candidate field becomes too settled – to jump into the race. Practically speaking, they begin campaigning the day after the midterm election, though most spend many more years positioning for a run. Aspirants compete with one another for money, media attention, professional consultants, and campaign staff. On the trail, they look to win the support of party notables, affiliated interest groups, and rank-and-file activists. Generally, the better the aspirants do in all of these competitions, the more likely they are to prevail in the nomination contests. Thus, aspirants work hard and start early, trying to earn the front-runner label.

During the invisible primary, these competitions are the focus of the media's coverage. Journalists report on the "horserace" (who is leading, gaining, or falling behind in the polls – where, and by how much) and rely a great deal on what may be thought of as campaign gossip (who has endorsed whom, who is working for whom, and whose positions are winning over the party's activists) for evidence. They also use the candidates' quarterly fundraising reports and the public opinion polls as evidence of the aspirants' standing in the campaign. The problem with these measures, however, is that they tend to reinforce the frontrunner's advantage. Poll favorites – frontrunners – have an easier time obtaining political contributions and media attention, which then leads to higher poll numbers, more money, and more media attention. This snowballing effect tends to continue through a front-loaded calendar until the numerous rapid-fire contests affirm that frontrunners tend to win party nominations. Augmenting this

Table 12.1 Comparison of the 2000 and 2008 Presidential Nomination Contest
Calendars

2000	State Contest	2008	State Contest
		January 3	Iowa
		January 5	Wyoming (R)
		January 8	New Hampshire
		January 15	Michigan
		January 19	Nevada
			South Carolina (R)
January 24	Iowa		
	Alaska (R)		
		January 26	South Carolina (D)
		January 29	Florida
February 1	New Hampshire	February 1	Maine (R)
February 5	Delaware (D)	February 5	Alabama
			Alaska
			Arizona
			Arkansas
			California
			Colorado
			Connecticut
			Delaware
			Georgia
			Idaho (D)
			Illinois
			Kansas (D)
			Massachusetts
			Minnesota
			Missouri
			Montana (R)
			New Jersey
			New Mexico (D)
			New York
			North Dakota
			Oklahoma
			Tennessee
			Utah
			West Virginia (R)
February 8	Delaware (R)		
		February 9	Kansas (R)
			Louisiana
			Nebraska (D)
			Washington*
		February 10	Maine (D)
		February 12	District of Columbia
			Maryland
			Virginia

(Continued)

Table 12.1 *Continued*

2000	State Contest	2008	State Contest
February 19	South Carolina (R)	February 19	Hawaii (D) Washington Wisconsin
February 22	Arizona (R) Michigan (R)		
February 27	Puerto Rico (R)		
February 29	North Dakota (R) Virginia (R) Washington		
		March 4	Ohio Rhode Island Texas Vermont
March 7	California Connecticut Georgia Hawaii (D) Idaho (D) Maine Maryland Massachusetts Minnesota (R) Missouri New York North Dakota (D) Ohio Rhode Island Vermont		
		March 8	Wyoming (D)
March 9	South Carolina (D)		
March 10	Colorado Utah Wyoming		
March 11	Arizona (D) Michigan (D) Minnesota (D)	March 11	Mississippi
March 12	Nevada (D)		
March 14	Florida Louisiana Mississippi Oklahoma Tennessee Texas		
March 21	Illinois		
March 25	Alaska (D)		
April 4	Pennsylvania Wisconsin		
April 15–17	Virginia (D)		
April 22	Kansas (D)	April 22	Pennsylvania
May 2	District of Columbia Indiana		

(Continued)

Table 12.1 *Continued*

2000	State Contest	2008	State Contest
	North Carolina		
		May 6	Indiana
			North Carolina
May 9	Nebraska		
	West Virginia		
		May 13	Nebraska (R)
			West Virginia
May 16	Oregon		
		May 20	Kentucky
			Oregon
May 23	Arkansas		
	Idaho (R)		
	Kentucky		
		May 27	Idaho (R)
		June 3	New Mexico (R)
			Montana*
			South Dakota
June 6	Alabama		
	Montana		
	New Jersey		
	New Mexico		
	South Dakota		
		June 7	Puerto Rico (D)

* Washington held caucuses on February 9, 2008, in which 51 percent of Republican delegates were selected and 100 percent of Democratic delegates were selected. The state also held a primary election on February 19, 2008. Similarly, Republicans held caucuses and selected delegates in Montana on February 5, 2008. The state also held its primary on June 3, but the outcome of this contest for Republicans was non-binding.

Sources: Information adapted from the National Association of Secretaries of State, *Primary Calendar*, January 15, 2008 update, see http://nass.org/index.php?option=com_content&task=view&id=74&Itemid=210 (accessed February 8, 2008) and from *Presidency2000: Calendar of Elections and Events*, see http://www.politics1.com/ primaries2k.htm (accessed February 8, 2008).

effect, frontrunners are better able than their opponents to capitalize on any momentum generated from winning (or beating expectations) and/or rebound from any stumble, because they are better positioned both financially and organizationally.[34]

It could, however, be worse. Not the front-loading, which is likely to continue, but its results: that well-known, experienced politicians who are strategically inclined, tactically competent, tireless workers, are those who tend to win their party's nomination. It is also fair to say that while the reforms have encouraged front-loading and have led to a less deliberative process, they have also managed to increase the representation of the delegates at the national party conventions and the number of partisans engaged in the nomination process, which were two of the reformers' goals.[35] Thus, although many are still dissatisfied with the process, because they believe that they either do not influence their party's decision (i.e., those who participate in contests that occur later on the calendar often are not able to affect the nomination) or do not have many choices (few aspirants continue to campaign after Iowa and New Hampshire), more Americans have more opportunities to weigh in on the choice of their president than at any time in the country's history.

An Unstoppable Ride: The Republican Nomination of George W. Bush in 2000

Mr. Bush's candidacy began like a rumor, evanescent and insubstantial but growing on thousands of tongues. Partly, on its own, and partly orchestrated by Mr. Bush's political strategist, Karl Rove, the bandwagon began to move: Governors dropped by to pay their respects, speaking invitations poured in, policy experts and Republican gurus came by to bless the noncandidacy, and abruptly he found himself under much greater scrutiny than ever before.

–The New York Times *Journalist Nicholas Kristof*[36]

By the time George Walker Bush won his gubernatorial reelection in November of 1998 in Texas, he had been the clear frontrunner for the Republican nomination for the 2000 presidential election for over a year.[37] He had led in the first poll, which was conducted in the summer of 1997.[38] He had garnered "the top billing, and the coveted Saturday night speaking slot, at a three-day Republican gathering" in Indianapolis, Indiana, in August of 1997, about which a journalist noted that his time slot had not gone "to the Speaker of the House [Newt Gingrich] or to a former Vice President from this state [Dan Quayle] or to the party's Vice Presidential nominee from last year [Jack Kemp]."[39] Bush had cemented his position by amassing "a campaign war chest of $13 million" by the end of the year.[40] Thus, long before the presidential race kicked off, Bush had earned frontrunner status.

Bush made his reputation and became a politician to watch (for a presidential run) during the 1994 election, when he defeated Ann Richards who was "a popular and savvy incumbent."[41] According to Stanley A. Renshon, Bush "orchestrated the removal of all his potential Republican opponents. He did it quickly with a series of rapid behind-the-scenes maneuvers . . . It was over before most people realized it was happening."[42] Bush ran on "four major themes: educational reform, reforming the juvenile justice system, welfare reform, and tort reform," which were not the typical Republican issues of lower taxes and less government.[43] When he won, Bush's governing strategy impressed most observers. He reached out to the Democratic Lieutenant Governor Bob Bullock as he developed his legislative program. Together, these aspects played into the notion that Bush was a bridge-builder and a different kind of conservative who bore little resemblance to the "radical" Republicans leading the Congress under Speaker Newt Gingrich.[44]

Bush sought to enhance this image during his reelection campaign in 1998. At an event in Midland, Texas, in August of 1997, he told the crowd that he lived on the "sunrise side of the mountain . . . I've been true to my philosophy, which is conservative and compassionate and full of hope."[45] On election night, he earned 69 percent of the vote and did well among constituencies not typically favorable to Republicans, including African-Americans, women, and Hispanics.[46] Thus, Bush provided "light to Republicans after a dreary [1998] election," when the Democrats gained seats in the House of Representatives, bucking the historical trends, which predict losses for a president's party in the midterm elections.[47]

To his credit, Bush did more than bask in the media glory lauding his gubernatorial successes. In fact, it is fair to say that he catapulted himself into the frontrunner position by aggressively preparing for the presidential race and not waiting until he announced his exploratory committee in March of 1999 to get to work. As Judith S. Trent explains:

> Bush undertook a series of tutorials to learn more about federal and foreign policy, he spoke at selected Republican state and regional conferences, and he raised money – a lot of money. In 1997 and 1998 Bush began building a financial network by inviting groups of eight fund-raisers to have lunch with him in Austin. The group was called "the Pioneers," and they consisted of 150 supporters who each agreed to raise $100,000 to help finance the governor's exploratory committee . . . long before the primaries began, Bush had raised $23 million, breaking all previous Republican records. Moreover, by September of 1999, the governor had collected endorsements from 23 of the 31 Republican governors and 169 of 277 Republican members of Congress.[48]

Bush's significant achievements on the presidential campaign front likely intimidated his rivals and helped him to clear the field. For while Elizabeth Dole (former Senator Robert Dole's wife and former cabinet member), former Tennessee Governor Lamar Alexander, Representative John Kasich from Illinois, and former Vice President Dan Quayle had launched presidential exploratory committees in 1999, each pulled out of the race before the end of the year – before the Iowa caucus. As a result, Bush had only two serious competitors heading into the nomination contests: businessman, publisher Steve Forbes and Senator John McCain of Arizona. While both Gary Bauer, former head of the Family Research Council, and former Ambassador Alan Keyes, continued pursuing the Republican nomination and pushing the social conservative message, each were polling in the low single digits and were not considered serious contenders.

George W. Bush also surrounded himself with a dedicated and experienced team of professionals. First and foremost was Karl Rove, a well-known Texas political consultant whom Bush had met more than 20 years earlier and who had worked for him when he was governor. Second was Karen Hughes who met Bush when she was the executive director of the Texas Republican Party from 1992 to 1994. She went to work on his 1994 gubernatorial campaign, and afterward she worked for Bush as his communications director in the governor's office. Third was Joe Allbaugh who came on board in 1994 and who "was to be the enforcer [in Bush's presidential effort]. His job was to make sure the campaign ran flawlessly, and it did. He took care of the internal systems of the campaign. Rove took care of the road map, and Hughes handled the driving."[49]

Although Bush campaigned only six days in Iowa between March 15 and August 2, 1999, he won the straw poll in August, defeating Steve Forbes and Elizabeth Dole.[50]

On January 24, 2000, Bush won the Iowa caucuses with 41 percent of the vote, and Forbes came in second. Interestingly, neither aspirant garnered much momentum from their Iowa wins, because neither had exceeded the media's expectations, which had been raised because both had similarly placed in the straw poll months earlier. Over the next eight days as the focus turned to New Hampshire, John McCain, who had come in fifth in Iowa, because he had largely ignored the state, began to "receive a large amount of favorable media attention."[51] Appealing to Independents and moderate Republicans, McCain pulled off an upset in New Hampshire on February 1, beating Bush by over 18 percentage points (48 to 30 percent). Shortly thereafter, Forbes and Bauer pulled out, which left Bush and McCain in mostly a two-way race (Keyes stayed in and participated in a few debates).

Though McCain was riding a wave of support, the Bush campaign had been prepared for such an occurrence. According to *The Washington Post* Journalist Terry M. Neal, by December 1999, Bush had "a volunteer army approaching 4,000 people to organize events, work the phones, hand out fliers, and get people to the polls in each of the early primary states." His advisors believed that McCain would "have little time to take advantage of that momentum [from a win in an early primary] and mount an effective campaign in other states, where Bush ha[d] an overwhelming money and organizational advantage." Further, when "Bush was asked about McCain's 'two state-strategy' of focusing on New Hampshire's primary on February 1 and South Carolina's on February 19," he responded: "I have a fifty-state strategy," and with over two weeks to regroup and redeploy their assets before the next contest, Bush proved that his campaign was unstoppable.[52]

As Bush and McCain moved into South Carolina, the campaign messages became more frequent and more negative. Bush had a strong base of support among evangelical Christians and when he spoke at Bob Jones University, a religious fundamentalist college, McCain attacked him for implicitly endorsing the school's known intolerance toward Catholics and its policy against interracial dating.[53] The Bush campaign allegedly responded with a "push poll"[54] that used a racially charged attack to smear McCain.[55] Additionally, both Bush and McCain "spent millions of dollars in South Carolina . . . [as did] at least twelve different interest groups."[56] McCain, however, went too far in his attacks and his "intemperate outburst instantly alienated large blocs of Christian conservatives, delivering them en masse to Bush in subsequent primaries."[57] Even though McCain won Michigan, Massachusetts, Arizona, Rhode Island, Connecticut, and Vermont, Bush beat him in the rest of the early contests, including California, New York, Missouri, and Ohio, which secured the nomination. By the end of June, Bush had also raised $96 million and had broken all fundraising records up to that point.

George W. Bush's nomination campaign provides the textbook example of an aspirant who established himself as the frontrunner early during the invisible primary and used his formidable resources to ensure that he would prevail nationwide once the contests got underway. As Stephen J. Wayne points out, aspirants who want to win the delegate race should, "plan far ahead, concentrate efforts in the early contests, raise and spend big bucks early, gain media attention, develop a deep and wide organization, monitor public opinion, and design and target a distinctive appeal."[58]

Though Bush lost New Hampshire to McCain, the window of time between New Hampshire and South Carolina (18 days) was not long enough for McCain's campaign to capitalize on his win. Although there is the possibility that had these contests been scheduled more closely together (i.e., the calendar was *more* front-loaded) that momentum alone could have put McCain over the top, it seems unlikely for the reasons discussed by Busch and Mayer, which relate to the fundraising and organizational advantages of frontrunners.[59] At the end of the day, Bush had to fight fiercely to capture his party's nomination. Still, he won and this could have been predicted by his frontrunner status as early as the summer of 1997.

A Demolition Derby: The Democratic Nomination of John F. Kerry in 2004[60]

By late January of 2003, Senate Minority Leader Tom Daschle and former Democratic Presidential nominee Al Gore had bowed out of the 2004 presidential contest, while Senator John Kerry of Massachusetts, Senator John Edwards of North Carolina, Representative Dick Gephardt of Missouri, and former Vermont Governor Howard Dean had established exploratory committees, declaring their intentions to run for the Democratic nomination. Once again, the previous year's midterm election had served as an unofficial launch date for the presidential aspirants who were taking their campaigns seriously, though unlike the 2000 Republican contest, there was not a clear frontrunner. Even so, a *The New York Times*/CBS poll of Democratic National Committee Members – party insiders – taken in December of 2002 showed Kerry leading the field with 23 percent, Edwards at 8 percent, Gephardt at 5 percent, Dean at 4 percent, and former Vice Presidential nominee Joseph Lieberman at 2 percent.[61] In short, Kerry was an early favorite, but he was far from being the prohibitive favorite.

Like Bush, Kerry had been laying the groundwork for a presidential campaign for some time. In February of 2002, *New York Times* Journalist Richard Berke covered the California State Democratic Convention and noted the already large number of likely presidential aspirants in attendance. He wrote: "Of those here, Mr. Kerry has been the most unabashed about his plans, and his address showed it. He joked: 'A number of you have asked me if I had any interest in running for the most powerful office in the land. But I want to make it clear to all of you today, I have no interest at all in being secretary of state of Florida.'"[62] With Kerry at the convention in Los Angeles were other talked about potential candidates like Edwards, Daschle, and California Governor Gray Davis. Kerry even made fun of the situation, saying: "Gore would have been here, folks, but to make sure Democrats are protected for '04, somebody had to be moved to an undisclosed location."[63] Aside from being humorous, Kerry's comment suggests what many political observers thought at that time: that if there was a front-runner in the Democratic Party, then that individual was Al Gore, the former vice president and Democratic nominee who had lost the 2000 presidential election in the Supreme Court, rather than in the Electoral College. Even Daschle had admitted that when it came to discussing potential 2004 presidential aspirants, Gore "deserve[d] to be in the mix."[64] The contours of the Democratic nomination contest were, therefore, formed as much by the large number of credible presidential aspirants running as by Gore's silence about his own plans. Working in concert, these factors kept party insiders from decisively coalescing behind a candidate during the invisible primary.

Nevertheless, as the campaign progressed through the first part of 2003, the top tier aspirants became more pronounced (Kerry, Edwards, Gephardt, Dean, and Lieberman) and Kerry was tentatively named the frontrunner. On February 26, 2003, *The New York Times* Journalist Adam Nagourney wrote that Kerry was "the leading candidate" in the Democratic race for the nomination, and he proceeded to explain the importance of such a designation: "Perceptions matter in these early days of a presidential campaign . . . They are what drive contributors to write checks, elected officials and activists in places like Iowa and New Hampshire to make endorsements and political professionals to decide which presidential candidate to sign up with."[65] Kerry had maneuvered into the top spot "with a combination of bluster and a calculated burst of early spending on a big staff, including some of the more respected names in Democratic politics. Mr. Kerry is about to announce that he has hired the Washington media consultant Bob Shrum, along with his partners Tad Devine and Mike Donilon."[66] Thus, early in the race, Kerry appeared to be on his way to earning his party's nomination for president.

Kerry's new status did not last long. He became embroiled first in a three-way fight for money and media attention, and then in a five-way brawl for endorsements and standing in the polls in New Hampshire and Iowa. The first person to take him down a notch was Edwards, whose fundraising was slightly stronger than Kerry's in the first financial quarter ($7.4 versus $7.0, respectively), ending on March 30, 2003. Throughout the spring, Kerry managed to remain the insider favorite – largely because of his 19 years of service in the Senate, his relationship to Senator Edward M. Kennedy, and his distinguished military service in Vietnam – and win the support of spouses of elected officials in key primary states. In Michigan, Governor Jennifer Granholm's husband endorsed Kerry. In New Hampshire, former Governor Jeanne Sheeheen's husband endorsed Kerry. In Iowa, Governor Tom Vilsack's wife came out in support of Kerry. These spousal endorsements provided the elected officials, who were also super delegates (PLEOs) with a way to hedge their nomination bets. If the aspirant for whom their spouse openly worked became the nominee, the elected official could claim credit. If the endorsed candidate lost, they could distance themselves from their spouses, asserting that they are their own persons.[67] For Kerry, this support allowed him to continue his claim on the frontrunner mantle, helping his fundraising through the second quarter.

In July, however, the race turned upside down as Dean's second quarter fundraising report knocked Kerry out of his precarious frontrunner spot. Dean not only more than doubled his own first quarter take, but he beat every other top tier aspirant, raising $7.6 million. For the rest of the summer and most of the fall, Dean became the new frontrunner and he led in money, endorsements, public opinion polls, and media attention. His was the only name that continued to echo even amidst the unexpected tumult of California's gubernatorial recall election. Still, questions lingered among insiders about Dean's ability to beat Republican incumbent George W. Bush and his suitability for the Oval Office, which left the door open for former General Wesley Clark to jump into the race in the fall.[68] By November, the nomination was a toss-up: Kerry, Dean, Edwards, and Gephardt were within the margin of error of each other in most of the Iowa polls, while Dean and Clark were ahead of Kerry and Edwards in New Hampshire. The national polls continued to show Dean leading the nomination race.

In the weeks leading up to Iowa – scheduled for January 19 – Kerry made three decisions that changed the course of his campaign. First, he chose to forgo public financing and the limits on primary spending imposed by them.[69] Second, he mortgaged his Beacon Hill home to provide over $6 million for his campaign. Third, he pulled the majority of his staff out of New Hampshire and relocated them to Iowa. Although this strategy involved substantial risk, he believed that winning Iowa would provide him with enough momentum to win New Hampshire because they were only eight days apart. Kerry's bet paid off: He earned over 38 percent of the vote in the Iowa caucus. Edwards came in second, and Dean ended up in third place. Gephardt withdrew after coming in fourth. Although Dean's third place finish had hurt him, but his reaction to the loss hurt him even more. Dean had been attempting to rally his supporters after his disappointing showing in Iowa, and as he was describing their future path to victory through the other contests, he began "screaming" the names of the states. The speech was televised, and the media leapt on the story of Dean's apparently un-presidential behavior. For most of the next few weeks, they played (and replayed) portions of the aspirants' speeches, alternating between criticizing Dean and lauding Kerry and Edwards. Kerry went on to win New Hampshire, besting Dean, Edwards, and Clark. On February 3, Kerry won five of the seven contests and as was noted in the week before, he was "the only candidate battling in all seven states, taking advantage of the high visibility he gained with big victories over Howard Dean in New Hampshire and Iowa and the flood of contributions his aides reported receiving the moment Democratic donors sensed he might be the horse to bet on."[70] The race effectively ended on March 2, when 11 states voted, and all but Vermont went for Kerry. Edwards withdrew that day – before California had even closed its polls. Thus, a mere six weeks after the contests had begun, Kerry had won the nomination.

While Kerry's nomination was not predictable, in hindsight, his early support (fundraising, media attention, and poll standing) and his decision to provide his campaign with enough resources to win Iowa, appear to have placed him in a position to capitalize on the results from that state. In essence, Kerry's top tier status and his strong outreach early on had provided him with a broad national support base of donors, volunteers, and staff, which meant he could scale up his organization quickly when the infusion of funds and attention arrived in late January. Kerry's path to the nomination, however, was volatile and chaotic, and few could have envisioned that Dean would flame out so spectacularly (after raising and spending more than $50 million, he won only the Vermont primary). In the end, the 2004 Democratic nomination looked less like a car chase and more like a demolition derby where Kerry's car – perhaps more appropriately, four-wheel drive vehicle – was the last one running.

The 2008 Election and a Few Conclusions about Future Presidential Campaigns

The 2000 and the 2004 nomination campaigns appear dull when compared to the 2008 presidential contests. There were nomination battles on both sides of the partisan aisle – the first time since 1952 – because there was no heir apparent to President George W. Bush. This open presidential seat drew nine aspirants in each of the party races. These aspirants – aiming at frontrunner status – started their campaigns as early as they ever had. By the end of January 2007, most had launched official committees (exploratory committees were thought passé) and had announced their campaign teams. They rolled out their Web sites and actively courted potential donors, endorsers, and voters over one year before Iowa's caucus on January 3, 2008.

Contributing to the chaos, the national political parties lost control of the nomination calendar. In previous cycles, the national political parties had been able to persuade the states to schedule their contests during the established window, which usually opened up a few weeks after the New Hampshire primary. In 2008, however, as late as 50 days before the originally scheduled date for the Iowa caucus (January 14), the order and the dates of the early contests were still fluctuating. Although 24 states complied with national party rules, scheduling their primaries or caucuses on February 5, having all of them do so on the first Tuesday in the window made this day the most important for winning delegates (nearly half of all pledged delegates in both parties were available on this day alone (1,676 out of 3,512 for Democrats and 1,038 out of 2,454).[71] Thus, the front-loading was extraordinary and unprecedented.

Another race among the states – for January dates – played out during the cycle and evinces just how much the national parties had lost control. The Democratic Party voted to allow South Carolina and Nevada – states whose electorates were more diverse than Iowa or New Hampshire – to hold early contests. This decision fostered envy and resentment among several other states, which led to more battles between the states and the national parties. Florida Democrats sued the Democratic National Committee (DNC) over the date of their primary (January 29), which had been scheduled by a Republican-controlled state legislature and signed into law by a Republican governor (with the tacit support of the state's Democrats), but had been placed on a day before the national party's established nomination window opened on February 5. Republicans in South Carolina, displeased by the actions of their fellow partisans in Florida, moved up their primary (January 19) and voted on a different day than the Democrats in their state (January 29). Annoyed with the leapfrogging of Florida and South Carolina, the Republicans and the Democrats in Iowa moved up their caucuses from January 14 to January 3. Michigan, which had been one of the states that had started the push for more representative states (ones that included urban centers with large minority populations) voting early, moved up its primary to a date (January 15) before not only the Democratic window, but also the established date for the Nevada caucus (January 19). New Hampshire's Secretary of State William Gardner waited until Michigan's State Supreme Court had ruled that Michigan would be allowed to hold its primary on January 15 before he announced in late November the date of the Granite state's primary (January 8). Complicating the situation further,

both Iowa and New Hampshire operate under state laws that required them to schedule their contests at the front of the calendar and in this cycle, thus forcing them to
move up their contests.

In response to these maneuvers, the Democratic National Committee asked the
presidential aspirants not to campaign in either Michigan or Florida (but they were
allowed to raise funds). It then told both rogue states that if they proceeded with
their plans, they risked not having their delegates seated at the Democratic Party's
national convention. The Republican National Committee followed suit and told
these states that they would lose half of their convention delegates. The states ignored these warnings and admonitions: They knew that their delegates would not be
displaced at the convention because either party nominee would restore the delegates' convention credentials. In short, the states (and their delegates) knew that
they would not be displaced at the convention because neither party nominee would
be able to afford angering a state's most active partisans just a few months before the
general election.

The early start and the large number of early contests, not surprisingly, led to the
large number of early contests led to skyrocketing campaign costs for presidential aspirants. Some experienced contenders (Senator John McCain of Arizona, Senator
Joseph Biden of Delaware, and Senator Chris Dodd of Connecticut) found it difficult
to keep their campaign coffers full. However, top-tier aspirants (Democratic Senators
Hillary Clinton from New York and Barack Obama from Illinois on the Democratic
side and former Governor Mitt Romney from Massachusetts on the Republican side),
more than met the challenge, partly because of their high "celebrity" status and the ease
of Internet fundraising. These top-tier aspirants pulled in around $25 million dollars in
each of the financial quarters of 2007. Unlike previous election cycles, almost all of the
candidates opted out of the public financing system (among the credible aspirants, only
former Senator John Edwards (D-NC) chose to participate with it). Thus, what may be
regarded as the entry fee for credible aspirants reached $100 million in 2008.

The front-loaded nomination process after 2008 appears headed for its own fiery
crash.[72] Three commonly discussed reforms to the nomination process include a rotating regional primary, the delegate bonus plan, and a national primary. In the rotating regional primary, the country would be divided into four geographic regions;
the first region would begin voting in March and the others would follow in April,
May, and June. Rotating each cycle, a different part of the country would begin the
voting every 16 years after the Iowa and New Hampshire contests.[73] Others have suggested — and in 2000 the Republicans attempted — a modest reform intended to
stretch out the calendar by providing states with additional delegates for scheduling
their nomination contests later in the window.

Unfortunately, as Andrew E. Busch and William G. Mayer note, this reform was
not effective in preventing front-loading.[74] The reform most likely to be implemented
before the next presidential election is a single national primary day that either allows
Iowa and New Hampshire to go first, or that encompasses all of the states and is set for
a date in early spring of the presidential election year. There are several reasons why a
national primary is likely to prevail over the other alternatives. First, it is the most
democratic and egalitarian (equally participatory) for all voters, even though it would

not necessarily place all of the states on an equal footing because of how presidential campaigns allocate their resources) – considerations that have mattered to presidential aspirants and party leaders who have argued for earlier reforms. Second, it would allow the national political parties to set a date later in the year (possibly in late April), reducing the length of the campaign, which would also presumably reduce the intra-party conflict that occurs between competing aspirants. Third, a shorter cycle might lead to a renewal of the public financing system because there would no longer be the lengthy time period between the end of the nomination contests and the national party conventions. Undoubtedly, a national primary would also allow more citizens and a more diverse citizenry to participate in the selection of the presidential nominees (which was the stated purpose for allowing both Nevada and South Carolina to vote prior to the opening of the "window" in 2008). Finally, a national primary would give more advantage to frontrunners.

A national plan would reinforce the trends already in place. Not only would a national primary campaign cost more, but it would likely create fewer opportunities for retail politics, where candidates attend small events and voters get to thoroughly question them on their issues of concern. A national primary campaign would turn into a national advertising blitz, where the wealthiest (largest campaign war chest) and the most popular (highest level of name recognition) aspirant won.[75] Beyond this, the aspirants would not campaign in every state. Instead, they would develop strategies based upon winning the states that are the most favorable to them and/or are delegate-rich, meaning that they would likely ignore many small and/or rural states on their paths toward their party's nomination. Still, it seems likely that a national primary will be in place by 2012. Thus, the politics of presidential nominations are likely to continue down the road that they have been on since the political parties first took over for the Electoral College – becoming simultaneously more democratic and less deliberative (more chaotic, yet more predictable) over time.

Endnotes

1. The author wishes to thank both James P. Pfiffner and Roger H. Davidson for the invitation to write this essay and for their many helpful suggestions to improve it.
2. Primaries are elections in which voters cast ballots to choose party nominees for elective office. Different states hold different types of primaries, but most states hold what are known as "closed" primaries, in which only registered partisans may vote in their party's primary. Caucuses are meetings of voters at which candidates are collectively chosen as party nominees for elective office. Both are nomination contests, but typically, caucuses have far fewer voters turnout, because they not only take more time, but they are scheduled at a specific time and as such, many voters find it difficult to participate. After 1972, states began using these types of contests to allocate pledged delegates (who were bound to support a specific candidate) to the parties' national conventions. Before 1972, many states held non-binding primaries or caucuses, where the delegates selected were able to switch their votes at the conventions. Before 1912, parties mostly staged local (or county) conventions to select delegates to a state convention who in turn would choose national convention delegates. Most of the local and state delegates were party leaders or elected officials, and few voters (or many partisans) had a role in selecting these delegates.

3. In 2008, 33 states held contests (most of them binding) by February 6, 2008, (National Association of Secretaries of State, Primary Calendar, January 15, 2008 update, see http://nass.org/index.php?option=com_content&task=view&id=74&Itemid=210). As recently as two cycles ago, the Iowa caucus was not scheduled to take place until January 24, 2000, and it would have taken until March 11 for 33 states held contests (see Table 1).

4. See Larry Bartels, *Presidential Primaries and the Dynamics of Public Choice* (Princeton, NJ: Princeton University Press, 1988). See also William G. Mayer and Andrew E. Busch, *The Front-Loading Problem in Presidential Nominations* (Washington, DC: Brookings Institution Press, 2004). See also William G. Mayer, ed., *The Making of the Presidential Candidates 2004* (Landham, MD: Rowman & Littlefield, 2004). See also Nelson W. Polsby and Aaron Wildavsky, *Presidential Elections: Strategies and Structures of American Politics*, eleventh edition (Lanham, MD: Rowman & Littlefield, 2004). See also Stephen J. Wayne, *The Road to the White House 2004: The Politics of Presidential Elections* (Belmont, CA: Wadsworth/Thomson Learning, 2004). See also Michael J. Goff. *The Money Primary: The New Politics of the Early Presidential Nomination Process* (Lanham, MD: Rowman & Littlefield, 2004). See also Marty Cohen, David Karol, Hans Noel, and John Zaller, "Beating Reform: The Resurgence of Parties in Presidential Nominations, 1980–2000," (Paper presented at the Annual Meeting of the American Political Science Association, 2002). See also Marty Cohen, David Karol, Hans Noel, and John Zaller, "Political Parties in Rough Weather," in *The Forum*, Vol. 5, Issue 4, Article 3 (2008), available at http://www.bepress.com/forum/vol5/iss4/art3. See also William G. Mayer, "Handicapping the 2008 Nomination Races: An Early Winter Prospectus," *The Forum*, Vol. 5, Issue 4, Article 2 (2008), available at http://www.bepress.com/forum/vol5/iss4/art2.

5. During the Constitutional Convention, several of the Framers believed that that the Electoral College would act as a nominating process for regional candidates and that the House of Representatives (or the Senate in the early drafts of the selection proposal) would make the final choice. George Mason stated, "Nineteen times out of twenty, the President would be chosen by the Senate" in Max Farrand, ed., *The Records of the Federal Convention*, volume II (New Haven, CT: Yale University Press, 1966), p. 500, and for further discussion, pp. 496-543. See also Forrest McDonald, *The American Presidency: An Intellectual History* (Lawrence, KS: University of Kansas Press, 1994).

6. The presidential selection method was one of the most debated topics at the Constitutional Convention. Though several components of the Electoral College are the result of compromise (i.e., the number of electors awarded to each state; the House, voting by state delegation and making the final decision, rather than the Senate, etc), the Framers did not enter into these bargains without substantial debate about what they might mean for executive power and the federal government, more generally. Thus, while some have argued that the Electoral College may be thought of as an arrived at middle-ground solution, which satisfied most delegates, it is more appropriate to think of it as an institution invented to reflect the Framers' values about the nature and purpose of an executive in a separated powers scheme. See Forrest McDonald, *The American Presidency: An Intellectual History* (Lawrence, KS: University of Kansas Press, 1994). See also Max Farrand, ed., *The Records of the Federal Convention*, volume I and II (New Haven, CT: Yale University Press, 1966), especially vol. II, pp. 496–543. See also Gary Glenn, "The Electoral College and the Development of American Democracy," in *Perspectives on Political Science*, vol. 32, no. 1 (2003), pp. 4–8.

7. A number of provisions (voting separately for president and vice president; limiting the number of eligible candidates should the House decide; placing the vice presidential decision with the Senate; providing for death and disability; and limiting the number of terms of service) were modified or added to the Constitution by the Twelfth, Twentieth, and Twenty-Second Amendments. For a discussion of the flaws in the Framers' design, see Bruce Ackerman, *The Failure of the Founding Fathers: Jefferson, Marshall, and the Rise of Presidential Democracy*, (Cambridge, MA: The Belknap Press of Harvard University Press, 2005).

8. Not incidentally, Washington's precedent and the Framers' expectation have constrained the behavior of most presidential aspirants. Early seekers of the office went out of their way to

feign indifference, while they simultaneously engaged in fierce politicking and partisan maneuvers. See Richard P. McCormick, *The Presidential Game: The Origins of American Presidential Politics* (New York, NY: Oxford University Press, 1982), pp. 41–75.

9. According to Alexander Hamilton, "nothing was more to be desired, than that every practicable obstacle should be opposed to cabal, intrigue, and corruption" in Joanne Freeman, *Alexander Hamilton: Writings* (New York, NY: The Library of America, 2001), *Federalist 68*, p. 364. Gouvernor Morris also noted at the Constitutional Convention on September 4, 1787, that the "principle advantage aimed at [by an electoral college] was that of taking away the opportunity for cabal" in Max Farrand, ed., *The Records of the Federal Convention,* volume II (New Haven, CT: Yale University Press, 1966), p. 501.

10. "The process of election affords a moral certainty, that the office of President will never fall to the lot of any man who is not in an eminent degree endowed with the requisite qualifications. Talents for low intrigue, and the little arts of popularity, may alone suffice to elevate a man to the first honors in a single State; but it will require other talents, and a different kind of merit, to establish him in the esteem and confidence of the whole Union, or of so considerable a portion of it as would be necessary to make him a successful candidate for the distinguished office of President of the United States," so wrote Alexander Hamilton in Joanne Freeman, *Alexander Hamilton: Writings* (New York, NY: The Library of America, 2001), *Federalist 68,* p. 364. Gary Glenn also explains that, "The Founders' electoral college knowingly gave greater weight to presidential candidates who made broad appeals to all parts of the country and across the inevitable small state-large state, rural-urban, and agricultural-commercial conflicts of interest. They regarded choosing a president as more about reconciling interests, or at least not exacerbating the natural and inevitable conflicts of interest, than about simple arithmetic equality," in "The Electoral College and the Development of American Democracy," in *Perspectives on Political Science,* vol. 32, no.1 (2003), p. 6.

11. Richard P. McCormick, *The Presidential Game: The Origins of American Presidential Politics* (New York, NY: Oxford University Press, 1982). See also John H. Aldrich, *Why Parties? The Origin and Transformation of Political Parties in America* (Chicago, IL: The University of Chicago Press, 1995).

12. John H. Aldrich, *Before the Convention: Strategies and Choices in Presidential Nomination Campaigns* (Chicago, IL: The University of Chicago Press, 1980), p. 5.

13. Jefferson wrote about the upcoming presidential election in a number of letters in 1795–1796, including those addressed to James Madison, James Monroe, and Edward Rutledge. In the letters, he wrote that he was not interested in the presidency and he suggested to Madison that he make the run for the office. Eventually, in May of 1796, Jefferson was made the nominee by James Monroe and his fellow partisans. See Thomas Jefferson Randolph, *Memoir, Correspondence, and Miscellanies from the Papers of Thomas Jefferson* (Charlottesville, VA: F. Carr, and Co 1829), pp. 337–353. See also Joseph J. Ellis, *American Sphinx: The Character of Thomas Jefferson* (New York, NY: Vintage Books), p. 194.

14. Though the Twelfth Amendment altered this provision, originally, each elector cast two ballots for president and the person with the most (so long as it was a majority) became president, while the second highest vote earner became the vice president.

15. In 1824, representatives from four states made up two-thirds of those attending the caucus. See Stephen J. Wayne, *The Road to the White House 2004: The Politics of Presidential Elections* (Belmont, CA: Wadsworth/Thomson Learning, 2004), p. 7.

16. See John H. Aldrich, *Before the Convention: Strategies and Choices in Presidential Nomination Campaigns* (Chicago, IL: The University of Chicago Press, 1980), p. 7. See also Stephen J. Wayne, *The Road to the White House 2004: The Politics of Presidential Elections* (Belmont, CA: Wadsworth/Thomson Learning, 2004), p. 8.

17. The southern delegates had mostly been ignored because the Republicans had no chance of winning electoral votes in the South. The southern delegates' votes (all 191½;) put McKinley over the top at the convention. For further discussion, see Wayne H. Morgan, *William McKinley and His America*, revised edition, (Kent, OH: The Kent State University Press, 2003), p. 146–147.

18. John H. Aldrich, *Before the Convention: Strategies and Choices in Presidential Nomination Campaigns* (Chicago, IL: The University of Chicago Press, 1980), p. 8.

19. In 1921, Franklin Roosevelt proposed in a letter that the Democratic National Committee employ a full-time staff at a national headquarters. He suggested that they hold national conferences (separate from the national conventions) where more activists could be involved with party issues and the development of a common ideology. In 1924, after the disastrous convention and election, he wrote another letter proposing "a permanent headquarters for the Party and a more democratic, participatory decision-making process for determining positions on issues and public policy . . . [he then copied it to] over 3,000 Democrats, including delegates at the recent convention," according to Sean Savage, *Roosevelt: The Party Leader, 1932–1945,* (Louisville: University of Kentucky Press, 1991), p. 6. Roosevelt continued these and other efforts (e.g., altering the number of delegates needed to win the nomination from two-thirds to a simply majority) throughout his presidency.

20. On the final ballot, Humphrey earned more than 1,000 delegates more than Senator George McGovern and Senator Eugene McCarthy (both anti-war candidates) combined.

21. The reform commission proposed "a rule requiring that all states represent these particular groups (African Americans, women, and youth) in reasonable relationship to their presence in the state population . . . [while the rule] was subsequently modified . . . beginning with its 1980 nominating convention, the party required that each state delegation be equally divided between the sexes," according to Stephen J. Wayne, *The Road to the White House 2004: The Politics of Presidential Elections* (Belmont, CA: Wadsworth/Thomson Learning, 2004), p. 106.

22. Larry Bartels, *Presidential Primaries and the Dynamics of Public Choice* (Princeton, NJ: Princeton University Press, 1988), p. 20.

23. It was thought that the early states held a disproportionate advantage over the later states, strict proportional representation had fostered too many factions, and the party leaders felt that they had too little sway in the process and that the rank-and-file partisans were not focused enough on the electability of the candidate. For further discussion, see Stephen J. Wayne, *The Road to the White House 2004: The Politics of Presidential Elections* (Belmont, CA: Wadsworth/Thomson Learning, 2004), p. 108.

24. See Stephen J. Wayne, *The Road to the White House 2004: The Politics of Presidential Elections* (Belmont, CA: Wadsworth/Thomson Learning, 2004), pp. 12, 103–117.

25. Andrew E. Busch and William G. Mayer, "The Front-Loading Problem," and William G. Mayer, "The Basic Dynamics of the Contemporary Nomination Process: An Expanded View" in Mayer, ed., *The Making of the Presidential Candidates 2004* (Landham, MD: Rowman & Littlefield, 2004).

26. Journalist Arthur Hadley coined this phrase, which refers to the campaign period before the contests get underway. See Arthur T. Hadley, *The Invisible Primary* (Englewood Cliffs, NJ: Prentice Hall, 1976).

27. See William G. Mayer and Andrew E. Busch, *The Front-Loading Problem in Presidential Nominations* (Washington, DC: Brookings Institution Press, 2004). See also Andrew E. Busch and William G. Mayer, "The Front-Loading Problem," and William G. Mayer, "The Basic Dynamics of the Contemporary Nomination Process: An Expanded View" in Mayer, ed., *The Making of the Presidential Candidates 2004* (Landham, MD: Rowman & Littlefield, 2004), pp. 1–43; 83–132. See also Nelson W. Polsby and Aaron Wildavsky, *Presidential Elections: Strategies and Structures of American Politics,* eleventh edition (Lanham, MD: Rowman & Littlefield, 2004), pp. 89–115. See also Stephen J. Wayne, *The Road to the White House 2004: The Politics of Presidential Elections* (Belmont, CA: Wadsworth/Thomson Learning, 2004), pp. 103–158. See also Michael J. Goff. *The Money Primary: The New Politics of the Early Presidential Nomination Process* (Lanham, MD: Rowman & Littlefield, 2004). See also Marty Cohen David Karol, Hans Noel, and John Zaller, "Beating Reform: The Resurgence of Parties in Presidential Nominations, 1980–2000," (Paper presented at the Annual Meeting of the American Political Science Association, 2002).

28. Andrew E. Busch and William G. Mayer, "The Front-Loading Problem," and William G. Mayer, "The Basic Dynamics of the Contemporary Nomination Process: An Expanded View" in Mayer, ed., *The Making of the Presidential Candidates 2004* (Landham, MD: Rowman & Littlefield, 2004), p. 23.

29. Importantly, these "outsiders" and "dark horses" were top-tier candidates. Further, some polls even showed them as frontrunners. For example, in December of 2003, John Kerry stood in the middle of the pack in most national polls, but he was leading in most of the statewide polls that were conducted in Iowa. As will be discussed shortly, his win there catapulted him into first place nationally, and he went on to win all but four states' contests (North Carolina, Oklahoma, South Carolina, and Vermont).

30. Although participation and awareness of party nominating contests has increased since before the institution of the McGovern-Fraser reforms, average turnout is often less than 35 percent of the voting age population.

31. Several studies have traced the tangible benefits awarded to states that hold their contests early in the process. For an overview of the findings, see: Andrew E. Busch and William G. Mayer, "The Front-Loading Problem," and William G. Mayer, "The Basic Dynamics of the Contemporary Nomination Process: An Expanded View" in Mayer, ed., *The Making of the Presidential Candidates 2004* (Landham, MD: Rowman & Littlefield, 2004), pp. 9–15.

32. While New Hampshire has been holding primary elections since 1920, it did not grow in its importance until the 1950s. New Hampshire allowed voters to express a presidential preference (no longer only selecting delegates to the national convention) in 1952, and with that, General Dwight D. Eisenhower beat Senator Robert Taft, the party's frontrunner for the nomination. The Iowa caucus, set up in 1972, came to national attention because it was another way for a state to abide by the Democratic Party reforms without holding a primary election (often more expensive).

33. Super Tuesday was the name given to the date (traditionally in March) when several southern states would hold their primary elections. As Nelson Polsby and Aaron Wildavsky explain: "The idea behind the creation of Super Tuesday primaries are twofold: (1) to give the South a larger voice in presidential nominating politics, and (2) by switching from caucuses to primaries, and by holding primaries relatively early in the campaign (i.e., before it was all decided), they hoped some more moderate or conservative Democratic politicians would be in the race, thereby attracting voters into the primaries." See Nelson W. Polsby and Aaron Wildavsky, *Presidential Elections: Strategies and Structures of American Politics*, eleventh edition (Lanham, MD: Rowman & Littlefield, 2004), p. 109.
This phrase, however, has now come to be applied to any early date with a large number of states holding contests. In 2008, there were so many states holding contests on February 5, some pundits renamed it "Tsunami Tuesday."

34. *Ibid.*, pp. 21–32

35. See William G. Mayer, ed., *The Making of the Presidential Candidates 2004* (Landham, MD: Rowman & Littlefield, 2004). See also Stephen J. Wayne, *The Road to the White House 2004: The Politics of Presidential Elections* (Belmont, CA: Wadsworth/Thomson Learning, 2004).

36. Nicholas Kristof, "For Bush, His Toughest Call Was the Choice to Run at All," (*The New York Times Magazine*, October 29, 2000).

37. *Ibid.*

38. Judith S. Trent, "And They All Came Calling: The Early Campaign of Election 2000," *The 2000 Presidential Campaign*, ed. By Robert Denton, (New York: Praeger/Greenwood, 2002), p. 26.

39. Richard Berke, "Governor Bush Becoming One to Watch in G.O.P.," *The New York Times*, August 25, 1997.

40. Sam Verhovek, "Bush Runs in Texas, But Bigger Quest Is Suspected," *The New York Times*, December 4, 1997.

41. Stanley A. Renshon, *In His Father's Shadow: The Transformations of George W. Bush*, (New York: Palgrave/MacMillan, 2004), p. 49.

42. *Ibid.*, p. 50.

43. *Ibid.*, p. 96.

44. Bryan LaBerge, *George W. Bush: In the Whirlwind*, (New York: Trafford Publishing, 2003), p. 22.

45. Sam Verhovek, "Bush Runs in Texas, But Bigger Quest Is Suspected," *The New York Times*, December 4, 1997.

46. Richard Berke, "Grand Old Problem; The Republican Middle Looks for an Edge," *The New York Times*, November 8, 1998.

47. Richard Berke, "Bush Brothers Provide Light to Republicans After a Dreary Election," *The New York Times*, November 19, 1998.

48. Judith S. Trent, "And They All Came Calling: The Early Campaign of Election 2000," *The 2000 Presidential Campaign*, ed. By Robert Denton, (New York: Praeger/Greenwood, 2002), p. 26.

49. Bryan LaBerge, *George W. Bush: In the Whirlwind*, (New York: Trafford Publishing, 2003), p. 25.

50. Nelson W. Polsby and Aaron Wildavsky, *Presidential Elections: Strategies and Structures of American Politics*, eleventh edition (Lanham, MD: Rowman & Littlefield, 2004), p. 101. See also Judith S. Trent, "And They All Came Calling: The Early Campaign of Election 2000," *The 2000 Presidential Campaign*, ed. By Robert Denton, (New York: Praeger/Greenwood, 2002), p. 25.

51. Nelson W. Polsby and Aaron Wildavsky, *Presidential Elections: Strategies and Structures of American Politics*, eleventh edition (Lanham, MD: Rowman & Littlefield, 2004), p. 100. See also Judith S. Trent, "And They All Came Calling: The Early Campaign of Election 2000," *The 2000 Presidential Campaign*, ed. By Robert Denton, (New York: Praeger/Greenwood, 2002), p. 18.

52. Terry M. Neal, "Bush Campaign Counts on Vast Network," *The Washington Post*, December 22, 1999.

53. Gary A. Jacobson, *A Divider, Not a Uniter: George W. Bush and the American People*, (New York: Pearson Education), p. 51.

54. A "push poll" is a poll that is designed not to survey the public about their opinions, but to persuade the public of an opinion. Usually, the callers pretend to be conducting a survey, but then pass on information that is erroneous or amounts to attack on one of the candidate.

55. This "push poll" was designed to negatively influence voters' opinions of McCain. For further discussion, see: James Moore and Wayne Slater, *Bush's Brain: How Karl Rove Made George W. Bush President*, (New York: Wiley Publishers, 2003), p. 257.

56. Bill Moore and Danielle Vinson, "The South Carolina Republican Presidential Primary," *PS: Political Science and Politics*, 2001, vol. 34, no. 2 (June), p. 274.

57. Gary A. Jacobson, *A Divider, Not a Uniter: George W. Bush and the American People*, (New York: Pearson Education), p. 51.

58. Stephen J. Wayne, *The Road to the White House 2004: The Politics of Presidential Elections* (Belmont, CA: Wadsworth/Thomson Learning, 2004), p. 148.

59. They explain that: (1) dark horse or "outsider" aspirants are not scrutinized to the same level as front-runners during the invisible primary and as a result, when they experience some success, they often garner a significant amount of negative media coverage; and (2) dark horse or "outsider" aspirants are also not able to raise enough money, quickly enough for it to be effective (i.e., there is limited time for media buys, for printing mailers, for conducting polls, etc.) in taking down the front-runner. Andrew E. Busch and William G. Mayer, "The Front-Loading Problem," and William G. Mayer, "The Basic Dynamics of the Contemporary Nomination Process: An Expanded View" in Mayer, ed., *The Making of the Presidential Candidates 2004* (Landham, MD: Rowman & Littlefield, 2004), pp. 1–43; 83–132. See also William G. Mayer and Andrew E. Busch, *The Front-Loading Problem in Presidential Nominations* (Washington, DC: Brookings Institution Press, 2004).

60. Portions of this section are drawn from Lara M. Brown and Mark Wrighton, "Leeches, Lemmings, and Pet Rocks: The 2004 Democratic Nomination Campaign," presented at the Northeastern Political Science Association Conference, Boston, November 11–13, 2004.

61. Adam Nagourney and Janet Elder, "National G.O.P. Members Weigh Against Lott in Poll," *The New York Times*, December 20, 2002.

62. Richard Berke, "Democrats Start Early on the Presidential Trail," *The New York Times*, February 18, 2002.

63. *Ibid.* Kerry's joke referred to the official statements that were made frequently in the months following the September 11, 2001 attacks about Vice President Dick Cheney, whom the public was told was in a "secure, undisclosed location" in case something were to happen to President George W. Bush.

64. Richard Berke, "Gore Rebukes Bush, and Tries to Mend Fences at Home in Tennessee," *The New York Times*, February 3, 2002.

65. Adam Nagourney, "In the First Mile of a Marathon, Kerry Emerges as the Front-Runner," *The New York Times*, February 26, 2003.

66. *Ibid.*

67. A few other early endorsements helped set the tone for the race. Former Democratic governors Jim Hunt of North Carolina and Roy Barnes of Georgia endorsed Senator Edwards, while U.S. Representative Harold Ford, Jr. of Tennessee endorsed Senator Kerry. For the most part, members of the House of Representatives – such as California Democrats Loretta Sanchez and Nancy Pelosi – backed Missouri Representative Richard Gephardt, the former caucus leader.

68. Adam Nagourney, "In the Candidacies of Clark and Dean, Democrats Confront Issues of Electability," *The New York Times*, October 30, 2003.

69. The Federal Election Campaign Act (1974 amendments) established a "partial" public financing system for presidential elections. During the primary period, presidential aspirants who raise at least $5,000 in contributions of $250 or less from individuals in at least 20 states are eligible to receive matching funds from the federal government. The funds are disbursed to campaigns on the first of January of the election year. While many candidates have taken these funds in the past, most of the 2008 aspirants have decided to forgo these funds. Aspirants have begun passing up this "free money" because along with the funds come spending limits for each state and an overall limit for the nomination period that are adjusted each electoral cycle, but which tend to amount to far less than many aspirants would like to spend on the race. While these limits are not as problematic during the primary contests themselves, they can become a burden during the late spring and the early summer period when the aspirant has secured enough delegates to have won their party's nomination, but they have not yet been made the nominee at the national convention. In other words, some aspirants have been forced to "go dark" (effectively shut down) during this time frame because they cannot yet access party money in support of their campaign, nor can they spend any more from their nomination account.

70. Adam Nagourney and Jim Rutenberg, "With More Contests Looming, Candidates Make Some Tough Decisions," *The New York Times*, February 1, 2004.

71. Numbers taken from *The New York Times* "Election Guide" Web site at http://politics. nytimes.com/election-guide/2008/calendars/republicanprimaries/index.html, accessed on October 14, 2007.

72. For further discussion, see: Bruce E. Altschuler, "Selecting Presidential Nominees By National Primary: An Idea Whose Time Has Come?" in *The Forum*, Vol. 5, Issue 4, Article 5 (2008), available at http://www.bepress.com/forum/vol5/iss4/art5.

73. For further information, see the National Association of Secretaries of States *Rotating Regional Presidential Primary Plan*: http://nass.org/index.php?option=com_content&task=view&id=74&Itemid=210 (accessed February 9, 2008).

74. Andrew E. Busch and William G. Mayer, "The Front-Loading Problem," and William G. Mayer, "The Basic Dynamics of the Contemporary Nomination Process: An Expanded View" in Mayer, ed., *The Making of the Presidential Candidates 2004* (Landham, MD: Rowman & Littlefield, 2004), p. 36.

75. Walter A. Shapiro, "My Letter to the Most Important Man in Politics," *Salon.com*, available at http://www.salon.com/opinion/feature/2007/10/15/new_hampshire/, accessed on October 15, 2007.

Peter L. Francia, Gregory Fortelny, and Clyde Wilcox

The Obama Juggernaut: Presidential Fundraising in 2008

In February, 2007, Hillary Clinton's campaign hosted a meeting of some 250 top fundraisers, most promising to raise $25,000 for her campaign, with her top fundraising team promising to raise $1 million apiece. Clinton had already transferred $10 million from her Senate committee and asked her fundraising team to raise an additional $15 million by the end of the first quarter – nearly twice what the leading Democratic candidate had done during the same months of 2003 (Fouhy 2007). Clinton fundraisers declared that she had an unstoppable machine.

Clinton's strategy was based on earlier successful campaigns, and it worked even better than she had expected. By the end of December, she had raised nearly $100 million – more than two-and-one-half times the amount that Howard Dean had raised in 2003. But Barack Obama led all fundraisers in 2007 receipts, and he went on to raise more than Clinton in every month of 2008. Obama raised $35 million in January, 2008 – primarily from small donations. More than 90 percent of Obama's donors in January gave $100 or less, and more than 40 percent gave $25 or less. Just a few days later, the Obama campaign announced that it had raised more than $7.5 million in just 36 hours on the Internet (Wilcox 2008).

By the end of the nomination period, Clinton had raised more than $214 million – a figure that shattered all previous records. But Barack Obama raised more than $424 million, with $217 million in contributions of $200 or less (Malbin 2009). Obama was not alone in raising small Internet contributions. Ron Paul, a mere footnote in the polls, raised more money in a single day on the Internet in January 2008 than John Kerry had during the entire month four years before.

More importantly, in 2008, Obama became the first candidate to decline accepting federal funds for the general election, allowing him to raise and spend unlimited amounts. John McCain, a longtime supporter of campaign finance reform, accepted the $84 million grant. Obama raised more than $150 million in September alone, and outspent McCain and the Republican Party committees by two to one in the early weeks of October (Malbin 2009).

In the last week of the campaign Obama was able to air a 30-minute ad on major networks. In response, John McCain appeared on a *Saturday Night Live* sketch with Tina Fey playing his running mate, Sarah Palin. McCain pretended that he was countering Obama's massive ad buy by hosting a QVC television program in which he would try to sell such goods as McCain's Fine Gold or special knives to cut pork.[1]

Obama's fundraising approach and its success have profound implications for future presidential campaigns. To understand what happened in the 2008 campaign and what it portends for future campaigns it is first useful to understand the basic rules that regulate fundraising, and past practices to raise money within these rules.

The Rules of the Presidential Finance System

Money has long been an important and controversial element in American presidential elections. In 1896, the Ohio industrialist Mark Hanna gave $100,000 to Republican nominee William McKinley—the equivalent of more than $1,000,000 today—and additionally raised between $3.5 and $10 million by assessing banks and corporations a fee based on their assets. Standard Oil and J. P. Morgan each gave $250,000, with other corporations, banks, and industrialists also giving large sums to the McKinley campaign (Baida 1992). While Democratic nominee William Jennings Bryan mobilized farmers, workers, and evangelical Christians, the Republican Party tapped the deep pockets of corporate America, outspending the Democrats by perhaps as much as 20 to one.

The abuses of the McKinley campaign led Congress to ban direct contributions by banks and corporations in national elections; later Congress also banned direct gifts from labor unions. Although these bans were routinely evaded, in 1972 President Richard Nixon's Committee to Reelect the President (CREEP) took a page from Hanna's playbook and asked for direct corporate contributions, implying that companies that did not comply might be denied access to administration policy-making circles. Illegal corporate contributions to CREEP were laundered through the Grand Caymen Islands and smuggled into the United States. Eventually the head of corporate fundraising for the Nixon campaign went to jail. Other large donors were made ambassadors, in spite of their apparent lack of anything remotely resembling a qualification for the job—an unseemly if not illegal reward for their gifts. These abuses led Congress to pass in 1974 the Federal Election Campaign Act (FECA) – a comprehensive system of campaign finance regulation described following.

The Federal Election Campaign Act

In 1974, Congress passed comprehensive amendments to the Federal Election Campaign Act, which provided a regulatory framework for congressional and presidential elections. The presidential campaign system had four main elements:

1. **Contribution limits.** Individuals were limited to contributions of $1,000 to any one candidate during the primary election campaigns under FECA and were not permitted to give to the presidential candidates during the general elections if the candidate accepted the public grant. Interest groups could form political action committees (PACs), which could raise money up to $5,000 from each of their members and give up to $5,000 per candidate in

the primary elections. Parties could give money to candidates in the primary election campaigns and spend on behalf of the candidates in the general elections. Candidates could give their own campaign $50,000 of their personal wealth, but later Court rulings allowed candidates who did not accept matching funds to spend unlimited amounts from their family's fortunes.

2. **Public funding.** Presidential candidates can accept partial funding of the primary election campaigns, partial funding of the nominating convention, and full funding of their general election campaigns. To receive public funds, a candidate must: (1) seek nomination by a political party to the office of president; (2) raise more than $5,000 in each of at least 20 states; and (3) agree to spending limits (described below). Taxpayers may direct some of their tax payments to the funding of presidential campaigns without increasing their tax burden by checking a box on their income tax form. This fund provides candidates with a subsidy matching the first $250 of any contribution from an individual during the primary season (e.g., a contribution of $1,000 is worth $1,250, while a gift of $25 is worth $50 because of the federal match). There is a maximum limit to how much any candidate can receive in matching funds: in 2008 that limit was $21.025 million. Candidates can receive these matching funds even if they run unopposed in their party's primaries, as Ronald Reagan did in 1984 and Bill Clinton did in 1996. Candidates can borrow from banks against the promise of matching funds, making that money available early in the campaign. The public fund is also used to finance the Republican and Democratic party conventions (more than $16.8 million each in 2008). Finally, the public fund is used to finance the general election campaigns of the two major parties by providing equal-sized grants: In 2008, the McCain campaign received the maximum $84.1 million (Obama declined the public grant). Minor-party candidates who receive at least 5 percent of the popular vote can receive a portion of the overall grant in the next election. For instance, Reform Party candidate, Ross Perot, who won 19 percent of the popular vote in the 1992 general election, received approximately $29 million for the 1996 election (compared to $61 million apiece for Democrat Bill Clinton and Republican Robert Dole).

3. **Spending limits.** During the primary election campaign, candidates who accept public funds agree to an overall spending limit, which is indexed for inflation. In 2008, the limit was approximately $50.46 million per candidate, not including some legal and accounting costs associated with compliance with the law, and some fundraising costs, which the law defines as excluded from totals. There are also spending limits for each individual state that vary with the state's population, although not with its importance in the electoral calendar. This means that critical states like Iowa and New Hampshire, which hold early caucuses and primaries, but have relatively few citizens, have low spending limits. However, nearly all candidates have evaded these early-state limits with a wide variety of creative bookkeeping arrangements, such as having campaign workers sleep and buy supplies in Nebraska, while campaigning in Iowa. Additionally, there are limits on the amounts that individuals and groups may spend to help promote particular candidates or

parties. Candidates who accept federal funds in the general election agree to forgo additional fundraising and spending by their campaign committees, although the national party committees can raise money and spend it to help their campaigns.

4. **Disclosure.** FECA created a new federal agency, the Federal Election Commission (FEC), to audit the presidential campaigns, disburse the federal fund, and maintain records of the fundraising and spending of candidates, parties, and PACs. Candidates, parties, and PACs must file regular reports detailing the names, occupations, and addresses of their contributors and also the way they have spent their money. This information is made available to the public by the FEC in a variety of formats, enabling reporters to determine when there is a coordinated effort by a particular industry to support a given candidate. The FEC maintains a Web page, which provides a great deal of summary information at http://www.fec.gov.

FECA Unravels

Although the FECA amendments provided a comprehensive framework for financing presidential campaigns, they were never fully implemented. Almost immediately an unusual coalition of liberal and conservative actors challenged the new FECA regime in court, and in the 1976 *Buckley v. Valeo* decision, the Supreme Court made important changes to the law. The Court sought to balance the importance of campaign spending as a form of free speech with the need to control corruption. The Court upheld contribution limits, but ruled that there could be no limits on the amount that individuals, groups, or candidates could spend. Any candidate who accepted federal matching funds, however, could be bound by the aggregate and statewide spending limits of the FECA. The Court reasoned that limiting *contributions* was needed to help prevent corruption or the appearance of corruption, but that limits on *spending* were an unconstitutional abridgement of free speech.

This ruling meant that groups and individuals were limited in the amounts they could give to a candidate, but could independently spend unlimited amounts to advocate the election or defeat of that candidate. Thus, a company or labor union could form a PAC and directly give $5,000 to a candidate such as Hillary Clinton or Barack Obama during the primary election. However, the same PAC could also spend, hypothetically, $10,000,000 in advertising urging voters to support either (or both) of the candidates. Such spending cannot be coordinated with the individual candidate and must be kept strictly independent of the campaign. In 1980, such independent spending in the New Hampshire primary helped Ronald Reagan win a critical victory.

In 1996, the Court made possible an additional type of spending when it ruled that groups could spend unlimited amounts to advocate issues—even mentioning candidates by name and showing their pictures, so long as they do not use specific phrases such as "vote for" or "reelect." This *issue advocacy* spending can be done through a PAC, but it can also be done with treasury money that comes from membership dues or corporate profits. Individuals and political parties can also engage in issue advocacy campaigns. Most importantly, issue advocacy campaigns need not be disclosed to the FEC. These issue advocacy campaigns, like independent expenditures, must not be coordinated with the candidate's campaign.

Although court decisions have greatly changed the FECA regulatory regime, legislation passed by Congress in 1979 opened up the greatest loophole in presidential fundraising. Congress allowed individuals and interest groups to make contributions of unlimited size to political parties. This "soft money" was to be used in party-building activities such as infrastructure, hiring staff, and mobilizing voters and in nonfederal elections for state and local offices. Almost immediately, parties discovered that presidential candidates are the best soft-money fundraisers. The two major parties combined raised more than $263 million in soft-money in 1996 and nearly $490 million in 2000.

By 2001, it was clear that the FECA framework was eroding. Contribution limits were evaded by soft money, which allowed individuals, corporations and unions to give unlimited sums. Spending limits were voided by the courts, except for candidates who accept matching funds. The matching fund system was in place, but George W. Bush proved in 2000 that some candidates could decline matching funds and raise far more than the spending limits that come with these funds. Finally, disclosure was becoming problematic as issue advocacy spending, and the contributions that financed them, were not transparent.

The Bipartisan Campaign Reform Act

In 2002, Congress passed the Bipartisan Campaign Reform Act (BCRA), seeking to deal with some of the problems that had developed in the FECA framework. The law sought to eliminate soft money, regulate issue advocacy, and improve disclosure. The act did not primarily focus on presidential campaigns, but its provisions did affect fundraising by presidential candidates.

The new law initially doubled the contribution limits from $1,000 to $2,000 from any individual donor per election (or $4,000 for the primary and general election combined). This limit is indexed for inflation and in 2008 had increased to $2,300. The law, however, did not increase the portion of individual contributions matched by the federal government in presidential elections. As noted earlier, under the original FECA provisions of 1974, the government matched the first $250 of contributions that were capped at $1,000; now it matches the first $250 of contributions capped at $2,300.

The presidential public finance system also has failed to keep pace with the escalating costs of presidential campaigns, and BCRA did not address this problem. Because candidates who take matching funds are bound by spending limits for individual states, especially the Iowa caucuses and the New Hampshire primary, and to an overall spending limit that applies to the entire primary election process, more and more serious candidates have opted against participating in the program, especially with the higher contribution limit. Additionally, candidates who accept matching funds can invest no more than $50,000 of their own money into their campaign, providing another reason – at least for independently wealthy candidates – to decline public funds.

Steve Forbes, a Republican, was the first serious candidate not to seek matching funds in 1996, spending $42.6 million, mostly of his own money, in a year when the spending ceiling was $37.3 million. George W. Bush followed Forbes' lead in 2000 by rejecting public funding and raising some $96 million in a year when the cap was less than half that amount. Bush became the first candidate to win the presidential nomination of a major political party after refusing public funds during the primaries and caucuses. He rejected matching funds again in 2004, as did two of the Democrat's leading contenders: Howard Dean and John Kerry. Dean and Kerry recognized that Bush had no Republican challenger for the GOP nomination in 2004. This gave Bush a potentially huge strategic advantage. If Dean or Kerry accepted federal matching funds, they would be bound by spending limits set by federal law that would be far less than Bush would be able to spend. Moreover, if the Democratic nomination was competitive, then the eventual winner might well have spent the entire amount allowed by the law in his efforts to win the primary, and be barred from further spending until the late summer when the Democratic national convention freed up funding for the general election campaign. In that scenario, Bush could air unanswered broadcast ads for months, building an insurmountable lead. This calculus undoubtedly influenced Dean's and Kerry's decision to decline matching funds.

Kerry went on to become the first Democrat to win the party's presidential nomination without accepting public funds during the primaries and caucuses. Perhaps, not surprisingly in light of the strategic considerations explained above and the fact that voters failed to punish Bush or Kerry for their financing decisions, many of the leading candidates in both parties in 2008 refused public matching funds, including Democrats Barack Obama and Hillary Clinton, and Republicans Rudolph Giuliani, Mitt Romney, and John McCain.

BCRA also banned soft-money contributions to political parties. In 1996, Republican Bob Dole's campaign relied heavily on party soft-money spending to keep his campaign afloat after the primaries ended and before he received the general election public grant. Dole had spent his legal limit winning his party's nomination, while President Clinton had been able to use his primary election funds for general election purposes because Clinton faced no opposition in the Democratic primaries. In 2004, Bush enjoyed the same advantage Clinton had in 2000. The Democratic challenger, John Kerry, did not accept matching funds during the nomination phase of the election and was able to raise enough money to compete with Bush on a relatively level playing field.

In 2008, John McCain and Barack Obama both rejected matching funds during the nomination phase of the election. During this phase, McCain raised $216 million while Obama took in $424 million – amounts that exceeded those raised by both Bush and Kerry during the same period four years earlier. However, unlike McCain, Obama became the first major-party nominee since 1976 to reject public funds in the general election as well. McCain's acceptance of the general election grant limited him to $84.1 million. Meanwhile, Obama was able to raise $318 million during the general election, outspending McCain by large margins in key battleground states during the final months of the campaign.

The Money Chase: How the Internet Changed Fundraising in 2008

Over the past several election cycles, fundraising and spending by presidential candidates have soared (Magleby 2008). Most of this money comes from individual contributors, who were limited to giving no more than $2300. In the 2008 election cycle, the combined presidential candidates raised more than $1.1 billion from individual contributors – nearly twice the total raised in 2003-04 (Malbin 2009). Barack Obama alone raised more than $600 million from individuals, and even candidates with no real chance at the nomination raised several million dollars in individual contributions. This means that the least serious candidates had tens of thousands of donors, and the leading candidates had millions of donors.

The contributors who finance elections have different motives for giving, and campaigns have developed different methods to connect their solicitation of a contribution with the motives of the donor. Some donors are ideologues, who care deeply about issues like abortion, health care, the war in Iraq, or small government. Others are investors, who give to candidates in order to gain access to help pursue policies that will further their business interests. Still others are intimates, who enjoy the social contacts that come with big fundraising events (Francia, Green, Herrnson, Powell, and Wilcox 2003).

Candidates differ in their ability to appeal to these different pools of donors. Moderates have a difficult time appealing to ideologues, and candidates who are not public officials (such as Al Sharpton in 2004 and Pat Buchanan in 2000) have a difficult time attracting money from investors. Minor-party candidates have a difficult time as well. The three most prominent minor-party candidates in 2008 – independent Ralph Nader, Green Party candidate Cynthia McKinney, and Libertarian Bob Barr – all raised minimal sums of money. Nader brought in only $3 million from individual contributors, Barr just $1.4 million, and McKinney less than $200,000.

Most serious campaigns solicit large contributions from investors and intimates by building networks of personal solicitation. Hillary Clinton's top fundraisers, described earlier, each asked hundreds of others to give to Clinton, and after they gave they asked them to also help raise even more. Large fundraising networks therefore resemble pyramids, in which each fundraiser has other fundraisers who are seeking to help them raise money for the candidate. Clinton's top fundraisers pledged to raise $1 million apiece, and some then sought out others who would pledge to help raise $100,000.

Top solicitors frequently are recognized with titles: George W. Bush called his top solicitors "Pioneers" in 2000; John Kerry called his top fundraisers "Chairs" in 2004; and in 2008, John McCain had his "Trailblazers" while Hillary Clinton had her "Hill Raisers" (Luo and Drew 2008). Often these solicitation networks are based on personal relationships more than ideology. Donors may give to a candidate not because they support him or her, but because they do not want to refuse the person who asked them. Clinton, Romney, Giuliani, and other leading candidates in 2007 spent a good deal of time at large fundraising events where all in attendance paid large sums. In 2004, Bush raised $3.5 million at a single event on June 17, 2003, charging $2,000 a plate for a dinner of hot dogs, hamburgers, and nachos.

In addition, candidates raise money by contacting potential contributors imper-sonally—usually through the mail, often by telephone, and more recently through the Internet. In past elections, candidates found lists of ideologically motivated donors by "renting" the mailing lists of sympathetic organizations such as the NRA or the Sierra Club, and "prospecting" the list by mailing solicitations to people on the list. Those who respond are added to the candidate's "house list" and asked to give again, but those who do not respond to the first mailing may not be contacted again.

In earlier elections, direct-mail fundraising often raised substantial sums on money for ideologically extreme candidates. In 1988, televangelist Pat Robertson raised more money than the sitting vice president, George H. W. Bush, in the first months of the campaign, primarily in small contributions raised through the mail. Robertson's donors gave repeatedly, and his campaign responded with another letter asking for more (Brown, Powell, and Wilcox 1995).

Direct mail was used primarily by strongly ideological candidates because most direct mail letters are thrown in the recycle bin. Only strong emotions can make most Americans of modest means consider contributing to a candidate, and issues such as abortion and the war in Iraq elicit those emotions. Fundraising letters typi-cally use extreme language, and are aimed at individuals who are known to give in response to such letters. Direct mail fundraising costs money for each letter sent, and mailings to moderates have typically lost money.

The Internet has allowed candidates to develop new techniques for impersonal solicitations of small contributions. John McCain used the Internet successfully in 2000, but it was Howard Dean in 2004 who first understood the potential of the medium. Dean raised more than $600,000 in 2003 alone over the Internet. He devel-oped e-mail solicitation lists and invested in large and interesting Web sites, on which people could surf the site and eventually give without being solicited. He also attracted donors and volunteers through "meet up" sessions where they could interact in a vir-tual space that added great excitement to younger, technologically savvy citizens.

Dean showed that the Internet could deliver more complex ideological infor-mation, because Web sites can convey a far deeper and more nuanced position than a five-page letter. His campaign showed that the Internet could also provide social benefits by allowing activists to meet each other online, and then later arrange for meetings to do work for the campaign. But Barack Obama took Internet fundraising and organizing to a new level in 2008.

Fundraising in 2008

In the 2008 campaign, most of the leading candidates expected to forgo matching funds and rely instead on networks of large donors, supplemented with narrowly tar-geted direct mail. This approach had raised record amounts for George Bush and John Kerry. At the start of the campaign, conventional wisdom suggested that Clinton and Mitt Romney had the fundraising advantage. Clinton could tap into a well-established network of Democratic fundraisers who had worked for her husband and her Senate campaign, as well as fundraising experts for women's organizations. She asked fundrais-ers to commit to her early, so that her rivals would have fewer options, and told the fundraising team to ask donors to give only to her and not to any other Democratic candidate. Clinton sought to build an aura of inevitability to her campaign, so that potential donors might not bother to give to a rival who had no chance of winning. She expected her most serious rival to be John Edwards, who had run as vice president in 2004 and had access to solicitors and donor lists from that campaign.

Romney had an estimated net worth of roughly $200 million at his disposal, and a network of fundraisers who were impressed by his business background and success as governor in Massachusetts. But Romney faced serious rivals who might be expected to raise significant sums – including John McCain, who had run for the GOP nomination in 2000, Rudy Giuliani, former mayor of New York and leading in the polls, and former Senator Fred Thompson, whose television star status had many Republicans hoping he might be the next Ronald Reagan.

Table 13.1 shows Clinton led all Democratic candidates with $35 million in the first quarter of 2007, but to her surprise, Barack Obama raised nearly as much. In fact, Clinton's advantage came because she was able to transfer unused money from her Senate Campaign Committee – Obama outraised Clinton in new contributions at the start of the year. By the end of the third quarter of 2007, Obama was ahead in fundraising. More importantly, Clinton had spent lavishly early in the campaign, and had less money in hand to spend as the campaign accelerated.

In January, Obama raised $35 million and Clinton managed to raise slightly over half that amount only because she loaned her campaign $5 million. The Clinton campaign increased their efforts, raising $35 million in February, only to have Obama raise $57 million. Throughout the early primaries and caucuses Obama had more cash on hand and less debt and was able to outspend Clinton and more importantly to spend large sums as polling data showed shifting sentiments. Clinton raised more money in 2007-2008 than any candidate in past elections, and far more than any Democratic candidate had ever done, but Obama raised well over twice her total in individual contributions.

Obama's fundraising success depended heavily on creative use of the Internet. Obama maximized these strengths by reaching out to the "tech class" of Silicon Valley – something that was not done by the Clinton campaign with the same level of enthusiasm and intensity as the Obama campaign. Obama's Silicon Valley supporters provided not only their own money in the form of campaign contributions, but more importantly, the knowledge of how to make the most efficient use of the latest communications technology (Green 2008). The Web site, My.BarackObama. com, provided an array of social networking tools to allow visitors to participate in the campaign, including directions on how to register, and then various ways to volunteer and to contact others. It also contained information about Obama's biography; it allowed users to download an Obama news widget; and offered text-message updates and ring tones with Obama offering his signature campaign line, "Yes we can."

Like Pat Robertson's direct mail fundraising, Obama's fundraising included repeated e-mail solicitations, asking for small amounts. But the campaign also encouraged small donors to become solicitors. Supporters who visited the Obama Web site could create their own fundraising Web site with their own fundraising goals. The site showed a thermometer that became warmer as the solicitor moved toward

Table 13.1 Contributions to Primary Election Campaigns of Leading Presidential Candidates, Jan. 2007–Aug. 2008

	Total Receipts ($ millions)	Indiv Contrib. ($ millions)	In Amounts $200 or less	In Amounts $201– $999	In Amounts $1000– $2299	In Amounts of $2300
Democrats						
Obama						
Jan.–Mar. 2007	24.7	24.7	23%	10%	23%	44%
Apr.–Jun. 2007	30.9	30.7	28%	14%	22%	36%
Jul.–Sep. 2007	19.9	19.2	35%	13%	20%	31%
Oct.–Dec. 2007	22.2	21.7	47%	19%	18%	16%
Jan. 2008	35.2	35.0	47%	22%	16%	15%
Feb. 2008	54.3	54.2	57%	22%	12%	10%
Mar. 2008	40.4	40.2	60%	21%	12%	8%
Apr. 2008	30.3	30.2	65%	19%	10%	6%
May 2008	21.4	21.3	63%	18%	13%	6%
Jun. 2008	48.5	46.9	66%	18%	10%	6%
Jul. 2008	46.9	34.0	69%	19%	11%	1%
Aug. 2008	54.6	42.0	75%	15%	9%	1%
	429.2	**400.0**	**55%**	**18%**	**14%**	**13%**
Clinton						
Jan.–Mar. 2007	29.1	18.8	12%	7%	20%	62%
Apr.–Jun. 2007	21.4	20.4	12%	10%	27%	52%
Jul.–Sep. 2007	23.9	22.0	22%	11%	29%	38%
Oct.–Dec. 2007	24.3	22.9	20%	13%	24%	42%
Jan. 2008	18.1	12.8	36%	18%	21%	25%
Feb. 2008	33.5	33.1	53%	23%	13%	11%
Mar. 2008	19.7	19.4	59%	20%	14%	7%
Apr. 2008	25.7	20.3	23%	21%	11%	45%
May 2008	14.6	12.1	74%	18%	7%	1%
	210.3	**181.8**	**34%**	**16%**	**19%**	**32%**
Edwards						
Jan.–Mar. 2007	12.8	12.7	16%	10%	41%	33%
Apr.–Jun. 2007	8.1	7.9	43%	15%	21%	21%
Jul.–Sep. 2007	6.5	6.3	51%	19%	17%	13%
Oct.–Dec. 2007	13.7	4.6	63%	20%	10%	7%
Jan. 2008	4.5	3.8	72%	19%	6%	3%
Feb. 2008	3.1	0.0	28%	27%	2%	42%
	48.8	**35.5**	**40%**	**15%**	**24%**	**20%**
Richardson						
Jan.–Mar. 2007	6.2	6.2	10%	11%	24%	56%
Apr.–Jun. 2007	6.9	6.8	21%	16%	25%	38%
Jul.–Sep. 2007	4.7	4.6	33%	17%	20%	30%
Oct.–Dec. 2007	4.8	3.7	41%	20%	16%	23%
	22.7	**21.2**	**24%**	**15%**	**22%**	**39%**

(Continued)

Table 13.1 *Continued*

	Total Receipts ($ millions)	Indiv Contrib. ($ millions)	In Amounts $200 or less	In Amounts $201– $999	In Amounts $1000– $2299	In Amounts of $2300
Republicans						
McCain						
Jan.–Mar. 2007	12.9	12.6	18%	7%	34%	41%
Apr.–Jun. 2007	10.1	9.9	19%	11%	24%	46%
Sep.–2007	5.2	4.9	42%	23%	23%	13%
Oct.–Dec. 2007	9.5	6.3	42%	24%	22%	12%
Jan. 2008	12.3	11.3	27%	18%	22%	32%
Feb. 2008	10.7	10.5	23%	14%	20%	43%
Mar. 2008	18.0	14.8	26%	11%	21%	42%
Apr. 2008	18.2	17.5	36%	13%	20%	31%
May 2008	20.9	16.4	46%	16%	17%	22%
Jun. 2008	22.4	17.1	48%	18%	15%	19%
Jul. 2008	26.4	20.4	52%	18%	14%	16%
Aug. 2008	52.8	43.7	47%	21%	16%	15%
	219.3	**185.2**	**39%**	**16%**	**19%**	**26%**
Romney						
Jan.–Mar. 2007	23.3	20.6	6%	6%	50%	38%
Apr.–Jun. 2007	20.6	13.6	19%	13%	27%	40%
Jul.–Sep. 2007	18.4	9.5	21%	16%	25%	38%
Oct.–Dec. 2007	27.1	8.8	22%	13%	24%	42%
Jan. 2008	13.5	6.4	35%	19%	18%	28%
	102.9	**59.0**	**17%**	**12%**	**33%**	**38%**
Huckabee						
Jan.–Mar. 2007	0.5	0.5	11%	12%	21%	57%
Apr.–Jun. 2007	0.8	0.7	20%	17%	30%	33%
Jul.–Sep. 2007	1.0	1.0	37%	22%	20%	20%
Oct.–Dec. 2007	6.7	6.6	39%	17%	18%	26%
Jan. 2008	4.0	4.0	51%	17%	17%	15%
Feb. 2008	3.0	2.9	57%	16%	14%	13%
	16.0	**15.8**	**43%**	**17%**	**18%**	**22%**
Paul						
Jan.–Mar. 2007	0.6	0.6	39%	15%	26%	21%
Apr.–Jun. 2007	2.4	2.4	50%	17%	16%	17%
Jul.–Sep. 2007	5.3	5.2	52%	20%	18%	10%
Oct.–Dec. 2007	20.0	19.9	68%	18%	10%	5%
Jan. 2008	4.4	4.4	73%	17%	7%	2%
Feb. 2008	1.8	1.7	64%	30%	5%	1%
	34.5	**34.2**	**64%**	**19%**	**11%**	**6%**

(*Continued*)

Table 13.1 *Continued*

	Total Receipts ($ millions)	Indiv Contrib. ($ millions)	In Amounts $200 or less	In Amounts $201–$999	In Amounts $1000–$2299	In Amounts of $2300
Giuliani						
Jan.–Mar. 2007	15.5	13.5	9%	7%	26%	58%
Apr.–Jun. 2007	15.0	14.6	9%	9%	24%	58%
Jul.–Sep. 2007	10.3	9.9	15%	14%	31%	40%
Oct.–Dec. 2007	13.8	13.3	10%	12%	32%	46%
Jan. 2008	2.8	2.7	20%	16%	29%	35%
	57.4	**53.9**	**11%**	**11%**	**28%**	**51%**

Note: As contributions of $200 or less are typically not itemized, this category may contain funds marked for the general election. Total receipts includes individual contributions, loans, federal funds, and other receipts, minus offsets. Individual contributions account for refunds. Values in contribution categories are percents of total individual contributions.

Sources: Analysis of data obtained from the Federal Election Commission

the goal (Green 2008). Many of those who were asked to give this way themselves created fundraising Web pages. They went on to create links through Facebook, and many created personal videos that they displayed there or in some cases, posted to YouTube.

While Clinton spent time in smaller fundraising events where all in attendance had given a large sum, Obama often appeared at stadium rallies with thousands of people who were not charged any money. Obama not only asked for votes, but also that those in attendance make a small contribution. Those who sent a specific text message to the Obama campaign were then contacted with a request to contribute (Green 2008). Those who gave were later asked to raise money for the campaign. Many were contacted repeatedly by e-mail, and some of these messages included video attachments that provided much more excitement than any direct mail letter.

In comparison to the neat pyramidal networks of large donor fundraising, the Obama network grew virally, with individual donors contacting their Facebook friends or texting everyone in their cell phone list. Anyone who ended up on the Obama list was asked not just to give, but also to work for the campaign. During the final days, the campaign asked its small donors to contact specific neighbors, or to download a program that would automatically text message anyone on their cell phone list who lived in a closely contested state (Dunham and Silverman 2008).

Late in the campaign, the Clinton team discovered Internet fundraising and used it effectively. But Clinton ran a very good 2004 fundraising campaign in a year when a candidate rewrote the playbook.

On the Republican side, Giuliani led early fundraising, in part because Romney did not contribute from his own funds until later. McCain's early fundraising faltered in 2007, and his end-of-the-year report in 2007 to the Federal Election Commission actually showed his campaign in the red, with $3 million on hand and $4.5 million in debts. But the surprising leader in fourth quarter receipts was long-shot candidate, Representative Ron Paul of Texas, who raised a stunning $19.8 million largely through Internet donations that came about from motivational YouTube videos and social networking techniques similar to those of the Obama campaign. The Paul campaign failed to win a Republican caucus or primary and never posed a serious challenge for the Republican nomination. However, it did prove that the techniques that worked for Obama can work for at least certain types of Republican candidates.

In the early months of the campaign, Romney loaned his own campaign $45 million from his personal wealth – the highest sum on record. Romney outspent his rivals in Iowa and New Hampshire by large sums. Romney spent a record $7 million on TV ads in Iowa alone, only to lose to former governor and Baptist minister Mike Huckabee who spent far less (Hull 2008). Huckabee used a network of evangelical churches first created by Pat Robertson in the 2008 caucuses. A few days later, John McCain won the New Hampshire primary despite being outspent by a wide margin by Romney. The Republican race demonstrated clearly that money alone does not determine election outcomes.

After his victory in New Hampshire, McCain went on to win in South Carolina and Florida, and his successes bolstered his fundraising. He clinched the nomination early and continued to raise money throughout the campaign, eventually raising nearly $220 million – a remarkable figure roughly equal to the amount raised by Clinton in a more competitive campaign. Yet McCain's primary election fundraising was nearly doubled by Obama's $424 million raised by Barack Obama during the same period.

The 2008 General Election: Obama's $84 Million Gamble

After some hesitation, Barack Obama became the first major-party nominee to decline public funding in the general election in 2008. Obama had earlier promised to accept the $84.1 million public subsidy that McCain had agreed to accept. Obama gambled that he could raise far more than this amount during the general election by returning to donors who had given during the primaries. Under campaign finance rules, even those primary election donors who had given the maximum $2,300 during the nomination phase could give again in the general election. Obama was counting on not only being able to raise far more money than McCain, but also that the voters would not punish him for breaking his earlier promise.

Obama raised an additional $318 million during the general election campaign, a figure nearly four times the public grant that McCain accepted. McCain benefitted from significant spending by Republican party committees, but Obama's vastly larger budget allowed him to spend a record $240 million on television advertising including the 30-minute ad mentioned previously (Schouten 2008). He was able to invest money in traditionally Republican states such as Indiana, Virginia, and North Carolina – three states Obama's campaign likely would have ignored absent his fundraising success.

This posed major strategic problems for the more limited McCain budget. As polls began showing competitive contests in Indiana, Virginia, and North Carolina, McCain was forced to decide between whether to move his resources there or whether to continue spending huge money sums of money on advertising in the critical battleground states of Ohio, Florida, and Pennsylvania. By expanding the battlefield, Obama made the most of his considerable money advantage. It allowed his campaign to go on offense in states where Bush had won in 2004, forcing McCain to spend most of his time defending these states instead of the contested battleground states.

In the increasingly purple state of Virginia, Obama spent $24 million in television advertising, more than three times the $7.4 million spent by McCain (Schouten 2008). Obama went on to win Virginia in 2008 – the first Democrat to do so since Lyndon Johnson in 1964. He also carried seven more states that went Republican in 2004: Indiana, North Carolina, Florida, Iowa, Colorado, New Mexico, and Nevada.

McCain's financial disadvantage was partially offset by an aggressive fundraising effort by the Republican National Committee (RNC). While most Democratic contributions went directly to the Obama campaign, Republican donors gave to party committees that could legally spend to help McCain. The RNC had a substantial cash advantage over its Democratic counterpart.

Independent groups spent heavily in the final months of the campaign. Republican groups organized primarily through 501 (c) committees that are not required to disclose expenditures or receipts (Weisman 2009). The U.S. Chamber of Commerce led the Republican groups, claiming more than $35 million in spending. Democratic 527 committees were also active, especially labor unions. Two of the top three spenders among 527 groups in 2008 were labor groups: AFSCME ($32.9 million) and the SEIU ($27 million). The third top spender, America Votes ($17.6 million) was a coalition made up of various progressive groups, but with organized labor again playing a significant role. Many groups did electioneering without spending much money, placing ads on their Web sites and e-mailing links to members and to the press. MoveOn.Org sponsored a contest for college students to design innovative ads for Obama, many of which can still be seen on the organization's Web site. It also created a viral e-mail that members could send to friends, inserting the friend's name in a fake news story that McCain had won the election by a single vote, because the friend had not elected to cast a ballot (Lukovitz and Lentini 2008).

The Future of Presidential Fundraising

Until recently, public financing of presidential elections had been a largely successful program, having disbursed nearly $1.5 billion since its inception in 1976 (Federal Election Commission 2009). In 2000, however, the system developed its first serious crack when George W. Bush opted out of the primary phase and went on to raise far more money than the spending limit that would have applied had he accepted public funds. Bush's subsequent victory and willingness to bypass the primary phase again in 2004 drove even two liberal Democrats – Howard Dean and John Kerry – away from the primary phase of the system four years later. By 2008, most of the leading candidates declined public funds in the primaries. The 21.7 million in public funds that were distributed during the primary contest was the lowest since the government began matching contributions in 1976 (Federal Election Commission 2009). Barack Obama duplicated Bush's feat in the general election, raising far more than the public grant would have provided without an apparent penalty among voters. This precedent leaves the public financing system in serious jeopardy.

Obama claimed that his fundraising effort was "a parallel public financing system," because many of his contributors gave small contributions (Overby 2008). He claimed that his campaign was financed by people of modest means and, therefore, was a different type of public fund. Yet many of those who made small contributions went on to give large aggregate sums (Malbin 2009). A donor who gave $100 a month for 10 months would have given $1,000 total to the campaign, a large contribution by anyone's definition. By one standard, the majority of Obama's contributions came in small amounts, but much of his money came from those who contributed (over time) large sums.

Some scholars have suggested a variety of reforms to the federal funding system, including increasing spending limits during the primaries or even eliminating them, which might induce some candidates to accept matching funds and in doing so reach out to less affluent donors. Still other proposals include matching small contributions at a higher rate; for example, at a rate of three to one (Campaign Finance Institute 2005).

Meanwhile the basic rules of campaign finance remain in question, as the Supreme Court has continued to overturn portions of the regulatory framework. In 2007, the Court ruled in *Wisconsin Right to Life v. FEC* that BCRA's provision banning issue ads in the month preceding the primary and the two months preceding the general elections was unconstitutional violation of free speech. In issuing the majority decision, Chief Justice John Roberts offered an ominous tone for future reforms, declaring, "Enough is enough." The Court may hear a series of challenges to the key provisions of campaign finance law over the next year, and possibly radically change the rules of the game. During the next year, the Court will decide whether airing an attack film on Hillary Clinton on television stations would constitute electoral spending, and the Court has invited opposing sides to argue again over the constitutionality of BCRA, perhaps signaling that it will overturn earlier decisions.

Obama's fundraising (and also that of Ron Paul) suggests that it is now possible to finance campaigns by drawing significant sums in small contributions. Meanwhile, political groups have continued to spend large sums in advertising not controlled by the candidates or parties. Future court rulings may well open the floodgate to more spending by these kinds of groups, which would allow wealthy individuals and interests to spend even more on campaigns. At this point, the future of presidential campaign finance is less certain than at any recent time. What is clear, however, is that in 2008 creative campaign teams used technology to invent new fundraising models, which when placed atop their use of existing techniques, allowed them to raise sums unimaginable 10 years ago.

References

Baida, Peter, 1992. "The Legacy of Dollar Mark Hanna." In Stephen J. Wayne and Clyde Wilcox (ed) *The Quest for National Office* New York, St. Martins.

Campaign Finance Institute, 2005. "So the Voters May Choose: Reviving the Presidential Matching Fund System." http://www.cfinst.org/president/pdf/VotersChoose.pdf

Dunham, Richard S. and Dwight Silverman. 2008. "Favored Obama Address Begins with http, Not 1600." *Houston Chronicle*, November 8. Accessed on September 7, 2009. Available at http://www.chron.com/disp/story.mpl/nation/6102843.html.

Federal Election Commission. 2009. "2008 Presidential Campaign Financial Activity Summarized: Receipts Nearly Double 2004 Total." Accessed on August 15, 2009. Available at http://www.fec.gov/press/press2009/20090608PresStat.shtml.

Fouhy, Beth. 2007. "Clinton Aims to Raise $75M Before 2008." *Associated Press*, February 7, 2009. Accessed on September 7, 2009. Available at http://www.foxnews.com/printer_friendly_wires/2007Feb07/0,4675,ClintonFundraising,00.html.

Francia, Peter, John Green, Paul Herrnson, Lynda Powell, and Clyde Wilcox. 2003. *The Financiers of Congressional Elections: Investors, Ideologues, and Intimates.* New York: Columbia University Press.

Green, Joshua. 2008. "The Amazing Money Machine." *The Atlantic*, June. Accessed on September 7, 2009. Available at http://www.theatlantic.com/doc/200806/obama-finance.

Hull, Christopher C. 2008. "Why Obama and Huckabee Won Iowa: Inside the 2008 Caucuses." Presented at the 2008 Annual Meeting of the American Political Science Association. Boston, MA.

Lukovitz, Karlene and Nina M. Lentini. 2008. "Moveon.org Shows Viral's Power with Obama Vid." *Marketing Dailey*, October 30. Accessed on September 7, 2009. Available at http://www.mediapost.com/publications/?fa=Articles.showArticle&art_aid=93643.

Luo, Michael and Christopher Drew. 2008. "Obama and McCain Lag in Naming 'Bundlers.'" *New York Times*, July 11. Accessed on September 7, 2009. Available at http://www.nytimes.com/2008/07/11/us/politics/11bundlers.html?pagewanted=print.

Magleby, David B. 2008. "Rolling in the Dough: The Continued Surge in Individual Contributions to Presidential Candidates and Party Committees." *The Forum* 6 (1): Article 5.

Malbin, Michael J. 2009. "Small Donors, Large Donors and the Internet: The Case for Public Financing after Obama." The Campaign Finance Institute, April. Accessed on August 3, 2009. Available at: http://www.cfinst.org/president/pdf/PresidentialWorkingPaper_April09.pdf.

Overby, Peter. 2008. "McCain Pressures Obama on Public Financing." *NPR*, April 10. Accessed on September 7, 2009. Available at http://www.npr.org/templates/story/story.php?storyId=89538146.

Schouten, Fredreka. 2008. "Obama's Fundraising Obliterates Records." *USA Today*, Dec 2. Accessed on September 7, 2009. Available at http://www.usatoday.com/news/politics/election2008/2008-12-02-obama-money_N.htm.

Weissman, Stephen R. 2009. "Soft Money Political Spending by 501(c) Nonprofits Tripled in 2008 Election." Campaign Finance Institute, Feb 25.

Wilcox, Clyde. 2008. "Internet Fundraising in 2008: A New Model? *The Forum* 1 (6). Article 6.

Endnote

1. These referenced the McCain-Feingold campaign finance law, and McCain's promises to pare "pork" spending from the national budget.

James W. Ceaser and Daniel DiSalvo

The Magnitude of the 2008 Democratic Victory: By the Numbers*

People commonly exaggerate the magnitude of events that take place in their day, probably to flatter themselves about the significance of their own lives and times. Journalists, keen to feed the public what it wants, contribute mightily to this amplification. This tendency to inflate was on vivid display in many interpretations of the Democrats' 2008 electoral victory, which ranged from claims that it was "unprecedented" and "historic" to unqualified assertions that it was "a genuinely realigning election." *Time* magazine went so far as to suggest a likeness to Franklin Roosevelt's victory of 1932, printing a cover that morphed Barack Obama's head onto a iconic photo of FDR sporting his '30's-style "lid" and driving a convertible.[1]

The 2008 Democratic triumph was no doubt impressive—how much so will be seen shortly—but it was far from being massive, or even unusual, by historical standards. Looking at the record, even if that proves tedious, provides some perspective. There have been 29 presidential contests since 1896, a year many scholars use as the starting point of "modern politics." Barack Obama won the presidency with a share of the popular vote of just under 53 percent, which ranks 14th, or at the median (Table 1).

Jim Ceaser and Daniel DiSalvo, "The Magnitude of the 2008 Democratic Victory: By the Numbers" in *The Forum*. http://www.bepress.com/journals

His margin of victory over his rival (6.9 percent) ranks as the 19th largest, or slightly below the median. Finally, his electoral vote percentage (a figure almost always magnified relative to the popular vote) was 67.8, or 17th among the 29 contests.

The most helpful figure in determining the magnitude of a presidential victory is the popular vote margin because it "controls" for the problem of third-party candidacies. On the basis of this figure, presidential elections can be sorted into five different categories: (1) the near-to-dead heats (a margin of less than two percent), which must include George W. Bush's election of 2000, when he lost the national popular vote; (2) the squeakers (a margin of 3 to 5 percent), of which George W. Bush's 2004 victory was the squeakiest; (3) the moderately competitive races (6 to 9 percent); (4) the big wins (10 to 12 percent), with Ronald Reagan's 1980 victory over Jimmy Carter being the most recent; and (5) the landslides (more than 13 percent), the largest and also the least memorable of which was Warren G. Harding's 26-point thumping of James M. Cox in 1920.[2]

Obama's victory fits squarely into the moderately competitive category, which happens to correspond to the "feel" of the race as experienced by the American public. As the election neared, all the major polls had Obama ahead, but a few were at or near the margin of error. A last-minute swing of only two or three points, in just the right places, could have produced an upset.[3] This outside possibility gave the last weeks of the 2008 election an air of expectation that kept many riveted to the press coverage and the blogosphere. Some appear to be suffering symptoms of withdrawal to this day.

The actual outcome was in no way surprising. When the television networks reported early on election eve that Obama won Pennsylvania, a state that John McCain needed in order to pull off his improbable inside straight, it was clear the race was over. Unlike 2004 (or 2000), there would be no waiting until the wee hours of the morning (or for five weeks) to learn who had won. Better still, there was no talk of recounts or of litigation; the armies of lawyers that were at the ready, their briefs fixed like bayonets, were demobilized and sent back to their barracks. Something happened that Americans who had come of political age since 1996 had never seen: the election of a president without accusations of perfidy or ballot manipulation.

To take a more fine-grained measure of Barack Obama's victory, it is helpful to look at the subset of elections of *first-term* presidential victories (Table 14.2). Not surprisingly, the larger victory margins have tended to occur in cases when a popular incumbent is re-elected, such as Ronald Reagan in 1984 or Franklin Roosevelt in 1936, while more of the narrower margins, including all of the "dead heats," take place in elections involving candidates ascending to the office for the first time. In this more limited group, Obama fares slightly better, ranking 10th among the 16 first-term presidents. His victory was not as large as Ronald Reagan's in 1980 or George H. W. Bush's in 1988, but it was greater than Jimmy Carter's in 1976, Bill Clinton's in 1992, and, of course, George W. Bush's in 2000. Indeed, Obama had the largest margin of victory of any incoming *Democratic* president since FDR in 1932.

Analyzing the scope of congressional victories in a historical perspective is trickier, as much depends on the position from which a party begins:[4] It is harder to pick up seats when a party already has many of them than when it is starting from a low base. In addition, more has changed in the system of congressional elections across time, including the direct election of senators, which began in 1914, and the rules and practices governing the drawing of district boundaries for House seats. For what it suggests, however, the Democratic congressional victory of 2008, relative to the midterm election of 2006, falls in the upper range of congressional victories in a presidential year (see Table 14.1). The pickup of seats in the Senate (now at seven, with the Minnesota seat still undeclared) is the sixth largest since 1896 (although tied with five other elections), and the 10th largest for the House (23 seats with one seat still being decided).[5] Looking at the results of the Senate and the House together, there have been only six presidential election years in which a party has either held its own or gained more seats in both the Senate and the House (1948, 1980, 1912, 1928, 1932, and 1920).

The Bigger Story

The statistical portrait just provided depicts what is on its own terms a substantial Democratic victory in 2008. Yet to grasp the full significance of the election, it needs to be looked at in light of what happened since the previous presidential contest. The combined impact of 2008 with the 2006 midterm election dramatically transformed the political scene in America, turning a red nation into a blue one. Yet this reversal of party fortunes is all the more important because of what the 2004 election meant for the Republican Party. That election represented the high-water mark for the GOP since 1952, when Dwight Eisenhower was chosen (and arguably since 1928, when Herbert Hoover won).

Granted, the Republicans since 1952 had won the presidency by much greater margins, including three landslides (Eisenhower in 1956, Nixon in 1972, and Reagan in 1984). But unless one counts 2000, when the Republicans limped into control of all three institutions while losing the popular vote for the presidency and managing only a tie in the Senate, 2004 was the only election since 1952 in which Republicans emerged holding a majority in all three branches. (By contrast, Democrats had majorities in all institutions following the elections of 1960, 1964, 1976, 1992, and now, of course, 2008.) And 2004 was the only time since 1952 that Republicans won each branch and gained ground in each institution. With 55 senators, Republicans equaled their largest number in that chamber since 1929 (the GOP had achieved that number on three other occasions, from 1987 to 1989, 1997 to 1999, and 1999 to 2001), and they secured their largest majority in the House since 1929.

The Republican victory in 2004 fulfilled at long last one of the hopes of the "new" Republican Party that had been born under Ronald Reagan in 1980. Beginning in 1980, the Republicans achieved some notable victories: Reagan's own election along with a Republican Senate (but still a Democratic House), and the stunning 1994 GOP congressional victory in both the House and Senate during Bill Clinton's first presidential term. Yet they had never attained a majority across the board. Many Republicans, and not just Republicans, looked at 2004 as a plateau on which the GOP would consolidate and begin a climb to a more commanding majority status. The titles of some of the books published after the election, including One Party Country and Building Red America, were indicative of this assessment.[6]

Table 14.1 The Magnitude of Presidential Victories

Margin	Election	Winning Candidate	Losing Candidate	Winners %	Electoral College %	Senate Midterm	House Midterm	Senate - 4yrs	House - 4yrs
Dead Heats									
-0.5	2000	G. W. Bush (R)	Gore (D)	47.9	**50.4**	-5	-2	-5	-7
0.2	1960	Kennedy (D)	Nixon (R)	49.7	**56.4**	-1	-20	13	29
0.7	1968	Nixon (R)	Humphrey (D)	**43.4**	55.9	7	4	11	52
2.1	1976	Carter (D)	**Ford (R)***	50.1	55.2	1	1	5	50
Squeakers									
2.5	2004	**G. W. Bush (R)**	Kerry (D)	50.7	53.2	4	3	5	11
3.1	1916	**Wilson (D)**	Hughes (R)	49.2	52.2	-2	-16	3	-77
4.3	1896	McKinley (R)	Bryan (D)	51	60.6	5	-48	9	*
4.5	1948	**Truman (D)**	Dewey (R)	49.6	57.1	9	75	-3	21
Moderately Competitive									
5.6	1992	Clinton (D)	**Bush (R)**	43	68.8	1	-9	2	-2
6.1	1900	**McKinley (R)**	Bryan (D)	51.7	65.3	0	13	7	-6
6.9	2008	OBAMA(D)	McCain (R)	52.9	67.8	7	23	12	54
7.5	1944	**F. Roosevelt D**	Dewey (R)	53.4	81.4	0	20	*	-25
7.7	1988	G. Bush (R)	Dukakis (D)	53.4	79.2	1	-2	-8	-7
8.5	1908	**Taft (R)**	Bryan (D)	51.6	66.5	-1	-4	2	-32
8.5	1996	**Clinton (D)**	Dole	49.2	**70.4**	-3	2	-12	-52
Big Wins									
9.7	1980	**Reagan (R)**	**Carter (D)**	50.8	90.9	12	34	15	49
10	1940	**F. Roosevelt (D)**	Willkie (R)	54.7	84.6	-3	5	-10	*
10.8	1952	Eisenhower (R)	Stevenson (D)	55.2	83.2	1	22	6	50

Landslides

Landslides	Year								
14.4	1912	Wilson (D)	**Taft (R)****	41.8	82.0	7	61	19	119
15.4	1956	**Eisenhower (R)**	Stevenson (D)	57.4	86.1	0	–2	–1	–20
17.5	1928	Hoover (R)	Smith (D)	58.2	83.6	8	32	2	23
17.7	1984	**Reagan (R)**	Mondale (D)	58.8	97.6	–1	16	0	–.0
17.8	1932	F. Roosevelt (D)	**Hoover (R)**	57.4	88.9	12	97	20	149
18.8	1904	**T. Roosevelt (R)**	Parker (D)	56.4	70.6	1	44	2	51
22.6	1964	Johnson (D)	Goldwater (R)	61.1	90.3	2	36	4	32
23.2	1972	**Nixon (R)**	McGovern (D)	60.7	96.7	–2	12	–1	0
24.3	1936	**F. Roosevelt D**	Landon (R)	60.8	98.5	7	12	17	21
25.2	1924	**Coolidge (R)**	Davis (D)	54	71.9	1	22	–5	"55
26.2	1920	Harding (R)	Cox (D)	60.3	76.1	10	62	17	88

*Incumbents are in **Bold**.

** In 1912, although Taft was the incumbent, Theodore Roosevelt actually came in second to Woodrow Wilson. Wilson's margin of victory is thus calculated for the differences between him and Roosevelt.

Sources: Dave Leip's Atlas of U.S. Presidential Elections, http://www.uselectionatlas.org/; Changes in Senate party strength were calculated from the official U.S. Senate Web site, http://www.senate.gov/pagelayout/history/one_item_and_teasers/partydiv.htm; Changes in House party strength were calculated from: http://www.emailthecongress.com/partv-strength-house.html; *Biographical Directory of the U.S. Congress;* Congressional Research Service; Office of the Clerk of the U.S. House of Representatives, http://clerk.house.gov/arthistory/househistory/partvDiv.html

Table 14.2 First Term Presidential Victories Ranked by Margin of Victory

Rank	Election	Winner	Loser	Winners Percentage	Margin of Victory	Electoral College Percentage
1.	1920	Harding (R)	Cox (D)	60.3	26.2	76.1
2.	1924	Coolidge (R)	Davis (D)	54	25.2	73.8
3.	1932	F. Roosevelt (D)	Hoover (R)	57.4	17.8	88.9
4.	1928	Hoover (R)	Smith (D)	58.2	17.7	83.6
5.	1912	Wilson (R)	Taft (R)	41.8	14.5	82.0
6.	1952	Eisenhower (R)	Stevenson (D)	55.2	10.8	83.2
7.	1980	Reagan (R)	Carter (D)	50.8	9.7	90.9
8.	1908	Taft (R)	Bryan (D)	51.6	8.5	66.5
9.	1988	G. Bush (R)	Dukakis (D)	53.4	7.7	79.2
10.	2008	Obama (D)	McCain (R)	52.9	6.9	67.8
11.	1992	Clinton (D)	Bush (R)	43	5.6	68.8
12.	1896	McKinley (R)	Bryan (D)	51	4.3	60.6
13.	1976	Carter (D)	Ford (R)	50.1	2.1	55.2
14.	1968	Nixon (R)	Humphrey (D)	43.4	0.7	55.9
15.	1960	Kennedy (D)	Nixon (R)	49.7	0.2	56.4
16.	2000	G. W. Bush (R)	Gore (D)	47.8	−0.5	50.5

There was much speculation that the GOP could win that most coveted and elusive of prizes in American politics (if it exists at all): the holy grail of a favorable partisan realignment.

By 2006, these GOP hopes had been dashed, and entering 2008 Republicans were fighting just to hang on. The explanation for the decline and fall of the Republican empire, short-lived as it was, is to be found largely on the streets of Baghdad and New Orleans. George W. Bush lost the mandate of heaven sometime in the period between 2005 and 2006, and the Republicans in Congress never mastered the art of being a responsible governing party. The magnitude of the partisan change that occurred in the consecutive elections of 2006 and 2008 is the conclusion to this story. Democrats gained 12 Senate seats and 49 House seats, moving in the process—in 2006—from minority to majority status in both chambers. After the 2008 elections, the Democratic congressional majorities surpassed by a significant margin the Republican majorities after 2004 (Table 14.3). Since 1932, Republicans have barely had a moment in the sun.

There are many ways to assess congressional gains made since the last presidential election (see the final two columns of Table 1 or Table 3). But however one looks at it, the 2008 Democratic "surge" for consecutive elections (with gains in both elections) is striking. It would be ranked about fifth, on a rough par with what Republicans achieved with Reagan's victory in 1980, but well short of the party gains that occurred at the time of FDR's triumphs in 1932 or 1936, Harding's in 1920, and Wilson's in 1912.

As is well known, the domestic policy-making process in the U.S. is normally characterized by slow action, a result that derives from the structural requirement of consent by three power centers (the presidency, the Senate, and the House).

Table 14.3 Changes in Congressional Party Strength: 2000–2008

Republicans-Democrats-Independents				
Year	Senate		House	
2000	50R-50D		221R-212D	2 I
2002	51R-48D	1I	229 R-204D	1 I
2004	55R-44D	1I	232 R-201D	1 I
2006	49R-50D	1I	198 R-234D	
2008	41R-59D	1I	178 R-257D	

There are occasional exceptions, such as Wilson's New Freedom, FDR's New Deal, and LBJ's Great Society, when the policy process temporarily resembles parliamentary governments and huge new legislative programs are enacted. These periods are associated with some of the surge elections noted previously. Of course, the incoming president must be one who wants an active agenda, which excludes Harding and Eisenhower, as well as one who controls a solid majority in both houses, a factor that slowed Reagan in 1980. Add a crisis (or at least talk of one) and the conditions that favor a major policy shift are enhanced still further. Obama will enter the White House with some of these conditions fulfilled, but with nothing approaching the size and scope of the personal victory of these other presidents.

It is a sobering lesson to some of those who experienced these surges to discover how quickly they can be reduced or overturned. The Eisenhower government elected in 1952 won control of all three national electoral institutions by picking up one seat in the Senate and 22 in the House. Two years later, the Republicans were in the minority in both chambers, losing 18 seats in the House and one in the Senate. In 1982, two years after Reagan won the White House and Republicans gained 12 seats (and the majority) in the Senate plus 34 in House, the GOP gained one seat in the Senate but gave back 26 seats in the House. In 1920, Harding's landslide brought in its wake 10 new Republican senators and 62 House members, only to see the party lose six seats in the Senate two years later and a whopping 77 in the House (though still enough in both cases to keep the majority).

Democrats in comparable circumstances have had more luck, or shown better skill. In 1912, Wilson's coattails brought in seven new senators and 61 representatives. The 1914 election produced mixed results, as Democrats picked up four more seats in the Senate but slipped back in the House to where they were before 1912, losing 61 seats but still controlling the chamber. The elections of the 1930s were so overwhelmingly favorable to one party as to set this period apart from all others. In 1934, Democrats continued their rout of the GOP, winning nine more seats in the House and 10 seats in the Senate. Just when it looked as if the Democrats could go no higher, Roosevelt's second landslide of 1936 led to a gain of 12 more seats in the House, reducing the GOP to a paltry 88 members, and seven more seats in the Senate, shrinking Republican Conference meetings to the size of a modest dinner party (at 16 members).[7]

It is no wonder, then, that some of President-Elect Obama's enthusiasts in the media have him riding in FDR's convertible. Even if more frequent historical patterns hold, and Democrats should slip in the 2010 congressional elections, they would have to suffer a huge reversal to lose control of either chamber. The most likely scenario at the moment is that Democrats will probably lose some House seats but hold or improve their position in the Senate. The House GOP has nowhere to go but up, as there is a fairly large quotient of Democrats holding seats in districts that voted for Bush and McCain. It is also hard to see how the number of Republicans in the House can get much smaller, as there are only five members that won seats in districts that voted for Kerry and Obama. The 2010 Senate elections look much more favorable to the Democrats, as some older Republicans are likely to retire and very few of the Democrats up for reelection appear (for now at least) to be vulnerable.[8] In this respect, although Obama's victory was less impressive than Wilson's, 2008 appears structurally to be closest to 1912 in terms of the large Democratic congressional majorities that can sustain some losses and still be workable governing entities.

Is 2008 a Realigning Election?

Party realignment is currently among the most contested concepts in political science, with some arguing that the idea should be retired altogether, and others holding that, shorn of certain outsized connotations, it remains helpful.[9] Whatever the state of the academic debate, journalists and pundits have not retreated from hauling the bounty of political science theorizing into the political arena. Many liberal commentators, not surprisingly, were quick to declare the Obama victory a realignment. According to *The Washington Post* columnist Harold Meyerson, Obama's margins "among decisive and growing constituencies make clear that this was a genuinely realigning election."[10] For John Judis of *The New Republic*, the election "is the culmination of a Democratic realignment that began in the 1990s, was delayed by September 11, and resumed with the 2006 election."[11]

Dispensing with the more fantastic notions that some of the originators of the concept ascribed to it, a realignment can be conceived as a major electoral shift in the relative strength of the political parties (and therefore likely to endure for awhile), accompanied or sealed by a shift in the reigning political ideas that set government's agenda, plus a major change in the direction of public policy. By this definition, it is clear that a "realigning election" can only be determined well after the fact: it is something projected backward in light of an assessment of the performance of an administration following an election like 1932.

Yet even if there are such things as realignments, their significance for electoral outcomes can be greatly exaggerated. They are only part of the story. A realignment is not a guarantee—nowhere close to it—that the favored party will win future elections. American presidential elections are influenced both by an alignment (meaning the tendency of partisans to vote their party preference) *and* by a relatively freestanding assessment by many voters at each election of the performance of the incumbent and the incumbent party, weighed against the merits of an alternative. With the exception of one or two periods in American history, when the alignment may have provided one party with a truly commanding lead over the other, the aligned portion of the electorate is too small relative to the assessing portion to determine the outcome.

What an alignment in a party's favor provides, therefore, is an advantage, all things being equal. But all things are almost never equal in politics. And because the alignment itself is influenced by ongoing assessments, it too may not endure for very long. The advantage is even countered slightly by the apparent political law that after a certain point, holding power means accumulating grievances more than winning plaudits. If one were to apply, albeit prematurely, the elements of a partisan realignment to the 2008 Democratic victory, then, a case by and *against* the claim can be made.

In favor is the argument that Obama's 7 percent margin has greater significance than usual, because it occurred on the first truly "open" presidential election (one in which no sitting president or vice-president was running) since 1952; because it was accompanied by expanded Democratic congressional majorities; because it comes amid survey evidence of fall-off in Republican party identification; and finally, because the coalition that helped elect Obama portends longer term Democratic dominance, because the constituencies that comprise it are growing segments of the electorate. Those constituencies are Latinos, youth, and professionals. According to exit polls, Obama won 66 percent of the Latino vote, a group that is growing, and which was a key to his victories in states such as New Mexico, Colorado, and Florida. Obama won 66 percent of voters between the ages of 18 and 29, which some believe signals their allegiance to the Democratic party for the longer term. Obama also appealed enormously to the highly educated (or well-schooled), doing extremely well among voters with advanced degrees.[12]

On the flip side, it has been said that while Obama won in an "open" election, the unpopularity of the incumbent was in fact a huge factor pulling against John McCain; that, as noted, a 7-percent victory in the popular vote was hardly a rout and that but for the (contingent) financial crisis that struck in mid-September, McCain had a good shot; that Obama enjoyed a massive advantage in campaign funds; and that the electoral map did not change all that decisively. Although Obama won striking victories in three states that were not competitive in 2000 or 2004 (Virginia, North Carolina, and Indiana), most of the states (Florida, Ohio, New Hampshire, and New Mexico) that were competitive in the prior two elections remained battlegrounds this year.

In terms of new governing ideas, it appears less that the Democratic Party has anything particularly new on tap than that it is more self-confident in asserting its traditional liberal agenda. One of the striking things about the Obama campaign was that he did not propose a new programmatic direction, such as claiming to be a "New Democrat." His appeal was largely based on valence issues and themes (like change and post-partisanship) rather than on clearly stated positions. This leaves much to be filled in, which is what is happening as this is written. What cannot be said at this point is that there is evidence of a decisive ideological shift in Americans' thinking. Exit polls showed that 51 percent of Americans believed government "should do more"—a reversal of the Reagan-era majorities that thought government should do less. But the proportion of voters describing themselves as liberal, moderate, and conservative stayed roughly the same compared with four years ago. Andrew Kohut of the Pew Research Center argues that: "This was an election where the middle asserted itself," and that there was "no sign" of a "movement to the left."[13]

Events are often more important than elections in shaping the strategies of presidents once they are in office. The current economic crisis has opened the door for an activist agenda far wider than anyone earlier might have imagined. Already, Obama's newly appointed Chief of Staff Rahm Emanuel, has claimed: "You never want a serious crisis to go to waste." To avoid any misunderstanding, he went on, "What I mean by that is an opportunity to do things you think you could not do before."[14] With an extended honeymoon period about to begin, all await what the marriage between Barack Obama and the American public will beget.

Endnotes

1. *Time Magazine,* Vol. 172, No. 24, November 24, 2008; Ryan Lizza, "How Obama Won," *The New Yorker,* November 17, 2008.
2. For a categorization of presidential elections on a similar basis, see, Lee Sigelman and Emmet Buell, *Attack Politics: Negative Campaigning in Presidential Elections Since 1960* (Lawrence: University Press of Kansas, 2007).
3. None of the major polls had McCain ahead, but a few of them had him within or just beyond the margin of error. For those interested in the polling industry, solace could be found in the fact that an average of the polls, taken by RealClearPolitics, reflected almost exactly the election result. But individual polls were spread out widely.
4. Such determinations are also complicated by the fact that during some periods, especially the late 19th and early 20th centuries, a fair number of candidates ran on party tickets other than the Republicans and Democrats. To avoid methodological complications, our calculations are based solely on the gains or losses for Republicans and Democrats.
5. The number for the comparisons between 2006 and 2008 are derived from the CNN Election Center. http://www.cnn.com/ELECTION/2006/ and http://www.cnn.com/ELECTION/2008/results/main.results/tfvaHH.
6. Tom Hamburger and Peter Wallsten, *One Party Country: The Republican Plan for Dominance in the 21st Century* (New York: Wiley, 2007); Thomas Edsall, *Building Red America: The New Conservative Coalition and the Drive for Permanent Power* (New York: Basic Books, 2006).
7. As in Table 1, changes in Senate party strength were calculated from the official U.S. Senate Web site, http://www.senate.gov/pagelavout/history/oneitemandteasers/partvdiv.htm. Changes in House party strength were calculated from http://www.emailthecongress.com/partv-strength-house.html; http://www.emailthecongress.com/partv-strength-house.html;*Biographical Directory of the U.S. Congress;* Congressional Research Service; Office of the Clerk of the U.S. House of Representatives, http://clerk.house.gov/art_history/house_history/partyDiv.html. Candidates who ran under other labels than Republican or Democrats were left out of the calculations.
8. Thomas Schaller, "The Republican Comeback of 2010," *Salon.com,* December 8, 2008. Accessed at http://www.salon.eom/news/feature/2008/l2/08/2010/print.html: Amy Walter, "Is the Democrats' Momentum Already Sagging?" *National Journal.com,* December 9, 2008.
9. David Mayhew, *Electoral Realignments: A Critique of An American Genre* (New Haven: Yale University Press, 2004); James W. Ceaser and Andrew Busch, *Red Over Blue: The 2008 Elections in American Politics* (Lanham: Roman & Littlefield Publishers, 2005).
10. Harold Meyerson, "A Real Realignment," *The Washington Post,* November 7, 2008, A19.
11. John B. Judis, "America the Liberal," *The New Republic,* November 5, 2008.
12. Exit polls accessed at: http://www.cnn.com/ELECTION/2008/results/polls/tfUSP00p1.

13. Remarks on The News Hour with Jim Lehrer, November 5, 2008. See also, Andrew Kohut, "Post-Election Perspectives," 2nd Annual Warren J. Mitofsky Award Dinner on Behalf of the Roper Center Newseum, Washington DC, November 13, 2008.
14. Quoted in Gerald F. Seib, "In Crisis, Opportunity for Obama," *The Wall Street Journal,* November 21, 2008. A video of the interview with Emanuel can be accessed at http://www. realclearpolitics.com/video_log/2008/ll/emanuel_says_crisis_is_an_oppo.html.

Robert A. Dahl

The Myth of Presidential Mandate

On election night in 1980, the vice president elect enthusiastically informed the country that Ronald Reagan's triumph was

> . . . not simply a mandate for a change but a mandate for peace and freedom; a mandate for prosperity; a mandate for opportunity for all Americans regardless of race, sex, or creed; a mandate for leadership that is both strong and compassionate . . . a mandate to make government the servant of the people in the way our founding fathers intended; a mandate for hope; a mandate for hope for the fulfillment of the great dream that President-elect Reagan has worked for all his life.[1]

I suppose there are no limits to permissible exaggeration in the elation of victory, especially by a vice president elect. He may therefore be excused, I imagine, for failing to note, as did many others who made comments in a similar vein in the weeks and months that followed, that Reagan's lofty mandate was provided by 50.9 percent of the voters. A decade later it is much more evident, as it should have been then, that what was widely interpreted as Reagan's mandate, not only by supporters but by opponents, was more myth than reality.

In claiming that the outcome of the election provided a mandate to the president from the American people to bring about the policies, programs, emphases, and new directions uttered during the campaign by the winning candidate and his supporters, the vice president elect was like other commentators echoing a familiar theory.

Source: Political Science Quarterly 105 (Fall 1990), pp. 355–366.

Origin and Development

A history of the theory of the presidential mandate has not been written, and I have no intention of supplying one here. However, if anyone could be said to have created the myth of the presidential mandate, surely it would be Andrew Jackson. Although he never used the word mandate, so far as I know, he was the first American president to claim not only that the president is uniquely representative of all the people, but that his election confers on him a mandate from the people in support of his policy. Jackson's claim was a fateful step in the democratization of the constitutional system of the United States—or rather what I prefer to call the pseudo-democratization of the presidency.

As Leonard White observed, it was Jackson's "settled conviction" that "the President was an immediate and direct representative of the people." Presumably as a result of his defeat in 1824 in both the electoral college and the House of Representatives, in his first presidential message to Congress, in order that "as few impediments as possible should exist to the free operation of the public will," he proposed that the Constitution be amended to provide for the direct election of the president.[2]

> To the people," he said, "belongs the right of electing their Chief Magistrate: it was never designed that their choice should, in any case, be defeated, either by the intervention of electoral colleges or by . . . the House of Representatives.[3]

His great issue of policy was the Bank of the United States, which he unwaveringly believed was harmful to the general good. Acting on this conviction, in 1832, he vetoed the bill to renew the bank's charter. Like his predecessors, he justified the veto as a protection against unconstitutional legislation; but unlike his predecessors in their comparatively infrequent use of the veto, he also justified it as a defense of his or his party's policies.

Following his veto of the bank's charter, the bank became the main issue in the presidential election of 1832. As a consequence, Jackson's reelection was widely regarded, even among his opponents (in private, at least), as amounting to "something like a popular ratification" of his policy.[4] When, in order to speed the demise of the bank, Jackson found it necessary to fire his treasury secretary, he justified his action on the grounds, among others, that "The President is the direct representative of the American people, but the Secretaries are not."[5]

Innovative though it was, Jackson's theory of the presidential mandate was less robust than it was to become in the hands of his successors. In 1848, James Polk explicitly formulated the claim, in a defense of his use of the veto on matters of policy, that as a representative of the people the president was, if not more representative than the Congress, at any rate equally so.

> The people, by the constitution, have commanded the President, as much as they have commanded the legislative branch of the Government, to execute their will. . . . The President represents in the executive department the whole people of the United States, as each member of the legislative department represents portions of them. . . ."
> The President is responsible "not only to an enlightened public opinion, but to the people of the whole Union, who elected him, as the representatives in the legislative branches . . . are responsible to the people of particular States or districts. . . .[6]

Notice that in Jackson's and Polk's views, the president, both constitutionally and as representative of the people, is on a par with Congress. They did not claim that in either respect the president is superior to Congress. It was Woodrow Wilson who took the further step in the evolution of the theory by asserting that in representing the people the president is not merely equal to Congress but actually superior to it.

Earlier Views

Because the theory of the presidential mandate espoused by Jackson and Polk has become an integral part of our present-day conception of the presidency, it may be hard for us to grasp how sharply that notion veered off from the views of the earlier presidents.

As James Ceaser has shown, the Framers designed the presidential election process as a means of improving the chances of electing a *national* figure who would enjoy majority support. They hoped their contrivance would avoid not only the populistic competition among candidates dependent on "the popular arts," which they rightly believed would occur if the president were elected by the people, but also what they believed would necessarily be a factional choice if the president were chosen by the Congress, particularly by the House.

In adopting the solution of an electoral college, however, the Framers seriously underestimated the extent to which the strong impulse toward democratization that was already clearly evident among Americans—particularly among their opponents, the anti-Federalists—would subvert and alter their carefully contrived constitutional structure. Because this is a theme I shall pick up later, I will mention only two such failures that bear closely on the theory of the presidential mandate. First, the Founders did not foresee the development of political parties nor comprehend how a two-party system might achieve their goal of ensuring the election of a figure of national rather than merely local renown. Second, as Ceaser remarks, although the Founders recognized "the need for a popular judgment of the performance of an incumbent" and designed a method for selecting the president that would, as they thought, provide that opportunity, they "did not see elections as performing the role of instituting decisive changes in policy in response to popular demands." In short, theory of the presidential mandate not only cannot be found in the Framers' conception of the Constitution; almost certainly, it violates that conception.

No president prior to Jackson challenged the view that Congress was the legitimate representative of the people. Even Thomas Jefferson, who adeptly employed the emerging role of party leader to gain congressional support for his policies and decisions,

> was more Whig than . . . the British Whigs themselves in subordinating [the executive power] to "the supreme legislative power." . . . The tone of his messages is uniformly deferential to Congress. His first one closes with these words: "Nothing shall be wanting on my part to inform, as far as in my power, the legislative judgment, nor to carry that judgment into faithful execution."[7]

James Madison, demonstrating that a great constitutional theorist and an adept leader in Congress could be decidedly less than a great president, deferred so greatly to Congress that in his communications to that body, his extreme caution rendered him "almost unintelligible"[8]—a quality one would hardly expect from one who had been a master of lucid exposition at the Constitutional Convention. His successor, James Monroe, was so convinced that Congress should decide domestic issues without presidential influence that throughout the debates in Congress on "the greatest political issue of his day . . . the admission of Missouri and the status of slavery in Louisiana Territory," he remained utterly silent.[9]

Madison and Monroe serve not as examples of how presidents should behave but as evidence of how early presidents thought they should behave. Considering the constitutional views and the behavior of Jackson's predecessors, it is not hard to see why his opponents called themselves Whigs in order to emphasize his dereliction from the earlier and presumably constitutionally correct view of the presidency.

Woodrow Wilson

The long and almost unbroken success of mediocrities who succeeded to the presidency between Polk and Wilson for the most part subscribed to the Whig view of the office and seem to have laid no claim to a popular mandate for their policies—when they had any. Even Abraham Lincoln, in justifying the unprecedented scope of presidential power he believed he needed in order to meet secession and civil war, rested his case on constitutional grounds and not as a mandate from the people. Indeed, because he distinctly failed to gain a majority of votes in the election of 1860, any claim to a popular mandate would have been dubious at best. Like Lincoln, Theodore Roosevelt also had a rather unrestricted view of presidential power; he expressed the view then emerging among Progressives that chief executives were also representatives of the people. Yet the stewardship he claimed for the presidency was ostensibly drawn—rather freely drawn, I must say—from the Constitution, not from the mystique of the mandate.

Woodrow Wilson, more as political scientist than as president, brought the mandate theory to what now appears to be its canonical form. His formulation was influenced by his admiration for the British system of cabinet government. In 1879, while still a senior at Princeton, he published an essay recommending the adoption of cabinet government in the United States. He provided little indication as to how this change was to be brought about, however, and soon abandoned the idea without yet having found an alternative solution. Nevertheless, he continued to contrast the American system of congressional government, in which Congress was all-powerful but lacked executive leadership, with British cabinet government, in which Parliament, though all powerful, was firmly led by the prime minister and his cabinet. Because Americans were not likely to adopt the British cabinet system, however, he began to consider the alternative of more powerful presidential leadership. In his *Congressional Government*, published in 1885, he acknowledged that "the representatives of the people are the proper ultimate authority in all matters of government, and that administration is merely the clerical part of government." Congress is "unquestionably, the predominant and controlling force, the center and source of all motive and of all regulative power." Yet a discussion of policy that goes beyond "special pleas for special privilege" is simply impossible in the House, "a disintegrate mass of jarring elements," while the Senate is no more than "a small, select, and leisurely House of Representatives."

By 1908, when *Constitutional Government in the United States* was published, Wilson had arrived at strong presidential leadership as a feasible solution. He faulted the earlier presidents who had adopted the Whig theory of the Constitution.

> . . . [T]he makers of the Constitution were not enacting Whig theory. . . . The President is at liberty, both in law and conscience, to be as big a man as he can. His capacity will set the limit; and if Congress be overborne by him, it will be no fault of the makers of the Constitution,—it will be from no lack of constitutional powers on its part, but only because the President has the nation behind him, and Congress has not. He has no means of compelling Congress except through public opinion. . . . [T]he early Whig theory of political dynamics . . . is far from being a democratic theory. . . . It is particularly intended to prevent the will of the people as a whole from having at any moment an unobstructed sweep and ascendancy.

And he contrasted the president with Congress in terms that would become commonplace among later generations of commentators, including political scientists:

> Members of the House and Senate are representatives of localities, are voted for only by sections of voters, or by local bodies of electors like the members of the state legislatures. There is no national party choice except that of President. No one else represents the people as a whole, exercising a national choice. . . . The nation as a whole has chosen him, and is conscious that it has no other political spokesman. His is the only national voice in affairs. . . . He is the representative of no constituency, but of the whole people. When he speaks in his true character, he speaks for no special interest. . . . [T]here is but one national voice in the country, and that is the voice of the President.[10]

Since Wilson, it has become commonplace for presidents and commentators alike to argue that by virtue of his election the president has received a mandate for his aims and policies from the people of the United States. The myth of the mandate is now a standard weapon in the arsenal of persuasive symbols all presidents exploit. For example, as the Watergate scandals emerged in mid-1973, Patrick Buchanan, then an aide in the Nixon White House, suggested that the president should accuse his accusers of "seeking to destroy the democratic mandate of 1972." Three weeks later in an address to the country Nixon said:

> Last November, the American people were given the clearest choice of this century. Your votes were a mandate, which I accepted, to complete the initiatives we began in my first term and to fulfill the promises I made for my second term.[11]

If the spurious nature of Nixon's claim now seems self-evident, the dubious grounds for virtually all such pretensions are perhaps less obvious.

Critique of the Theory

What does a president's claim to a mandate amount to? The meaning of the term itself is not altogether clear. Fortunately, however, in his excellent book *Interpreting Elections*, Stanley Kelley has "piece[d] together a coherent statement of the theory."

Its first element is the belief that elections carry messages about problems, policies, and programs—messages plain to all and specific enough to be directive. . . . Second, the theory holds that certain of these messages must be treated as authoritative commands . . . either to the victorious candidate or to the candidate and his party. . . . To qualify as mandates, messages about policies and programs must reflect the *stable* views both of individual voters and of the electorate. . . . In the electorate as a whole, the numbers of those for or against a policy or program matter. To suggest that a mandate exists for a particular policy is to suggest that more than a bare majority of those voting are agreed upon it. The common view holds that landslide victories are more likely to involve mandates than are narrow ones. . . . The final element of the theory is a negative imperative: Governments should not undertake major innovations in policy or procedure, except in emergencies, unless the electorate has had an opportunity to consider them in an election and thus to express its views.

To bring out the central problems more clearly, let me extract what might be called the primitive theory of the popular presidential mandate. According to this theory, a presidential election can accomplish four things. First, it confers constitutional and legal authority on the victor. Second, at the same time, it also conveys information. At a minimum it reveals the first preferences for president of a plurality of votes. Third, according to the primitive theory, the election, at least under the conditions Kelley describes, conveys further information: namely that a clear majority of voters prefer the winner, because they prefer his policies and wish him to pursue his policies. Finally, because the president's policies reflect the wishes of a majority of voters, when conflicts over policy arise between president and Congress, the president's policies ought to prevail.

While we can readily accept the first two propositions, the third, which is pivotal to the theory, might be false. But if the third is false, then so is the fourth. So the question arises: Beyond revealing the first preferences of a plurality of voters, do presidential elections also reveal the additional information that a plurality (or a majority) of voters prefer the policies of the winner and wish the winner to pursue those policies?

In appraising the theory, I want to distinguish between two different kinds of criticisms. First, some critics contend that even when the wishes of constituents can be known, they should not be regarded as in any way binding on a legislator. I have in mind, for example, Edmund Burke's famous argument that he would not sacrifice to public opinion his independent judgment of how well a policy would serve his constituents' interests, and the argument suggested by Hanna Pitkin that representatives bound by instructions would be prevented from entering into the compromises that legislation usually requires.

Second, some critics may hold that when the wishes of constituents on matters of policy can be clearly discerned, they ought to be given great and perhaps even decisive weight. But, these critics contend, constituents' wishes usually cannot be known, at least when the constituency is large and diverse, as in presidential elections. In expressing his doubts on the matter in 1913, A. Lawrence Lowell quoted Sir Henry Maine: "The devotee of democracy is much in the same position as the Greeks with their oracles. All agreed that the voice of an oracle was the voice of god, but everybody allowed that when he spoke he was not as intelligible as might be desired."

It is exclusively the second kind of criticism that I want now to consider. Once again I am indebted to Stanley Kelley for his succinct summary of the main criticisms.

Critics allege that 1) some particular claim of a mandate is unsupported by adequate evidence; 2) most claims of mandates are unsupported by adequate evidence; 3) most claims of mandates are politically self-serving; or 4) it is not possible in principle to make a valid claim of a mandate, since it is impossible to sort out voters' intentions.

Kelley goes on to say that while the first three criticisms may well be valid, the fourth has been outdated by the sample survey, which "has again given us the ability to discover the grounds of voters' choices." In effect, then, Kelley rejects the primitive theory and advances the possibility of a more sophisticated mandate theory according to which the information about policies is conveyed not by the election outcome but instead by opinion surveys. Thus the two functions are cleanly split: presidential elections are for electing a president, opinion surveys provide information about the opinions, attitudes, and judgments that account for the outcome.

However, I would propose a fifth proposition, which I believe is also implicit in Kelley's analysis:

> 5) While it may not be strictly impossible in principle to make a reasoned and well-grounded claim to a presidential mandate, to do so in practice requires a complex analysis that in the end may not yield much support for presidential claims.

But if we reject the primitive theory of the mandate and adopt the more sophisticated theory, then it follows that prior to the introduction of scientific sample surveys, no president could reasonably have defended his claim to a mandate. To put a precise date on the proposition, let me remind you that the first presidential election in which scientific surveys formed the basis of an extended and systematic analysis was 1940.[12]

I do not mean to say that no election before 1940 now permits us to draw the conclusion that a president's major policies were supported by a substantial majority of the electorate. But I do mean that for most presidential elections before 1940 a valid reconstruction of the policy views of the electorate is impossible or enormously difficult, even with the aid of aggregate data and other indirect indicators of voters' views. When we consider that presidents ordinarily asserted their claims soon after their elections, well before historians and social scientists could have sifted through reams of indirect evidence, then we must conclude that before 1940 no contemporary claim to a presidential mandate could have been supported by the evidence available at the time.

While the absence of surveys undermines presidential claims to a mandate before 1940, the existence of surveys since then would not necessarily have supported such claims. Ignoring all other shortcomings of the early election studies, the analysis of the 1940 election just mentioned was not published until 1948. While that interval between the election and the analysis may have set a record, the systematic analysis of survey evidence that is necessary (though perhaps not sufficient) to interpret what a presidential election means always comes well after presidents and commentators have already told the world, on wholly inadequate evidence, what the election means.[13] Perhaps the most famous voting study to date, The American Voter, which drew primarily on interviews conducted in 1952 and 1956, appeared in 1960.[14] The book by Stanley Kelley that I have drawn from so freely, which interprets the elections of 1964, 1972, and 1980, appeared in 1983.

A backward glance quickly reveals how empty the claims to a presidential mandate have been in recent elections. Take 1960. If more than a bare majority is essential to a mandate, then surely Kennedy could have received no mandate, because he gained less than 50 percent of the total popular vote by the official count— just how much less by the unofficial count varies with the counter. Yet "on the day after election, and every day thereafter," Theodore Sorenson tells us, "he rejected the argument that the country had given him no mandate. Every election has a winner and a loser, he said in effect. There may be difficulties with the Congress, but a margin of only one vote would still be a mandate."

By contrast, 1964 was a landslide election, as was 1972. From his analysis, however, Kelley concludes that "Johnson's and Nixon's specific claims of meaningful mandates do not stand up well when confronted by evidence." To be sure, in both elections some of the major policies of the winners were supported by large majorities among those to whom these issues were salient. Yet "none of these policies was cited by more than 21 percent of respondents as a reason to like Johnson, Nixon, or their parties."

In 1968, Nixon gained office with only 43 percent of the popular vote. No mandate there. Likewise in 1976, Carter won with a bare 50.1 percent. Once again, no mandate there.

When Reagan won in 1980, thanks to the much higher quality of surveys undertaken by the media, a more sophisticated understanding of what that election meant no longer had to depend on the academic analyses that would only follow some years later. Nonetheless, many commentators, bemused as they so often are by the arithmetical peculiarities of the electoral college, immediately proclaimed both a landslide and a mandate for Reagan's policies. What they often failed to note was that Reagan gained just under 51 percent of the popular vote. Despite the claims of the vice president elect, surely we can find no mandate there. Our doubts are strengthened by the fact that in the elections to the House, Democratic candidates won just over 50 percent of the popular vote and a majority of seats. However, they lost control of the Senate. No Democratic mandate there, either.

These clear and immediate signs that the elections of 1980 failed to confer a mandate on the president or his Democratic opponents were, however, largely ignored. For it was so widely asserted as to be commonplace that Reagan's election reflected a profound shift of opinion away from New Deal programs and toward the new conservatism. However, from this analysis of the survey evidence, Kelley concludes that the commitment of voters to candidates was weak; a substantial proportion of Reagan voters were more interested in voting against Carter than for Reagan; and despite claims by journalists and others, the New Deal coalition did not really collapse. Nor was there any profound shift toward conservatism. "The evidence from press surveys . . . contradicts the claims that voters shifted toward conservatism and that this ideological shift elected Reagan." In any case, the relation between ideological location and policy preferences was "of a relatively modest magnitude."

In winning by a landslide of popular votes in 1984, Reagan achieved one prerequisite to a mandate. Yet in that same election, Democratic candidates for the House won 52 percent of the popular votes. Two years earlier, they had won 55 percent of the votes. On the face of it, surely the 1984 elections gave no mandate to Reagan.

Before the end of 1986, when the Democrats had once again won a majority of popular votes in elections to the House and had also regained a majority of seats in the Senate, it should have been clear and it should be even clearer now that the major social and economic policies for which Reagan and his supporters had claimed a mandate have persistently failed to gain majority support. Indeed, the major domestic policies and programs established during the 30 years preceding Reagan in the White House have not been overturned in the grand revolution of policy that his election was supposed to have ushered in. For eight years, what Reagan and his supporters claimed as a mandate to reverse those policies was regularly rejected by means of the only legitimate and constitutional processes we Americans have for determining what the policies of the United States government should be.

What are we to make of this long history of unsupported claims to a presidential mandate? The myth of the mandate would be less important if it were not one element in the larger process of the pseudo-democratization of the presidency—the creation of a type of chief executive that, in my view, should have no proper place in a democratic republic.

Yet even if we consider it in isolation from the larger development of the presidency, the myth is harmful to American political life. By portraying the president as the only representative of the whole people and Congress as merely representing narrow, special, and parochial interests, the myth of the mandate elevates the president to an exalted position in our constitutional system at the expense of Congress. The myth of the mandate fosters the belief that the particular interests of the diverse human beings who form the citizen body in a large, complex, and pluralistic country like ours constitute no legitimate element in the general good. The myth confers on the aims of the groups who benefit from presidential policies an aura of national interest and public good to which they are no more entitled than the groups whose interests are reflected in the policies that gain support by congressional majorities. Because the myth is almost always employed to support deceptive, misleading, and manipulative interpretations, it is harmful to the political understanding of citizens.

It is, I imagine, now too deeply rooted in American political life and too useful a part of the political arsenal of presidents to be abandoned. Perhaps the most we can hope for is that commentators on public affairs in the media and in academic pursuits will dismiss claims to a presidential mandate with the scorn they usually deserve.

But if a presidential election does not confer a mandate on the victor, what does a presidential election mean, if anything at all? While a presidential election does not confer a popular mandate on the president—nor, for that matter, on congressional majorities—it confers the legitimate authority, right, and opportunity on a president to try to gain the adoption by constitutional means of the policies the president supports. In the same way, elections to Congress confer on a member the authority, right, and opportunity to try to gain the adoption by constitutional means of the policies he or she supports. Each may reasonably contend that a particular policy is in the public good or public interest and, moreover, is supported by a majority of citizens.

I do not say that whatever policy is finally adopted following discussion, debate, and constitutional processes necessarily reflects what a majority of citizens would prefer, or what would be in their interests, or what would be in the public good in any other sense. What I do say is that no elected leader, including the president, is uniquely privileged to say what an election means—nor to claim that the election has conferred on the president a mandate to enact the particular policies the president supports. . . .

Endnotes

1. Stanley Kelley, Jr., *Interpreting Elections* (Princeton, NJ: Princeton University Press, 1983), p. 217.
2. Quoted in Leonard D. White, *The Jacksonians: A Study in Administrative History, 1829–1861* (New York: Free Press, 1954), p. 23.
3. Cited in James W. Ceaser, *Presidential Selection: Theory and Development* (Princeton, NJ: Princeton University Press, 1979), p. 160, fn. 58.
4. White, *Jacksonians,* p. 23.
5. *Ibid.,* p. 23.
6. *Ibid.,* p. 24.
7. Edward S. Corwin, *The President: Offices and Powers, 1789–1948,* 3rd ed. (New York: New York University Press, 1948), p. 20.
8. Wilfred E. Binkley, *President and Congress* (New York: Alfred A. Knopf, 1947), p. 56.
9. Leonard D. White, *The Jeffersonians: A Study in Administrative History, 1801–1829* (New York: Free Press, 1951), p. 31.
10. Woodrow Wilson, *Constitutional Government in the United States* (New York: Columbia University Press, 1908), pp. 67–68, 70, 202–203.
11. Kelley, *Interpreting Elections,* p. 99.
12. Paul F. Lazarsfeld, Bernard Berelson, and Hazel Gaudet, *The People's Choice* (New York: Columbia University Press, 1948).
13. The early election studies are summarized in Bernard R. Berelson and Paul F. Lazarsfeld. *Voting* (Chicago, IL: University of Chicago Press, 1954), p. 331ff.
14. Angus Campbell et al, *The American Voter* (New York: Wiley, 1960).

Roger H. Davidson

Changing Tides: Public Opinion, Campaigns, and Governance, 2004–2009

There is a tide in the affairs of men, Which, taken at the flood, leads on to fortune; Omitted, All the voyage of their life Is bound in shallows and in miseries. On such a full sea are we Now afloat, And we must take the current when it serves, Or lose our ventures.

—William Shakespeare, *Julius Caesar*

Source: Original essay written for this volume.

"Public opinion stands out, in the United States, as the great source of power, the master of servants who tremble before it."[1] James Bryce, perhaps the most astute foreign observer of our political life, wrote those words in 1888. Among the "servants" controlled by opinion, Bryce noted, were the president, Congress, and the political parties' vast machinery.

Electoral contests bear out Bryce's axiom. Journalists, pundits, and attentive citizens, not to mention the candidates and their handlers, understand the commanding role of public opinion and strive to understand and even to shape it. People's attitudes and habits frame presidential and congressional elections and pose the central dilemmas of strategy and governance. Many of our concerns about contemporary policymaking, in fact, are best understood by posing two of the most enduring questions about U.S. public opinion: First, how are public attitudes distributed among political elites and within the attentive publics? Second, how intensely are those attitudes held by each grouping?

The nation's quadrennial presidential selection processes are long and tortuous—especially compared to the more tidy and compact methods of most of the world's democracies. They command nonstop media coverage both in the U.S. and around the world. In contrast to these presidential battles, thousands of other electoral contests of varying significance take place at the state and local level. Most important for national policy are races for seats in the Senate and House of Representatives. Every two years, all House members and a third of all Senators face the voters. These electoral contests can turn out to be as complex and time-consuming as the presidential struggles. But they remain a mystery to most citizens. They normally pass under the radar screens of the national media; the races often receive scant media coverage even in the localities where they are fought out.

Presidential and congressional elections ought to be considered together. They reflect public viewpoints—in party choice and policy preferences. These elections—congressional as well as presidential—equally influence the patterns of governance that follow. Examining both sets of elections during the early 2000s illuminates a tidal change that occurred in public attitudes and affected the parties' electoral fortunes. This tide favored the Democrats and eventually swamped the Republicans. After the 2000 elections, Republicans controlled both the White House and Capitol Hill. Elections in 2006, however, ended the GOP's control of the House and Senate. Another two years brought what may well have been the peak of the Democrats' flood tide: further House and Senate gains and election of the party's presidential nominee. But will there also be a Democratic ebb tide? By late 2009, the party's honeymoon seemed over as the public grew restive and skeptical.

The Elections of 2004

The broad contours of the 2004 presidential election are easily summarized. The race between incumbent President George W. Bush and Massachusetts Senator John F. Kerry was always viewed as a close call, with victory well within the grasp of either candidate. Daily tracking polls during the final month of the campaign showed the race "too close to call," although the numbers tilted toward Bush.

Partisan Loyalties and Issue Preferences

Potential voters in 2004 were closely divided yet farther apart in their partisan loyalties than at any time since the Vietnam War era. The Pew Research Center reported that partisan identification was split fairly evenly three ways: Democrats claimed 33 percent, Republicans 31 percent, and Independents 36 percent. Such partisan parity was judged "a relatively new phenomenon" in American politics. From the 1930s through 2001, Democrats had led the GOP in party identification (with a few short-lived exceptions). But the terrorist attacks of September 2001 brought a major Republican surge; "the shift [was] seen in most major demographic and social groups in the population, and [was] fairly consistent in size." Thus the 2004 playing field was virtually level.

Moreover, Pew's longitudinal measures (which began in 1987) of political, economic, and social values showed that

> political polarization is now as great as it was prior to the 1994 midterm elections that ended four decades of Democratic control of Congress. But now, unlike then, Republicans and Democrats have become more intense in their political beliefs.[2]

So the agreed-upon story line for the 2004 campaign and election was the deep rift within the U.S. public concerning pressing national concerns—the Iraq war and the state of the economy, not to mention such hot-button social issues as abortion, gay marriage, and stem-cell research.

Yet such intense divisions of opinion are found mainly among politically active citizens: the very people, to be sure, who are most likely to contribute time and money to parties and candidates—and, of course, to turn out on election day. The larger public—which includes apathetic or occasional voters—tends to cluster nearer the center of the ideological spectrum. The National Election Survey (NES) reported that, as in prior years, respondents in 2004 basically conformed to a normal bell-shaped curve, which means that the populace contained a plurality of moderates—at least four out of every 10 citizens.[3] The networks' exit polls of voters found also that 45 percent of voters pegged themselves as moderates while 34 percent called themselves conservatives, and 21 percent said they were liberals.

The election was also thought to be about "values." One exit poll reported that a plurality of all voters (22 percent) ranked values as the top response to a vaguely worded question, "Which one issue mattered most in deciding how you voted for president?" Four out of five of those voters went for President Bush. Most purveyors of the "values" hypothesis honed in on a few divisive social issues—abortion, gay marriage, and the like. Yet personal values or priorities underlie the behavior of all voters: A nationwide poll by Zogby International found that 42 percent of voters cited the war in Iraq as the "moral issue" that most influenced their candidate choice—more than triple the number who mentioned abortion and quadruple the number who mentioned same-sex marriage.

Ironically, however, the issue of legalizing gay marriage may well have been decisive in the election's final Electoral College outcome. Citizens at that time rejected the notion of same-sex marriage by a margin of 57 to 32 percent; but the issue was most salient for opponents—especially GOP stalwarts, religious conservatives, and older voters. Encouraged by White House strategists, anti-gay groups in 11 states sponsored constitutional referendums defining marriage as solely the union of a man and a woman. Anti-gay sentiment swelled the ranks of voters in those states, especially in the pivotal states of Michigan, Oregon, and Ohio. Kerry narrowly won the first two states, but Bush took Ohio in a close contest involving disputed voting procedures and tallies. So Ohio became the 2004 tie-breaking equivalent of Florida four years earlier. "That was probably the deciding factor in the race," boasted the head of a "pro-family" lobby—and he may well have been right.

The Candidates' Personal Qualities

A final variable in the voting equation is the candidates themselves: their issue positions, their personalities, their character, their leadership strengths, and their ways of connecting with the electorate. Bush's public approval was already trending downward as the 2004 ballots were cast: *The Washington Post*/ABC News poll in January 2004 found that, with the conspicuous exceptions of the fight against terrorism and the Iraqi venture, the public believed the Democrats would do a better job on a wide range of domestic issues—such as the economy, health care, Medicare, the budget deficit, immigration, and taxes. On the question of who was most trusted to handle the nation's leading problems, Bush enjoyed a statistical one-point advantage—down from 18 points the year before.

Likely voters in 2004 saw different qualities in the two candidates: Kerry's supporters connected with his stands on issues, whereas Bush's followers discerned character and leadership. A plurality of potential voters favored Kerry rather than Bush to handle leading domestic issues, even contentious social questions. But despite his lackluster job ratings, Bush won the image contest: He "kept the nation safe from terrorism," and he came across as the more likeable, approachable person—a 20-percent advantage over his challenger.

Campaigning: Core Voters versus Swing Voters

Presidential campaigns must mobilize the parties' most loyal followers, the "core voters." These people are more attuned to the parties' objectives and most likely to act upon their convictions—to volunteer, to donate money, and to turn out on election day. Many campaign professionals, and not a few political scientists, thus advise that campaigners work primarily to raise the enthusiasm and the turnout of such loyalists.

In presidential elections, however, campaign managers cannot afford to ignore the uncommitted middle of the ideological spectrum. In June 2004, the Pew Research Center reported that about one-fifth of the "certain voters" remained undecided about their choice, a segment of the electorate large enough to affect election outcomes. But winning over such voters presents a twofold challenge: They are more likely to be swayed by candidates than by the parties and their programs; and of course, they are less likely than dedicated partisans to show up on election day.

Faced with this partisan and issue landscape, the president's handlers opted for targeting core voters over swing voters, even in states considered in play by both camps. So the president bettered his 2000 performance among many GOP-leaning groups—including men, whites, older voters, married people, white Protestants, Catholics, suburban dwellers, affluent voters, and those with less formal education. He even cut Kerry's share among traditionally Democratic groups: for example, Blacks, Hispanics, Jews, and city dwellers. *Los Angeles Times* analyst Ronald Brownstein concluded that Bush "triumphed more by solidifying than expanding his coalition—more by deepening than broadening his support. . . . The conservative surge to the polls consolidated the Republican hold on the portions of the country where the party was already strongest."[4] Thus, exit polls found that the president had actually *lost* ground among Independent voters between 2000 and 2004.

Democratic campaigners countered with efforts to register thousands of new voters, mainly young people. This no doubt paid off. New voters and those 18 to 29 years of age were among the strongest Kerry supporters. Within the party's base, also, there were some bright spots: Kerry improved upon Gore's performance among ideological liberals and moderates, small towns, rural Democrats, highly educated voters, and those from the economic underclass. Among most other Democratic-leaning groupings, however, Kerry fell behind Gore's margins of 2000.

Unresolved Issues after the Balloting

When the actual votes were tallied, President Bush received 50.7 percent to Senator Kerry's 48.3 percent. The Electoral College margin was a bit wider: Bush, 286 (53 percent) to Kerry's 252 (47 percent). It was an uncontested but narrow victory for the incumbent president—the smallest margin of any reelected president in recent memory. (Four years earlier Bush, the disputed Electoral College winner, trailed Democrat Al Gore by half a million votes.) Bush's chief strategist, Karl Rove, proclaimed that a permanent Republican majority had arrived. But for a president whose fortunes had been carried aloft in the aftermath of the September 2001 terrorist attacks, the closeness of his reelection might well have signaled mounting troubles during his second four years.

President Bush's image as a wartime leader won him just enough centrist voters to win—even though many of them disagreed with his policies. But his reelection did nothing to heal the sharp divisions among political activists. After the balloting, 72 percent of the voters said the nation was more deeply divided on major issues than in recent years—up from 64 percent who felt that way four years earlier. During his second term, therefore, he and his party were faced with the dilemma that the 2004 election failed to resolve: how to recapture the political center while retaining the party's ideological core supporters.

The Congressional Races

As with most congressional elections, the overall outcomes in 2004 were mostly determined months and even years before the actual balloting. A large majority of House seats, and many Senate seats, are safe for one party or the other; they are even safer if they are held by incumbents seeking reelection. Fewer than one in 10 House districts and no more than a third of Senate seats to be voted upon (that is, about one-ninth of all Senate seats) were truly in play. With a three-seat Senate margin and a 24-seat House margin during the previous 108th Congress (2003-2005), the Republicans enjoyed a statistical head start going into the 2004 campaign season.

The four Capitol Hill parties (that is, the House and Senate Democratic and Republican campaign committees) nowadays play an active role in recruiting, supporting, and even funding House and Senate candidates.[5] First, the parties' successes or failures over the recruitment season—starting just as soon as the previous elections' ballots are counted and extending through the state and district primaries—determine whether quality candidates (mostly incumbents) or long-shot contenders are on the ballot. Incumbents begin with large advantages—in visibility, in fundraising, and in records of service to their constituents. In many cases, House districts have been artfully designed to protect their careers. Incumbents (especially if recently elected) who face closely contested races are provided by their parties with extra resources: for example, a prominent committee assignment, a role in passing popular bills, or extra campaign funds. To retain their control of the two chambers, Republicans (aided by the Bush White House) and Democrats therefore worked first to dissuade their incumbents from retiring.

The party committees then directed their efforts toward seats that were open or held by retiring or vulnerable members: recruiting promising candidates, "clearing the field" by elbowing rivals aside to forestall divisive primaries, and channeling resources to campaigns. Democrats pursued a similar course, also targeting states or districts deemed winnable. For 2004, then, the two parties fought over a small minority of congressional races.

Party leaders tend to be pragmatists, above all identifying and supporting winners. Thus, Democrats sometimes court anti-abortion or pro-gun figures in swing states or districts; the GOP leans toward moderates rather than extremists for such races. In 2004, both parties were able to recruit big-name contenders and other quality candidates. Sometimes controversial figures were shunned—for example, Representative Katherine Harris, the presumed GOP frontrunner for Florida's open Senate seat, was persuaded to postpone her bid, because as Florida's secretary of state she had been at the vortex of the 2000 presidential election controversy. The ultra-right Club for Growth promoted conservative candidates in several contests—backing a Colorado Senate candidate who ultimately lost the general election, and spending more than $2 million against moderate Senator Arlen Specter—who narrowly won nomination with help from the White House and the party establishment. (Six years later, Specter switched to the Democrats to avoid overwhelming right-wing opposition in the state's GOP primary.)

Not all nationally sponsored choices win nomination. Although 2004 was a good year for Republicans, they suffered a major embarrassment in Illinois' open Senate seat. Their vulnerable incumbent having retired, their wealthy frontrunner withdrew in the wake of a marital scandal; several prominent substitutes (especially Chicago Bears' legendary linebacker Dick Butkus) shunned the race. Lacking a credible candidate, the party finally had to stand aside for a self-promoting nominee, an out-of-state ideologue too extreme for the state. So the young Democratic contender walked to victory, winning seven out of 10 general election votes. He was Barack Obama, only the third black senator to be elected in 100 years.

As in presidential elections, party identification is the most powerful factor at the congressional balloting—even more so, because congressional contenders are usually less well known than presidential candidates. This is especially true of non-incumbents, who normally lack the visibility of sitting House and Senate members. Lacking deep information about the candidates, voters use party affiliation as a short cut to reaching their decisions. Issue preferences also play a role: candidates and their party backers stress them, but again citizens tend to subsume their preferences to partisanship.

The 2004 elections rewarded Republicans with four more Senate seats and three more House seats, giving them a 55-45 Senate majority (counting one Independent with the Democrats) and a 232-202 margin in the House. This was probably the result of high Republican turnout in states already in the party's fold. The most spectacular example was South Dakota Republican John Thune's narrow victory (by 1.2 percentage points) over Senate Majority Leader Tom Daschle—a race that drew national attention and lavish funding from a variety of interest groups. In this normally Republican state, Thune cast the race as a referendum on Daschle's role in thwarting President Bush's programs.

Regionally, the South and Great Plains and Rocky Mountain states—all but one of which went for Bush that year—formed the backbone of the congressional GOP. In the eleven southern states, the party claimed nearly two-thirds of the House seats and all but five senators. In the plains and mountain states the party boasted two-thirds of the representatives and nearly three-quarters of the senators. The upper Midwest—from Ohio to Wisconsin—remained competitive. Democrats were strongest at the edges of the national map—the two coasts along with the upper Midwest. The 11 states of the eastern "Amtrak corridor," from Boston to the nation's capital, were increasingly Democratic. In those states (all in Kerry's column) the party claimed two-thirds of the House seats and a nine-seat Senate margin. Similarly, the left-hand coast—the four Pacific-rim states (excluding Alaska), again all in the Democratic presidential column in 2000 and 2004—had a Democratic margin of 20 House seats and seven out of eight Senate seats. In these areas, the Democrats had about run out of future gains; to expand their holdings, the party needed to find new openings in midwestern, mountain, and southern states.

The 2006 Electoral Turnaround

Two years later, the two parties faced a vastly altered political landscape. These were midterm elections, waged without the president at the top of the ticket. Historically, the president's party typically loses ground, with the balloting serving as a kind of referendum on the administration's policies (1998 and 2002 were rare exceptions). Following a brief post-election surge, President Bush's public support resumed its downward path: citizens were equally divided on his job performance by April 2005, but by fall a majority or respondents judged him negatively. By the time of the 2006 elections, only 38 percent of the general public approved of Bush's presidency, whereas 53 percent disapproved.[6] The president's eroding public support weakened his leverage on Capitol Hill; his reelection strategy of "feeding the [GOP] base" limited his policy options. His most fervent and time-consuming crusade—Social Security reform—went nowhere; even immigration reform, his one major effort to expand his coalition (to Latinos) was thwarted, because the bill that emerged tilted too heavily toward the conservatives' goal of stricter border protections. Ron Brownstein concludes: "[M]ostly Bush spent his second term in retreat."[7]

Conversely, Democratic prospects had visibly brightened. The party rose to a double-digit advantage, with a lead of 49 to 38 percent among registered voters, and 50 to 39 percent among likely voters. The Democrats' public image was on the upswing (53 percent viewed the party favorably, compared to 41 percent for the GOP); and the party was more trusted to handle most issues (with the exception of terrorism and possibly immigration). The Democrats' advantage extended to contested House districts, and was felt even in GOP strongholds.[8] Not that people were thrilled with either Capitol Hill party; but as the ruling party, Republicans bore the brunt of the disaffection.

Both parties struggled to gain the edge in recruiting candidates. Given the state of public opinion, the Democrats had little trouble finding quality candidates. Successful Senate contenders included Pennsylvania's state treasurer (Bob Casey, an anti-abortion moderate and son of a revered late ex-governor); Montana's Jon Tester, a farmer and state senate president; and Virginia's Jim Webb, a Marine combat veteran and former Navy secretary in the Reagan administration who shed his GOP identity because of the Iraq war. Successful House candidates included two former House members, eight state senators, six city or county officials, and at least 10 former candidates for state or federal office.

Republicans were hard-pressed to find viable replacements for several scandal-ridden House members who withdrew at the last moment. They were also unable to find top-flight challengers to Democratic incumbents—most notably, New York Senator Hillary Rodham Clinton, who won by 1.5 million votes. In Florida, Representative Harris—pushed aside two years earlier—could not be denied the nomination this time around; but she lost to Democratic incumbent Bill Nelson by more than a million votes.

The parties' various campaign committees raised some $848 million to underwrite their efforts and disperse to candidates. Republican committees, traditionally successful fundraisers, raised about 55 percent of this money. Surprisingly, though, the Democratic Senate Campaign Committee, chaired by New York's Charles E. Schumer, outspent its Republican counterpart by some $32 million. This unusual shortfall in the GOP campaign committee's fundraising was clearly a miscalculation, in view of the razor-thin margins that marked several Senate contests.

The electoral results gave Democrats control of both chambers: a 233-202 margin in the House, and a nominal 51-49 edge in the Senate (actually a 49-49 tie, but two Independents who caucus with the Democrats enabled them to organize the chamber). California's Representative Nancy Pelosi became history's first female speaker, while Senator Harry Reid of Nevada moved from minority to majority floor leader.

Electoral outcomes are shaped both by local and national forces. Top-down trends seemed to prevail in 2006, led by the Iraq war (25 percent of citizens counted it the "most important problem") followed by terrorism, the economy, and energy costs. Anti-incumbent sentiment was another factor: nearly half of those surveyed said they did not want "most incumbents" reelected. Ethical issues (the Republicans' scandals were more visible) fed popular unrest.

The Democrats' geographic reach extended beyond the party's usual strongholds to include some traditionally Republican battlegrounds—the Virginia and Montana Senate victories, for example. While the two parties' Hill committees continued to focus their attention on open or contested seats, Democratic National Committee chair Howard Dean was launching a "50-state strategy"—the goal of which was to build the party's strength nationwide by reaching beyond the 18 to 20 "blue" [Democratic] states"—not just for presidential and congressional races, but also for local and state offices, where potential candidates for federal office gain experience and visibility. Dean's broad strategy clashed with the narrower focus of the congressional committees; but he proved himself to be "a pragmatic and visionary political field general," whose initiatives would reach fruition two years later.[9]

The 2008 Presidential Election: "The Best Campaign"

The 2008 presidential election drew near-record levels of interest and involvement. Not in nearly half a century—the Kennedy-Nixon race of 1960—had so many Americans recognized the importance of the contest, paid such rapt attention to the process, volunteered to participate, and cast their votes. The contest, moreover, engaged the attention—occasionally awestruck, more often befuddled—of onlookers in Europe, the South Pacific, Africa, and elsewhere around the globe. It had all the drama and uncertainty of a long-running athletic rivalry. "What a show it's been!" enthused David S. Broder, the revered political analyst who proclaimed it "the best campaign I've ever covered."[10]

Leading up to the 2008 balloting, the citizens' mood was even bleaker than two years previously. Large majorities believed the nation was headed "on the wrong track": a compilation of national surveys found some 70 percent felt this way in early 2008, and by election day that figure had swelled to almost 90 percent.[11] The economic crisis of autumn 2008—the largest downturn since the Great Depression—further eroded public confidence in the nation's wellbeing. Just before the election, the Conference Board's Consumer Confidence Index fell to an all-time low.[12]

Citizens tended to blame the president and the Republican party for the nation's woes: Bush's positive job ratings tumbled to 29 percent just before the election.[13] And the GOP's deficit in party identification—a mere 2 percent in 2004—grew to 12 percent. Democratic party identifiers accounted for nearly four in 10 voters (38 percent), according to Pew Center surveys.[14] And Independents (unreliable as they might be) were expected to favor Democratic candidates by at least a 60-40 ratio.

The Democratic tide occurred among voters of all ages; but the greatest gains were among younger voters. Democrats outnumbered Republicans by nearly a two-to-one margin (61 to 32 percent) among voters aged 18 to 29.[15] The party's strength extended beyond traditional Democratic states and into pivotal GOP-leaning states. They claimed margins in such battleground states as Colorado, Florida, Indiana, Iowa, Missouri, North Carolina, and Virginia (among these, only Missouri voted—narrowly—for the GOP's presidential candidate).

The public's policy attitudes and values, moreover, were drifting toward long-standing Democratic party positions. Twenty years after launching its surveys of Americans' political values in 1987, the Pew Center found the policy landscape more favorable to Democrats: "[i]ncreased public support for the social safety net, signs of growing public concern about income inequality, and a diminished appetite for assertive national security policies."[16] The surveys found more approval of government programs for the disadvantaged, less social conservatism, less rigid religious beliefs, and more tolerance for racial, cultural, and sexual minorities. Younger people seemed to be leading the way to more liberal social and political values.

Massive registration drives by the parties and their allied groups in the run-up to the election enlarged the number of potential voters. Again, Democrats ran ahead of the pack: traditionally "blue" Democratic states became more so, and many "red" GOP states morphed to pink or purple. An attitudinal measure closer to actual voting decisions is the surveys' "general ballot question": If the election were held today, which party's candidate would they choose? On the eve of the election, the registered voters polled by Gallup favored the Democrats, 54 to 30 percent.[17]

The Candidates and Their Campaigns

The nominating phase of presidential elections—far more protracted than the general election phase—is dizzyingly complex and subject to quadrennial change. The basic pattern is laid down by the national parties, but the precise rules—for example, who can participate, and how delegates are selected—vary from state to state, and between the parties within each state. Between January 2007 and June 2008, this was the most fascinating but puzzling part of the process. While the nomination contests are somewhat tangential to our central narrative, a few basic elements should be mentioned—especially because they laid the groundwork for Senator Obama's eventual victory.

Delegates to the national nominating conventions are selected, state-by-state, by caucuses, conventions, or primaries, or some combination of the three. Broadly speaking, GOP state contests proceed on a *winner-take-all* (or at least winner-take-most) basis. But the Democrats' rules, at least since the McGovern-Fraser Commission reforms of 1970, tilt decidedly toward *proportional representation*, also encouraging states to choose their delegates through primary elections.[18] Serious presidential contenders (or rather, their managers) are thus well advised to study procedures adopted by all the states and territories, and to organize their efforts accordingly. The California Democratic Party, for example, published in July 2007 a 30-page handbook detailing procedures for selecting the state's 503 delegates and alternates, including a list of affirmative action goals.[19]

Recent presidential nominees have tended to be *frontrunners* "established either by lining up endorsements and contributions before the voting started or by performing well in the early contests."[20] Such advantages can provide enough "momentum" to propel them to the nomination. This pattern applied not only to such Republicans as Robert Dole (1996) and George W. Bush (2000), but also to such Democrats as Jimmy Carter (1976), Walter Mondale (1984), Bill Clinton (1992), and John Kerry (2004).

Arizona's Senator John McCain, considered the 2008 GOP frontrunner, went on to win his party's nomination—overcoming several strong rivals and a financial meltdown within his campaign in summer 2007. McCain's delegate count piled up as a result of virtually unbroken victories in state contests. By the time his last serious rival, former Arkansas Governor Mike Huckabee, withdrew in early March, McCain had amassed enough delegates for the nomination—only a month after the first-in-the-nation Iowa caucuses and with 11 states yet to vote.

The Democratic race, in contrast, turned into a close, bitter five-month struggle between New York Senator Clinton and freshman Illinois Senator Obama. Clinton won her frontrunner status through media visibility, poll numbers, and support from notable Democrats (many of them veterans of Bill Clinton's presidency). Obama, however, inspired audiences with his theme of "change" and led one of history's most brilliantly executed campaigns. The core insight of his effort was that, under the party's proportional representation rule, the nomination would hinge on gaining delegates, not just on statewide wins or losses. Winning a state's "beauty contest" captures media attention and ensures a certain majority of delegates; but even a loss can still reap a sizeable share of delegates. The news media, for example, reported that by winning the California Democratic primary Senator Clinton "captured the biggest prize of all." In fact, her margin—51 to 48 percent—awarded her only 55 percent of the 370 delegates at stake (proportionately allocated statewide and within congressional districts). So Obama's statewide "defeat" actually netted him 45 percent of California's delegates.[21] As for those 12 states that chose delegates by caucuses (some in combination with primaries), Obama reaped a rich harvest—amounting to nearly 20 percent of his pledged delegates. "His average margin of victory in those contests was 34 percent. He won almost twice as many delegates in caucuses as did Clinton."[22]

Senator Clinton's campaign—led by many of her husband's campaign veterans—found itself outmatched, outmaneuvered, and outspent. Her campaign resources were spent in winning statewide races—according to the prevailing frontrunner-momentum model—rather than concentrating on actual delegate selection procedures. (Perhaps the campaign's managers were simply ill-informed: Her chief strategist reportedly declared in a campaign meeting that a California victory would give her all the delegates.[23]) Moreover, Obama's commanding financial resources enabled him to open more local offices and send more workers into communities across the country—even in Republican-leaning states—than any other contender. Obama raised a record three-quarters of a billion dollars for his 2008 campaign—two-thirds of which came from online contributions. Of the total, Obama allocated $414 million to his nomination campaign. (Senator Clinton raised a total of $224 million, and Senator McCain $221 million.) For the first time since the advent of the presidential public financing system, Obama opted to rely on private donations and decline public funds for the nomination (he collected eight times more than the federal spending limit) as well as the general election.

Compared with the exciting Democratic nomination battle, the general election contest was mostly a letdown. One exception was McCain's vice presidential choice: Rejecting several candidates he preferred (presumably because their pro-choice stands would alienate the party's conservative core), he chose instead first-term Alaska Governor Sarah Palin. This surprise choice excited GOP stalwarts; but Democrats and many moderates (64 percent of whom thought her unqualified) were repelled by her inexperience and weak grasp of national issues. Despite an early bounce in the polls, the Palin nomination ultimately harmed McCain's cause: "She may have helped shore up the Republican base, but she made it far more difficult for McCain to broaden his appeal," two seasoned reporters concluded.[24] Obama's vice-presidential choice of six-term Delaware Senator Joseph E. Biden was generally applauded (two-thirds of voters believed Biden was qualified to step into the presidency, whereas 60 percent thought Palin was unqualified).

The decisive blow to McCain came when the nation's deteriorating economy was jolted by a Wall Street crisis beginning on September 15, when the stock-trading company Lehman Brothers failed. That day, McCain repeated at a Florida rally his often-expressed claim that "the fundamentals of our economy are strong." Obama quickly mocked this as evidence that his opponent, along with Bush and the rest of the GOP, were clueless about the economy. McCain tried several tactics to recover his footing—suspending his campaign briefly to return to Washington to help craft a financial bailout package, and then introducing the nation to "Joe the Plumber," a working-class hero. Nothing worked. Obama's poll numbers climbed: Three weeks before the balloting, a *Los Angeles Times*/Bloomberg poll found Obama had expanded his lead from four to nine points.

Obama's November 4 victory was a broad-based, clear-cut win, but no landslide.[25] Obama commanded the popular-vote majority by a 6.3-point margin (52.5 percent to McCain's 46.2 percent). He also gained more than two-thirds of the Electoral College votes (365 to 173)—far below the landslides of Franklin Roosevelt, Eisenhower, or Reagan, but well ahead of Truman, Kennedy, and Carter—not to mention both of George W. Bush's elections.

Obama's election fulfilled the campaign goal of reaching beyond the reliably Democratic states: his edge in such contested states as Colorado, Florida, Indiana, Iowa, Nevada, New Hampshire, North Carolina, Ohio, and Virginia meant that the election did not hinge upon just one or two pivotal states. And he had improved the party's vote among young people, women, Blacks and Hispanics, city and suburban residents, and political moderates and Independents (not to mention liberals). Nonetheless, given the election's context—political, social, and finally economic—its result was highly predictable. Two seasoned observers put it this way:

> In many ways, the actual results . . . were as expected; they were quite unremarkable if one understood how the fundamentals of the political landscape so favored the Democrats throughout all of 2008. Obama's victory margin was what it should have been for a generic Democrat against a generic Republican.[26]

The Congressional Races

DNC Chair Howard Dean's 50-state strategy harmonized in 2008 not only with Senator Obama's outreach to traditional GOP strongholds, but also (unlike 2006) with the Capitol Hill campaign committees' stepped-up recruitment and financing efforts.

The Republicans' outlook looked bleak from the very outset of the 2008 congressional election cycle (that is, as soon as the 2006 ballots had been counted). After a dozen years the GOP had lost its majority status—a deprivation felt especially by House members. Of course, the GOP was not without defensive weapons: the Senate's 60-vote barrier to close filibusters and President Bush's veto pen. But future prospects looked grim, given the declining popularity of the party and its president.

Many Republicans therefore decided that 2008 was a good time to retire. All six Senate retirees were Republicans, as were all but three of the 26 House retirees. Three of the Senate retirees were replaced by Democrats, as were 11 House retirees. Some newly reelected members—including former House Speaker Dennis Hastert (Illinois) and former Senate Majority Leader Trent Lott (Mississippi)—simply resigned without bothering to serve out their terms.

Even though the outcome fell short of a landslide, Democrats were able to expand their Capitol Hill majorities beyond their 2006 levels. The party gained 24 seats in the House, giving them a 257-178 majority—only two votes shy of the 259 seats the party held before the GOP took control of Congress in 1995. More than a dozen House Republicans were defeated, including the GOP's only remaining New England member, Representative Christopher Shays of Connecticut. In New York State, only one Republican was left standing.

As for the Senate, the party barely attained the supposedly filibuster-proof 60-seat majority—counting the two Independents who caucus with the Democrats (Senators Bernard Sanders of Vermont and Joseph I. Lieberman of Connecticut), one party-switcher (Senator Arlen Specter of Pennsylvania), and Senator Al Franken, belatedly named winner of Minnesota's razor-tight contest (only 325 votes out of nearly 3 million cast). The death of Senator Edward M. Kennedy later in the year resulted not only in a temporary deficit for the Democrats, but also an incalculable loss of his legendary tactical and bargaining skills.

The Democratic High Tide?

President Obama and his party's House and Senate leaders face immense domestic and global policy challenges—including a serious financial crisis, numerous unmet domestic needs, and two long-term wars. In crafting legislative responses to such contentious issues, Democratic majorities—especially the 60 votes needed to shut down Senate filibusters—are by no means guaranteed. The irony of the party's House and Senate successes is that they have given it a more diverse membership, and with it greater resistance to the party's traditional progressive goals. Democratic victories in 2006 and 2008 were achieved in large part by overthrowing Republicans in moderate and even conservative states and districts. These Democratic newcomers naturally worry about holding their seats, which means appealing to moderate voters. (The House "Blue Dog" group, composed of moderate to conservative Democrats, has 52 members.) In both chambers, such members push back against activist policy initiatives, such as huge financial bailout packages and innovative health care plans.

Constituents—whose generic call for "change" helped put the Democrats in power—might well turn against the legislative products that the party is able to enact into law. Seven months into the Obama administration, surveys recorded doubts and concerns about the rapid pace of the Democrats' ambitious policy agenda, along with continued generalized support for reform. The midterm 2010 elections loom as a challenge for the majority party. "Democrats no longer have the momentum they once possessed," independent campaign analyst Stuart Rothenberg declared. "[T]he landscape has shifted again, this time improving significantly for Republicans."[27] Another respected nonpartisan commentator, Charlie Cook, observed that Democratic fortunes had "slipped completely out of control" and speculated that the party would risk losing 20 or more House seats in 2010.[28]

Political fortunes, like the ocean tides described in Shakespeare's *Julius Caesar*, flow but also ebb. Between 2004 and 2008, Democrats were borne aloft by a remarkable tide "which, taken at the flood, leads on to fortune." But ebb tides may also occur, in which fortune "is bound in shallows and in miseries." Alas, no one can confidently foretell what the future political tides may bring to the nation's two political parties.

Endnotes

1. James Bryce, *The American Commonwealth* (New York: Capricorn Books, 1959), Vol. 1, p. 296.
2. Pew Research Center for the People and the Press, "Survey Report: The 2004 Political Landscape: Evenly Divided and Increasingly Polarized" (November 5, 2003), p. 1.
3. The National Election Survey (NES) is a survey and data-dissemination organization— affiliated with the University of Michigan's Survey Research Center (SRC) and supported by the National Science Foundation (NSF)—that has conducted biennial election-year surveys since 1952. The NES has since 1972 included an item asking respondents to place themselves on a seven-point ideological scale running from "extremely liberal" on the left to "extremely conservative" on the right.
4. Ronald Brownstein, *The Second Civil War: How Extreme Partisanship Has Paralyzed Washington and Polarized America* (New York: Penguin Books, 2007), p. 295.
5. For the record, the two House committees are the House Democratic Congressional Campaign Committee (DCCC) and the National Republican Campaign Committee (NRCC). Their Senate counterparts are the Democratic Senatorial Campaign Committee (DSCC) and the National Republican Senatorial Committee (NRSC). They are aided by the national party organizations: the Democratic and Republican National Committees (DNC and RNC).
6. Pew Center for the People & the Press, *Democrats Hold Double-Digit Lead in Competitive Districts* (October 26, 2006), p. 5.
7. Brownstein, p. 298
8. Pew Center, pp. 1–2.
9. Ben Benenson, "Muscling Up the Majorities," *CQ Weekly* 66 (October 27, 2008), pp. 2866-2885.
10. David S. Broder, "The Amazing Race," *Washington Post* (November 2, 2008), p. B1.
11. Polling Report, *Direction of the Country*, (November 2, 2008). Polling Report.com.
12. The Conference Board, "The Conference Board Consumer Confidence Index Plummets to an All-Time Low," Press release (October 28, 2008). Conferenceboard.org.
13. Gallup Poll, "Bush Approval Rating Doldrums Continue," Press release (October 30, 2008). Gallup.com.
14. Pew Research Center, "Democrats Hold Party ID Edge Across Political Battleground" Press release (October 30, 2008). Pewresearch.org/pubs/1018.

15. Pew Research Center, "Democrats Post Gains in Affiliation across Age Cohorts," Press release (October 31, 2008). Pewresearch.org/pubs/1018.

16. Pew Research Center for the People and the Press, *Trends in Political Values and Core Attitudes: 1987–2007* (March 22, 2007). People-press.org/report/?reportid=312.

17. Chris Cillizza, "Democrats Carry Big Generic Ballot Lead," *Washington Post* (November 2, 2008), p. A1.

18. After the initial experience with the McGovern-Fraser rules, the party's officeholders complained that they were left out of the delegate selection process unless they pledged to vote for a specific candidate; so the rules were changed to create a class of "Superdelegates" apart from the formal selection process.

19. The affirmative action goals included: Latinos 26%, African Americans 16%, GLBT 12%, youth (under 30) and disabled persons, 10% each, and Native Americans 1%. California Democratic Party, *California Delegate Selection Plan for the 2008 Democratic National Convention* (Sacramento, Calif., July 2007).

20. Alexander George Theodoridis, "The Nominating Process in 2008: A Look Inside the Rube Goldberg. Did the Rules Decide?" in Larry J. Sabado, ed., *The Year of Obama* (New York: Longman, 2010), p. 231. The subsequent discussion relies substantially on Theodoridis's insightful account.

21. The delegates derived from the primary vote excluded 133 Superdelegates and local officials, pledged or not pledged to a given candidate.

22. Theodoridis, p. 239.

23. Karen Tumulty, "Five Mistakes Clinton Made," *Time* (May 8, 2008), cited in Theodoridis, p. 238.

24. Chuck Todd and Sheldon Gawiser, *How Barack Obama Won* (New York: Vintage Books, 2009), p. 23.

25. Michael Cooper, "A Blowout? No, But a Clear-Cut Win, for a Change," *The New York Times* (November 7, 2008), p. A22.

26. Todd and Gawiser, p. 25.

27. Stuart Rothenberg, "Sizing Up the 2010 Senate Contests in the Summer of 2009," *Roll Call* (August 3, 2009), p. 5.

28. Cited in David Brooks, "The Obama Slide," *The New York Times* (September 1, 2009), p. A29.

THE PUBLIC PRESIDENCY: PRESS, MEDIA, AND PUBLIC APPROVAL

F or better or worse, the public presidency envisioned and embodied by Theodore Roosevelt and Woodrow Wilson has become an essential part of the modern presidency—grafted onto, as it were, the constitutional presidency as defined by the Framers. It was Roosevelt who called the office "a bully pulpit."[1] His cousin, Franklin D. Roosevelt (who served 1933–1945), put the same thought differently. "The presidency is not merely an administrative office. That is the least of it," he said. "It is preeminently a place of moral leadership."[2] Their successors in the Oval Office have the responsibility of managing press and public relations as a constant and challenging part of the job.

For presidents, "going public" is inevitable and unavoidable. They are expected to honor the nation's traditions, stir hope and confidence, and foster a sense of national unity and purpose. Moreover, as the quotes from the two Roosevelts imply, they can exploit their unique visibility as a strategy of presidential leadership. "Going public" is defined by political scientist Samuel Kernell as "a strategy whereby a president promotes himself and his policies in Washington by appealing to the American public for support."[3] According to Kernell, modern presidents make extensive use of this strategy because they confront mounting difficulties in bargaining directly with their constitutional counterparts (especially members of Congress) at the same time that new communications media make it easier for them to appeal to the general public over the heads of rival politicians.

An important link between presidents and the mass public is through their leadership in a political party. It is true that significant numbers of citizens claim independence from the two major parties, and that presidents themselves oftentimes want to break free of their party moorings. President Barack Obama, for example, fashioned himself as a "post-partisan" figure, appealing to members of both parties. But his initiatives revealed deep partisan divisions. After all, the major parties are still the largest and most inclusive political groupings in the country. Equally important from the president's perspective, the parties have cultivated firm and mutually beneficial alliances with many influential interest groups and mass-membership organizations. For the Democrats, such organizations include those claiming to represent African Americans, women, environmentalists, and many trade unions. Republicans, in contrast, collaborate with groups claiming to speak for large and small businesses, the defense establishment, and cultural conservatives.

One aspect of the public presidency that is not of modern origin is the role of reporters and the press. In the early decades of the republic, many newspapers were stridently partisan in tone. The very first president, George Washington, complained bitterly about opposition papers' vicious attacks upon his administration. The Federalists were so vexed by these attacks that in 1798 they enacted the infamous (and almost certainly unconstitutional) Sedition Act, which classified as criminal libel any criticism or attempts to organize any criticism of the government or its leaders.

The Jacksonian era coincided roughly with the rise of the press as a mass phenomenon: new high-speed presses supplied cheap newspapers to an increasingly literate public. For nearly a century, the daily newspaper was the chief conveyer of public information. (New York City had 14 mass circulation daily newspapers in 1920; today it has only three.) Theodore Roosevelt, the very model of a modern president, understood that the press craved news from authoritative sources. So he began the practice of inviting small groups of reporters to the White House for informal exchanges of information about his policies. Formal press conferences were initiated by Woodrow Wilson. Since Wilson, every occupant of the presidential office has endeavored to maintain good relations with the press, although with widely varying success. Today, presidential effectiveness is often measured in terms of their mastery of electronic media. For example, Franklin Roosevelt communicated forcefully through radio in the 1930s, and television was exploited effectively by John F. Kennedy in the 1960s, Ronald Reagan in the 1980s, and Bill Clinton in the 1990s.

Observers now realize that presidential campaigns are not confined to the months leading up to the quadrennial elections. Presidents, and indeed other federal elected officials, campaign virtually nonstop. In his elegant and thoughtful essay, "Viewing the 'Permanent Campaign,'" Hugh Heclo begins this section by showing how this permanent state of contested politics came about, seemingly inevitably from the changing nature of American public life: the decline of parties, the rise of special-interest groups, innovations in media technology, the advent of political professionals (public relations, polling, and the like), the need to finance the enterprise, and the continuing high stakes in national policies.

In an original essay written for this volume, political scientist Mark J. Rozell reviews the recent history of White House–press relations, identifying high points and low points and indicating general trends. "Presidents spend a great deal of time worrying about the press," he notes. He recounts the highlights of the modern media-savvy White House: Franklin Roosevelt, "master of the media," and the televised presidency of John F. Kennedy (which included his rise to power, his seemingly glamorous presidency, and his tragic death). Then he assesses the impact of presidential "failures": the Vietnam War entanglement (1965–1974) and the so-called Watergate scandal (perpetrated during the 1972 presidential campaign and uncovered bit by bit in 1973–1974). He concludes with an analysis of the Clinton and George W. Bush presidencies. In his two terms, Clinton faced a press that was almost unrelentingly negative—starting just after his inauguration and continuing throughout the many scandals attributed to his administration. George W. Bush's tight control of press relations succeeded in his first term, buoyed by a post-9/11 surge in public support; his second term image was blurred by economic troubles, post-Katrina missteps, and public weariness with the Mideast wars.

A central attribute of all occupants of the White House is what Jeremy D. Mayer terms (in his essay, "The Presidency and Image Management") the "presidential image"—defined as "the impression Americans have of their leader as a leader and a human being." This image is partly true and partly false, partly realistic and partly fantasy. It is concocted out of four elements: (1) the president's actual appearance, character, and actions; (2) image management by the White House staff; (3) counter-images raised by the president's foes; and (4) media "takes" about who the president is really is and what he represents.

George W. Bush provides a case study for Mayer's concept of presidential imagery and image making. Bush and his advisors were remarkably disciplined at shaping the president's image and placing him in public settings that enhanced that image. Although Bush performed reasonably well in more or less open-ended events (presidential debates, for example), he was uncomfortable in unstructured situations, especially before audiences that included inquisitive or hostile individuals (press conferences, for example). Scripted, structured events were therefore preferred: the chief executive was usually seen speaking or interacting with selected audiences—often in military settings—in front of backdrops containing simple slogans drawn from the topic at hand.

Prevalent Bush's images were those of the "regular guy" and the "wartime leader." Although Bush was by any definition the privileged offspring of a notable upper-class family, he won the likeability contest hands down against the geeky Al Gore in 2000 and the elegant but preachy John Kerry in 2004. After the terrorist attacks of September 11, 2001, Bush refashioned his persona to become a war leader. Although his remarks on the day of the tragedy were unmemorable, his prepared speeches over the following weeks were high points in the history of presidential rhetoric. His steadfastness in pursuing military options burnished his leadership image and linked him with an institution highly regarded by the American public. But the American public eventually tired of the war, pulling Bush's job ratings to modern low points. How his grafting of an Iraq war onto the terrorism effort will affect his long-term historical standing is, of course, still unknown.

George Edwards begins his analysis in "The Presidential Pulpit: Bully or Baloney?" by noting our popularly held assumption that presidents achieve their policy goals by persuading the public and Congress about the wisdom of presidential preferences. Theodore Roosevelt's "bully pulpit" supposedly enabled the president to lead public opinion in the direction he thought best. Edwards challenges Roosevelt's maxim and our conventional wisdom by taking up the case of Ronald Reagan, who was known as the "Great Communicator" because of his impressive powers of persuasion. He argues that Reagan in fact was not very effective at all in changing public attitudes about the policies he favored. Edwards also argues that despite his many roll-call victories in Congress, Bill Clinton was not very successful in convincing Congress to pass his major legislative initiatives. Edwards goes on to analyze the major factors that affect a president's ability to influence public opinion and, in turn Congress, and he concludes that the cards are stacked against a president who hopes to change public attitudes. Edwards maintains that as in leading Congress, presidents can only lead the public "at the margins."

The ultimate reckoning of the public presidency is of course the reactions and sentiments of the public itself. But how do we find out what people are thinking about the president? Elections are but a crude measure of public sentiment: They are infrequent and, as we saw in Section 3, they often convey a murky picture of what citizens really expect or want from the president. However, for the past 50 years or more, public opinion surveys have frequently probed presidential popularity. In such surveys, citizens are typically asked to rate the job the president is doing—excellent, pretty good, only fair, or poor. The responses are then dichotomized into "favorable" or "unfavorable" ratings. As a result, "we now have a continuing monthly referendum on the president's public support." By comparing this long-running string of data with contextual events (for example, wars, crises, economic conditions, issues of current saliency), we gain a clearer picture of how people assess presidents and their performance.

Presidents themselves are extremely conscious of their standing in the polls. However much they may belittle poll results, they are eager to take advantage of favorable ratings and work to explain away low ones (a variety of spin control). High approval ratings, it is said, may compel other politicians to follow the president's leadership or at least mute their criticisms; conversely, low ratings supposedly embolden criticism and encourage politicians to seek their own courses of action. Such claims are hard to prove empirically, but there is no doubt they are widely believed in the political community.

Endnotes

1. "Bully" was a favorite Rooseveltian term expressing great enthusiasm. Students inform us that "awesome" or "rad" conveys something of the same meaning.
2. Quoted by Edward S. Corwin, *The President: Office and Powers 1787–1957* (New York: New York University Press, 1957), p. 273. The text of Roosevelt's remarks on the presidency was found in *The New York Times* (November 13, 1932), Sect. 8, p. 1.
3. Samuel Kernell, *Going Public. New Strategies of Presidential Leadership,* 4th ed. (Washington, DC: CQ Press, 2006), p. 2.

Hugh Heclo

The "Permanent Campaign"

The term *permanent campaign* was first widely publicized early in the Reagan presidency by Sidney Blumenthal, a journalist who went on to work in the Clinton White House—and then was caught up in the semi-permanent campaign to impeach the president. Calling it "the political ideology of our age," Blumenthal described the permanent campaign as a combination of image making and strategic calculation that turns governing into a perpetual campaign and "remakes government into an instrument designed to sustain an elected official's popularity."

Should Campaigning and Governing Differ?

In one sense—a promissory sense—it seems clear that campaigning and governing should have much in common. Any democratic political system is based on the idea that what happens in government is related to people's electoral choices. Elections and their attendant campaigns are not a thing apart from, but integral to, the larger scheme of democratic government, both in guiding responses to the past election and in anticipating reactions to the next. In the long run, without good-faith promise making in elections and promise keeping in government, representative democracy is unaccountable and eventually unsustainable.

Source: Reprinted from *The Permanent Campaign and Its Future*, Norman Ornstein and Thomas Mann, eds. (Washington: American Enterprise Institute and Brookings, 2000).

Although the two necessarily relate to each other, good reasons exist to think that campaigning and governing ought not to be merged into one category. Common sense tells us that two different terms are necessary, because we know that promise making is not promise keeping, any more than effective courtship is the same thing as well-working marriage. . . .

While the designers of the U.S. Constitution had little use for parties and popular electioneering, the campaign analogy was not threatening in the 19th century, precisely because popular appeals had to be shaped to the constitutional system the framers had designed. On the one hand, it was a system brimming with elections—eventually hundreds for the federal House of Representatives, dozens in state legislatures for the Senate, and dozens more for the presidency (through the state electors), not to mention the thousands of elections for the state governments of the federal system. On the other hand, no one election or combination of elections was decisive. No election could trump any other as the one true voice of the people. The people, through elections shaped to the multiplex constitutional structure, were held at arm's length. Governing was what had to happen inside the intricately crafted structure of the Constitution. Every part of that structure derived its authority from—and was ultimately dependent on—the people. But the people never all spoke at the same time, and they never had residence in any one part or in the whole of the government quarters. Inside those quarters institutions were separated, and powers were shared, so that there would be a lot going on inside—a rich internal life to governing, a place of mutual accommodation and deliberation—if only because no one could do anything on his or her own, although each could defend his or her own turf. The people were outside—in the open countryside to which their governors would have to come to give account of their stewardship. . . .

In at least three important ways campaigning and governing point in different directions—that is to say, not always in opposite but in sufficiently divergent directions to matter.

First, campaigning is geared to one unambiguous decision point in time. In other words, campaigning must necessarily focus on affecting a single decision that is itself the outcome, the event determining who wins and who loses. Governing, by contrast, has many interconnected points of outcome through time—the line decision, so to speak, of the "going concern." Anyone who has worked in a political campaign will probably recall the initial enthusiasms of launching the campaign, the accelerating pace and growing intensity, the crashing climax of election day, and the eerie stillness of cleaning out the campaign offices in the period immediately following. Governing is different. It is a long persistence with no beginning or final decision point, something like a combination of digging a garden in hard ground and the labors of Sisyphus. The time scale for campaigning has historically been short and discontinuous, while that for governing stretches beyond the horizon.

Second, within its fixed time horizon, campaigning is necessarily adversarial. Nineteenth-century political writers borrowed the military metaphor precisely because it captures the essential idea of a contest to defeat one's enemy. The competition is for a prize that cannot be shared, a zero-sum game. In comparison with a campaign, governing is predominantly collaborative rather than adversarial. While campaigning would willingly drown out its opponent to maximize persuasion, genuine governing wishes an orderly hearing of many sides, lest the steersman miss something important. In that sense, campaigning is self-centered, and governing is group-centered.

In the third place, campaigning is inherently an exercise in persuasion. The point of it all is to create those impressions that will yield a favorable response for one's cause. In contrast, governing places its greatest weight on values of deliberation. While good campaigning often persuades by its assurance and assertions, good governing typically depends on a deeper and more mature consideration. This is so because whatever conclusions governing comes to will be backed by the fearsome power of the state. Taking counsel over what to do and how to do it lies at the heart of the governing process. Of course, it has to be acknowledged that *deliberation* may sound too genteel a term for the knife fights that are often associated with governing, especially along the banks of the Potomac. Nevertheless, the men and women governing public policy do make up a going concern as they bargain and seek to persuade each other inside the constitutional structure. The deliberation in view here means nothing more profound or high-minded than that.

Creating the Permanent Campaign

As noted at the outset, *permanent campaign* is shorthand for an emergent pattern of political management that the body politic did not plan, debate, or formally adopt. It is a work of inadvertence, something developed higgledy-piggledy since the middle of the 20th century, much as political parties became part of America's unwritten constitution in the 19th century. The permanent campaign comprises a complex mixture of politically sophisticated people, communication techniques, and organizations—profit and nonprofit alike. What ties the pieces together is the continuous and voracious quest for public approval. Elections themselves are only one part of the picture, where the focus is typically on personalities and the mass public. Less obvious are the thousands of orchestrated appeals that are constantly underway to build and maintain favor of the certain publics and targeted elites for one or another policy cause.

What we can identify and discuss without doing excessive injustice to the subject are the political instrumentalities that give expression to the deeper development of political culture. Those features proved important in creating the permanent campaign, and one can conveniently group them into six categories. The point is not to describe each in detail but to show the logic that has connected those emergent properties into a coherent pattern during the past 50 or so years— the pattern of campaigning so as to govern and even governing so as to campaign.

The Decline of Political Parties

Where parties have become much weaker is at the level of political fundamentals— generating candidates for office and being able predictably to mobilize blocs of people to vote for them. The cumulative effect of many changes from the late 19th century onward—ending the "spoils" system in public employment, electoral reforms and party primaries, suburbanization, and television, to name a few examples—was largely to destroy the parties' control over recruitment and nomination of candidates for office. Concurrently, the general trend since the middle of the 20th century has been a gradual decline in the strength of voters' identification with the two major parties. The 20th-century change in American parties represents a general shift from party-centered to candidate-centered elections, in an "every man for himself" atmosphere. Because politicians cannot count on loyalties from party organizations, voting blocs of the New Deal coalition, and individual voters, after the 1950s, politicians have had every reason to try to become the hub of their own personal permanent campaign organizations.

Although much weaker on the recruitment side, political parties have also become stronger in other dimensions that intensify the permanent campaign. In the last quarter of the 20th century, party coalitions grew more ideologically and socially distinctive. Simultaneously, the national party organizations' ability to raise and distribute money vastly increased. The central headquarters of each party also became more adept at constructing national election strategies and campaign messages to attack the other party. At the same time, two-party conflict in Congress became more ideologically charged and personally hostile. With that development came congressional leaders' growing use of legislative campaign committees to raise money, set agendas, and define the party image. All that has provided the financial wherewithal and career interest for more sustained and polarized political warfare. In short, both where parties have become weaker and where they have become stronger, the effect has been to facilitate a climate of endless campaigning.

Open Interest-Group Politics

A second feature creating the permanent campaign is the rise of a much more open and extensive system of interest-group politics. "Opening up the system" became a dominant theme of American politics after the Eisenhower years. On the one hand, to open up the system meant that previously excluded Americans—minorities, women, youth, consumers, and environmentalists, for example—demanded a voice and place at the table. The civil rights movement was in the vanguard, followed by many others. With the politics of inclusion came more advocacy groups and a nurturing environment for that minority of Americans who were inclined to be political activists. On the other hand, opening up the system also meant exposing all aspects of the governing process to public view. In the name of good government and participatory democracy, barriers between policy-makers and the people were dismantled. Open committee meetings, freedom-of-information laws, publicly recorded votes, televised debates, and disclosure and reporting requirements symbolized the new openness. The repeal of public privacy had a sharp edge. After Vietnam, Watergate, and other abuses of government power, deference to public officials became a thing of the past. Replacing that deference were investigative journalism and intense media competition for the latest exposé. People in public life became themselves the object of a new regime of strict ethics scrutiny and exposure—and thus tempting targets in a permanent campaign.

New Communications Technology.   A third feature is the new communications technology of modern politics. The rise of television after the 1940s was obviously an important breakthrough in personalizing direct communication from politicians and interest groups to a mass public. Candidates for office could move from retailing their appeals through party organizations to direct wholesaling with the voting public. Likewise, groups could use protests and other attention-grabbing media events to communicate their causes directly to a mass audience. For both politicians and advocacy groups, communication with the public bypassed intermediaries in the traditional three-tiered "federal" structure of party and interest-group organizations, where local, state, and national commitments complemented each other. In place of the traditional structure could grow something like a millipede model—direct communication between a central body and mass membership legs. Of course, the story did not stop with broadcast television but went on to include cable TV, talk radio, the 24-hour news cycle, "narrowcasting" to target audiences, and the Internet. Explosive growth in the electronic media's role in Americans' lives provided unfathomed opportunities to crossbreed would-be campaigners and governors. . . .

As Walter Lippmann saw in analyzing the popular print media in the early 20th century, communication must be of a kind that translates into audience shares and advertising dollars. That has meant playing up story lines that possess qualities of dramatic conflict, human interest, immediacy, and strong emotional value. The easiest way for the media to meet such needs has been to frame the realities of governing in terms of political contests. The political-contest story about government makes complex policy issues more understandable, even if the "understanding" is false. It grabs attention with short and punchy dramas of human conflict. It has the immediacy of a horse race and a satisfying resolution of uncertainty by naming winners and losers. In addition, of course, it does much to blur any sense of distinction between campaigning and governing. . . .

New Political Technologies.   The fourth feature underlying creation of the permanent campaign is what we might call new political technologies. At the same time as changes in parties, interest groups, and electronic media were occurring, the twin techniques of public relations and polling were invented and applied with ever growing professional skill in the public arena. Together, they spawned an immense industry for studying, manufacturing, organizing, and manipulating public voices in support of candidates and causes. The cumulative result was to impart a much more calculated and contrived quality to the whole political process than anything that prevailed even as recently as the 1950s.

Over time, consultants and pollsters moved into the political front office. After the 1960s, increasingly specialized political consultant services developed and were fortified by professional polling to cover every imaginable point of contact among politicians, interest groups, and the people being governed. The basic features of the political marketing landscape include the following services: poll and focus-group research, strategic planning, image management, direct-mail marketing, event management, production of media materials, "media buys," opposition research against competitors, and orchestration of "grassroots" citizen campaigns. . . .

Need for Political Money.   The fifth factor in the creation of the permanent campaign amounts to a logical consequence of everything else that was happening. It is
the ever-growing need for political money. It turns out that most of what political
marketing does resolves into spending money on itself—the consultants—and the
media. Hence, after the 1960s, an immense new demand grew for politicians and
groups to engage in nonstop fund-raising. Even if the people managing the new
technologies—media, polling, and public relations—were not in profit-oriented
businesses, the new forms of crafted politics would have cost huge amounts of money
to create and distribute. As it was, the splendid profits to be made helped add to even
larger political billings. For example, in 1994, the 15 most expensive Senate campaigns in the United States devoted almost three-quarters of their funds to consultants' services.

Stakes Involved in Activist Government.   To close the circle of forces behind the
permanent campaign, we need to revisit the obvious. Granted a massive and growing need for more political money exists. But why should anyone pony up the money?
What we might easily overlook is the obvious point that the permanent campaign
exists, because there is something big and enduring to fight about. The stakes involved in activist government are what make it worthwhile to pay out the money
that keeps the permanent campaign going and growing. At the simplest level, one
might call that the Microsoft effect. Only after Bill Gates found that the federal government had an Antitrust Division did Microsoft lobbyists and contributions to both
parties begin appearing to demonstrate the company's commitment to civic education and participation.

If the federal government were as small a part of people's lives and of the economy as it was during the first half of the 20th century, we can be sure that there would
be far less interest in the continual struggle to influence the creation, administration,
and revision of government policies. Campaigning has become big and permanent,
because government has become big and permanent. One is speaking here of more
than the obvious benefits to be derived from influencing spending and taxation. . . .
It is not even a matter of the federal government's growing regulatory power over society and the economy. The deeper reality is a pervasive presence of public policy
expectations. . . .

To say it another way, conceptions of who we are as a people became increasingly translated into arguments about what Washington should do or should stop
doing. . . .

* * *

The campaign without end is not a story of evil people's planning and carrying
out nasty designs on the rest of us. Rather, it is more like a story of things all of us
would do, given the incentives and what it takes to win under changing circumstances. The story's central narrative is the merger of power-as-persuasion inside
Washington with power-as-public-opinion manipulation outside Washington.
The two, inside and outside, governing and campaigning, become all but
indistinguishable—as they now are in any one of the big-box lobbying or consulting

firms in Washington. The paradox is that a politics that costs so much should make our political life feel so cheapened.

Concluding Unscientific Postscript

. . . The permanent campaign is not the way Americans do politics, but the way politics is done to them. Without calling it by that name, the way most Americans do politics is by not doing what they consider "political" but by engaging in a myriad of local volunteer activities—politics in particular. That is all to the good and worth remembering. However, it is also true to say that the handiwork of professional consultant-crafted politics is now probably the only version of nonlocal politics that the average American ever experiences.

The pervasiveness of political marketing means that all national politics take place in a context of permanent, professionally managed, and adversarial campaigning to win the support of those publics upon whom the survival of the political client depends. Into the media are poured massive doses of what historian Daniel Boorstin discerned in the 1960 birth of TV politics and called *pseudo-events*. They are not spontaneous, real events but orchestrated happenings that occur because someone has planned, incited, or otherwise brought them into being for the purpose of being observed and swaying opinion. Leaks, interviews, trial balloons, reaction stories, and staged appearances and confrontations are obvious examples that most of us hardly recognize as "pseudo" anymore. It is difficult to know anything about national affairs that is not subject to the ulterior motives of professionals in political management or in the media, a distinction that itself is tending to dissolve.

What is the result of transforming politics and public affairs into a 24-hour campaign cycle of pseudo-events for citizen consumption? For one thing, the public is regularly presented with a picture of deeper disagreements and a general contentiousness about policy issues than may in fact be true when the cameras and microphones are turned off. Second, immense encouragement is given to the preexisting human tendency to overestimate short-term dramatic risks and underestimate the long-term consequences of chronic problems. Third, public thinking is focused on attention-grabbing renditions of what has gone wrong for which somebody else can be blamed. Thus, any attempt to debate policy continually reinforces a culture of complaint and victimization where seemingly dramatic conflicts never really settle anything or lead anywhere. . . .

The term that perhaps best describes what happens in the permanent campaign is *instrumental responsiveness*. It is a hands-on approach to leveraging and massaging opinion to make it serve one's own purposes. The campaigners do not engage the public to teach people about real-world happenings and thereby disabuse them of false hopes or encourage forbearance against harsh realities. Rather, the permanent campaign engages people to tell them what they want to hear in ways that will promote one's cause against others. Such instrumental responsiveness appears to be the system's functional philosophy, even while mimetic responsiveness—doing the people's will—is its confessional theology.

Why should one care? Because our politics will become more hostile than needed, more foolhardy in disregarding the long-term, and more benighted in mistaking persuasions for realities. The case for resisting further tidal drift into the permanent campaign rests on the idea that a self-governing people should not wish to become more vile, myopic, and stupid. Apart from that, there probably is not much reason to care.

Mark J. Rozell

The Press and the Presidency

For most Americans, understanding the presidency is a mediated experience. People learn about their president—his goals, strategies, leadership style, and even many details of his personal life—from the news media.

Although some suggest that journalistic scrutiny of the chief executive today is too intense, presidents nonetheless need the media both to communicate their objectives to the public and to lead the nation. Presidents often complain that their news coverage is biased or unfair, but they understand that to lead effectively requires persuasion of the general public as well as the elite. Through the media, they can most effectively reach the public.

Constitutionally there is no requirement—or even expectation—that the president try to lead public opinion. The Framers worried about the potentially harmful consequences of public appeals by presidents, and they devised a constitutional scheme that guarded against popular leadership.

Indeed, throughout the nation's first century, Congress—not the president—generally set the nation's policy agenda. Presidents were not expected to "lead" in the modern sense of the word; that is, they were not expected to establish and publicly promote a broad-based, national policy agenda. Presidents did not need the press in the way that they do today, because they did not rely on mass support to promote their more modest goals.

Today, no president can adequately lead without "going public." By reaching out to the public through the media, presidents seek to overcome the stalemate engendered by

---

Source: Original essay written for this volume.

the constitutional scheme of separation of powers. Rather than defer to Congress, modern presidents set national priorities, promote their goals before the public, and try to entice Congress into following their lead.

Nonetheless, the record of presidential press relations is mixed. Despite the fears of some that the constitutional scheme can be thwarted by a charismatic president who masters the media and charms the public, presidents in reality find their relations with the media to be, at best, a mixed blessing—and many have suggested actually a curse. They know they must reach out to the public through the media to lead, but ultimately, they find that journalists are anything but allies in this cause.

Presidential Press Relations in the 20th Century

In the 20th century, a view of presidential leadership different from that of the founding era began to emerge. The newer outlook—one in which the president advances his agenda through direct popular leadership—developed both out of the perceived necessity of bold national leadership (because of dramatic changes at home and abroad) and the words and deeds of "strong" presidents.

Theodore Roosevelt maintained that the president must act as a "steward" of the people. In other words, he must define for the public the national interest and advance programs to achieve that end. Roosevelt envisioned the presidency as a "bully pulpit" from which the chief executive leads the people.

Roosevelt may have been the first media savvy president in the modern sense. He held numerous informal press conferences, had reporters visit him for discussions while he shaved, made strategic use of reporters to leak information and float "trial balloons," instructed his personal secretary to feed reporters a steady diet of Roosevelt family stories, and traveled more than any of his predecessors to reach the people directly through speeches. Roosevelt was acutely aware of the import of the news media to a presidential image and how a positive image could help him to be an effective steward of the people.

As a political scientist, Woodrow Wilson theorized that a president who earned the admiration and confidence of the people could be as powerful as he wished to be. Wilson challenged the wisdom of the constitutional Framers' admiration of separation of powers and checks and balances. To break the debilitating stalemate—or "gridlock"—of the national government, he believed, required the leadership of a strong, popular president.[1]

Wilson's tenure as president certainly revealed the possibilities and limitations of direct popular leadership. Although Wilson was less cordial than Roosevelt with much of the press corps, during a period of war—when the media had customarily softened presidential criticism—he proved to be superbly adept at rallying popular opinion to a common endeavor. Even the victorious wartime president, however, could not rally his people later for Senate ratification of the Treaty of Versailles, which contained provisions for the creation of a League of Nations. The president who had earned the admiration and confidence of the people could not move them to support an unpopular initiative.

FDR: Master of the Media

Perhaps no president has been—or ever will be—as adept at news management and direct popular leadership as Franklin D. Roosevelt. In part, the willingness of reporters to slant coverage in favor of his administration reflected the nature of the times. The nation faced economic calamity at home, and then foreign aggression, and reporters did not exhibit the same skepticism of official Washington that is customary today. None of that, however, detracts from FDR's accomplishment.

By force of personality and media savvy, FDR captivated reporters and used them with great effect to promote the White House slant on events. For press conferences, reporters abided by White House rules that today would be dismissed as unacceptable: the president determined what information was on-background, off-the-record, or not-for-attribution. Reporters who did not follow the president's rules could be cut off from access to the White House. He requested that reporters who asked what he considered to be foolish questions to wear a figurative dunce cap. FDR also made a point of flattering reporters by using their first names, soliciting their advice on matters of state, and even inviting some to the White House to join the Roosevelts' small family dinners.

This deference given to the president is remarkable by today's standards. Newspapers strictly abided by the White House rule that FDR, who was disabled from polio, not be photographed in a wheelchair or when being carried by his aides. When the president fell down face-forward in the mud just before he was to deliver his 1936 nomination speech at Philadelphia's Franklin Field, no photographs were taken, and no one reported the mishap. James E. Pollard wrote some 50 years ago that

> [in] sum, here was an administration with a concept of public relations far beyond that of any predecessor. The times called for candor and frankness with the public. Much of the early success of the New Deal was undoubtedly due to the constant steady stream of organized information from the White House and to the fact that most of the working correspondents were on the side of Mr. Roosevelt. He played their game and very often they were inclined to play his.[2]

The New Deal policies of FDR were enormously unpopular with newspaper publishers, however, and they exerted more control over editorial writers than reporters. FDR maneuvered around the Republican-leaning editorialists and his other critics by reaching out to the people directly through the more liberal-minded reporters. He used the language of class warfare to denounce the "Tory press," which he claimed had used its economic power to try to derail the New Deal. He derided editorialists as insignificant, claimed that the vast majority of people did not read or care about newspaper editorials, and thereby tried to undermine their authority.

His most innovative medium for reaching the people was radio. Carefully prepared and scripted, his performances were masterly. The president's words, presented with just the right touch of drama, captivated the public and helped to give him the political leverage he needed to take bold action in domestic and foreign policy.

That FDR was liked by reporters and admired by the people redounded to the benefit of his programs. No chief executive since has succeeded so well at turning the working press practically into presidential sycophants. And none—with the possible exception of Ronald Reagan—has had FDR's gift of eloquence and ability to lead the people. To be sure, although none of the White House personalities since could match FDR, the changing nature of the times profoundly influenced presidential press relations.

JFK and the Television Presidency

The powerful medium of television first became a major factor in presidential politics during the 1960 election. Broadcast both by radio and television, the presidential debates between Vice-President Richard M. Nixon and Senator John F. Kennedy may well have been decisive to the outcome of that close race. To television viewers, Kennedy—youthful appearing, polished, and articulate—bettered Nixon, who failed to cut such an appealing presence on screen (radio listeners, however, judged Nixon's performance to be stronger). Kennedy's televised appearances, and the immediate stature conferred on him by appearing alongside the incumbent vice-president, undercut Republican claims that he was not presidential material.

Television gave candidate Kennedy the electoral boost that he needed. JFK often has been called our "first television president." Indeed, he deftly used the emerging medium as a vehicle to promote himself and his presidency. JFK personalized the presidency by allowing television cameras to film both him and his family at the White House. Although afflicted with chronic back pain, the president staged family football games and other outdoor activities to convey to the public an active, energetic, and physically fit chief executive.

More than any other modern president, JFK was adept at off-the-cuff responses that were succinct and often witty. The public relations event that JFK commanded was the televised press conference. He used these events as a vehicle for public communication of his goals and objectives. His performances were superb—even entertaining—as the president offered just the right mix of serious presentation and humorous bantering with reporters to keep viewers interested and convey the information that he wanted to reach the public.

Although Kennedy demonstrated the potential of television as an instrument of mass persuasion, his presidency also demonstrated the separation pf popular leadership from the policymaking process. Despite his personal popularity, JFK had difficulty transferring that support into congressional votes for his policies. Many of his most cherished, progressive legislative initiatives never made it out of the conservative-led House Rules Committee for a vote.

In part because of his popularity with the press, and in part because of the nature of the times, journalists did not report information they possessed about JFK that would have destroyed his finely honed image as a vigorous athlete and good family man. They were well aware of his poor health (his chronic bad back and adrenal insufficiency) as well as his many marital infidelities; yet they did not consider such matters as being important to the public.

The Impact of Vietnam and Watergate

Journalists who allowed themselves to get close to FDR or JFK undoubtedly believed that such access was good for their careers. In so doing, however, many had become conduits for presenting the presidential slant on events to the public. The revelation that journalist Theodore White accepted "dictation" from Jackie Kennedy about the "Camelot" image is a case in point. Any reporter today who so lost his or her professional objectivity would rightfully be derided by colleagues. During the 1960s and 1970s, journalists learned the hard way the costs of being so easily seduced by their political leaders: sometimes those leaders concealed information and lied. And nothing so angered the reporters as being turned into unwitting agents of official deception.

The events of the Vietnam War and Watergate resulted in heightened media cynicism toward official Washington that still is felt today. Much of that cynicism has focused on the presidency and the occupants of that office, because reporters who for a long time had trusted official White House sources discovered that they had been lied to and deceived. Relations between reporters and the White House broke down.

During the Lyndon Johnson administration, reporters wrote of the "credibility gap"—the distance between reality and government projections about the progress of the Vietnam War. Unlike his predecessor, who had charmed the media, LBJ was combative with reporters. He was obsessed with the media to the point of having three television screens—one for each major network—and wire-service feeds installed in the Oval Office so that he could monitor his coverage. Johnson felt that the steady drumbeat of media criticism about his wartime policies undermined public support for U.S. actions and, ultimately, brought down his presidency.

Antagonism between the White House and the media achieved new heights during the Richard M. Nixon years. Nixon had always believed that the national media were overwhelmingly liberal, and that they had despised him ever since his first campaign for Congress in California and for his vigilant efforts to expose State Department employee Alger Hiss as a communist. Because he believed that he could never get a fair hearing from the press on the merits of his actions, Nixon went to unusual lengths to combat negative national news coverage and get his message to the public.

Among the Nixon White House innovations discussed by John Anthony Maltese was the creation in 1969 of the Office of Communications—a unit that was established to promote the president's actions through letters-to-the editor campaigns, generating letters to the White House in favor of the president's actions, encouraging opposite-editorial essays in newspapers to promote the administration view, and reaching out to the usually more pro-administration local media, among others.[3] Unlike the White House Press Office, which handles the day-to-day needs of the press corps, the White House Office of Communications engages in long-term public relations strategies. Although it was unable to save Nixon from himself or Watergate, the Office of Communications left a lasting imprint on presidential media relations, especially during the Reagan years.

Ignoring the old adage, "never get in a fight with someone who buys ink by the barrel," the Nixon White House tried to combat negative news coverage with confrontational tactics. The leading administration spokesman against the allegedly hostile press was Vice President Spiro Agnew, who made speeches denouncing national reporters as elitist "snobs" and, most memorably, "nattering nabobs of negativism."

As the Watergate scandal unfolded, Agnew was forced to resign his post under charges of bribery and tax evasion; Gerald R. Ford was named in his place. And when Watergate brought down the Nixon presidency, the relationship between the White House and the press corps had deteriorated to the point where reporters were openly delighted to see the president and his people leave Washington.

Perhaps most galling to the White House press corps was the fact that two young *Washington Post* "Metro" (local affairs) reporters—Bob Woodward and Carl Bernstein—uncovered the Watergate scandal. The White House reporters who had been toiling for years in the press room—about 30 feet from the Oval Office—had missed the story of a lifetime. Many concluded that their mistake had been that they were too reliant on, and trusting of, official sources of information in the White House. If only they had been more skeptical of official pronouncements and dug beneath the surface of White House activities, many speculated, they might have uncovered the scandal first.

The White House press corps responded by treating Nixon's immediate successors, Gerald R. Ford and Jimmy Carter, with the skepticism that reporters wished that they had exhibited toward Nixon. As David Broder reported, "Watergate changed many of the fundamentals in the White House–press relationship." Reporters became more skeptical of official pronouncements, and their questioning at White House briefings was "almost more prosecutorial than inquisitive."[4] President Ford explained that "We inherited a very bad rapport between the White House press corps and the presidency as a result of Watergate and the Vietnam war. It was difficult to quickly change that negative attitude of the White House press corps."[5] Ford's first press secretary, Jerald F. terHorst, described the immediate post-Watergate atmosphere:

> You couldn't talk about policy and the need for continuity without someone questioning whether there was a devious plot behind it all. The press had been feeding on Watergate and Vietnam for so long that it was hard for them to shift gears.[6]

For most of the public, the image of a president as presented through the media is reality, whether it is accurate or not. There probably is no better example of a presidential image at odds with reality than that of Gerald Ford. Perhaps the most athletically gifted man ever to serve in the Oval Office—a former college football All-American who was drafted by two professional teams and an expert skier and swimmer—Ford's image was that of a clumsy, uncoordinated "stumbler." A high academic achiever and graduate of Yale Law School, Ford was portrayed as an intellectual lightweight. This negative presidential image grew out of the media's emphasis on such trivial events as the president losing his footing while exiting an airplane and an oft-repeated story that LBJ once called Ford too dumb to walk and chew gum at the same time.

Jimmy Carter also suffered a press image problem as president, in part because of the post-Watergate cynicism of those covering the White House. Reporters treated allegations of wrongdoing—some petty, some unsubstantiated—with Watergate-like inquisitiveness. And because Carter's election meant that a Democratic president would be working with strong partisan majorities in Congress for the first time since

LBJ, press expectations for his leadership were initially very high. Carter's press image suffered irreparably when he battled with congressional Democrats over policy priorities and when his image fell short of the kind of commanding presence that the media define as "presidential."

Because media relations are so paramount to presidential leadership in the modern era, journalists often judge a chief executive's leadership acumen according to how well he handles the public presidency. Furthermore, journalists most often view the incumbent administration through the operations of the White House Press Office. When the president's press relations are not smooth and the Press Office operates chaotically—common complaints during the Ford and Carter years—the White House image is one of poor leadership.

By the late 1970s, scholars began to write of the presidency as an "imperiled" rather than "imperial" institution. A succession of "failed" presidencies led some to conclude that public expectations of the office had become so unrealistic—and media scrutiny so debilitating—that no one could adequately do the job.

The Reagan–Bush Years

Ronald Reagan proved that it was still possible for the modern president to win the battle of imagery with the media. Reagan, a former movie actor, came to the White House with a unique set of skills conducive to image-crafting. His administration gave high priority to the public relations aspects of the presidency.

To a large extent, the president's daily activities were driven by the needs of the news media, especially television. The White House worked hard to stay "on message" by generating its "line of the day" and "theme of the week," and by ensuring that administration spokespersons reinforced one another—a marked contrast to the Carter administration, in which, for example, White House spokespersons and Cabinet officials often contradicted one another in public.

Also unlike his immediate predecessor, Reagan did not divorce imagery from policy substance. Both he and his press relations staffers well understood the relationship between positive coverage and moving forward a policy agenda. Through the Legislative Strategy Group, the White House coordinated its political and press strategies. As the White House Office of Communications Director, David Gergen, explained:

> We molded a communications strategy around a legislative strategy. We very carefully thought through what were the legislative goals we were trying to achieve and then formulated a communications strategy which supported them.[7]

During crucial periods of his tenure, Reagan consequently was able to sustain enough public support to pressure Congress into approving his agenda and politically protect himself from the kinds of scandals and investigations that surely would have crippled other presidencies.

Reagan's successor—George H. W. Bush—could not match the media and public relations skills of the "Great Communicator." Acutely aware that he lacked Reagan's skills, Bush downplayed the public relations presidency. According to his press secretary, Marlin Fitzwater, Bush resisted running a Reagan-style, stage-managed presidency.

> It represented a kind of phoniness to him, or fakery, that repelled him. There was the basic old-New England, Yankee honesty of spirit about George Bush that made him distrustful of anything that was staged. He used to say to me, "don't tell me what to do Marlin, I'm not a piece of meat. . . ." So he just resisted any efforts to stage manage him or to do the basic public relations things that we wanted him to do.[8]

It is debatable whether better public relations could have saved the George H. W. Bush presidency. During a period of recession and high public anxiety about the future, few were prepared in 1992 to reward Bush with a second term merely because of his legislative achievements in such areas as clean air and civil rights for the disabled. It is no small testimony to the importance of press and public relations, however, that Bush received little credit for these domestic accomplishments, or that his reputation for foreign policy acumen was untarnished despite some major setbacks for U.S. policy in Eastern Europe, the Middle East, and Africa.

The New Media and the Presidency: Bill Clinton and George W. Bush

President Clinton often complained that the press denied him the customary "honeymoon" period of positive coverage. He was unarguably correct. Indeed, every president expects that when he first enters the White House, journalists will withhold their criticism—at least for several weeks.

Eleven days after his inauguration, the *Washington Post* featured a front-page story entitled "Coverage Quickly Turns Sour as Media Highlight Troubles." The article listed various media descriptions of Clinton that had already been used: "incredibly inept," "slowness and vacillation," "stumbling," and "common sense of a gnat," among others.[9]

From the very beginning, Clinton found himself under a barrage of media criticism for inadequate leadership. At the 100-day juncture, a common media benchmark for sizing up the president, numerous reports and commentaries declared the Clinton presidency in peril.[10] The major criticisms were that Clinton's agenda lacked "focus," that his administration had failed to expediently move much of its policy agenda through Congress, and that consequently, "gridlock" still ruled Washington. Just four months into Clinton's term, *Time* featured a cover story "The Incredible Shrinking President" (with a picture of a miniaturized Clinton), and *Newsweek*'s cover screamed "What's Wrong?"[11]

Compounding the problem were perceived slights of the media by the Clinton White House. Journalists complained of not having adequate access to the president and his staff, of being temporarily cut off from the West Wing of the White House, and of not having their inquiries answered in a timely fashion. Reporters began to sense that the new administration did not like them. After a deluge of negative stories about Clinton, *Newsweek* declared: "The press has now had its revenge. Clinton never gets the benefit of the doubt."[12]

Despite some efforts to improve its press relations, the Clinton White House made no secret of its feeling that news coverage was unfairly hostile. Whether Clinton's news coverage was worse than that of other presidents, joining the drumbeat of criticism about his actions were an increasingly influential and growing "alternative media," led by the predominantly conservative talk-radio format. Of course, presidential scandals and impeachment fueled the frenzy of the anti-Clinton coverage led by conservative media and eventually followed by the mainstream press. The modern media thrive on scandal coverage, and the Clinton White House gave journalists a steady stream of material for their stories.

President George W. Bush attempted perhaps more aggressively than any president since Nixon to control the media through limited access and outright manipulation. Bush conveyed an open hostility to the mainstream media, and his administration engaged in such tactics as paying conservative commentators to write favorable columns and giving extraordinary press access to a partisan Republican who held a White House media credential under a phony name. More than anything, Bush closed off access to reporters as much as possible and even stated that he liked to get his news unfiltered from staff rather than from the media. In his first term in office, Bush held a mere 17 press conferences. Clinton had held 44 by that stage, and George H. W. Bush 84.[13]

Through much of his first term, presidential efforts to control the media did not seem to matter. After the September 11, 2001 terrorist attacks on the U.S. the country rallied behind its president and media coverage of his leadership was quite naturally soft. With the GOP in control of Congress, moreover, there were fewer voices of opposition speaking loudly against the administration than during the era of divided government. But early in Bush's second term, circumstances changed, and so did his press coverage. His widely acknowledged poor response to Hurricane Katrina, a slumping economy, and soaring gasoline prices all resulted in a spate of negative coverage that contributed to his plummeted approval ratings by fall 2005.

What, if anything, can a president do to recover from media criticism and improve his image with the public? Ford's presidential press secretary, Ron Nessen, claimed that "no White House can do much about a president's image." In his view, if the economy is sound and people feel secure about their future, the president does not need much stage managing or a crafty media strategy to look good. If the economy falters, and people are anxious about the future, however, the president's image suffers, no matter how articulate he may be or how much he glad-hands the press.[14] Carter press secretary Jody Powell, responding to criticism that Carter's common-man symbolism was at the heart of the administration's image problem, stated that "a president might look good in blue jeans if it is going well and not so good if things are bad."[15]

Indeed, during a recession in 1982–1983, even Reagan—the "Great Communicator"—suffered poor press coverage and declining public support. George H. W. Bush, whose popularity reached 91 percent in early 1991 following the Gulf War, saw his fortunes plunge later that year during an economic downturn. Bill Clinton could not count on a good economy alone to revive his public standing. Questions about Clinton's character kept the president under a steady firestorm of tough media coverage. President George W. Bush achieved unprecedented approval ratings after 9-11 and achieved tight control over media coverage throughout his first term. But a highly successful White House strategy of media control could not rescue the president from a spate of negative stories about his leadership and the state of the economy after 2005.

Nonetheless, all of these presidents believed that relentlessly negative media coverage compounded their problems and made leading the country unduly difficult. Nessen and Powell certainly are correct to argue that forces larger than presidential press relations (e.g., the inevitable swings of the economy) significantly influence the public's perception of a president's leadership acumen, but the ways in which the public views those larger forces and the adequacy of the president's responses largely are determined by the media. As the political scientist Murray Edelman wrote in his classic 1967 text, *The Symbolic Uses of Politics*,

> For most people most of the time politics is a series of pictures in the mind, placed there by television news, newspapers, magazines and discussions. . . . Politics for most of us is a passing parade of abstract symbols.[16]

Nearly four decades later, this parade of symbols is joined by the cacophonous sound of a larger marching band of cable-television stations, talk radio, Internet sites, Web-blogs, town-hall meetings, and numerous other means of communications. Presidents cannot control these various means, but they have many different venues today through which they can get their messages out to the public. Fitzwater believed that despite all the complaints of unfair media coverage,

> the president has the upper hand in press relations. You control the information, you control the time-table, you control the schedule. If the president has bad press relations, he's doing something wrong. . . . The communications tools at the disposal of a president are so immense, that no one can compete with him. When you have 100 to 150 reporters there every day to record everything you say as president, that's an incredible power. . . . A president can get out any message that he wants.[17]

President Clinton tried to get his message to the public in many unconventional ways, including the Internet, specialty cable-television programs, talk shows, and town-hall meetings. He moved well beyond his predecessors into innovative areas of communications, but his presidency has been testimony to the enduring, preeminent importance of the traditional Washington press corps to the White House image. Alternative means of communications have not displaced the White House press corps.

Conclusions

Presidents spend a great deal of time worrying about the press. They employ large numbers of press officers, communications aides, and image-makers to try to promote a favorable view of the administration's activities. Despite all of their efforts to manage the news and project a favorable image, presidents inevitably are frustrated with the press coverage that they receive.

Is the president's image, as Nessen and Powell implied, nearly a prisoner to forces over which he has little control? Or, as Fitzwater argued, is the president able to control his message and communicate whatever he wants?

The answer is not clear-cut. Both views are accurate to some extent. There are factors that bear on presidential press relations over which a White House has little or no control; yet a White House can improve its fate in some respects.

Uncontrollable events and circumstances often drive the presidential agenda and make it difficult for the White House to stay "on message." Bill Clinton's 1992 campaign boasted the unmistakable message of the candidate's priorities: "It's the economy, stupid." On entering office, several complex foreign policy crises demanded the president's attention and cluttered his agenda. When the president also tried to move forward his tax and budget policies, the media criticized his leadership, maintaining that he was trying to do "too much, too soon." President George W. Bush seemed to have better control over the media than any modern president – until a natural disaster and a faltering economy shifted the tone of his news coverage significantly for the worse.

Public perceptions of the state of the economy have an enormous impact on the presidential image, as George H. W. Bush learned the hard way. In 1991, he had a 91 percent approval rating. In 1992, in the midst of a recession, he received 38 percent of the vote. In reality, presidents have very little control over the direction of the domestic economy, yet they are held accountable for current economic conditions.

The White House also has little control over how journalists define and evaluate presidential leadership. Those who cover the presidency admire the almost larger-than-life image of the activist, visionary leader—an idealized, FDR-type figure with an aggressive, 100-day plan to confront the nation's problems. This standard is almost impossible to live up to, and it poses special problems for a president such as Bush, who favored a cautious, status-quo leadership approach.

Presidents nonetheless are able to influence their relations with the press corps. Although a positive, cordial relationship does not guarantee favorable coverage, White House efforts to accommodate journalists and tend to their needs can help a great deal. Clinton learned that by antagonizing reporters, a president may suffer the press' "revenge."

Presidents also are able to control, to some extent, how they communicate with the public through the media. It is true that television networks may refuse to carry a presidential speech or commentators may pan a press conference performance, but there is no excuse for a president failing to communicate a message to the public. As Fitzwater commented, "there is no such thing as the president not getting his message out." The president "may be getting the wrong message out. Or, he may not have a message. But something is being communicated. In our case, it was that President Bush was out of touch with the economy."[18]

In addition, presidents can lower somewhat the expectations of their performance. Presidents often promise that they will achieve great things, and it is reasonable for the press to evaluate whether they have made good on those promises. Being more realistic about likely achievements can go a long way in breaking the debilitating cycle of promises made, expectations unfulfilled, media criticism, and public cynicism.

For most Americans, understanding the presidency occurs primarily through the daily reporting and commentary of the media, not through textbooks. Most people know the political world only through messages conveyed to them by the media. For that reason, presidents and their aides are profoundly concerned about, and try to influence, their media coverage, because for the public, the image of the president *is* reality. Presidents cannot control how they are viewed through media coverage of their activities, but they have many means by which to influence coverage and get their message to the public. In the mass-media age, no president can afford to ignore this powerful force in American politics.

Endnotes

1. Woodrow Wilson, *Constitutional Government* (New York: Columbia University Press, 1908).
2. James E. Pollard, *Presidents and the Press* (New York: MacMillan, 1947), p. 774.
3. See John Anthony Maltese, *Spin Control: The White House Office of Communications and the Management of Presidential News* (Chapel Hill, NC: University of North Carolina Press, 1992).
4. David Broder, *Behind the Front Page: A Candid Look at How the News Is Made* (New York: Simon & Shuster, 1987), p. 167.
5. Author interview with President Gerald R. Ford, December 13, 1989.
6. Author interview with Jerald F. terHorst, June 27, 1990.
7. Quoted in Mark Hertsgaard, *On Bended Knee: The Press and the Reagan Presidency* (New York: Farrar Straus Giroux, 1988), p. 108.
8. Author interview with Marlin Fitzwater, July 9, 1994.
9. Howard Kurtz, "Coverage Quickly Turns Sour as Media Highlight Troubles," *The Washington Post,* January 31, 1993, p. A1.
10. See, for example, Jeffrey H. Birnbaum and Michael K. Frisby, "Clinton's Zigzags Between Politics and Policy Explain Some Problems of His First 100 Days," *Wall Street Journal,* April 29, 1993, p. A16; Richard Cohen, "Mr. Clinton Goes to Washington," *The Washington Post,* May 6, 1993, p. A23; Matthew Cooper, "The Next 100 Days: Stress Test," *U.S. News and World Report,* May 10, 1993, pp. 26–32; Thomas B. Edsall, "Clinton Loses Focus—And Time," *The Washington Post,* May 2, 1993, pp. C1, 5; David Gergen, "After 100 Days, a President in Distress," *U.S. News and World Report,* May 3, 1993, p. 51; and Kenneth T. Walsh and Matthew Cooper, "Great Expectations Meet Bleak House," *U.S. News and World Report,* May 3, 1993, p. 11.
11. Both issues were June 7, 1993.
12. Joe Klein, "What's Wrong?" *Newsweek,* June 7, 1993, p. 19.
13. Lori Robertson, "In Control," *American Journalism Review* (February/March 2005), http://www.ajr.org/Article.asp?id=3812 (accessed on October 8, 2005); Howard Kurtz, "Is Bush Targeting the Media?" *Washington Post,* March 3, 2005, http://www.washingtonpost.com/wp-dyn/articles/A3421-2005Mar3.html (accessed on October 8, 2005).
14. Author interview with Ron Nessen, July 5, 1990.
15. Quoted in George C. Edwards III, *The Public Presidency: The Pursuit of Popular Support* (New York: St. Martin's Press, 1983), p. 70.
16. Murray Edelman, *The Symbolic Uses of Politics* (Urbana, IL: University of Illinois Press, 1967), p. 5.
17. Fitzwater interview.
18. Fitzwater interview.

Jeremy D. Mayer

The Presidency and Image Management: Discipline in Pursuit of Illusion

"Presidential government is an illusion. . . ." Heclo and Salamon (1981, 1).

Scene One: A triumphant president lands in a jet on an aircraft carrier, to celebrate with loyal troops a stunning victory over a tyrannical despot. The sailors greet him with boisterous cheering, and he gives a speech from the deck as the sun sets perfectly in the Pacific, the last golden rays of the sun illuminating a patriotic banner reading "Mission Accomplished."

Scene Two: In the midst of a photo opportunity with Florida second-graders about reading, a president is told in whispers by his chief of staff that the second tower at the World Trade Center has been hit by a terrorist attack. As two other hijacked planes speed toward Washington, the confused president picks up "The Pet Goat" and stays on photo-op autopilot for at least seven long minutes, chatting about goats and literacy (Paltrow 2004).

These two images of the same president, George W. Bush, illustrate the challenges of presidential image management in the 24-hour video era. One shows the president in a carefully planned setting of patriotism, victory, masculinity, and daring. The other shows a president taking no actions, making no decisions, as crucial minutes tick away. The Bush administration's success at image management is demonstrated by the fact that most Americans have seen the unprecedented carrier landing, while almost none have seen the complete footage of Bush complimenting Ms. Daniels's children on their reading abilities while the towers burned.

The image of the president—the impression Americans have of their chief executive as a leader and a human being—is vitally important to the success of any modern president. Public views about their leaders' personal characteristics have been been part of successful governance since before the Athenian age of Pericles, and certainly pervade the long history of the American presidency. Image has become more

Source: Presidential Studies Quarterly, Vol. 34, No. 3 (September 2004), p. 620–631.

central to the presidency in the decades since television became the primary mode of political communication. Image is both a source of power and a measure by which presidents and their staffs are judged. This essay will briefly explore how presidential images are created and assess how the Bush image managers are doing at their task. It will conclude by raising questions about the future of presidential image management.

The Components of Presidential Image

What is image? It is both truth and lie, both accurate perception and the gap between reality and perception. It is not policy or substance. It is, however, connected to both. Image is built up day by day, slowly accreting sediment at the bottom of the lake of public opinion. Images can be startlingly resilient, in part because of the media's tendency to reinforce whatever the public image has become. At a certain point in a presidency, it becomes easier to change policy than it is to change image, for this very reason. As one of the great presidential image managers, Reagan aide Michael Deaver, observed, "in the television age, image sometimes is as useful as substance" (Waterman, Wright, and St. Clair 1999, 53).

The public image of a president is produced in a complex interaction among four elements: the "reality" of the president's character, actions, and policies; the image management of his staff; the attempted redefinitions of his political opponents; and the cacophony of media assessments of the man in the White House. Together, they create the inchoate and shifting image within the collective minds of Americans.

The "reality" that is the supposed root of image begins with the president's character, talents, worldview, and style. It also encompasses, in the no-privacy modern era, such things as family life and sexual behavior. The president's policies and political background are relevant as well, to the extent that they color the public's perception of the president as a man. Policies that are seen as mean spirited, thoughtless, or dangerous have all affected the personal image of presidents. It also includes his physical appearance, as well as his diction and his accent.

Consider how the exigencies of image politics limit who can actually be president. While the American general population is perhaps the most obese in the world, the last president to be truly overweight was William Howard Taft in 1912.[1] The last bald man elected president was Dwight Eisenhower. Given that estimates of the number of bald or mostly bald men older than 35 in the general public range from 40 to 70 percent, it should astound us that the 16 men who ran for the major party nominations in 2000 and 2004 were all follicularly gifted.[2] Not one of them was overweight, and the eventual winner in 2000 was remarkably svelte. Washington may be, as one quip has it, Hollywood for ugly people, but at the top, it is now run by people who are quite attractive, or at least not unattractive. If we consider Kennedy the first president of the television age, the trend toward physical attractiveness becomes clear. The last five presidents (Reagan, Bush I, Clinton, Bush II, Obama) are far more attractive than the preceding four (Johnson, Nixon, Ford, Carter). The reality of personal appearance may be the clearest example of the power of image in politics.[3]

The image manager's task begins with deciding which of these aspects of the president to emphasize and which to submerge. Sometimes, reality must be directly contradicted. A divorced president who has dysfunctional relationships with some of his own children is portrayed as a benevolent father figure (Reagan). A famously unfaithful husband lectures American teenagers about sexual propriety (Clinton). A president raised in wealth and privilege lets it be known that his favorite food is pork rinds and his favorite music is the Oak Ridge Boys (Bush I). The danger of such tactics is that image manipulation that directly contradicts reality may strike the public as fake—a perception corrosive to all future attempts at image repair and manipulation (Waterman et al. 1999, 186). The best image management leaves no traces, no fingerprints of public relations professionalism. Thus, the call to "let Reagan be Reagan" or its equivalent is often heard. The typical protest from image managers is that their job is to let the public get to know the "real" president. In truth, the job is to let the public believe they know the real person.

Political opponents of the president know if they can increase the number of Americans who hold unfavorable impressions of the president as a person, they will have much greater success at defeating his policies. Many observers remark on the increasingly vituperative tone of politics in the nation; the main cause is the emphasis on personal image. Politics became more personal because the personal is far more potent today than ever before. Thus, image politics have had concrete effects. Because so many in both parties have come to believe that the opposition party's leaders are not just wrong on policy but are actually bad people, it is difficult for leaders to reach across the gulf between the parties without potentially alienating core supporters. Campaign finance reform may be to blame. By making parties and candidates dependent on thousands of upper-middle class donors, rather than the ultra-wealthy few, campaign finance reform has forced fundraisers to demonize their opponents. For example, a hypothetical partisan letter emphasizing the positive aspects of Barack Obama's platform would raise much less money than one that disparaged the personalities of John McCain or Sarah Palin. The politics of personal destruction pays as well as plays.

The ability of a White House to maintain a relatively neutral or positive personal image for the president has been changed by these increased incentives for opponents to wage war against the president as an individual. This can be done through a number of different venues. First, changes in the media permit "narrowcasting" messages to partisan groups. When Americans watched three broadly marketed television networks, the need to appear objective and even respectful toward the office of the presidency limited the dissemination of truly egregious and partisan characterizations of the president. Those who seek to distribute a negative image of the president will find many willing viewers on the Internet if not somewhere on cable television.

The media serve as referees of the ongoing fight over the president's image, adjudicating which depictions are credible through their decisions about what to broadcast. The media have also changed their standards as to what is news and what is private. In 1962, a woman picketed outside the White House, carrying a sign stating that John Kennedy was an adulterer and that she had photographic proof. Not a single media outlet broadcast her allegations, or even investigated them, even though many reporters and editors were aware of such rumors, and some knew them to be accurate

(Reeves 1997, 242–43). Today, a half-baked, nearly unsourced allegation of adultery is on the Web within a few hours of its emergence, as occurred with John Kerry in 2004. The quality of a president's marriage is widely discussed in parts of the media, down to the sincerity of a kiss between husband and wife (for example, Tipper and Al Gore in 2000, and the media's obsessive interpretations of public physical gestures between Bill and Hillary Clinton). While the partisan press era of the early republic did feature some scandalous assertions about the sexual practices and characters of occupants of the White House, the personalized coverage today is far more intrusive.

Some of the most powerful media shapers of presidential image are not even journalists. The monologues and sketches on *Leno, Letterman,* and *Saturday Night Live* are at least as important as the nightly news broadcasts when it comes to the image of our leaders. These shows, which focus on the most simplified aspects of the public face of the president, both influence the presidential image and are perhaps the best barometer of the public's current judgment about him.

These media depictions of presidents and their challengers quickly become hardened into almost irrefutable realities: George W. Bush—dumb; Bill Clinton—letch; Al Gore—wooden prig and serial liar; Bob Dole—old and cold. Through selective reporting, the media's own practices help set these images in concrete. Perhaps the best example of this was Bush I's encounter with a grocery store scanner. Widely perceived as an aloof patrician, Bush found this image particularly damaging when the economy was doing badly in 1990–1992. Bush was alleged by the media to have looked at a checkout laser scanner with the wonder befitting a multi-millionaire insulated from the daily concerns of average Americans—when the economy was in recession. While the first reporter who wrote of Bush's apparent bewilderment was not even there, it quickly became a hardened "fact" repeated endlessly, even by scholars (Waterman et al. 1999, 61–62). However, a videotape of the event shows Bush was not surprised at all by the scanner, as an apology from the publisher of *The New York Times* conceded (Kurtz 1992).

In a complicated and shifting interaction, these four forces (reality, image management, image attack from the opposition, and the media) shape the image of every president. What methods did the Bush White House use to convince Americans to perceive Bush positively?

The Bush Image Team: Discipline and Set Design

The Bush White House was tremendously successful at image management in his first term. Two components stand out: the message discipline of the White House, and the quality of the set design that served as the backdrop for the president.

Although Bush seldom claimed to have profited from his sterling education, it was unquestionably to his advantage to be our country's first MBA president. Bush ran his administration like a CEO. "This is the most disciplined White House in history," said an admiring Michael Deaver (Auletta 2004). Particularly in its staff conduct and ethos, a White House reflects the values and priorities of the president. Clinton, famously addicted to open-ended debate, had a White House that leaked constantly. Bush, by contrast, was a martinet for loyalty and discipline. Nearly every account of the internal operation of Bush's White House included a testimony to its leak-proof nature (Millbank 2002).

How did Bush manage to do what every president attempts? In addition to his MBA and his obvious administrative talents, Bush was the only modern president to have had a ground-level view of the operations of a White House staff. (During his father's term in office, Bush was an informal enforcer of discipline and a loyalty checker; York 2001a.) He inspired a tremendous sense of personal loyalty in staffers, as well as some level of intimidation, which worked together to stop self-aggrandizing or policy-based leaking. The Bush White House also wisely limited the number of people who regularly interact with the press. In previous White House administrations, top aides were frequently made available to give interviews or at least make comments on stories. At the Bush White House, top staffers boasted about being inaccessible to the media. President Bush somehow inspired a selfless White House staff that put his image ahead of their own celebrity (Auletta 2004). Indeed, the men and women of the Bush White House came closer to achieving the ideal "passion for anonymity" than any other recent presidential staff.[4]

The Bush White House was also remarkably successful at convincing the rest of the executive branch to work with the White House on image management. The centrifugal forces of Washington bureaucracies and the personal ambitions of Cabinet secretaries often defeated such efforts in the past (Maltese 1992). To combat these tendencies, the Bush administration appointed loyalists throughout the communications offices of the various agencies and departments (Kumar 2003a, 384). Adding to the uniformity of positive depictions of the president and his policies was a new level of coordination and control of message with the Republican leadership on Capitol Hill and with linked interest groups.

All of the discipline on image control gives the White House extraordinary ability to force the media to cover the pictures and narratives it provides. If no one from the White House contributes to a negative image of the president, then the media are almost forced to cover the portrait of the president designed for them by Bush's image handlers.

Presidential Set Design

How a president should be shown to the public is the heart of presidential image management. Believing that most Americans will not read a newspaper article on any given day, or perhaps even watch through an entire news story, the Bush staff crafted an image of the president that suited the person flipping channels (Kumar 2003a, 387). The attention to detail, which became legendary, was thus to be expected; if Americans only see one picture of their president each day, it had better be a good one. At some events, wealthy Republican supporters in the shot behind the president were instructed by the advance team to remove their ties, so that an image of normal Americans supporting Bush would be conveyed (Shella 2003). The backdrop was often composed of repetitive slogans, far too small for the live audience to see, but just right for television. Whether there was any marginal "subliminal" effect on the viewer of seeing slogans associating Bush with jobs, security, and strong families was un-known, but it again served the busy channel-shifting American, who got the White House message of the day. As Dan Bartlett, communications director put it:

> Americans are leading busy lives, and sometimes they don't have the opportunity to read a story or listen to an entire broadcast. But if they can have an instant under-standing of what the president is talking about by seeing 60 seconds of television, you accomplish your goals as communicators (Bumiller 2003).

In pursuit of the perfect video shot, events were scheduled like Hollywood movies, to get the cherished director's "golden hour" of setting sunshine. When the timing or weather prevented this, the staff was known to spend tens of thousands of dollars on renting rock concert quality lighting sets for single televised events (Bumiller 2003).

Perhaps any White House would adopt this strategy today. Surveys suggest that amid the cacophony of the Internet and dozens of cable options, few Americans watch presidential speeches, and even when they do, few retain more than one sim-ple message from a 30-minute speech (Welch 2003, 353). If the public has a bias to-ward absorbing information through pictures, then the White House will work to feed that preference. But in Bush's case, it was also an inevitable response to the weaknesses of his presentation of self. Unlike Reagan or Clinton, Bush was a poor public speaker. On rare occasions, he could fill a room with passion and inspire a na-tion with his vision and courage, as he did in his seminal September 20, 2001, speech to Congress. With a good speech, a supportive audience, and inspiration, Bush was frequently competent. He was, however, at his worst in unscripted interactions with non-supporters. Thus, perhaps the most crucial image-handling decision in his first term was to insulate him as much as possible from questions and conflict (Suskind 2004, 147–48). When Bush held an economic conference in Waco early in his ad-ministration, the president "spontaneously" wandered from panel to panel, with his comments prepared for each session. The conference was a Potemkin's village of dis-course. Instead of actually discussing the economic issues of the day—as presidents as diverse as Ford and Clinton had done at similar events—the points to be made were pre-screened, the conclusions about the policies already reached before discus-sions began (Suskind 2004, 269–73). How could there be any debate at this "con-ference"? Almost all participants were fervent Bush supporters.

Deft awareness of Bush's limitations explains why Bush had fewer solo press con-ferences than any other recent president (Kumar 2003b). But it went beyond avoid-ing tough questions from reporters. Bush enveloped himself in a security bubble in all of his public appearances. Those with anti-Bush signs or chanting anti-Bush slo-gans were relegated to distant areas with the Orwellian title of "free speech zones," far from television cameras. Although the claim of security was made, Bush support-ers with similar-sized signs were permitted to stay on the motorcade route, or outside a presidential event (Lindorff 2003). If the danger were assassination, surely those who wish the president harm would be smart enough to carry a sign that says "Bush-Cheney." The claim that the post-9/11 security environment required such control of dissent also rings hollow: Bush as governor was known for forbidding pro-testers outside his mansion in ways no previous occupant had ever done (Baldauf

1999). The picture of Bush confronting a hostile demonstrator or even driving by angry crowds has rarely if ever been on American television. This image management conveyed, wordlessly, subtly, and powerfully, the impression that those who disagreed with the president were irrelevant and weak. They must be fringe elements: they were physically on the outskirts of every presidential event.

Bush's Two Main Images: Presidential Media Roles

What images did the Bush White House convey of the president of the United States? While several were tried—such as First Christian, Racial Uniter, and President CEO—the two major ones were the Average American and the War Leader.

Average American with Common Values

President Bush boasted one of the most elite backgrounds of any president, and was only the second son of a president to become president. As of November 2004, the Bush family name had been on six of the last seven presidential ballots. Bush also had an educational record far above the American norm, or even the average for presidents: Andover, Yale, and a Harvard MBA. Yet this man of such rarefied background successfully sold himself to the public as a man of the people, a person of typical values and simple small-town beliefs.

In part, the reality of Bush made it easy for the image to be conveyed. Even in comparatively harsh accounts of his presidency, the fact that he made time for secretaries, cooks, and others shines through.[5] Bush did not pretend to dislike intellectuals in order to woo voters. His disdain toward intellectuals, particularly East Coast intellectuals, is one of the most constant themes in Bush biographies, dating back to his time at Yale if not earlier. Unlike his father, who shielded the fact that he spoke French from the press until after his election, Bush gave little evidence of academic gifts in need of hiding. Confronted with questions about the failure to find weapons of mass destruction in Iraq, Bush brushed them aside as of concern only to those in "elite circles"—as if Bush had not spent his life in such circles.

One of the ways Bush demonstrated his everyman status was through his eager and sincere enthusiasm for sports, especially baseball. One of the major image initiatives of the first nine months of his presidency was hosting tee-ball games at the White House. By inviting small children to play an iconic American sport on the lawn of the White House, Bush was sending a simple message, according to a senior administration official:

> . . . tee ball isn't the reason people like him, but it's initiatives like this . . . that show the wholesomeness factor and will allow him to be one of the more successful presidents (York 2001b).

The percentage of Americans who believed that Bush "shares your values" never dropped below 50 percent in his first term, according to Gallup, and often ranged much higher. The cause lay not only with the adroit handling of his image by his staff.

Rather, it was also a product of his opponents' inability to broadcast a consistent counter-image. Those who opposed Bush could never decide whether he was a dumb man pretending to be sophisticated and failing, or if he was a sophisticated man pretending to be dumb for political reasons. It seems likely that Bush's tendency to fail at subject-verb agreement, to mangle relatively simple words, and to regularly demonstrate an inability to handle nuance served as much to insulate him from the charge of privilege as it did to support the charge that he lacked the intellectual depth some see as vital to the presidency. The best image for a president suits his personality as well as his political needs. Bush clearly believed that he was in many significant ways a typical American, and this lent sincerity to the depiction, regardless of its accuracy.

War Leader

One of the chief constitutional duties of president is to lead the armed forces. Every recent American president has had to deploy the American military into hostile areas. However, the scope and intensity of the conflicts that Bush has launched made it a far more central part of his presidential image, perhaps more so than any president since Roosevelt. As the president during the most significant attack on the country since Pearl Harbor, Bush's image inevitably became mixed with the perception of his handling of military leadership.

Bush put himself into many positive military settings, including the high-profile aircraft carrier landing. When "major hostilities" were ended in Iraq in April of 2003, President Bush's communications staff wanted to arrange a compelling event to celebrate the good news of rapid victory over Iraq. They chose to put the president on an aircraft carrier full of sailors returning from the Mideast. In an unprecedented step, the commander in chief landed on the deck of the carrier in a pilot's uniform; shifting to civilian gear, Bush spoke in front of a banner reading "Mission Accomplished." The entire event was full of the mood of victory and celebration. Some Democrats complained initially about the jingoism and use of the military for partisan purposes, alleging that the event unnecessarily delayed the sailors return to port, and that Bush had been showboating to land by airplane. However, the event was generally viewed as wonderful politics, and evidence of the skill of the White House image team. As television pundit Chris Matthews asked: "Why are the Democrats so stupid to attack the best presidential picture in years?" (Whitney 2003).

The other iconic image of Bush as War President occurred in Thanksgiving of 2003. The president secretly traveled to Iraq to celebrate the classic American holiday with the troops, an act of personal courage given the security situation in Baghdad. The trip resulted in the perfect photo of Bush offering the troops a turkey on a platter. In this dramatic image, most of the tactics of the Bush image management team were on display. Few White Houses would have had the discipline to undertake such a surprising and risky gesture with no leaks. As with Bush's economic conference or the words posted behind him at public events, the turkey on the platter did not actually nourish any living person at the event—a display turkey, it only nourished the president's image at home.[6] Finally, the military screened all non-Bush-supporting troops out of the event, thus extending Bush's no-dissent bubble even to the overseas environment

(Sealey 2004). Had a single soldier challenged the president about weapons of mass destruction, extended deployments, or simply said, "Send me home, Mr. President," all the positive outcomes for the president's image would have evaporated. Instead, the president's standing in polls improved significantly following the trip (Jacobson 2003).

Bush's image as a war leader was an essential aspect of his popularity. Bush hovered just above 50 percent approval in the polls for the first eight months of his presidency. Following the attacks of 9/11, his popularity soared to unprecedented heights and remained lofty for months as he led a successful and remarkably swift and low-casualty invasion of Afghanistan. A few months after the removal of the Taliban, a slow bleed began in his popularity. Just at the point where it was reaching its pre-9/11 levels, hostilities with Iraq loomed. Once the Iraq war began, Bush's numbers soared again, although not to the heights of September–February 2001–2002. Following that war, once again Bush's numbers began a slow decline (Jacobson 2003). While Americans "rally 'round the flag'" and the president during any conflict, conflict seemed to be crucial to Bush's popularity.[7]

The Future of Presidential Image Management

The centrality of image to the American presidency is likely to grow. We may be only at the dawn of the era of the "short attention-span presidency," in which substantive policy proposals become entirely props in the pursuit of effective image conveyance. It is difficult to think of a countervailing political, technological, or cultural force that could stop the increasing salience of images to the voting preferences of the American public. In this sense, the gloomy jeremiads of Neil Postman (1985) and other communication scholars appear to have been confirmed in the decades since their baleful predictions were first aired.

Some might agree with Postman that Americans are thus "amusing themselves to death," the title of Postman's most important book. Will modern presidents pursue gossamer and ephemeral images, at the expense of long-term historical accomplishments? Consider Truman and Eisenhower, the last two presidents before the image became the dominant means of political communication. No American president has been lower in the polls at the end of his term than Truman was in 1953.[8] Yet despite the image of a country bumpkin too small for the presidency, which he took with him back home to Independence, Missouri, Truman's stock has risen in the esteem of historians in every poll on presidential greatness since 1953. In Eisenhower's case, he was apparently content to let the public think he was less sharp than he actually was, in order to achieve substantive policy goals of moderate conservatism. One might observe that Truman and Eisenhower correctly put their time and efforts into matters of substance. Yet their presidency is not the one George W. Bush was sworn into on January 20, 2001. Image is now so directly linked to the ability to achieve substantive policy goals that tactics such as Eisenhower's may no longer be feasible. Even a president committed to achieving substantive goals will have to follow the logic of image management.

Yet there is another possibility, more hopeful than the inevitable subjugation of substance to image. Critical theorist Walter Benjamin, writing in the 1930s, made two key claims for the virtues of mechanically reproduced images: They would free the masses from elite filters because of the immediacy of their conveyance, and they would reveal previously hidden aspects of life. In the case of one iconic image of George W. Bush—the aircraft carrier shot—we can see evidence of Benjamin's prescience. Although widely viewed at the time as a brilliant exploitation of Bush's victory over Saddam, by June of 2006, many more Americans had died in the occupation of Iraq than in its liberation. Unlike the largely positive pictures that came out during the initial war in Iraq, the images of young Americans burned alive in Fallujah, bombed in Ramadi, or maimed in Mosul were very tough for the Bush White House to spin; their immediacy was far less subject to elite filtering, as Benjamin would have anticipated.

Similarly, one aspect of life that has been largely hidden from most citizens during the nation-states era is the true face of warfare and occupation. No matter how vivid the text of a Stephen Crane, a Leo Tolstoy, or an Ernest Hemingway, print could never take a nation to the frontlines the way video can. Previous presidents could occupy the Philippines or Haiti and fight a long bloody guerrilla war, secure in the knowledge that the public would never see the inevitable human costs of occupation. The images of death and upheaval in "liberated" Iraq forced a slow retreat from "Mission Accomplished" by the Bush White House. What had looked like the acme of image management later became an image blunder.[9] At first, the president implied that the Navy, not his staff, had chosen the banner, (Conason 2003a). Eventually, the White House admitted that they had planned and produced the banner, although the Navy had physically put it up on the ship (Conason 2003b). Karl Rove, the man most responsible for Bush's image, conceded in an interview that "Mission Accomplished" had not been a wise move. Largely because of dissatisfaction with the war in Iraq, Bush eventually sank lower in presidential popularity than all but three postwar presidents. Contra Postman, the triumph of image over substance, of spin over reality, may be farther off than it initially seemed.

Endnotes

1. Although our anorexic media (particularly David Letterman) often labeled Clinton as "fat," in fact, he was among our more telegenic presidents. Indeed, his image handlers probably did not mind the label, because it gave him something in common with millions of Americans, much the same way Bush's fractured diction does. Clinton got the best of both worlds—he did not look fat on television, which would have been disastrous, but got to be seen sympathetically by obese Americans regardless.
2. Obviously, we are not considering the two female candidates, and we are also not getting picky about those two candidates with thinning hair problems.
3. And as seen by the rumors of plastic surgery swirling around John Kerry, even this reality is subject to alteration.
4. The phrase is political scientist Louis Brownlow's, from his 1937 commission report on administrating the executive branch. Quoted in Allen Felzenberg, "The Transition: Guide for the President-Elect." *Policy Review* 103 (October/November 2000).
5. See, for example, the letter by former White House staffer John Dilulio, which makes clear Bush's common touch, as well as Paul O'Neil's account as told in Ron Suskind, *The Price of Loyalty* (New York: Simon and Schuster, 2004).

6. The White House denies that it knew the decorative turkey would be there, or that Bush picking it up for the cameras was planned. Mike Allen, "The Bird Was Perfect but Not for Dinner: In Iraq Picture, Bush Is Holding the Centerpiece," *Washington Post*, December 4, 2003, p. A33.
7. The Bush administration may also be controlling the image of the president at war in a subtle way, by enforcing with new vigor a policy denying media access to the arrival of military casualties from Iraq and Afghanistan at Dover Air Base. These images of coffins draped in flags had been emblematic of the costs of previous military conflicts.
8. This does not include Nixon, who left office before completing his term. James Pfiffner, *The Modern Presidency* (New York: St. Martins, 1994), 221.
9. It has even been compared to Michael Dukakis's head bobbling over the top of an M-1 tank, the previous nadir of self-inflicted image wounds.

References

Auletta, Ken, 2004. "Fortress Bush," *The New Yorker*, January 19.

Baldauf, Scott,1999. Lawsuit May Test Bush's Free-Speech Views," *Christian Science Monitor*, August 31, 1999.

Bumiller, Elizabeth, " 'Top Gun' and His Image-Makers," *The New York Times*, May 16, p. A1.

Conason, Joe, 2003a. "The Enlisted and the Entitled," *Salon*, October 23.

Conason, Joe, 2003b. "The Banner Stops Here," *Salon*, October 28.

Felzenberg, Allen, 2000. "The Transition: Guide for the President-Elect," *Policy Review* available at www.policyreview.org/oct00/felzenberg.htm/.

Heclo, Hugh, and Lester M. Salamon, 1981. *The Illusion of Presidential Government*, Boulder: Westview.

Jacobson, Gary C, 2003. "The Bush Presidency and the American Electorate," *Presidential Studies Quarterly* 33 (4): 701–29.

Kumar, Martha Joynt, 2003a. "Communications Operations in the White House of President George W. Bush: Making News on His Terms," *Presidential Studies Quarterly* 33 (2): 366–93.

Kumar, Martha Joynt, 2003b. "Does This Constitute a Press Conference? Defining and Tabulating Modern Presidential Press Conferences," *Presidential Studies Quarterly* 33 (1): 221–37.

Kurtz, Howard, 1999. The Story That Just Won't Check Out," *The Washington Post*, February 19, p. C1.

Lindorff, Dave, 2003. "Keeping Dissent Invisible: How the Secret Service and the White House Keep Protesters Safely out of Bush's Sight—and off TV," *Salon*, October 16.

Maltese, John A, 1992. *Spin Control: The White House Office of Communication and the Management of Presidential News*, Chapel Hill: University of North Carolina Press.

Millbank, Dana, 2002. "Bush Loses Closest Political Aide," *The Washington Post*, April 24.

Paltrow, Scot J., 2004. "Government Accounts of 9/11 Reveal Gaps, Inconsistencies," *Wall Street Journal*, March 22, p. A1.

Pfiffner, James, 1994. *The Modern Presidency*, New York: St. Martins.

Postman, Neil, 1985. *Amusing Ourselves to Death*, New York: Vintage.

Reeves, Thomas C., 1997. *A Question of Character*, New York: Prima.

Sealey, Geraldine, 2004. "Look Who Couldn't Come to Dinner," *Salon*, March 10.

Shella, Jim, 2003. "Some Audience Members Told Not to Wear Ties for Bush Speech," WISH TV (Indianapolis), June 2. Available from http://www.wishtv.com/Global/story.asp?s%20%201278487.

Suskind, Ron, 2004. *The Price of Loyalty*, New York: Simon and Schuster.

Waterman, Richard W., Robert Wright, and Gilbert St. Clair, 1999. *The Image-Is-Everything Presidency*, Boulder: Westview.

Welch, Reed L., 2003. Presidential Success in Communicating with the Public through Televised Addresses," *Presidential Studies Quarterly* 33 (2).

Whitney, Gleaves, 2003. "George W. in the Flight Suit," *National Review Online*, May 8.

York, Byron, 2001a. "Leakproof? At the Bush White House, Mum's the Word," *National Review*, October 21.

York, Byron, 2001b. "Bush to a 'Tee': The President's Most Heartfelt Values Initiative," *National Review*, September 3.

George C. Edwards, III

The Presidential Pulpit: Bully or Baloney?

We do not think of presidents as passively accepting the current state of public opinion. Theodore Roosevelt proclaimed, "People used to say of me that I . . . divined what the people were going to think. I did not 'divine' . . . I simply made up my mind what they ought to think, and then did my best to get them to think it."[1]

On the other hand, when asked about his "biggest disappointment as president," George Bush replied, "I just wasn't a good enough communicator."[2] In a discussion of his problems in governing, President Clinton declared that he needed to do a better

---

Source: Original essay written for this volume.

job of *communicating*. "[I]t's always frustrating to feel that you're misunderstood . . . and you can't quite get through."[3]

What is happening here? Leading the public is perhaps the ultimate resource of the political leader. It is difficult for others who hold power to deny the legitimate demands of a president with popular support. Theodore Roosevelt declared the White House to be a "bully pulpit," yet contemporary presidents typically find the public unresponsive to many issues at the top of the White House agenda and unreceptive to requests to think about, much less act on, political matters.

How should we evaluate the presidential pulpit as a tool for achieving passage of the president's programs in Congress? Should we accept the assumption of many journalists and scholars that the White House can persuade and even mobilize the public if the president simply is skilled enough at using the "bully pulpit"? Or have these commentators mistakenly attributed failures of presidential leadership to presidents' rhetorical deficiencies while ignoring broader forces in American society that may influence the leadership of public opinion? More broadly, are we looking in the right direction as we seek solutions to the problems of governing?

In another work, I outlined two contrasting views of presidential leadership.[4] First, the president is the *director of change*, establishing goals and leading others where they otherwise would not go. The second perspective is less heroic. In this view, the president primarily is a *facilitator of change*, reflecting, and perhaps intensifying, widely held views and exploiting opportunities to help others go where they want to go anyway.

The director creates a constituency to follow his lead, whereas the facilitator endows his constituency's views with shape and purpose by interpreting and translating them into legislation. The director restructures the contours of the political landscape and paves the way for change, whereas the facilitator exploits opportunities presented by a favorable configuration of political forces.

This essay explores the potential of the presidential pulpit for leading the public—and thus increasing the chances of the president's policies passing in Congress. We will try to determine whether the presidential pulpit allows the president to be a director rather than a facilitator of change.

A Tale of Two Presidents

To obtain a better grasp of the challenges that presidents face in using the presidential pulpit to lead the public, let us examine the experiences of two recent presidents, Ronald Reagan and Bill Clinton, in attempting to lead the public.

Ronald Reagan

Ronald Reagan often was called "the Great Communicator." Was he able to move the public to support his policies if it were not already inclined to do so? Like presidents before him, Reagan was a facilitator rather than a director of change. The basic themes that Reagan espoused in 1980 were ones he had been articulating for many years: Government was too big; the nation's defenses were too weak, leaving it vulnerable to intimidation by the Soviet Union; pride in country was an end in itself, and public morals had slipped too far. In 1976, conditions were not yet ripe for his message. It took the Carter years—with their gasoline lines, raging inflation, high interest rates, Soviet aggression in Afghanistan, and hostages in Iran—to create the opportunity for victory. By 1980, the country was ready to listen.

But not for long. In his memoirs, Reagan reflected on his efforts to ignite concern among the American people regarding the threat of communism in Central America and mobilize them behind his program of support for the Contras (rebels fighting the leftist government in Nicaragua):

> For eight years the press called me the "Great Communicator." Well, one of my greatest frustrations during those eight years was my inability to communicate to the American people and to Congress the seriousness of the threat we faced in Central America.[5]
>
> Time and again, I would speak on television, to a joint session of Congress, or to other audiences about the problems in Central America, and I would hope that the outcome would be an outpouring of support from Americans who would apply the same kind of heat on Congress that helped pass the economic recovery package.
>
> But the polls usually found that large numbers of Americans cared little or not at all about what happened in Central America—in fact, a surprisingly large proportion didn't even know where Nicaragua and El Salvador were located—and, among those who did care, too few cared enough about a Communist penetration of the Americas to apply the kind of pressure I needed on Congress.[6]

Reagan was frustrated not only in his goal of obtaining public support for aid to the Contras in Nicaragua;[7] his leadership problem was broader than this. On other national security issues, including military spending, arms control, military aid and arms sales, and cooperation with the Soviet Union, public opinion by the early 1980s had turned to the left—*ahead* of Reagan.[8]

Numerous national surveys of public opinion have found that support for regulatory programs and spending on health care, welfare, urban problems, education, environmental protection, and aid to minorities increased—contrary to the president's views—during Reagan's tenure.[9] On the other hand, support for increased defense expenditures was decidedly lower at the end of his administration than when he took office.[10] (This may have resulted from the military buildup that did occur, but the point remains that Reagan wanted to continue to increase defense spending, and the public was unresponsive to his wishes.)

Americans did not follow the president and move their general ideological preferences to the right.[11] Indeed, rather than conservative support swelling once Reagan was in the White House, there was a movement *away* from conservative views almost as soon as he took office.[12] According to Mayer, "Whatever Ronald Reagan's skills as a communicator, one ability he clearly did not possess was the capacity to induce lasting changes in American policy preferences."[13]

Thus, Ronald Reagan was less a public relations phenomenon than conventional wisdom indicates. He had the good fortune to take office on the crest of a compatible wave of public opinion, and he effectively exploited the opportunity that voters had handed him. When it came time to change public opinion or to mobilize it on his behalf, however, he typically met with failure. As his press secretary, Marlin Fitzwater, put it, "Reagan would go out on the stump, draw huge throngs, and convert no one at all."[14]

Bill Clinton

Ronald Reagan's difficulties in changing public opinion stretched over an eight-year period. Even in the short run, however, presidents face just as great a challenge. An examination of President Clinton's efforts to lead the public demonstrates this fact.

When the president's first major economic proposal, the fiscal stimulus plan, was introduced, it ran into strong Republican opposition. During the April 1993 congressional recess, Clinton stepped up his rhetoric on the bill; he counted on a groundswell of public opinion to pressure moderate Republicans into ending the filibuster on it. (Republicans, meanwhile, kept up a steady flow of sound bites linking the president's package with wasteful spending and Clinton's proposed tax increase.) The groundswell never materialized, and the Republicans found little support for any new spending in their home states. Instead, they found their constituents railing against new taxes and spending. The bill never came to a vote in the Senate.[15]

The president's next major legislative battle was over the budget. On August 3, 1993, he spoke on national television on behalf of his budget proposal, and Senate Republican leader Robert Dole spoke against the plan. A CNN overnight poll following the president's speech found that support for his budget plan *dropped*.[16] Several million calls were made to Congress in response to both Clinton and Dole, and the callers overwhelmingly opposed the president's plan.[17]

When the crucial rule regarding debate on the 1994 crime bill was voted down in the House, the president immediately went public. Speaking to police officers with flags in the background, he blamed special interests (the National Rifle Association) and Republicans for a "procedural trick," but his appeal did not catch fire. Meanwhile, Republicans were talking about pork-barrel spending and tapping public resentment. Clinton's public push yielded the votes of only three members of the Congressional Black Caucus, so he had to go to moderate Republicans and cut private deals.

Most painful of all to President Clinton was his inability, despite substantial efforts, to sustain the support of the public for health care reform. Nevertheless, the White House held out against compromise with the Republicans and conservative Democrats, hoping for a groundswell of public support for reform. Again, it never came.[18] Indeed, by mid-August 1994, only 39 percent of the public favored the Democratic health care reform proposals, while 48 percent opposed them.[19]

An Unusual Success

Presidents are not always frustrated in their efforts to obtain public support. In rare instances, the White House is able to move the public to communicate support for a president's policies directly to Congress. Mobilizing the public can be a powerful weapon to influence Congress. When the people speak, and especially when they speak clearly, Congress listens attentively.

Perhaps the most notable recent example of a president mobilizing public opinion to pressure Congress is Ronald Reagan's effort to obtain passage of his bill to cut taxes in 1981. Shortly before the crucial vote in the House, the president made a televised plea for support of his tax cut proposals, and he asked the public to let their representatives in Congress know how they felt. Evidently this worked, because thousands of phone calls, letters, and telegrams poured into congressional offices. How much of this represented the efforts of the White House and its corporate allies rather than individual expressions of opinion probably never will be known. Even so, on the morning of the vote, House Speaker Thomas P. ("Tip") O'Neill (D-Mass.) declared, "We are experiencing a telephone blitz like this nation has never seen. It's had a devastating effect."[20] With this kind of response, the president easily carried the day.

Of course, the White House is not content to rely solely on presidential appeals for a show of support. It may take additional steps to orchestrate public pressure on Congress. For example, Samuel Kernell described the auxiliary efforts at mobilization of Reagan's White House in 1981:

> Each major television appeal by President Reagan on the eve of a critical budget vote in Congress was preceded by weeks of preparatory work. Polls were taken; speeches incorporating the resulting insights were drafted; the press was briefed, either directly or via leaks. Meanwhile in the field, the ultimate recipients of the president's message, members of Congress, were softened up by presidential travel into their states and districts and by grass-root lobbying campaigns, initiated and orchestrated by the White House but including RNC and sympathetic business organizations.[21]

Reagan's White House tapped a broad network of constituency groups. Operating through party channels, its Political Affairs Office, and its Office of Public Liaison, the administration generated pressure from the constituents of congressional members, campaign contributors, political activists, business leaders, state officials, interest groups, and party officials. Television advertisements, letters, and attention from the local news media helped to focus attention on swing votes. Although these pressures were directed toward Republicans, Southern Democrats received considerable attention as well, which reinforced their sense of electoral vulnerability.

The administration's effort at mobilizing the public on behalf of the tax cut of 1981 is significant not only because of the success of the presidential leadership but also because it appears to be a deviant case—even for Ronald Reagan. His next major legislative battle was over the sale of AWACS planes to Saudi Arabia. The White House decided that it could not mobilize the public on this issue, however, and adopted an "inside" strategy to prevent a legislative veto.[22]

During the remainder of his tenure, President Reagan went repeatedly to the people regarding a wide range of policies, including the budget, aid to the Contras in Nicaragua, and defense expenditures. Despite his high approval levels for much of the time, he never again was able to arouse many in his audience to communicate their support of his policies to Congress. Most issues hold less appeal to the public than do substantial tax cuts.

Why the Public Is Difficult to Lead

Why did two outstanding American politicians such as Ronald Reagan and Bill Clinton have so much trouble influencing the public to support their policies? There are many answers, but to understand presidential leadership, we must first understand the nature of the president's potential followers.

Gaining the Public's Attention

To influence the public directly, the president must first obtain its attention. This usually poses a substantial challenge. On April 18, 1995, President Clinton gave his fourth prime-time news conference. Only CBS covered it live, while ABC and NBC showed reruns of the popular sit-com shows. We should not be surprised that only a small portion of the public saw the president.

Obtaining an audience is difficult, even when television coverage is greater. On August 3, 1993, President Clinton made a nationally televised address on the budget. Only 35 percent of the public saw even "some" of the speech.[23] A month later, he gave a major address on the defining issue of his administration: health care. Forty-three percent of the public saw little or none of the speech.[24] In general, the size of the audience for televised presidential speeches has declined over time.

Even if presidents gain the public's attention, they must hold onto it if they expect to change opinion and get Congress to respond accordingly. Keeping the public focused is very difficult, however. Focus requires limiting attention to a few priority items, and success in this endeavor will be determined to a large extent by the degree to which issues, including international crises, impose themselves on the president's schedule and divert attention from his priority agenda.

In the summer of 1994, as the White House entered the final negotiations over its high-priority bills on crime and health care reform, it had to deal first with the Whitewater hearings and then a huge influx of Cuban refugees. When the White House tried to put off focusing on welfare so as not to undermine its massive health care reform proposal, Senator Daniel Patrick Moynihan (D-N.Y.), then chairman of the Senate Finance Committee that had to handle much of health care reform, threatened to hold health care hostage until the White House devoted at least some attention to welfare reform.[25]

Often, the White House can do little in such situations. As Clinton advisor George Stephanopolous put it,

> On the campaign trail, you can just change the subject. But you can't just change the subject as President. You can't wish Bosnia away. You can't wish David Koresh away. You can't just ignore them and change the subject.[26]

The Public's Receptivity

No matter how effective presidents may be as speakers, or how well their speeches are written, they still must contend with the receptivity of the audience. Unfortunately for the White House, Americans rarely are attentive listeners and most are not very interested in politics.

Television is a medium in which visual interest, action, and conflict are most effective, and presidential speeches are unlikely to have these characteristics. Although some addresses to the nation occur at moments of high drama, such as President Johnson's televised demands for a voting rights act before a joint session of Congress in 1965, this is not typical. Style sometimes can give way to substance because of circumstances, but it usually is an uphill battle.

The relative importance that the typical person attaches to a president's address is illustrated by the attention that presidential staffs give to setting a date for the president's annual State of the Union message. They must be careful to avoid preempting prime time on the night that offers the current season's most popular shows while at the same time trying to maximize their national viewing audience.

The public's lack of interest in political matters can be very frustrating for the White House. It is difficult to get a message through; the public may misperceive or ignore even the most basic facts regarding a presidential policy. As late as 1986, 62 percent of Americans did not know which side the United States supported in Nicaragua despite extensive, sustained coverage of the president's policy and the congressional debate by virtually all news media.[27] Similarly, in June 1986, only 40 percent of the public had heard or read at least something about Reagan's highest domestic priority, the tax reform bill before the Senate.[28]

Americans are difficult to persuade and mobilize, not only because of their apathy but also because of their predispositions. Most people usually hold views and values that are anchored in like-minded social groups of family, friends, and fellow workers. Both their cognitive needs for consistency and their uniform (and protective) environments pose formidable challenges for political leaders to overcome. In the absence of a national crisis—which fortunately is a rare occurrence—most people are not open to political appeals.[29]

Instead, citizens have psychological defenses that screen the president's message and reinforce their predispositions. A study of persons watching Ronald Reagan speak on television found that those who were previously supportive of him had a positive response to his presentation, whereas those who were previously disapproving became irritated.[30]

Finally, although Americans are attracted to strong leaders, they do not seem to feel a corresponding obligation to follow their leadership. Cultural predispositions continue to bedevil presidential leadership.

Presentation

One factor that may affect the ability of presidents to obtain public support is the quality of their presentations to the people. Not all presidents are effective speakers, and not all look good under the glare of hot lights and the unflattering gaze of television cameras. All presidents since Truman have had advice from experts on lighting, make-up, stage settings, camera angles, clothing, pacing of delivery, and other facets of making speeches. Despite this aid, and despite the experience that politicians inevitably have in speaking, presidential speeches aimed at directly leading public opinion typically have not been very impressive. Only Kennedy, Reagan, and Clinton have mastered the art of speaking to the camera.

Presidents not only must contend with the medium but also must concern themselves with their messages. The most effective speeches seem to be those whose goals are general support and image building rather than specific support. They focus on simple themes rather than complex details. Calvin Coolidge successfully used this method in his radio speeches, as did Franklin Roosevelt in his famous "fireside chats." The limitation of such an approach, of course, is that general support cannot always be translated into public backing for specific policies.

Speeches also seem to be more successful when the political climate surrounding the policy topic at hand serves to reinforce the image of the president as a national leader and problem-solver. When the situation presents the president as inept or controversial, the image is not matched and the results are not favorable for the president.[31] Most legislative matters on which the president seeks public support fall into the "controversial" category.

Presidents may be hindered by their inability to project clear visions of public policy. The need for simplicity in public messages places a premium on coherence and consistency, both in the presentation of the administration's goals and the means for meeting them. Presidents often find this demand on their rhetoric difficult to satisfy, however. With the exception of Ronald Reagan, most recent presidents have been criticized for lacking a unifying theme and cohesion in their programs and for failing to inspire the public with a sense of purpose. Democratic presidents typically have large, diverse agendas, while Republicans such as Nixon and Bush I may combine a complex blend of traditional values and moderate policy stances, thus making it difficult to establish central organizing themes for their administrations.

Conclusions

A belief in the importance of obtaining public support for legislation is not surprising for presidents who have attained their office through lengthy campaigns and virtually constant communications, and for White House political advisers who have employed communications techniques adeptly during the preceding presidential campaign. There are important differences between campaigning and governing, however, and presidents must adjust if they are to succeed.

The transition between campaigning and governing rarely is smooth. As Charles O. Jones put it, "After heading a temporary, highly convergent, and concentrated organization" in a presidential campaign, the winner moves into the White House and becomes the "central figure in a permanent, divergent, and dispersed structure."[32] Communication becomes more difficult as the president loses control of his agenda and has to convince people not that he is superior to his opponent(s)—a relatively simple comparative judgment—but that his calls for specific policies deserve support.

Public support is not a dependable resource for the president, nor one that he can easily create when needed to influence Congress. Most of the time, the White House can do no more than move a small portion of the public from opposition or neutrality to support, or from passive agreement to active support. Even a seemingly modest shift in public opinion, however, can be very useful to the president. For example, a change of 6 percentage points could transform a split in public opinion to a presidential advantage of 56 percent to 44 percent. Presidential leadership operates at the margins of the basic configurations of American politics, but these margins can be vital to a president's success.

There also are some occasions in which the president may wish to keep a low public profile. To attract fence sitters in Congress on issues of relatively low visibility, the White House may choose to "stay private." By doing so, the president may be able to avoid arousing opposition to some of his proposals. He also may avoid the appearance of defeat if he loses. Finally, staying private eases the path of reaching agreement with Congress, because to eschew public posturing provides maneuvering room for concessions and avoids the appearance of inconsistency when compromises are made.[33]

In the end, the cards seem to be stacked against a president who tries to influence public opinion. John Kennedy once sardonically suggested an exchange from *King Henry IV, Part 1*, as an epigraph for a famous work on the presidency:

Glendower: I can call spirits from the vasty deep.

Hotspur: Why, so can I, or so can any man. But will they come when you do call for them?[34]

Endnotes

1. Quoted in Emmet John Hughes, "Presidency vs. Jimmy Carter," *Fortune,* December 4, 1978, pp. 62, 64.
2. Victor Gold, "George Bush Speaks Out," *The Washingtonian,* February 1994, p. 41.
3. Quoted in Jack Nelson and Robert J. Donovan, "The Education of a President," *Los Angeles Times Magazine,* August 1, 1993, p. 14. See also "The President at Midterm," *USA Weekend,* November 4–6, 1994, p. 4.
4. George C. Edwards III, *At the Margins: Presidential Leadership of Congress* (New Haven, CT: Yale University Press, 1989).
5. Ronald Reagan, *An American Life* (New York: Simon and Schuster, 1990), p. 471.
6. Reagan, *An American Life,* p. 479.
7. Reagan, *An American Life,* pp. 471, 479; Page and Shapiro, *The Rational Public,* p. 276. See also *CBS News/The New York Times Poll* (News release, December 1, 1986), Table 5; *CBS News/The New York Times Poll* (News release, October 27, 1987), Table 17; and "Americans on Contra Aid: Broad Opposition," *The New York Times,* January 31, 1988, sec. 4, p. 1.
8. Benjamin I. Page and Robert Y. Shapiro, *The Rational Public* (Chicago, IL: University of Chicago Press, 1992), pp. 271–281; John E. Reilly, ed., *American Public Opinion and U.S. Foreign Policy 1987* (Chicago, IL: Chicago Council on Foreign Relations, 1987), Chapters 5–6; and William G. Mayer, *The Changing American Mind* (Ann Arbor, MI: University of Michigan Press., 1992), Chapters 4 and 6.
9. Seymour Martin Lipset, "Beyond 1984: The Anomalies of American Politics," *PS* 19 (1986), pp. 228–229; Mayer, *The Changing American Mind,* Chapters 5–6; Page and Shapiro, *The Rational Public,* pp. 133, 136, 159; and William Schneider, "The Voters' Mood 1986: The Six-Year Itch," *National Journal,* December 7, 1985, p. 2758. See also "Supporting a Greater Federal Role," *National Journal,* April 18, 1987, p. 924; "Opinion Outlook," *National Journal,* April 18, 1987, p. 964; "Federal Budget Deficit," *Gallup Report,* August 1987, pp. 25, 27; and "Changeable Weather in a Cooling Climate," pp. 261–306. See also *CBS News/The New York Times Poll* (News release, October 27, 1987), tables 16, 20.

10. Lipset, "Beyond 1984," p. 229; Mayer, *The Changing American Mind,* pp. 51, 62, 133. See also "Defense," *Gallup Report,* May 1987, pp. 2–3; "Opinion Outlook," *National Journal,* June 13, 1987, p. 1550; and *CBS News/The New York Times Poll* (News release, October 27, 1987), Table 15.

11. See, for example, John A. Fleishman, "Trends in Self-Identified Ideology from 1972 to 1982: No Support for the Salience Hypothesis," *American Journal of Political Science* 30 (1986), pp. 517–541; Martin P. Wattenberg, "From a Partisan to a Candidate-centered Electorate," in Anthony King, ed., *The New American Political System* (Washington, DC: American Enterprise Institute, 1990), pp. 169–171; and Martin P. Wattenberg, *The Rise of Candidate-Centered Politics* (Cambridge, MA: Harvard University Press, 1991), pp. 95–101.

12. James A. Stimson, *Public Opinion in America: Moods, Cycles, and Swings* (Boulder, CO: Westview, 1991), pp. 64, 127.

13. Mayer, *The Changing American Mind,* p. 127.

14. R. W. Apple, "Bush Sure-Footed on Trail of Money," *New York Times,* September 29, 1990, p. 8.

15. "Democrats Look to Salvage Part of Stimulus Plan," *Congressional Quarterly Weekly Report,* April 24, 1993, p. 1002–1003.

16. Bob Woodward, *The Agenda: Inside the Clinton White House* (New York: Simon and Schuster, 1994), p. 285. A *CBS News/New York Times Poll* with before and after samples on August 2 and 3 found that support for the president's budget remained unchanged even in the immediate aftermath of the speech, but that opposition weakened.

17. "Switchboards Swamped with Calls Over Tax Plan," *The New York Times,* August 5, 1993, p. A18.

18. "Health Care Reform: The Lost Chance," *Newsweek* September 19, 1994, p. 32.

19. Gallup poll of August 15–16, 1994.

20. Quoted in "Tax Cut Passed by Solid Margin in House, Senate," *Congressional Quarterly Weekly Report,* August 1, 1981, p. 1374. See also Samuel Kernell, *Going Public* (Washington, DC: Congressional Quarterly Press, 1986), pp. 120–121.

21. Samuel Kernell, *Going Public,* p. 137. See also p. 116.

22. See "Reagan's Legislative Strategy Team Keeps His Record of Victories Intact," *National Journal,* June 26, 1982, p. 1130.

23. Gallup poll of August 3, 1993.

24. Gallup poll of September 3, 1993.

25. Jason DeParle, "Moynihan Says Clinton Isn't Serious About Welfare Reform," *The New York Times,* January 8, 1993, p. 8.

26. Quoted in Thomas L. Friedman and Maureen Dowd, "Amid Setbacks, Clinton Team Seeks to Shake Off the Blues," *The New York Times,* April 25, 1993, Sec 1, p. 12.

27. *CBS News/The New York Times Poll* (News release, April 15, 1986), Table 15.

28. *CBS News/The New York Times Poll* (News release, June 24, 1986), Table 9.

29. For a discussion of the social flow of information, see Robert Huckfeldt and John Sprague, "Networks in Context: The Social Flow of Political Information," *American Political Science Review* 81 (December 1987): 1197–1216.

30. Roberta Glaros and Bruce Miroff, "Watching Ronald Reagan: Viewers' Reactions to the President on Television," *Congress and the Presidency* 10 (Spring 1983): 25–46.

31. Lyn Ragsdale, "Presidential Speechmaking and the Public Audience: Individual Presidents and Group Attitudes," *Journal of Politics* 49 (August 1987): 704–736.

32. Charles O. Jones, *The Presidency in a Separated System* (Washington, DC: Brookings Institution, 1994), p. 294.

33. Cary R. Covington, "'Staying Private:' Gaining Congressional Support for Unpublicized Presidential Preferences on Roll-Call Votes," *Journal of Politics* 49 (August 1987): 737–755.

34. Theodore C. Sorensen, *Kennedy* (New York: Bantam, 1966), p. 440.

5

THE INSTITUTIONAL PRESIDENCY

• • • • • • • • • • • • •

The idea of an institutional presidency is a modern one. During the 19th century, presidents played a limited role in routine national policymaking, in accordance with the Framers' expectation that Congress would be the primary policymaking body in the new American government. Although the Constitution did not provide for any formal advisory structure for the president, it did provide that the president could require reports from the officers of the executive branch. George Washington began to seek advice from the heads of the departments, and this group of department heads began to be known as the "Cabinet." It was not until 1857 that Congress even provided a government-paid secretary for the president, and by the time of President Hoover (1929–1933) the president's staff was still limited to only several professionals paid by the government. All of this changed, however, with the creation of the modern presidency during the terms of Franklin D. Roosevelt.

With the growth of domestic agencies as the government geared up to fight the Great Depression, FDR felt that he needed more administrative power to control and direct the many new agencies created during his first term. In 1936, he asked three public administration scholars, headed by Louis Brownlow and known as the Brownlow Committee, to provide a report that would justify an expanded presidential apparatus along with the necessary legal power to take much more direct control of the executive branch. Although the initial report was rejected by Congress, the president's efforts finally came to fruition in 1939, when Congress gave him six new professional White House staff positions and the authority to reorganize parts of the executive branch (subject to congressional veto). Roosevelt used his new power to create by executive order the

Executive Office of the President (EOP), which would be the basis for the expansion of White House staff over the next half century.

The first selection in this section is the part of the Brownlow Committee Report that lays out the rationale for an expanded, professional White House staff. It stands today as the classic statement of the appropriate role of White House staffers regardless of how Brownlow's ideals have been ignored by many presidential aides.

President Truman's administration saw the expansion of the institutional apparatus of the presidency with the creation by Congress of the Council of Economic Advisers. More far-reaching, however, was the National Security Act of 1947, which created the Department of Defense, the Central Intelligence Agency, and the National Security Council (NSC). The NSC and its small staff was neglected by Truman during the 1940s, but when the Korean War began in 1950, he came to rely on NSC meetings to formulate strategy for the war. President Eisenhower used the NSC by creating a formalized system of committees to develop national security policy options and coordinate implementation of his decisions. Eisenhower also created a formal superstructure to control the organization of the White House through a staff secretary and chief of staff who would oversee its operation.

With this base, the office of the presidency expanded to include a White House Office (WHO) of more than 500 people by the 1970s, which in turn was part of the larger Executive Office of the President (EOP), which included about 2,000 people by the 1980s and remained about that size into the 21st century. This section deals with the institutional presidency, emphasizing especially how presidents can best ensure that all of these offices in fact do what presidents want. The broader purpose of the EOP is to enable the president to manage a huge executive branch, which has grown to more than 1.8 million civilian employees.

The president's primary formal advisory mechanism for the first century and a half of the republic was the president's cabinet, composed of the heads (secretaries) of the major departments of the executive branch. But with the increasing number of departments in the mid-20th century and the expanding role of government, the cabinet has atrophied as the major advisory mechanism for presidents. Cabinet meetings are still important in the presidency, but more as informational and team-building mechanisms than as policy deliberation. The function of advising the president has shifted to the White House staff, which is closer to the president. Cabinet secretaries are important as implementers of policy and managers of their departments, but they advise the president primarily as individuals, not as a collective body.

In "Can the President Manage the Government?" James P. Pfiffner analyzes the presidency as a managerial problem. Although he admits that presidents are much more than managers, he argues that implementation of presidential priorities is essential to the political legacy of any president. Hence, presidents must pay attention to management, even though they should not attempt to personally manage the White House themselves. Pfiffner examines how recent presidents have chosen to manage the White House regarding the choice to have a chief of staff or to act as their own chief of staff. After examining recent experience, he concludes that some form of chief of staff is essential to the successful management of a contemporary

White House. He also cautions that presidents should be selective in choosing those issues in which to take a personal role; if presidents try to control too much of executive branch operations, the White House will become overwhelmed.

Hugh Heclo, a professor at George Mason University, argues that new presidents have the ability to reorganize the presidential office to their personal desires — but only at a superficial level. In "The Changing Presidential Office," Heclo explains that the "deep structure" of the office is shaped not by personal preferences but by the expectations that others have of each president. Thus, presidents cannot easily decide *not* to deploy their personal lobbyists on Capitol Hill (Office of Congressional Liaison), or *not* to rely upon personal agents coordinate the policies of the State and Defense Departments (NSC staff), or *not* to provide press releases and information about the president's program to the press (press secretary). As presidential power has increased, it also has become diffused and shared by many presidential helpers. Thus, the problem is how to ensure that all of these aides serve presidential needs and prevent them from using the president for their own purposes. Presidents must be very selective in what they allow their staffs to undertake, Heclo concludes, or they will be overwhelmed by the demands to run all of the government from the center.

In the next selection, Bradley Patterson (a veteran White House staffer of the Eisenhower, Nixon, and Ford Administrations) and James Pfiffner outline the range of political appointments available to presidents. They argue that the volume of appointments is so great—with a total of more than 6,000—that preparation for recruiting these people must begin before the election. They outline the development of the White House capacity to control these appointments in the Office of Presidential Personnel and how it should be organized for the president. Finally, they explain the sources of conflict that each new administration faces in deciding whom the president should appoint to lead the executive branch.

President Bush and attorneys in his administration propounded an approach to executive authority known as the "unitary executive" theory. In his article, Richard Waterman argues that such an approach would leave Congress out of major areas of public policy that have traditionally been shared between Congress and the president. Proponents of the theory argue that Congress can have no voice in any administrative matters in the executive branch because the president alone is given complete control of the executive. This claim seems to run counter to Madison's observation in Federalist 47; in commenting on the intermixture of governing powers set forth in the Constitution, he cites Montesquieu: "he [Montesquieu] did not mean that these departments ought to have no *partial agency* in, or no *control* over, the acts of each other" (emphasis in original). The war power and the spending power alone, as set forth in the Constitution, ought to signify that the Framers intended for the three branches to share power.

Selected Bibliography

Arnold, Peri, *Making the Managerial Presidency: Comprehensive Reorganization Planning, 1905–1989* (Knoxville, TN: University of Tennessee Press, 1989).

Burke, John P., *The Institutional Presidency* (Baltimore, MD: Johns Hopkins University Press, 1992).

Campbell, Colin, *Managing the Presidency* (Pittsburgh, PA: University of Pittsburgh Press, 1986).

Fenno, Richard, Jr., *The President's Cabinet* (New York: Vintage Books, 1959).

Fisher, Louis, *The Constitution Between Friends: Congress, the President, and the Law* (New York: St. Martin's Press, 1978).

Hess, Stephen, with James Pfiffner *Organizing the Presidency*, 3rd ed. (Washington, DC: Brookings, 2002).

Kumar, Martha J. and Terry Sullivan, *The White House World: Transitions, Organizations, and Office Operations* (College Station, TX: Texas A&M University Press, 2003).

Nathan, Richard P., *The Administrative Presidency* (New York: John Wiley and Sons, 1983).

Pfiffner, James P., *The Managerial Presidency* 2nd ed. (College Station TX: Texas A&M University Press, 1999).

Pfiffner, James P., *The Strategic Presidency*, 2nd ed. (Lawrence, KS: University Press of Kansas, 1996).

Seidman, Harold, and Robert Gilmour, *Politics, Position and Power*, 4th ed. (New York: Oxford University Press, 1986).

Szanton, Peter, ed. *Federal Reorganization: What Have We Learned?* (Chatham, NJ: Chatham House, 1981).

Walcott, Charles E., and Karen M. Hult, *Governing the White House: From Hoover Through LBJ* (Lawrence, KS: University Press of Kansas, 1995).

The President's Committee on Administrative Management (Brownlow Committee)

The White House Staff

In this broad program of administrative reorganization the White House itself is involved. The President needs help. His immediate staff assistance is entirely inadequate. He should be given a small number of executive assistants who would be his direct aides in dealing with the managerial agencies and administrative departments

---

Source: Report of The President's Committee on Administrative Management in the Government of the United States, January 1937 (Washington: Government Printing Office, 1937), pp. 5–6.

of the Government. These assistants, probably not exceeding six in number, would be in addition to his present secretaries, who deal with the public, with the Congress, and with the press and the radio. These aides would have no power to make decisions or issue instructions in their own right. They would not be interposed between the President and the heads of his departments. They would not be assistant presidents in any sense. Their function would be, when any matter was presented to the President for action affecting any part of the administrative work of the Government, to assist him in obtaining quickly and without delay all pertinent information possessed by any of the executive departments so as to guide him in making his responsible decisions; and then when decisions have been made, to assist him in seeing to it that every administrative department and agency affected is promptly informed. Their effectiveness in assisting the President will, we think, be directly proportional to their ability to discharge their functions with restraint. They would remain in the background, issue no orders, make no decisions, emit no public statements. Men for these positions should be carefully chosen by the President from within and without the Government. They should be men in whom the President has personal confidence and whose character and attitude is such that they would not attempt to exercise power on their own account. They should be possessed of high competence, great physical vigor, and a passion for anonymity. They should be installed in the White House itself, directly accessible to the President. In the selection of these aides the President should be free to call on departments from time to time for the assignment of persons who, after a tour of duty as his aides, might be restored to their old positions.

This recommendation arises from the growing complexity and magnitude of the work of the President's office. Special assistance is needed to insure that all matters coming to the attention of the President have been examined from the over-all managerial point of view, as well as from all standpoints that would bear on policy and operation. It also would facilitate the flow upward to the President of information upon which he is to base his decisions and the flow downward from the President of the decisions once taken for execution by the department or departments affected. Thus such a staff would not only aid the President but would also be of great assistance to the several executive departments and to the managerial agencies in simplifying executive contacts, clearance, and guidance.

The President should also have at his command a contingent fund to enable him to bring in from time to time particular persons possessed of particular competency for a particular purpose and whose services he might usefully employ for short periods of time.

The President in his regular office staff should be given a greater number of positions so that he will not be compelled, as he has been compelled in the past, to use for his own necessary work persons carried on the pay rolls of other departments.

If the President be thus equipped he will have but the ordinary assistance that any executive of a large establishment is afforded as a matter of course.

In addition to this assistance in his own office the President must be given direct control over and be charged with immediate responsibility for the great managerial functions of the Government which affect all of the administrative departments. . . . These functions are personnel management, fiscal and organizational management, and planning management. Within these three groups may be comprehended all of the essential elements of business management.

The development of administrative management in the Federal Government requires the improvement of the administration of these managerial activities, not only by the central agencies in charge, but also by the departments and bureaus. The central agencies need to be strengthened and developed as managerial arms of the Chief Executive, better equipped to perform their central responsibilities and to provide the necessary leadership in bringing about improved practices throughout the Government.

The three managerial agencies, the Civil Service Administration, the Bureau of the Budget, and the National Resources Board should be a part and parcel of the Executive Office. Thus the President would have reporting to him directly the three managerial institutions whose work and activities would affect all of the administrative departments.

The budgets for the managerial agencies should be submitted to the Congress by the President as a part of the budget for the Executive Office. This would distinguish these agencies from the operating administrative departments of the Government, which should report to the President through the heads of departments who collectively compose his Cabinet. Such an arrangement would materially aid the President in his work of supervising the administrative agencies and would enable the Congress and the people to hold him to strict accountability for their conduct.

James P. Pfiffner

Can The President Manage The Government?

The 20th century was marked by increasing activism on the part of presidents and by the rising importance of the institutional staff of the presidency in controlling the government. The formal landmarks of institutional power have been the 1921 Budgeting and Accounting Act, which established the Bureau of the Budget, and the Brownlow Committee Report of 1937, which led to the creation of the Executive Office of the President in 1939. The steady growth of the presidential apparatus since

Source: James P. Pfiffner, The Managerial Presidency, 2nd ed. (College Station, TX: Texas A&M University Press, 1999).

then has been a response not only to the expansion of the size and scope of the federal government, but also to the feeling by presidents that they need more control of the government to fulfill their promises and control their political fortunes. This essay will examine the degree to which presidents should become involved with the management of the major components of the executive branch: the White House, the cabinet, political appointments, and the career services.

Presidents have felt the need to gain personal control over the government because of the relative decline of political parties over the past several decades. Working in tandem with the decline of parties have been changes in the selection processes for president. A series of reforms of the presidential nominating system since 1968 have led to presidential candidates who are more dependent on their personal appeal to voters than on political parties or other centers of power in Washington.[1]

In addition to the breakdown of traditional political institutions and practices, rising public expectations of presidents have led to the centralization of power and the "politicization" of the federal government. Terry Moe argues: "The expectations surrounding presidential performance far outstrip the institutional capacity of presidents to perform." And thus "the president will find politicization irresistible."[2]

As a result, presidents now try to do for themselves things that were previously done by others. Cabinet secretaries used to dominate high-level political appointments. Harry Truman assigned one aide to deal with political personnel. By the 1980s, President Reagan's personnel assistant had 100 people working for him, and all levels of political appointments were dominated by the White House.[3] Franklin Roosevelt was able to handle his press relations by holding an informal briefing for a handful of reporters. In the 1980s, the White House Communications Office had a sizable number of aides supervising five separate subunits.[4] The deals and accommodations that the president used to make by talking with a few "whales" in the congressional leadership now have to be "retailed" to many members in a more fragmented Congress. The Office of Congressional Liaison now has a sizable staff dedicated to the care and feeding of members of both Houses of Congress.[5]

Presidents used to depend on the secretaries of state and defense to be their principle spokespeople and advisers for national security matters. Over the past several decades, the president's assistant for national security affairs and the National Security Council staff have come to dominate national security policy making.[6] The Office of Management and Budget in the Executive Office of the President has centralized control of executive branch budgets and personnel as well as central clearance powers over regulatory matters.[7] This dynamic of centralization has greatly increased the importance of organizing, managing, and controlling the apparatus of the presidency.

The Presidency as a Managerial Problem

Conventional wisdom holds that the structure of the White House and organization of the presidency is entirely dependent on the personality and style of the incumbent. Scholars and practitioners have analyzed the variety of presidential styles and structures in the modern presidency from the informally organized approaches of

Roosevelt and Kennedy to the much more formal structures of Eisenhower and Nixon, and concluded that there is no one best way to organize the presidency.

On the face of it, this is self-evident. There is no one style of organization that characterizes "successful" presidencies. Each president has stamped his administration with his own personality. There are, nevertheless, deep structural continuities in the modern presidency. "At first blush," argues Hugh Heclo, "it would seem that the internal arrangements of his own office are simply a matter of presidential taste. And so they are in most unimportant respects. . . . In terms of its *deep structure*, however, the office is largely a given that a president can change slowly if at all. This structure is a web of other people's expectations and needs."[8] These expectations and needs have been met by the increasing size and complexity of the White House. The White House staff grew from 250 aides in the 1950s to 550 aides two decades later; from one level and 11 subunits in the Eisenhower administration to four levels and 29 subunits in the Reagan administration.[9] Presidents can ignore the managerial implications of this structural complexity only at their own peril. There may be no one best way to organize a presidency, but there are predictable organizational issues that must be faced anew by each president.

Some scholars, however, feel that presidents should not be involved in managerial issues. Stephen Hess, for instance, argues that "Presidents have made a serious mistake, starting with Roosevelt, in asserting that they are the chief managers of the federal government. . . . Rather than chief manager, the President is chief political officer of the United States."[10] Hess makes the point that Congress gives department heads the authority to run programs, not the president.

While Hess is right that the president should not become enmeshed in the details of managing departments and programs, managerial issues are crucial to the political leadership of the government. The constitutional basis for presidential intervention is the provision that the president "take care that the laws be faithfully executed." Thus the president has the constitutional right to delve into administrative matters at any level of the executive branch. Whether it is wise or administratively advisable to do this depends on the circumstances but should not be dismissed out of hand.

Recent presidents have learned through hard lessons that managerial matters are important. The Bay of Pigs blunder, Watergate, President Carter's initial problems with Congress, and the Iran–Contra affairs all involved the White House directly. Their negative effects might have been avoided or mitigated with more attention to management. President Eisenhower's dictum is on point: "Organization cannot make a genius out of incompetence. . . . On the other hand, disorganization can scarcely fail to result in inefficiency and can easily lead to disaster."[11]

In the aftermath of the Iran–Contra affair Brent Scowcroft, assistant to the president for national security affairs in the Ford and Bush administrations, argued that it is not the president's responsibility to accommodate himself to some abstract ideal of organization, but rather the staff's responsibility to accommodate itself to the president's personality and style. While Scowcroft is certainly right about the appropriate responsibilities, a president cannot afford to assume that his staff will adapt itself to his strengths and weakness. The president has to set up a staff structure that will guard against error and get him the information he needs when he needs it.

The president must set up, or have set up, a managerial structure that will ensure that he is not at the mercy of others' priorities. That is, he needs to "manage" the White House. "To manage," writes Hugh Heclo, "is something that falls between administering in detail and merely presiding in general."[12] The National Academy of Public Administration, in its 1988 report, *The Executive Presidency,* called for "management by design," rather than by inadvertence.[13]

But merely saying that the president should pay attention to management does not solve the problem. What level of managerial detail is appropriate for each level of the president's responsibility? Obviously, different levels of presidential attention are required for the White House, the cabinet, personnel appointments, and the career bureaucracy. This essay argues that the president should not try to manage much *directly,* but he must be concerned with managerial *issues* and have deputies pay attention to the details.

So management and administration are crucial to the modern presidency. But what does this mean to presidents? Peri Arnold argues that managerial issues are essential to the president's "ability to transform ideas and commitments into policies."[14] Although management is an essential component of presidential leadership, presidents should not necessarily try to control everything nor make management the central focus of their administrations. The right balance must be struck between management and political leadership.

The answer to Hess's argument that the president ought to be concerned not with management of the government but with political leadership is Arnold's point that the first is essential to the second: good management is essential to political leadership. "Thus the president ought to be concerned with administration, not because he is a manager but because administration is part of the system through which his choices become policy. . . . The president's political and policy concerns come first and lead him to administration. . . . In this view the president is not so much a manager of administration; he is a tactician using it."[15]

The previous points bring us to the question of what is the appropriate stance of the president with respect to management in the main areas of presidential authority. There are four central paradoxes of the managerial presidency.

With respect to the White House:

> The greatest threats to the reputation and political interests of recent presidents have come from overenthusiastic loyalists rather than from political "enemies."

With respect to the cabinet:

> The best way for a president to "control" the executive branch is to delegate most issues that are not clearly presidential to department and agency heads. Presidential involvement should be very selective.

With respect to political personnel:

> The president should play a positive role in setting the tone for recruiting political appointees, but should delegate the selection of most subcabinet appointees to department and agency heads. Personal or ideological loyalty to the president does not guarantee the effective implementation of presidential priorities.

With respect to the permanent bureaucracy:

> The career bureaucracy is often seen by new presidents as an obstacle to the achievement of presidential priorities. But a cooperative relationship with the career services is essential to accomplishing presidential goals, and enlisting the bureaucracy's enthusiastic support can enhance the probability of presidential success.

Managing the White House

It is notable that many of the embarrassing blunders that have done the most damage to recent presidencies were not the result of external "enemies" sabotaging the president but resulted from the actions of loyal subordinates in the White House. Thus presidents must pay attention to management of the White House, and this management should fall somewhere between detailed administration and presiding in general. For instance, presidents do not need to be involved in the fine points of policy proposals at early stages in the policy development process, nor do they need to decide who will play on the White House tennis courts. On the other hand, they should be aware of the major elements of administration proposals, they should make major staffing decisions, and they should be aware of what their immediate staff aides are doing in their names.

Modern presidents have demonstrated a range of styles of White House management. Franklin Roosevelt used a competitive approach to keep his small White House staff in line and responding to his needs. He gave overlapping jurisdictions and incomplete grants of authority to his staff and enjoyed watching the conflict that inevitably developed. Dwight Eisenhower was at the other end of the spectrum of management style. His was a much more formal and structured approach, derived in part from his experience with staff systems in the military.

John Kennedy consciously rejected the Eisenhower approach to managing his presidency and took the advice of Clark Clifford and Richard Neustadt in deciding to be his own chief of staff. Neustadt urged that Kennedy should be closer to Roosevelt's pattern than to Eisenhower's: "You would be your own 'chief of staff.' Your chief assistants would have to work collegially, in constant touch with one another and with you. . . . There is room here for a *primus inter pares* to emerge, but no room for a staff *director* or arbiter, short of you. Neither is there room for sheer, unguided struggle. . . . *you* would oversee, coordinate, and interfere with virtually everything your staff was doing."[16]

Richard Nixon decided to return to a more structured White House and designated H. R. Haldeman to be his chief of staff. Haldeman set up a system that protected the president's time and ensured that all presidential decisions were "staffed out" before being presented to the president.

In trying to distance himself from the legacy of the Nixon administration, President Ford decided to act as his own chief of staff in a "spokes of the wheel" or "knights of the Round Table" fashion. It soon became clear, however, that with 9 people reporting directly to the president and a White House staff of over 500 that someone short of the president had to be in charge. Ford designated Donald

Rumsfeld and later Richard Cheney to act as his chiefs of staff. "Someone, I decided, had to be responsible for scheduling appointments, coordinating the paper flow, following up on decisions I had made and giving me status reports on projects and policy development. I didn't like to idea of calling this person chief of staff, but that was the role he would fill."[17]

For the same reasons as Ford, President Carter began his administration without a chief of staff, and for the same reasons, he eventually abandoned the spokes-of-the-wheel approach to managing the White House. Jack Watson concluded that Carter's lack of a chief of staff early in the administration was "a fatal mistake," and Stuart Eizenstat concluded that "It is critical to have one person in charge."[18]

Ronald Reagan's style of managing the White House was at the polar opposite from Roosevelt and Kennedy with respect to presidential engagement. While President Reagan was very active in the promotion of his political and policy agendas, he was perhaps the most passive of modern presidents with respect to White House management. His approach to management was ". . . you surround yourself with the best people you can find, delegate authority, and don't interfere as long as the overall policy that you've decided upon is being carried out."[19]

"The Reagan presidency," concluded Hedrick Smith, "has probably been simultaneously the most centralized and staff-dominated presidency in history. . . . the Reagan presidency could be called a staff presidency because Reagan gave so much authority and latitude to his senior staff aides."[20] This style of staff management of the White House worked reasonably well in Reagan's first term. Many of the administration's initial goals were achieved, and major changes of policy direction were accomplished. Much of the credit for these victories must be given to the political skills of chief of staff James Baker and his deputy, Richard Darman. Baker's fine political sense allowed him to not only orchestrate the Reagan administration's dealings with Congress, but also to run the White House in the context of the "troika" of the first term. Even though Baker was chief of staff, Edwin Meese, as counselor to the president, and Michael Deaver, who had worked for Reagan for many years, had direct access to Reagan, and all three had to be involved in any major decision.

During Reagan's second term, Donald Regan took over as chief of staff. He controlled all avenues of access to the president at the same time that other strong aides to the president were leaving the White House. Regan personally approved virtually everything concerning the president: speeches, schedule, paper flow, appointments, and phone calls.[21] But Regan's tight control over the White House and his domineering style of management left him without allies to defend him when the Tower Commission laid the blame for much of the Iran–Contra scandal at his feet. "He must bear responsibility for the chaos that descended on the White House. . . ."[22]

George Bush had a chief of staff as vice-president and did not hesitate to take the same approach when he became president in 1989. His choice, John Sununu, had played a key role in Bush's come-from-behind victory in the New Hampshire primary election of 1988. Sununu played the roles of liaison for the president with the conservative wing of the Republican Party and of promoter of their policy values. As chief of staff, he did his best, often in tandem with Richard Darman, to dominate the

White House policy process. His style of leadership often irritated members of the cabinet and their subordinates, because he used his position, intelligence, and domineering personality to win his way. He also alienated Republican members of Congress as well as the Washington press corps.

At long last, President Bush felt compelled to fire him after a series of public indiscretions in which Sununu used Air Force and White House transportation for what appeared to be personal trips. Sununu's approach to the chief of staff position was clearly in line with the domineering chiefs of the past: Sherman Adams, H. R. Haldeman, and Donald Regan.

When Bill Clinton became president, he knew intellectually that a chief of staff was necessary in the White House, but his personal style of leadership resisted the delegation of very much authority to anyone. His first chief of staff, Thomas "Mack" McLarty, had been a boyhood friend who combined personal graciousness with a low key approach to the job that suited Clinton's personality. He spent much of his time acting as a personal emissary for the president and trouble-shooting special problems. In contrast to other chiefs of staff, he spent only about two-thirds of his time actually managing the White House.

The Clinton White House also was a special challenge in that the First Lady, Hillary Rodham Clinton, also played an important role in policy development. While other First Ladies had been powerful in selective areas and issues, Mrs. Clinton was active across the policy and management spectrum. The vice-president, Al Gore, also played a more active policy role than previous vice-presidents. A chief of staff for President Clinton had to negotiate with two power centers in the White House in addition to the president. Thus the Clinton White House was a special challenge to a chief of staff.

By the summer of 1994, President Clinton realized that McLarty was the wrong person for the position and replaced him with his OMB director, Leon Panetta. Panetta tightened up some of the policy-making process by controlling access to the president, clearing staff work before it went to the Oval Office, and limiting the size and scope of White House staff meetings. That Panetta imposed more discipline on the White House was not due only to his personality, but also to Clinton's realization that more power had to be delegated to the chief of staff to run the White House.

When President-elect Bush organized his White House during his transition to the presidency, there was no chance that he would have a free-wheeling staff structure that characterized Bill Clinton's early White House. His would be a buttoned-down, traditional Republican administration, with a clear hierarchy. But as he was reacting against the (early) Clinton model, Bush also learned the lesson from his father's administration that a domineering chief of staff, like John Sununu, would also be problematic, if not a disaster. As his old friend and personnel director, Clay Johnson said, Bush "did not want someone to be chief of staff who was over-territorial or was a control freak."[23]

Thus his choice of Andrew Card for chief of staff fit into Bush's plans for the White House. Card had been with the Bush family since 1980 and had been Secretary of Commerce in George H.W. Bush's administration. Perhaps more importantly, he had been deputy chief of staff to John Sununu in the Bush 41 administration and had seen first hand the effects of a domineering chief of staff. His personal style was so low-key and effective, that he was the one who told his boss that the president had decided that he had to go. He was called "the Human Alka-Seltzer" because of his ability to smooth over troubled sensibilities. Because of this and because President Bush depended on his skills so much, he was the longest serving chief of staff since Sherman Adams.

Card's role in the administration throughout the first term and into the second term was as a low-visibility manager who made the trains run on time. He did not seek the limelight, and he served with quiet efficiency. Although he was in on all of the major policy and political decisions of the administration, he did not dominate the policy process. Even if he had wanted to, this would have been difficult in an administration in which the Vice President played such a central role. Vice President Cheney, with a staff of more than 50, was intimately involved with the full range of national security and most domestic policy decisions of the administration, in addition to liaison with Capitol Hill.

So in deciding how to organize the White House, presidents must choose along a continuum between a hierarchical organization with a chief of staff and the less structured collegial alternative of multiple advocacy. Each has its strengths and weaknesses. If the intention is to ensure that directives are carried out and that staff work is thorough and coordinated, the hierarchical model is preferable. If the intention is to ensure that creative ideas are brought to the fore and that many sides of issues are argued by their advocates, the collegial model is preferable. If you want information and alternatives presented in a logical, coherent manner, hierarchy is better. If you want to ensure that presidents are not trapped by their channels of information, collegiality is better.[24]

The drawbacks to the more open system are that it makes heavy demands on the president's time and energy. This approach may bring up issues before they are ready for presidential resolution. It is vulnerable to domination by strong personalities that may overshadow rational argument. If no one short of the president is in charge, more than the usual amount of conflict may result. On the other hand, the chief of staff system is subject to the potential information distortions of hierarchies. The process may "overcook" decisions, and the chief of staff may act as too strict a gatekeeper and screen out those whom the president should see.

In recent years a consensus has emerged that a chief of staff is necessary to the management of the modern presidency. The essential elements of the chief-of-staff role are: imposing order on the White House by coordinating paper flow, ensuring that decisions are staffed out, regulating access to the president, acting as arbiter among other White House staffers, and negotiating with cabinet members on issues that are not important enough for the president's personal attention. Chiefs of staff are also stuck with the "dirty work" of delivering bad news to subordinates of the president, for example, firing them. "If there's a dirty deed to be done," said Richard Cheney, "it's the chief of staff who's got to do it."[25] In Jack Watson's words, the chief of staff is the president's "javelin catcher." Finally, one of the chief of staff's most important functions is to be an "honest broker" who will accurately represent the views of other White House staffers and cabinet officers to the president. If the chief of staff is not perceived to be an honest broker, powerful people in the administration will establish back channels to the president, and order will be undermined.

Even Richard Neustadt, who had urged John Kennedy to be his own chief of staff, finally admitted that it is a practical impossibility. "I've given up long opposition to the formal designation of a Chief of Staff, on grounds that in administrative terms it, or something like it, has become a practical necessity. . . . The accumulated experience [since President Truman] is quite enough, I think, to bind future Administrations, as a matter not of law but of convenience and common sense."[26] But Neustadt also argued that the chief of staff should not emulate the strong chiefs: Adams, Haldeman, Regan, and Sununu. They should not control all access to the president and they should not be the only person with direct and regular access to the president. Presidents have often had three or four top aides with whom to consult. Presidents need to have persons with whom they can interact as peers. Someone must say so when the president is wrong. Chiefs of staff in the past have performed this function, but they should not be the only ones that the president can turn to for frank advice.

Just as someone short of the president needs to be in charge of administrative matters and settling lower level disputes, the president should have the benefit of someone who shares a presidential perspective. That is, someone who has access to the same information and is aware of the same pressures should be available to give an alternative perspective for presidential consideration. For this reason, the chief of staff should not be excluded from national security matters. This does not mean that the president's assistant for national security should report to the president through the chief of staff, but that the chief of staff should be apprised of all national security matters so the president can have the benefit of someone with a comparable scope of perspective.[27]

However, the existence of a chief of staff is no substitute for personal presidential monitoring of the White House staff system, as the Iran–Contra affair demonstrated. Even though presidents should not act as their own chiefs of staff, they must take an active role in assuring that an effective staff system is in place. They must monitor it constantly to make sure that it gives them the type of support that they need to do their job. Presidents must make sure they get the bad news as well as the good. They must make sure that there is a devil's advocate. And they must make sure that overzealous subordinates do not do things the presidents do not want done, in the name of accomplishing their goals.

Neustadt frames this question: "How can the President use his circle so that it informs his choices in every dimension relevant to him, political and substantive alike, without relying on his intimates so passively that they, or some of them, make him the instrument of their bad judgment regardless?"[28] Heclo states, "The management aim cannot, therefore, simply be to create a unified team; it must be to create the counter-pressures that will be useful to him, lest he become victimized by his own helpers."[29]

White House experience over the past several decades has taught us that if the president opts for a chief of staff who plays too domineering a role, there will be trouble. At the very least, other members of the administration will try to set up back channels of communication with the president. At worst, the domineering chief of staff will—as in the cases of Adams, Haldeman, Regan, and Sununu—run roughshod over potential presidential allies. Each of these domineering chiefs of staff alienated the press, members of Congress, members of the administration, and had the reputation for lack of civility in their jobs. And *each* of them ended up resigning in disgrace after hurting their presidents. On the other hand, those chiefs of staff who acted as neutral brokers—such as Donald Rumsfeld, Richard Cheney, Jack Watson, James Baker, Erskine Bowles, and Andrew Card—served their presidents firmly and well.

So the president must be involved in the management of the White House to establish a responsive staff system. A chief of staff in the facilitating tradition (as opposed to the strong chiefs) can relieve the president of much "administrivia," but the president must monitor the system to assure that it is not over-protective. This monitoring can never be delegated; it is the responsibility of the president, because the president's legacy and political fortunes depend on it.

Managing the Cabinet

At times in U.S. history, the cabinet has been a major source of advice to the president and has played a dominant role in policy formulation and enunciation. But in the second half of the 20th century power has slipped from the cabinet to the White House staff. White House staffers wield this power because of their proximity to the president and their control over the president's basic needs.

> The White House staff's leverage derives from control of the most rudimentary elements of the president's life: whom he sees, what he reads, what business and what events are worth his time, when he will give speeches and what he will say, what will be said in his name by his press spokesman, and what messages will be conveyed by his staff to his cabinet and congressional allies.[30]

The president usually develops trust and support with White House staffers because of long and close association. This relationship is nearly impossible with cabinet officers who are selected because of their independent political standing and must spend most of their time running their departments.

Presidents come to depend on White House aides because of this trust and because of the aides' responsiveness and proven loyalty. Presidential staffers are concerned primarily with their boss's political interests and will respond immediately. White House staffers do not have divided loyalties since they are not encumbered with legal or bureaucratic obligations to departments or agencies. For these reasons presidents are tempted to run everything that is important to them directly out of the White House. But ironically, presidents cannot maximize control of the government without delegating much to their cabinets.

Presidents' use of their cabinets has been declining since 1960. Eisenhower's approach to managing his cabinet was to use it as a deliberative body and to delegate much of what was "not presidential" to his cabinet secretaries. His military background made him sensitive to the distinctions between "staff" positions, which were advisory, and "line" positions, which were the locus of operational authority. White House aides were clearly part of the staff with no authority except that derived from the president; cabinet officers had legal responsibility for their departments. This does not mean that the cabinet made the major administration decisions or that Eisenhower did not actively control policy.[31] It means that he did not choose to centralize control of the government in the White House to the extent that his successors have.

John Kennedy consciously rejected Eisenhower's approach to White House organization and structure. He discarded the position of chief of staff as well as Eisenhower's elaborate NSC machinery. Nor did Kennedy have any use for the cabinet as a consultative mechanism. He felt that more work could get done in small groups or task forces of officials and advisers who were most directly involved with the problem at hand. He also wanted to maximize his personal control over policy options and did not want to be presented with a bureaucratic consensus. The Kennedy and Johnson administrations also marked the beginning of the rise of the president's assistant for national security affairs to a prominence and visibility rivaling and eclipsing the secretary of state.

Richard Nixon began his presidency with intentions of "cabinet government." He intended to delegate most domestic matters to his cabinet appointees. "I've always thought this country could run itself domestically without a President. All you need is a competent cabinet to run the country at home. You need a President for foreign policy."[32] In foreign affairs, Nixon intended to be his own secretary of state.

However, disillusionment soon set in for Nixon when he felt that his cabinet appointees were not as concerned with his re-election as they should have been. White House suspicion of cabinet members was reflected by cabinet secretaries who thought they did not have the access to the president that befitted their status as the first officers of the government. In his second term, Nixon replaced a number of his appointees and proposed a major reorganization of the executive branch to give him more control over his appointees and the government.

Jimmy Carter came to office with promises of cabinet government. But as with his initial decision not to designate a chief of staff, Carter soon became disillusioned with cabinet government. He felt that his cabinet secretaries were advancing their own agendas rather than his. The White House staff felt there was no discipline in the administration, and in the summer of 1979, Carter decided to dismiss four of his cabinet secretaries and designate a chief of staff.

The Reagan administration also came to office with promises of cabinet government, but from the beginning it centralized policy making, personnel selection, and budget formulation more tightly in the White House than had any other administration. The White House staff dominated the administration, sometimes to the frustration of cabinet secretaries. Alexander Haig complained that he did not have enough access to the president: "During the transition from the election to the inauguration, I saw the president alone once! . . . That's all. That began to worry me very, very much, early on."[33] Donald Regan also felt that, as secretary of the treasury, he did not get much guidance from the president. "In the four years that I served as

Secretary of the Treasury, I never saw President Reagan alone and never discussed economic philosophy or fiscal and monetary policy with him one-on-one. From first day to last at Treasury, I was flying by the seat of my pants. . . . After I accepted the job, he simply hung up and vanished."[34]

While the Reagan administration was one very much centered around the White House staff, this centralization was moderated by the establishment of cabinet councils. The system was intended to bring together those cabinet secretaries who were concerned with a particular area of policy and had overlapping jurisdictions. The councils were staffed in the White House and provided a useful forum to bring together White House staffers and cabinet members to deliberate on policy issues.

While President Reagan established a cabinet-council system that is an important contribution to the organization of the presidency, he also presided over one of the major scandals of the modern presidency: the Iran–Contra affair. He had criticized the Carter administration for letting Zbigniew Brzezinski, the president's assistant for national security affairs, dominate foreign policy making. Accordingly, Reagan's first adviser for national security was Richard Allen, who adopted a low-visibility role. The initial intention was to let Secretary of State Alexander Haig run foreign policy. But distrust soon developed between Haig and the White House staff. Haig was seen by the White House staff as self-aggrandizing and power hungry, and Haig felt he was being kept from the president by the White House staff.

Ironically, after Reagan appointed George Shultz in whom he did have confidence, the Iran–Contra initiatives by the National Security Council staff undercut the secretary of state, leaving him out of the loop in major areas of U.S. foreign policy. The administration that began its term with a national security assistant clearly subordinate to the secretary of state and with broad declarations of "cabinet government" ended up with unprecedented operations being run by the NSC staff without the knowledge of (diversion of funds to the contras) or against the advice of (arms to Iran) the secretaries of state and defense.

It is easy to understand why recent presidents have been tempted to run foreign policy from the White House and give primacy to their national security advisers and the NSC staff. White House aides have the advantage of proximity to the president and can respond immediately to presidential desires. They can operate without the cumbersome interagency task forces, bureaucratic consultation, and red tape associated with the state or defense departments. White House aides can assure secrecy, speed, and concentration. They do not have other institutional loyalties or turf interests to distract them from the president's priorities.

In the case of the Iran–Contra affair, the disadvantages of a system overly centralized in the White House became apparent. When the NSC staff is advocate and executor as well as coordinator of policy, its analytical capacity is undermined. The President's Special Review Board (the Tower Commission) concluded: "The NSC staff assumed direct operational control. The initiative fell within the traditional jurisdictions of the Departments of State, Defense, and CIA. Yet these agencies were largely ignored."[35]

The NSC staff, which was created to be a coordinating mechanism, had in the 1980s come to dominate and even exclude the official foreign-policy-making apparatus. The Iran–Contra affair grew out of a profound distrust of and contempt for the governmental policy-making apparatus in the departments of state and defense.

In 1986, the president's national security assistant, Admiral John Poindexter, deliberately misled the secretary of state about U.S. relations with Iran and kept important information from the secretaries of state and defense concerning U.S. aid to the contras in Nicaragua. Poindexter even declared that he kept crucial information from the president: "On this whole issue, you know, the buck stops here with me."[36] The Tower Commission disagreed:

> Setting priorities is not enough when it comes to sensitive and risky initiatives that directly affect U.S. national security. [The president] must assure that the content and tactics of an initiative match his priorities and objectives. He must insist upon accountability. For it is the president who must take responsibility for the NSC system and deal with the consequences.[37]

President George H. W. Bush's approach to his cabinet moderated some of the centralization of the Reagan administration. He appointed cabinet officers he knew personally and trusted to run their departments. He allowed his cabinet secretaries to have more say in the appointment of their political subordinates, and he involved them more regularly in policy development. He also had a much better grasp of policy implementation issues than President Reagan had and was willing to pick up the phone to stay in touch with his cabinet members.

Bush did not, however, return to Eisenhower's approach to the cabinet. His top White House staffers—Chief of Staff Sununu and OMB Director Richard Darman—did their best to keep policy control in the White House. Thus, Bush pulled back slightly but did not reverse the long-term centralization of control over policy development in the White House at the expense of the cabinet.

Bill Clinton came to office with no promises of cabinet government to keep. He did spend a considerable amount of time carefully selecting cabinet nominees during his transition into office, but he did not attempt to delegate much policy development authority to his cabinet. The most important policy initiatives of the Clinton administration were run from the White House. The first-year-deficit-reduction package dominated the early agenda and was formulated in the White House, as was the NAFTA initiative. The farthest-reaching Clinton policy initiative—the health-care reform proposal—was run from the White House by the First Lady and a team of 500 detailees and specialists. The Department of Health and Human Services played an important role but clearly did not have the lead. Thus, Clinton continued the trend toward White House staff domination of administration policy development at the expense of cabinet secretaries. The Clinton cabinet met as a body only seven times in 1993.

President Bush recruited a cabinet of talented and diverse members but did not reverse the trend toward centralization of policy making in the White House. In keeping with recent past practice, Bush did not use his cabinet for collective deliberation and advice. In his first 100 days in office, he met with his cabinet only three times, similar to Clinton's four meetings and his father's three times. The principal role of cabinet secretaries continued to be implementation rather than initiation or primary advice.

For instance, the administration's education initiatives were handled by the domestic policy adviser, Margaret LaMontagne Spellings rather than Education Secretary Roderick Paige. On medial issues, such as government financing of prescription drugs, the patients' bill of rights, and stem-cell research, the action was in the White House rather than with Health and Human Services Secretary Tommy Thompson. The administration's tax cut proposals were not led by Treasury Secretary Paul O'Neill but by White House staffers, such as National Economic Adviser Lawrence Lindsey. Vice President Cheney, rather than Secretary of Energy Spencer Abraham, dominated the administration's energy policy proposals. Exception to the general rule of White House staff preemption of cabinet input was Attorney General John Ashcroft who played a major role in internal security after 9-11 and in other social conservative policies of the administration. Also, Donald Rumsfeld played a major role in the administration's national security policy. Colin Powell, while playing important roles in national security policy, was not a Bush intimate.

President Bush had one of the most stable (post-WWII) cabinets, with only two positions changing hands. Yet in shifting to his second term, President Bush replaced more of his cabinet than had his predecessors, changing nine cabinet secretaries. In the second term shifts, Bush placed several of his close White House advisers in the cabinet to assure adherence to his priorities. Condoleezza Rice became secretary of state, Margaret Spellings became secretary of education, and Alberto Gonzales became attorney general. The perceived role of the cabinet, from the White House perspective however, did not change after Bush's reelection. According to one presidential adviser, "The Bush brand is few priorities, run out of the White House, with no *interference* from the Cabinet. . . . The function of the Bush Cabinet is to provide a chorus of support for White House policies and technical expertise for implementing them." (emphasis added)[38]

White House staff domination of policy making is partially inevitable and partially desirable, but pulling too much into the White House risks overload and can lead to negative consequences. The president needs to create a balance between the White House staff and the department secretaries so that administration policy making is coordinated and not unduly conflictual.

With respect to managing the cabinet, the president should expect to establish administration policy and should have a policy development mechanism that ensures White House control but facilitates input from cabinet secretaries who will reflect departmental perspectives. The Iran–Contra affair is an extreme case that demonstrates the need for presidents to insist on a balance between White House and cabinet input.

Ironically, the best way for presidents to control the executive branch is to delegate most of what they want done to their cabinet appointees. There is no way the White House staff has the capacity or the expertise to run the government from the White House. The only way for the White House to be in control is through great selectivity. The president, as elected head of the executive branch, should be able to direct policy and its execution, but he cannot exercise this right too often or the White House will be stretched too thin.

In addition, the more that the White House staff interferes with the execution of policy, the more problems are brought into the White House. The president must keep a distance from as many problems as possible while retaining the option of intervening when it is important to presidential interests to do so.

A useful illustration is the military doctrine of delegation to the tactical commander. The commander on the scene of the battle is supposed to have the discretion to determine the tactics of the battle without second guessing or control from higher authority far removed from the scene of battle. Thus, the complaints from military commanders when their judgments are overruled by headquarters are soundly based in military doctrine. While this makes sense from a tactical point of view, the president is concerned with the strategic implications of military actions.

Following this reasoning, John Kennedy's insistence that he have direct control over the blockade of Cuba in 1962 was appropriate, because there was more at stake in the missile crisis than the tactics of a blockade. President Johnson asserted direct control over bombing targets in North Vietnam. Regardless of the merits of his judgments about bombing targets, the principle that the president should have control is valid, because strategic concerns, such as U.S. relations with China, were affected by the choice of bombing targets. Modern communications technology, however, presents presidents with the temptation to take personal control over any situation in which the stakes are high. While in principle, the president should be able to take control, wisdom dictates that this option of direct presidential control be exercised selectively. The dangers are that the president, far removed from the scene, may make poor decisions and that any problems or failures, even if they are not under his control, will be blamed on the president.

Another reason to delegate as much as possible to departments and agencies is that cabinet officers will be frustrated with frequent White House "interference." Cabinet officers have the legal obligation to implement the law in their areas of jurisdiction. The president can also use cabinet appointees in order to keep White House staff in line. In Hugh Heclo's judgment:

> Paradoxically, one of the most effective ways for the president to manage his own office is through the use of his appointees in the departments and agencies. If these department heads are known to have intimate knowledge of the president's thinking, and therefore seem likely to be backed by the president in disputes with White House staffers, White House aides will likely be kept in their proper place as assistants to the president rather than as assistant presidents.[39]

In addition to being better situated to implement presidential policy, cabinet officers are likely to be tied into sources of information that the White House staff cannot possibly monitor. Centralizing too much control in the White House shuts off the president from these valuable sources of information.

Conclusions

This essay has argued that presidential control of the government is legitimate and essential, but that presidents are tempted to define the necessary amount of control too expansively. Construed too broadly, presidential control will overwhelm the president with detail and bring unnecessary problems into the White House.

Viewed with enlightened self-interest, however, presidential control of the government means ensuring that presidential priorities are effectively formulated into policy directions and that policies are carried out with efficiency and dispatch. Effective implementation of policy demands competence as well as loyalty from subordinates.

A president, therefore, should not become involved in any detailed way with staff management but should designate a chief of staff to worry about the hundreds of staffers in the White House. However, the president must be involved sufficiently to ensure that his interests are being well served. The president must probe enough to guard against the overzealous subordinate who is willing to bend the laws or the Constitution in what is thought to be the president's interest. No one should be allowed to think that the buck stops short of the president.

With respect to the cabinet, the president should delegate as much as possible to cabinet secretaries. This delegation should include a significant role in policy development through cabinet councils and the primary role in policy implementation. White House control over major policy decisions must be assured, but intervention at lower levels will be most effective if pursued selectively and only when the president's personal interests are at stake. With respect to political appointments, presidents should not abdicate control, but should exercise it sparingly. With respect to the career services, presidents should realize that civil servants are essential to presidential success and engage them as allies rather than treat them as adversaries.

From a broader perspective, presidential control of the government means realizing that the president leads better by persuasion than by command.[40] Our fragmented separation of powers system will not allow the type of tight presidential control over the government that some presidents seem to want. Effective presidential control derives from the realization that real power in the U.S. political system grows out of political consensus forged by true political leadership, not stratagem or management techniques.[41]

Acknowledgments

The author would like to thank Peri Arnold and Michael Genovese for helpful comments on an earlier version of this essay.

Endnotes

1. See Samuel Kernell, *Going Public* (Washington, DC: CQ Press, 1986).
2. Terry Moe, "The Politicized Presidency," in James P. Pfiffner, ed. *The Managerial Presidency* (Pacific Grove, CA: Brooks/Cole, 1991), p. 142.
3. See James P. Pfiffner, *The Strategic Presidency* (Pacific Grove, CA: Brooks/Cole, 1988), chapter 4.
4. See Samuel Kernell, "The Evolution of the White House Staff," in James P. Pfiffner, ed. *The Managerial Presidency* (Pacific Grove, CA: Brooks/Cole, 1991), p. 142.
5. See James P. Pfiffner, "The President's Legislative Agenda," *The Annals* Vol. 499 (September 1988).

6. See Kevin Mulcahy and Cecil V. Crabb, "Presidential Management of National Security Policy Making: 1947–1987," in James P. Pfiffner, ed. *The Managerial Presidency* (Pacific Grove, CA: Brooks/Cole, 1991), p. 142.

7. See James P. Pfiffner, "OMB: Professionalism, Politicization, and the Presidency," in Margaret Wyszomirski and Colin Campbell, eds., *The Executive Establishment and Executive Leadership: A Comparative Perspective* (Pittsburgh, PA: University of Pittsburgh Press, 1991).

8. Hugh Heclo, "The Changing Presidential Office," James P. Pfiffner, ed. *The Managerial Presidency* (Pacific Grove, CA: Brooks/Cole, 1991), pp. 34–35.

9. Samuel Kernell, "The Evolution of the White House Staff," in John E. Chubb and Paul E. Peterson, eds., *Can the Government Govern?* (Washington, DC: Brookings, 1989) p. 191.

10. Stephen Hess, *Organizing the Presidency* (Washington, DC: Brookings, 1976), p. 10; in the revised edition of 1988, see p. 6.

11. Quoted by Fred I. Greenstein, *Leadership in the Modern Presidency* (Cambridge, MA: Harvard University Press, 1988), p. 83. For an insightful analysis of Eisenhower's management approach, see Phillip Henderson, *Managing the Presidency* (Boulder, CO: Westview Press, 1988).

12. Hugh Heclo, "The Changing Presidential Office," in James P. Pfiffner, ed. *The Managerial Presidency* (Pacific Grove, CA: Brooks/Cole, 1991), p. 39.

13. National Academy of Public Administration, *The Executive Presidency: Federal Management for the 1990s* (Washington, DC: NAPA, 1988), p. 2.

14. See Peri E. Arnold, *Making the Managerial Presidency.* (Princeton, NJ: Princeton University Press, 1986), p. 363.

15. *Ibid.,* p. 363.

16. Memorandum on "Staffing the President—Elect" (October 30, 1960), James P. Pfiffner, ed. *The Managerial Presidency* (Pacific Grove, CA: Brooks/Cole, 1991), p. 21.

17. Gerald R. Ford, *A Time to Heal* (New York: Harper and Row, 1979, p. 147.

18. For Watson quote, see Samuel Kernell and Samuel Popkin, eds., *Chief of Staff,* (Berkeley, CA: University of California Press, 1986), p. 71. Interview with Stuart Eizenstat, Washington, DC, July 14, 1983.

19. Quoted by Ann Dowd, "What Managers Can Learn from Manager Reagan," in *Fortune* (September 15, 1986), p. 36.

20. Hedrick Smith, *The Power Game* (New York: Random House, 1988), p. 300.

21. See Bernard Weinrub, "How Donald Regan Runs the White House," *New York Times Magazine,* January 5, 1986, p. 12.

22. *The Tower Commission Report* (New York: Bantam Books, 1987), p. 81.

23. Stephen Hess with James P. Pfiffner, *Organizing the Presidency* (Washington: Brookings, 2002), p. 165.

24. See Samuel Kernell, "How Can the President Be a National Leader and a Chief Executive at the Same Time?" unpublished paper, December 1987.

25. Samuel Kernell and Samuel Popkin, eds., *Chief of Staff* (Berkeley, CA: University of California, 1986), p. 62.

26. Richard E. Neustadt, "Does the White House Need a Strong Chief of Staff?" in James P. Pfiffner, *The Managerial Presidency* (Pacific Grove, CA: Brooks/Cole, 1991), pp. 29–30.

27. While the vice president might seem like a natural candidate for this function, the political dynamics of selecting the vice-presidential candidate are such that we cannot count on there being a close and trusting relationship between the president and vice president. On the appropriate scope of purview of the chief of staff, former President Ford said in response to a question about the Iran–Contra scandal: "I would make my Chief of Staff the controlling official in the operation of the White House staff. There would be no bypassing of that individual by NSC. The Chief of Staff has to be the focal point for management. I would not exclude Cabinet members of the head of the NSC or other top officials from having access, but it has to be through a responsible Chief of Staff who knows what's going on." (Quoted in *The Next President,* interviews by David Frost. Washington, DC: U.S. News, 1988, p. 39).

28. Neustadt, "Does the White House Need a Strong Chief of Staff?" in James P. Pfiffner, ed. *The Managerial Presidency* (Pacific Grove, CA: Brooks/Cole, 1991), p. 31.

29. Hugh Heclo, "The Changing Presidential Office," in James P. Pfiffner, ed. *The Managerial Presidency* (Pacific Grove, CA: Brooks/Cole, 1991), p. 42.

30. Hedrick Smith, *The Power Game* (New York: Random House, 1988), p. 303.

31. See Fred L. Greenstein, *The Hidden-Hand Presidency* (New York: Basic Books, 1984).

32. Rowland Evans, Jr. and Robert D. Novak, *Nixon in the White House* (New York: Random House, 1971), p. 11.

33. Quoted by Hedrick Smith, *The Power Game,* p. 310.

34. Donald Regan, *For the Record* (New York: Harcourt, Brace & Jovanovich, 1988), pp. 142–143.

35. *The Tower Commission Report,* p. 62.

36. *Washington Post,* July 16, 1987, p. 1.

37. *The Tower Commission Report,* p. 80.

38. Jim VandeHei and Glenn Kessler, "President to Consider Changes for New Term," *Washington Post* (November 5, 2004), p. 1, A8.

39. Hugh Heclo, "The Changing Presidential Office," in James P. Pfiffner, ed. *The Managerial Presidency* (Pacific Grove, CA: Brooks/Cole, 1991), p. 41.

40. See Fred I. Greenstein, "In Search of a Modern Presidency," in *Leadership in the Modern Presidency,* Greenstein, ed. (Cambridge, MA: Harvard University Press, 1988).

41. See Donald F. Kettl, "Presidential Management of the Economy," in this volume.

Hugh Heclo

The Changing Presidential Office

The office of the president has become so complex, so propelled by its own internal bureaucratic dynamics, that it now presents every new president with a major problem of internal management. Without a conscious effort to the contrary, he may not even perceive the prison that his helpers erect around him.

To tackle this problem successfully, a president must be aware of how "his" office can constrain him and must use "his" staff at least as effectively as they use him. He must be aware of the management impact of everything he does. He must choose his priorities carefully and pursue them tenaciously lest he become dependent on the

Source: Arnold Meltsner, *Politics and the Oval Office* (San Francisco, CA: Institute for Contemporary Studies, 1981).

priorities of everyone else around him. He must have a good sense of how his staff act and interact. He must maintain a delicate balance between the executive office and his appointees in the departments and agencies. Above all, he must set himself at the center of a web of pressures and counter-pressures that ultimately serves his purposes.

The Internal Management Problem of the Presidency

Our most familiar image of the presidency finds a man, sitting alone, in the dimly lit Oval Office. Against this shadowy background the familiar face ponders that ultimate expression of power, a presidential decision.

It is a compelling and profoundly misleading picture. Presidential decisions are obviously important. But a more accurate image would show a presidency composed of at least 1,000 people—a jumble of personal loyalists, professional technocrats, and bureaucratic staff with one man struggling, often vainly, to stay abreast of it all. What that familiar face ponders in the Oval Office is likely to be a series of conversations with advisers or a few pages of paper containing several options. These represent the last distillates produced from immense rivers of information flowing from sources—and condensed in ways—about which the president probably knows little. The great irony is that, as more and more forces combine to program the president, he sees only people who are trying to help him do what he wants.

In 1980, the Executive Office of the President (EOP) is composed of 10 disparate major units, including a White House office with its own two dozen or so basic subdivisions. The number of people involved is subject to a variety of inventive accounting methods, but a reasonable approximation would be 500 or so people attached to the White House and another roughly 1,500 people in the rest of the EOP.[1] There seems little doubt that a trimmer, more rational, staffing arrangement would help a president meet national needs as well as substantially simplify any president's job of managing his own office.

Yet, however the presidency is equipped with staffs and processes, the president's personal management problem remains. His choice is to run or to be run by his office. No conceivable staffing arrangement will meet all his needs, and yet every arrangement carries the potential of submerging his interests into those of his help and their machinery. All the trends suggest that the grip of this well-intentioned machinery on the president is likely to grow, just as it has grown in the past two decades. The president's great danger lies in thinking that by making decisions he is actually managing. His internal management problem—the underside of the presidency—is to use those who serve him without becoming dependent on them. He must avoid being victimized by their loyalty to him or by his loyalty to them. To put it most directly, I do not see how, given contemporary demands on the office, a president can exercise leadership without being quietly manipulative within that office.

Constraints on Internal Management

At first blush, it would seem that the internal arrangements of his own office are simply a matter of presidential taste. And so they are in most unimportant respects. Apart from matters of style, the president's main area of discretion is the choice as to what personalities he will deal with directly in the everyday running of his office. Even this choice is likely to be constrained by personal commitments to familiar aides, particularly since no modern candidate can hope to negotiate the long drawn-out campaign process without a bevy of loyal aides. Those who manage the campaign bureaucracy inevitably have a claim on the White House bureaucracy.

In terms of its *deep structure*, however, the office is largely a given that a president can change slowly if at all. This structure is a web of other people's expectations and needs. On the surface, the new president seems to inherit an empty house. In fact, he enters an office already shaped and crowded by other people's desires. What the would-be presidents seem to be reaching for on the nightly news is simply the top prize in our ultimate contest as a competitive society. What the winner grasps is an office that is the raw, exposed ganglion of government where immense lines of force come together in ways that no single person can control. The total effect is to program the modern president.

Legal and Political Pressures

One set of constraints arises from a growing number of statutory requirements placed on the office. Core advisory units of the presidency (Council of Economic Advisers, National Security Council, Domestic Council) were established by laws passed by Congress and can be altered only by persuading Congress to change these laws. A president can, of course, use or bypass this formal machinery, but the fact is that over the years these units have generally been accepted as important parts of the presidency and have generated expectations that presidents will not simply ride roughshod over their operations. For example, as President-elect Reagan prepared to take office, a key issue discussed was who would bring to him the work of staffs from the national security and domestic councils, not whether to have and to use these units in the first place.

Legal constraints also arise from statutory requirements which that tell a president what he must do. At last count there were 43 separate requirements for annually recurring presidential reports (environmental impacts, foreign arms sales, and so on). None of these reports are things about which a president bothers himself personally except in the rarest of circumstances. What they require are more staff work, more specialists, and more routines within the presidency. Each process gives someone a proprietary interest in that process—in other words, someone other than the president with a claim on what must get done in the presidency.

A second part of the web preventing a president from designing his own office is the political interest of outsiders. Many people, it turns out, have a stake in the internal arrangements of the presidency. Even a hint of major increases in presidential staff arouses immediate and intense congressional criticism. Thus President Carter in his first few months in office, for example, in order to avoid future trouble with his reorganization plans, had to informally promise a leading congressional committee chairman that he would not increase the size of the EOP even though important, nonpolitical parts of the presidency were seriously undermanned.

Congressional committees hold the purse strings for every major unit in the EOP; they can and have made life miserable for the head of a unit such as the president's Office of Management and Budget (OMB), requiring exhaustive and exhausting testimony, cutting funds for unfavored projects, and adding staff for functions bearing no relation to a president's interests. Since the Nixon administration, moreover, Congress has been far more reluctant to grant funds in special emergency or "management improvement" accounts which presidents could formerly use largely at their discretion. Even a president's papers are no longer his. Under a recent congressional enactment, President Reagan will be the first chief executive in our history who will not be able to take his papers away with him when he leaves office.

Congress is only the most obvious of the political constituencies constraining presidential management of the presidency. Various specialized communities have an interest in staking out claims to particular pieces of the Executive Office. This applies, for example, to the Office of Science and Technology Policy (disbanded in 1973 and reinstated in 1976 at the demand of the scientific community), environmentalists (Council on Environmental Quality), and many others in the recent past. More subtly, the Council of Economic Advisers serves as the voice of the economics profession and the National Security Council does likewise for professional students of foreign and military affairs. Even though each of these communities contains different viewpoints from which a president can pick and choose, he is not free to deny someone from these professional groups a major advisory role in the highest councils of his administration.[2]

Legal constraints and political constituencies in the presidency have grown in the past two decades, but a president can try to "manage around" them by observing the formalities. Whatever the statutory requirements, a president's real management system consists of whom he consults, where he bestows trust, and how he polices those in his trust. There are two remaining sets of constraints that have grown in recent years and that strike at the very heart of this real-life management system. Because they spring from deep-seated social and political trends, these two forces are not elements that can be managed around. Indeed, presidents under the necessity of responding to these twin pressures become the agents for programming their own office. The more that recent presidents have thought they were putting their personal stamp on the office and events, the more they have affirmed a larger design that they cannot control and can rarely comprehend.

The Requisites of a Presidential Party

As far as one can tell from the historical record, the five presidents since Eisenhower did not consciously plan to create their own political parties. Yet that, in embryo, is what has come to exist in the White House. Consider for a moment some of the specialized subdivisions that existed in the Carter White House *before* the active start of the 1980 presidential campaign:

- Assistant to the President (Women's Affairs)
- Assistant to the President (Organizational Liaison)
- Special Assistant for Hispanic Affairs
- Special Assistant for Ethnic Affairs
- Special Assistant for Civil Rights
- Counselor to the President on Aging [ours, not his]
- Special Assistant for Consumer Affairs
- Assistant for Intergovernmental Affairs
- Assistant for Congressional Liaison
- Special Assistant to the President (Press and Public Relations)

Taken as a whole, the list indicates something more important than the desire of particular groups to have their representatives at the president's elbow. What these and similar political operatives for other presidents suggest is an attempt to reach out from the White House and to build at least some lines of reliable political support for presidents. If one were inventing a political party, these are exactly the types of offices at branch headquarters that one would want to create. What is lacking is only the local cells that would give such an organization feet and hands. As President Carter discovered, fireside chats, town meetings, and convocations with local publishers and editors are no substitute for *that*.

The fact is that each president during the last 20 years has felt increasingly compelled to mobilize the White House to build the equivalent of a presidential party for governing. To some presidents (such as Johnson or Nixon) the inclination comes naturally but, whatever the vagaries of personality, every contemporary president has been under pressure to move in the same direction. The reason is clear: a more politically volatile public, a less-manageable Congress, a disappearing party hierarchy, proliferating groups of single-minded activists which merge with the networks of policy experts discussed later. All these add up to a shifting political base of support for presidents. This is not atomization—a breaking down of our political life into tiny elemental particles. It is rampant pluralism, with groups crosscutting the political landscape into incoherent patterns. Atomization would produce anomie and anarchy. Rampant pluralism produces what we in fact have: unnegotiable demands, political stagnation, and stalemate.

People in the White House have had little choice but to try and cope with this trend by shoring up the president's own base of support. Given the succession of one-term presidents since the Kennedy assassination, no one would want to claim great success for these efforts, but that is not the point. What modern president could reasonably be expected to give up the attempt at using the White House to build a presidential party?

Once that fact is admitted, we can begin to see how even the most loyal aides and the presidents themselves cooperate in the programming of the modern presidency. When mayors or governors have problems, it is not enough to refer their calls to some departmental appointee or bureaucrat. Doing that will not build the strong relations which a president needs. Hence, someone in the White House is tasked to keep an eye on "intergovernmental relations." A small staff develops. The mayors' and governors' telephone calls are returned from the White House, their entreé to the bureaucracy smoothed a little. By helping them, the president helps himself. In the longer run, however, the president acquires a staff with a vested interest in continuing to process such problems, and he confirms the larger expectation that he is somehow responsible for seeing to it that a fiendishly complex federal system works to the satisfaction of all concerned.

There is no need to belabor the point. The same dynamic applies in one area of presidential activity after another. Will the president work exclusively through top congressional leaders, none of whom can control the actions of the legislature? Or will the president try to string together the many pieces of Congress that are in business for themselves? All the pressures of the moment dictate the latter course. Accordingly, the president acquires an extensive congressional liaison staff, doing favors and attracting demands for more. President Carter in his first year showed little willingness to be programmed as a builder of his own party in Congress, and he paid dearly for following his preferences. Can a president rest content in channeling relations he needs with all the interest groups in our mobilized society through his party's national committee or a federal department? The answer began to come clear as early as 1940 when Franklin Delano Roosevelt, in seeking a third term, had one aide working part-time on relations with ethnics and unions and another preparing materials on what the New Deal had done "for the benefit of Negroes."[3] Since then, a veritable political technocracy of such people has developed, entangling the presidential office in extensive networks of activists interested in this and that issue.

There is—or seems to be—a way out of all these entanglements produced by the need of presidents to create a quasi party for themselves. Richard Neustadt described it in late 1979:

> While national party organizations fall away, while congressional party discipline relaxes, while interest groups proliferate and issue networks rise, a President who wishes to compete for leadership in framing policy and shaping coalitions has to make the most he can out of his popular connection. Anticipating home reactions, Washingtonians. . . are vulnerable to any breeze from home that presidential words and sights can stir. . . . The President with television talent will be likely to put his very talent at the center of his hopes when he takes office.

As viewers of the past four presidents can attest, even chief executives with a definite untalent for television are likely to seize on the tube to deploy their leadership. Unfortunately, by trying to do a little programming of their own on TV, presidents do not escape their personal management problem and may (especially if talented) only add to it by mistaking a successful screen image for the substance of leadership.

The tube is a blunt instrument. It allows a president to explain himself, catch a mood, create a persona. These are important, but they are not things through which a president escapes the programming that crowds in on his leadership. On the contrary. The generalized utility of television for the president has a counterpart in the media's need for its own kind of presidency. The increasingly powerful news media needs stories, preferably with a White House backdrop. They need presidential statements to help create the story, favored access, and background information from the White House staff to give them an edge in the competition for stories. When all else fails, the media need care and feeding by the White House press office with a steady stream of handouts to those who cannot find a story. This communications industry complex of the presidency is a far cry from the early off-the-record chats that presidents used in order to give the "boys in the press" an idea of their thinking and activities. The media's expectations run against the grain of the president's managerial needs for private deliberations, for discretion as to when to get into or out of the news, and for an administration that appears united. Television language accurately captures the disutility of the medium for presidential management purposes. The tube *follows* stories, but the president must first manage a process for choosing where *he* wants to go. TV *covers* events in general, but the president's office needs to give sustained attention to specific, often technical, matters where there is never a clear story line.

The requisites for a presidential party, including television, are probably with the White House to stay. The members of his political technocracy will be a constraint or an opportunity—usually some weighting of both—for a president, depending on how he maneuvers among them. But if they are not to be pure constraint, the watchword must be active presidential maneuvering, not lying in repose or trusting in his aides' undoubtedly sincere professions of loyalty. Yet this section has referred only to the political base of the president's office. Another trend strikes even deeper into the presidency than has our growing political fragmentation and volatility. This is a massive social diffusion of policy-making powers.

The Hemorrhage of Presidential Power

The classic question to ask about the presidential office is what has happened to its power. It is a question that invites a thumbs up or thumbs down vote: increasing or decreasing? More imperial or more post-Watergate? The developments of the last 20 years call for a more complicated answer. Presidential power has increased by becoming more extended, scattered, and shared; it has decreased by becoming less of a prerogative, less unilateral, and less closely held by the man himself. The right word for what has happened to the power of the office is diffusion, not dissipation. This condition exists, not basically because Congress or other groups have made successful grabs at the president's power but because of the very nature of modern policy-making and the growth of federal activity.

Consider for a moment the anti-bureaucracy Reagan transition bureaucracy. This effort, writ small, is a good snapshot of what has happened to presidential power. The president-elect begins before inauguration with a $2 million, taxpayer-funded budget, a building, a motor pool, a minimum of seven dozen advisory committees, a communications system, and official stationery for the "Office of the President-Elect."

What, a person may well ask, is going on here? Certainly some of this is intended only for public consumption, some as a political liaison job for building the relations necessary to a presidential party. But there is more than that, and it shows up in the substantive work of the various policy groups and "issue clusters." The president-elect may have a few general themes in mind but to have any impact on complex modern policies he needs to have specific, usually highly technical, proposals. Moreover, whatever he might want to do to increase *or* to decrease federal government activity, he is automatically entangled in a web of relations with other people who can have a decisive impact on the same issue—not just congressmen, but a bureaucracy of congressional staffs numbering well over 13,000 professionals; not just mayors and governors, but analysts and lobbyists to represent these elected officials in Washington; not just grasping interest groups, but a mini-industry in the nation's capital employing 15,000 or more full-time professionals.

The exact numbers are less important than the fact that the federal government has acquired responsibilities requiring successful linkages between all manner of public, semi-public, and private groups. This applies not only to functions acquired in the last two decades—consumer protection, medical and school financing, mass transportation, and so on—but also to older tasks enhanced with more demanding goals: occupational safety, natural resource use and protection, economic management and industrial revitalization, and so on. Can the president, with a few themes and a handful of aides, negotiate his ideas through these linkages and past the many other knowledgeable participants with a stake in what he is doing? Not likely. And so the helpers, offices, and briefing books pile up on the president-elect no less than on the presidency.

The United States does not have a high-level, government-wide, civil service that could (as in European countries) help a new chief executive and his top team turn their ideas into administrative realities; there is scarcely even a low-level civil service in the White House to help with the paperwork. The increasing resort to transition bureaucracies is one accommodation to this fact, thereby loading onto the presidency more of the responsibility for turning themes into playable scores than would otherwise be the case. But with or without a competent civil service, the very nature of federal activity impels the presidency to become a predictable bureaucracy so that other participants can play their parts.

Imagine, for example, a president committed to replacing government regulation with market competition and incentives in various policy areas. Having grown accustomed to the old regulations and possessing the power to make or break any proposed "market solution" that affects them, people in Congress, the departments, interest groups, and sub-national governments need to know what, in detail, the president proposes to do. To create a market where none has been implies some forethought about how far it will extend, what transitional arrangements with the affected groups will be made, how this will affect programs in related areas, what rules of competition will be enforced, and who will enforce them. Because markets typically impose some costs and spillovers that many people consider unfair, thought must also be given to compensations, subsidies, and other kinds of protections (more regulations). All of this implies presidential helpers who can work knowledgeably with planners, analysts, economists, administrators, inspectors, lawyers, not to mention all the political legwork involved. To survive in this kind of world, the president needs to be surrounded by policy technocrats no less than by the political technocrats of his quasi-party. But how can the president know that all these bright, committed, and (like the rest of us) self-interested people are doing what *he* would want?

The President as Manager

Whoever the president and whatever his style, the political and policy bureaucracies crowd in on him. They are there in his office to help, but their needs are not necessarily his needs. Delegation is unavoidable; yet no one aide or combination of aides has his responsibilities or takes his oath of office. However much the president trusts personal friends, political loyalists, or technocrats, he is the person that the average citizen and history will hold accountable.

If this diagnosis of the presidential office is close to the truth, then there is one big prescription. The president must take responsibility for deprogramming himself. Since the deep structure of the office is shaped by trends well outside his control, the president must try to preserve his maneuverability within this structure—a maneuverability not just in the images of personal style, but in the substance of work that gets done around him. Trusting a chief of staff or a few senior aides is not enough. Behind the scenes, the president must manage and manipulate if he is not to be suffocated by the political and policy technocrats of Washington.

To manage is something that falls between administering in detail and merely presiding in general. At most, the president himself can directly administer one or two major issues and half a dozen or so senior aides. And to preside is a dangerous abdication to the momentum of forces around him. It is difficult to put the president's management chore into words without seeming to be cynical or sinister. To speak of the president's manipulation of the people in his office should not summon up Nixonian memories, for if ever there was a president cut off from (though criminally responsible for) what was going on in his own office, it was Richard Nixon. The appropriate mentor is still the first inhabitant of the modern presidency, Franklin Roosevelt. For a paraplegic president, his appreciation for the primary task of internal management came almost instinctively: to use those who waited on him without becoming dependent on them.

Roosevelt had his tactics; other presidents will have theirs. But the basic necessity for personal management remains and grows as modern presidents become increasingly penned in. Programmed more than paralyzed, today's president needs many different eyes and ears for the things he should know, legs to take him where he should be, and protective devices to avoid situations that leave him vulnerable.

How to do all this? The exact structure and personalities are less important than sometimes thought. Given the record of recent administrations, there are some useful guidelines to be drawn from experience, usually of the painful variety. These guidelines are as follows:

1. *Self-awareness is the place to begin.* The president, by his own actions and even more by the anticipations of his actions that he creates in other people, generates a kind of *de facto* management system. The more he is willing to do, the more he will be asked to do. The more questions he will take rather than passing them to others, the more he will be asked. The more unconditional his support of his staff seems, the less the incentive for good performance. The more widely spread his trust, the less its value. These are obvious points familiar to any executive, but under the crush of daily emergencies and decisions in the presidency, they become more important and easier to overlook.

2. *Selectivity needs to be a part of self-awareness.* Because the president can personally administer only a few issues and can manage only a handful of aides, he needs to know the one or two things that matter to him most, subject to changing circumstances. Without this selectivity, there are no goals to work toward and disorientation quickly spreads throughout his office and administration. Most of the rest of his presidency, to put it bluntly, will consist of managing for damage control in the history books.

3. *Self-awareness and selectivity have to be linked to a consciousness of the bureaucratic terrain in his own office through which the president is moving.* A presidential bureaucracy—rather, a collection of bureaucracies—seems to be with us to stay, and its workings pose special hazards for the president. The following are perhaps the most common hazards:

   - Presidential staffs tend to bring into the presidency conflicts and controversies raging among departments, congressional committees, and interest groups. This means that the president, unless he makes a conscious effort to the contrary, is likely to be closely identified with the inevitable ebb and flow of debate that occurs on complex policy matters—a tentative finding this way, an interim decision that way. Even the most firm-minded president is bound to appear indecisive in this situation. Perhaps the best safeguard is for the president to allow a great deal of "precooking" of policies some distance away from him, with low-visibility participation by presidential staff members to protect his interests. This approach seems most appropriate for the bulk of issues that are not among his few priority concerns.
   - Each presidential staff, in order to carry weight inside the office and with outsiders, seeks to invent ways that allow it to claim that its members are acting "at the direction of the president." And each such invention ties the president more closely to the work of unfamiliar helpers. Because all these people have a stake in generating presidential decisions, his influence and public standing are likely to be on the line in more places than he might wish. A president can help himself by making sure that issues coming to him really are matters on which he, rather than someone else, has to make

a formal decision. The exact machinery is less important than the need for the president to choose some particular system—an administrative secretary, a chief of staff, a secretariat, a formal procedure of decision memoranda—for disciplining the way he gets into decisions and for keeping tabs on what he, rather than anyone else, wants done. It is only the president who, by his own actions, can enforce and sustain any such system.

- The presidential bureaucracy has a natural desire for self-preservation. Internal conflicts which would convey more information to the president by being openly fought out tend to be submerged in *sub rosa* court politics inside the White House and the rest of the EOP. Rather than a free-for-all among presidential staffs, what typically exists is a kind of truce by which each staff settles for a piece of the president's attention and decision-making. This hardly helps the president to know what is going on. To overcome this tendency the president, again by his own behavior, needs to make it clear that he expects in-house disagreements, that suppression of contrary views is punished, and that all can live to fight another day—as long as the battle does not continue once the president has made up his own mind. The same staff procedures used to keep the president out of unnecessary decisions can probably be used to create a fair hearing and due process for such internal conflicts.

- Because of the trends identified earlier, the presidential office tends to be divided into two large hemispheres: a political technocracy and a policy technocracy. On almost every conceivable issue the president needs to hear, unvarnished, the facts from both sides. In general, the competition between the two hemispheres for presidential attention has tended to become unequal as media attention has increased and political fragmentation grown. Political staff work tends to drive out longer-term, institutional interests in policy and administration. This tendency is amplified if the president makes it clear that he gives serious attention only to his short-term personal stakes in the issues coming before him.

4. *Paradoxically, one of the most effective ways for the president to manage his own office is through the use of his appointees in the departments and agencies.* If these department heads are known to have intimate knowledge of the president's thinking, and therefore seem likely to be backed by the president in disputes with White House staffers, White House aides will likely be kept in their proper place as assistants to the president rather than as assistant presidents.

Unfortunately, every new administration seems to raise false expectations by proclaiming that the president intends to manage through his cabinet officers, or words to that effect. In fact, their individual frames of reference are too narrow to give the president all the perspective he needs, and their collective interests are a fiction without active presidential support and guidance. Hence, the president must manage through both his own office's bureaucracies *and* his department and agency heads. In general, the cabinet is a communication—not a decision-making—device. It carries information to and from the president. At their best, cabinet officers help the president by telling him things he would not otherwise hear, by conveying his sense of a unified administration, by keeping presidential staff in line. It is the president's management job to see that when department and agency heads fight among themselves—as they inevitably will—it is done in front of him and tells him something worth knowing.

5. *In addition to his political staffs, policy offices, and cabinet officers, the president typically has access to his closest personal friends: the Kitchen Cabinet.* Experience suggests that it is safest to keep these advisers outside his office staffs or official departmental family. The reason is simple and practical. If the president is to protect himself as he manages, any other person must be dispensable. Because not everyone wishes the president well, putting a close personal friend in an official position leaves both that person, and through him, the president, vulnerable. Informal advisers attract less attention, are changed more easily, and perform their greatest services precisely because they are not caught up in the daily grind of government machinery. Exceptions can, of course, be found; President Eisenhower and President Kennedy made effective use of their brothers in official positions, as did President Truman of his friend John Snyder. But for every Snyder there is a Bert Lance, and it is just as well to recognize the risks at the outset. Only the president can decide whether it is worth having someone so close that his presidency will be gravely wounded through that person's loss to scandal, the appearance of scandal, or larger policy ends.

Cautions about these five hazards add up to an approach to presidential management that tries to use the various tensions and counter-pressures inherent in the job. The counter-pressures within his own office staffs, between them and cabinet officers, and between all these and the president's closest personal loyalists are opportunities as well as constraints. A president with some self-awareness can use this cat's cradle of tensions to help see to it that he is at the center of things when he wants to be and "out of it" when he needs to be. The management aim cannot, therefore, simply be to create a unified team; it must be to create the counter-pressures that will be useful to him, lest he become victimized by his own helpers.

Others, no doubt, will see things differently, but this much seems clear: a modern president who cannot govern his own office is unlikely to be able to govern anything else.

Endnotes

1. A brief description is contained in National Academy of Public Administration, *A Presidency for the 1980s* (Washington, DC: NAPA, 1980), Chapter 2.
2. The current advisory mechanisms available to the president are surveyed in Richard Pious, *The American Presidency* (New York: Basic Books, 1979), Chapters 7–10.
3. From the Wayne Coy Paper, "Memorandum of October 26, 1940," in the Franklin D. Roosevelt Presidential Library, Hyde Park.

Bradley H. Patterson and James P. Pfiffner

Presidential Appointments And The Office Of Presidential Personnel

In order for a new president to take effective control of the government, he or she must appoint people to head the executive branch. Consequently, one of the first things that a president-elect must worry about is having in place an effective personnel recruitment operation. This function is so important that the planning for it must begin well before the election, even though there is a danger that setting up the operation may appear presumptuous if news of it gets into the press. As Pendleton James, President Reagan's personnel recruiter in 1980–81 said, "The guys in the campaign were only worried about one thing: the election night. I was only worrying about one thing: election morning."[1] "Presidential personnel cannot wait for the election, because presidential personnel has to be functional on the first day, the first minute of the first hour." But "it has to be behind-the-scenes, not part of the campaign and certainly not known to the public."[2]

This essay will present an overview of the Office of Presidential Personnel (OPP) and how it functions during the transition and early months of a new presidential administration. We will first set out the scope of the job by specifying the number and types of political appointments for which OPP is responsible. Next, some background on how the office has developed in recent years will be presented along with the responsibilities of its director. Each administration's OPP faces predictable challenges in the form of pressures for appointments from Congress, the campaign, and cabinet secretaries; these typical areas of concern will be examined. Our conclusion is that the responsibilities of the OPP are crucial to the success of each president and that the better prepared the new director is, the better he or she will serve the president.

Scope of Presidential Appointments

What categories of positions are filled by political appointment, and how many positions are there in each category? The following table lays out different types of presidential appointments and the number of positions in each category.[1]

Source: Presidential Studies Quarterly, Vol. 31, No. 3 (September 2001).

Table 24.1. Presidential Appointments and the Office of Presidential Personnel

I. Full time presidential appointments	
A. PAS appointments requiring Senate confirmation (e.g., cabinet secretaries, agency heads, ambassadors)	1,177
B. "PA" presidential appointments not requiring Senate confirmation	21
II. Full-time political appointments (Appointed by agency heads but only with White House approval)	
A. "Schedule C" positions, mid-level management and below (GS 1–15)	1,428
B. Non-career senior executive service, upper-level management	796
III. Part-time presidential appointees (advisory boards and commissions)	
A. "PAS"—requiring Senate confirmation	579
B. "PA"—not requiring Senate confirmation	2,509
IV. White House staff positions (not handled by OPP)	
A. Receiving formal, signed commissions from the president (assistant and deputy assistants to the president)	154
B. Appointed under presidential authority (Special assistants to the president and below)	<u>790</u>
Total positions that can be filled by the White House in a typical term	7,454

(Source of table: Adapted from Bradley Patterson, To Serve the President (Washington, D.C. Brookings, 2008), pp. 93-94.

The "PAS" and "PA" positions in Category I, most federal judgeships (Category I), and the memberships on part-time advisory boards and commissions (Category III) are created in statute. (Ambassadorships and a few judgeships are authorized not in statute but in the Constitution itself.) The number of statutory posts can be increased or decreased only by congressional action. The president personally approves each of these appointments.

The Senior Executive Service (SES) is the corps of professional federal managers just below the level of assistant secretary. By law, only 10 percent of the positions in the SES may be filled on a noncareer basis. A department or agency head may propose a political candidate to be appointed to such a position, but it is also standard practice that each noncareer SES appointment is to be cleared with the director of the OPP. Once White House approval has been signaled, the Office of Personnel Management (OPM) grants "noncareer appointing authority" to the agency for the placement.

Schedule C positions are established by departments and agencies, but each such post must first be certified by the director of the Office of Personnel Management as being "policymaking" or "confidential." Once a Schedule C job is thus authorized, the department or agency head may appoint a person to the post. It has been standard presidential practice since 1981, however, that the White House—usually the director of the Office of Presidential Personnel—approves each Schedule C appointment. That practice is likely to continue.

While both Schedule C and noncareer SES appointees are employees of the agencies in which they work, with their service being at the pleasure of the respective agency heads, the White House cannot be oblivious to the quality and the commitment of these noncareer people.

Development of the Office of Presidential Personnel

Presidents have made political appointments of the officers of the executive branch of government ever since the administration of George Washington. Throughout most of the 19th century the "spoils system" dominated the executive branch, with much of the whole federal workforce changing upon the election of a new president from the other political party. After the Pendleton Act of 1883 created the merit system, the executive branch was gradually changed so that civil servants were hired by the Civil Service Commission and only the top levels of the government would be politically appointed.

But for most of the century after the Pendleton Act, the White House had no institutional capacity to recruit political appointees. The cabinet and top levels were of course determined by the president, but lower levels were often influenced heavily by patronage demands originating in political parties and Congress. As the scope of government expanded and the technical complexity of the functions of the government increased, the qualifications for appointees began to change to include technical and policy expertise as well as political loyalty. However, the ability of the White House to recruit actively slowly developed over time.

After World War II, the White House capacity to control appointments for the president was gradually created. President Truman was the first president to assign one person the duty to take care of all presidential appointments, and President Eisenhower used a special assistant for personnel management. President Kennedy designated three people to conduct his "talent hunt" for the "best and brightest" to serve in his administration. Kennedy did not expect political appointments to be too much of a challenge, but his perspective changed after he assumed office. "I thought I knew everybody and it turned out I only knew a few politicians."[3]

The presidential capacity to recruit political appointees took a jump in professionalism when Fred Malek became President Nixon's director of the White House Personnel Office in 1970 and established an executive search capacity with about 30 people working for him.[4] The Malek operation handled all presidential appointments but not schedule Cs.

President Carter was the first president to begin planning for personnel recruitment before the election, but conflict between the campaign operation (headed by Hamilton Jordan) and the transition preparation (headed by Jack Watson) foreshadowed an uncoordinated personnel recruitment process once he was in office. In addition, Carter intended to delegate to his cabinet secretaries broad authority to recruit their own management teams, as Nixon had initially.

Pendleton James was put in charge of the incoming Reagan administration's personnel recruitment operation and undertook systematic preparations in the summer of 1980. The incoming administration concluded that Nixon and Carter had delegated too much recruitment authority to their cabinet secretaries and had abdicated White House control. They thus established immediately after the election that the Office of Presidential Personnel would control all presidential appointments (PAS). But in addition, they decided to establish White House control over noncareer Senior Executive Service (SES) appointments and Schedule C appointments, which are technically appointed by cabinet secretaries and agency heads. Pen James was given the title of assistant to the president (the highest designation of White House staffers) and an office in the West Wing. James maintains that these two indicators of status are crucial for the authority necessary to do a good job of presidential recruiting.[5] The OPP under Reagan used ideological agreement with the president as a major criterion for selection of appointees. At the beginning of the administration, James had more than 100 people working with him, including volunteers.

President Bush continued to control appointments in the White House and chose Chase Untermeyer to head his OPP. The main criterion for a Bush administration appointment was personal loyalty to George Bush, and two special groups were set up to assure that demonstrated loyalty was rewarded. The president's nephew, Scott Bush, was put in charge of drawing up lists of those who had worked in the Bush campaign whose names would be sent to departments to be appointed to Schedule C positions. The president's son, George W. Bush, was put in charge of a group called the "Silent Committee," which drew up lists of those who had been loyal to George Bush over his career and made sure that they were "taken care of" in the appointments process.[6]

President Clinton continued White House control of presidential appointments, but his Office of Presidential Personnel got off to a slow start when its initial director, Richard Riley, after several weeks on the job, was named by Clinton to be secretary of education. OPP was then headed by Bruce Lindsey who was also responsible for many other duties for Clinton and could not devote the full time necessary for the job. The office was finally headed by Robert Nash who continued in the position through most of the administration. The hallmark of the Clinton personnel recruitment effort was "diversity," and they were successful in appointing greater numbers of women and ethnic minorities than any other administration had.

III. Setting Out the Ground Rules

Inauguration day arrives. Lucky is the personnel director who will even have time to witness the inaugural parade, because of the other parade—of supplicants—into the director's White House reception room. Typically, the director's 100-person team of assistants during the transition moves over to the White House too. What have heretofore been plans now become actions. The months-ago calculations must now be transformed into decisions.

In the new White House itself, the director of the Office of Presidential Personnel will want to make sure that several traditional rules are reaffirmed:

(1) No other person or office in the White House is to make personnel *commitments*. The new presidential personnel specialists will likely turn to the domestic or economic or national security offices in the White House for advice about the selection of

candidates. The political and legislative liaison staffs will funnel in streams of additional resumes from their own respective constituencies. Other members of the new White House staff, fresh from the campaign, will feel obligated to help their erstwhile buddies find jobs in the new administration. The first lady will refer to the director the mail from office-seekers who are writing to her. But when it comes to decision-making, there can be only one point from which the final recommendation goes to the president: the director of the Office of Presidential Personnel.

(2) Cabinet heads are to be informed: The White House is to govern the selection of the political appointees in the departments "all the way down." Some new cabinet and agency heads likely will want to boast that the president has given them free hand to pick departmental subordinates, but that will simply not be the case; it is clearly in the interest of the director of the Office of Presidential Personnel to make sure of this. What is meant by "all the way down"? It means that not only does the White House make the final decision on presidential appointments within each department, but that the director of the Office of Presidential Personnel usually signs off on *all* the political appointments that a department or agency head wishes to make, i.e. on Schedule C and noncareer SES positions as well. Does that mean every single one?

President Bush's second presidential personnel director, Constance Horner, warns:

> Absolutely—every single one. I was quite fierce about this, because I saw it as a process of building future leadership. So it mattered to me what the quality of the appointee was, and it mattered to me what their decisional level was, and what their loyalty was, and their intellectual capability.[7]

In practice, this rule means that the director will engage in negotiations with the cabinet or agency head and come to an (almost always) amicable agreement as to the person to be chosen.

The first weeks and months of a new presidential personnel director's tenure will be a period of constant, supercharged pressures, sticky, tangled bargaining, of making as many folks disappointed/mad as one makes appreciated/pleased— and overall a smattering of chaos. The OPP staff must be competent enough and energetic enough to push its way through the intricate negotiations and preparations that are needed to put the director in a position to make final recommendations to the president. In each case, all eight of the previously described sets of criteria must be applied. The White House Political Affairs Office will help in ascertaining from party headquarters how active candidates were in the campaign and how much reward is appropriate. The Legislative Affairs Office will assist with informal checks on the Hill. (If federal judges are being proposed, it is the counsel, rather than the director of the Office of Presidential Personnel, who will carry the prime responsibility for the necessary vetting of judicial candidates.)

In many instances, the OPP director will insist on interviewing some candidates personally: to satisfy himself or herself that the men and women being recommended to the president are of top quality. The director will ask the final question:

> Are there ANY skeletons in your closet? I want to know. And if you DON'T reveal them now, and leave me to make a judgment call not knowing about them, finding some way to handle them, I will STILL find out about them, and then you are out, REALLY OUT.[8]

The personnel director must ascertain from the president the answers to three procedural questions: (1) whether the president wants a single name proposed for each position, or a group of alternative candidates (with one of them recommended by the director); (2) to what extent the president wants the vice president consulted about personnel recommendations; and (3) what the role is to be of the White House Chief of Staff on personnel matters. With respect to the third point, Untermeyer's memoranda to the president would begin "The Chief of Staff and I recommend . . ."

The president's initials on a personnel memorandum are only the intermediate step in the process. Next are the formal clearance procedures: It is at this point that the FBI starts its security and suitability investigation (which could take weeks), and the candidate produces his or her financial and tax records in minute detail. It is the counsel, not the personnel director, who will scrutinize the resulting reports and who will notify the OPP director if there is anything negative in those findings that would affect the candidate's suitability. If a candidate's financial holdings, for instance, reveal a possible conflict of interest with the job for which he or she is destined, the counsel or the independent Office of Government Ethics will require the candidate to work out a divestiture or similar "insulating" arrangement with the ethics officer of the department involved.

During this investigative period, the position will appear to be still unfilled—and thus may attract new supplicants (and their supporters). It is difficult to tell them that the job is, in fact, no longer available. A final memorandum is sent to the president recommending his signature on the nomination papers. When that happens, the papers are dispatched to the Senate, and a White House press announcement is released. These actions mark the conclusion of the recruitment phase for presidential appointments that require Senate confirmation.

IV. The Challenges and Pressures Facing the Director of OPP

One of the first challenges for the Office of Presidential Personnel is to deal with the volume of resumes and requests for appointments that flood into the White House immediately after the election. In recent administrations, this flood has reached 1,500 per day.[9] The Bush administration had received 16,000 before the inauguration and by the end of May 1989, it had received more than 70,000 applications and recommendations (though 25,000 may have been duplicates).[10]

According to Pendleton James, the pressures on the OPP director are tremendous. "There's not enough time in the day to get it done . . . my job was like drinking water from a fire hydrant. There is so much volume coming at you. . . . There just isn't enough time."[11] He continued, ". . . being the head of presidential personnel is like being a traffic cop on a four-lane freeway. You have these Mack trucks bearing down on you at sixty miles an hour. They might be influential congressmen, senators, state committee chairmen, heads of special interest groups and lobbyists, friends of the president's, all saying 'I want Billy Smith to get that job'."[12]

Pressure from Congress is considerable. Pen James said that he received some advice from the legendary Bryce Harlow, who had run congressional relations for President Eisenhower during the Reagan transition. Harlow told him, "The secret to good government is never, ever appoint a Hill staffer to a regulatory job. That Hill staffer will never be the President's appointee. He or she will always be the appointee of that congressman or that senator who lobbied you for that job. And they will be beholden to that senator or to that congressman." After James's talk with Harlow, a senator came to talk with James, and after mentioning that 64 of the Reagan nominations had to go through his committee, demanded that several of his staffers be appointed to regulatory positions. Remembering Harlow's advice, James went back to the White House and asked chief of staff James Baker how to handle the situation. Baker said, "Give it to him." Some pressures from Congress cannot be ignored.[13]

Some friends of the president may have strong claims based on their political support but may not be qualified for high level managerial positions. This is a predictable challenge for the OPP director. But there is an art to dealing with the people who must be turned down for positions with the new administration. According to Constance Horner, one possibility is to appoint people to part-time and honorary positions. ". . . for every person you choose you're turning down ten, fifteen, twenty people who want the job. . . . [T]here is no way to do this and make everybody happy. . . . there are numerous part-time boards and commissions that offer advice on environmental matters where people come to Washington four times a year and they discuss the issues and make recommendations."[14] So if a person is not qualified for a position of great authority, Chase Untermeyer advises: "That person can also be rewarded in other ways with advisory commissions or invitations to State dinners or other things that are within a gift of the president to do short of putting that person in charge of a chunk of the federal government."[15]

While all PAS appointments are constitutionally the president's decision, the practical and prudential approach to sub-cabinet appointments (deputy, under, and assistant secretaries) is not quite so clear-cut. In the 1950s and 1960s, when the White House did not have the recruitment capacity it has now, it was most often the cabinet secretary who suggested to the president the preferred nominee, and most often the president went along. In battles between the White House staff and the cabinet secretary, most often the cabinet secretary won.[16]

From the perspective of the cabinet secretary, the issue is one of building a management team for the department. Each person has to be chosen carefully, with full consideration for how that person fits into the structure and how they will get along with the others on the team. Those in the cabinet are suspicious that the White House Office of Presidential Personnel will weigh very heavily the political service of the appointee and will neglect the expertise, managerial ability, and compatibility of the nominee with the other executives in the department. Frank Carlucci, secretary of defense in the Reagan administration, advised new cabinet members: "Spend most of your time at the outset focusing on the personnel system. Get your appointees in place, have your own political personnel person, because the first clash you will have is with the White House personnel office. And I don't care whether it is a Republican or a Democrat. If you don't get your own people in place, you are going to end up being a one-armed paper hanger."[17]

The White House staff has just the opposite perspective. They are afraid that cabinet secretaries are likely to recruit people who are loyal to the cabinet secretary but not necessarily to the president. For this reason, the Reagan administration decided to control political appointments tightly in the White House. Pen James explained that earlier presidents had failed to make sure that sub-cabinet appointments were controlled by the White House. "Nixon, like Carter, lost the appointments process."[18] One danger is that a newly selected cabinet nominee will ask the president for the authority to appoint his/her own team. But agreeing to that is a big mistake. So, according to James,

> We didn't make that mistake. When we appointed the cabinet member, he wasn't confirmed yet. We took him in the Oval Office; we sat down with the President. . . . And we said, 'All right . . . we want you to be a member of the cabinet but one thing you need to know before you accept is we, the White House, are going to control the appointments. You need to now that.'[19]

Each new administration must reach a balance between the OPP and cabinet secretaries about recommending nominations to the president. What is important is that this accommodation be made explicitly and at the direction of the president rather than through drift.

In recruiting political appointees, the primary criterion is loyalty, but the definition of loyalty is not a fixed target. Some interpret loyalty as service to the political party over the years; others see it as ideological compatibility with the president; others see it as personal service to the candidate in the past or in the most recent campaign. Others argue that competence, professionalism, and the ability to manage ought to be primary criteria for appointment.

According to Chase Untermeyer, ". . . the primary responsibility of the personnel office is to get those who are loyal to the president," rather than appointing a person who is loyal "to the person who hired you such as a cabinet secretary or such as an important senator who insisted on your getting a job."[20] This may mean turning away loyal partisans from previous administrations. Untermeyer was sympathetic to the "baleful looking veterans of the Nixon and Ford administrations, and even in one case the Eisenhower Administration, who felt that because they had been wonderful civil servants and devotees of George Bush that they, of course, would be prime candidates to be in our administration." But the political reality was that "our job was to find places for people who had worked in the 1988 campaign."[21] This calls attention to the strains created during a transition to a new administration of the same party. The new president may want his own people and thus have to "throw out" of office loyal incumbents of the same party.[22]

Chase Untermeyer warns that some newly appointed cabinet secretaries who are politically sophisticated and come to talk with the director of OPP "pre-armed with lists of those whom they want in various positions" and will refer to them as "my appointments."[23] So it is important for OPP to have an "inventory of names" of those who helped in the campaign when the cabinet secretary comes to talk about appointments. The secretary can then be told: ". . . while you were in your condo in Palm Beach during the New Hampshire primary, these people helped [the president] get elected so you could become cabinet secretary."[24]

Fred Malek, the head of the White House Personnel Office for President Nixon, has a slightly different perspective on loyalty. He argues that loyalty is certainly central in making political appointments, but construing that loyalty too narrowly might prematurely narrow the pool of talented candidates. ". . . Don't assume that somebody who hadn't worked for you in the past isn't loyal to you. Maybe they didn't know they could work for you. Maybe they haven't been involved in politics but there can be developed loyalty; it doesn't have to be proven loyalty."[25]

> "Too many administrations, *too many* administrations get staffed by the campaign. The qualities that make for excellence in a campaign are not necessarily the same as make for excellence in governing. . . . To govern you need, I think, people who are of a somewhat more strategic and substantive bent than you necessarily need in a campaign. Campaigns are more tactical. . . . In governing I think you need a better sense of strategy and a better sense of management."[26]

Thus many tough personnel choices will have to be made by the director of OPP, and many of them will hinge upon which kind of loyalty to weigh more heavily. But it should be kept in mind that the long term success of the president's administration will depend heavily upon the substantive competence of the people appointed to manage the departments and agencies of the executive branch.

Conclusion

A presidential candidate and the director-to-be of presidential personnel have to reflect that they face a daunting responsibility. Within a few short months after taking office, the winner must select, persuade, thoroughly evaluate, and install some 2,000 extraordinarily capable men and women who will suddenly have to take on the management of the most complicated and demanding enterprise on earth: governing the United States. A few of that cohort may be experienced in this endeavor; most, though, will be untutored. Many will accept financial sacrifice and leave quiet, comfortable lives only to be swallowed up in what they will rapidly discover is a roiling tempest of competition, cacophony, and contention: the environment of public life. They will be scrutinized and criticized from all sides; pressures and demands on them will be merciless, praise and recognition meager. A few will stumble; some will become world-famous. All of them, laggards and unsung heroes alike, will see themselves collectively vilified as "power-hungry Washington bureaucrats," but they must soldier on, helping faithfully to execute the laws, and to "promote the general welfare" unto the least of their fellow citizens. They will need—and almost all of them will earn—the president's loyalty and support. In the end, they will have had the opportunity—and the honor—of adding to the promise and to the goodness of their country, and of the world itself. Can there be a more ennobling challenge?

Endnotes

All quotations, unless otherwise specified, come from transcripts of the White House Interview Program and were conducted by Martha Kumar in 1999 and 2000.

1. James interview, p. 6.
2. Pendleton James interview, p. 21.

3. Quoted in Calvin Mackenzie, *The Politics of Presidential Appointments* (NY: The Free Press, 1981), p. 83.
4. Malek interview, p. 3.
5. James interview, p. 10.
6. Untermeyer interview, pp. 25, 26, 41.
7. Author's interview with Constance Horner, September 29, 1997.
8. Jay Matthews, quoting Frederick W. Wackerle, an executive recruiter with thirty-one years experience, in "Are There ANY Skeletons in Your Closet," *The Washington Post,* May 2, 1995, p. D-1.
9. James P. Pfiffner, *The Strategic Presidency,* 2nd ed. (Lawrence, KS: University Press of Kansas, 1996), p. 57.
10. See Pfiffner, *The Strategic Presidency*, p. 138.
11. James interview, p. 38.
12. James interview, p. 7.
13. James interview, p. 12.
14. Horner interview, pp. 12-13.
15. Untermeyer interview, p. 12.
16. Pfiffner, *The Strategic Presidency*, p. 66.
17. Pfiffner, *The Strategic Presidency*, p. 66.
18. Pfiffner, *The Strategic Presidency*, p. 67.
19. James interview, p. 6.
20. Untermeyer interview, p. 11.
21. Untermeyer interview, p. 37.
22. Pfiffner, *The Strategic Presidency*, p. 138.
23. Untermeyer interview, p. 9.
24. Untermeyer interview, p. 10.
25. Malek interview, p. 14.
26. Malek interview, p. 13.

Richard W. Waterman

The Administrative Presidency, Unilateral Power, and the Unitary Executive Theory

The administrative presidency strategy originally was initiated by the Richard M. Nixon administration as an attempt to accomplish administratively what it could not do legislatively (Nathan 1983; Waterman 1989). While the idea of the administrative

Source: Presidential Studies Quarterly (Vol. 39, no. 1 (March 2009).

presidency remains politically controversial, it is mostly based on solid constitutional principles. The strongest constitutional foundation is the president's ability to appoint loyalists to positions throughout the bureaucracy. While the debate over whether a president should promote loyalty rather than competence as the main criterion for making appointments is certainly controversial, there is a sound constitutional basis for this practice, even when presidents use their recess power to make late-term appointments.

Presidents have been on solid legal ground as well in removing officials who were judged to be insufficiently loyal to them or to their policies. As long as these officials held appointments that ultimately were responsible to the president and served at the president's pleasure, they could be legally subject to removal at any time. Abuses of power occurred, however, when the Nixon administration attempted to remove civil servants or to deploy them to remote locations. Later, though, Ronald Reagan was able to use newly emerging powers emanating from Jimmy Carter-era civil service reform legislation to transfer career employees to less amenable locations, which forced them to resign if they wished not to relocate. These steps, taken during the Reagan administration, while politically controversial, were nonetheless legal, and the results often advanced the policy interests of the president. While controversial and maybe even undesirable, these personnel actions were legally permissible and fell within the ambit of executive authority delegated by the Civil Service Reform Act.

A different idea, however, arose in the form of the unitary executive theory. It posits that the president has sole responsibility for the control and maintenance of the executive branch, further extending the debate on the scope of the president's removal power (Calabresi and Yoo 1997, 2003; Fitts 1996). Proponents of the theory have sought to repudiate the Supreme Court's decision in *Humphrey's Executor v. United States* (1935), which prohibits presidents from removing officials, such as the commissioners of the independent regulatory commissions, from office for political reasons. The unitary executive theory proclaims the president to be the sole responsible official for all that occurs within the executive branch. In consequence, all of the executive branch must be responsible to its chief executive. This new theory of presidential leadership, propounded in some conservative legal circles (the Federalist Society) and regularly cited by the George W. Bush administration in signing statements, has been presented as a legal justification for more expansive presidential power. In particular, it has increased the traditional authority presidents have employed since Nixon's presidency with regard to the administrative presidency strategy. It raises serious legal questions about the boundaries of presidential power and Congress's ability to limit presidential discretion. By asserting that Congress does not have the right to enact laws that limit the president's powers as chief executive or commander in chief, the unitary presidency provides presidents with broad unchecked power in the personnel removal area. This is but one way in which the unitary executive theory changes what, to date, has been a practice based on accepted constitutional premises.

Another component of the administrative presidency approach is the use of the budget to control agencies. Presidents are on solid constitutional ground when they do so in consort with Congress by approving new spending limits in congressionally en-acted legislation. Presidents also can and have aggressively used the provisions of the Budget and Impoundment Act of 1974 to defer or rescind spending. While the 1974 law outlawed impoundments—whereby a president refuses to spend congressionally allo-cated funds without congressional permission—it also created the deferral and rescis-sion process, which provides presidents with extraordinary flexibility to control bureaucratic spending, particularly when the president and Congress are in the hands of the same political party. The Reagan administration flooded Congress with such re-quests. It also used the same law's reconciliation process to force Congress to accept budget reductions the administration favored. Thus, presidents have a series of consti-tutionally and legally prescribed ways to control spending on bureaucratic agencies.

The unitary executive theory and other instruments of unilateral power further expand the realm of presidential power. In his extravagant use of signing statements, for example, George W. Bush unilaterally created what essentially amounted to a line-item veto. This allowed the president to sign a particular bill and then quietly, in a signing statement that generally received less public scrutiny, assert that the president would ignore certain provisions of the bill with which he disagreed. This mechanism provides yet another means of skirting the constitutional structure and avoids the per-ils of governing in a world of separated powers. If a president does not like a bill's pro-vision, rather than withhold funding, presidents can merely assert that they will not enforce the law, a dubious claim given the mandate of their oath of office and their duty to "take care" that laws are faithfully executed. Although much time and effort has been focused on the constitutional mechanisms at the president's disposal, to date, less attention has been paid to the implications of this new and expansive theory of presidential power. What, then, are the implications of the greater use of unilateral power and the unitary executive theory for the administrative presidency?

Unilateral Power and the Administrative State

Presidents have consistently used their unilateral powers to influence the bureau-cracy. Presidents can create agencies through executive orders. According to How-ell and Lewis (2002) and Lewis (2003), when they do so, they create structures that are more amenable to presidential control. On the other hand, agencies tend to be more insulated from presidential power when they are created by Congress.

Presidents also use executive orders to directly influence policy making at the administrative level. Reagan used executive orders to devise a system, managed through the Office of Management and Budget, by which all major rules and regula-tions had to pass a cost-benefit test before they could be implemented. Not surpris-ingly, most proposed regulations were rejected because of cost concerns, particularly in policy areas that were not favored by the Reagan administration (e.g., the envi-ronment). Reagan also used an administrative order to set up a more efficient cen-tral clearance procedure for all new rules and regulations, again monitored by the Office of Management and Budget and again generally stifling new policy initiatives. Reagan's innovations, with some modifications, have been enacted and implemented by his successors, thus establishing clear precedents for presidential action using executive orders to control the bureaucracy.

Since the Reagan administration, presidents also have made greater use of presidential signing statements. Journalist Charlie Savage, first in a series of articles that garnered the Pulitzer Prize, then later and more expansively in a book (Savage 2007), had noted that presidents use signing statements to directly inform the bureaucracy as to how it is expected to enforce laws passed by Congress. In many cases, bureaucrats are specifically advised *not* to enforce the law. This goes far beyond the practice of using executive orders to prescribe who in the bureaucracy is responsible for policy implementation, a long-standing practice. The use of signing statements essentially orders bureaucrats not to enforce the law, on the authority of the president.

Signing statements provide a bold new mechanism for controlling the bureaucracy, one with dubious constitutional support. Savage writes:

> Among the laws challenged included requirements that the government provide information to Congress, minimum qualifications for important positions in the executive branch, rules and regulations for the military, restrictions affecting the nation's foreign policy, and affirmative action rules for hiring. In his signing statements, Bush instructed his subordinates that the laws were unconstitutional constraints on his own inherent power as commander in chief and as head of the 'unitary' executive branch and thus need not be obeyed as written. (2007, 237)

Bush also said he "could bypass laws requiring him to tell Congress before diverting money from an authorized program in order to start a secret operation, such as funding for new 'black sites,' where suspected terrorists were secretly imprisoned around the world."

While scholars focus on the traditional mechanisms of the administrative presidency strategy, a revolution of sorts has occurred without much notice or comment, one that employs unilateral powers to impact bureaucratic behavior in ways that often are not subject to public scrutiny. With laws passed and monies appropriated, most policy makers turn their attention to other issues, not noticing the significance of the president's signing statement declarations.

The main theoretical basis for such broad presidential action is the unitary executive model. The theory posits that, by creating a single president, the founders intended for the president to have complete and unfettered control over all aspects of the executive branch. This reasoning ignores the clear constitutional powers that Congress possesses over the executive branch, such as its legislative and appropriation powers, as well as those inferred from the "necessary and proper" clause of Article I of the Constitution. It also threatens the ability of the legislative branch to perform meaningful oversight, as the president can order bureaucrats to refuse to comply with congressional requests for information. Particularly interesting is the theory's central assumption that any law passed by Congress that seeks to limit the president's ability to communicate or control executive branch relations is unconstitutional and therefore need not be enforced. The theory also posits that the president has the same authority as the courts to interpret laws that relate to the executive branch. Thus, the president can interpret the law and unilaterally decide to ignore it, without legal sanction or redress.

In this process, legal memoranda written by the Justice Department's Office of Legal Counsel provide presidents and their executive branch subordinates with a legal shield from prosecution. Any official who is challenged by Congress can assert that he or she is following a direct dictate from the president and that it is the Office of Legal Counsel's opinion that it is legal to do so.

This new and expanded use of presidential power represents a quantum expansion of the president's administrative authority, moving us far beyond the constitutionally prescribed boundaries of the initial administrative presidency approach to control of the bureaucracy. Initially, the administrative presidency model provided presidents with greater responsiveness at the bureaucratic level. As Moe (1985) correctly notes, this is both a reasonable and a rational response for presidents who seek greater control of the bureaucracy. As much empirical research has demonstrated, the tools of the administrative presidency indeed increased presidential power and influence (see Wood and Waterman 1991).

But if the ideas of the administrative presidency are conjoined with the expansive claims of inherent presidential power as represented by the unitary executive theory, then the concept of presidential accountability will be sacrificed. In terms of future empirical research on the bureaucracy, then, scholars need to pay greater attention to the content of presidential signing statements and executive orders, as well as to the number of citations of the unitary executive theory as a justification for presidential control. They also need to scrutinize the opinions of the Justice Department's Office of Legal Counsel—that is, when these opinions are available for public scrutiny. Unilateral power and the unitary executive represent the new frontier of presidential attempts to control the bureaucracy. While the George W. Bush administration greatly expanded presidential power in this realm, it is likely that his successors (from both parties) will invoke these precedents, when politically convenient, to further maximize their authority—that is, unless the courts decisively reject the assumptions of the unitary executive. Greater attentiveness to this important change in presidential-bureaucratic relations should be high on the agendas of those who focus on the nexus between the presidency and the executive branch.

References

Calabresi, Steven G., and Christopher S. Yoo. 1997. "The Unitary Executive during the First Half-Century." *Case Western Reserve Law Review* 47: 1451–61.

2003. "The Unitary Executive during the Second Half-Century." *Harvard Journal of Law and Public Policy* 26: 668–801.

Fitts, Michael A. 1996. "The Paradox of Power in the Modern State: Why a Unitary, Centralized Presidency May not Exhibit Effective or Legitimate Leadership." *University of Pennsylvania Law Review* 144: 827–902.

Howell, William G., and David E. Lewis. 2002. "Agencies by Presidential Design." *Journal of Politics* 64: 1095–114.

Lewis, David E. 2003. *Presidents and the Politics of Agency Design: Political Insulation in the United States Government Bureaucracy, 1946–1997.* Stanford, CA: Stanford University Press.

Moe, Terry M. 1985. "The Politicized Presidency. In *The New Direction in American Politics*, edited by John E. Chubb and Paul E. Peterson. Washington, DC: Brookings Institution, 235–71.

Nathan, Richard P. 1983. *The Administrative Presidency*. New York: Wiley.

Savage, Charlie. 2007. *Takeover: The Return of the Imperial Presidency and the Subversion of American Democracy*. Boston: Little, Brown.

Waterman, Richard W. 1989. *Presidential Influence and the Administrative State*. Knoxville: University of Tennessee Press.

Wood, B. Dan, and Richard W. Waterman. 1991. The Dynamics of Political Control of the Bureaucracy. *American Political Science Review* 85: 801–28.

SECTION

6

THE SEPARATION OF POWERS

Although the focus of this volume is on the presidency, it is obvious from the readings so far that the president does not operate alone in the U.S. government. In writing the Constitution, the Framers created a system that was explicitly designed to thwart the accumulation of power. According to James Madison, "Ambition must be made to counteract ambition." In fact, they expected that Congress would dominate the national government. When structuring the system, however, they created an executive branch that was independent of the legislature and potentially able to act as a counterweight to legislative power.

Even so, historical circumstances change, and the changes brought to the United States by the industrial revolution as well as the crises of the mid-20th century—World War I, the Great Depression, World War II, and the Cold War—conspired to allow power to shift to the executive branch. Despite this general trend, the power of the national government has always been in relative balance, with either branch leading the national agenda depending on the particular historical circumstances.

The selections in this section focus attention on this shifting equilibrium in the balance-of-powers system in the United States. Debates over institutions often center on whether the president or Congress has the edge at any given time, and whether changes in the structure of the system would bring better policy outcomes. The final article illuminates the dynamics of the separate institutions as they contend over the nomination of Supreme Court justices, with the president having the initiative to nominate but the Senate having the power to ratify or deny the president's choice.

In "Presidential Relations with Congress," Roger H. Davidson examines some of the strategies and tactics which presidents use in attempting to accomplish their policy preferences: He sees the president's legislative duties as requiring both agenda-setting and bargaining to achieve programmatic goals. This bargaining, he notes, must occur on at least four levels: with party leaders, with Capitol Hill work groups, with rank-and-file lawmakers, and with the public at large. A president's greatest asset is a hefty partisan majority in Congress; however, he cautions that unified party control of the two branches does not guarantee full support from the president's party in Congress, as Barack Obama found out during the first year of his presidency.

In the latter decades of the 20th century and the first years of the 21st, politics in Congress has been particularly divisive, increasingly polarized, and marked by "gridlock." The difficulty that Congress and the president have in addressing important public policy issues has often been attributed to divided government, that is, when one political party controls the House, Senate, or the presidency, but not all three. This sets up a situation in which each of the institutions has an effective veto on public policy that is hard to overcome. Political scientist Sarah Binder examines the consequences of divided government, but discovers that even more important than the division of power between the two parties is the ideological distance between them and the ideological distance between the two houses of Congress. Under such circumstances, policy making does not grind to a halt, but it becomes more contentious and difficult.

The relationship between the presidency and the courts has always been delicate. Federal judges have been aware that the judiciary has little leverage in enforcing a decision that the executive might decide to resist. The executive has the power of the sword, the legislature has the power of the purse to curb the executive, but the judiciary has only the power of judgment and legitimacy. Even though the power of the Supreme Court extends to the interpretation of the laws and the Constitution, it has taken on many contentious issues of public policy, some of which have changed the direction of national policy.

Thus the stakes are high when presidents nominate men and women for lifetime positions on the Supreme Court. In the next selection, John Anthony Maltese analyzes the politics of Supreme Court nominations. He notes that although most presidential nominations are confirmed by the Senate, a significant number fail because of political conflict. Conflict over nominations has occurred ever since the Senate's rejection of George Washington's nomination of John Rutledge, and Maltese documents the broader politicization of court nominations in the 20th century. He concludes that presidents can avoid major political fights by nominating moderate people for the court, but the polarization of American politics makes this difficult to do, as was evident in the political contention over President Obama's nomination of Justice Sonia Sotomayer.

In the final selection, Mark Rozell and Mitchel Sollegberger analyze the confrontation between President Bush and the Democratic 110th Congress over the firing of some U.S. attorneys. The principle of executive privilege rests on the principle that presidents need to be able to rely on frank advice from their advisers and that that frank advice will not be forthcoming if it is subject to congressional investigation and publication. But congressional demands for testimony by executive branch officials rest on the principle that investigations are a necessary incident of carrying out Congress's role in the legislative process. Rozell and Sollenberg conclude that if confrontations like this are not settled by political compromises between the two branches, there is the danger that the courts will impose a rigid legal rule that will result in benefitting one branch at the expense of the other and preclude the type of political compromises that are so important in maintaining a balance in the separation of powers system.

Roger H. Davidson

Presidential Relations with Congress

The designer of the nation's capital, Major Pierre L'Enfant, followed logic and advice when he placed the president and Congress on opposite sides of the city. Congress would occupy a single large building on Jenkins Hill, the highest promontory. On a flat plain a mile or so to the northwest would be the executive mansion. A broad avenue was planned to permit ceremonial exchanges of communication; but a bridge linking them by spanning Tiber Creek was not built for some 40 years. Thus the capitol faced eastward and the executive mansion northward, their backs turned on each other.[1]

Linkages between the two elective branches lie at the heart of the policy successes—and failures—of our government. The relationship is sometimes benign but more often conflict-ridden. Although cooperation is required to pass and implement policies, the two branches have different duties and serve divergent constituencies. Constitutional scholar Edward S. Corwin was referring to foreign policy when he described the Constitution as "an invitation to struggle" between the two elected branches, but the phrase applies even more to domestic policies.

Source: Original essay written for this volume.

The Constitutional Formula

Following history and philosophical principles, the Constitution's writers devoted Article I to the legislative branch. Congress is granted an awesome array of powers, embracing most of the government functions known to 18th-century thinkers. Reflecting the founders' Whig heritage of legislative supremacy—not to mention the founders' own legislative experiences—Congress's prerogatives embrace the historic parliamentary power of the purse in addition to sweeping supervision over money and currency, interstate and foreign commerce, and public works and improvement projects. Congress also plays an active part in foreign and defense policies, which traditionally had been prerogatives of the Crown. It is charged with declaring war, ratifying treaties, raising and supporting armies and navies, and setting rules governing military forces—including rules governing "captures on land and water" (Article I, Section 8). Finally, Congress is granted an elastic power "to make all laws which shall be necessary and proper" for carrying out its enumerated powers.

In contrast to Article I's precise listing of powers, Article II—the executive article—is quite loosely drawn. (However experienced the Founders were in legislative affairs, they had no clear models for the republican chief executive they envisioned.) In working out both legislative and executive policies, however, the Constitution spreads authority across both elected branches.

Even though Congress is vested with "all legislative powers herein granted" (Article I, section 1), other provisions make it clear that these powers must be shared with the executive. Presidents can convene one or both houses of Congress in special session. Although they cannot personally introduce legislation, presidents "shall from time to time give to the Congress information on the state of the Union, and recommend to their consideration such measures as [they] shall judge necessary and expedient." In other words, presidents can shape the legislative agenda, even if they cannot ensure that their proposals will be taken seriously, much less enacted into law. Since Franklin D. Roosevelt in the 1930s, all presidents have taken an active agenda-setting role. Although presidents compile widely varying legislative success records, all of them are now expected to submit their legislative programs and strive to gain their acceptance.

Modern presidents have struggled to dominate executive-branch agencies in the face of Capitol Hill and interest group efforts to capture them. During George W. Bush's administration, his proponents of presidential power contrived the "unitary executive" doctrine: that presidents ought to have complete control over all the entities within the executive branch. The text and intent of the Constitution, however, lend little support to this theory. Although the president is vested with "the executive power" (Article II, Section 1), the charter never defines that power. Thus, a presidential administration is, in Edward S. Corwin's careful words, "a more or less integrated body of officials through whom he can act."[2]

Presidents also have the power to veto congressional enactments. Once a bill or resolution has passed both houses of Congress and been presented to the president, the president must sign or return it within 10 days, excluding Sundays. A two-thirds vote is required in both houses to overrule a president's veto.

The veto power makes the president a major player in legislative politics. Out of more than 2,500 vetoes from George Washington through George W. Bush, only about 4 percent have been overridden by Congress. (Many vetoed bills eventually resurface in another form, however.) Presidents commonly explain their vetoes in one of the following ways: (1) the measure is deemed unconstitutional; (2) it encroaches on the president's powers; (3) it is unwise public policy; (4) it cannot be administered effectively; or (5) it either costs too much or does not cost enough (that is, it falls far short of what the president requested).

The most powerful vetoes are usually those that are threatened but not employed. Lawmakers constantly look to the White House to ascertain whether or not the president is likely to sign the bill. Therefore, enactments usually embody tradeoffs between provisions desired by the president and those favored by drafters on Capitol Hill. That is the leading reason why vetoes are relatively infrequent: throughout our history, presidents have vetoed only about 3 percent of all the measures presented to them. George W. Bush exercised no vetoes in his first six years in office; but when the opposition Democrats took over Congress in 2007, he began to wield his veto pen.

Throughout his administration, however, Bush issued more than 800 "signing statements" explaining his interpretation of the laws he signed—often controversial and sometimes at odds with the measures' purposes or even their plain texts. (Such statements do not have the force of law; but they are printed in the Federal Register and are intended to guide executives who implement the laws, not to mention judges who interpret them.) One of the more notorious examples involved Senator John McCain's (R-AZ) anti-torture amendment to the 2006 defense appropriations act. The provision reads:

> No individual in the custody or under the control of the United States government, regardless of nationality or physical location, shall be subject to cruel, inhuman, or degrading treatment or punishment.

McCain's amendment, which was widely discussed on Capitol Hill and in the press, passed overwhelmingly in both chambers. The president had agreed to sign it, and he did so.[3] However, the White House then put out two signing statements. The first—for public consumption—praised the bill and even referred favorably to the anti-torture provision. Later that evening, a second statement was issued—it was the Friday before the New Year's holiday, when few reporters were on duty—specifying how interrogators were to interpret the new torture ban law. According to this statement,

> The executive branch shall construe [the torture ban] in a manner consistent with the constitutional authority of the president to supervise the unitary executive branch and as Commander in Chief consistent with the constitutional limitations on the judicial power, which will assist in achieving the shared objective of the Congress and the president . . . of protecting the American people from further terrorist attacks.

In other words, the commander in chief would ignore the law as he saw fit. Senator McCain—reached in Antarctica where he was studying global warning—issued a statement taking issue with the White House's interpretation and promising "strict [congressional] oversight to monitor the administration's implementation of the new law."[4] So the inter-branch conflict was joined.

Although President Barack Obama vowed to depart from the Bush record on signing statements, he issued his own in several instances—sometimes to the dismay of Capitol Hill leaders. The president's minor objections to the 1,132-page 2009 appropriations bill were, he said, "subject to well-founded constitutional objections." A later statement appended to a State Department funding bill held that it might "interfere with [the president's] ability to conduct foreign policy." In response, the House in July 2009 passed a follow-up amendment—by a margin of 429-2—warning the president that if he ignored the provisions, he risked a congressional cut-off of funds. "We do this not just on behalf of this institution, but on behalf of democracy," declared Representative Barney Frank (D-Mass). "There's a kind of unilateralism, an undemocratic, unreachable way about these signing statements."

Congress nonetheless shapes the executive branch in many ways. Virtually alone among the world's national assemblies, Congress has the capacity to write, process, and refine its own legislation, relying largely upon "in-house" staff to augment executive initiatives and outside sources of information. Executive agencies receive their mandates, missions, programs, and even structures through congressional authorizations (as influenced and signed by presidents, of course). Key executive officers, as well as federal judges, are nominated by the president, but confirmed only "by and with the advice and consent of the Senate" (Article II, Section 2). Through its appropriations bills, Congress can then expand or contract executive agencies' programs and personnel.

In short, the Constitution blends executive and legislative authority, even though each branch is assigned special duties. The resulting scheme is popularly known as *separation of powers*. However, theory and historical practice point to something rather different: an arrangement in which separate institutions share the same powers. The relationship was designed, as James Madison explained in Federalist No. 48, so that "these departments be so far connected and blended as to give to each a constitutional control over the others."[5] Inter-branch relations are the product of compromise and accommodation, not of isolation or precise metes and bounds.

Growth of the "Legislative Presidency"

History bears out Madison's practical approach to presidential-congressional relationships. Rigid lines of demarcation between the White House and Capitol Hill are repeatedly trespassed. Alexander Hamilton, the first Treasury Secretary, aggressively sought mastery over Congress, as did Thomas Jefferson as president a decade later. For its part, Congress lost no time delving into the details of executive-branch operations—a habit that persists to this day and is often denounced as "micro-management" by frustrated executive managers.

Executive-legislative contacts, however, have expanded in volume, intensity, and formal structure. During the 19th century, presidents and Congresses tended to work at arm's length, although strong presidents such as Jefferson, Andrew Jackson, and Abraham Lincoln took an active part in legislative business. After Lincoln's death in 1865, there ensued an era of presidential eclipse that lasted for more than a generation: "Congressional government," political scientist Woodrow Wilson called it in 1885—long before he himself served in the White House. Still, the underlying post-Civil War trends—among them industrial growth, economic and social complexity, and an expanding public sector—laid the groundwork for later presidential activism in the legislative arena.

The modern legislative role of the president is primarily a 20th-century phenomenon. Wilson and the two Roosevelts—Theodore and Franklin Delano—all sent lengthy legislative agendas up to Capitol Hill. Wilson revived the practice of delivering his State of the Union address in person to capture public attention and media coverage. Since the end of World War II, everyone—Congress, the press, and the public—expects vigorous leadership from the White House. Presidents are judged in the media and elsewhere by their win-and-loss records on Capitol Hill. Presidents who neglect to present and promote their legislative priorities, or who appear simply to defer to congressional initiatives, invite criticism that they are weak or ineffective.

Framing agendas is what the presidency is all about. Within the White House, priorities have to be established for using the president's precious commodities of time, energy, and influence. Setting a national policy agenda poses the same problem writ large: how to guide or control the key actors rather than being swept along by other people's initiatives. This is the leadership challenge for all presidents with ambitious program goals—among them Wilson, the two Roosevelts, Lyndon Johnson, Ronald Reagan, and Barack Obama.

Reagan's first year in the White House (1981), for example, was a modern-day model of leadership through strict agenda control. Acting swiftly and communicating skillfully, the new president imposed his priorities at both ends of Pennsylvania Avenue—focusing on economic measures while pushing aside divisive social issues (for example, abortion and school prayer) urged by his conservative allies. The Reagan program swept through the nation's capital not because it was necessarily the right idea, but because at that moment it was the most compelling idea in town.

Despite his contested victory in 2000, George W. Bush quickly launched a bold set of agenda items—most of them calculated to appeal to the Republican Party's core supporters, mainly economic and cultural conservatives. Like Reagan, Bush kept his legislative agenda narrow and focused. As a result of his active salesmanship and refusal to back down, Bush was able in June 2001 to sign a 10-year $1.35 trillion tax cut, which became the touchstone of his presidency—the first of several such tax measures. Other victories followed: a major bill federalizing school reform, passed with bipartisan support; and "faith-based initiatives"—channeling federal grants to religious groups—an objective that appealed to religious supporters and achieved primarily through funding bills and revised agency regulations.

After the terrorist attacks of September 11, 2001, a panicky Congress quickly passed a series of bills supported by the administration. Three days after the attacks, lopsided majorities in both houses passed S. J. Res. 23, authorizing the president "to use all necessary and appropriate force" against the perpetrators. (This authorization was later used by the White House to justify actions not envisioned by Congress, including domestic wiretapping without court-approved warrants.) There followed the Patriot Act—an unprecedented domestic anti-terrorism law—intended to strengthen the government's hand in spotting and catching residents suspected of being potential terrorists.

The following fall, as the 2002 congressional elections loomed, the White House pushed two more fateful measures. First, sizable majorities in the House and Senate approved a blanket authorization for the president to intervene militarily in Iraq (H. J. Res. 114), bowing to the White House's argument equating the war on terror with toppling Saddam Hussein's autocratic regime. Some congressional skepticism, however, surfaced in a requirement that the president consult first with allies and the United Nations, and that before taking military action he certify that peaceful options had failed. A second White House priority—a new 180,000-employee Department of Homeland Security (DHS)—was stalled by Democrats' worries over the status of the agency's federal employees. Campaigning for GOP congressional candidates, Bush was able to berate Democrats for foot-dragging on DHS—which was approved shortly after the elections. Members on both sides of the aisle, however, eventually had reason to regret their haste in giving the executive the sweeping grants of authority that were contained in such bills.

Bush's aggressive agenda setting was the outcome of his advisors' view that the presidency had been greatly weakened by "unwise compromises" made by past occupants of the Oval Office. "I've seen a constant, steady erosion of the power and the ability of the president to do his job," declared Vice President Dick Cheney, "and time after time, administrations have traded away the authority of the president to do his job. We're not going to do that in this administration."[6] Cheney's view no doubt underlay the White House's refusal, among other things, to share documents with Congress, permit certain executive officers to testify before congressional committees, or otherwise cooperate with investigative or oversight efforts.

Cheney's view, unfortunately, rested upon a serious misreading of executive-legislative relations: It squared neither with the Framers' design nor with more recent historical trends. Despite a short-lived resurgence of congressional initiative in the 1970s—following the Watergate scandal and the Vietnam War—the overall story of contemporary legislative power is one of ebb, not flow.[7] Louis Fisher's careful study of the historical record concerning war powers, for example, reveals that a combination of presidential hubris and congressional abdication has caused an "unmistakable . . . drift away from Capitol Hill."[8]

Presidents communicate their agendas in a variety of ways—not only in State of the Union addresses, but in special messages, reports, required documents such as annual budgets, and public speeches of all kinds. Through these devices presidents can highlight priorities, provoke public debate, stimulate congressional deliberation, and exhort for attention and support.

Presidential Coalition Building

If modern presidents have no choice but to undertake legislative leadership, they nonetheless compile widely differing records of success. More than anything else, success or failure hinges on whether the president's party controls the House and

Senate, as well as how many votes the parties and their component factions command. Unified party control of the two branches nearly always produces higher levels of agreement than does divided party control. A president's skills or popularity with the public have less impact, although they do enhance or shrink a president's legislative record "at the margins."[9]

In the current era of what political scientists call "conditional party government," party officers in both chambers enjoy the advantage of leading like-minded partisans who—because of their ideological and policy consensus—are willing to accept their direction on a large number of broad policy questions.[10]

Despite the prevalence of quasi-party government, however, we must not forget that members of Congress are still independent players. Most of the time, their party loyalty is reflexive, expressed out of deep conviction and political socialization. Legislators' core goals, however, are advancing their constituency and career interests. As long as these goals coincide with the party's priorities, members will follow the party line. But when the two sets of values deviate, members grow restless and balk at their party leaders' demands.

As a result of recent elections, moreover, party government is noticeably weaker—in scholarly parlance, more "conditional"—among Democrats than among Republicans. Historically, even until recent years, the GOP embraced a small but active group of moderate lawmakers—mostly from the Northeast, but scattered elsewhere as well—who were prepared to break party ranks on, for example, social, environmental, and human rights issues. Because of retirements or defeats at the hands of Democrats, however, the numbers of these moderates gradually dwindled. Congressional elections finally eliminated almost all of these middle-of-the-road Republicans. The 111th Congress (2009-2011) contained no GOP representatives and only two senators from New England—once a bastion of moderate Republicanism; only one Republican congressman remained from New York State. In other regions, many suburban constituencies—whose constituents combine fiscal caution with social liberalism—have chosen Democrats rather than Republicans to represent them. Hence the current GOP is more monolithic than the majority Democrats—a number of whose recently elected members represent middle-of-the-road and even conservative voters.

Initially President Obama waved the banner of bipartisanship, making a point of inviting Republicans to the White House and promising to heed their concerns. But GOP solidarity repeatedly thwarted cross-party alliances. A handful of Republicans supported Obama's first financial stimulus packages and his first Supreme Court nominee, Judge Sonia Sotomayor. However, Republicans tended to close ranks on the president's prime legislative objectives: health care and energy reform.

Viewed from the White House, these realities mean that coalitions must repeatedly be forged in order to achieve legislative victories. In persuading and bargaining with Congress, presidents work on at least four levels: with congressional leaders (especially those of the majority party); with the numerous committee, issue, and factional work groups on Capitol Hill; with individual members, sometimes one by one; and with Congress as a whole, through media appeals and grassroots support.

Dealing with Congressional Leaders

Congress is organized by its two major parties, whose leaders supervise the legislative schedule and seek to guide the flow of legislation through the committees and on the floor. Leadership in the larger House of Representatives emerged early in the nation's history; the speaker is a partisan as well as a parliamentary officer, with potent organizing and scheduling powers. The Senate's party floor leadership emerged in the Wilson era (1913–1921)—primarily, scholars have concluded, in order to coordinate Senate actions with White House initiatives.

To achieve legislative results, party leaders have been tempted to violate what members and scholars regard as "the regular order"—traditional rules and courtesies needed to preserve comity among parties and factions. Thus House leaders are able to preempt committee deliberations, craft new versions of bills, and arrange floor debate and amendments so as to assure favorable outcomes. In contested House floor votes, the balloting period is sometimes stretched beyond the normal 15 minutes, so that members' arms can be twisted. During House consideration of the conference report on the 2003 Medicare prescription drug bill—a prize item in President George W. Bush's reelection strategy—House GOP leaders kept the balloting open for nearly three hours (a modern record). Finally, the leaders squeezed out a 220–215 victory, after three members from each party switched their votes to "yes." Bitter complaints about the leaders' tactics were heard from both sides of the aisle. After promising to work cooperatively on legislation, Democrats in the 110th and 111th Congresses (2007–2011) sometimes used the rules to prevent the opposition from offering alternative measures—prompting Republican complaints that nothing had changed.

In the Senate, cross-party harmony is more common. But over the last decade, committee and floor votes are often as partisan as those in the House. And minority -party senators—Democrats (1995–2006) and then Republicans (2007–)—resort to delaying tactics—including threats of filibusters, which under chamber rules require 60 votes to quell. The result is often stalemate—to the anger of the House's majority-party leaders, who can more easily produce floor victories for their bills.

The White House often seeks out individual leaders who command special subject-matter expertise or bargaining skills. Such a leader was Senator Edward M. Kennedy (D-MA), whose 47-year career made him one of the giants of the modern Senate. Although a liberal (a frequent target of negative GOP ads), he was regarded on both sides of the aisle as an "honest broker": someone adept at finding compromises and reliable in keeping his word. During the Obama administration's first year, Kennedy's losing battle with brain cancer kept him away from the Hill and the Senate's Health, Education, Labor, and Pensions (HELP) Committee, which he chaired. His absence was felt acutely during delicate negotiations over multiple House and Senate committee bills on health care reform, a signature Kennedy issue. A GOP colleague, Iowa's Senator Charles E. Grassley, confessed that "[i]f Kennedy were here, it would make melding the Finance Committee bill and the HELP Committee bill that much easier."[11]

Presidents meet frequently with House and Senate leaders from both parties. However, enlisting the leaders' support is only one purpose of such meetings. Party leaders bring reports and warnings about the likely fate of presidential initiatives. They take back equally valuable hints about the president's plans and intentions that can be turned into the coin of influence in dealing with their colleagues. Relationships are obviously more cordial when Congress is led by the president's party—for example, the supportive Republican majorities of George W. Bush's first six years. After the opposition Democrats took over in 2007, relations with leaders—notably Senate Majority Leader Harry Reid (D-NV) and House Speaker Nancy Pelosi (D-CA) were chilly and formal. Barack Obama's election in 2008 restored single-party control, with the president relying on mostly sympathetic leaders. Needless to say, however, formal meetings are only the tip of the iceberg. White House staff members and congressional leaders' staffs are in daily—sometimes even hourly—contact on a wide range of legislative matters.

What do presidents get out of their contacts with congressional leaders? At best they gain loyalty and support. More commonly, they glean timely intelligence about Congress' mood as well as advice about where to look in seeking votes. Messages from the Hill are not always what the president wants to hear. For example, it was through candid sessions with key Republicans, especially then-Senate Majority Leader Bill Frist (R-TN), that the Bush White House learned in October 2005 that the Supreme Court nomination of presidential counsel Harriet Miers was doomed—primarily because of opposition within GOP ranks.

Capitol Hill Work Groups

Bargaining with a few influential leaders no longer ensures passage of the president's program. The specific provisions of bills are normally hammered out in congressional committees or subcommittees. Today's Congress embraces a large number of work groups—including committees, subcommittees, party entities, task forces, and informal caucuses. In the 111th Congress (2009–2011), there were some 200 standing (that is, more or less permanent) work groups—House and Senate committees and their subcommittees, along with four joint committees.

The jurisdictional boundaries among these entities are complex, often overlapping, and sometimes the object of competitive bidding. Today 11 House committees deal with aspects of environmental policy; the Senate has an Environment and Public Works Committee, but at least nine other panels share jurisdiction over related topics. The Department of Homeland Security, created in 2002, faces a jurisdictional jungle on Capitol Hill. Claiming that at least 88 committees and subcommittees had some jurisdiction over DHS, the independent 9/11 Commission urged each chamber to create a single authorizing committee for the agency.[12] The House decided to do so, but the Senate demurred; its lead authorizing committee was Governmental Affairs—whose former chair, Senator Susan Collins (R-ME) complained that her panel controlled only 38 percent of the DHS budget and 8 percent of its personnel.

To untangle committee jurisdictional barriers posed by President Obama's wide-ranging agenda, House Democratic chairs managed to coordinate their efforts. To straddle health care reform, three committees worked to put together an omnibus bill: Energy and Commerce (chaired by California's Representative Henry Waxman), Education and Labor (chaired by another Californian, George Miller), and Ways and Means (chaired by Charles B. Rangel of New York). The climate change bill—American Clean Energy and Security Act, or ACES)—was referred to Representative Waxman's committee and no less than eight other panels (all of which were eventually discharged from considering the measure). In the end, Waxman and Agriculture Chair Collin C. Peterson of Minnesota struck a deal embodied in a substitute bill pushed through the Rules Committee and reported to the floor. Six hours later, the rule was called up and the bill passed by the narrow margin of 219 to 212. Former Rules Committee staff director Don Wolfensberger pronounced the result "an impressive display of a well-oiled and energy-efficient political machine that maximized majority strengths while avoiding minority resistance by process of exclusion."[13]

Party task forces and informal voting-bloc groups outside the standing committee system also allow members to involve themselves in policies of interest to them. Before 1970, there were only a handful of informal caucuses; today there are more than 100.

Persuading Individual Lawmakers

Despite the prevalence of party-line behavior, senators and representatives are basically autonomous. Of course, they are not free of outside influences. Partisan influences are surprisingly strong: Party-line voting on Capitol Hill has soared to modern-day highs in recent years, and party leaders wield sanctions to discourage those who too often stray from the fold. But constituents put their own concerns first and expect their representatives to defend those interests, even if it means straying from the party line. Indeed, given the multiplicity of interested citizens and groups, as well as their unprecedented invasion into electoral politics, "special interests" probably are more powerful and certainly more pervasive than they have ever been. As a result, members march to many different drummers—first one, then another. An evocative metaphor was used by former Senator John Breaux (D-LA), who as a representative joined other southerners to support President Reagan's 1981 budget package in exchange for reconsideration of sugar price supports—which the administration had opposed as inflationary. Asked if his vote could be bought, Breaux replied: "No, but it can be rented."[14]

Sooner or later, presidents and their aides must "retail" their appeals, engaging individual members of Congress in order to sell the White House position, ask for votes, and offer inducements for support. Presidents have always had to make these personal, informal overtures. Washington dispatched Treasury Secretary Hamilton to consult with members; Jefferson socialized at the White House with congressional allies. With their stress on legislative achievements, modern presidents assign White House staffers to conduct day-to-day relations with Capitol Hill. Franklin Roosevelt and Harry Truman dispatched close aides to contact members and help build support for legislation. Dwight Eisenhower set up the first separate congressional liaison office, under Wilton B. "Jerry" Persons and then Bryce Harlow.[15] Eisenhower's legislative goals were modest, and the style of his liaison staff was low-key and mainly bipartisan.

In 1961, President Kennedy expanded legislative liaison (renamed the Office of Congressional Relations) to advance his New Frontier legislative program. Its head, Lawrence F. O'Brien, who is regarded as the father of modern legislative liaison, dispatched staff aides to Capitol Hill to familiarize themselves with members from each geographic area, learn their interests, and plan how to win their votes for the president's program. Departmental and agency liaison activities were coordinated to complement White House efforts.

Presidents since Kennedy have added their individual touches, but all have continued the liaison apparatus. Nixon elevated his first liaison chief, Bryce Harlow, to cabinet status; Ford enlarged the staff; Carter added computers to analyze congressional votes and target members for persuasion. In other respects, Carter's liaison operation drew less than rave reviews. House Speaker Thomas P. "Tip" O'Neill (D-MA) was furious when his guests received inferior seats at Carter's inaugural concert; he claimed to have met with top Carter aide Hamilton Jordan (whom he dubbed "Hannibal Jerkin") only three times in four years.[16] While the inexperience of Carter's initial liaison staff contributed to the appearance of ineptitude, Carter's own indifference to Congress probably was more to blame. When a president gives only sporadic attention to one of his duties, staff productivity is bound to suffer.

Effective congressional liaison involves granting or withholding resources in order to cultivate support on Capitol Hill. This includes not only patronage—executive and judicial posts—but also construction projects, government installations, offers of campaign support, access to strategic information, even plane rides on Air Force One, White House dinners and social events, signed photographs, and countless other favors both large and small that can be traded for needed votes. Some of these services may seem petty or even tawdry; but legislative majorities are oftentimes built out of a patchwork of such appeals.

Some presidents relish the persuasive challenges of their office. Lyndon Johnson was known for "the treatment," a face-to-face assault that ranged the whole gamut of human emotions and often left its targets emotionally battered. Ronald Reagan was known for dispensing gift cuff links and theater tickets along with brief homilies, prompted by index cards, concerning the issue at hand. Both George Bushes engaged in a variety of informal contacts, ranging from White House social events to mobile phone conversations. A few presidents, such as Richard Nixon and Jimmy Carter, disliked asking for votes and preferred to leave the task to others.

Clinton employed a variety of tactics in desperate efforts to win approval of his chief legislative proposals. In several instances, he named an individual to serve as "lobbying czar" for a particular issue; White House aides worked feverishly out of a Capitol Hill "war room" to coordinate their lobbying efforts. Clinton's 1993 budget—which raised taxes on fuels and upper-income individuals, cut the defense budget, and hiked funds for some social and antipoverty programs—was perhaps his greatest victory. Campaigning intensely and in person, Clinton and his allies managed to overcome defections from conservative Democrats. The plan barely passed the House (218 to 216) and the Senate (51 to 50, with Vice President Al Gore casting the tie-breaking vote). It was an important achievement: by raising taxes, especially in the higher-income brackets, the measure helped produce large budget surpluses by the late 1990s.

A legislative high point of Clinton's first term—congressional approval of the North American Free Trade Agreement (NAFTA) in late 1993—was the result of a bipartisan effort. Many Democrats, among them leaders of organized labor and such House figures as the House Democratic Whip, opposed the treaty. Clinton launched a high-profile public relations campaign, trumpeted the treaty's job-creation benefits, welcomed support from Republican leaders, and cut deals to meet individual legislators' objections. The legislation implementing NAFTA was a huge patchwork of provisions aimed at placating disparate interests. It included a program to retrain U.S. workers who lost their jobs because of competition from low-wage foreign firms. In the end, only 40 percent of House Democrats supported the president; but along with those of 132 Republicans, their 102 votes were enough to gain House approval. NAFTA then easily passed the Senate.

The NAFTA victory contained a valuable lesson in winning votes on Capitol Hill. The president's partisan allies cannot always be counted on for support, so opposition party lawmakers should never be written off in searching for votes. This maxim is even more important when supermajorities are required for passage—as in the 60 votes needed to end a Senate filibuster. As one reporter explained it, the White House

> had learned from the budget negotiations, in which each concession had led to demands for another, that it needed to be firm. And yet it could not be too combative, because it needed to attract two more Republican votes to break the filibuster.[17]

As a minority president working first with a fractious Capitol Hill majority (1993–1994) and then with a minority that was by turns disheartened (1995–1996), resurgent (1997), defensive (1998), and again emboldened (1999–2000), Clinton and his aides were obliged to forage for votes wherever they could find them. Threatening to veto congressional measures sometimes is needed to get members of Congress to see things the president's way. Over his first two years, Clinton was able to keep his veto pen in his pocket, becoming the first president since Millard Fillmore in the 1850s to not veto a single bill during an entire Congress (George W. Bush became the second).

Facing an aggressive GOP majority after 1994, Clinton actively played the veto card as a last-resort bargaining device. His tough bargaining goaded the Republicans into calling his bluff and shutting down the government on two occasions during the winter of 1995–1996—an impasse which the public blamed mainly on the GOP Congress. Resolving not to let this happen again, Republican leaders thereafter dealt more cautiously with the White House on spending bills. Anxious to end the divisive and unproductive 105th Congress in October 1998, GOP strategists opted to settle the funding disputes quickly while reminding voters of President Clinton's transgressions. It turned out, however, that citizens were impressed neither by Congress's productivity nor by the GOP's drive toward impeachment proceedings against Clinton.

George W. Bush, whose presidency rested on a contested election and who then faced Capitol Hill parties that were in virtual parity, had no choice but to build winning coalitions one at a time as congressional votes took place. As his legislative program was seemingly unraveling in mid-2001, he risked defeat on a popular "patients' rights" bill—setting federal rules in support of patients in suits against their health maintenance organizations (HMOs). The House was poised to enlarge patients' right to sue their HMOs beyond what Bush's corporate backers could support; yet Bush could not afford to veto such a popular measure. So the White House reached out to Representative Charlie Norwood (R-GA), a former dentist who had staked his career on this issue, even bucking his party leaders by cosponsoring a bipartisan HMO bill with, among others, senior Democrat John D. Dingell (MI).

When the two met in the Oval Office, President Bush opened with several minutes of lavish praise for Norwood's skill in outmaneuvering the administration. "So now that I've kissed your [rear end], what do I have to do to get a deal?" Bush asked.[18] They explored the two unresolved issues, and a deal was cut; the entire meeting lasted no more than 15 minutes. "Norwood told Bush he wanted to take the deal back to the Hill and discuss it with allies. 'The President wasn't going to let him off the property without going by the press first,' a Bush aide said." Norwood's allies from both parties were dismayed or angry at his decision to freelance behind their backs. "The deal had to be cut by somebody," Norwood said in defending his decision to go to the president and say, "What do we need to do to get your signature?"

The Bush-Norwood agreement was a textbook legislative bargain: A key legislator compromised in order to ensure that the president would not veto the measure, and the president modified his demands to ensure passage of the bill. "Norwood gives you the Good Housekeeping seal of approval," remarked an aide to then-Speaker J. Dennis Hastert (R-IL). "He will bring along a lot of undecided House members."[19] Norwood's reputation as a champion of the issue gave many moderate Republicans "political cover" to support the president and their party leaders. The crucial amendment—setting forth patients' rights in damage suits against HMOs—was adopted 218 to 213, with only six Republicans breaking ranks.

Mobilizing Public Pressure

In their efforts to goad members of Congress into agreement, presidents strive to mobilize public opinion.[20] White House staffs devote much time to gaining media attention and stimulating popular support. Presidents are better than Congress at exploiting the media, so they assume that media coverage will enhance their influence. The hope is that a "fireside chat," a nationally televised address, a carefully planned event, or a nationwide tour might be able to tap a vast reservoir of support "outside the beltway" that members of Congress dare not defy.

"Going public" on behalf of an issue is not without its risks. If the president already enjoys overall support on Capitol Hill, such extreme tactics are redundant. The president may raise expectations that cannot be fulfilled, make inept appeals, lose control over the issue, alienate legislators whose support is needed, or put forward hastily conceived proposals. Public persuasion can be a potent tactic, but overuse will dull its impact. Finally, although presidents enjoy unique advantages in capturing media and public attention, they are not the only political actors striving to sell their positions or programs. Many members of Congress attempt to bend public debate in their direction by staking out an issue or voicing a viewpoint in such a way that it attracts attention. Lobbying groups with deep pockets can mount media campaigns that mobilize not only their own members but the general public as well.

The meltdown of the Clinton administration's 1994 health care reform initiative showed the limitations of public appeals. President Clinton had trouble keeping the public spotlight on his message, especially after months were consumed in drafting the White House's bulky proposal. That delay gave skeptical lawmakers and threatened lobbying groups time to ferret out the plan's weaknesses and raise public doubts. Moreover, health-care providers and insurers—who comprise one of the nation's largest, wealthiest, and most predatory industries—outspent and outgunned the White House in reaching the public. A consortium of large insurance firms called the Health Insurance Association of America (HIAA) launched a simple but effective series of ads and media spots featuring "Harry and Louise," an average couple who voiced their worries over the complicated Clinton plan.

George W. Bush had mixed success in making public appeals. His moderately successful tenure was invigorated by the terrorists' attacks of September 11, 2001—when he assumed leadership by declaring a "war on terror" and thereafter launched attacks on Afghanistan, a known terrorist base of operations. But a prolonged second war against Saddam Hussein's regime in Iraq eventually faced mounting opposition—as had occurred in the wars in Korea (early 1950s) and Vietnam (late 1960s). Repeated speeches and events—that had initially evoked patriotic responses—eventually fell on indifferent ears. A major Bush domestic priority—reforming Social Security by privatizing individuals' accounts—utterly failed to catch fire despite scores of presidential speeches, statements, and staged meetings with citizens.

At the outset of his presidency, Barack Obama enjoyed personal public support hovering around 60 percent. And although citizens expressed misgivings about his specific policy initiatives, they still wanted him to press for action on such major issues as the economy, health care, and the deficit.[21]

The Obama White House sponsored appearances, speeches, and public forums highlighting the president's wide-ranging agenda. Organizing for America, a Democratic grass-roots group that grew out of the Obama campaign apparatus, launched a television ad campaign that recast the "Harry and Louise" ads that had helped scuttle the Clinton health care reforms in 1994. This time around, Harry and Louise favored Obama's effort to enact a universal health care plan. The TV spots targeted states represented by centrist Democrats as well as some Republicans.[22]

Affected industry groups—of which there are dozens in the money-rich health care field—challenged the president and aired their own viewpoints. The U.S. Chamber of Commerce, the nation's leading business lobby, launched a campaign against what it called "government-run health care." The chamber's Campaign for Responsible Health Reform ran print and online ads and flooded lawmakers' offices with letters and phone calls. Meanwhile, a more targeted campaign came from a biotechnology and pharmaceutical industry group called BIO—many of the same firms that had fought the Clinton health plan—that lobbied to give drug manufacturers longer periods of exclusive patent rights ("exclusivity") for their products, delaying their release as lower-cost generic compounds. (The opposing coalition, composed of seniors, consumer groups, pharmacy benefit managers, and health insurers, hoped to bring down drug costs through shorter "exclusivity" periods for manufacturers.)[23] Such conflicts—waged by multiple groups with deep pockets—may well be the central challenge of the Obama presidency.

Cultivating public favor and support will continue to figure prominently in White House efforts to prevail in legislative-executive struggles. Newly elected presidents are told to act quickly in order to capitalize on their early support and enact their agendas.

Every modern president, no matter how popular, faces the prospect that the initial "honeymoon period"—when public hopes and approval run high—can quickly fade. Popularity usually slips as the administration remains in office, repeatedly making decisions that alienate one group after another. For some presidents, such as Eisenhower and Reagan, the decline was minimal; for others—among them Truman, Johnson, Nixon, Ford, Carter, and Bush (father and son)—the decline was precipitous. Clinton's honeymoon hardly survived the wedding night. The second Bush endured a lackluster first nine months, but after 9/11 soared on the updraft of a prolonged public "rally" effect, which added luster to a number of his legislative initiatives; only in his second term did that support dissipate. Obama risked the same decline when his numerous initiatives confronted problems of cost and support.

Patterns of Inter-Branch Control

Of all the factors that affect inter-branch relations, partisan control is the most powerful. Both branches may be controlled by the same single party—party government, as this situation is commonly termed. Divided government occurs when Congress and the White House are in the hands of opposing parties—as happened over the final two years of George W. Bush's presidency. A third pattern, truncated majority, leaves the president's party controlling one but not both houses of Congress. Historically, this pattern has been rather rare. But for six years of Reagan's presidency—1981–1987—Republicans claimed the Senate but not the House. And after less than six months in office, George W. Bush saw the Senate shift from Republican to Democratic control until the 2002 elections restored full party control.

Party Government

For much of our history, the same party has tended to control the White House and both chambers of Congress. This was the case during about two-thirds of all the congresses throughout the 20th century. However, this orderly state of affairs has become less common than it once was: One-party control marked only 12 of the 29 Congresses that convened between 1945 and 2007. During much of this period, tensions between White House and Capitol Hill were high.

Eras of true legislative harmony—party government in the parliamentary sense of the term—are relatively rare in this country. There have been only four over the last century: Wilson's first administration (1913–1917); Franklin Roosevelt's celebrated

"New Deal" (1933–1936); the balmiest days of Lyndon Johnson's "Great Society" (1963–1966); and George W. Bush's six-year mastery of Congress (2001–2007). These flowed from unique convergences of a forceful chief executive, a popular but unfulfilled policy agenda, and a Congress responsive to presidential leadership. For good or ill, these were periods of active lawmaking that produced landmark legislation and innovative governmental programs.

Periods of party government as productive as these four are not free of problems, of course. Lawmaking may be so fast-paced and sweeping that political and governmental entities require years to absorb the new programs and their costs. Succeeding generations may reconsider, retrench, or even reverse over-ambitious or ineffective programs.

Nor does partisan control of the two branches guarantee legislative success. Although Congress boasted Democratic majorities during all but four years from the late 1930s until the mid-1960s, its affairs actually were dominated by a conservative coalition of southern Democrats and Republicans. The coalition's ascendancy over domestic policy outlasted several presidents of varying goals and skills. It succeeded in thwarting civil rights and social legislation pushed by Roosevelt, Harry S. Truman, and later John F. Kennedy. The later case of Jimmy Carter is more complicated; but despite huge Democratic majorities in both chambers his legislative record was mixed. George W. Bush's legislative majorities were more modest. His first four years in office were quite successful; but his second, lame-duck term found his fellow Republicans splintered over the course of public policies. The Obama administration's record with Democratic majorities on Capitol Hill has yet to play out.

Divided Government

Divided government has been more common in modern times. It marked all of Nixon's, Ford's, Reagan's, and George H. W. Bush's presidencies, all but two years of Eisenhower's and Clinton's, and two years of Harry Truman's and George W. Bush's. Under divided government, inter-branch relationships range from lukewarm to hostile. During the Eisenhower administration, Democratic Congresses usually refrained from attacking the popular president, developing instead modest legislative alternatives and pushing them in election years. Hostility marked relations between Truman and the Republican Congress of 1947–1948, which he labeled the "awful 80th Congress" during his barnstorming 1948 reelection campaign. The same hostility marked relations between Nixon and Democratic Congresses (1969–1974), between Clinton and Republican ones (1995–2001), and between George W. Bush and the Democratic 110th Congress (2007–2009).

The most recent period of divided control underscores the frustration and stalemate that can result. Believing that their successes in the 2006 elections flowed from public weariness over the Iraq war, Democratic leaders sought to act upon their policy disagreements by pushing a series of measures aimed at setting timetables for withdrawing troops and other conditions for continued funding. All were thwarted by presidential vetoes or the failure to curb GOP filibusters in the Senate. The Democrats' achievements were few but significant: a new ethics package, a long-overdue hike in the minimum wage, and a significant energy bill. But Congress's public image continued to sag: 70 percent of the respondents in a *NBC News / Wall Street Journal* poll in January 2008 disapproved of performance on Capitol Hill, and only 18 percent approved—scores almost as bad as just before the 2006 elections, and not very different that the president's own dismal ratings.[24]

Even if Congress does not prevail in situations of divided control, it has weapons that can embarrass the administration and stall its initiatives. One weapon is legislative oversight—the ability to hold public hearings and issue reports concerning alleged mismanagement of federal programs. Assessing the new Democratic Congress in 2007, Thomas E. Mann and his colleagues observed that "[A]fter years of inattention, congressional oversight of the executive has intensified, most sharply regarding the war in Iraq."[25] Domestically, charges that partisan politics governed the removal of several U.S. attorneys, for example, damaged George W. Bush's administration and led to the resignation of several key Justice Department officials, including Attorney General Alberto Gonzales. Another is withholding action on presidential nominations. During Bush's final two years, Senate committees declined to act upon dozens of appointees, especially federal judgeships. Democrats' hopes for a partisan shift in the White House after the 2008 elections were part of the story, but the conflict went deeper. "This is a natural consequence of insults to the Senate over five or six years," noted Paul C. Light, a leading scholar. "The process has just completely broken down."[26]

Divided government does not preclude inter-branch cooperation or legislative productivity. Despite divided party control, legislative activity was extraordinarily high during the Nixon and Ford presidencies and during Reagan's first year. Some scholars contend that the supposed benefits of unified party control have been exaggerated. David R. Mayhew found that unified or divided control made little difference in enactment of important legislation or launching of high-profile congressional investigations of executive-branch misdeeds. His follow-up study of the Clinton and George W. Bush presidencies seemed to confirm this conclusion: "On the lean evidence," he writes, "unified party control was not a superior supplier of legislative volume."[27] My own examination of legislative productivity levels revealed, as well, that they corresponded imperfectly with presidential administrations, whether with united or divided party control.[28]

Yet, divided government exacts a long-term price in terms of policy stalemate. Uncommon leadership and skillful inter-branch bargaining are required to overcome divergent political stakes and resultant inertia. Frustration in achieving their policy goals psychologically wears down presidents, legislators, and their staffs. Policy decisions may be deferred or compromised so severely that the solutions have little impact. Voters find it difficult to hold presidents and lawmakers accountable, as each blames the other for failing to resolve pressing national problems or enact coherent policies.

Assessing Presidential Influence

Shifts of influence between the White House and Capitol Hill are a recurrent feature of American politics. Scholars are tempted to designate certain eras as times of "congressional government" and others of "presidential dominance." There is surely an ebb and flow of power between the two branches, but one must be cautious in generalizing about them.

Passage of presidentially supported measures is a starting point. Indeed, the rate at which such measures are passed is a common index of presidential success. Influence over legislation is difficult to measure with certainty, however. Who really initiates legislation? A president can draw publicity by articulating a proposal and giving it currency, but its real origins are likely to be embedded in years of political agitation, congressional hearings, or academic discussion.

What exactly is "the president's program"? Major proposals are adopted and trumpeted by the president; but what of minor proposals? Franklin Roosevelt's New Deal successes of the 1930s are regarded as a high-water mark of presidential leadership; but aside from emergency measures approved quickly during his first hundred days, his legislative agenda drew heavily on proposals already introduced and incubated on Capitol Hill. Lyndon Johnson liked to announce support for measures already assured of passage in order to boost his record of success. Bill Clinton's first year (1993) boasted the most successful post-Johnson legislative record, but some of the enactments were long-standing Democratic party agenda items stalled by White House vetoes during the Reagan-Bush years—for example, the Family and Medical Leave Act, the "Motor Voter" registration plan, and the Brady handgun control bill.[29] A number of George W. Bush's most publicized achievements—for example, creation of the 9/11 Commission and the Department of Homeland Security, as well as reforming the government's intelligence network—were initiated on Capitol Hill; some were at first stoutly resisted by the White House. In other words, not all White House–endorsed measures really "belong to" the president; not all weigh equally in the president's agenda.

Finally, who actually wields the decisive influence in enacting a piece of legislation? Presidential lobbying may tip the scales, but no legislation passes Congress without help from many quarters. Lawrence H. Chamberlain's pioneering study of 90 laws (1873–1940) found that presidential influence predominated in only about one-fifth of the cases; more than half of those occurred during the New Deal years of the 1930s.[30] Congressional influence dominated in almost 40 percent of the laws, and joint presidential-congressional influence in about one-third. In a few cases, mainly tariff laws, interest groups were the dominant force. Chamberlain's findings demonstrate "the joint character of the American legislative process."[31]

The seemingly inexorable growth of the presidency in the modern era has done little to alter these findings. From their examination of 12 categories of laws (1940–1967), Ronald C. Moe and Steven C. Teel concluded that "Congress continues to be an active innovator and very much in the legislative business."[32] More recent investigations have yielded identical conclusions.[33] Because lawmaking is such a cooperative enterprise in our system, White House influence over legislation should not be exaggerated.

The legislative-executive balance of power is in constant flux. The influence of either branch can be affected by issues, circumstances, or personalities. Exhibit A was Clinton's roller-coaster ride with Congress and the American people—which produced several distinct phases of executive-legislative relations. Exhibit B was his successor's regime, which passed through at least three phases: a moderately productive pre-9/11 period, an extremely successful post-9/11 period, and a conflict-laden second term. So even within a single administration, the pendulum of power can swing back and forth several times.

Nor are legislative-executive struggles necessarily zero-sum games. If one branch gains power, it does not necessarily mean that the other loses it. Even when one branch is eclipsed, it may exert potent influence. When Clinton's agenda-setting role atrophied, for example, his veto and rule-making powers could still be deployed skillfully and cunningly. Bush, his successor, declared war on terrorists and then linked the war to a discretionary invasion of Iraq; in the process Congress ceded much of its constitutional authority over military matters. When the public tired of the Iraqi venture and its side effects, however, Congress began to insist upon its right to set conditions and even timetables for the conflict.

Expanded governmental authority since World War II has augmented the authority of both branches. Yet believers in representative democracy now confront troubling times. "The default position between presidents and Congress has moved toward the presidential end of the inter-branch spectrum—and irreversibly so," is Andrew Rudalevige's bleak judgment. "Presidents have regained freedom of unilateral action in a variety of areas, from executive privilege to war powers to covert operations to campaign spending."[34] Congress's prerogatives are under siege not only from aggressive executive officials but also from activist federal judges and elite opinion makers—who repeatedly belittle its capacities and evade its scrutiny.

Yet lawmakers themselves are to blame for yielding all too often to the initiatives of executives (and others)—for failing to ask hard questions and to demand straight answers. Congress too frequently retreats from its constitutional stature as an initiator of national policy and an overseer of government operations. It has ceded too much ground to executives, bureaucrats, courts, and even private entities. As a result, Congress has fallen distressingly—but hopefully not irreversibly—short of the Founders' vision that it should be the "first branch of government."

Endnotes

1. James Sterling Young, *The Washington Community, 1800–1828* (New York: Columbia University Press, 1966), pp. 75–76.
2. Edward S. Corwin, *The President: Office and Powers, 1787–1957* (New York: New York University Press, 1957), p. 69.
3. Charlie Savage, *Takeover: The Return of the Imperial Presidency and the Subversion of American Democracy* (New York: Little, Brown & Co, 2007), pp. 224–227. Savage, a national legal reporter for the Boston Globe, won a 2007 Pulitzer Prize for his exposure of White House signing statements.
4. Savage, "Three GOP Senators Blast Bush Bid to Bypass Torture Ban," *Boston Globe*, (January 5, 2006).
5. Alexander Hamilton, James Madison, and John Jay, *The Federalist Papers*, Clinton Rossiter, ed., (New York: Mentor, 1961), p. 308.
6. Susan Page, "GAO Chief, Cheney Barreling toward Showdown," *USA Today* (February 18, 2002), p. 6A.
7. On the pre-modern history of inter-branch relations, see James L. Sundquist's masterful survey, *The Decline and Resurgence of Congress* (Washington, DC: The Brookings Institution, 1981).

8. Louis Fisher, *Presidential War Power*, 2nd revised ed., (Lawrence: University Press of Kansas, 2004), p. 261.
9. George C. Edwards, *At the Margins* (New Haven: Yale University Press, 1989).
10. John H. Aldrich, *Why Parties? The Origin and Transformation of Party Politics in America* (Chicago: University of Chicago Press, 1995); Aldrich and David W. Rohde, "The Consequences of Party Organization in the House: The Role of the Majority and Minority Parties in Conditional Party Government," in Jon R. Bond and Richard Fleisher, eds, *Polarized Politics: Congress and the President in a Partisan Era* (Washington, DC: CQ Press, 2000), pp. 31–72.
11. Mark Liebovich, "Absent Voice on Health Bill Is Resonating," *The New York Times* (July 17, 2009), p. A 1.
12. National Commission on Terrorist Attacks Upon the United States, *The 9/11 Report* (New York: St. Martin's Paperbacks, 2004), pp. 596–599.
13. Don Wolfensberger, "Climate Change Bill Wins on Political Energy Boost," *Roll Call*, (July 7, 2009), p. 6.
14. Quoted in *Congressional Quarterly Weekly Report* 39 (July 4, 1981): 1169.
15. Stephen J. Wayne, *The Legislative Presidency* (New York: Harper & Row, 1978), p.142.
16. The incident is entertainingly recounted in Thomas P. O'Neill, Jr. (with William Novak), *Man of the House: The Life and Political Memoirs of Speaker Tip O'Neill* (New York: St. Martin's Press, 1987), pp. 371–372.
17. Steven Waldman, *The Bill* (New York: Viking Books, 1995), p. 213.
18. Dana Milbank and Juliet Eilperin, "On Patients' Rights Deal, Bush Scored with a Full-Court Press," *The Washington Post* (August 3, 2001) p. A9.
19. Robert Pear, "Bush Strikes Deal on a Bill Defining Rights of Patients," *The New York Times* (August 2, 2001), p. A16.
20. Samuel Kernell, *Going Public: New Strategies of Presidential Leadership*, 3rd ed. (Washington, DC: CQ Press, 1997).
21. Dan Balz and Jon Cohen, "Poll Shows Obama Slipping on Key Issues," *The Washington Post* (July 20, 2009), p. Al.
22. Christi Parsons and Noam N. Levey, "Obama Takes Health Care Debate and Runs with It," *Los Angeles Times* (July 21, 2009), p. Al; Christi Parsons, "Amid Criticism, Obama Kicks Health Care Drive Up a Gear," *Los Angeles Times* (July 22, 2009), p. A18.
23. Kate Ackley, "An Ad Blitz that Really Worked?" *Roll Call* (July 15, 2009), p. 9.
24. "Current Opinion," *Roll Call* (January 31, 2008), p. 4.
25. Thomas E. Mann, Molly Reynolds, and Peter Hoey, "Is Congress on the Mend?" *The New York Times* (April 28, 2007), p. A27.
26. Quoted in James Gerstenzang, "Prospects Are Dim for Bush Nominees," *Los Angeles Times* (February 7, 2008), p. A12.
27. David R. Mayhew, *Divided We Govern: Party Control, Lawmaking and Investigations, 1946–2002*, 2nd ed. (New Haven: Yale University Press, 2005), p. 215.
28. Roger H. Davidson, "The Presidency and Congressional Time," in James A. Thurber, ed., *Rivals for Power: Cooperation and Conflict between the President and Congress*, 2nd ed. (Lanham, MD: Rowman & Littlefield, 2006), pp. 125–149.
29. Phil Duncan and Steve Langdon, "When Congress Had to Choose, It Voted to Back Clinton," *Congressional Quarterly Weekly Report* (December 18, 1992), pp. 3427–343l.
30. Lawrence H. Chamberlain, *The President, Congress and Legislation* (New York: Columbia University Press, 1946), pp. 460–462.
31. Chamberlain, p. 453.
32. Ronald C. Moe and Steven C. Teel, "Congress as Policy-Maker: A Necessary Reappraisal," *Political Science Quarterly* 85 (September 1970): p. 469.
33. Mark A. Peterson, *Legislating Together: The White House and Capitol Hill from Eisenhower to Reagan* (Cambridge: Harvard University Press, 1990); Mayhew, *Divided We Govern.*
34. Andrew Rudalevige, *The New Imperial Presidency* (Ann Arbor: University of Michigan Press, 2005), p. 261.

Sarah A. Binder

The Disappearing Political Center

Thus far, one of the big stories of [recent] congressional elections is not who is running, but who is quitting. Most notably, these retirements are speeding along the thinning of the political center—the "incredible shrinking middle," as one senator calls it.

Within the Republican party, the moderate wing occupies the political center—that is, it is closer ideologically to the midpoint between the two parties than to its own party's ideological center. And retirements threaten to eliminate Republican moderates from Capitol Hill. . . . Among Democrats the party's conservative wing is closest to the political center. And it too is being depleted.

The result, many worry, is an unprecedented disappearance of the political center. In a political system that demands compromise and accommodation to bring about change, the center is considered vital to the moderate, bipartisan public policymaking generally preferred by the American public. Absent a political center, increased partisanship and ideological polarization are inevitable—and sure to feed public distrust of and distaste for politicians and the political process.

Whither the Center?

The political center in Congress has shrunk markedly over the past 15 years (Figure 27.1). Hovering around 30 percent of House and Senate members in the 1960s and 1970s, the percentage of centrists in each chamber began slipping in the 1980s, and it has fallen to about 10 percent today. Centrists now can claim 11.3 percent of the House, down from 20 percent or more during the 1980s. And after peaking at 32.3 percent of the Senate during 1969–70, the first term of the Nixon administration, centrists make up less than 10 percent of today's Senate.

The broadly similar declines in both chambers conceal several notable differences between the House and Senate and their two parties. In the House, both conservative Democrats and moderate Republicans have seen their ranks gradually thin

Source: Reprinted from *The Brookings Review* 15 (Fall 1996), 36–39

Figure 27.1 Size of the Political Center, 1959–96

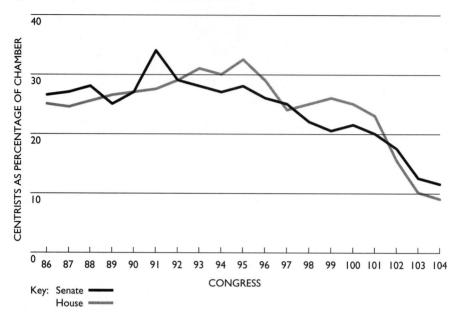

Note: "Centrists" are defined as those members or senators whose ideological positions on a liberal conservative dimension place them closer to the ideological mid-point between the two parties than in the median member of their own party. Ideological scores are drawn from first dimension coordinates of D NOMINATE and W NOMINATE scores calculated by Keith Poole and Howard Rosenthal from congressional roll call data. NOMINATE scores for the 104th Congress (1995–96) are based on the roll call votes through December 1995. See Keith T. Poole and Howard Rosenthal, "Patterns of Congressional Voting," *American Journal of Political Science*, February 1991.

since the early 1970s. But the conservative Democratic faction has consistently been larger than the moderate wing of the Republican conference since the late 1950s. Today conservative Democrats in the House still outnumber moderate Republicans three to one.

In the Senate, centrists of both parties actually increased sporadically from the mid–1960s to the mid–1970s before starting to decline during the late 1970s. However, the most striking development in the Senate has been the depletion of conservative Democrats, whose numbers made up nearly a quarter of Senate Democrats during the late 1980s but in recent years claim only a handful.

Are Retirements to Blame?

The conventional wisdom is that voluntary retirements are newly driving the demise of the middle as House and Senate centrists find themselves too out of step with their parties to seek reelection.

As it turns out, the retirement of conservative Democrats in the House is nothing new. Conservative Democrats consistently made up the lion's share of their party's House retirements in every election save two between 1968 and 1978. But though conservative Democrats retired at very high rates during the 1970s, their contingent shrank only incrementally, suggesting that retiring conservative Democrats tended to be replaced by like-minded lawmakers. What *is* new is that Democratic conservatives who are once again showing an increased tendency to retire—particularly in the 1994 election and in the upcoming fall elections—are no longer being replaced by their own kind. Southern voters instead are electing conservative Republicans. The overall size of the Democrats' right-leaning wing is steadily shrinking.

Out of step with their more liberal colleagues, often unable to swallow the policy prescriptions of the new Republican majority, and facing voters who now prefer conservative Republicans to themselves, House Democratic conservatives (save those who jumped ship and switched to the Republican party) have little incentive to stay in the House. Observed retiring Pete Peterson (D-FL), "I have worked as a bridge-builder to find bipartisan solutions to our nation's problems. Unfortunately, the current political climate has rendered this approach ineffective."

Unlike their Democratic colleagues, moderate House Republicans have shown little distinctive inclination to retire, either now or in the past. . . . The steady decline of moderate Republicans since the early 1970s suggest that electoral defeat and replacement by more conservative Republicans, not retirement, has been at work. Although moderate Republicans make up less than 10 percent of the House Republican conference, they are not showing their discouragement by retiring. . . . The Republicans' slim majority in the House clearly enhances the leverage of their small moderate wing. In times past, recalled moderate Sherwood Bochlert (R-NY) early this year, Republican moderates got "more attention and consideration from the Democratic majority side than they did from the leadership of the Republican majority. That has changed."

In the Senate, most retirements among centrists are by Republicans, not Democrats. In fact the thinning of conservative Democratic ranks does not appear to have been driven by voluntary retirements. . . . The abrupt drop in the number of conservative Senate Democrats in recent years appears to be, again, more the result of the emergency of a conservative Republican electorate in the South than of voluntary retirements. To be sure, over time these two forces are likely to complement each other: As conservative Democrats are replaced by Republicans or in some cases by liberal Democrats, the more isolated their remaining political soul mates likely feel and the more likely they are to retire.

Among Senate Republicans, the retirement of moderates has only lately begun taking its toll on the dwindling center. The gradual rightward shift of Senate Republicans in the past, it seems, has primarily been driven by election results, not voluntary retirements. This year is an important exception, as Republican moderates are calling it quits before testing the electoral waters. Seeing their numbers shrunk by electoral forces in recent years and finding themselves increasingly isolated by their more conservative and homogeneous Republican colleagues, moderate Republicans are strongly inclined to give up their Senate seats. Democratic Senator John Breaux of Louisiana described their predicament best: ". . . Those in the middle, [he] noted, have to have someone to meet with. You can't meet with yourself in a phone booth."

A Congress without a Political Center

The shrinking political center has left Congress increasingly polarized (Figure 27.2). Democrats are perched on the left, Republicans on the right, in both the House and the Senate as the ideological centers of the two parties have moved markedly apart. The change since the late 1980s is most extreme for the Senate, but striking for both chambers. From the late 1950s until well into the 1980s, the ideological distance between the centers of the two parties became more homogeneous. Since the 1980s, the distance between the two parties has essentially doubled.

Some observers might see the parties' movement toward ideological extremes as a benign, if not positive, development. Advocates of stronger political parties, for example, have bemoaned a political system that encourages the two major parties to drift toward the center. A disappearing center reflects to some extent the emergence

Figure 27.2 Ideological Distance between Congressional Parties, 1959–96

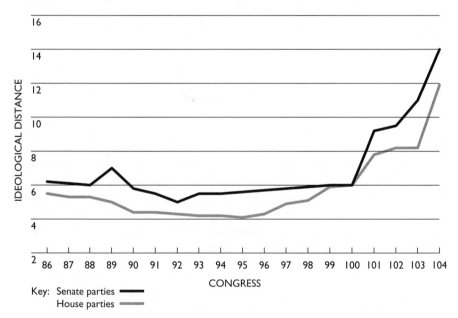

Note: Ideological distance is the absolute difference between the median Democrat and median Republican in each chamber, based on Poole and Rosenthal's NOMINATE scores (see notes to Figure 1).

of more cohesive and homogeneous legislative parties. And as the distance between the two parties grows, their philosophical differences on such matters as the appropriate role and reach of the federal government become more pronounced, giving voters a real choice between political agendas.

But the movement away from the center has been accompanied by a coarsening of politics and bitter partisanship—leaving voters increasingly disenchanted with Washington politics. Political discord has played itself out in part in an apparent decline in congressional comity. Senator Robert Byrd noted scathingly last year, "There have been giants in this Senate, and I have seen some of them. Little did I know when I came here that I would live to see pygmies."

The polarized environment has also made it hard for members of both parties to meet in the center to forge compromise. As former majority leader Bob Dole lamented in retiring from the Senate, "None of us has a perfect solution. But there's got to be some solution of where we can come together, Republicans and Democrats." The farther apart the two parties, the tougher it is to negotiate compromise, partly because fewer members are positioned in the center and partly because there is little incentive for others to reach into the middle. In the Senate, for example, Republicans this year adopted a new party rule that requires party leaders and committee chairs (who now must be confirmed by secret ballot) to pledge allegiance to a legislative agenda at the start of each Congress. Reaching across party lines is unlikely to be rewarded in such a partisan climate—something Senator John Chafee discovered after trying unsuccessfully to negotiate a bipartisan solution to the health care debate in 1994. In the House, several moderate Republicans were passed over for committee chairmanships when their party captured the majority in 1994. Carlos Moorhead, a conservative Republican from California with a reputation for conciliation, was in line to chair both the Commerce Committee and the Judiciary Committee and failed to get either—because, his chief aide contended, Speaker Newt Gingrich had let it be known that Moorhead was "just not mean enough."

Increased polarization may have the most profound effects in the Senate. Unlike the House, where simple partisan majorities can prevail over minority opposition, bipartisan agreement is all but essential in the Senate. Unless the majority in the Senate has a filibuster-proof roster of 60 senators consistently willing to cut off debate, it will continually be stymied by minority opposition. Much of the legislation that grew out of the House Republican Contract with America in 1995 languished and died in the Senate despite the support of the majority—a fate that illustrates well the effects of ideologically distant parties in the Senate.

Of course, the ideological centers of the two parties are not fixed in stone. In fact, as the congressional elections approach, many voters seem apprehensive about the excesses of the Republican majority, and congressional Democrats seem determined to moderate their platform and image. It may be that voters will nudge the two parties back to the center—giving the political center a reprieve from its predicted demise.

John Anthony Maltese

Presidents and the Judicial Appointment Process

As the controversy over Barack Obama's nomination of Sonia Sotomayor reminded us, Supreme Court justices are among the most important (and contentious) nominations that presidents send to the Senate. As a tool for influencing judicial policymaking, Supreme Court appointments are an important exercise of presidential power. They are also a test of presidential strength, because the Senate retains the constitutional power to offer "advise and consent" (and thus confirm or reject) nominees.

Sotomayor was eventually confirmed by a vote of 68 to 31 in August 2009. George W. Bush's nominees also provoked controversy and garnered a substantial number of negative votes (Samuel A. Alito, Jr. was confirmed by a vote of 58 to 42, and John G. Roberts, Jr. was confirmed by a vote of 78 to 22). In stark contrast, the earlier nominations of Antonin Scalia and John Paul Stevens (both whom would surely provoke controversy if they faced the confirmation process today) sailed through the Senate by a votes of 98 to 0.

Such lopsided votes were common until Ronald Reagan's controversial nomination of Robert Bork in 1987. Bork was nominated to replace a "swing" voter on the nine-member Court who broke the tie between two blocks of four justices. Bork's predecessor leaned toward the more liberal block of four justices; Bork did not. Therefore he was a potentially "transformative" appointment: one that could have led to the reversal of a number of closely decided liberal-leaning 5-4 decisions including the 1973 abortion rights decision, *Roe v. Wade*, 410 U.S. 113. Interest groups mobilized with fury and the Senate rejected Bork by a vote of 58 to 42, not because he was unqualified but simply because of how he would vote if he got on the Court. Many justices had been defeated before Bork, but never so openly because of how they would vote if confirmed. The fact that the Senate now considered it legitimate to judge confirmation on such a basis transformed the process and led to the close votes of many recent nominees.

More recently, Harriet Miers (nominated by George W. Bush in 2005) withdrew her nomination before the Senate could even hold hearings on her. Like Bork in 1987, Miers was nominated to replace a "swing" voter on the Court, thereby making

Source: Original essay written for this volume.

her a potentially "transformative" appointment who could move the Court to the right. President Bush's conservative base had waited years for this opportunity. They were stunned when Bush failed to nominate a tried and true conservative and instead turned to the unknown Miers, a longtime friend.

William Kristol, a leading conservative, wrote that the Miers nomination left him "disappointed, depressed, and demoralized." "It is very hard to avoid the conclusion that President Bush flinched from a fight on constitutional philosophy," Kristol wrote, adding that the nomination appeared to reflect "a combination of cronyism and capitulation on the part of the president." "Surely," he concluded, "this is a pick from weakness."[1] George Will went even further, arguing that Miers was unqualified for a post on the Supreme Court. "It is not important that she be confirmed," he wrote, "because there is no evidence that she is among the leading lights of American jurisprudence, or that she possesses talents commensurate with the Supreme Court's tasks. The president's 'argument' for her amounts to: Trust me. There is no reason to. . . ."[2]

In the coming days, the White House did nothing to improve Miers' standing. President Bush, in a clumsy attempt to win over conservatives, pointed to her religious faith as a justification for her nomination.[3] Meanwhile, former Indiana Senator Dan Coats, who led the White House effort to shepherd the Miers nomination through the Senate, made an embarrassing attempt to turn charges of Meirs' mediocrity into a virtue: "If a great intellectual powerhouse is a requirement to be a member of the court and represent the American people and the wishes of the American people and to interpret the Constitution, then I think we have a court so skewed on the intellectual side that we may not be getting representation of America as a whole."[4] In the end, both the Republican and Democratic leaders of the Senate Judiciary Committee publicly rebuked Miers for her "incomplete" and "inadequate" answers to a detailed questionnaire from the committee.[5] A week later, she withdrew and Bush nominated a tried a true conservative: Samuel Alito.

Miers and Bork are just the latest in a long list of failed Supreme Court nominations. If one excludes consecutive nominations of the same individual by the same president for the same seat on the Supreme Court,[6] there have been 151 nominations to the Supreme Court submitted to the Senate through President Obama's 2009 nomination of Sotomayor. Of these 151 nominations, seven of the nominees declined,[7] one died before taking office,[8] and one expected vacancy failed to materialize.[9] Yet another (Bush's nomination of John Roberts to fill Sandra Day O'Connor's associate justice seat) was withdrawn before Senate action and then re-submitted to fill a different seat. Of the 141 remaining nominations, 115 were confirmed by the Senate. The other 26 may be classified as "failed" nominations, because Senate opposition blocked them: The Senate rejected 12 by roll-call vote,[10] voted to postpone or table another five,[11] and passively rejected five others by taking no action.[12] Presidents withdrew the remaining four in the face of strong opposition.[13] The number of "failed" nominations rises to 27 if Douglas Ginsburg (whose nomination was announced by Ronald Reagan, but withdrawn before it was officially transmitted to the Senate) is included.[14]

The failure rate of Supreme Court nominees is the highest for any appointive post requiring Senate confirmation.[15] That is indicative of the profound effect that

Supreme Court appointments can have on public policy. By defining privacy rights, interpreting the First Amendment, setting guidelines for the treatment of criminal defendants, and exercising its power of judicial review in a host of other areas, the Supreme Court establishes public policy. So do the more than 800 judges who serve on lower federal courts (and who are also nominated by the president and subject to the "advice and consent" of the Senate).

In theory, impartial judges objectively applying the law according to set standards of interpretation should all reach the same "correct" outcome in cases that come before them. But, in practice, there are very different views among judges about how to interpret legal texts. Moreover, judges are human beings who are influenced, at least in part, by their backgrounds, personal predilections, and judicial philosophies. Quite simply, different judges can–and do–reach different conclusions when confronted with the same case. Thus, participants in the federal judicial appointment process often use it as a way to influence policy outcomes.

In a 1969 memo to President Richard Nixon, White House aide Tom Charles Huston noted that judicial nominations were "perhaps the least considered aspect of Presidential power. . . . *In approaching the bench, it is necessary to remember that the decision as to who will make the decisions affects what decisions will be made.* That is, the role the judiciary will play in different historical eras depends as much on the type of men who become judges as it does on the constitutional rules which appear to [guide them]." Thus, Huston urged Nixon to set specific criteria for the types of judges to be nominated in an effort to influence judicial policy making. If the president "establishes *his* criteria and establishes *his* machinery for insuring that the criteria are met, the appointments will be *his*, in fact, as in theory."[16] In response, Nixon wrote: "RN *agrees*. Have this analysis in mind when making judicial nominations."[17]

Despite Nixon's approval, it was not until Ronald Reagan that presidents created formal institutional mechanisms for screening federal judicial nominees to ensure that they reflected the administration's ideology. Reagan created the President's Committee on Federal Judicial Selection, staffed by representatives of the White House and the Justice Department, to conduct the screening. Political scientist Sheldon Goldman called the innovation "the most systematic judicial philosophical screening of candidates ever seen in the nation's history."[18] Critics deemed the screening an ideological litmus test, and members of his administration did not seem to disagree. White House counsel Fred Fielding said the system was designed to choose "people of a certain judicial philosophy," and Attorney General Edwin Meese III said that it was a way to "institutionalize the Reagan revolution so it can't be set aside no matter what happens in future elections."[19] And so, faced with judicial nominees chosen by Republicans because of their conservative ideology, Democrats in the Senate began to exert their power to withhold consent based on ideology. That is what led to the 1987 defeat of Robert Bork.

The Bork nomination was unprecedented in the history of Supreme Court confirmation politics in terms of the breadth of involvement by organized interests, the degree of grassroots support that these groups generated, the extensive use of marketing techniques in the confirmation struggle, the length and detail of Bork's public testimony before the Senate Judiciary Committee, and the number of witnesses appearing at the televised hearings. The process even generated a new verb: to *bork*, which means unleashing a lobbying and public relations campaign designed to defeat a nominee.

Bork's defeat was the culmination of a series of factors that came together to create an epic battle. His was certainly not the first contentious confirmation battle.[20] His was not even the first nomination to be "borked" (George Washington's nomination of John Rutledge in 1795 arguably has that distinction),[21] nor was he the first nominee to face active interest group opposition (groups had actively opposed nominees at least as early as the nomination of Stanley Matthews in 1881,[22] and had been largely responsible for defeating several nominees before Bork, including John J. Parker in 1930 and Clement Haynsworth in 1969).[23] Still, as similar as some early confirmation battles were to Bork's in various ways, there was an important difference: throughout the nineteenth century, Senate consideration of Supreme Court nominees had usually taken place behind closed doors. In 1881, *The New York Times* reported that the "Judiciary Committee of the Senate is the most mysterious committee in that body, and succeeds better than any other in maintaining secrecy as to its proceedings."[24] Even floor debate on nominees was usually held in executive session. Under Senate rules, floor debate on all nominations remained closed unless two-thirds of the Senate voted to open it – a rare occurrence. In addition, the Senate usually acted quickly on nominations, with both committee action and floor debate often taking place with little discussion and no roll-call votes. This meant that external actors, such as interest groups, seldom had either the time or the opportunity to influence the Senate confirmation process. Secrecy, and the fact that senators were not popularly elected but chosen by state legislatures, meant that retaliation against senators after the fact was also difficult: Interest groups might not even know how senators voted and, when they did, the method of choosing senators undermined the potent threat of electoral retaliation that interest groups now possess.

Both of these impediments to interest group involvement were removed in the 20th century. The ratification of the Seventeenth Amendment to the Constitution in 1913 led to the direct election senators, and Senate rules changes in 1929 opened floor debate on nominations on a regular basis. In turn, the Senate Judiciary Committee opened its hearings to the public. By the time Bork was nominated, the hearings were routinely televised. All this gave interest groups more power. Not only did they now have access to information, they could generate free publicity for their position by sending representatives to testify at the televised hearings. And, by the 1980s, the number of interest groups had increased dramatically, their rhetoric concerning nominees had intensified, and what had once been sporadic involvement in the Supreme Court appointment process was now routine.

Modern presidents reacted to changes in the confirmation process by developing their own strategic resources to help secure confirmation of their nominees. Presidents now have an unprecedented – though not always successful – ability to communicate directly with the American people, to mobilize interest groups, and to lobby the Senate. For each of these areas, specialized White House staff units have evolved to advise presidents and to implement strategic initiatives. The modern institutional presidency is a system of government centered in the White House, a system in which presidents and their staff oversee the formulation and implementation of policy.

Increasingly contentious confirmation battles have made presidents even more reliant on centralized resources to mobilize public opinion, generate group support, and lobby senators to combat opponents of their judicial nominees. Still, there are examples of the failure of such resources. Many suggested, for example, that initial attempts by the Bush administration to sell its nomination of Harriet Miers in 2005 were botched, and the resources at Reagan's disposal in 1987 did not save the Bork nomination.

Another significant change that affected the Bork battle was the emergence of nominee testimony. Until 1925, no Supreme Court nominee had ever testified. Most refused any public comment whatsoever. (Likewise, most presidents at that time refused publicly to discuss their nominees.) It is only since 1955 that every Supreme Court nominee has testified.[25] The Supreme Court's landmark school desegregation ruling in *Brown v. Board Education*, 347 U.S. 483 (1954), served as a catalyst for that change. After *Brown*, many southern Democrats insisted on questioning nominees about their judicial philosophy – part of an effort to denounce what they saw as the Court's activism in that case. Such questioning set a precedent for liberals to question Bork about his judicial philosophy.

The trend toward divided government, with one party controlling the White House and another controlling the Senate, also played an important role in the Bork defeat (when a Republican controlled the White House and Democrats controlled the Senate). Divided government was rare before World War II, but has been commonplace since 1969. From 1969 through 2005, the same party controlled the White House and the Senate for only 15 out of 37 years, and the same party controlled the White House and both houses of Congress for only nine of those 37. When the opposition party controls the Senate, the rejection rate of judicial nominees increases considerably.[26] At the Supreme Court level, the statistics are striking: close to 90 percent approval of nominees during unified government, but only about 55 percent approval when the White House and the Senate are controlled by rival parties. Arguably, divided government encourages both the president and Congress to have a stake in each other's failure.

Along with the recent trend of divided government has come a pronounced increase in partisanship. Parties in Congress have become more polarized, with a dramatic increase in partisan voting. Since the mid-1990s, the Senate, as measured by party votes, is even more partisan than the House of Representatives.[27] At the same time, partisanship is up among the electorate: Party loyalty has increased, ticket splitting has decreased, and the ideological gap between members of the two parties has widened.[28]

Polarized politics has contributed to the ongoing "confirmation mess,"and has led to a dramatic partisan wedge, illustrated by the gap in public support for President George W. Bush between Democrats and Republicans. An analysis by political scientist Gary C. Jacobson of 28 public opinion polls taken between Bush's inauguration and the terrorist attacks on September 11, 2001, showed that 88 percent of self-identified Republicans approved of Bush's performance, compared with only 31 percent of self-identified Democrats. September 11 temporarily narrowed that 57-point gap, but even after the Republican success in the 2002 midterm elections, the gap averaged 54 points.[29] A CBS News Poll taken October 3-5, 2005 (the week that President Bush nominated Harriet Miers to fill Sandra Day O'Connor's associate justice seat) showed a 65-point gap: Seventy-nine percent of self-identified Republicans approved of Bush's performance, compared with only 14 percent of self-identified Democrats.[30]

Along with polarized politics came a reluctance to give presidents clear mandates. Neither George W. Bush in 2000 nor Bill Clinton in either 1992 or 1996 received 50 percent of the popular vote. Though he claimed a mandate in 2004, Bush still only received 50.7 percent of the popular vote and 53.3 percent of the electoral vote (even Ronald Reagan's "landslide" in 1980 amounted to only 50.7 percent of the popular vote – the same as Bush in 2004 – although Reagan garnered 90.9 percent of the electoral vote). Initial approval ratings of presidents are down, too. Dwight Eisenhower and Lyndon Johnson both entered office with 78 percent approval ratings according to the Gallup Poll. Even John F. Kennedy, who won only 49.7 percent of the popular vote in 1960, had an initial approval rating of 72 percent. In contrast, Barack Obama was the first president since Jimmy Carter to have had an initial approval rating of more than 58 percent (George W. Bush had 57 percent approval and, at 25 percent, the highest *dis*approval rating since Gallup polling began; Obama entered office with a 68 percent Gallup approval rating, but that dwindled to 51 percent by August 2009).

This potent combination of interest group involvement, divided government, polarized politics, and lack of electoral mandates has given rise to modern confirmation battles. Those battles have spilled over into lower federal court appointments as well. Both opposition Republicans during Bill Clinton's presidency and opposition Democrats during the George W. Bush presidency used a variety of tactics to block confirmation of nominees to the lower federal courts.[31] The practice began in earnest after Clinton's 1996 re-election.

When Clinton first ran for president in 1992, he decried what he perceived to be the ideologically driven judicial appointments of Ronald Reagan and George H. W. Bush. Such ideologically narrow appointments, he wrote in 1992, "have resulted in the emergence of a judiciary that is less reflective of our diverse society than at any other time in recent memory. I strongly believe that the judiciary thus runs the risk of losing its legitimacy in the eyes of many Americans." In comparison, Clinton promised nominees who would be met by the Senate with "general approval." This, he added, should help to avoid confirmation delays.[32] Although he did promise to nominate judges with "a demonstrated concern for, and commitment to, the individual rights protected by our Constitution, including the right to privacy,"[33] he nonetheless started out his administration with an apparently genuine effort to present consensus nominees to the Senate. At the Supreme Court level, Clinton won the support of Senator Orrin Hatch of Utah, the ranking Republican member of the Senate Judiciary Committee, before nominating Ruth Bader Ginsburg to the Supreme Court in 1993.[34] Ginsburg had steered a centrist course as a judge on the U.S. Court of Appeals for the District of Columbia. She won easy confirmation as a Supreme Court justice, as did Stephen Breyer the next year. Again, Clinton sought a consensus nominee and won support from key Republicans, such as Hatch and Senator Strom Thurmond (R-S.C.).[35] Ironically, some liberals seemed more critical of Breyer than conservatives.

Clinton also worked closely with home-state senators, including Republicans, when nominating lower federal judges.[36] When the 2002 midterm election ushered in divided government, Clinton reportedly "evinced greater willingness to compromise," took pains to avoid forwarding controversial nominees to the Senate, and worked closely with the new Republican chairman of the Senate Judiciary Committee, Orrin Hatch of Utah.[37] But consensus did not continue in Clinton's second term. Republicans had made "activist liberal judges" a campaign issue in 1996. Republican presidential nominee Bob Dole called Clinton's appointees a "team of liberal leniency." Pat Buchanan, who had sought the Republican nomination had gone even further, lashing out at "judicial dictatorship" and accusing liberal federal judges of protecting "criminals, atheists, homosexuals, flag burners, illegal aliens (including terrorists), convicts, and pornographers."[38] Once re-elected, the conservative Judicial Selection Monitoring Project criticized Republicans for voting to confirm Clinton's nominees, whom they labeled extreme "judicial activists." In a fundraising letter, Robert Bork said that Clinton's nominees were "drawn almost exclusively from the ranks of the liberal elite" and that they had "blazed an activist trail, creating an out-of-control judiciary."[39] House Majority Whip Tom DeLay (R-Texas) also entered the fray, saying that Republicans should begin efforts to impeach liberal federal judges.[40]

The rhetoric emboldened Republicans to launch an unprecedented slowdown of the confirmation of Clinton nominees. Orrin Hatch interpreted Senate practice to allow Republican home-state senators to block hearings on nominees put forward by a Democratic president. By the end of 1997, one in 10 seats on the federal judiciary was vacant, with 26 of those seats vacant for at least 18 months. President Clinton declared a "vacancy crisis"[41] – a view that Chief Justice William Rehnquist reiterated in his 1997 year-end report to Congress on the federal judiciary, saying that continued delay threatened the nation's "quality of justice."[42]

Republicans backed off the slowdown in 1998, but revived it in 1999 as the prospect of a Republican victory in the 2000 presidential election loomed. Just 10 years after Reagan left office, Clinton was on the verge of appointing a new majority on the federal courts. Republicans wanted to prevent that. Once again, Judiciary Committee chairman Hatch allowed Republican home-state senators to block Clinton's judicial nominees. When Clinton left office in January 2001, 42 of his judicial nominees remained unconfirmed. Thirty-eight of them had never received a hearing. In Clinton's eight years in office, the Senate had blocked 114 of his lower court nominations and confirmed 366. In comparison, the Senate blocked none of Richard Nixon's lower court nominations and confirmed 224 (it did block two of his Supreme Court nominees). Even during the Reagan administration, the Senate blocked only 43 court nominees and confirmed 368.[43]

After the 2000 presidential election, when Republicans briefly controlled the Senate, Senate Judiciary Committee Chair Orrin Hatch announced a dramatic re-interpretation of Senate procedure. Although he had allowed Senate Republicans to block hearings on nominees when Clinton had been president, he now said that Senate Democrats could not block hearings with Bush as president. The turnabout was blatantly political, and Senate Democrats reacted with fury. All 50 signed a letter of protest.[44] Hatch's plan was temporarily averted when Senator James Jeffords of Vermont left the Republican party and became an independent, thereby throwing control of the Senate back to the Democrats. But when Republicans regained control after the 2002 midterm elections, Hatch imposed his re-interpretation of Senate procedure. That, in turn, prompted Democrats to use the filibuster against nominees who, under the old rules, would have been blocked by the opposition of a home-state senator. Although Republicans had mounted a filibuster against Lyndon Johnson's nomination of Abe Fortas to be chief justice of the Supreme Court in 1968, Senate Majority Leader Bill Frist of Tennessee now threatened to use of the so-called "nuclear option" – a procedural change designed to end the ability of Senators to use filibusters against judicial nominees. At the 11th hour, 14 moderate senators (seven from each party) brokered a compromise that at least temporarily averted the "nuclear option." When the Senate reverted to control by the Democrats in 2007, Republicans again complained that confirmations proceeded too slowly.

Delay tactics continued when President Obama took office. Six months into his first term, the Senate still had not confirmed a single federal judge. Opposition Republicans made it clear they were ready to fight. All 41 Republicans signed a letter to the president threatening to "preserve the rights of our colleagues" if home-state Republicans lost their power under senatorial courtesy to block nominees.[45] Some interpreted this as a threat to filibuster judicial nominees. In the end, Democrats did not alter the power of home-state senators, but they did abolish the use of the "anonymous hold": a practice whereby a senator could anonymously block a nomination. The change meant that senators who block a nomination must do so publicly.

Political expediency explains much of the behavior of participants in the federal judicial appointment process. At different times, both liberals and conservatives have supported strict scrutiny of judicial nominees and decried judicial activism. The conservatives' rallying cry against judicial activism in the early 21st century is exactly the same rallying cry used by liberals in the 1920s and '30s to decry the judicial activism of conservative judges who read economic rights into the constitution. Democrats supported the borking of nominees when Reagan was president, but urged a kinder, gentler treatment of nominees when Clinton was in office. Republicans embraced the confirmation slowdown of judicial nominees when Clinton was president, but condemned it when Bush became president. Conservatives declared that every nominee had a right to an "up or down vote" when Bush nominated John Roberts in 2005, but applauded the withdrawal of Harriet Miers just a few weeks later. Republicans decried the use of a filibuster they controlled the Senate, but may resort to its use now that Democrats control the Senate.

At root, the judicial appointment process is a political one, shaped by changing political dynamics and balances of power. As long as the balance of power remains closely divided, the process promises to be a contentious one.

Endnotes

1. William Kristol, "Disappointed, Depressed, Demoralized: A Reaction to the Harriet Miers Nomination," *The Daily Standard* (October 4, 2005), online edition.
2. George Will, Editorial, *Chicago Sun-Times* (October 6, 2005), p. 45.

3. Charlie Savage, "Bush, Promoting Miers, Invokes Her Faith," *Boston Globe* (October 13, 2005), p. A1.
4. Quoted in: "A Case of Foot-in-Mouth," *Hartford (Connecticut) Courant* (October 14, 2005), p. A12.
5. Kathy Kiely, "Senators Criticize Miers for 'Inadequate' Answers," *USA Today* (October 20, 2005), p. 4A.
6. The official U.S. Senate Web site lists eight consecutive re-submissions of nominations of the same person by the same president for the same seat (usually for merely technical reasons): William Patterson in 1793, Edward King in 1844, John Spencer in 1844 (though the re-nomination was withdrawn the same day that it was submitted), Reuben Walworth *twice* in 1844, William Hornblower in 1893, Pierce Butler in 1922, and John Harlan in 1955. Stanley Matthews, who was consecutively nominated by two *different* presidents in 1881, *is* counted twice for our purposes. A complete list of all nominations (including the eight re-nominations by the same president) can be found at the U.S. Senate Web site: http://www.senate.gov/ pagelayout/reference/nominations/Nominations.shtml. The 149 nominations do not include Douglas Ginsburg in 1987. Although Ronald Reagan publicly announced Ginsburg's nomination, Ginsburg withdrew before his name was formally submitted to the Senate.
7. Robert Harrison in 1789, William Cushing in 1796, John Jay in 1800, Levi Lincoln in 1811, John Quincy Adams in 1811, William Smith in 1837, and Roscoe Conkling in 1882.
8. Edwin Stanton in 1869.
9. Homer Thornberry was nominated by Lyndon Johnson to fill Abe Fortas' associate justice seat in 1968 when Johnson nominated Fortas to be chief justice. Johnson subsequently withdrew Fortas' nomination. Because Fortas then remained an associate justice, the Senate took no action on Thornberry's nomination.
10. John Rutledge in 1795 (10–14), Alexander Wolcott in 1811 (9–24), John Spencer in 1844 (21–26), George Woodward in 1845 (20–29), Jeremiah Black in 1861 (25–26), Ebenezer Hoar in 1869 (24–33), William Hornblower in 1893 (24–30), Wheeler Peckham in 1894 (32–41), John J. Parker in 1930 (39–41), Clement Haynsworth, Jr. in 1969 (45–55), G. Harrold Carswell in 1970 (45–51), and Robert Bork in 1987 (42–58).
11. John Crittendon in 1828, Roger Taney in 1835, Ruben Walworth and Edward King in 1844, and George Badger in 1853.
12. John Read in 1845, Edward Bradford in 1852, William Micou in 1853, Henry Stanbery in 1866, and Stanley Matthews in 1881.
13. George H. Williams in 1873, Caleb Cushing in 1874, Abe Fortas in 1968, and Harriet Miers in 2005.
14. It rises still further if one counts the unsuccessful re-nominations of individuals already blocked by the Senate: John Spencer (after his Senate rejection), Edward King (after his nomination was blocked by postponement), and Reuben Walworth (twice re-nominated: first after a Senate vote to postpone, and then again after no action being taken by the Senate).
15. P. S. Ruckman, Jr., "The Supreme Court, Critical Nominations, and the Senate Confirmation Process," *Journal of Politics* 55 (August 1993), p. 794.
16. Tom Charles Huston to President Richard Nixon, March 25, 1969, pp. 1 and 2, in WHCF ExFG 50, the Judicial Branch (1969–1970), Box 1, White House Central Files, FG 50, Nixon Presidential Materials Project, College Park, Maryland [hereafter "NPMP"].
17. John D. Ehrlichman to Staff Secretary, March 27, 1969, in News Summaries, March 1969, Box 30, President's Office Files, NPMP.
18. Sheldon Goldman, "Reagan's Judicial Legacy: Completing the Puzzle and Summing Up," *Judicature* 72 (April-May 1989), pp. 319–20.
19. Quotes found in David M. O'Brien, *Judicial Roulette* (New York: Priority Press, 1988), pp. 61–62 and 21–24.
20. Between 1835 and 1885, 15 Supreme Court nominees were rejected by the Senate— a number unmatched in any 50-year period since then.
21. See John Anthony Maltese, *The Selling of Supreme Court Nominees* (Baltimore: Johns Hopkins University Press, 1995), pp. 26–31 for an account of Rutledge's defeat.

22. See Scott H. Ainsworth and John Anthony Maltese, "National Grange Influence on the Supreme Court Confirmation of Stanley Matthews," *Social Science History* 20 (1996), pp. 41–62.
23. For detailed accounts of both Parker and Haynsworth, see Maltese, *The Selling of Supreme Court Nominees*, chapters 4 and 5.
24. "The Electoral Count," *New York Times* (January 30, 1881).
25. Douglas Ginsburg did not, but he withdrew before his nomination was ever formally sent to the Senate.
26. Jeffrey Segal, Charles Cameron, and Albert Cover, "A Spatial Model of Roll Call Voting: Senators, Constituents, Presidents, and Interest Groups in Supreme Court Nominations," *American Political Science Review* 36 (1992), p. 111.
27. Richard Fleisher and Jon R. Bond, "Congress and the President in a Partisan Era," in *Polarized Politics: Congress and the President in a Partisan Era*, ed. Jon R. Bond and Richard Fleisher (Washington, DC: CQ Press, 2000), pp. 3–4.
28. Gary C. Jacobson, "Party Polarization in National Politics: The Electoral Connection," in *Polarized Politics*, ed. Bond and Fleisher, pp. 19–23.
29. Gary C. Jacobson, "The Bush Presidency and the American Electorate," in *The George W. Bush Presidency: An Early Assessment*, ed. Fred Greenstein (Baltimore: Johns Hopkins University Press, 2003), pp. 197–227.
30. The poll can be found at www.pollingreport.com.
31. For a full account of the process, see: John Anthony Maltese, "Confirmation Gridlock: The Federal Judicial Appointments Process under Bill Clinton and George W. Bush," *Journal of Appellate Practice and Process* 5 (Spring 2003), pp. 1–28.
32. "The Candidates on Legal Issues," *American Bar Association Journal* 78 (October 1992), p.2 of online LexisNexis version.
33. "The Candidates on Legal Issues," p. 1 of online LexisNexis version.
34. Carl Tobias, "Choosing Judges at the Close of the Clinton Administration," *Rutgers Law Review* 52 (Spring 2000), p. 831.
35. Tobias, "Choosing Judges," p. 835.
36. Federal judicial districts all fall within the confines of a single state. By tradition, judges who staff district courts reside in the state where the district sits and the senators from that state (the so-called "home-state" senators) exert considerable power in the confirmation process.
37. Tobias, "Choosing Judges," p. 837.
38. Quoted in: James Bennet, "Judicial Dictatorship" Spurns People's Will, Buchanan Says," *The New York Times* (January 30, 1996), p. A9.
39. Quoted in Henry Weinstein, "Drive Seeks to Block Judicial Nominees," *Los Angeles Times* (October 26, 1997), p. A3.
40. Michael Kelly, "Judge Dread," *New Republic* (March 31, 1997), p. 6.
41. Ronald Brownstein, "GOP Stall Tactics Damage Judiciary, President Charges," *Los Angeles Times* (September 28, 1997), p. A1.
42. William H. Rehnquist, *1997 Year-End Report on the Federal Judiciary*, p. 7 [copy available at www.supremecourtus.gov].
43. Statistics for Franklin Roosevelt through George W. Bush can be found in a chart accompanying Neil A. Lewis, "Bitter Senators Divided Anew on Judgeships," *The New York Times* (November 15, 2003), p. A1.
44. Thomas B. Edsall, "Democrats Push Bush for Input on Judges," *The Washington Post* (April 28, 2001), p. A4.
45. Letter from all 41 Republican senators to President Obama, March 2, 2009.

Mark Rozell and Mitchel Sollenberger

Executive Privilege
and the U.S. Attorneys Firings

President George W. Bush's penchant for secrecy is widely acknowledged by his detractors and even many of his supporters. Although the president says that the war on terror and other contemporary threats to U.S. interests necessitate his expanded use of various powers, even prior to September 11, 2001, Bush had made significant strides to enhance secrecy in the executive branch. His early efforts to expand executive privilege to conceal presidential records and Department of Justice deliberative documents from past administrations set off firestorms of protests. Criticism from Congress and from outside interests has not dampened Bush's commitment to protecting presidential secrecy. Thus, in 2007, Bush fueled more firestorms when he made multiple claims of executive privilege to conceal White House documents and to prevent presidential aides from testifying before Congress about the controversial decision to force the resignations of a number of U.S. attorneys.

Before examining the events of the controversial firings, it is necessary first to put these into the broader context of the academic debate over executive privilege, which recognizes the right of the president and his high-level advisors to withhold information from Congress, the courts, and the public under certain circumstances. At this point, there is not much of a debate over the legitimacy of executive privilege, as the overwhelming majority of legal scholars and some important court decisions acknowledge the existence of this presidential power. Yet there is considerable contention over the scope and limits of this power, and thus some presidents have tried to expand their authority to claim executive privilege, although usually not without a fight from Congress, independent counsels, and public interest groups.

The controversy over the forced resignations or firings of the U.S. attorneys highlights an enduring issue in debates over executive privilege—that is, whether some legislative or judicial line drawing would help in the future to resolve such battles. Although it is tempting to constrain the future use of executive privilege, we see things differently. That is, this latest controversy instead showcases the necessity of leaving the definition of executive privilege broad enough to allow for a process

Source: Presidential Studies Quarterly Vol. 38, no. 2 (June 2008).

of give and take between the branches, even if it means an occasional game of brinks-manship that locks the different sides in a protracted battle. The theory of separated powers envisions the inevitability of occasional conflicts between the branches, which is far preferable to resorting to narrow legalisms that would constrain the flexibility built into the system. Some background on past executive privilege controversies is instructive.

Controlling Executive Privilege

What we have traditionally seen in the exercise of executive privilege is a classic balancing of the competing interests of the president and Congress. Presidents maintain that they have the right to candid advice without fear of public disclosure of every Oval Office utterance. Some have been more aggressive than others in asserting this principle.

When confronted with the threat of congressional subpoena to compel testimony by a White House aide during the Army-McCarthy hearings of 1954, President Dwight D. Eisenhower famously said, "Any man who testifies as to the advice that he gave me won't be working for me that night." Ike proceeded to characterize a close aide's work as "really a part of me" (Greenstein 1982,204). *The Washington Post* weighed in with editorial support for the president, writing that the president's right to withhold information and testimony from Congress "is altogether beyond question" (*The Washington Post* 1954).

Two decades later, the *Post* and the Supreme Court fashioned a very different response to executive privilege when President Richard M. Nixon tried to use the principle to shield evidence of criminal conduct in the White House. In *United States v. Nixon*,[1] the Court ruled that executive privilege is subject to limits and to the competing interests of the other branches. In the case of Watergate, access to evidence in a criminal investigation overrode the president's generalized claim to confidentiality.

Just as presidents have legitimate needs to keep information secret, Congress has a legitimate need to access information in order to carry out its duty to investigate executive branch actions. Moreover, in a democratic republic, the presumption strongly favors openness. Despite Solicitor General Paul D. Clement's suggestion that Congress has failed to show a "demonstrably critical" need for information on the U.S. attorney firings, the burden generally rests with the president to prove that he requires secrecy rather than with Congress to show that it has a right to investigate.

But if both branches have legitimate claims, which one prevails? Often the answer does not come from the courts, which take a long time to resolve legal issues that are, in fact, political questions. Because the answer is not usually or appropriately decided by legalistic definitions, political compromises often win out. Two examples from the past—involving Presidents Nixon and Reagan—help us judge the current controversy.

During the Watergate investigation, a Senate committee requested the testimony of White House Counsel John Dean. The president contended that executive privilege shielded his aides from compulsory testimony. Nixon made the extraordinary claim that, because of the separation of powers, the president's exercise of his powers cannot be questioned by another branch—an assertion as sweeping as current White House counsel Fred Fielding's claim of "absolute immunity" from compelled testimony for present and former presidential aides (Fielding served in the White House counsel's office from 1970 to 1974 and 1981 to 1986). Nixon also stated, "If the president is not subject to such questioning, it is equally inappropriate that members of his staff not [sic] be so questioned, for their roles are in effect an extension of the president" (U.S. House 1973, 308).

Congress was not convinced. In the face of strong opposition, Nixon backed down and consented to allow Dean and other White House aides to testify. Most significant to the current debate, Nixon further conceded that, in investigations of possible criminal conduct, executive privilege would "no longer be invoked for present or former members of the White House staff" (Fisher 2004, 60).

In the 1980s, Reagan claimed executive privilege several times in response to congressional demands. In every case, the president asserted some principled need to protect the republic from the damaging effects of disclosure of secret executive branch information. Each time Congress pushed hard, and eventually the two branches reached an accommodation whereby Reagan released almost everything he had tried to conceal. Most germane to Bush's dilemma today was Reagan's refusal to allow Anne Gorsuch, administrator of the Environmental Protection Agency (EPA), to appear bearing certain documents before two congressional committees. In his second stint in the office, Fielding directed Gorsuch not to comply with congressional subpoenas and assured her that the White House would stand firmly behind its claim of privilege. Gorsuch later said that she had favored full disclosure but had felt constrained by the White House. Because she had followed the president's orders, Congress voted Gorsuch in contempt—the same fate that has fallen on Harriet Miers and White House Chief of Staff Joshua Bolten.

Yet after much posturing (including filing suit to block the contempt action), the White House eventually caved in to the political pressure and let Congress see the disputed EPA documents. Once again, a president settled politically after initially insisting on his plenary constitutional authority to unilaterally withhold information from Congress (Rozell 2002, 100-02).

Bush, too, has made sweeping claims of executive privilege before. In one remarkable case in late 2001 and early 2002, the president tried to withhold from Congress some Justice Department documents that were more than 20 years old. A House committee investigating the Federal Bureau of Investigation for probable allegations of wrongdoing during the 1960s and 1970s was demanding access to key papers. Bush insisted that deliberative documents from the Department of Justice are always protected by executive privilege, even in cases that were closed down years ago.

Though the House was then run by the Republicans, the committee stood firm in its opposition to executive privilege in that instance and threatened to take the matter to court. Bush's actions also elicited substantial editorial and public criticism. And before the committee could pursue the matter further, the White House agreed to a compromise, turning over most of the contested documents. Both sides declared victory, as the committee received the materials it needed and the White House was able to protect a small category of documents from full disclosure (Rozell 2002, 151–54).

This is what generally happens in these battles between the president and Congress: The two sides posture for a while, and then some accommodation is reached before the matter goes to court. Each branch recognizes that it could lose a lot if a court decides the dispute, and thus they both have an incentive to cut a deal. Of course, a compromise is not always reached. Sometimes one side backs down entirely. At those times, it is politics rather than law that settles the matter. For example, if Congress were still controlled by Republicans, it is possible that we would not even be having a debate over executive privilege in the U.S. attorneys case (although, as noted, presidents are not immune from challenge by their own party).

With this background, we can now turn to the latest executive privilege controversy. We first explain the process of appointing U.S. attorneys and then consider why the Bush White House actions became a matter of inter-branch contention.

The Process of Appointing U.S. Attorneys

U.S. attorneys function as chief prosecutors for violations of federal criminal and civil law and act as defense counsel on behalf of the United States in civil actions brought against the government in the districts to which they are appointed.[2] There are currently 93 U.S. attorneys serving in the 94 federal judicial districts (one U.S. attorney is appointed to serve the Guam and the Northern Mariana Islands districts). Congress has given the responsibility of appointing U.S. attorneys to the president with the advice and consent of the Senate.[3]

Although presidents have the authority to nominate whomever they choose, the custom of senatorial courtesy has produced a system in which the decision has been transferred to the home-state senator of the president's political party. If there are no friendly senators in the state, then the responsibility usually falls on the senior House member, state governor, or party chairman to recommend a candidate. However, even minority party members of the Senate are routinely consulted about appointment changes in the federal judicial districts within their states.

Two recent changes to the method of appointing U.S. attorneys directly relate to the controversy in question. On March 9, 2006, Congress passed the reauthorization of the USA PATRIOT Act, which, among other things, modified the way interim U.S. attorney appointments were managed. Prior to the passage of this law, the attorney general could make interim appointments for no more than 120 days. Once the appointment term expired, the district court could appoint a U.S. attorney until the president and Senate filled the vacancy.[4] However, the PATRIOT Act eliminated the time limit, giving the attorney general the authority to fill a vacancy indefinitely. Those changes lasted from March 9, 2006, to June 14, 2007, when President Bush signed into law the Preserving United States Attorney Independence Act of 2007.[6]

The Plan to Replace the U.S. Attorneys

After Bush's reelection in 2004, the White House began to consider removing and appointing new U.S. attorneys (Goldstein 2007). On February 3, 2005, Alberto Gonzales replaced John Ashcroft as attorney general. Less than a month after taking office, Gonzales signed a confidential memorandum that reorganized the process for hiring and firing U.S. attorneys and other political appointees. He gave the primary vetting responsibility to his chief of staff, D. Kyle Sampson, and to the deputy director of the Executive Office for U.S. Attorneys (EOUSA), Monica M. Goodling. During this time, Goodling, Sampson, and John Nowacki, deputy director and acting counsel in the EOUSA prepared a list of U.S. attorneys to be dismissed (Lipton 2007), which Sampson sent to the White House (Johnston and Lipton 2007a).

Not until January 2006 did the process to replace U.S. attorneys heat up again. At that time, Sampson recommended to White House Counsel Harriet Miers that the Department of Justice and the White House work together to determine which U.S. attorneys to replace. Sampson thought that a "limited number of U.S. attorneys could be targeted for removal and replacement, mitigating the shock to the system that would result from an across the board firing." He also provided a list of candidates to be removed (Eggen and Solomon 2007). The next month, Goodling sent an e-mail with an attached spreadsheet that listed all U.S. attorneys and included information on, among other things, their political activities and whether they were members of the conservative Federalist Society (Johnston and Lipton 2007c).

By September, Sampson urged a plan not only to dismiss various U.S. attorneys but to do so by using the newly passed interim appointment law. He wrote that, by avoiding Senate confirmation, "we can give far less deference to home state senators and thereby get 1) our preferred person appointed and 2) do it far faster and more efficiently at less political cost to the White House" (Eggen and Solomon 2007).

On November 15, 2006, Sampson sent his dismissal plan to the White House for approval. A final meeting with Justice Department officials to discuss the U.S. attorney matter occurred on November 27, attended by Gonzales; Paul J. McNulty, deputy attorney general; Sampson; Goodling; William Moschella, assistant attorney general for legislative affairs; and Michael A. Battle, then director of the EOUSA (Johnston and Lipton 2007b). A week later, the White House gave its final approval. On December 7, the Justice Department phoned seven U.S. attorneys informing them of their removal (Johnston and Lipton 2007 a). Although the formal list of dismissals only included these seven, the Justice Department had removed several other individuals during the previouspast two years (AP 2007).

Congress Responds; a Scandal Brews

Initially Congress barely reacted, but then after a number of news reports, several members questioned the administration's actions. On January 9, 2007, Senators Patrick Leahy and Dianne Feinstein wrote to Gonzales and expressed their concerns. They requested that he refrain from "moving forward with" the changes and to "provide information regarding all instances in which you have exercised the authority to appoint an interim United States Attorney." The senators also asked for all "information on whether any efforts have been made to ask or encourage the former or current U.S. Attorneys to resign their position" (Feinstein 2007). Two days later, Senators Leahy, Feinstein, and Mark Pryor introduced legislation to prevent Gonzales from circumventing the Senate's advice and consent authority (Pryor 2007).

A January 18 Senate Judiciary Committee hearing was the first time Congress formally questioned the attorney general about this matter. Gonzales, in a rather heated exchange with Feinstein, responded to several questions related to the controversy. Gonzales said he did not deny that the Justice Department had asked the U.S. attorneys to resign, but that such a request was part of a performance evaluation. "I think I would never ever make a change in a U.S. Attorney position for political reasons or if it would in any way jeopardize an ongoing serious investigation. I just would not do it" (U.S. Senate 2007a, 24).

Not satisfied with such answers, the committee held additional hearings. In opening the February 6 hearing, Senator Charles Schumer intoned, "I am committed to getting to the bottom of [this matter]. If we do not get the documentary information that we seek, I will consider moving to subpoena that material, including performance evaluations and other documents" (U.S. Senate 2007b, 2). He added, "[W]hat happened here does not sound like an orderly and natural replacement of underperforming prosecutors; it sounds more like a purge . . . it appears more reminiscent of a different sort of Saturday Night Massacre" (U.S. Senate 2007b, 2).

Deputy Attorney General McNulty testified that the Justice Department had removed the U.S. attorneys for reasons of job performance, not political considerations. He added that the "indisputable fact is that United States attorneys serve at the pleasure of the president. They come and they go for lots of reasons" (U.S. Senate 2007b, 14). When pressed to explain the removals of the U.S. attorneys in question, McNulty was evasive and said that he would not "discuss specific issues regarding people" because that would be "unfair to individuals to have a discussion like that in this setting in a public way" (U.S. Senate 2007b, 17). Senator Arlen Specter replied that the committee routinely investigates personal aspects of people's lives during confirmation hearings.

Gonzales tried to diffuse the scandal with an op-ed column in *The Washington Post*, in which he repeated that the reasons for the firings were "related to policy, priorities and management" and not political retaliation. He ended, "Like me, U.S. attorneys are political appointees, and we all serve at the pleasure of the president. If U.S. attorneys are not executing their responsibilities in a manner that furthers the management and policy goals of departmental leadership, it is appropriate that they be replaced" (Gonzales 2007a).

Gonzales chief of staff Sampson resigned on March 12, 2007, saying that "information given Congress that minimized White House involvement in the firings was the result of [Gonzales's] failure to tell key Justice Department officials about the extent of his communications with administration officials about the plan" (Carr and Herman 2007). His replacement, Chuck Rosenberg, proceeded to ask the Justice Department's inspector general to investigate whether the career prosecutor appointments had been politicized (Eggen and Leonnig 2007).

Bush and Congress Dig In

On March 20, 2007, President Bush called the announcement and subsequent explanation of the U.S. attorney changes "confusing and, in some cases, incomplete. Neither the Attorney General nor I approve of how these explanations were handled. We're determined to correct the problem" (Bush 2007, 359). Bush announced the implementation of several steps to show the administration's "willingness to work with the Congress." These included allowing the attorney general and some of his staff to testify; permitting "relevant committee members, on a bipartisan basis, to interview key members of my staff to ascertain relevant facts"; and disclosing "all White House documents and e-mails involving direct communications with the Justice Department or any other outside person, including Members of Congress and their staff, related to this issue" (Bush 2007, 359-60). Bush maintained that he was offering a "reasonable solution" and concluded that he would "not go along with a partisan fishing expedition aimed at honorable public servants" (Bush 2007, 360). The proposal did not permit White House officials to testify about the U.S. attorney controversy. Asked by a reporter whether he was willing to "go to the mat" and "take this to court," Bush replied, "Absolutely" (Bush 2007, 361).

Thus, what Bush had characterized as a good faith compromise was instead an open defiance of Congress's requests for certain relevant documents and for meaningful testimony. And he effectively dared Congress to take him to court.

On March 21, the House Judiciary Committee approved subpoenas for Karl Rove, deputy White House chief of staff; Sampson; Miers; William Kelley, deputy White House counsel; and J. Scott Jennings, special assistant to the president in the Office of Public Affairs (Hulse 2007). On March 22, the Senate Judiciary Committee approved subpoenas for Rove, Miers, and Kelley. However, Senator Specter realized that "[i]f we have the confrontation, we're not going to get this information for a very long time" (Kane 2007a). Neither committee actually issued any subpoenas at this point, as Congress wanted to give the president time to respond.

At a Justice Department press conference, Gonzales said he had no prior knowledge of the process: "Mr. Sampson was charged with directing the process to ascertain who were weak performers, where we could do better in districts around the country. That is a responsibility that he had during the transition." He added, "I never saw documents. We never had a discussion about where things stood. What I knew was that there was ongoing effort that was led by Mr. Sampson, vetted through the Department of Justice, to ascertain where we could make improvements in U.S. attorney performances around the country" (Gonzales 2007b). Yet at the March 29 Senate Judiciary Committee hearing, Sampson responded that "I don't think the attorney general's statement that he was not involved in any discussions of U.S. attorney removals was accurate. . . . I remember discussing with him this process of asking certain U.S. attorneys to resign" (Eggen and Kane 2007).

On April 10, the House Judiciary Committee served the first subpoena for documents, ordering that Gonzales turn over all information relating to the removals of U.S. attorneys. "We have been patient in allowing the (Justice] department to work through its concerns regarding the sensitive nature of some of these materials," Representative

John Conyers, Jr., the panel's chairman, wrote to Gonzales in a letter that accompanied the subpoena. "Unfortunately, the department has not indicated any meaningful willingness to find a way to meet our legitimate needs" (Eggen 2007). Two weeks later, the committee passed a resolution that authorized House lawyers to apply for a court order granting Goodling immunity in exchange for her testimony. The District of Columbia district court granted that immunity. In May, the Senate Judiciary Committee subpoenaed Gonzales and demanded that he turn over all the relevant e-mails (Leahy 2007a). In June, the Senate and House judiciary committees issued subpoenas to Miers and the former deputy assistant to the president and director of political affairs, Sara Taylor.

President Bush Invokes Executive Privilege

On June 27, 2007, Solicitor General and Acting Attorney General Clement notified the president that it was his "considered legal judgment that you may assert executive privilege over the subpoenaed documents and testimony." Clement believed that these related to "internal White House communications about the possible dismissal and replacement of U.S. Attorneys," and thus such information falls "squarely within the scope of executive privilege." He reasoned that one "of the underlying purposes of the privilege is to promote sound decisionmaking by ensuring that senior Government officials and their advisers speak frankly and candidly during the decisionmaking process." Clement claimed that the deliberations in question "relate to the potential exercise by the President of an authority [nomination and removal] assigned to him alone." He declared Congress's oversight interest "sharply reduced by the thousands of documents and dozens of hours of interviews and testimony already provided to the Committees by the Department of Justice as part of its extraordinary effort at accommodation" (U.S. Department of Justice 2007a).

The next day, White House counsel Fielding wrote to Conyers and Leahy that Bush was claiming executive privilege, and thus "the White House will not be making any production in response to [the] subpoenas for documents." Fielding said that "the President attempted to chart a course of cooperation. It was his intent that Congress receive information in a manner that accommodated presidential prerogatives." He added that more than "8,500 pages" of Justice Department documents had been released, and numerous department personnel "have testified in public hearings." The president, he said, was willing to go further to allow White House staffers to testify and to produce additional communications between the White House and Justice Department. This offer "took care to protect fundamental interests of the Presidency and the constitutional principle of separation of powers." Fielding maintained that the president would be constrained in his ability to "receive candid and unfettered advice" if White House advisors were constantly afraid of being compelled to testify or to release documents to Congress (White House 2007a).

On July 9, Fielding again wrote to Conyers and Leahy, and this time he asserted executive privilege regarding the testimony of Miers and Taylor. He claimed that the White House had acted "to protect a fundamental interest of the presidency" by not revealing internal decision-making processes (White House 2007b). Two days after this latest executive privilege claim, the Senate Judiciary Committee held another oversight hearing and Taylor testified, although she refused to answer questions that she considered protected by the privilege. Miers refused to testify and agreed to follow Bush's request not to appear before the committee.

House and Senate Judiciary Committees Vote for Contempt

On July 25, 2007, the House Judiciary Committee voted 22-17 to cite Miers and Bolten for contempt of Congress (Lewis 2007). Conyers said that this measure was taken "not only to gain an accurate picture of the facts surrounding the U.S. attorneys controversy, but to protect our constitutional prerogatives as a co-equal branch of government" (Lewis 2007). A Justice Department official said that contempt charges would not be enforced because "the House or Senate would have to ask the United States attorney for the District of Columbia to convene a grand jury with the aim of indicting Ms. Miers and Mr. Bolten" (Lewis 2007).

The following day, Leahy issued subpoenas for Rove and Jennings to appear before the Senate Judiciary Committee at an August 2 hearing (Ward 2007). In addition, Schumer and other Democratic senators called for the appointment of a special prosecutor to determine whether Gonzales had "misled Congress or perjured himself during his July 24 testimony before the Senate Judiciary Committee (Ward 2007).

On August 1, Bush invoked executive privilege for a third time in this controversy within a month, this time to prevent Rove from testifying (White House 2007c). Leahy protested that someone "who is now refusing to comply with Senate subpoenas, spoke publicly in speeches about these firings when the scandal first broke, but is suddenly unable to talk it about when he is under oath?" (Leahy 2007b). Two weeks later, in a letter to Bush, Leahy expressed his frustration at the lack of cooperation from the White House and the "political corruption of law enforcement" in the scandal. Leahy ended with the warning, "The stonewalling leaves me and the Senate Judiciary Committee with few options other than considering citations for contempt of Congress against those who have refused to provide relevant testimony and documents to the Congress" (U.S. Senate 2007c).

On August 16, Leahy requested that the Justice Department's inspector general, Glenn A. Fine, "investigate and evaluate potential misleading, evasive, or dishonest testimony by Attorney General Alberto Gonzales before the Senate Judiciary Committee on July 24, 2007" (U.S. Senate 2007d). A few weeks later, Fine said that there were ongoing investigations of the questionable testimony of Gonzales (U.S. Department of Justice 2007b). Under fire, Gonzales resigned his post and Bush nominated former circuit court judge Michael B. Mukasey to serve as attorney general. Then, in December, the Senate Judiciary Committee voted to hold Bolten and Rove in contempt of Congress. The White House remained defiant, as Press Secretary Dana M. Perino said: "The constitutional prerogative of the president would make it a futile effort for Congress to refer contempt citations to U.S. attorneys" (Kane 2007b). Leahy fumed, "White House stonewalling is unilateralism at its worst, and it thwarts accountability. Executive privilege should not be invoked to prevent investigations into wrongdoing" (Kane 2007b). Nonetheless, the legislative session ended and Senate majority leader Harry Reid declared that the chamber would not take up the issue again until 2008 (Kane 2007b).

Nearly a month into the second session of the 110th Congress, the House voted 223-32 to issue contempt citations against Miers and Bolten (Kane 2008, A4). The White House stood its ground and responded: "This action is unprecedented, and it is outrageous. . . . It is also an incredible waste of time—time the House should spend doing the American people's legislative business" (Schmitt 2008, A13). The resolution calls on the U.S. attorney for the District of Columbia to enforce the contempt charges. However, if no action is forthcoming then the chairman of the Judiciary Committee can seek in federal court a declaratory judgment "affirming the duty of any individual to comply with any subpoena" of the House (H. Res. 980 (2008).

At the time of this writing, Attorney General Mukasey has said that Miers' and Bolten's refusal to comply with the subpoenas does "not constitute a crime" and as such the Justice Department "will not bring the congressional contempt citations before a grand jury or take any other action" (Eggen 2008, A2). House Democrats had disagreed and filed a lawsuit in federal court to enforce the contempt charges (Lewis 2008, A17). "There is no authority," House Speaker Pelosi declared, "by which persons may wholly ignore a subpoena and fail to appear as directed because a President unilaterally instructs them to do so" (Pelosi 2008).

The controversy reveals the primary weakness in the procedures that Congress relies on when issuing a contempt citation. Enforcement traditionally comes from the executive branch. When Congress cites an executive official for contempt, a U.S. attorney is the one who enforces it. However, when the Justice Department has already taken a position on the constitutionality of the administration's action (as is the case here), any action might be slow in coming, if at all.

Administrations rarely push such a confrontation so far. For example, in 1998, the Clinton Justice Department eventually compromised with a Republican-controlled House committee after the committee had issued a contempt citation for Attorney General Janet Reno (*The Washington Post* 1998; Fisher 2004, 132-33). In at least one case, the executive branch did not initially see the need to cooperate with Congress, and the judicial branch had to intervene. Under an order from President Reagan, EPA administrator Gorsuch refused to provide documents to a House committee. Only after a federal court urged compromise between the branches did the Justice Department agree to release the documents.[7]

After the Gorsuch incident, the executive branch has guarded against future legislative incursions. In a 1984 opinion, the Office of Legal Counsel stated that, based on a separation-of-powers analysis, no U.S. attorney is required to enforce a contempt citation of Congress that is directed against an executive official who is carrying out the president's claim of executive privilege. However, the opinion did state that its conclusions were limited "to controversies similar to the one to which this memorandum expressly relates, and the general statements of legal principles should be applied in other contexts only after careful analysis."[8]

The Bush White House is following a similar path as the Gorsuch case. If the Justice Department refuses to enforce contempt charges, Congress could respond by using its own power to issue a warrant and detain individuals instead of seeking a declaratory judge from the courts. This right was first employed in 1795 when the speaker of the house ordered the sergeant-at-arms to arrest and detain two men accused of "bribery, libel, and failure to appear before committees." In 1800, the Senate asserted the same right when the editor of a Republican newspaper, William Duane, failed to appear before the Senate. During this episode, the Senate debated its inherent power at some length. As Richard E. Levy explains, "the argument in favor of such a power rested on the inherent authority of public bodies 'to do all acts necessary to keep themselves in a condition to discharge the trusts confided in them.'" Levy explains that this "inherent authority was reflected in the historical practices of the British Parliament, state legislatures, and courts." Yet the power could only be exercised "through enactment of necessary and proper laws pursuant to Article I" (Levy 2006, 33).

In 1821, the Supreme Court upheld this power in *Anderson v. Dunn*. The Court concluded that if such authority was refused, it would lead "to the total annihilation of the power of the House of Representatives to guard itself from contempts, and leaves it exposed to every indignity and interruption that rudeness, caprice, or even conspiracy, may meditate against it."[9] The principle underscored in *Anderson* is that Congress must possess certain powers necessary to protect the functioning of its own processes, even if such implicit powers do not appear to be expressly legislative in nature.

Of course, Congress does not have to rely on any direct authority in this area to enforce its will. Rather, the legislative branch has a variety of constitutionally based powers at its disposal that it may use to pressure the executive branch to cooperate. The legislative power itself, control of the budget, the confirmation and treaty-approval powers, among others, are all at Congress's disposal should legislators want to challenge executive branch lack of cooperation or overreaching of authority. The usual problem for Congress is not a lack of authority but a failure to exercise its existing powers.

This appears to be the case in the present situation. At a press conference announcing the contempt citations, Representative Brad Miller remarked that the House voted for contempt and now must "let a court declare what the law is." He asked:

> Are we entitled in the exercise of our constitutional powers to get the information that we've asked for and then ask the court to require by an injunction the administration to provide that information so that Americans will see someone incarcerated by a court proceeding, not by a vote on the floor, on the floor of the House or the floor of the Senate?

The statement seemed to imply that the House would not use its own enforcement powers. Continuing, Representative Miller declared that "these questions have to be decided by a court. Questions of what the Constitution means, how the powers are allocated between the different branches of government should be decided by a court, not by decree of the president, not by an announcement" (Conyers et al. 2008). The House appears to be seeking institutional protection from the judiciary in a constitutional standoff against the White House.

Regrettably, President Bush is willing to push this controversy to the brink, perhaps in the hope of winning a judicial decision that will be a victory for his expansive definition of presidential powers. Yet both the president and Congress risk setting a precedent that will put unwarranted judicial parameters on the future exercise of executive privilege. Such an effort to confine constitutional practice in mid-development is regrettable. Perhaps that is what Bush wants, because he believes that he will win. And thus, what makes this controversy potentially different from past clashes is a lame-duck president with little to lose who believes deeply in the principle of expanding presidential powers and who may think that, if necessary, a conservative-leaning judiciary would give him a major victory. Goading Congress into a constitutional fight might be part of his plan.

The risk here is that President Bush realizes that he is playing for the future and lawmakers of both parties do not. Do the Republican members supporting the president understand the consequences of a definitive loss for Congress? Do they recognize that one day they may stand in the majority, facing off against a Democratic president and stuck with a vastly weakened hand because of their actions today? Neither party knows when and why another president may need or want to keep deliberations secret. A precise legislative or judicial line drawing on the use of executive privilege will inevitably constrain a future leader who needs secrecy—or free a future leader who should be constrained.

And there is no reason to suppose that that another administration faced by strict limits on executive privilege will inevitably choose greater transparency. Future presidents will be as likely to sidestep the principle altogether and find other statutory or constitutional bases for secrecy. The worst outcome in this battle would be a bad precedent that undercuts the delicate balance of negotiations that has long characterized disputes over executive privilege.

Endnotes

1. 418 U.S. 683 (1974).
2. 28 U.S.C. § 547 (2000).
3. 28 U.S.C. § 541(a) (2000).
4. 28 U.S.C. § 546 (2000).
5. P.L. 109-177 § 502, 120 Star. 246 (2006).
6. P.L. 110-34, 121 Stat. 224 (2007).
7. *U.S. p. House of Representatives,* 556 F. Supp. 150, 153 (D.D.C. 1983).
8. 8 O.L.C. 101 (1984).
9. 19 U.S. 204 (1821).
10. 19 U.S. 204 (1821), 228.

References

Associated Press (AP). 2007. List of 8 dismissed U.S. prosecutors. Boston.com, March 6. http://www.boston.com/news/nation/wash/articles/2007/03/06/list_of_8_dismissed_us_prosecutors/ [accessed March 18, 2008]. Bush, George W. 2007. Remarks on the Department of Justice and an exchange with reporters. *Weekly Compilation of Presidential Documents* 43, March 20, pp. 359–62.

Carr, Rebecca, and Ken Herman. 2007. "Gonzales, Rove Had Early Role in Firings; E-Mails Show High White House Interest." *Atlanta Journal-Constitution*, March 16.

Cohen, Adam. 2007. "Congress Has a Way of Making Witnesses Speak: Its Own Jail." *The Washington Post*, December 4.

Conyers, John, Louise M. Slaughter, Brad Miller, Sheila Jackson Lee, and Michael Arcuri. 2008. "House Democrats Hold a News Conference on Contempt Citations." *CQ Transcriptions*, Feb. 14.

Eggen, Dan. 2007. "House Panel Issues First Subpoena Over Firings." *The Washington Post*, April 11.

———. 2008. "Mukasey Refuses to Prosecute Bush Aides." *The Washington Post*, March 1.

Eggen, Dan, and Paul Kane. 2007. "Ex-Aide Contradicts Gonzales on Firings." *The Washington Post*, March 30.

Eggen, Dan, and Carol D. Leonnig. 2007. "Officials Describe Interference by Former Gonzales Aide." *The Washington Post*, May 23.

Eggen, Dan, and John Solomon. 2007. "Firings had Genesis in White House; Ex-Counsel Miers First Suggested Dismissing Prosecutors 2 Years Ago, Documents Show." *The Washington Post*, March 13.

Feinstein, Dianne. 2007. Letter from Patrick Leahy and Dianne Feinstein to Alberto Gonzales, January 9. http://feinstein.senate.gov/public/index.cfm?FuseAction=NewsRoom.PressReleases&ContentRecord_id=18a696d7-7e9c-9afV-7a2b-397a786a69fc&Region_id=&Issue_id= [accessed March 18, 2008].

Fisher, Louis. 2004. *The Politics of Executive Privilege*. Durham, NC: Carolina Academic Press.

Goldstein, Amy. 2007. "Report Suggests Laws Broken in Attorney Firings." *The Washington Post*, July 25.

Gonzales, Alberto. 2007a. "They Lost My Confidence." *USA Today*, March 7.

———. 2007b. Transcript of media availability with Attorney General Alberto R. Gonzales, March 13. http://www.usdoj.gov/ag/speeches/2007/ag_speech_070313.html [accessed March 18, 2008].

Greenstein, Fred I. 1982. *The Hidden-Hand Presidency: Eisenhower as Leader*. New York: Basic Books.

Hulse, Carl. 2007. "Panel Approves Rove Subpoena on Prosecutors." *The New York Times*, March 22.

Johnston, David, and Eric Lipton. 2007a. "'Loyalty' to Bush and Gonzales Was Factor in Prosecutors' Firings, E-Mail Shows." *The New York Times*, March 13.

———. 2007b. "Gonzales Met with Advisers on Dismissals." *The New York Times*, March 24.

———. 2007c. "E-Mail Identified G.O.P. Candidates for Justice Jobs." *The New York Times*, April 13.

Kane, Paul. 2007a. "Senate Panel Approves Subpoenas for 3 Top Bush Aides." *The Washington Post*, March 23.

———. 2007b. "Rove, Bolten Found in Contempt of Congress; Senate Committee Cites Top Bush Advisers in Probe of U.S. Attorney Firings." *The Washington Post*,

December 14. 2008. "West Wing Aides Cited for Contempt." *The Washington Post*, February 15.

Leahy, Patrick. 2007a. "Chairman Leahy Issues Subpoena for 'Lost' Karl Rove E-Mails." News release, May 2. http://leahy.senate.gov/press/2OO7O5/O5O2O7.htmWLetter [accessed March 18, 2008].

———. 2007b. Comment of Sen. Patrick Leahy on White House letter regarding testimony of Karl Rove and J. Scott Jennings. *News release, August 1.* http://leahy.senate.gov/press/200708/080107c.html [accessed March 18, 2008].

Levy, Richard E. 2006. *The Power to Legislate: A Reference Guide to the United States Constitution.* Westport, CT: Greenwood Press.

Lewis, Neil A. 2007. "Panel Votes to Hold Two in Contempt of Congress." *The New York Times,* July 25.

Lipton, Eric. 2007. "Colleagues Cite Partisan Focus by Justice Official." *The New York Times,* May 11.

———. 2008. "Panel Asks Judge to Rule in Contempt Case." *The New York Times,* March 11.

Pelosi, Nancy. 2008. Letter to Michael B. Mukasey. Available at http://www.house.gov/pelosi/press/releases/FebO8/mukasey.html [accessed March 18, 2008].

Pryor, Mark. 2007. "Senators Feinstein, Leahy, Pryor to Fight Administration's Effort to Circumvent Senate Confirmation Process for U.S. Attorneys." News release, January 11. http://ptyor.senate.gov/newsroom/details.cfm?id=267495 [accessed March 18, 2008].

Rozell, Mark J. 2002. *Executive Privilege: Presidential Power, Secrecy, and Accountability.* Lawrence: University Press of Kansas.

Schmitt, Richard B. 2008. "House Oks Contempt Citations for Bush Aides." *Los Angles Times,* Feb. 15. White House. 2007a. Letter from Fred F. Fielding to John Conyers and Patrick Leahy, June 28. http://www.whitehouse.gov/news/releases/2007/06/LetterfromCounseltothePresident06282007.pdf [accessed March 18, 2008].

———. 2007b. Letter from Fred F. Fielding to John Conyers and Patrick Leahy, July 9. http://www.whitehouse.gov/news/releases/2007/07/Memo_070907.pdf [accessed March 18, 2008]. 2007c. Letter from Fred F. Fielding to Patrick Leahy and Arlen Specter, August 1. http://leahy.senate.gov/press/200708/07-08-01%20white%20house%20rove.pdf [accessed March 18, 2008]. U.S. Department of Justice, Office of the Solicitor General. 2007a. Letter from Paul D. Clement to George W. Bush, June 27. http://www.whitehouse.gov/news/releases/2007/06/LetterfromSolicitorGeneral06272007.pdf [accessed March 18, 2008].

———. 2007b. Letter from Glenn A. Fine to Patrick Leahy, August 30. http://leahy.senate.gov/press/200708/8-30-07%20fine%20to%20pjl.pdf [accessed March 18, 2008].

U.S. House of Representatives. 1973. *Availability of information to Congress.* Hearings before a Subcommittee of the Committee on Government Operations. 93rd Cong., 1st sess., April 3, 4, 19. U.S. Senate. Committee on the Judiciary. 2007a. *Department of Justice oversight.* 110th Cong., 1st sess., January 18.

——. 2007b. *Preserving Prosecutorial Independence: Is the Department of Justice Politicizing the Hiring and Firing of U.S. Attorneys?* 110th Cong., 1st sess., February 6.

——. 2007c. Letter from Patrick Leahy to George W. Bush, August 14. http://leahy. senate.gov/press/200708/081407LetterToPresident.pdf [accessed March 18, 2008].

——. 2007d. Letter from Patrick Leahy to Glenn A. Fine, August 16. http://leahy. senate.gov/press/200708/8-16-7%20PJL%201tr%20to%20Glenn%20Fine-AG. pdf [accessed March 18, 2008]. Ward, Jon. 2007. "Democrats Seek Gonzales Probe, Subpoena Rove." *Washington Times*, July 27.

The Washington Post. 1954. "Presidential Discretion." Editorial, May 18.

S E C T I O N

POLICY LEADERSHIP

• • • • • • • • • • • •

A t the end of the 20th century, Americans were accustomed to presidents with active domestic policy agendas—whether to expand governmental programs or contract them. The large governmental programs to which we have become accustomed, however, are a product of the 20th century after the previous century of narrow governmental scope. Likewise, few presidents in the 19th century were assertive in their actions toward Congress or in their domestic policy ambitions.

Things began to change during the late 19th century with the rise of the progressive movement and the increasing role the federal governmental began to play in the life of the nation. As with so many other aspects of the modern United States, however, the big change came with the presidency of Franklin Roosevelt. Just as World War II transformed forever the place of the United States in the world, so did coping with the Great Depression transform the role of the federal government in the economy and the stance of presidents toward Congress.

The initial salvo that began this revolution of governmental and presidential activism was the famous first "Hundred Days" of Franklin Roosevelt's first term. In the depths of the Great Depression, the country was gripped by fear and virtual panic—from the heads of financial institutions, who saw the banking system collapsing around them, to the wage earners, 25 percent of whom were unemployed. But FDR's jaunty spirit and sense of humor, communicated in several "Fireside Chats," set the stage and engendered enough public confidence and support for the flurry of legislation that would be passed in his first 100 days in office. Congress passed 15 major laws that transformed the role of the federal government in the economy and set the country on the road to eventual recovery from the Depression.

The selection by Richard Neustadt takes up the expectations that FDR's legislative achievements have created in the press. Since FDR, most newly elected presidents have been given scorecards for their first 100 days in office. Neustadt argues that the FDR 100-day scorecard is not appropriate for subsequent presidents. For one thing, FDR had until March 4 of 1933 before he took office; this was changed to January 20 by the 20th Amendment to the Constitution. In addition, the emergency of the Great Depression has not been replicated at the beginning of any presidential term since then. Even the political unanimity provided by the 9/11 terrorist attacks on the United States created a consensus only with respect to national security and only for a short period of time. The financial meltdown of 2008–2009 provided support for decisive governmental intervention in the economy, but the ameliorative measures taken prevented the economy from matching the disaster of the Great Depression, and political support for President Obama did not give him the same leerage that FDR got out of the Great Depression.

Richard Neustadt's classic book, *Presidential Power*, first published in 1960, changed the way we look at modern presidents. Traditionally, the emphasis in presidency scholarship was on the formal powers of the presidency and the legal and constitutional aspects of the office. In his path breaking analysis, Neustadt changed the focus to the personal influence of the individual president. He did not ignore the formal aspects of presidential power, but rather he used these as a constant given, and analyzed how individual presidents were able to use those formal powers.

John Burke's essay examines the first six months of President Obama in office. He emphasizes the important connections between the preparation for office that occurs before the election and during the transition period and how successfully a new president can "hit the ground running." Burke gives Obama high marks for his carefully planned transition into office and his early policy initiatives. But Burke also points out the great challenges that faced Obama and his very ambitious policy agenda, including health care reform, financial bailouts, and energy independence. At the time he wrote his essay (in the summer of 2009), the success of Obama's early presidency was still up in the air.

William Howell, in the following selection, argues that in emphasizing the president's need to persuade members of Congress and others with political power to support him, we often overlook the many direct powers that presidents possess that can be exercised unilaterally. Presidents have at their disposal a range of unilateral tools that can be used to accomplish their policy goals. Among these are executive orders, executive agreements, memoranda, proclamations, and reorganization plans. Howell calls attention to these important powers that are likely to be used increasingly by presidents frustrated by the unwillingness of Congress to do their bidding.

In the next selection, Richard Pious examines the policy leadership of President George W. Bush in the "War on Terror." In his policy choices in response to the terrorist attacks of 9/11, President Bush could have chosen to deal with suspects of terrorism as criminals or as sources of intelligence. Pious argues that the Bush administration chose to adopt the intelligence model and interrogate suspects for information about possible future terrorist attacks. In rejecting the criminal approach, the administration ignored a number of due process rights of defendants and thus created precedents that were challenged in court. In his essay, Pious examines the consequences of President Bush's choice and points out some of the drawbacks, including the erosion of some civil liberties and some reversals of the administration's policies by the Supreme Court.

The final selection by James Pfiffner analyzes how decisions were made in the George W. Bush White House. He argues that several important decisions (the decision to topple the Taliban in Afghanistan and the "surge" in Iraq) were made with the deliberation of the president's main advisers and that the president consulted widely before making his decisions. In other decisions, however, President Bush did not consult widely and sometimes made important decisions without informing or consulting top members of his administration in the Cabinet and White House. Pfiffner concludes that careful deliberation about important decisions does not guarantee good outcomes, but the lack of consultation can often lead to mistakes.

Selected Bibliography

Cooper, Philip, *By Order of the President* (Lawrence, KS: University Press of Kansas, 2002).

Fishel, Jeff, *Presidents and Promises* (Washington, DC: CQ Press, 1985).

Hargrove, Erwin C., and Michael Nelson, *Presidents, Politics, and Policy* (New York: Knopf, 1984).

Howell, William. *Power Without Persuasion* (Princeton, NJ: Princeton University Press, 2003).

Kellerman, Barbara, *The Political Presidency* (Oxford: Oxford University Press, 1984).

Kingdon, John, *Agendas, Alternatives, and Public Policies,* 2nd ed. (New York: HarperCollins, 1995).

Lewis, David, *Presidents and the Politics of Agency Design* (Stanford, CA: Stanford University Press, 2003).

Light, Paul, *The President's Agenda* (Baltimore, MD: Johns Hopkins University Press, 1982).

Light, Paul, *A Government Ill Executed* (Cambridge, MA: Harvard University Press, 2090),

McKay, David, *Domestic Policy and Ideology* (New York: Cambridge University Press, 1989).

Milkis, Sidney, Michael Nelson,, and Greg Giroux, *The American Presidency,* 5th ed. (Washington, DC: CQ Press, 2010).

Polsby, Nelson, *Congress and the Presidency* (Englewood Cliffs, NJ: Prentice-Hall, 1986).

Shull, Steven. *Domestic Policy Formation: Presidential–Congressional Partnership* (Westport, CT: Greenwood Press, 1983).

Spitzer, Robert J., *The Presidency and Public Policy* (University, Al: University of Alabama Press, 1983).

Sundquist, James, *Politics and Policy* (Washington, DC: Brookings, 1968).

Wildavsky, Aaron, *The New Politics of the Budgetary Process* (Glenview, IL: Scott, Foresman, 1988).

Richard E. Neustadt

The Presidential "Hundred Days"

The "Hundred Days" of 1933, a term the American media had borrowed from French history, was used to denote Franklin D. Roosevelt's great success with Congress in and after that year's banking crisis. Ever since, the term has been used analogically by journalists to measure the effectiveness of newly elected presidents in their first legislative session and also has been used by certain presidents-elect to plan their post-inaugural strategies.

The analogy, however, is not apt. Roosevelt's Congress had come into special session at his call, amid emergency conditions, widely perceived as such. Subsequent presidents have dealt with Congresses in regular session, facing lesser problems, while 100 days reaches only to the Easter recess of a modern Congress, not a date for finishing most bills. Even LBJ in 1964, though not a president then elected, faced only a psychological emergency created by his predecessor's murder. And that he rode to early legislative triumphs at the later cost of escalation in Vietnam, imprisoned by his own initial pledge, "let us continue." The next year, newly elected in his own right, Johnson's coattails carried with him the largest Democratic majorities in both Houses since Roosevelt's heyday. With these, in the course of two regular sessions, Johnson launched and carried through the measures for his Great Society.

The original "Hundred Days" had nothing whatever to do with the United States. In the spring of 1815, the former emperor of the French, Napoleon I, escaped from Elba, where he had been exiled after his abdication of the year before. Returning to France, he rallied the army, regained Paris, restored his rule, prepared to fight the rest of Europe still arrayed against him, and at Waterloo in Belgium was decisively defeated. Thereupon, he had to abdicate again and this time was transported far away, to St. Helena in the South Atlantic. This coda to his reign in France lasted 100 days and was so labeled by historians.

In 1933, when Americans swiped that label, FDR had been sworn in on March 4 (under constitutional provisions before the Twentieth Amendment), while the

Source: *Presidential Studies Quarterly* Vol 31, no. 1 (March 2001).

"lame-duck" session of Congress had adjourned the day before, and the new Congress was not scheduled to meet until the following December. But in March, the country was gripped by financial disaster crowning three years of deepening depression. Banks were failing on every hand. Desperate depositors were losing their life's savings. Desperate businesses were short of cash. Roosevelt at once took executive measures, but he needed legislative authority for more and so called the new Congress into special session. Somewhat to his surprise, he found it so compliant in the face of the emergency that he kept it in session for three months and bargained through it 16 major bills, many of them newly improvised, such as the National Industrial Recovery Act, and some previously kicked around for years, such as the Tennessee Valley Authority. In sum, they constituted what became known as the "First New Deal."

When FDR ran low on measures and found members running out of steam, he prudently dismissed them and from June until December governed with the Congress out of town. From his call until adjournment, that special session had lasted 100 days. The press affixed to it the Napoleonic designation.

Ever since, journalists have speculated in advance and summed up after a new president's first 100 days—with Congress routinely in session (thanks to the Twentieth Amendment)—while his legislative success, compared to Roosevelt's, is often at the heart of their stories. And not journalists alone, but also incoming presidents and still more their staffs have often adopted this yardstick, prospectively, before their inaugurations, in commenting on what they hoped to do. Bill Clinton was notorious for this after the 1992 election. Some of them, moreover, have centered their planning on the first three months in office. Ronald Reagan's staff is a notable example. Scholars also have tended to generalize: claiming the early months of a new term as the most advantageous time for presidents to make their mark on Congress. Avowedly or implicitly, Roosevelt—and Reagan—are frequently invoked.

Journalists and scholars read each other, while presidents-elect, or at least their aides, read both. Accordingly, in Rooseveltian, not Napoleonic terms, the tag "100 Days," as measurement and opportunity alike, now seems to be entrenched in the conventional wisdom of our politics.

Analytically, this is unfortunate for at least three reasons. The first relates to conditions produced by the Twentieth Amendment itself. The second relates to the character and timing of congressional "honeymoons" with newly elected presidents. The third relates to their usual ignorance about the ways and means of some (or all) institutions "inside the Beltway." Let me take these three in turn.

The Twentieth Amendment to the Constitution was designed to ensure that the four months of Herbert Hoover's lame-duck status after FDR's election, in the midst of a burgeoning financial crisis, would never occur again. Henceforth, the new Congress would meet in regular session on January 3 of the year after November's election, with the new president inaugurated on January 20. This might have helped with the banking emergency of 1932–1933. It also put an end to lame-duck sessions of the outgoing Congress, which had long been thought unsatisfactory. But in other respects, the new timing was profoundly disadvantageous for incoming presidents.

Formerly, elected presidents had had four months before the inauguration to choose their cabinets and personal aides, while appraising the condition of the country, and then nine months in office to accustom themselves to one another, learn the ropes in the executive establishment (and in press relations), review policies, and ponder budgets—all before Congress and its committees hove on the scene. If Congress arrived earlier, it would do so only in special session on the president's call, for the limited purposes he chose. Even Abraham Lincoln, with the Union dissolved and hostilities beginning, gave himself and his associates from March until June before calling Congress into special session.

How good that looks now, from the standpoint of an incoming administration, and how unattainable! Instead, the new Congress is in session three weeks before the inauguration, with its committees organized, impatiently awaiting the new president's initiatives. Moreover, because for half a century, one or both Houses have usually been organized by the political party opposed to the president, impatience has an undertone of negativity.

This brings me to my second point. Congress, institutionally, is suspicious of "downtown," being competitive with the White House for control of federal agencies, their programs, and their budgets and licensed by the Constitution to compete. So Congress does, in modern times most notably through its extensively staffed subcommittees and its partisan floor leaderships. Because the latter are so frequently opposed to the White House in national politics, the competition is necessarily heightened, with party-enhancing institutional motives. Constituency motives heighten it still further. "All politics is local," as a recent speaker said, and all congressional constituencies differ, not alone from one another but also from the president's.

Thus, the presumed advantages, in legislative terms, of the first 100 days for new administrations cannot be said to rest on any special institutional, partisan, or constituency preferences binding congressmen and senators to newly installed presidents. On the contrary, those underlying motives to compete with the White House seem as much a factor in congressional life at the outset of a presidency as later. What, then, explains the widely reported readily observable "honeymoon"— by way of courteous manners and procedural accommodations—most incoming presidents appear to get from Congress? The answer seems to lie in public opinion or, more accurately, in public sentiment as gauged by congressmen themselves and by their party leaders, drawing on polls and on press treatment of the new regime downtown.

From long experience, the judgment on the Hill appears to be that in the first weeks after the inauguration, most Americans wish their new president well and want him to succeed, with partisanship relatively low, interest in him relatively high, and interest fueled by curiosity about him in his new, never-before-seen capacity, not as one party's candidate but as the country's magistrate. The congressional instinct, therefore, crossing party lines, is to repress most overt signs of rampant competition until that public mood is seen to fade, as judged by media reactions, constituent expressions, and polls. Then, as an institution, Congress bounces back to its accustomed stance of vocal, procedural, and substantive competitiveness with the president.

In modern times, the congressional reflection of a public "honeymoon" has not endured for more than about six months. In the air-conditioned era, the first session of a Congress far exceeds that limit, with final action on most controversial bills occurring later. So "honeymoons" are marginal, at best, in deciding a new president's success with legislation. The Reagan case, so often cited as exceptional, is less different than it seems, although his gallant response to attempted assassination, coupled with his concentration on a nominally single target, the budget, and Democratic shock after losing the Senate, changed both public and congressional parameters for the time being.

The third reason to discount the efficacy of a newly elected president's first 100 days is ignorance, his own and that of his associates. If he has not already held high executive office at the federal level—as only Dwight D. Eisenhower, Richard M. Nixon, and George H. W. Bush have done since FDR—he will be ignorant of many things he urgently needs to know yet can learn only by experience all through the 100 days and for months after. So those early months are exceptionally hazardous as well as marginally advantageous. Hazards transcend the legislative sphere and include executive operations, where even a vice president's experience is not a certain guide to presidential knowledge.

A classic case of ignorance-as-hazard is that of John F. Kennedy in planning for the Bay of Pigs, the covert invasion of Cuba, which exiles attempted under CIA direction on the 87th day of his incumbency. When the director of the CIA urged his approval, Kennedy did not know that the man spoke for only one part of it, the covert operations that had made the plan and loved it. The agency's analysts, who would have scoffed, had been kept uninformed, as not needing to know. Moreover, being told by the joint chiefs of staff, to whom he had insisted on referring the plan, that it had a "fair" chance of success, he took "fair" as next to good, whereas the chiefs of staff, evidently, meant next to poor. When Kennedy then chanced the plan, moving the landing site to lessen the "noise level" (thereby unintentionally placing it on the wrong side of a swamp from the mountains, a site that the invaders were to use as their escape hatch), he assumed that the joint chiefs of staff would comment on the change without being asked. Because it was not their operation, they would not and did not. Finally, JFK thought that when he barred use of American forces, the CIA and joint chiefs of staff would take him at his word. Having dealt some years before with Eisenhower, who had been prepared to eat such words, if necessary, they assumed Kennedy would do the same and acquiesced in further changes that made overt U.S. intervention all but essential. There upon, to their horror, Kennedy pretty much kept his word and let the invasion fail.

From all that, Kennedy learned a great deal, which was and is important compensation.

Ignorance, in this sense of personally not knowing, is complemented by ignorance in the sense of institutional inexperience. With the Bay of Pigs, the CIA had never before attempted a covert operation on such a scale, nor had the joint chiefs of staff been called on to comment hastily on someone else's war plan. Ignorance in this second sense is no respecter of the line between executive and legislative branches. In June 1977, when President Carter allowed Budget Director Bert Lance to go to the Senate Committee to seek modification of the terms of his confirmation, neither they, nor indeed the committee chairman, seemed aware how exceptional such a request would be and thus how likely to intrigue at least some journalists in an otherwise slow summer.

And in February 1981, when Reagan sent to Congress the most sweeping revisions of the budget and of taxes ever attempted by an incoming administration, he rationalized it with an economic scenario, termed "rosy" by associates, that suffered from the haste with which the package had been put together and within weeks was acknowledged by his budget director as plain wrong. Faced by the choice of repudiating that scenario, hence modifying his proposals, Reagan understandably decided to stick with both. This set the stage for outsized budget deficits in later years. He then found virtues in them but would not have planned them consciously. They were the unintended consequences of a huge and novel effort, pursued in haste by his incoming aides on top of hard-pressed civil servants.

Ignorance of the first sort will be inescapable for many or most presidents-elect. This is all the more reason why ignorance of the second sort should be avoided whenever possible by new administrations. Innovations, to be sure, will be desired and desirable in its first months. But those requiring the relevant parts of government to act in wholly unfamiliar ways perhaps should be delayed at least until the major players' personal ignorance has been overcome. How else to deal with the shortcomings of Reagan's budget director?

For that rarity, a newly elected president with vice presidential experience, such as in Nixon's case, there has been a long interval between one post and the other; past experience is not a guarantee of understanding every facet of the presidency he inherits. If the vice presidency has been the incoming president's immediate preceding office, separated only by his campaign, he may know everything about his new job except how it feels to be in it, which he undoubtedly will have imagined, sitting on the side, watching mistakes made, but perhaps imagined wrongly, as compared with how he would perform if actually in—and on—the spot. His early months will thus involve not "learning" so much as adjustment of perspective—which is best done consciously.

For a newly elected president fresh from the vice presidency, there is, besides, a special hazard in his first 100 days and even after. At least I judge so, on the strength of tales told by associates of our sole modern example, George H. W. Bush. In late 1988 and early 1989, all sorts of people in the Reagan administration, cheered by their party's victory, with all sorts of views and plans for their departments on their own next steps, had to be disappointed, gently moved aside, or quietly disposed of so the incoming president could interject his views and plans with people of his choice. What for new presidents of other sorts is an open changing of the guard was for Bush an almost covert one, involving far less brashness and decidedly more tact than usual—and stretching far into the spring. Coping with his problems is presumably a challenge for any successor in a comparable situation.

John P. Burke

Obama Becomes President: Policy Development and Leadership

Presidential transitions to office have increasingly become recognized as consequential to the performance and effectiveness of new presidential administrations.[1] Jimmy Carter and Bill Clinton both had transitions that weakened the policy efforts of their early presidencies; Ronald Reagan and George W. Bush, by contrast, used that time more productively.

Efforts to plan for a possible transition now begin well before Election Day, sometimes even before the presidential candidates have cinched their party's nomination. At a minimum, candidates and their transition advisers must begin to think about the organization of the transition, its leadership and personnel, budgetary constraints, legal issues, financial disclosure requirements and other ethics matters for potential administration appointees, as well as gathering information about a range of tasks that will confront them, after Election Day. Some transitions have been more robust in their pre-election efforts: consideration of possible appointments to key cabinet and White House positions as well as beginning to plan for the new administration's policy agenda. But there are often trade-offs: The more that is done can sometimes raise concerns of the campaign war room that a new group is taking over, potentially deflecting efforts at the immediate goal at hand: winning the presidential election. A more ambitious effort might also raise the attention of the news media and lead to negative press reports about "measuring the White House drapes" too early.

After Election Day, the pace quickens, to say the least. Expectations are high—and speculation is rampant—concerning the announcement of key cabinet and White House positions. Not only does this involve selection of candidates for cabinet slots, but steps must start in filling some 500 subcabinet jobs requiring Senate confirmation (This is a process that will last months, and sometimes longer, into the new administration). Work must also begin to fill another 2,500 or so jobs that are subject to presidential appointment. The White House staff must also be assembled—another 2,000 or so slots that must be filled. Even more importantly, the staff's internal core must be organized and defined. There is virtually no statutory or legal

---

Source: Original essay written for this volume.

constraint on how the "West Wing" is structured or operates, and this is usually one of the main tasks for the chief of staff-designate, among others, to work out. Very few positions are subject to Senate confirmation, so there is a greater degree of freedom in making appointments (especially the two most important—White House chief of staff and NSC advisor). The catch is that the chief of staff must be named early (so too for the NSC advisor in that policy area) enabling the rest of the staff to be put in place and White House internal organization set by Inauguration Day.

For journalists and political pundits, transitions mark a period of intense scrutiny of the new team as it shifts from campaigning to governing. Mistakes made are taken as signs of a lack of preparation and inexperience, but, more importantly and potentially damaging, as a signal of possible problems in "presidential management" of a new administration. Any initial perceptions of incompetence are hard to disabuse later on. For the public, transitions are a time to become acquainted with their new national leader, no longer a partisan candidate. Public perceptions, in turn, have increasingly become the object of the transition team's attention; a turn to governing has begun, but the "campaign" is not quite over. Indeed, it is never really over given the extensive communications apparatus needed to "sell" a president's program that is now an ongoing part of the institutional presidency.

Policy development is another—and for us an important—piece of the puzzle. During the transition, policy teams are created to hone a myriad of campaign promises into a more limited agenda for the new Congress. Errors during this time can really hurt a new presidency: Carter's laundry list of proposals when he took office; Clinton's distraction over the gays in the military issue and the misstep in tapping Hillary Clinton to lead a closed process for engineering a comprehensive health-care proposal to Congress. Other teams are created for each department, agency, and commission. The effort is to get a sense of the lay of the bureaucratic land, but also to assess policy needs. What legislation is up for reauthorization? What policy changes need to be made?

In short, presidential transitions to office are a daunting task. Their most obvious concern is to put—as best they can—an administration in place by day one. Yet policy development and achievement are the ultimate aim, wrapping themselves around all these efforts and serving as their horizontal goal. Cabinet and White House appointments figure into the creation of a presidential decision-making process, one directed at policy deliberation and choice. In addition, announcement of appointments are now often "rolled out" in policy-thematic public events, emphasizing agenda concerns and beginning to spell out policy proposals. Molding public and media perceptions about the transition are aimed at building wider support, and avoiding any weakening of the soon-to-be president's power position. So too are events with a variety of constituency groups. Efforts to court Congress during the transition—to "build bridges"—are a more direct instrument to secure policy success.

Transition efforts in all these areas are also framed by the "internal time" of a presidency. Budgetary and tax priorities must be set by February, in time for the president's economic address to Congress and the beginning of its budget process for the federal government's new fiscal year in October. A successful policy-defining effort also might take advantage of the early "honeymoon" period with Congress. There is no guarantee of congressional receptiveness, but the president is better positioned to achieve success than later on: In year two of a presidency the mid-term congressional elections loom, potentially deflecting congressional concerns towards re-election and the folks back home; later on, the presidential election is on the horizon, again potentially weakening the president's power position, especially if bipartisan support is needed.

External constraints also matter. Because of these, the Obama transition faced the most difficult and uncertain environment since Franklin D. Roosevelt took office in 1933. Economic conditions were grave: Financial institutions and the domestic auto industry on the verge of collapse, a stock market in its worst decline since the 1930s, growing budget deficits, and an economy headed toward the deepest and longest recession since World War II. Nor was foreign policy clear sailing. Although the war in Iraq was winding down, increased effort in Afghanistan appeared likely. The nuclear ambitions of Iran and North Korea still loomed. That all noted, how did Barack Obama and his team perform?

The Obama Pre-Election Transition and Policy Development

It is not entirely clear when Obama began to plan for a possible presidential transition. Some reports indicated that preliminary efforts began in the spring of 2008. But, at the very least, a formal effort was underway under the direction of John Podesta by the summer of 2008. Podesta had been the fourth and last chief of staff under Clinton and had directed the outgoing Clinton transition in 2000; he was thus someone knowledgeable about White House and personnel matters, as well as presidential transitions. He was a Democratic Party insider, and he understood Congress and the ways of Washington. In addition, as the founder and head of the Center for American Progress think tank, he could draw on a wealth of policy-related studies and an organized cadre of policy-informed associates. Many of the latter served in the transition and eventually in the new administration. His efforts were aided by the candidate's own recognition of the importance of early transition planning. According to Podesta, Obama "understood that in order to be successful he had to be ready. And he had to be ready fast" (Tumulty 2008, 27).

Notable were the lack of media reports of tension between the transition group and the Obama campaign staff. The latter had developed a reputation for internal order during the campaign, as well as strong interpersonal harmony and a rather cautious, "tight-lipped" relation with the media. So, too, on the transition side: Podesta "runs a tight ship," and he has calmed "rancor. . . . by ensuring that people aren't free-lancing in the newspapers by anonymous quotes" (Crowley 2008, 27). No leaks to the media suggested any friction between the two groups. Nor would any have likely sat well with the candidate, who during the campaign had earned the nickname of "No-drama Obama" and a reputation for low tolerance of interpersonal competition, back-biting, or self-serving press leaks.

The lack of conflict is all the more remarkable given the rather robust pre-election effort that Podesta and his team were undertaking. In the Reagan, G. H. W. Bush, and G. W. Bush efforts—which are generally regarded as among the more successful of recent transitions—the pre-election period was largely devoted to preparing for the post-election transition; policy development and appointments were largely off the table before Election Day.[2] In fact, Podesta's efforts were closer in scope to the more expansive operations run for Carter in 1976 and Clinton in 1992. But there was one crucial difference: They did not generate the friction and infighting with the campaign war rooms that negatively affected those earlier transitions, both before and after Election Day.

Potential nominees for key positions began to be considered, albeit discretely (Rucker 2008). The pre-election group also took a look at their predecessors' early successes and mistakes. Preliminary planning for the Obama administration's first 100 days was also undertaken. For this, Podesta's ready access to his own think tank proved important: "Much of its staff has been swept into planning for Obama's first 100 days in office," including a 26-page report detailing the day-to-day activities of an early Obama presidency (Connolly and Smith 2008). No pre-election effort in the past has had a director who could so easily and directly tap into such a policy and planning resource.

The need to hone down an array of campaign promises to a leaner presidential agenda especially was explored. In particular, addressing the declining economy through an economic stimulus package was raised, both as to substance and timing. These debates, one account noted shortly after Election Day, have "flavored the discussion among Mr. Obama's transition advisers *for months, even before his election.*" Should the policy focus be largely on the economy or include other agenda items? This too was explored: "The tension between these strategies has been a recurring theme in the memorandums prepared for him on various issues, advisers said" (Baker 2008, emphasis added).

Reviews of President Bush's executive orders, as well as other rules and regulations, were also undertaken: "The Obama transition team has identified executive orders he can sign in the first hours and days of his presidency to demonstrate action, even as the more ambitious promises take more time. Among other things, he can reverse a variety of Bush policies, like restrictions on abortion counseling [in foreign-aid programs abroad] and stem-cell research" (Baker 2008). According to another account, a team of some 50 people, mostly lawyers, "working for months in virtual solitude," compiled a list of approximately 200 regulatory actions and executive orders that could be rescinded, thereby positioning "the incoming president to move fast on high-priority items without waiting for Congress" (Connolly and Smith 2008).

An especially important step was the early selection of a White House chief of staff. Obama had begun thinking about Representative Rahm Emanuel (D-IL) for the position for a considerable time. As campaign adviser David Axelrod later recalled, "It was months before the election when Barack said to me, 'You know, Rahm would make a great chief of staff.'" Emanuel, "spent six years in the White House, knows this place inside and out, spent four or five years in Congress, and became a leader in a short period of time. He really understands the legislative process, he's a friend who the President has known for a long time from Chicago, and whose loyalty is beyond question, and who thinks like a Chicagoan" (Lizza 2009, 28). Two days after the election, Emanuel's appointment was announced. By contrast, it was not until December 12, 1992, that Clinton named his chief of staff, which delayed other White House appointments and the staff's role in developing the new administration's policy agenda.

Post-Election: The Transition and Policy Development

Pre-election work enabled the Obama transition to get off to a quick start. Podesta continued in his central role, but he was now assisted by two other co-directors, both from the Obama camp: Peter Rouse, Obama's Senate chief of staff, and Valerie Jarrett, a longtime confidante from Chicago. By November 12, teams were announced to continue work on the early policy initiatives of the Obama presidency.[3] Groups were also assigned to bore into departments and agencies, with oversight provided by an eleven-person review group.

Walking a Fine Line

Obama's transition efforts benefited from close cooperation with the Bush team assigned to transition matters. Contact had been made with the pre-election teams of both presidential candidates over the summer. Briefing materials were ordered prepared in each agency and department. After the election, there were regular meetings between the key members of the incoming and outgoing administrations.

Economic policy obviously was of special concern. Space was provided in the Treasury Department for Obama aides to remain in close contact with department officials in dealing with the banking crisis and the economic downturn. However, efforts at the very top also mattered. Bush was prepared to take some presidential steps to make it a bit easier for his successor, such as requesting that Congress release the second half of the $700 billion in bank bailout funds and agreeing to emergency funds of $17.4 billion to avert the bankruptcy of General Motors and Chrysler. Reports also indicated that Obama and his economic advisers were working "closely with President Bush to inject confidence into the trembling financial markets . . . The coordination between Mr. Obama and Mr. Bush was taking place among aides, as well as in direct talks about the rescue plan for Citigroup and unresolved details of the overall Treasury bailout plan." President Bush also told reporters that Obama would be informed of every "big decision" made, and that "It's important for the American people to know that there is close cooperation" (Zeleny 2008b).

Obama walked a fine line given the increasing magnitude of economic difficulties. He and his aides did not wish to follow FDR's path in the 1932 transition by distancing themselves too much from the ongoing crisis of the Great Depression, as FDR had done. At the same time, they recognized that they did not want to get closely yoked to Bush administration policies. Throughout the post-election period, Obama repeatedly emphasized that we have "only one president at a time," a posture which led him to decline to attend President Bush's global economic summit meeting on November 15 (Zeleny and Calmes 2008; Balz and Murray 2008). Yet he did not shy away from discussion of his own proposals for a stimulus package, aid to the automobile industry, or energy, environmental, and health care policies. He was also sometimes critical of the Bush administration's failure to deal with the declining housing market and mortgage foreclosure crises (Kornblut 2008).

Indeed, some of the economic issues were matters he pressed in his meeting with Bush. That the economy was suffering was becoming increasingly clear: data released only a few days after the election indicated that the unemployment rate had increased to 6.5 percent in October from 6.1 percent in September. It was but an early sign of increasing economic decline: by autumn 2009, the unemployment rate had risen to 10.2 percent.

Appointments, Policy, and Publicity

Starting on November 15—and for roughly a week after—the Obama transition began to announce key White House appointments. Emanuel's (and Podesta's earlier) efforts paid off: there would be no delay in the White House staff's role in the Obama policy agenda. Of particular note was the appointment of three individuals close to Obama—Axelrod, Rouse, and Jarrett—to a newly defined positions: senior advisors to the president. The announcement events that Obama presided at served not only as occasions for the nominees to make brief remarks, but as points at which the president-elect took advantage of the occasion to emphasize his policy agenda and seize the "bully pulpit," the one-president-at-a-time maxim notwithstanding.

The interwoven relationship of appointments, policy, and publicity was especially apparent as Obama then turned to his cabinet and other positions. Throughout the ensuing weeks, announcements were made in waves, with each wave designed to emphasize a particular area of policy concern. It was not the first time that this had been done (Reagan and Clinton had done so as well), but it was perhaps the most sustained and focused, and, at the time, seemingly successful.

The economic team came first, starting on November 24 and continuing over the next two days. Obama began with his principals: Timothy F. Geithner, president of the New York Federal Reserve, as treasury secretary; Lawrence Summers, former Clinton treasury secretary and former president of Harvard University, as director of the White House National Economic Council (NEC); and Berkeley economist Christina D. Romer as chair of the White House Council of Economic Advisers.

The group—which also included Melody Barnes, the new director of the White House's Domestic Policy Council—was unveiled at Obama's second news conference after the election. The president-elect also used the occasion to announce that he and his economic team would begin work immediately to put together a stimulus package to "jolt" the economy out of a "vicious cycle" affecting both Wall Street and Main Street; reports indicated the proposed package would be in the $700 billion range. By including Barnes's appointment, Obama sought to link economic issues with domestic policy: "We know that rebuilding our economy will require action on a wide array of policy matters—from education and health care to energy and Social Security. Without sound policies in these areas, we can neither enjoy sustained economic growth nor realize our full potential as a people" (Fletcher 2008). Those domestic areas foreshadowed items that would appear in his first budget proposal presented in late February. They also indicated that he would pursue an ambitious policy agenda, not simply a focus on economic issues.

The rollout continued the next day: Peter R. Orszag, director of the Congressional Budget Office, was tapped as director of the Office of Management and Budget (OMB), with Rob Nabors as his deputy. The third day of emphasis on the economy centered on the announcement of a new President's Economic Recovery Advisory Board (PERAB, which was modeled after the President's Foreign Intelligence Advisory Board created by President Eisenhower in 1956) to be chaired by former Federal Reserve chairman Paul Volcker.

The next week, foreign policy was emphasized: Senator Hillary Clinton (D-NY) at State; the continuation of Defense Secretary Robert Gates at the Pentagon; General James L. Jones as NSC advisor; Governor Janet Napolitano of Arizona at Homeland Security; Eric Holder as Attorney General; and longtime Obama foreign policy adviser Susan Rice as UN ambassador. The group included three women and two African Americans: an opportunity to emphasize diversity was not ignored.

Other cabinet appointments quickly followed.[4] By December 19, selection of the cabinet at least *appeared* to be complete. No recent transition, since Nixon's in 1968, had made swifter progress in filling out the cabinet. According to data compiled by Prof. Terry Sullivan, five of the 15 cabinet appointments were the earliest on record starting with the Carter transition in 1976 (White House Transition Project 2009a). A number of cabinet nominees, however, ran into difficulty as the confirmation process moved forward.[5] Replacements were eventually found, although the appointment of subcabinet members was delayed a bit and attention was periodically deflected away from the early Obama policy agenda.

White House staff appointments also set records. The White House Transition Project found that of 13 top staff positions, seven appointments were announced at an earlier point than in any transition going back to Carter in 1976 (White House Transition Project 2009a). The importance of having a White House staff quickly in place cannot be underestimated. Only a handful of positions require Senate confirmation (some 26 slots in various Executive Office of the President's units created statutorily—but not jobs in what we generally think of as the "West Wing," such as NSC advisor, chief of staff, or other members of the White House Office). Given the delay in filling subcabinet positions, the White House staff usually serves as the incubator of early policy initiatives and is the primary agent in making sure a new administration "hits the ground running" in its policy initiatives. Almost immediately, for example, the members of the White House economic team (plus Geithner, the only treasury official yet named) were at work on the stimulus plan, and key meetings with Obama were held in mid-December (Wilson 2009). In addition, over the early months of the new administration, White House "czars" were designated to lead key policy initiatives, eventually more than 30 such positions by some counts.

Congress: Building Bridges?

The transition also served as a time to meet with members of Congress, with the aim of building support for the new administration's political agenda. Two days after the election, reports indicted that Obama and chief of staff-designate Emanuel were working with Democratic congressional leaders on a stimulus package. According to one account, they were working "behind the scenes" on a plan that included "more jobless benefits, food stamps, aid to financially strapped states and cities, and spending for infrastructure projects that keep people at work" (Zeleny and Calmes 2008).

Elements of the plan largely matched the stimulus package that would pass Congress on February 13. Other policy areas of prime discussion were the bailout of the auto industry and expansion of the children's health insurance program, which President Bush vetoed twice (Hulse and Herszenhorn 2008).

Republicans in Congress were also approached; despite increased Democratic majorities in both the House and the Senate, reaching out to the opposition and building bridges was pursued. Obama met with rival Senator John McCain (R-AZ) on November 17. Obama then made calls to Republican leaders, and he instructed Emanuel to meet with them on Capitol Hill. In January, Emanuel and NEC director Summers met privately with Senate Republicans on a number of occasions to discuss economic recovery plans and freeing the remaining $350 billion in the bank bailout fund. According to one account of these efforts, "Some Republicans say they hear more than they ever did from the Bush administration" (Hulse 2009). Would this courtship yield sufficient votes for passage of the Obama agenda? One advantage the Obama camp had was that—in addition to Obama's, Vice President Joe Biden's, and Emanuel's own service in Congress — a significant number of transition members had served on congressional staffs. So, too, had many members of the Obama White House staff (see: Burke 2009, 587).

Obama in Office: A Robust Policy Agenda

The work undertaken by the Obama transition—both before and after Election Day—paid off. Within two weeks of taking office, the president issued a number of executive orders rescinding Bush's orders and putting new ones in place. Most notable of later efforts was a March 9 order lifting a ban on federal funding for most types of stem-cell research.

As for legislative efforts—attempts to reach across the aisle during the transition notwithstanding—Obama's relationship with Republicans in Congress was not noticeably different from that of his predecessors' dealings with members of the opposite party on the Hill: normal—if at times divisive—partisanship. His early executive orders permitting states to toughen auto-emissions standards, allowing federal funding for abortion-providers overseas, and, initially, proposing closure of the Guantanamo Bay detainee camp abroad drew Republican fire. Bipartisanship proved elusive.

Early Successes

There were some early successes. Two were leftovers from the Bush presidency. In late January, President Obama signed the "Lilly Ledbetter Act"; expanded the time for employees to sue for various types of work-based discrimination. The bill had been blocked by Senate Republicans the previous spring, but the increased Democratic majority led to passage in the new 111th Congress (the vote was 250-177 in the House and 61-36 in the Senate). On February 4, the president signed legislation renewing and expanding the State Children's Health Insurance Program (SCHIP), which had been vetoed twice by President Bush; the legislation added an additional

4 million children to the program. Forty House Republicans voted in favor, and the margin in the Senate was 66 to 32. The administration attracted some bipartisan support on both measures, but that was not to last.

Given the dire state of the economy and rising projections of budget deficits, Obama's team was divided about how and whether they should pursue a robust or more economy-focused policy agenda. Some favored emulating FDR's expansive approach in 1933,[6] others were more cautious and drew lessons from the failed health-care initiative during the early Clinton presidency. But over time there were signs that, although not fully following the FDR model and putting everything immediately on the front burner, the new administration was planning steps for major policy initiatives during the first year. The price, however, was bipartisanship, and Republicans quickly and vociferously distanced themselves from the administration's proposals.

Early Proposals

The most important early legislation initiative was the White House's economic stimulus plan. Obama actively lobbied for bipartisan support, but in the end it was a Democratic initiative. A $787 billion package bill finally passed both chambers of Congress on February 13, in a highly partisan vote (no House Republicans, and only three Senate Republicans, supported iteover, its components raised controversy. It aimed to create millions of jobs through spending on transportation and other infra-structure projects, energy, health–care, and education spending. But was it an effort best designed to stimulate the economy? Was it the "best bang for the buck"?

The second major initiative was funding for the remainder of FY2009. Continuing congressional resolutions had been in place since October; no agreement could be reached between the Bush White House and the Democratic-controlled Congress. In 2009, the new congressional proposal especially drew criticism as it contained more than 8,500 "earmarked" projects. Although Obama had urged restraint on pet bills, he signed what he called "imperfect" legislation on March 11. The legislation's effects—plus those of the bank bailout and the stimulus plan—on federal deficits were staggering. In FY 2007, the deficit was $162 billion, in FY 2008 $458 billion, and in FY 2009 $1.8 trillion, if not more. Still, economic circumstances were severe, and federal spending may prove wise in the end.

A third early initiative was the president's own budget proposal for FY2010, presented in a televised address to a joint session of Congress on February 26. The plan included $150 billion in new energy projects; new environmental policies directed at global warming, especially a "cap-and-trade" system on carbon emissions; expansion of grants for college students; and a major, 10-year, $634 billion initiative (by summer 2009, the price-tag would raise to nearly $900 billion, if not more) to extend health-care coverage on a universal basis. On the revenue side, the plan proposed a variety of tax increases and changes in itemized deduction rules for the top 5 percent of tax-payers, as well as letting the Bush tax cuts lapse. The White House resisted, however, even more expansive steps, such as House Speaker Nancy Pelosi's (D-CA) hope for immediately rescinding the Bush tax cuts on the wealthy rather than waiting for them to lapse. Still, it was an ambitious policy agenda, wrapped in an omnibus budget and tax plan, and with a projected deficit of $1.2 trillion, if not more. A preliminary budget reconciliation vote—close to the administration's request but divided along party lines—passed both houses of Congress in early April.

An Agenda in Progress

Obama and his advisers chose to roll the dice on an ambitious agenda, rather than just focusing on the economy. By the end of summer 2009, the fate of two major agenda items remained outstanding: a comprehensive health-care reform proposal and an environmental policy aimed at "cap and trade," an ambitious system for limiting air pollutants. However, another key proposal to eliminate private ballot elections for union representation—relying instead on a signed "card check" in favor of unionization—proved too divisive and fell by the wayside. Time will tell whether the White House's health care and environmental proposals will reach fruition. Of particular note will be the fate of White House's strategy of letting Congress flesh out the details on health care reform while emphasizing broad parameters and goals rather than a White House-directed plan. But there were some important victories: The Obama administration successfully secured the appointment of federal appeals court judge Sonia Sotomayor to the U.S. Supreme Court without much controversy. She will serve as the first female Hispanic judge on the high court, replacing Associate Justice David Souter.

Conclusion

Unfocused laundry lists can get new presidents in trouble, as occurred for Carter in 1977; so too for the closely held health care reform plan offered by Clinton. More targeted and more transparent efforts seem smarter politics, especially if they take advantage of a president's initial popularity and honeymoon with Congress to press important initiatives that may be more difficult to achieve later on (even as early as 2010 when the midterm congressional elections loom). Time is rarely on a president's side. The economic crisis might have worked to the administration's advantage: demands for a response were pressing, in ways they might not have been later on. Moreover, as Rahm Emanuel observed shortly after the election, "Never allow a crisis to go to waste. They are opportunities to do big things" (Zeleny 2008a). The legislative success of the Obama policy agenda would be an important test for the early Obama presidency, including repercussions of the bank bail-out plan, health care reform, and "cap and trade" environmental policy.

Although not perfect, the Obama transition to office did reasonably well in laying the ground work for the Obama presidency. The pre-election effort is especially notable. It not only put in place the necessary steps for organizing the post-election transition effectively, but it also undertook a robust effort to plan for his presidency. Both before and after Election Day, discipline prevailed; the infighting and media leaks that had plagued some earlier transitions were absent. The post-election transition moved quickly in appointing and organizing the White House staff; how its internal dynamics work out, however, remained to be seen. Vetting of some cabinet nominees was clearly problematic and contributed to delay in sub-cabinet appointments.

President Obama signaled his intention to make a clean break from the unpopular Bush presidency with his executive orders and early policy and budget proposals. At the same time, he sought to tamp down public expectations for quick results on the economy. Early—and ambitious—actions were taken, but as he cautioned in his inaugural address, "The challenges we face are real" and they "will not be met easily or in a short span of time." His initial political capital seemed high.

But was the right course of action chosen? The decision was made to embrace a broad range of policy reforms, not just focus on the economy. Moreover, it was a controversial agenda. His early efforts to gain bipartisan support in Congress—much like those of his predecessors—seem largely for naught and forced the administration to rely on narrow partisan majorities. The question that remained was whether his political capital, both in Congress and with the public, would bring him legislative—and ultimately policy—success.

Good transition planning is propitious, but it offers no guarantees. Still, without it, political and policy disaster likely awaits. President Obama seemed to reside largely on the positive side of the equation. But whether his early efforts would result in success remained uncertain in the summer of 2009.

Endnotes

1. For a fuller analysis of the Obama transition, see Burke (2009). On the Carter through Clinton transitions, see Burke (2000); on the George W. Bush transition and early presidency, see Burke (2004).
2. Among the very few exceptions were James A. Baker's selection as secretary of state in 1988 and Andrew Card Jr. as chief of staff for G. W. Bush in 2000.
3. On November 19, seven additional groups were announced.
4. December 3, New Mexico governor and former presidential candidate Bill Richardson at Commerce; December 7, Gen. Eric Shinseki, former Army Chief of Staff, at Veterans Affairs; December 11, former Sen. Tom Daschle at HHS; December 13, Shaun Donovan, New York City's housing commissioner, at HUD; December 15, Steven Chu, a physicist at the University of California, at Energy, and Lisa Jackson, former New Jersey commissioner of environmental protection, at EPA; December 16, Arne Duncan, chief executive of Chicago public schools, at Education; December 17, Sen. Ken Salazar (D-CO) at Interior, and former Iowa Gov. Tom Vilsack at Agriculture; December 19, Rep. Ray LaHood (R-IL) at Transportation, Rep. Hilda Solis (D-CA) at Labor, and former Dallas mayor Ron Kirk as U.S. Trade Representative. The only two key positions that experienced some delay were Dennis Blair's selection as director of National Intelligence and Leon Panetta's as director of the CIA; both were announced on January 9.
5. Those withdrawing included Richardson at Commerce, Daschle at HHS, and Senator Judd Gregg's (R-NH) as the initial replacement for Richardson. The loss of Daschle to the Obama team was especially costly in terms of its health care initiatives. Daschle had been selected to head up a special White House unit in that policy area, and reports indicated he might be given an office in the White House as well as attend morning staff meetings. There were delays in naming sub-cabinet nominees, especially in the Treasury Department (for a fuller analysis, see Burke 2009, pp. 591-93). However, by the 100-day mark on April 29—according to data compiled by Terry Sullivan—221 nominations to Senate-confirmed positions had been announced (compared to 201 for G. W. Bush), 183 had been sent to the

Senate (compared to 87 for Bush), and 67 had been confirmed, compared to 33 for Bush. Furthermore, Obama was ahead of G. H. W. Bush and Clinton (both with 45 confirmations) but behind Reagan's record of 83 (White House Transition Project 2009b).

6. It is interesting to note, however, that some of FDR's most important initiatives were enacted later in his first term—after his initial focus on the economic crisis—especially key components of the "Second New Deal" such as the Social Security Act, the National Labor Relations (Wagner) Act, and bills creating the Works Progress Administration and the National Youth Administration. FDR also benefited from increased Democratic majorities in Congress following the 1934 midterm elections.

References

Baker, Peter, 2008. "Obama Team Weighs What to Take on First," *The New York Times*, November 9.

Balz, Dan and Shailagh Murray, 2008. "President-Elect Meets the Press, Cautiously," *The Washington Post*, November 8.

Burke, John P., 2000. *Presidential Transitions: From Politics to Practice*, (Boulder: Lynne Rienner).

———. 2004. *Becoming President: The Bush Transition, 2000-2003*, (Boulder: Lynne Rienner).

———. 2009. "The Obama Transition: An Early Assessment," *Presidential Studies Quarterly* 39 (September 2009): pp. 572-602.

Connolly, Ceci and R. Jeffrey Smith, 2008. "Obama Positioned to Quickly Reverse Bush Actions," *The Washington Post*, November 9.

Crowley, Michael, 2008. "The Shadow President: How John Podesta Invented the Obama Administration," *New Republic*, November 19, pp. 26–28.

Fletcher, Michael A., 2008. "Domestic Adviser May Play Greater Role," *The Washington Post*, November 25.

Hulse, Carl, 2009. "Obama Team Makes Early Efforts to Show Willingness to Reach Out to Republicans," *The New York Times*, January 20.

Hulse, Carl and David M. Herszenhorn, 2008. "Obama Team and Congress Are Hoping to Have Bills Ready by Inauguration," *The New York Times*, November 27.

Kornblut, Anne E., 2008. "Obama Warns Economy Will 'Get Worse,'" *The Washington Post*, December 8.

Lizza, Ryan, 2009. "The Gatekeeper: Rahm Emanuel on the Job," *The New Yorker*, March 2, pp. 24-29.

Rucker, Philip, 2008. "Potential Obama Appointees Face Extensive Vetting," *The Washington Post*, November 18.

Tumulty, Karen, 2008. "Change: What It Looks Like ," *Time*, November 24, pp. 26–29.

White House Transition Project, 2009a. "Transition Roundup: Cabinet Record; WH Staff Record," www.whitehousetransitionproject.org (accessed March 1, 2009).

———. 2009b. Appointments Summary. www.whitehousetransitionproject.org (accessed April 8, 2009).

Wilson, Scott, 2009. "Bruised by Stimulus Battle, Obama Changed His Approach to Washington," *The Washington Post*, April 29.

Zeleny, Jeff, 2008a. "Obama Weighs Quick Undoing of Bush Policy," *The New York Times*, November 10.
——. 2008b. "Obama and Bush Working to Calm Volatile Market," *The New York Times*, November 25.

William G. Howell

Unilateral Powers: A Brief Overview

To advance their policy agenda, presidents have two options. They can submit proposals to Congress and hope that its members faithfully shepherd bills into laws; or they can exercise their unilateral powers—issuing such directives as executive orders, executive agreements, proclamations, national security directives, or memoranda—and thereby create policies that assume the weight of law without the formal endorsement of a sitting Congress. To pursue a unilateral strategy, of course, presidents must be able to justify their actions on some blend of statutory, treaty, or constitutional powers; and when they cannot, their only recourse is legislation. But given the ambiguity of Article II powers and the massive corpus of law that presidents can draw upon, as well as the well-documented travails of the legislative process, the appeal of unilateral powers is readily apparent.

Not surprisingly, almost all the trend lines point upward. During the first 150 years of the nation's history, treaties (which require Senate ratification) regularly outnumbered executive agreements (which do not); but during the last 50 years, presidents have signed roughly 10 executive agreements for every treaty that was submitted to Congress (Margolis 1986; Moe and Howell 1999b). With rising frequency, presidents are issuing national security directives (policies that are not even released for public review) to institute aspects of their policy agenda (Cooper 1997, 2002). Since Truman fatefully called the Korean War a "police action," modern presidents have launched literally hundreds of military actions without first securing a formal congressional authorization (Blechman and Kaplan 1978; Fisher 2004b). Though the total number of executive orders has declined, presidents issued almost four times as many "significant" orders in the second half of the 20th century as they did in the first (Howell 2003, 83). Using executive orders, department orders, and reorganizations plans, presidents have unilaterally created a majority of the administrative agencies listed in the *United States*

Source: Presidential Studies Quarterly Vol. 35, No. 3 (September 2005).

Government Manual (Howell and Lewis 2002; Lewis 2003). These policy mechanisms, what is more, hardly exhaust the options available to presidents, who regularly invent new ones or redefine old ones in order to suit their own strategic interests.

The nation's recent experience under the last two presidential administrations makes the subject all the more timely. From the creation of military tribunals to try suspected "enemy combatants" to tactical decisions made in ongoing conflicts in Afghanistan and Iraq to the freezing of financial assets in U.S. banks with links to bin Laden and other terrorist networks to the reorganization of intelligence gathering domestically and abroad, Bush has relied upon his unilateral powers in virtually all facets of his "war on terror." And to the considerable consternation of congressional Democrats, Bush has issued numerous rules that relax environmental and industry regulations concerning such issues as the amount of allowable diesel engine exhaust, the number of hours that truck drivers can remain on the road without resting, and the logging of federal forests.

During his tenure, Bill Clinton also "perfected the art of go-alone governing."[1] Though Republicans effectively undermined his 1993 health care initiative, Clinton subsequently managed to issue directives that established a patient's bill of rights for federal employees, reformed health care programs' appeals processes, and set new penalties for companies that deny health coverage to the poor and people with preexisting medical conditions. While his efforts to enact gun control legislation met mixed success, Clinton issued executive orders that banned various assault weapons and required trigger safety locks on new guns bought for federal law enforcement officials. Then, during the waning months of his presidency, Clinton extended federal protections to literally millions of acres of land in Nevada, California, Utah, Hawaii, and Arizona.

Nor are Bush and Clinton unique in this respect. Throughout the modern era, presidents have used their powers of unilateral action to intervene in a whole host of policy arenas. Examples abound: By creating the Fair Employment Practices Committee (and its subsequent incarnations) and desegregating the military in the 1940s and 1950s, presidents defined federal government involvement in civil rights decades before the 1964 and 1965 Civil Rights Acts; from the Peace Corps to the Bureau of Alcohol, Tobacco, and Firearms to the National Security Agency to the Food Safety and Inspection Service, presidents unilaterally have created some of the most important administrative agencies in the modern era; with Reagan's executive order 12291 being the most striking example, presidents have issued a long string of directives aimed at improving their oversight of the federal bureaucracy; without any prior congressional authorization of support, recent presidents have launched military strikes against Grenada, Libya, Lebanon, Panama, Haiti, Bosnia, and Somalia. A defining feature of presidential power during the modern era, one might well argue, is a propensity, and a capacity, to go it alone.

Power and Persuasion

What theoretical tools currently allow us to discern when presidents exercise their unilateral powers, and what influence they glean from doing so? For answers, scholars habitually turn to Richard Neustadt's seminal book *Presidential Power*, originally published in 1960 and updated several times since. This book not only set an agenda for research on the American presidency, it structured the ways scholars conceived of presidential power in America's own highly fragmented system of governance.

When thinking about presidents since FDR, Neustadt argues, "Weak remains the word with which to start" (Neustadt 1990, xix). The modern president is more clerk than leader, struggling to stay atop world events, congressional dealings, media cycles, and dissension within his party, cabinet, and White House. Though held responsible for just about everything, the president controls almost nothing. Congress, after all, enacts laws and the bureaucracy implements them, placing the president at the peripheries of government action. The pursuit of his policy agenda is marked more by compromise than conviction; and his eventual success ultimately depends upon the willingness of others to do things that he cannot possibly accomplish on his own.

Neustadt identifies the basic dilemma facing all modern presidents: The public expects them to accomplish far more than their formal powers alone permit. This has been especially true since the New Deal when the federal government took charge of the nation's economy, commerce, and the social welfare of its citizens. Now, presidents must address almost every conceivable social and economic problem, from the proliferation of terrorist activities around the globe to the "assaults" on marriage posed by same-sex unions. Armed with little more than the powers to propose and veto legislation and recommend the appointment of bureaucrats and judges, however, modern presidents appear doomed to failure from the very beginning. As one recent treatise on presidential "greatness" describes it, "Modern presidents bask in the honors of the more formidable office that emerged from the New Deal, but they find themselves navigating a treacherous and lonely path, subject to a volatile political process that makes popular and enduring achievement unlikely" (Landy and Milkis 2000, 197).

If a president is to enjoy any measure of success, Neustadt counsels, he must master the art of persuasion. Indeed, for Neustadt, power and persuasion are synonymous. As George Edwards notes, "Perhaps the best known dictum regarding the American presidency is that 'presidential power is the power to persuade.' This wonderfully felicitous phrase captures the essence of Neustadt's argument in *Presidential Power* and provided scholars with a new orientation to the study of the presidency" (2004, 126). The ability to persuade, to convince other political actors that his interests are their own, defines political power and is the key to presidential success.[2] Power is about bargaining and negotiating; about convincing other political actors that the president's interests are their own; about brokering deals and trading promises; and about cajoling legislators, bureaucrats, and justices to do his bidding. The president wields influence when he manages to enhance his bargaining stature and build governing coalitions—and the principal way to accomplish as much, Neustadt claims, is to draw upon the bag of experiences, skills, and qualities that he brings to the office.[3]

The image of presidents striking out on their own to conduct a war on terrorism or revamp civil rights policies or reconstruct the federal bureaucracy contrasts sharply with scholarly literatures that equate executive power with persuasion and, consequently, places presidents at the fringes of the lawmaking process. Conducting a secretive war on terrorism, dismantling international treaties brokered by previous administrations, and performing end runs around some of the most important environmental laws enacted during the past half-century, Bush has not stood idly by while committee chairs debated whether to introduce legislation on his behalf. Instead, in each instance he has seized the initiative, he has acted boldly (some would say irresponsibly, or even unconstitutionally), and then he has dared his political adversaries to counter. Having issued a directive, Bush sought not so much to invigorate Congress's support as to neutralize its criticism. An inept and enervated opponent, rather than a cooperative and eager ally, seemed to contribute most to this president's powers of unilateral action.

The actions that Bush and his modern predecessors have taken by fiat do not fit easily within a theoretical framework of executive power that emphasizes weakness and dependence, and offers as recourse only persuasion. For at least two reasons, the ability to act unilaterally is conceptually distinct from the array of powers presidents rely upon within a bargaining framework. First, when presidents act unilaterally, they move policy first and thereby place upon Congress and the courts the burden of revising a new political landscape. If they choose not to retaliate, either by passing a law or ruling against the president, then the president's order stands. Only by taking (or credibly threatening to take) positive action can either adjoining institution limit the president's unilateral powers. Second, when the president acts unilaterally, he acts alone. Now of course, he relies upon numerous advisers to formulate the policy, to devise ways of protecting it against congressional or judicial encroachment, and to oversee its implementation (more on this below). But in order to issue the actual policy, the president need not rally majorities, compromise with adversaries, or wait for some interest group to bring a case to court. The president, instead, can strike out on his own. Doing so, the modern president is in a unique position to lead, to break through the stasis that pervades the federal government, and to impose his will in new areas of governance.

The ability to move first and act alone, then, distinguishes unilateral actions from other sources of influence. Indeed, the central precepts of Neustadt's argument are turned upside down, for unilateral action is the virtual antithesis of persuasion. Here, presidents just act; their power does not hinge upon their capacity to "convince [political actors] that what the White House wants of them is what they ought to do for their sake and for their authority" (Neustadt 1990, 30). To make policy, presidents need not secure the formal consent of Congress. Instead, presidents simply set public policy and dare others to counter. And as long as Congress lacks the votes (usually two-thirds of both chambers) to overturn him, the president can be confident that his policy will stand.

Institutional Constraints on Presidential Power

Plainly, presidents cannot institute every aspect of their policy agenda by decree. The checks and balances that define our system of governance are alive, though not always well, when presidents contemplate unilateral action. Should the president proceed without statutory or constitutional authority, the courts stand to overturn his actions, just as Congress can amend them, cut funding for their operations, or eliminate them outright.[4] Even in those moments when presidential power reaches its zenith—namely, during times of national crisis—judicial and congressional prerogatives may be asserted (Howell and Pevehouse 2005, forthcoming; Kriner, forthcoming; Lindsay 1995, 2003).

In 2004, as the nation braced itself for another domestic terrorist attack and images of car bombings and suicide missions filled the evening news, the courts extended new protections to citizens deemed enemy combatants by the president,[5] as well as noncitizens held in protective custody abroad.[6] And while Congress, as of this writing, continued to authorize as much funding for the Iraq occupation as Bush requested, members have imposed increasing numbers of restrictions on how the money is to be spent.

Though we occasionally witness adjoining branches of government rising up and then striking down presidential orders, the deeper effects of judicial and congressional restraints remain hidden. Bush might like to unilaterally institute a ban on same-sex marriages, or to extend additional tax relief to citizens, or to begin the process of privatizing aspects of Social Security accounts, but he lacks the constitutional and statutory basis for taking such actions, and he therefore prudently relents.[7] And so it is with all presidents. Unilaterally, they do as much as they think they can get away with. But in those instances when a unilateral directive can be expected to spark some kind of congressional or judicial reprisal, presidents will proceed with caution; knowing that their orders will promptly be overturned, presidents usually will not act at all.

Elsewhere, I survey the historical record on legislative and judicial efforts to amend and overturn executive orders issued by presidents (Howell 2003, Chapters 5 and 6). On the whole, Congress has had a difficult time enacting laws that amend or overturn orders issued by presidents, though efforts to either codify in law or fund an executive order enjoy markedly higher success rates; while judges and justices have appeared willing to strike down executive orders, the vast majority are never challenged, and for those that are, presidents win more than 80 percent of the cases that actually go to trial.

Information and Foreign Policy

In foreign affairs, the president enjoys important informational advantages. This is especially true in matters involving the use of force, when a massive network of national security advisers, an entire intelligence community, and diplomats and ambassadors stationed all over the globe report more or less directly to the president, and when nothing comparable supports members of Congress. Instead, members must rely on the president and those within his administration to share information that might bear upon contemporary foreign-policy debates. To deal with the fact that presidents are not always forthcoming, Congress has established a variety of oversight procedures, a complex rule-making process, and liaison offices throughout the federal bureaucracy (Kiewiet and McCubbins 1991; McCubbins and Schwartz 1984). But a more basic problem often goes unnoticed: the issuance of unilateral directives without Congress knowing, or without its membership finding out until it is too late to craft an effective response. Such sorts of informational breakdowns, plainly, corrode congressional checks on presidential power; so as to mitigate these specific effects, over the past century, Congress has enacted several important laws.

Before Franklin Roosevelt's first term, Congress could not take for granted that presidents would publicly release the contents of their policy directives. Though they issued literally thousands of executive orders, proclamations, rules, and regulations, presidents were not required to publish them, and no central clearinghouse existed for lawmakers to review them. With the growth of the federal government came considerable confusion, as legislative enactments conflicted with unilateral directives, as judges and bureaucrats wondered what the law of the day was, and as different departments within the executive branch struggled to keep track of each other's doings. Recognizing that the "number and importance of administrative regulations [had] enormously increased," and that no system was in place to classify or catalogue them, Harvard Law Professor E. N. Griswold warned that the very principles of limited government and checks and balances were imperiled. "It might well be said that our government is not wholly free from Bentham's censure of the tyrant who punishes men 'for disobedience to laws or orders which he had kept them from the knowledge of'" (1934, 213). To correct this state of affairs, in 1935 Congress enacted the Federal Register Act, which required the Government Printing Office in collaboration with the National Archives to publish all executive orders, proclamations, agency rules, and regulations; later, notices and proposed rules were added to the list. The act typically is understood as a pragmatic solution to a growing administrative problem—and for obvious reasons, given the pervasive inefficiencies that then existed. But the act also had important consequences for the workings of the nation's system of separated powers. For by promptly publishing and cataloging various kinds of unilateral directives, the act at last established a system for members of Congress to oversee, and hence to check, presidential policy making.

Almost 40 years later, Congress revisited these issues, this time addressing the issuance of executive agreements. As the Federal Register Act does not require presidents to publish accords reached with foreign countries, Congress often was left in the dark about new trade or security agreements brokered by the president.[8] During the 1950s and 1960s, for example, the Eisenhower, Kennedy, and Johnson administrations negotiated a series of executive agreements with the government of South Vietnam, but Congress did not learn of their existence until Nixon assumed office. Thus, in 1972, Congress passed the Case Act, requiring presidents to report every "international agreement, other than a treaty" within 60 days. In 1977, and again in 1979, Congress passed additional legislation that reduced the reporting period to 20 days and expanded the scope of the act to include international agreements brokered by executive agencies and departments. Unlike executive orders and proclamations, however, executive agreements still do not have a uniform classification or numbering scheme, making it more difficult for politicians (not to mention scholars) to track them.

The 1973 War Powers Resolution, the most renowned of the three laws considered in this section, dealt with related problems associated with the use of military force. Requiring presidents to consult with Congress "in every possible instance" before introducing military forces into foreign hostilities, and then requiring that troops be withdrawn if Congress does not authorize the action within sixty or ninety days, the resolution attempted to limit the president's ability to freely decide when, and for how long, troops would be sent abroad. Having to obtain congressional authorization, it was supposed, presidents would supply members of Congress with the information they so sorely lacked about the costs and benefits of military action. And should members disagree with the president's initial decision to enter into the conflict, they could then force him to withdraw.

Though the Federal Register Act, the Case Act, and the War Powers Resolution have helped Congress monitor the exercise of a president's unilateral powers, problems nonetheless persist. Presidents regularly ignore the War Powers reporting requirements (Fisher 2000, 2004b); they re-label "executive agreements" as "arrangements" or "accords" in order to circumvent the Case Act (Hall 1996, 267); and they declare executive privilege to conceal their efforts to construct and implement public policy (Fisher 2004a; Rozell 2002). Meanwhile, one of the most auspicious displays of executive secrecy continues unchecked: national security directives (sometimes called national security decision memoranda, national security decision directives, or presidential decision directives), which are kept confidential, making it virtually impossible for members of Congress to regulate them. In the past several decades, presidents have used national security directives to do such things as escalate the war in Vietnam, initiate support for the Nicaraguan contras in the 1980s, commission studies on the "Star Wars" missile defense system, direct the nation's efforts to combat the international drug trade, develop national policy on telecommunications security, and define the nation's relationship with the former Soviet Union.[9] These particular actions, moreover, come at the behest of orders that have recently been declassified. Many more continue to come down the pipeline, though Congress, and the public, will have to wait some time to learn about them.

Obviously, to check executive power, legislators and judges must know what presidents have done, or what they plan to do. It is of considerable consequence, then, that for stretches of American history, presidents did not always inform members of Congress about their unilateral dealings. And still today, presidents continue to issue classified directives that often have far-reaching policy consequences. With a nontrivial amount of freedom to craft new kinds of unilateral directives, citing national security concerns and executive privilege as justifications for concealing their actions, presidents have obstructed the efforts of members of Congress to keep pace.

Getting on to the Agenda

Amid the congestion of interest groups and government expansion, political actors struggle to place on the public agenda the issues they care most about. Given the sheer number of problems that Congress now must cope with, and the limited amount of time and resources available to legislators, it can be difficult just to secure a hearing for one's chosen issue. To be sure, by going public, introducing their annual budget proposals, or leaning on key committee members, presidents have unique advantages, especially on issues of national importance. By holding a summit or announcing a policy initiative in the annual State of the Union address, presidents often succeed in launching public deliberations on their legislative agendas. But on smaller matters, members of Congress can check presidential influence not so much by organizing and mobilizing coalitions in opposition, but rather by letting his proposals languish. Instead of taking the president head on and debating the merits of specific proposals, members simply preoccupy themselves with other policy matters. As a consequence, congressional inaction, often more than action, is occasionally the preferred response to White House entreaties, and the bane of a president banking his legacy on legislative victories.

Fortunately, from the president's perspective, unilateral directives provide a way out. For when presidents act unilaterally, they do not call into an expansive void, hoping that someone will respond. Quite the opposite, with the stroke of a pen, presidents instantly make gays in the military or arsenic in drinking water or military tribunals the news of the day. And if its members hope to affect the course of policy making, Congress had better spring to action, for an executive order retains the weight of law until, and unless, someone else overturns it. The strategy of ignoring the president is turned against Congress; the check on presidential power that complacency typically affords is instantly removed. Indeed, having issued a unilateral directive, presidents would just as soon pass unnoticed, for congressional inaction often is functionally equivalent to support.

By issuing a unilateral directive, however, presidents do more than capture the attention of members of Congress. They also reshape the nature of the discussions that ensue. The president's voice is not one of many trying to influence the decisions of legislators on committees or floors. The president, instead, stands front and center, for it is his order that motivates the subsequent debate. When members of Congress consider whether or not to fund a unilaterally created agency or to amend a newly issued order or to codify the president's action in law, discussions do not revolve lazily around a batch of hypotheticals and forecasts. Instead, they are imbued with the urgency of a world already changed; and they unavoidably center on all of the policy details that the president himself instituted. And because any policy change is difficult in a system of separated powers, especially one wherein transaction costs and multiple veto points line the legislative process, the president is much more likely to come out on top in the latter debates than in the former.

This fact is made abundantly clear when presidents consider sending troops abroad. Though Clinton faced a fair measure of opposition to his plans to intervene in Haiti and Bosnia—as Bush (41) did when he tried to make the case for invading Iraq, and as Reagan did when he considered action in Grenada—the terms of debate irrevocably changed the moment these presidents launched the military ventures. As soon as troops were put in harm's way, the exigencies of protecting American lives muted many of the reservations previously raised about military action. The domestic political world shifted the moment that presidents formally decided to engage an enemy. Though Congress retained important avenues of influence over the ongoing conduct of these military campaigns, opponents of the president, at least initially, were put on the defensive. By using force unilaterally, these presidents effectively remade the political universe, launching their policy initiatives toward the top of Congress's agenda and ensuring that they received a considerably fairer hearing than they would have during the weeks and months that preceded the actions.

We must not overstate the point, of course. There are many policy areas in which presidents lack the constitutional or statutory authority to act unilaterally; in these instances, the president's only option is to engage the legislative process. Moreover, even when they retain the option of an administrative strategy, presidents cannot be sure that Congress will abstain from amending or overturning his actions. The basic point, however, remains: If inattention and disregard are effective means of checking executive power, unilateral directives instill subsequent discussions with a renewed sense of urgency and alter the terms of debate in ways that are more favorable to the president.

Budgets

If it has one, the power to appropriate money for unilaterally created programs is Congress's trump card. When a unilateral action requires funding, considerable influence shifts back to the legislative branch—for in these instances, a president's directive requires positive action by Congress. Whereas previously, presidents needed only to block congressional efforts to amend or overturn their orders—something more easily done, given the well-documented travails of the legislative process—now they must build and sustain the coalitions that often prove so elusive in collective decision-making bodies. And should they not secure it, orders written on paper may not translate into action taken on the ground.

For at least three reasons, however, the obligations of funding do not torpedo the president's unilateral powers. First, and most obviously, many unilateral actions that presidents take do not require additional appropriations. Bush's orders took immediate effect when he decided to include farm-raised salmon in federal counts under the Endangered Species Act, removing 23 of 27 salmon species from the list of endangered species and thereby opening vast tracks of lands to public development;[10] when he issued rules that alter the amount of allowable diesel engine exhaust, that extend the number of hours that truck drivers can remain on the road without resting, and that permit Forest Service managers to approve logging in federal forests without standard environmental reviews;[11] and when he froze all financial assets in U.S. banks that were linked to bin Laden and other terrorist networks.[12] These orders were, to borrow Neustadt's term, "self-executing," and the appropriations process did not leave him open to additional scrutiny.

Second, the appropriations process is considerably more streamlined, and hence easier to navigate, than the legislative process. It has to be, for Congress must pass a continually expanding federal budget every year, something not possible were the support of supermajorities required. However, by lowering the bar to clear appropriations, Congress relaxes the check it places on the president's unilateral powers. There are a range of programs and agencies that lack the support of supermajorities that are required to create them but that have the support of the majorities needed to fund them. Just because the president cannot convince Congress to enact a program or agency does not mean that he cannot build the coalitions required to fund them.

Third, and finally, given the size of the overall budget and the availability of discretionary funds, presidents occasionally find ways to secure funding for agencies and programs that even a majority of members of Congress oppose. Presidents may request moneys for popular initiatives and then, once secured, siphon off portions to more controversial programs and agencies that were unilaterally created. They can reprogram funds within budgetary accounts or, when Congress assents, they may even transfer funds between accounts. And they can draw from contingency accounts, setasides for unforeseen disasters, and the like, in order to launch the operations of certain agencies that face considerable opposition within Congress. By Louis Fisher's account, "The opportunity for mischief is substantial" (1975, 88). While discretion is far from absolute, the president does have more flexibility in deciding how funds are spent than a strict understanding of Congress's appropriations powers might suggest.

As evidence of this last scenario, recall Kennedy's 1961 executive order creating the Peace Corps. For several years prior, Congress had considered, and rejected, the idea of creating an agency that would send volunteers abroad to perform public works. Republicans in Congress were not exactly thrilled with the idea of expending millions on a "juvenile experiment" whose principal purpose was to "help volunteers escape the draft"; Democrats refused to put the weight of their party behind the proposal to ensure its passage (Whitnah 1983). By unilaterally creating the Peace Corps in 1961, and then using contingency accounts to fund it during its first year, Kennedy managed to change all of this. For when Congress finally got around to considering whether or not to finance an already operational Peace Corps in 1962, the political landscape had changed dramatically—the program had almost 400 Washington employees and 600 volunteers at work in eight countries. Congress, then, was placed in the uncomfortable position of having to either continue funding projects it opposed, or eliminate personnel who had already been hired and facilities that had already been purchased. Not surprisingly, Congress stepped up and appropriated all the funds Kennedy requested.

These three caveats aside, the exigencies of funding recommend an important distinction. The president's powers of unilateral action are greatest when they do not require congressional appropriation. For when funding is required, inaction on the part of Congress can lead to the demise of a unilaterally created agency or program. And as a consequence, the president's power of unilateral action diminishes, just as congressional influence over the scope and operations of these agencies and programs expands.

* * *

Some Concluding Thoughts

Over the past several decades, the vast majority of quantitative work on presidential power has focused exclusively on the conditions under which presidents successfully guide their policy agenda through Congress. Whole literatures are devoted to whether presidents are more successful in convincing Congress to enact their foreign-policy than their domestic-policy initiatives (see, e.g., Wildavsky 1966, 1989); to the influence that presidents garner from wielding a veto at the end of the legislative game (Cameron 1999; Cameron and McCarty 2004); to the effects that presidential appeals to the public have on legislative deliberations (Canes-Wrone 2005; Kernell 1997); and to the incentives that presidents have to politicize and centralize the crafting of legislative proposals (Rudalevige 2002). More than any other yardstick, scholars measure presidential power by reference to his variable success at coaxing legislative processes in directions and distances they would not otherwise traverse.

All of this work is vital; much more remains to be done. But if we are to account for the full range of powers that presidents exercise, we need a comparable literature that scrutinizes the conditions under which presidents issue unilateral directives and the influence that they glean from doing so. The legislative arena is hardly the only venue in which presidents exercise power. Increasingly, they pursue their policy agenda not through laws, but instead through some combination of executive orders, executive agreements, proclamations, memoranda, and other sorts of unilateral directives. And until we have a firm understanding of the trade-offs associated with administrative and legislative strategies, and we more fully document the regularity with which presidents pursue one versus the other, our understanding of presidential power will remain incomplete.

As we build this literature, scholars should keep two considerations in mind. First, the theory that was (and is) used to explain presidential success within Congress may not accurately explain presidential success outside of Congress. Theories of lawmaking and theories of unilateral action will likely generate different expectations about the conditions under which policy change occurs. For instance, two recent pivotal politics models suggest that Congress and the president will produce more laws when the preferences within and across the two respective branches are relatively cohesive, but as preferences disperse, opportunities to enact legislation typically decline (Brady and Volden 1998; Krehbiel 1998). As we have seen, however, the production of significant executive orders follows a very different logic. When members of Congress are unified and strong, unilateral activity declines; when gridlock reigns, presidents seize the opportunity to issue policies through unilateral directives that would not possibly survive the legislative process. This particular empirical finding should not come as a surprise, for unilateral power varies according to the legislative and judicial checks placed upon the president. When these checks weaken, unilateral power expands; when they strengthen, unilateral power declines. So doing, though, presidential influence through legislation would appear to increase at precisely those times when, and in those areas where, presidential influence through unilateral directives dissipates.

This leads to the second point concerning the construction of a literature on unilateral action. That theories (and tests) of presidential power must be embedded within larger theories (and tests) of systems of separated powers is well understood (see Jones 1994). Few scholars would now argue that we can understand the American presidency outside of the larger political system that individual presidents inhabit. But when examining unilateral powers, the president's relationships with Congress and the courts shift in important ways. Specifically, when unilateral powers are exercised, legislators, judges, and executive do not work collectively to effect meaningful policy change, and opportunities for change do not depend upon the willingness and capacity of different branches of government to cooperate with one another. To the contrary, the system looks more like a system of pulleys and levers—as presidents issue unilateral directives, they struggle to protect the integrity of orders given and to undermine the efforts of adjoining branches of government to amend or overturn actions already taken. Rather than being a potential boon to presidential success, Congress and the courts represent threats. For presidents, the trick is to figure out when legislators and judges are likely to dismantle a unilateral action taken, when they are not, and then to seize upon those latter occasions to issue public policies that look quite different from those that would emerge in a purely legislative setting.

Endnotes

1. Francine Kiefer, "Clinton Perfects the Art of Go-Alone Governing," *Christian Science Monitor,* July 24, 1998, p. 3.
2. Neustadt certainly was not the only scholar to equate power with persuasion. Some seven years before Neustadt published his seminal tract on presidential power, Robert Dahl and

Charles Lindbloom observed that "like everyone else in the American policy process, the president must bargain constantly—with Congressional leaders, individual Congressmen, his department heads, bureau chiefs, and leaders of nongovernmental organizations" (1953, 333).

3. A number of scholars have challenged this last claim, namely that power is personal and depends upon a president's reputation and prestige. For one of the more trenchant critiques, see Moe (1993).

4. Future presidents, too, can overturn the unilateral directives of their predecessors. Incoming presidents regularly relax, or altogether undo, the regulations and orders of past presidents; and in this respect, the influence a sitting president wields is limited by the anticipated actions of their successors. As Richard Waterman correctly notes, "Subsequent presidents can and often do . . . reverse executive orders. Clinton reversed abortion policy established via executive order by the Reagan and G.H.W. Bush administrations. G. W. Bush then reversed Clinton's orders on abortion. . . . This is not a constraint if we think only within administrations, but for presidents who wish to leave a long-term political legacy, the fact that the next president may reverse their policies may force them, at least on occasion, to move to the legislative arena" (2004, 245). The transfer and exchange of unilateral directives across administrations, however, is not always as seamless as all this supposes. Often, presidents cannot alter orders set by their predecessors without paying a considerable political price, undermining the nation's credibility, or confronting serious, often insurmountable, legal obstacles (see Howell and Mayer in this volume).

5. *Hamdi v. Rumsfeld,* 03-6696, June 28, 2004; *Rumsfeld v. Padilla,* 03-1027, June 28, 2004.

6. *Bush v. Gherebi,* 03-1245, Ninth Circuit U.S. Court of Appeals, December 18, 2003. On June 30, 2004, the Supreme Court remanded the case back to the appellate level in light of the *Hamdi* and *Padilla* decisions.

7. For a discussion on the difficulties of constraining the president through crafting carefully worded statutes, see Moe and Howell (1999a, 1999b).

8. For more on the conditions under which presidents issue executive agreements versus treaties, see Lisa Martin's contribution to this volume.

9. The National Security Archive has recently assembled a sample of declassified national security directives issued by every president since Truman. See http://nsarchive.chadwyck.com/pdintro.htm (accessed January 6, 2005).

10. Timothy Egan, "Shift on Salmon Re-ignites Fight on Species Law," *The New York Times,* May 8, 2004, p. A1.

11. David Brinkley, "Out of Spotlight, Bush Overhauls U.S. Regulations," *The New York Times,* August 14, 2004, p. A1.

12. Carolyn Lochhead, "Bush Goes after Terrorists' Funds," *San Francisco Chronicle,* September 25, 2001, p. A1. Patrick Hoge, "U.S. List of Frozen Assets Gets Longer," *San Francisco Chronicle,* October 13, 2001, p. A8.

References

Blechman, Barry, and Stephen Kaplan. 1978. *Force without War: U.S. Armed Forces as a Political Instrument.* Washington, DC: Brookings Institution Press.

Brady, David, and Craig Volden. 1998. *Revolving Gridlock: Politics and Policy from Carter to Clinton.* Boulder, CO: Westview Press.

Brady, David, Joseph Cooper, and Patricia Hurley. 1979. "The Decline of Party in the U.S. House of Representatives, 1887–1968," *Legislative Studies Quarterly* 4(3): 381–407.

Cameron, Charles M. 1999. *Veto Bargaining: Presidents and the Politics of Negative Power.* New York: Cambridge University Press.

Cameron, Charles, and Nolan M. McCarty. 2004. "Models of Vetoes and Veto Bargaining," *Annual Review of Political Science* 7: 409–35.

Canes-Wrone, Brandice. 2005. *Who's Leading Whom?* Chicago: University of Chicago Press.

Cash, Robert. 1963. "Presidential Power: Use and Enforcement of Executive Orders," *Notre Dame Lawyer* 39(1): 44–55.

Cooper, Phillip. 1997. "Power Tools for an Effective and Responsible Presidency," *Administration & Society* 29(5): 529–56.

———. 2001. "Presidential Memoranda and Executive Orders: Of Patchwork Quilts, Trump Cards, and Shell Games," *Presidential Studies Quarterly* 31(1): 126–41.

———. 2002. *By Order of the President: The Use and Abuse of Executive Direct Action.* Lawrence: University Press of Kansas.

Dahl, Robert, and Charles Lindbloom. 1953. *Politics, Economics, and Welfare.* New York: Harper and Row.

Deering, Christopher, and Forrest Maltzman. 1999. "The Politics of Executive Orders: Legislative Constraints on Presidential Power," *Political Research Quarterly* 52(4): 767–83.

Edwards, George C. III. 2004. "In Memoriam: Richard E. Neustadt," *Political Science and Politics* 37(1): pp. 125–27.

———. ed. 2005. *Presidential politics.* Belmont, CA: Wadsworth.

Farris, Anne, Richard P. Nathan, and David J. Wright. 2004. *The Expanding Administrative Presidency: George W. Bush and the Faith-Based Initiative.* Washington, DC: Roundtable on Religion and Social Policy.

Fisher, Louis. 1975. *Presidential Spending Power.* Princeton, NJ: Princeton University Press.

———. 2000. *Congressional Abdication on War and Spending.* College Station: Texas A&M University Press.

———. 2004a. *The Politics of Executive Privilege.* Durham, NC: Carolina Academic Press.

———. 2004b. *Presidential War Power.* 2nd ed. Lawrence: University of Kansas Press.

Fleishman, Joel, and Arthur Aufses. 1976. "Law and Orders: The Problem of Presidential Legislation," *Law and Contemporary Problems* 40(Summer): 1–45.

Griswold, E. N. 1934. "Government in Ignorance of the Law: A Plea for Better Publication of Executive Legislation," *Harvard Law Review* 48(2): 198–215.

Hall, Richard. 1996. *Participation in Congress.* New Haven, CT: Yale University Press.

Hebe, William. 1972. "Executive Orders and the Development of Presidential Powers," *Villanova Law Review* 17(March): pp. 688–712.

Howell, William G. 2003. *Power without Persuasion: The Politics of Direct Presidential Action.* Princeton, NJ: Princeton University Press.

Howell, William, and David Lewis. 2002. "Agencies by Presidential Design," *Journal of Politics* 64(4): pp. 1095–114.

Howell, William, and Jon Pevehouse. 2005. "Presidents, Congress, and the Use of Force," *International Organization* 59(1): pp. 209–32.

———. Forthcoming. *While Dangers Gather: Congressional Checks On Presidential War Powers.* Princeton, NJ: Princeton University Press.

Huber, John, and Charles Shipan. 2002. *Deliberate Discretion? The Institutional Foundations of Bureaucratic Autonomy.* New York: Cambridge University Press.

Jones, Charles. 1994. *The Presidency in a Separated System*. Washington, DC: Brookings Institution Press.

Kernell, Samuel. 1997. *Going Public: New Strategies of Presidential Leadership*. Washington, DC: Congressional Quarterly Press.

Kiewiet, Roderick, and Mathew McCubbins. 1991. *The Logic of Delegation*. Chicago: University of Chicago Press.

Krause, George, and David Cohen. 1997. "Presidential Use of Executive Orders, 1953–1994," *American Politics Quarterly* 25(October): pp. 458–81.

Krause, George, and Jeffrey Cohen. 2000. "Opportunity, Constraints, and the Development of the Institutional Presidency: The Case of Executive Order Issuance, 1939–1996," *Journal of Politics* 62(February): pp. 88–114.

Krehbiel, Keith. 1998. *Pivotal Politics: A Theory of U.S. Lawmaking*. Chicago: University of Chicago Press.

Kriner, Douglas. Forthcoming. "Hollow Rhetoric or Hidden Influence: Domestic Constraints on the Presidential use of Force," Ph.D. diss., Department of Government, Harvard University, Cambridge, MA.

Landy, Marc, and Sidney Milkis. 2000. *Presidential Greatness*. Lawrence: University of Kansas Press.

Lewis, David E. 2003. *Presidents and the Politics of Agency Design*. Stanford, CA: Stanford University Press.

Lindsay, James M. 1995. "Congress and the Use of Force in the Post-Cold War Era," In *The United States and the Use of Force in the Post-Cold War Era*, edited by T. A. S. Group. Queenstown, MD: Aspen Institute.

——. 2003. "Deference and Defiance: The Shifting Rhythms of Executive-Legislative Relations in Foreign Policy," *Presidential Studies Quarterly* 33(3): 530–46.

Margolis, Lawrence. 1986. *Executive Agreements and Presidential Power in Foreign Policy*. New York: Praeger.

Mayer, Kenneth. 1999. "Executive Orders and Presidential Power," *Journal of Politics* 61(2): pp. 445–66.

——. 2001. *With the Stroke of a Pen: Executive Orders and Presidential Power*. Princeton, NJ: Princeton University Press.

Mayer, Kenneth, and Kevin Price. 2002. "Unilateral Presidential Powers: Significant Executive Orders, 1949–99," *Presidential Studies Quarterly* 32(2): pp. 367–86.

Mayer, Kenneth, and Thomas Weko. 2000. "The Institutionalization of Power," In *Presidential Power: Forging the Presidency for the Twenty-First Century*, edited by R. Shapiro, M. Kumar, and L. Jacobs. New York: Columbia University Press.

McCubbins, Mathew, and Thomas Schwartz. 1984. "Congressional Oversight Overlooked: Police Patrols versus Fire Alarms," *American Journal of Political Science* 28(1): pp. 165–79.

Moe, Terry. 1990. "The Politics of Structural Choice: Toward a Theory of Public Bureaucracy," In *Organization Theory: From Chester Barnard to the Present and Beyond*, edited by Oliver Williamson. New York: Oxford University Press.

——. 1993. "Presidents, Institutions, and Theory," In *Researching the Presidency: Vital Questions, New Approaches*, edited by G. Edwards, J. Kessel, and B. Rockman. Pittsburgh, PA: University of Pittsburgh Press.

———. 1999. "The Presidency and the Bureaucracy: The Presidential Advantage,"
In *The Presidency and the Political System*, edited by M. Nelson. Washington,
DC: Congressional Quarterly Press.

Moe, Terry, and William Howell. 1999a. "Unilateral Action and Presidential
Power: A theory," *Presidential Studies Quarterly* 29(4): pp. 850–72.

———. 1999b. "The Presidential Power of Unilateral Action," *Journal of Law,
Economics, and Organization* 15(1): pp. 132–79.

Moe, Terry M., and Scott A. Wilson. 1994. "Presidents and the Politics of
Structure," *Law and Contemporary Problems* 57(2): pp. 1–44.

Morgan, Ruth P. 1970. *The President and Civil Rights: Policy Making by Executive
Order*. New York: St. Martin's Press.

Neustadt, Richard E. 1990. *Presidential Power and the Modern Presidents*. New York:
Free Press.

Rockman, Bert, and Richard W. Waterman, eds. Forthcoming. *Presidential
Leadership: The Vortex of Power*. Los Angeles: Roxbury Press.

Rozell, Mark. 2002. *Executive Privilege: Presidential Power, Secrecy, and
Accountability*. Lawrence: University of Kansas Press.

Rudalevige, Andrew. 2002. *Managing the President's Program: Presidential Leadership
and Legislative Policy Formation*. Princeton, NJ: Princeton University Press.

Waterman, Richard W. 2004. "Unilateral Politics," *Public Administration Review*
64(2): pp. 243–45.

Whitnah, Donald R. 1983. *Government Agencies*. Westport, CT: Greenwood Press.

Wildavsky, Aaron. 1966. "The Two Presidencies," *Trans-Action* 4(December): pp. 7–14.

———. 1989. "The Two Presidencies Thesis Revisited at a Time of Political
Dissensus," *Society* 26(5): pp. 53–59.

Richard Pious

Prerogative Power and the War on Terrorism

"We will protect America," Bush promised the American people after the 9/11 attacks,
"But we will do so within the guidelines of the Constitution . . . the American people
got to understand that the Constitution is sacred as far as I'm concerned."[1] Bush had

---

Source: Original essay written for this volume.

at times taken a different stance, signaling a curtailment of civil liberties: "The enemy has declared war on us," he said, "and we must not let foreign enemies use the forums of liberty to destroy liberty itself."[2] Several years later George Tenet, the director of the CIA, wrote a memoir in which he defended extreme interrogation measures, claiming they had been required to gain information to protect the American people.[3] Does the Bush administration's response to terrorism mean that we are moving down a slippery slope that is eroding due process of law and international norms of human rights? Or is it a response consistent with historical precedents and the Constitution?

Presidential Prerogative

President Bush's administration had a choice of two approaches in dealing with the terrorist threats; one emphasized gathering intelligence in a "war" on terror, and the other viewed apprehending terrorists as an issue of international cooperation in police work, and would require adherence to due process of law.

The Intelligence Model

The "intelligence" model focuses on the enormity of the potential damage from weapons of mass destruction, the possibility of cyber-warfare against the infrastructure that controls physical or information systems, and the potential for martyrdom acts that can instill terror in the population.[4] Terrorism can lead to panic, with a "third day" scenario in which Americans would be stampeding out of cities, or away from nuclear reactors, so that the impact of a single act committed by a handful of terrorists—or even one—could be leveraged. Networks of operatives are loosely linked and dispersed throughout the world, making it difficult to monitor them. Weapons from the arsenals of the laboratories and stockpiles of the former Soviet Union may be stolen or sold to terrorists. American borders are porous, and people and weapons are likely to make it through. Threats of reprisal are meaningless and deterrent factors limited.[5]

The intelligence model (the television program *24* is based on it) seeks to limit those advantages through enhanced surveillance, infiltration by use of double-agents, early and preemptive detention, and aggressive interrogation, all designed to find the operatives who are planning new attacks and disrupt their plans. Trying conspirators or perpetrators is not nearly as important as preventing catastrophic events. What counts is to apprehend them before the next act of terrorism and obtain information from them.

The Due Process Model

The due process model starts with the premise that when a person (whether a citizen or not) is under surveillance or an investigation focuses on a suspect, that person must be accorded constitutional and legal rights of due process. These will be extensive for ordinary criminal suspects and involve the right to know the charges, to have the privilege of the writ of *habeas corpus* (the right to have a magistrate determine if the arrest and conditions of detention were lawful), the right to counsel, the right to question witnesses, the right to introduce evidence, the right to a trial, and the right of appeal. For aliens apprehended abroad, rights may be limited, but everyone must be dealt with according to the rule of law.

The False Dichotomy

Critics argue that the due process model fails to protect Americans, and that other approaches must be substituted, because the potential costs of terrorist actions are so catastrophic—including the doomsday use of nuclear weapons.[6] They argue that once weapons of mass destruction can be employed, prior calculations about the price society must pay to ensure the rights of the accused are outmoded.

Richard Posner, a distinguished jurist and legal scholar, has argued, "The safer the nation feels, the more weight judges will be willing to give to the liberty interest. The greater the threat that an activity poses to the nation's safety, the stronger will the grounds seem for seeking to repress that activity, even at some cost to liberty."[7] Posner argues that all that can reasonably be asked in considering the constitutionality of government action is that we weigh the costs as well as benefits in curtailing liberties.

Yet the "balancing" test may well be wrongheaded. Sometimes there may be a trade-off situation in which one must give up some of one thing of value in order to attain some of another; but sometimes the balance does not work, because the approach taken provides less of both valued things. In fighting terrorism, we want the best combination of guarantees of due process of law that protect our personal freedom and our privacy, and of strong government action that protects national security and our own personal security.[8]

Civil libertarians argue that protection of due process rights is *necessary* to maximize intelligence about terrorism. First, unless surveillance is targeted to the most likely threats, it wastes resources. If judges are required to approve surveillance requests, it is likely the government will concentrate its efforts on those searches most likely to produce results. Second, interrogations conducted with brutality or use of torture are likely to result in misleading information because detainees so treated will say anything. Third, the adversarial system produces better information than the interrogation system. A prisoner's counsel will develop a case, gather documentation, and organize testimony. Counsel may advise a client to plead to a lesser crime, turn state's evidence, and cooperate for leniency—cooperation the government cannot force with brutality. Above all else, due process of law protects the innocent, and when innocent people are set free, the government no longer diverts resources to combat nonexistent terrorist threats based on calculations of the *modus operandi* of those who had been suspects. Fourth, intelligence leads come from informers and with the cooperation of civic leaders, and this cooperation is more likely to be achieved under the rule of law than through brutalizing the population.

Bush's Choice

The Bush administration chose to employ the intelligence model in dealing with terrorists. To do so the government would go beyond the customary interpretations of international law, constitutional provisions, statutes, and existing military regulations, all of which were based on adherence to the due process model.[9] President

Bush would issue executive and military orders based on his constitutional prerogatives (as he defined them) to authorize aggressive gathering of intelligence through
expanded electronic surveillance not subject to judicial warrant, and through the
mistreatment of detainees; to hold detainees indefinitely and punish them, the federal courts and military courts martial would be supplanted by military tribunals.

Surveillance Authority

In the immediate aftermath of 9/11, President Bush authorized by a secret executive
order the National Security Agency (NSA) to target calls made in or out of the U.S.
when one party was abroad and there might be a link to al Qaeda, and to do so without obtaining a judicial warrant from the Foreign Intelligence Surveillance Court, as
the Foreign Intelligence Surveillance Act (FISA) required. The administration
briefed selected congressional leaders more than a dozen times, but swore them to secrecy and refused to let them consult with outside counsel on the legality of the program. Under another program, Verizon, Bell South, and ATT&T allowed the NSA
to conduct surveillance on domestic calls and e-mails without warrants. This
program was in violation of section 222 of the Communications Act of 1934, which
prohibits phone companies from giving out information about their customers' calls.
Two years later, Attorney General John Ashcroft and other senior officials threatened
to resign, believing the way the program was administered by NSA was illegal. President Bush intervened and reauthorized the program without Justice's concurrence,
and then made modifications (still classified) that averted the resignations.

Status of Enemy Combatants

President Bush asserted a prerogative power to reinterpret existing international obligations in order to detain indefinitely prisoners captured in Afghanistan and elsewhere and to mistreat them in order to obtain information. He applied the Geneva
Conventions to Taliban prisoners captured in Afghanistan but not to al Qaeda detainees (because al Qaeda is not a sovereign state and is not a party to the conventions), but determined that neither group would be granted prisoner-of-war status, and
both would be considered "unlawful combatants." Under the Geneva Conventions,
lawful combatants are granted significant due process guarantees, and they are entitled to defense by a qualified advocate or counsel of their own choice (Article 105),
right of appeal of conviction to civilian courts (Article 106), and right to the same
sentences as U.S. personnel, which would limit the death penalty (Article 87).[10] But
unlawful combatants are treated differently: Their status is supposed to be determined,
according to the Geneva Conventions, by a competent tribunal: President Bush,
without using the civilian courts or military courts, made the determination unilaterally for a whole class of detainees, thus acting as the "competent tribunal" himself. Unlawful combatants are granted some due process rights, set forth in the First Additional
Protocol to the Geneva Conventions.[11] But the United States is not a signatory to that
convention; thus, the Afghan and Guantanamo Bay prisoners were granted no rights
at all; their treatment depended completely on the sufferance of military authorities.

Indefinite Detention of Unlawful Combatants

Under international law, the United States has the right to detain and to try unlawful combatants for violations of the laws of war (battlefield atrocities), violations of humanitarian law (genocide), or violations of criminal law (airplane hijacking and murder). Some of the unlawful combatants were sent to a newly constructed prison facility (Camp X-Ray, later Camp Delta) at the Guantanamo Bay Naval Station in Cuba.[12]

American citizens were not brought to Guantanamo, but some were placed in solitary confinement and indefinite detention in military facilities in the United States. In the past, citizens had been subject to military detention and trial in military courts only when martial law had been proclaimed and when the military had occupied territory in secession or rebellion. They also had been subject to military justice, if they had been enemy combatants during hostilities and had violated the laws of war. In *Ex Parte Quirin*, involving German saboteurs captured in the United States, the Supreme Court took up the question of whether one of those captured, who held American citizenship, could be subject to a presidential proclamation denying him access to civilian courts. The Court held that "citizens who associate themselves with the military arm of the enemy government, and with its aid, guidance and direction enter this country bent on hostile acts, are enemy belligerents within the meaning of the Hague Convention and the law of war."[13] Therefore, whether citizen or not, violations of the laws of war are enough to give the military jurisdiction.

Absent such violations, civilians successfully had challenged military detention and trials. In *Ex Parte Milligan*, a citizen in Indiana was arrested and held by the military during the Civil War on charges of conspiracy. He was sentenced to death by a military commission and sought his release through a writ of *habeas corpus*. The Supreme Court held that the military commission did not have jurisdiction, because Indiana was not a state in rebellion, the federal civilian courts were open and unobstructed, and Milligan was a civilian and not subject to the laws of war.[14] In *Duncan v. Kahanamoku*, the Supreme Court reaffirmed its reasoning in *Milligan*. The court held that because civilian courts remained open in Hawaii during World War II, martial law could not replace their jurisdiction over civilians.[15] On the other hand, *Hirabayashi v. U.S.* and *Korematsu v. U.S.* upheld the right of the government to place Japanese-Americans on the West Coast under a curfew, and then to exclude them from the coast and intern them in concentration camps inland for the duration of the war. The Supreme Court, in upholding these actions, noted that they involved "joint concord," because Congress had acted as well as the president in developing the policy.[16] But there is more to the story than these two cases. The Supreme Court, as part of a package deal involving *Korematsu*, also decided *Ex Parte Endo*, a case in which it determined that without an *individual* determination that someone should be interned, there was no rational reason that could justify mass internments.[17] In all of these cases, the federal courts, not military authorities, had the final word on whether or not an action authorized by the president and carried out by military authorities was constitutional. And it had only ruled in favor of the government in the World War II cases, because Congress had provided authorization.

So far as the Bush administration was concerned, anyone involved in the war on terror was not a civilian, but was an "enemy combatant" who might be held without charges, denied access to an attorney, and "softened up" by being kept in solitary confinement indefinitely. The Pentagon did not abide by customary international law and Geneva Convention obligations to disclose the names of combatants to the Red Cross—violations of which constitute a war crime under the War Crimes Act of 1996. The government took the position that the president could order these actions on his own authority as commander in chief and that courts could not thereafter review such indefinite detentions; that presidential prerogative superseded congressional prohibitions against indefinite detention that would otherwise apply to American citizens; and that when it comes to combating terrorism, Congress had implicitly authorized the president to detain unlawful combatants when after 9/11 it had passed the Authorization to Use Military Force against terrorists.

Interrogation of Unlawful Combatants

Under the Geneva Conventions governing treatment of POWs, *lawful* combatants do not have to provide information to their captors beyond "name, rank and serial number" or other basic identification and may not be coerced or intimidated. However, the Bush administration argued that these Geneva protections would not apply to "unlawful combatants," although under the Geneva Conventions, even unlawful combatants have the right to humane treatment; there are limits on interrogations; and while imprisoned, they have the right to communicate with protective agencies such as the Red Cross and Red Crescent—none of which was granted to them.

Common Article 3 of the Geneva Conventions provides that detained persons "shall in all circumstances be treated humanely," and that "[t]o this end," certain specified acts "are and shall remain prohibited at any time and in any place whatsoever." What are termed "grave breaches" of the conventions by captors mistreating "protected persons" in their custody are considered to be war crimes. These include the following: (1) willful killing of protected persons such as injured combatants, POWs, and civilians under their control; (2) murder, mutilations, torture, inhumane treatment, outrages upon personal dignity, humiliating or degrading treatment, or causing great suffering or bodily injury to protected persons. Article I of the Convention Against Torture prohibits torture and defines it as any act intentionally inflicting severe pain or suffering (physical or mental) to obtain information or a confession from that person or someone else (e.g. a close relative).

It had always been an American military tradition, dating from George Washington's generalship in the Revolutionary War, that prisoners were not to be mistreated. Abraham Lincoln during the Civil War issued General Order Number 100, Article 16, which prohibited torture irrespective of any military necessity. Pursuant to the Convention Against Torture, Congress passed a law making it a criminal offense for a U.S. citizen or foreign national resident in the United States to commit or attempt to commit torture under color of law outside the United States.[18] The law defines torture as an "act committed by a person acting under color of law specifically intended to inflict severe physical or mental pain. . . ." Not covered under this anti-torture statute are U.S. diplomatic, military, and other government facilities located abroad, as well as detention centers under U.S. jurisdiction—a huge loophole. But another prohibition against torture is the War Crimes Act of 1996 passed by Congress, which makes it a criminal offense for an American citizen or a member of the U.S. Armed Forces (citizen or noncitizen) to commit in the U.S. or abroad a grave breach of the Geneva Conventions.[19]

With the recommendation of the Department of Defense and over the objections of the State Department, President Bush issued the following order: "The United States Armed Forces shall continue to treat detainees humanely and to the extent appropriate and consistent with military necessity, in a manner consistent with the principles of Geneva." This language invoked Geneva and pledged humane treatment, only to subvert that promise with the loophole of "military necessity." Department of Defense civilian legal counsel then prepared legal memoranda justifying brutal interrogation methods: They argued that prisoners were unlawful combatants and not entitled to protection under the Geneva Convention; if there were no violations of the Conventions, then the Uniform Code of Military Justiceprohibitions against war crimes would not be violated, because the Code requires that there be violation of theConventions in establishing that a war crime has been committed. Secretary of Defense Donald Rumsfeld appointed a task force that recommended a set of extremely brutal methods of questioning, which Rumsfeld approved. Only methods that would have *lasting* physical or mental effects akin to organ failure or *permanent* disability would be considered torture and would be prohibited. Tactics that inflicted *temporary* pain or suffering, or mental disorientation, would not be considered torture, no matter how painful.

Seasoned interrogators and military lawyers in the Judge Advocate Generals' Offices of the uniformed services argued that use of aggressive interrogation techniques would lessen the likelihood that they could obtain the surrender of enemy forces, or gain the cooperation of local communities, or the assistance of friendly nations. The information obtained would be of questionable value, because those subjected to torture will say anything if they are broken—or nothing accurate (or usually nothing at all) if they are not. Use of these methods would put American personnel at risk if they were captured. Their arguments were overruled by the civilian political appointees in the Pentagon. Later, the use of torture was condemned by the top American commander in Iraq, General David Petraeus, who wrote a letter to his troops, explaining, "Some may argue that we would be more effective if we sanctioned torture . . . to obtain information from the enemy. They would be wrong. Beyond the basic fact that such actions are illegal, history shows that they are also frequently neither useful nor necessary."[20]

In Afghanistan, interrogators of the 377th Military Police Company and interrogators under private contract (working for the CIA) used particularly brutal methods. Prisoners alleged that these techniques included administering beatings, keeping them in stress positions for long periods of time, immersing them in cold water, hanging them by chains, subjecting them to "waterboarding" (simulating drowning) and using sexual humiliations (taunting or violating Islamic strictures against seeing nude bodies). At least eight prisoners died while in American custody. At Guantanamo, more than 24,000 interrogation sessions were held in the first four years. Behavioral scientists had access to detainees to develop psychological profiles of Islamic radicals. The Justice Department argued that keeping prisoners in isolated confinement and using aggressive interrogation was the best way to obtain information.[21] Numerous congressional and private organizations conducted investigations that have established that maltreatment has been severe and systematic.[22] FBI agents at Guantanamo protested to their superiors after witnessing interrogations, as did some naval personnel, but their objections did not lead to changes. Years later, retired generals Charles Krulak and Joseph Hoar would condemn the defense of torture by former CIA director Tenet and by leading Republican candidates for the presidential nomination (in 2007 debates), when they warned: If we forfeit our values by signaling that they are negotiable in situations of grave or imminent danger, we drive those undecideds into the arms of the enemy. This way lies defeat, and we are well down the road to it.[23]

Military Tribunals

Evidence from these interrogations would be necessary to prosecute detainees, but it could not be admitted under the rules of military courts martial. The Bush administration decided that forums would be needed with different rules. On November 13, 2001, President Bush issued a military order based on his power as commander in chief.[24] It mandated the establishment of military tribunals (either inside or outside the territory of the United States), to be implemented subsequently through regulations developed by the Pentagon.[25] Those subject to the tribunals, at the discretion of the president, would be any noncitizen of the United States (including a resident alien) who was a member of al Qaeda, involved in "acts of international terrorism," or had "knowingly harbored" others in the first two categories. U.S. citizens would not be subject to their jurisdiction.

The president would appoint military judges to the tribunals. He would determine who would be tried by such commissions, and if defendants were found guilty, would determine the sentence. There were some elements of the due process model in the tribunal proceedings. Defendants would be presumed innocent, would be given notice of charges before trial, and would not have to testify against themselves, with no presumption being drawn from their refusal. They could choose their own counsel (if they could afford them) or military counsel would be provided for them. The burden of proof would remain with the government. Defendants could call witnesses in their defense. Two-thirds of the panel would have to vote to convict. According to Department of Defence rules, the death penalty would be recommended only with a unanimous verdict. There was a right of appeal to an independent appeals board, on which civilians might serve.

However, in many respects, due process protections were wanting. No definition of "international terrorism" was provided in the order or in subsequent regulations. Group association and membership, rather than commission of concrete acts, could be the basis for detention and trial. A person could be charged and tried solely at the discretion of the president, without any judicial review of that decision. (In civilian criminal proceedings, the Fourth Amendment requires a prompt judicial determination of probable cause after an arrest has been made, usually defined as 48 hours.) Anyone charged could be held indefinitely at any location in the world, a provision that went far beyond Congressional intent in the USA Patriot Act, which specified only a limited seven-day detention period, after which a person held must be charged with a crime or immigration violation, and which provides for judicial review in *habeas corpus* proceedings. The accused would be permitted a civilian lawyer of his choosing, but the attorney would have to be cleared for "secret" information under Defense Department guidelines. These lawyers would not have the right to be present if the commission or the President ordered "closed" proceedings. Even the accused could be ordered excluded from part or all of them. There would be no right to confront prosecution witnesses.

Perhaps most important, illegally and unconstitutionally obtained evidence would be permissible if it had "probative value to a reasonable person." This stands in sharp contrast to court-martials, in which strict rules of evidence similar to civilian courts apply. There would be no exclusionary rule for evidence illegally obtained, particularly by unreasonable search and seizure, or for illegally obtained confessions extracted by torture or maltreatment or other statements made by an accused or by witnesses.

Rights of appeal were limited: the appeals board could only examine the evidence, and could not apply the Constitution or federal laws. There would be no right of appeal to the civilian courts: this stands in contrast to courts-martial cases, which may be reviewed by the Court of Criminal Appeals, then by the Court of Appeals for the Armed Forces, and then by the U.S. Supreme Court. Finally, the Pentagon intimated that even a defendant acquitted by a tribunal might still be kept in custody if thought to be dangerous.[26]

The administration claimed the president had constitutional authority to establish such commissions by fusing his power as commander in chief with his oath of office to defend the Constitution. It pointed to what it considered to be past precedents under the constitution, including the establishment of military courts in the Civil War, in the Second World War, and in the Korean War (though in the last instance they were never used). The government also cited the Authorization for the Use of Military Force (AUMF) in which Congress that had authorized the president "to use all necessary and appropriate force against those nations, organizations, or person he determines planned, authorized, committed, or aided the terrorist attacks that occurred on September 11, 2001, or harbored such organizations or persons, in order to prevent any future acts of international terrorism against the United States by such nations, organizations or persons."[27] Using it for tribunals was a stretch, because the resolution contemplated military action against Afghanistan and was not passed in order to provide a framework for apprehending and trying terrorists. The administration also pointed out that the Uniform Code of Military Justice, established by Congress, refers to the establishment of military tribunals by the president.[28] But Congress had specifically provided in Section 36 of the law that such tribunals "may not be contrary to or inconsistent with the UCMJ."

Bush's military order drew rejoinders from critics, and not only from civil libertarians and partisan opponents: Rule-of-law centrists and right-of-center libertarians also opposed this expansion of governmental power. The American Bar Association House of Delegates, by a vote of 286 to 147, recommended that defendants tried before military tribunals be guaranteed traditional legal protections and resolved that the special courts be used only in limited circumstances and under established legal and constitutional rules. American allies abroad, including the British and Australian governments (who had sent forces to Iraq and Afghanistan) condemned the procedures approved by the president.

Defense Department officials discouraged private pro bono lawyers from defending detainees. The Justice Department proposed to limit lawyers to three visits at Guantanamo, and to allow government officials to deny counsel access to secret evidence without obtaining court authorization. It proposed monitoring attorney-client mail.[29] The Pentagon proposed barring lawyers who violated rules from visiting clients, without requiring approval from judges.

The Intelligence Model in the Courts

Private lawyers (some working for civil liberties organizations) and military counsel assigned to detainees moved to challenge many of the assertions of prerogative power.

Indefinite Detention of Unlawful Combatants

Shafiq Rasul, Asif Iqbal, and David Hicks, captured in Afghanistan and held at Guantanamo Bay, denied they were enemy combatants or members of al Qaeda. After interrogation, they confessed to having attended terrorist training camps in Afghanistan and identified themselves in a videotape taken of Osama bin Laden. Petitions for *habeas corpus* were brought in federal district court by the Center for Constitutional Rights, claiming that because the 1903 Lease Agreement with Cuba gave the United States "complete jurisdiction and control over and within Guantanamo," the United States had *de facto* sovereign powers, and therefore prisoners held there should be granted the same rights as if they had been held on U.S. territory, which would preclude indefinite detention without trial. When the Supreme Court accepted the case, the main issue was whether federal courts had jurisdiction to consider challenges to detention of foreigners at Guantanamo. That, in turn, would require the court to decide whether a 1950 case involving military trials outside the territory of the United States, *Johnson v. Eisentrager*, was a controlling precedent.[30] In that case, the court had decided that a combatant held after World War II had no *habeas corpus* rights if held outside the territory of the United States.

The majority opinion, written by Justice Stevens, distinguished the status of the detainees from the German prisoners of war in the *Eisentrager* case, who had been held on German soil. Rasul and others were not nationals of countries at war with the United States; they denied having plotted acts of aggression; they had not been afforded access to any tribunal or charged with any crime; and for more than two years, they had been imprisoned in territory over which the United States exercised exclusive jurisdiction and control. Congress had provided for the right of habeas review on American territory. Stevens held that Guantanamo was such territory, because the United States exercises plenary and exclusive jurisdiction, although not ultimate sovereignty, and so the petitioners had the right to *habeas corpus* review. He also held that in the absence of such a congressional statute the aliens would have had no constitutional right to such review. Shortly thereafter, British Intelligence demonstrated to American authorities that the two English nationals (Rasul and Iqbal) had been in England at the time the video alleging their involvement with bin Laden had been produced, and they were released and repatriated in 2005. Subsequently, the Pentagon instituted an unusual and secret "do-over" procedure: It can order a subsequent hearing if the first board makes a determination with which it disagrees and can continue until a review board approves the detention of a detainee.

In the next important case, the Supreme Court, in a 5-3 decision ruled in *Hamdan v. Rumsfeld* that the president had authority granted by Congress to establish military commissions.[31] The court ruled that trials in civilian courts were not required for detainees, and none of the justices insisted on closure of Guantanamo or other military detention facilities. Justice Stevens, writing for the majority (himself a veteran of World War II) noted that "Hamdan does not challenge, and we do not today address, the Government's power to detain him for the duration of active hostilities." The court's decision was not a complete victory for the government, because it then considered and rejected many of the procedures for the commissions established by the president. Stevens held that Congress had required that military commissions comply with the laws of war, and unless Congress otherwise provides, the president's conduct is subject to limitation by statutes and treaties and must comply with the international laws of armed conflict. Congress had also provided that rules and regulations for such commissions be uniform so far as practicable with rules for courts martial. But the military tribunals violated the UCMJ and the Geneva Conventions: A detainee could be excluded from the proceedings; the detainee or counsel could be denied the right to see evidence, and evidence obtained under duress could be admitted. The court ruled that only Congress had the authority to establish tribunals with such procedures; otherwise Common Article 3 of the Geneva Conventions applied to al Qaeda terrorists. They could be tried and punished only by a "regularly constituted court," which meant an "ordinary military cour[t]" that is "established and organized in accordance with the laws and procedures already in force in a country." A military commission can be "regularly constituted" only if some practical need explains deviations from court-martial practice. The court found that no such need had yet been demonstrated by the administration. Four justices agreed with Stevens that the phrase "all the guarantees . . . recognized as indispensable by civilized peoples" in Common Article 3 must be understood to incorporate at least some trial protections recognized by customary international law. Justice Breyer's concurring opinion invited Congress to clarify its intent about procedures for future trials of detainees.[32]

President Bush, putting the best face on the decision, claimed that the high court had approved the use of tribunals and announced that he would ask Congress to determine whether military tribunals would be the right approach, and to authorize the tribunals in statutory law.[33] The Pentagon then accelerated its policy of transferring detainees back to their home countries: It released nearly one-third of the prisoners at Guantanamo, because they posed no threat to U.S. security, and Pentagon officials indicated that most of the remaining would eventually be sent to their home countries or released because they no longer had any intelligence value. Hamdan, however, was charged with conspiracy and providing support for terrorism (He was a driver and bodyguard for Osama bin Laden) and faced trial in 2007. The Pentagon intended to charge only 60 to 80 of the more than 600 detainees it had held.

Indefinite Detention of American Citizens

A Saudi national, Yaser Esam Hamdi, was captured in Afghanistan on the battlefield by the Northern Alliance, was sent to Guantánamo Bay, but then quickly transferred to the Navy brig in Norfolk Naval Station in Virginia, (where he was held in solitary confinement with only the Red Cross and interrogators having access) after it was learned that he had been born in the United States and was an American citizen. Hamdi was an "enemy combatant," ineligible for protections under the rules regarding prisoners of war, and the Justice Department argued that he could be held without trial indefinitely. It furthered argued that the executive, and not the courts, had the right to make the final determination on his status, and therefore Hamdi had no need for or right to counsel. This was the first time that the government had argued that an American citizen could be detained *indefinitely* without charges, without access to a lawyer, and without access to courts for habeas corpus review.

A lower federal court ruled that Hamdi could not be held indefinitely, but a three-judge panel of the federal appeals court in Richmond, Virginia, upheld the government's view. Chief Judge J. Harvie Wilkinson characterized the detention as an intelligence gathering effort after a military operation, not as a part of the criminal justice process, although he did express concern that in the absence of such judicial review of the classification, "any American citizen alleged to be an enemy combatant could be detained indefinitely without charges or counsel." The panel's decision was affirmed by the full appeals court.

Hamdi's counsel appealed the ruling to the Supreme Court. In argument before the justices, Deputy Solicitor General Paul D. Clement insisted that "[no] principle of the law or logic requires the United States to release an individual from detention so that he can rejoin the battle," considering that the United States "still have 10,000 U.S. troops in Afghanistan." The Supreme Court decided in an 8-1 decision that even alleged "enemy combatants" have the right to a fair hearing to determine their status and that federal courts retain *habeas corpus* review of the fairness of such procedures.[34] Justice O'Connor, writing the majority opinion, crafted a set of guidelines for the military to use in developing its hearing procedures. The opinion was criticized by Justice Scalia, in dissent, who argued that the writ of *habeas corpus* should have been applied, and Hamdi should have been under the jurisdiction of federal courts, not the military tribunal system.

As a result of the Supreme Court decision, the government decided to end Hamdi's detention. He was deported to Saudi Arabia on condition that he renounce his American citizenship, which he did on October 11, 2004, shortly after he returned to Saudi Arabia, and agreed not to leave the Kingdom for five years, and never to travel to Afghanistan, Iraq, Israel, Pakistan, Syria, the West Bank, or the Gaza Strip.

The Illusion of Congressional Checks

Bush's use of prerogative power might have been checked by Congress. As it turned out, a Republican president could count on the support of Republican majorities in the House and Senate, and this partisan backing meant that congressional activity provided only the illusion of effective checks and balances for the first five years of the war on terrorism.

Statutory Authorization for Warrantless Surveillance

In the aftermath of revelations that President Bush had authorized the NSA to conduct warrantless electronic surveillance, bypassing the provisions of the Foreign Intelligence Surveillance Act, a Republican-controlled Congress talked about putting the program on a statutory basis. President Bush attempted to forge a compromise with moderate Senators on the Judiciary Committee, and Chairman Arlen Specter (R-PA) drafted S. 2453, the National Security Surveillance Act of 2006. The measure did not roll back presidential prerogatives but instead provided the White House with recognition of these presidential powers and legal protections for those implementing them. It provided retroactive legal immunity for the participants in the both the disclosed and any undisclosed (i.e., those not yet known by Congress) surveillance programs authorized by the president since 9/11. Any legal challenges alleging violations of civil liberties would be taken to the FISA Court of Review if the attorney general claimed grounds of national security, thus stopping a series of lawsuits in federal and state courts in their tracks. According to the Senate bill, the intelligence court, dominated by judges favoring the Intelligence Model, "may dismiss a challenge to the legality of an electronic surveillance program for any reason," and its proceedings and decisions would remain secret. The bill recognized a unilateral presidential authority for warrantless surveillance, even as it established procedures for judicial warrants: Section 801 stated that "Nothing in this Act shall be construed to limit the constitutional authority of the President to collect intelligence with respect to foreign powers and agents of foreign powers." It provided that electronic surveillance was to be authorized "under the constitutional authority of the executive or the Foreign Intelligence Surveillance Act of 1978" eliminating the prior provision of law that had prescribed FISA as being the "exclusive means" of electronic surveillance.[35] Finally, even if using FISA procedures, the NSA no longer would need to obtain a warrant to conduct surveillance on an individual, but rather needed to win court approval only for a "program" of surveillance.

Critics complained that Specter's bill acknowledged a presidential prerogative and did nothing to limit it. Specter countered that, "The bill does not accede to the president's claims of inherent presidential power; that is for the courts either to affirm or reject. It merely acknowledges them, to whatever extent they may exist."[36] Some Republicans felt the measure provided the administration with too much latitude: Senators Craig, Sununu, and Murkowski proposed removing the language referring to the president's inherent constitutional authority, as well as the provision involving "program" warrants.

Time ran out on the Republican Congress before it could pass a bill. As Democrats took control in 2007, Congress was likely to pass a measure that would reaffirm FISA procedures and curtail warrantless surveillance. But in order to overcome a Senate filibuster, it was also likely that such a bill would have to include some language allowing the president to certify the necessity for such surveillance; expand the scope of targets; provide an immunity clause for prior surveillance; and transfer existing lawsuits to the FISA courts. And once Congress passed such a measure, federal courts would be likely to uphold warrantless surveillance on the grounds that "joint concord" had been established by the president and Congress.

Oversight of Interrogation

Congressional oversight of CIA and Pentagon interrogations was *pro forma* until newspapers published accounts of prisoner abuse at the prison at Abu Ghraib in Iraq. But with the Senate and House controlled by Republicans, committees did not direct their investigations at top administration officials, and Democrats did not have the votes to force the issue. Only lower level "grunts" and junior and mid-level officers were prosecuted after military investigations.

Congress eventually passed Senator John McCain's (R-AZ) "anti-torture amendment" to a military authorization bill, a measure known as the Detainee Treatment Act (DTA), by a margin of 90 to nine. However, a close look indicates that this was a hollow gesture. McCain's bill required that detainees in the custody of the military could be subjected only to interrogation techniques authorized by the *Army Field Manual* and that "no individual in the custody or under the physical control of the United States Government, regardless of nationality or physical location, shall be subject to cruel, inhuman, or degrading treatment or punishment."[37] His initial version of the bill covered CIA interrogations as well. McCain would have allowed a presidential waiver, "if the president determines that such operations are vital to the protection of the United States or its citizens from terrorist attack," but after Vice President Cheney attempted to pressure him to withdraw the entire amendment, McCain stiffened his terms, removed the waiver provision, and got more than three dozen retired high-ranking military officers to sign letters of support. McCain met Bush in a "showdown" at the Oval Office, after which Bush agreed not to exercise his veto, but there was no reason for him to do so: The Pentagon was already in the process of revising the *Army Field Manual* to increase authority for extreme interrogations; the language of the amendment did not provide specific definitions of cruel, inhumane, and degrading treatment; and McCain had compromised on two key points: CIA officers and other civilians accused of abusive interrogation techniques could raise as a defense that they believed they were obeying a legal order; and interrogators charged with abuses would have the right to government counsel. Finally, a separate provision of the DTA sponsored by senators Lindsey Graham (R-SC) and Jon Kyl (R-AZ) was more to the Bush administration's liking: Graham changed a prior draft that had forbidden the use of evidence from coercive interrogations, into the following provision: "to the extent practicable" courts martial or military tribunals would assess whether testimony was obtained as a "result of coercion," consider the "probative value" of illegally obtained evidence, and have the power to admit it. This was the first time Congress had legitimated using the fruit of torture in the courts.[38] The DTA also stripped the federal courts of the right to review the legality of their indefinite detentions through *habeas corpus* petitions from detainees.[39] Guantánamo detainees could have access to the courts only to appeal their enemy combatant status determinations and their convictions by military commissions. When Bush signed the measure into law, he issued a "signing statement" that indicated that he was giving up none of his prerogatives: "'The executive branch shall construe [the law] in a manner consistent with the constitutional authority of the President . . . as Commander in Chief." Treatment of detainees under the Pentagon guidelines would continue.

Congress and Military Tribunals

In response to the Supreme Court's *Hamdan* decision the Republican Congress passed the Military Commissions Act of 2006.[40] Rather than check the president's assertions of power the bill retroactively legitimated all that the president had ordered. It amended the War Crimes Act in order to immunize the CIA from prosecution for its interrogation techniques. It prohibited detainees' counsel from speaking about any information they received from their clients (including interrogation treatment) until they obtained classification review. It broadened the definition of enemies that the president could identify (not only those who fought the United States, but those who "purposefully and materially supported hostilities"), hold indefinitely and try through military commissions. It allowed the CIA to continue to hold and interrogate terrorists in prisons outside of U.S. territory, where they would be exempt from the anti-torture statutes. And it would allow evidence from any interrogations conducted by the military before passage of the Detainee Treatment Act of 2005, even if the interrogations had involved mistreatment amounting to "cruel, inhumane, and degrading treatment" (though it did ban evidence gained through torture). It banned the president from authorizing torture, but it would allow the president to "interpret the meaning and application" of Geneva Conventions regarding cruel, inhumane, and degrading treatment (a provision that would reduce the interpretive role of the federal courts). The most controversial provision of the law was the prohibition against federal courts hearing *habeas corpus* petitions filed by any alien enemy combatant wherever detained, even in the United States. Congress, with this provision, stripped the federal courts of an entire category of habeas cases.

The law was subsequently challenged by Hamdan. In a decision by U.S. District Judge James Robertson, it was held that detainees do not have the right to challenge their imprisonment in U.S. federal courts, and a petition for a writ of *certiorari* (i.e. review by the Supreme Court) was denied by the justices.[41] Hamdan's military trial began thereafter. After the installation of a Democratic Congress in 2007, it seemed likely that a provision restoring *habeas corpus* review for federal courts would repeal the court-stripping provisions the Republican Congress had passed the year before, though it was doubtful that other provisions of the law would be repealed; if they were, there was hardly any chance they could pass over a likely veto by President Bush.

Parallel Governance

Presidents claim prerogatives based on their commander-in-chief powers, their inherent and implied executive powers, or their responsibilities stemming from the oath of office. When taken to its extreme, the result is not merely a "unitary executive" in which all executive powers are to be exercised by the president and his subordinates, but rather parallel governance, in which the executive also exercises quasi-legislative and quasi-judicial powers that bypass the powers of Congress and courts.

James Madison in *Federalist No. 47* observed, that the "accumulation of all powers legislative, executive and judiciary in the same hands, whether of one, a few or many, and whether hereditary, self appointed, or elective, may justly be pronounced the very definition of tyranny." He argued for a system of separation of powers, but pointed out that if a *complete* separation of power were achieved (so that Congress exercised all legislative power and only legislative power, the president exercised all executive power and only executive power, and the courts exercised all judicial powers and only judicial powers), the institution that was assigned all legislative power would be so powerful it would suck the other institutions into the "legislative vortex." Madison proposed *partial* separation of powers, in which some powers would overlap and some would blend, so one department could exercise powers considered to be a part of another department. And so, in spite of the fact that the Constitution assigned "the judicial power" to a Supreme Court, Congress has a power of subpoena;, it may hold witnesses at hearings in contempt; it conducts impeachments as a trial; and the president has a power to issue reprieves and pardons for offenses against the United States. Similarly, Congress does not exercise all legislative powers: Executive orders, executive agreements, military orders, and proclamations all have the force of law, and Supreme Court "landmark" decisions are as broad as legislation passed by Congress.

Partial separation doctrine allowed President Bush to cobble together a set of concurrent powers and institutional practices, first to set policies in the war on terror, then to implement them unilaterally, and finally to pass judgment, all the while claiming the power to avoid judicial review. He did so at a time when public opinion tended to be skeptical of the exercise of power yet insistent on strong measures for national security, when the judiciary acted at times to preserve its own jurisdiction but otherwise did not overturn presidential policies, and when Congress cared more about partisan solidarity than it did about insisting that framework laws it had passed to preserve civil liberties be faithfully executed by the President.

Endnotes

1. "60 Minutes II" *CBS Network,* September 11, 2002.
2. Quoted in Charles Lane, "Fighting Terror vs. Defending Liberties," *The Washington Post National Weekly Edition,* September 9–15, 2002, p. 30.
3. George Tenet, *At the Center of the Storm.* New York: Harper Collins, 2007.
4. "Means of Attack" in "National Strategy for Homeland Security" (Washington, DC: The White House, 2002).
5. Richard K. Betts, "The Soft Underbelly of American Primacy: Tactical Advantages of Terror," in Demetrios Caraley , ed., *September 11, Terrorist Attacks, and U.S. Foreign Policy* (New York: Academy of Political Science, 2002), pp. 33-50.
6. Laurence Tribe, "Trial by Fury," *The New Republic,* December 10, 2001, p. 12; and Ronald Dworkin, "The Threat to Patriotism," *The New York Review of Books,* February 28, 2002, p. 47.
7. Richard Posner, "Security versus Civil Liberties," *The Atlantic Monthly,* November 2001, p. 46
8. James Fallows, "How We Could Have Stopped It: The Plan We Still Don't Have," *The Atlantic Monthly,* January/February 2005, pp. 80–92.
9. For a defense of these policies see Viet D. Dinh, "Foreword: Law and the War on Terrorism, Freedom and Security After September 11,"*Harvard Journal of Law and Public Policy,* Vol. 25, No. 4, 2002 p. 399.
10. POWs are those who have engaged in open, announced combat in accordance with the customs of war. According to the Third Geneva Convention, they are members of armed forces or militia, or organized resistance groups against the established government if they

are under a chain of command and have a fixed recognition sign or uniform and carry arms openly, and conduct operations according to the laws and customs of war.

11. Unlawful combatants under Article 75 of the Geneva Convention are supposed to have trial by impartial and regularly conducted court, necessary rights and means of defense, presumption of innocence, the right to examine witnesses and right not to testify.
12. Diane Marie Amman, "Guantanamo," 42 *Colum. J. Transnat'l L.* (2004): 263.
13. *Ex Parte Quirin*, 317 U.S. 1 at 38.
14. *Ex Parte Milligan*, 71 U.S. 2 (1866).
15. *Duncan v. Kahanamoku, Sheriff*, 327 U.S. 304 (1946).
16. *Hirabayashi v. U.S.* 320 U.S. 81 (1943); *Korematsu v. US* 323 U.S. 214 (1944).
17. *Ex Parte Endo*, 323 U.S. 283 (1944).
18. 18. U.S.C. sec.2340A.
19. *War Crimes Act* 18 U.S.C. sec. 2441 (1996).
20. Petreaus Letter, cite TK
21. Neil A. Lewis, "Guantanamo Prisoners Seek to See Families and Lawyers," *The New York Times*, December 3, 2002, p. A22.
22. Steven Strassner, ed. *The Abu Ghraib Investigations* (NY: Public affairs, 2004; Karen J. Greenberg and Joshua L. Dratel, *The Torture Papers: the Road to Abu Ghraib*, (NY: Cambridge University Press, 2005); Generals Randall Schmidt and John Furlow on interrogations at Guantánamo, summarized at www.defenselink.mil/news/detainee_investigations.html. See also *Command Responsibility*, (NY: Human Rights First. 2006).
23. Charles C. Krulak and Joseph P. Hoar, "It's Our Cage Too: Torture Betrays Us and Breeds New Enemies," *The Washington Post*, May 17, 2007, p. A17.
24. "Military Order on Detention, Treatment and Trial of Certain Non-Citizens in the War Against Terrorism," 66 Fed. Reg. 57831 (2001). Note that this was a military order, and not an *executive* order.
25. *Procedures for Trials by Military Commissions of Certain Non-United States Citizens in the War Against Terrorism*, Department of Defense Military Commission Order No. 1, March 21, 2002. The rules promulgated by the Pentagon are available at: www.defenselink.mil/news/Mar2002/d20020321ord.pdf.
26. According to Pentagon official William J. Hayes, II, in Katharine Q. Seelye, "Pentagon Says Acquittals May Not Free Detainees," *The New York Times*, March 22, p. 13.
27. P.L. 107-40 Sec. 2(a) (2001).
28. The use of commissions has been recognized by Congress in the Articles of War in 1920, the *Uniform Code of Military Justice* in 1950, and the *War Crimes Act of 1996*.
29. American Bar Association, Task Force on Treatment of Enemy Combatants" Criminal Justice Section, Section of Individual Rights and Responsibilities, "Report to the House of Delegates, 2003."
30. 339 U.S. 763 (1950).
31. *Hamdan v. Rumsfeld* 126 S. Ct. 2749 (2006).
32. Jeremy Rabkin, "Not As Bad As You Think: The Court Hasn't Crippled the War on Terror," *The Weekly Standard*, July 17, 2006, Volume 11, Issue 41.
33. Sheryl Gay Stolberg, "Justices Tacitly Backed Use of Guantanamo, Bush Says," *The New York Times*, July 9, 2006.
34. *Hamdi v. Rumsfeld*, 542 U.S. 507 (2004).
35. 18 U.S.C. 2511(2)(e).
36. Arlen Specter, "Surveillance We Can Live With," *The Washington Post*, July 24, 2006, p. A19.
37. Title X, *Defense Appropriation Act, 2006* (H.R.2863); Sections 1402–1405, *Defense Authorization Act, 2006*.
38. This amendment contradicts the flat prohibition on the use of testimony secured through torture or extreme coercion, contained in the *Uniform Code of Military Justice*, 10 U.S.C. sec. 863.
39. The Graham amendment was designed to render the Supreme Court decision in *Rasul v. Bush* 542 U.S. 466 (2004), a nullity. The court held that detainees at Guantánamo could file habeas petitions to contest their detentions. The amendment limits such review to the

validity of decisions of the Combatant Status Review Tribunals, a preliminary proceeding. It would mean that federal courts could not determine if the McCain anti-torture amendment had been violated. Sec. 1005 of the *Detainee Treatment Act of 2005*, "Procedures for Status Review of Detainees Outside the United States."

40. P.L. 106-366, (2006).
41. *Hamdan v. Gates*, 127 S. Ct. 1507 (2007).

James P. Pfiffner

Decision Making in the Bush White House

The process of moving paper in and out of the Oval Office, who gets involved in the meetings, who does the president listen to, who gets a chance to talk to him before he makes a decision, is absolutely critical. It has to be managed in such a way that it has integrity.

—Dick Cheney

The staffing system on Presidential decisions must have integrity, and be known to have integrity. When the President is making a decision, either be sure he has the recommendations of the appropriate people, or conversely, that he knows he does not have their views and is willing to accept the disadvantages that will inevitably result.

—Donald Rumsfeld

A president must give people access. If everybody had the same opinion and the same prejudices and the same belief structure . . . I would not get the best advice. So I need people walking in here and saying, "You're not looking so good."

—George W. Bush

Dick Cheney and Donald Rumsfeld came to the foregoing conclusions after their experience as President Gerald Ford's chiefs of staff—Rumsfeld first and, after he was appointed secretary of defense, Cheney as his successor in the White House. President George W. Bush himself articulated the reasoning behind their observations,

Source: Presidential Studies Quarterly Vol. 39, no. 2 (June 2009).

yet he allowed some of his subordinates to circumvent the regular policy-making process. The integrity of the policy process is crucial, because a president can easily make a disastrous decision if he or she does not have the full range of informed judgment from the relevant senior people in the administration. The White House Office is so large and complex that a systematic process of policy evaluation is essential. Those who have expertise, authority, or implementation responsibilities must have a way to get their judgments to the president, or the president will act from an incomplete understanding of the implications of the policy decision.

In a conference of former chiefs of staff to several presidents, Cheney pointed out the danger of an "Oh, by the way" decision. That is, there is a danger of the president "making some kind of offhand decision that hadn't been carefully thought about, and then people took it and ran with it. It's what I called an 'Oh, by the way' decision. . . . That's when you really got into big trouble" (Kernell and Popkin 1986, 19-21). Commenting further on the importance of a systematic and open policy process, Cheney emphasized the centrality of trust:

> If you don't trust the process . . . all of a sudden you have people freelancing, trying to get around the decision-making process because they feel the process lacks integrity. So it's very, very important when you set up shop to make certain that you have a guaranteed flow. . . . that everybody's got their shot at the decision memo. You know if there's going to be a meeting, the right people are going to be in the meeting, that the president has a chance to listen to all of that and then make a decision. (Kumar and Sullivan 2003, 10)

Rumsfeld also articulated the principle that in order to make wise decisions, the president should not be shielded from those who disagree with the current consensus in the White House. "Avoid overly restricting the flow of paper, people, or ideas to the President. . . . Don't allow people to be cut out of a meeting or an opportunity to communicate because their views may differ from the President's views. . . . The staff system must have discipline to serve the President well" (Rumsfeld 1989, 37, 39). The problem in the George W Bush White House was that these rules were ignored at important junctures by each of these two administration officials, especially in the first term. The results were disastrous.

This article will focus on four important policy decisions to illustrate the lack of a regular policy process that characterized many important decisions of the Bush administration's first term: two on detainee policy—the military commissions order of November 13, 2001, and the February 7, 2002, decision to suspend the Geneva Conventions—and two about the war in Iraq—the initial decision to go to war and the decision to disband the Iraqi army in May 2003.

Decision Making in the White House

Both practitioners and scholars begin from the premises that no one individual can hope to understand all of the ramifications of the decisions facing the president and that staff structures and processes are thus necessary to enable the president to make informed decisions. Of course, well-organized advisory systems cannot guarantee good decisions. As President Dwight D. Eisenhower put it, "Organization cannot of course make a successful leader out of a dunce, any more than it should make a decision for its chief. But it is effective in minimizing the chances of failure and in insuring that the right hand does, indeed, know what the left hand is doing" (1965, 630).

One way to ensure that the decisions facing the president have undergone systematic analysis by the experts and professionals in the administration is to prescribe an orderly policy process. One veteran staffer of the National Security Council (NSC) put it this way:

> The idea is to have working-level officials from across the government meet to hammer out a policy, then move it up level by level, refining it at each step, until it reaches the national security cabinet known as the Principals Committee. The long road to a principals meeting in the White House Situation Room ensures, to the extent possible, that the government does its due diligence and that the affected agencies buy into the new policy. (Benjamin 2008)[1]

The principles of presidential management, gleaned from the practical experience of White House veterans, have been echoed in the political science literature on presidential decision making. The consensus in the scholarly literature is that presidents will make better decisions if they consider a range of realistic options and alternative policies brought to their attention. This is a primary function of a presidential advisory system and overall White House organization (Walcott and Hult 1995). And the key to eliciting these alternatives from aides is to encourage contrasting perspectives. Presidents need frank advice and unvarnished evaluations. If aides trim their advice to suit the perceived predispositions of their superiors, they will not serve the president well. If presidents discourage dissent, their aides will anticipate their wishes and self-censor conflicting views. This may lead to a narrow focus and the neglect of alternative courses of action. Meena Bose (1998) compared Eisenhower's more formal advisory system with Kennedy's less formal system and concluded that the Eisenhower approach was superior. In Eisenhower's words,

> I know of only one way in which you can be sure you've done your best to make a wise decision. This is to get all of the people who have partial and definable responsibility in this particular field, whatever it may be. Get them with their different viewpoints in front of you, and listen to them debate. (Burke et al. 1989, 54)

Students of presidential decision making have come to similar formulations of the elements of informed decision making in the White House.

Alexander George (1972; 1980) argued that presidents needed to ensure that their advisory systems provide them with a range of alternatives for any important decision and that the best way to ensure this was a system of "multiple advocacy." Irving Janis (1982) analyzed the effects of small-group solidarity in situations in which the stakes are high, pressure is great, and secrecy is important. The danger in these instances is that the group will develop the illusion of invulnerability and inherent morality, underestimate the enemy and chances of failure, and fail to reexamine their initial assumptions. Janis used the term "groupthink" to characterize such situations and analyzed cases of presidential decision making to illustrate the syndrome as well as cases when it was avoided.[2]

One way to ensure that the president is exposed to differing perspectives in national security policy is for the president's top aide to adopt an "honest broker" role. This concept implies that in any important decision-making situation, the staffer presents to the president in a neutral way the most important policy alternatives and represents faithfully the views of the advocates of different policy alternatives. The president can thus have confidence that the dice are not loaded in favor of only one or another alternative (or staffer). Playing the role of honest broker does not preclude the staffer from giving his or her best advice to the president, but it ensures that this judgment will not unfairly subvert the judgments of other staffers. Roger Porter described this approach as "a managed process relying on an honest broker to insure that interested parties are represented and that the debate is structured and balanced" (1980, 16). The honest broker role with respect to the assistant to the president for national security affairs has been analyzed by Burke (2005a, 2005b, forthcoming), Daalder and Destler (2009), Destler (1972, 1981), and Mulcahy and Crabb (1991), among others.

A central theme throughout the decision-making literature is that the president needs frank advice about alternatives and that an effective airing of that advice can come only if the president is exposed to contrasting perspectives. In the George W. Bush administration, however, national security advice to the president was dominated by Vice President Cheney, and he was effectively able to manage the policy process to ensure that his preferences prevailed.[3] In making many important decisions, the administration lacked an orderly policy-making process and the benefit of an honest broker. In Bush's case, such a process would have helped because, in Scott McClellan's words, "He is not one to delve deeply into all the possible policy options . . . before making a choice. Rather, he chooses based on his gut and his most deeply held convictions. Such was the case with Iraq" (2008, 127). President Bush's role was characterized by Alan Brinkley: "George Bush was an eager enabler, but not often an active architect, of the government's response to terror. His instinct was to be tough and aggressive in response to challenges, and Cheney's belligerence fit comfortably with the president's own inclinations" (2008).

Treasury Secretary Paul O'Neill thought that the Bush White House had no serious domestic policy process during its first years in office. "It was a broken process . . . or rather no process at all; there seemed to be no apparatus to assess policy and deliberate effectively, to create coherent governance" (Suskind 2004, 97). John DiIulio, who worked in the Bush White House on faith-based initiatives for the first eight months of the administration, said, "There is no precedent in any modern White House for what is going on in this one: a complete lack of a policy apparatus" (Suskind 2003). Jack Goldsmith, a Bush appointee as director of the Office of Legal Counsel, characterized the Bush administration's "concept of power" as entailing "minimal deliberation, unilateral action, and legalistic defense" (Goldsmith, 2007, 205).

Before examining the cases of flawed decision making and lack of deliberation that are the subject of this paper, it may be useful to mention two decisions by President Bush that were made after appropriate policy deliberation: the decision to go to war in Afghanistan and the decision to order the "surge" in U.S. troops in Iraq in 2007.

Despite the time pressure immediately after 9/11 to do something quickly, President Bush deliberated over the following two months, considered a range of options, and decided on a (militarily) successful policy. To plan the administration's response to the terrorist attacks, President Bush assembled his "war cabinet," which included Vice President Cheney, National Security Advisor Condoleezza Rice, Secretary of State Colin Powell, Secretary of Defense Donald Rumsfeld, Chief of Staff Andrew Card, and Director of Central Intelligence George Tenet (Woodward 2002, 37–38).

The war cabinet considered several options for the U.S. pursuit of al-Qaeda in Afghanistan: a strike with cruise missiles, cruise missiles combined with bomber attacks, or "boots on the ground"—that is, U.S. soldiers in Afghanistan (Woodward 2002, 79–80).[4] Although attacking Iraq in response to 9/11 was proposed by Deputy Secretary of Defense Paul Wolfowitz, the president decided to delay that option. During the deliberations, Condoleezza Rice demonstrated her skill acting as an honest broker and custodian of the decision-making process (Burke 2005a, 2005b). She did not often insert her own views or act as a policy advocate, but sharpened questions, focused the discussions, and clarified issues for presentation to the president. She gave her personal advice to the president privately, and at meetings acted as custodian of the process.

At times, Rice was even willing to challenge the president's judgment and urge caution. For instance, in early October, President Bush was impatient to get U.S. troops into Afghanistan. At one point, when Rice informed him that more time for planning and staging was needed by the military, he responded, "That's not acceptable!" (Woodward 2002, 157). But Rice prevailed by explaining the reasoning of military leaders. Contrasting views were presented, even though Bush did not encourage spirited debate over important issues.

Similarly, in his 2006 decision to increase the number of troops in Iraq (the "surge"), Bush considered a range of perspectives. The Baker-Hamilton Iraq Study Group had recommended several diplomatic initiatives, pressure on the Iraqi government, and a gradual disengagement of American troops in Iraq. Despite a broad range of sentiment supporting those proposals, President Bush decided to reject them and increase the number of troops in Iraq with the hope of turning the tide of the insurgency (Barnes 2008). Bush's plan to send more troops was not favored by the Joint Chiefs of Staff; Secretary of State Rice; the American commander in Iraq, General George Casey; or head of the Central Command, General John Abizaid (Woodward 2008, 279–321).

Bush went to the Pentagon to listen to the analysis of military leaders and to convince them that he was determined to carry out the surge. Bush told Fred Barnes that "[n]ot every meeting in the White House is a formal meeting, and a lot of times decisions can be formulated outside the formal process" (Barnes 2008, 3). Despite the lack of formal deliberation before his decision, President Bush did engage in a wide range of discussions with those who disagreed with his plans for a surge. Rejecting the advice of those who were against a surge, President Bush decided to go ahead with his plans to increase the number of troops in Iraq by about 20,000 over the next six months and made his decision public on January 10, 2007. Regardless of one's judgment about the wisdom of the surge, President Bush had considered an array of alternatives articulated by military and civilian administration leaders as well as outside experts.

The article will now turn to the more typical cases of decision making that did not resemble the relatively well-informed decisions about the war in Afghanistan and the 2007 troop surge in Iraq. The first two concern the detainee policies that led to the abuse and torture of prisoners by U.S. personnel; the second two will consider the decision to go to war and to disband the Iraqi army after the U.S. military victory.

Two Decisions on Detainee Policy

The Military Commissions Order of November 13, 2001, and the decision to suspend the Geneva Conventions on February 7, 2002, set the conditions for the abuse and torture of detainees at Guantánamo, at Bagram Air Force Base in Afghanistan, and at Abu Ghraib in Iraq (Pfiffner, forthcoming).

The Military Commissions Order

When a small group of lawyers was preparing President Bush's Military Order of November 13, 2001, they felt that normal trials (civilian or Uniform Code of Military Justice) would afford too many legal protections to terrorists, and thus were "not practicable" (Sec. 1[f]), so the order required that military commissions be established entirely within the executive branch to try suspected terrorists (Bush 2001). In the order, President Bush declared that any noncitizen "whom I determine" (Sec. 2[a]) was a terrorist or had abetted one, could be "detained at an appropriate place" by the secretary of defense and tried by military tribunals created by the secretary of defense (Fisher 2005, 168). The order also declared that no court would have jurisdiction to hear any appeal of a decision or for a writ of habeas corpus (Sec. 2[a]). Any evidence would be admitted that would "have probative value to a reasonable person" (Sec. 7[2]). Evidence obtained through torture might be considered reasonable to a presiding officer.

The Military Commissions Order was important because it created the new category of "enemy combatant" to avoid the "prisoner of war" category that would have invoked the Geneva Conventions. People could be labeled enemy combatants at the president's discretion. In conjunction with the president's decision in early 2002 to suspend the Geneva Conventions, enemy combatants would not be entitled to the protections of the Geneva rules, either for prisoners of war or for others held at the mercy of opposing forces. This determination led to the abuse and torture of detainees.

It may be reasonable to use lawfully established military commissions to try enemy belligerents. However, the procedures set out in the Defense Department's Military Commission Order No. 1 to implement President Bush's military order on March 21, 2002, contained a number of problems (Rumsfeld 2002). They provided no independent authority, other than the president's decision, to establish military tribunals. Military commissions established by previous presidents were created pursuant to acts of Congress, which has the constitutional authority to "define and punish . . . Offenses against the Law of Nations" (Article I, Section 8, clause 10). Neither did the commissions provide for any review outside the executive branch. That is, the person would be indicted by a subordinate of the president based on evidence provided by subordinates of the president; the defendant would be tried by subordinates of the president; the defendant would be sentenced by subordinates of the president; and the only appeal would be to the president.

The Military Commissions Order, which was later overturned by the Supreme Court, was the product of the secret work of a few individuals, rather than the result of any regular policy development process. In October 2001, an interagency working group had been examining the legal implications of how to handle detainees who might have been members of the Taliban or al-Qaeda. It was led by Pierre Prosper, who was ambassador at large for war crimes. But according to Timothy E. Flanigan (deputy White House counsel), David Addington felt that it would be useful to demonstrate that the president was not dependent on legal bureaucrats in making decisions "without their blessing—and without the interminable process that goes along with getting that blessing" (Gellman and Becker 2007a). National Security Advisor Rice and Secretary of State Colin Powell knew that the Prosper Committee was working on the issue and thought that they would have some input when the order was drafted. But in late October, Cheney felt that the process was taking too long, and he short-circuited the process and ignored the Prosper Committee work.

The order was drafted by David Addington, the vice president's lawyer, and was purposefully kept secret from the rest of the administration. Addington forcefully expressed his attitude toward consultation: "Fuck the interagency process" (Mayer 2008, 80). One of the few lawyers who did see the draft said that it "was very closely held because it was coming right from the top" (Gellman and Becker 2007a). Because President Bush had not yet seen the draft, "the top" must have meant Vice President Cheney. One might expect that such an important and far-reaching order would involve consultation with the national security advisor, the secretary of state, and military lawyers from the Judge Advocate General (JAG) Corps. But Vice President Cheney gave strict instructions that others in the White House and cabinet be bypassed before President Bush signed it. The head of the Criminal Division in the Justice Department, Michael Chertoff, was also excluded, as was John Bellinger, the top NSC lawyer.

The decision to write the draft without respect to the Uniform Code of Military Justice, enacted in law, was based on a November 6 legal memorandum written by John Yoo. When asked why the secretary of state (who has jurisdiction over treaties) was not shown the draft, Yoo said, "The issue we dealt with was: Can the president do it constitutionally? State—they wouldn't have views on that" (Gellman and Becker 2007a).

When Attorney General John Ashcroft saw the draft, he was upset that the Justice Department would not have a role in deciding which terrorist suspects would be tried by military commission and which in the criminal justice system. When he went to the White House to object, he found that the vice president was in charge of the order and that John Yoo of the Office of Legal Counsel, nominally Ashcroft's subordinate, had recommended that the U.S. court system be avoided. Ashcroft wanted to see the president about the issue, but Cheney denied him access to the president (Gellman and Becker 2007a).

Military lawyers were generally excluded from commenting on the draft of the military order. Rear Admiral Donald J. Guter, the U.S. Navy's judge advocate general, said, "I can't tell you how compartmented things were. This was a closed administration" (Golden 2004). On November 9, four days before the president signed the order, Defense Department General Counsel William J. Haynes II allowed a small group of lawyers, headed by Lawrence J. Morris, to look at a draft of the order, but he was not allowed to have a copy or take notes. At the last minute, U.S. Army JAG Major General

Thomas Romig called a group of military lawyers together over the weekend to try to make some changes, but their efforts were unavailing (Golden 2004; Ragavan 2006, 37).

On November 13, Cheney personally took the document to President Bush in his private dining room to clear it with him. After Bush's concurrence, Cheney made sure that no one could make any last-minute objections. Cheney gave it to Addington and Flanigan, who took it to Bradford Berenson, associate White House counsel, who was not told that it had come from Cheney. Berenson took it to the staff secretary, Stuart Bowen, Jr., who was told not to let other White House staffers see it and to prepare it for the president's signature. Despite Bowen's objections that other relevant staffers had not seen the document, he was told it was too sensitive, that there was no time for others to vet it, and that the president had already approved it (Gellman 2008, 167; Gellman and Becker 2007a). Cheney then took the document to the president in the Oval Office, and Bush signed it immediately. White House aides present said they did not know that the vice president had been involved in drafting the memo. Thus, Cheney had engineered President Bush's approval and signature without any regular policy process or sign-off by relevant White House and cabinet officials; most importantly, National Security Advisor Rice and Secretary of State Colin Powell were not consulted or informed.

On the evening of November 13, when CNN broadcast that the military order had been signed by the president, Colin Powell exclaimed, "What the hell just happened?" (DeYoung 2006, 367; Gellman and Becker 2007a). National Security Advisor Rice sent an aide to find out about the order. Staff Secretary Bowen later felt that the policy process had been short-circuited and that the president was not well served. "It is by no means a picky procedural matter. It is fundamental to advising the president. The staffing process exists to ensure the president receives complete and accurate advice that has been vetted by his most senior advisers, and therefore helps the president avoid mistakes" (Gellman 2008, 168).

One of the ostensible purposes of vetting important decisions with White House staffers and members of the cabinet who might have expertise or be involved with implementing orders is that they might know something that the vice president or his lawyers do not know about the issue. Vice President Cheney had been successful in excluding from the decision process anyone who might have disagreed with his draft of the order; he got his way, but the decision led to a flawed legal framework for dealing with detainees in the war on terror. The consequences of excluding outside input on the draft came when the Supreme Court, in *Hamdan v. Rumsfeld*, struck down the military commissions plan, because it was not set up in accord with U.S. law or the Uniform Code of Military Justice.[5]

Suspending the Geneva Conventions

In the fall of 2001, Bush administration officials felt tremendous pressure not only to pursue those who had committed the 9/11 atrocities but also to prevent future attacks, which they assumed were in planning stages. In order to obtain crucial intelligence, the United States would have to depend on the interrogation of prisoners to discover plans for future attacks. Thus, the traditional interrogation techniques developed by the U.S. military and limited by the strictures of the Geneva Conventions would not be sufficient, they thought. In late 2001 and early 2002, the administration went about exempting U.S. interrogators from the Geneva rules.

Top members of the Bush administration thought that terrorists did not deserve to be treated in accord with the Geneva rules, because they did not represent a state that had signed the agreement, and they were terrorists who did not act according to the rules of war. Accordingly, John Yoo at the Office of Legal Counsel, working with David Addington, wrote legal memoranda arguing that the United States was not bound by the Geneva Conventions (Yoo 2002; see also Bybee 2002).

The Judge Advocate Generals of the services (JAGs or TJAGs), however, were not consulted about the decisions (Sands 2008, 32). That is, those who, because of their training and years of experience, were among the most informed and qualified lawyers on the laws of war, were excluded from being consulted on this important decision. The reason they were left out of the loop was that they might have raised objections about the legal reasoning or the policy implications of this decision. Administration lawyers were careful to maximize the chances that their preferred policies would be adopted without change. As Addington reportedly said, "Don't bring the TJAGs into the process, they aren't reliable" (Sands 2008, 32).

On November 14, 2001, Vice President Cheney declared that terrorists do "not deserve to be treated" as prisoners of war (Gellman 2008, 168). On January 11, 2002, Secretary of Defense Rumsfeld said that the Guantánamo detainees would be "handled not as prisoners of war, because they're not, but as unlawful combatants [who] do not have any rights under the Geneva Convention" (DeYoung 2006, 367). State Department counsel William Taft replied to Yoo's memo, arguing that "[b]oth the most important factual assumptions on which your draft is based and its legal analysis are seriously flawed. . . . In previous conflicts, the United States has dealt with tens of thousands of detainees without repudiating its obligations. I have no doubt we can do so here" (DeYoung 2006, 368). Taft considered the issue to be in the process of policy development prior to its being considered by the NSC principals, but President Bush made his decision on January 8.

Taft learned that the president had determined that the Justice Department's interpretation would prevail, and Secretary Powell was informed of the decision on January 18, when he was in Asia (DeYoung 2006, 368; Mayer 2008, 123).

On January 25, a memo to the president from his counsel, Alberto Gonzales, reaffirmed the reasoning of the Justice Department memos and recommended that Geneva Convention III on Treatment of Prisoners of War should not apply to al-Qaeda and Taliban prisoners. He reasoned that the war on terrorism was "a new kind of war" and that the "new paradigm renders obsolete Geneva's strict limitations on questioning of enemy prisoners." Gonzales restated the previous memos' arguments that denying captured al-Qaeda and Taliban prisoners Geneva Convention protections would preclude the prosecution of U.S. interrogators under the U.S. War Crimes Act. "A determination that GPW is not applicable to the Taliban would mean that Section 2441 [War Crimes Act] would not apply to actions taken with respect to the Taliban" (Gonzales 2002).

Powell objected to the reasoning of Gonzales's January 25 memo recommending that Bush abandon Geneva. In a memo of January 26, 2002, Powell argued that the drawbacks of deciding not to apply the Geneva Conventions outweighed the advantages because "[i]t will reverse over a century of policy . . . and undermine the protections of the law of war for our troops, both in this specific conflict and in general; It has a high cost in terms of negative international reaction . . . ; It will undermine public support among critical allies" (Powell 2002). Powell also noted that applying the Convention "maintains POW status for U.S. forces . . . and generally supports the U.S. objective of ensuring its forces are accorded protection under the Convention." The memo also addressed the intended applicability of the Geneva Convention to nontraditional conflicts: "[T]he GPW was intended to cover all types of armed conflict and did not by its terms limit its application" (Powell 2002).

Although Powell felt that the proper place to make a formal recommendation to the president on such a crucial issue was in a principals' meeting, he asked Rice for a meeting with the president to discuss the issue personally. Treaty issues, particularly the abandoning of such an important international agreement, were within the jurisdiction of the State Department, but the decision had been made without Powell's advice and without any formal, high-level discussion of the issues. Powell met with the president on January 21, when he said, "I wanted everybody covered [by Geneva rules], whether Taliban, al-Qaeda or whatever, and I think the case was there for that" (DeYoung 2006, 369).

Though Bush rejected Powell's argument, he did call an NSC meeting for January 28. But before the meeting, a memorandum drafted by David Addington for Alberto Gonzales was leaked to the The Washington Times. The memo refuted Powell's arguments in advance of the NSC meeting and argued that the "new paradigm" of nonstate warfare rendered obsolete the Geneva Conventions. The Times said that the Office of Legal Counsel's opinions were definitive and reported that international administration "sources" said that Powell "was bowing to pressure from the political left" (Gellman and Becker 2007a). According to Powell, the leak was made "in order to try to screw me" and "blow me out of the water" (DeYoung 2006, 370; Gellman 2008, 170). Powell was right.

Despite Powell's memo, and in accord with the Justice Department and his counsel's recommendations, President Bush signed a February 7, 2002, memorandum that stated, "Pursuant to my authority as Commander in Chief. . . . I . . . determine that none of the provisions of Geneva apply to our conflict with al Qaeda in Afghanistan or elsewhere throughout the world because, among other reasons, al Qaeda is not a High Contracting Party to Geneva." The memo argued that the Geneva Convention applies only to states and "assumes the existence of 'regular' armed forces fighting on behalf of states," and that "terrorism ushers in a new paradigm" that "requires new thinking in the law of war." The memo also stated, "As a matter of policy, the United States Armed Forces shall continue to treat detainees humanely and, *to the extent appropriate and consistent with military necessity*, in a manner consistent with the principles of Geneva" (Bush 2002b; emphasis added).

The purpose of the suspension of the Geneva Conventions by the administration was to ensure that prisoners in Guantánamo did not have to be treated according to the Geneva rules; thus, interrogators could apply harsh interrogation techniques to gain intelligence on terrorist activities. The memo also sought to ensure that the U.S.

war crimes statute (which referenced the Geneva rules) did not apply to interroga-tors. President Bush's determination on Geneva allowed the use of aggressive tech-niques of interrogation by military intelligence at Guantánamo, which were later, in the fall of 2003, employed at the prison at Abu Ghraib.

The impact of the abandonment of the Geneva Conventions for the war on ter-rorism was emphasized by General Ricardo Sanchez, former head of U.S. forces in Iraq, who said that the president's decision "unleashed the hounds of hell" (Mayer 2008, 242). He explained,

> This presidential memorandum constitutes a watershed event in U.S. military history. Essentially, it set aside all of the legal constraints, training guidelines, and rules of in-terrogation that formed the U.S. Army's foundation for the treatment of prisoners on the battlefield since the Geneva Conventions were revised and ratified in 1949. (Sanchez 2008, 144)

The irony in this evaluation by Sanchez was that the Bush administration publicly and explicitly acknowledged that the Geneva Conventions *did* apply to Iraq, because it was a signatory to the treaty, as was the United States. That crucial distinction was lost on U.S. forces in Iraq, and it demonstrates how difficult it is to limit torture and harsh interrogation tactics once they are authorized. The other irony in Sanchez's statement was that he himself issued a memorandum in September 2003 that au-thorized the use of illegal interrogation practices in Iraq (Sanchez 2003).

In sum, the decision by President Bush to suspend the Geneva Conventions was engineered by Vice President Cheney and David Addington. Although William Taft of the State Department did write a dissenting memo and Colin Powell did have a chance to see President Bush and force an NSC meeting, the decision had already been made. The leak of the rebuttal of Powell's argument immediately before the NSC meeting undermined any chance for a serious consideration of the decision.

Iraq War Policy: Two Decisions

The next two decisions to be considered are President Bush's decision to go to war in Iraq and the decision to disband the Iraqi army made by Paul Bremer in May 2003. Both of these decisions had historic effects. The war in Iraq took essential resources away from the war against al-Qaeda and the Taliban in Afghanistan and alienated many of the nations of the world from U.S. policy. The decision to disband the Iraqi army undermined (and possibly doomed) the effort to maintain internal security in Iraq in the aftermath of the U.S. military victory in 2003. The momentous decision to go to war was not the subject of a formal decision-making process, and the deci-sion to disband the Iraqi army was slipped by President Bush without a conscious, de-liberate decision by the president.

The Decision to Go to War in Iraq

In the decision to go to war in Afghanistan, President Bush deliberated with his war cabinet and made the major decisions in a relatively short time period. In contrast, the decision to invade Iraq seems to have been made over the course of a year or so and was characterized by incremental decision making along the way. President Bush had probably made up his own mind about the war sometime early in 2002, but other members of his administration became aware of his decision at different times over the next year.

President Bush did not make public his decision to pursue Iraq until the State of the Union message on January 29, 2002, though even then, he was somewhat vague about the way in which he stated his intention. (In November 2001, he had ordered Donald Rumsfeld to prepare operational plans for a war against Iraq.) Bush announced his decision with a high level of generality, with his inclusion of Iraq, Iran, and North Korea in what he called an "axis of evil." In the speech Bush declared, "I will not wait on events while dangers gather. I will not stand by as peril draws closer and closer" (Bush 2002a). In April, the administration started talking about "regime change" in Iraq, and Bush told a British reporter, "I made up my mind that Saddam needs to go" (Woodward 2004, 119).

According to State Department's director of policy and planning, Richard Haass (who had worked on the NSC staff on Middle East issues under George H. W. Bush), Condoleezza Rice told him that the president had made up his mind by July 2002. Haass said that he broached the issue of war with Iraq with Rice: "I raised this issue about were we really sure that we wanted to put Iraq front and center at this point, given the war on terrorism and other issues. And she said, essentially, that that decision's been made, don't waste your breath" (Lemann 2003, 36).

On August 5, 2002, at Powell's initiative, Rice arranged for him to spend two hours with the president in order to explain his own reservations about war with Iraq. He argued that war with Iraq would destabilize the whole Middle East; an American occupation would be seen as hostile by the Muslim world; and an invasion of Iraq should not be undertaken by the United States unilaterally. Powell did not think the president understood the full implications of an American invasion. He told the president that if the United States invaded Iraq, it would tie down most of the army and the United States would be responsible for 25 million people: "You will become the government until you get a new government" (Woodward 2004, 150–51).

The relative informality of the decision-making process is illustrated by the way the president informed his secretary of state that he had made up his mind. The president asked Rice and White House counselor Karen Hughes their opinion about going to war with Iraq, but he did not ask Powell his opinion. Once he finalized the decision to go to war, Bush immediately informed Rumsfeld, but not Powell. In fact, the president informed Prince Bandar, the Saudi Arabian ambassador to the United States, of his decision before he informed Powell (Woodward 2004, 151–52, 165). The president had to be prompted by Rice to inform Powell that he had made up his mind to go to war. So, on January 13, the president brought Powell in for a 12-minute meeting to inform him of the decision to go to war and to ask him to support his decision. The president stressed that it was a "cordial" conversation and that "I didn't need his permission" (Woodward 2004, 269–74). The deliberations about war were not definitive enough or inclusive enough for the secretary of state (the only NSC principal with combat experience) to know that President Bush had made the decision.

Paul Pillar, national intelligence director for the Near East and South Asia from 2001 to 2005, noted "the absence of any identifiable process for making the decision to go to war—at least no process visible at the time. . . . There was no meeting, no policy-options paper, no showdown in the Situation Room when the wisdom of going to war was debated or the decision to do so made" (2007, 55). Central Intelligence Agency (CIA) director George Tenet agreed: "There was never a serious debate that I know of within the administration about the imminence of the Iraqi threat," or even a "significant discussion" about options for continuing to contain Iraq (Shane and Mazzetti 2007). By his own admission, President Bush did not ask for recommendations about the war from Secretary of State Colin Powell, Secretary of Defense Donald Rumsfeld, CIA director George Tenet, or his father, George H. W. Bush, three of whom had much more experience with U.S. war policy than he did (Woodward 2008, 432).[6]

The seeming lack of deliberation is striking. Though there were many meetings on tactical and operational decisions, there seemed to be no meetings at which the entire NSC engaged in face-to-face discussions of all the options, including the pros and cons of whether to go to war. In part, this may have been attributable to the shift in Rice's role away from the honest broker role she had played in the decisions about Afghanistan. According to John Burke (2005b), in the decisions about Iraq, Rice did not act as a broker. Instead, the president decided to use her talents as a confidant and articulator of his views.

In addition to the lack of deliberation, President Bush chose to ignore important human intelligence sources at the highest levels of Saddam Hussein's government. The French had recruited Naji Sabri, Saddam's foreign minister, who told them that Saddam had no weapons of mass destruction (Drumheller 2006; Pfiffner 2008). The British had recruited Saddam's intelligence chief, Tahir Jalil Habbush, who also told them Saddam had no weapons of mass destruction. Reports of each of these two intelligence breakthroughs reached President Bush, who decided that they were not relevant to his plans for war (Suskind 2008, 179–96).

In making the decision to invade Iraq, the administration might well have benefited from a more thorough deliberation of the issues, similar to the war cabinet meetings before the decision to invade Afghanistan. By contrast, Bush did not seem to consider fully dissenting opinions such as those of Powell, Haass, or Brent Scowcroft (national security advisor to George H. W. Bush) when making his decision on Iraq. Bush and his neoconservative advisors were committed to regime change in Iraq for a variety of reasons, and thus did not feel that an open process of deliberation would suit their purpose. President Bush was undoubtedly aware of disagreements about his intention to go to war, but most of these came from outside the administration. The only serious reservation expressed to Bush from within was voiced by Colin Powell during the dinner with President Bush in August 2002.

Disbanding the Iraqi Army

Early in the occupation of Iraq, two key decisions were made that gravely jeopardized U.S. chances for success in Iraq: (1) the decision to bar from government work those who ranked in the top four levels of Saddam's Baath Party and the top three levels of each ministry, and (2) the decision to disband the Iraqi army and replace it with a new army built from scratch. These two fateful decisions were made against the advice of military and CIA professionals and without consulting important members of the president's staff and cabinet.

Both of these decisions fueled the insurgency by (1) alienating hundreds of thousands of Iraqis who could not support themselves or their families; (2) undermining the normal infrastructure necessary for social and economic activity; (3) ensuring that there was not sufficient security to carry on normal life; and (4) creating insurgents who were angry at the United States, many of whom had weapons and were trained to use them. Before examining the disbanding order, a key decision should be mentioned.

The decision to give Paul Bremer sole authority in Iraq without the co-representative of the president, Zal Khalilzad, as had been planned, was made by the president during an informal lunch with Bremer. The decision to make Bremer, in effect, the viceroy of Iraq was made without consulting the secretary of state or national security advisor (Gordon and Trainor 2006, 475). According to Colin Powell, "The plan was for Zal to go back. He was the one guy who knew this place better than anyone. I thought this was part of the deal with Bremer. But with no discussion, no debate, things changed. I was stunned." Powell observed that President Bush's decision was "typical." There were "no full deliberations. And you suddenly discover, gee, maybe that wasn't so great, we should have thought about it a little longer" (Cohen 2007).

The decision by Bush to put Bremer fully in charge led to the first of the two blunders. In his de-Baathification order (Coalition Provisional Authority [CPA] Order No. 1, May 16, 2003), Bremer ordered that all senior party members were banned from serving in the government and the top three layers of all government ministries were removed, even if they were not senior members of the Baath Party. This included up to 85,000 people who, in Bremer's eyes, were "true believers" and adherents of Saddam's regime (Bremer 2006, 39; Ricks 2006, 160). The problem was that these mid-level technocrats constituted the professional capacity that was essential to running the electrical, transportation, education, and communications infrastructure of Iraq. The decision threw many thousands of Iraqis out of work and contributed significantly to Iraqi resentment of the U.S. occupation.

But more important than the de-Baathification of the civilian agencies of the Iraq government was the disbanding of the Iraqi army. President Bush had agreed with military planners and had decided in meetings on March 10 and 12 that the Iraqi army was essential for the internal and external security of the country (Gordon and Trainor 2006, 476; Ricks 2006, 160). The story of how President Bush's March decision got reversed is a tangled one, with many major participants trying to deflect responsibility from themselves.

Paul Bremer, against the advice of the army and the professional planners, issued CPA Order No. 2 on May 23, 2003, which dissolved the Iraqi security forces. The security forces included 385,000 in the armed forces, 285,000 in the Interior Ministry (police), and 50,000 in presidential security units (Ricks 2006, 162, 192). Of course, those in police and military units (e.g., the Special Republican Guard) that were Saddam's top enforcers had to be barred from working in the government. But many officers in the army were professional soldiers, and the rank-and-file enlisted solders constituted a source of stability and order. Bremer's decision threw hundreds of thousands out of work and immediately created a large pool of unemployed and armed men who felt humiliated and hostile to the U.S. occupiers. According to one U.S. officer in Baghdad, "When they disbanded the military, and announced we were occupiers—that was it. Every moderate, every person that had leaned toward us, was furious" (Ricks 2006, 164). The prewar plans of the State Department, the Army War College, and the Center for International and Strategic Studies had all recommended against disbanding the army (Fallows 2004, 74).

In disbanding most of the Iraqi bureaucracy, Bremer ignored Max Weber's insight from a century ago: "A rationally ordered system of officials [the bureaucracy] continues to function smoothly after the enemy has occupied the area; he merely needs to change the top officials. This body of officials continues to operate because it is to the vital interest of everyone concerned, including above all the enemy" (1946, 229). Despite the decisions in March that U.S. forces would use the Iraqi army to help provide internal and external security in postwar Iraq, they were disbanded (Gordon 2008). How did this crucial reversal come about?

Paul Bremer and Walt Slocombe planned to disband the security forces and create "an entirely new Iraqi army" (Feith 2008, 432). They worked on the policy when they were in the Pentagon, and according to Bremer, Rumsfeld approved an outline of the plan on May 9 (Bremer 2006, 54; Feith 2008, 428; Gordon 2008). On May 19, Bremer, in a memo, updated Rumsfeld about the final form of the plan (Bremer 2006, 57; Feith 2008, 432). The authority for the order seemed to come from the White House; Bremer told Garner that the decision was made "at a level 'above Rumsfeld's pay grade'" (Tenet 2007, 429).

After Feith reviewed the draft order on May 22, Bremer sent President Bush a three-page letter that was an update on conditions in Iraq. Near the end of the letter, he mentioned that he was going to dissolve "Saddam's military and intelligence structures" (Andrews 2007). In the NSC meeting that same day, Bremer *"informed the president of the plan in a video teleconference"* (Bremer 2006, 57; emphasis added). President Bush did not formally decide to reverse the decision he had made in March, and Bremer interpreted his lack of questions as approval. Bremer later said, "I don't remember any particular response from that meeting. If there had been an objection, I would have made note of it then" (Gordon 2008). Bremer also recalled, "I might add that it was not a controversial decision. The Iraqi army had disappeared" (Andrews 2007). Bremer concluded that "it was fairly clear that the Iraqi Army could not be reconstituted, and the president understood that" (Andrews 2007).

Bremer's impression that Bush had approved his order was reinforced in a May 23 letter that Bush wrote to Bremer (the day of the proclamation): "Your leadership is apparent. You have quickly made a positive and significant impact. You have my full support and confidence" (Andrews 2007). Despite Bremer's contention that the decision had been fully briefed and vetted by all necessary parties, others did not remember things the same way.

The decision by Bremer, seemingly approved by President Bush at the May 22 NSC meeting, was seen by other participants in policy making on Iraq as having been slipped by President Bush without the necessary vetting by other responsible parties in the government. Franklin C. Miller, a participant in NSC planning for postwar Iraq, said, "Anyone who is experienced in the ways of Washington knows the difference between an open, transparent policy process and slamming something through the system. . . . The most portentous decision of the occupation was carried out stealthily and without giving the president's principal advisers an opportunity to consider it and give the president their views" (Gordon 2008).

Importantly, Colin Powell was out of town (as he had been when the Geneva decision was initially made) when the decision was made, and he was not informed about it, much less consulted. One might expect that the secretary of state would have had the opportunity to comment on such an important policy change, but he was left out entirely. Powell later recalled, "I talked to Rice and said, 'Condi, what happened?' And her reaction was: 'I was surprised too, but it is a decision that has been made and the president is standing behind Jerry's decision. Jerry is the guy on the ground.' And there was no further debate about it" (Gordon 2008). The irony is that Powell, aside from being secretary of state, had spent his career in uniform and was the only one of the principals with combat experience. Bremer had not had any experience in the military, occupying countries, or the Middle East; and he had been "on the ground" for only 11 days (this was his first time in Iraq) when he gave the order. The order greatly upset military commanders who had not been consulted and who had planned all along to use most of the Iraqi army to help stabilize Iraq after the invasion.

The order had not been cleared through any normal policy process. Feith admitted he did not bring it up in the deputies meetings (Feith 2008, 433), but said that he had "received detailed comments back from the JCS [Joint Chiefs of Staff]" (Andrews 2007). But Richard B. Myers, then chair of the Joint Chiefs, said, "I don't recall having a robust debate about this issue, and I would have recalled this" (Gordon 2008). In Iraq, U.S. Army Colonel Greg Gardner was tasked by Slocombe to get the reaction of General David D. McKiernan (then head of coalition forces in Iraq) to the plan the day before it was issued (McKiernan was at Baghdad airport, while Bremer was in the Green Zone). Gardner said that a member of McKiernan's staff told him over the phone that McKiernan accepted the policy decision (Gordon 2008). McKiernan, however, denied that he was consulted: "I never saw that order and never concurred. That is absolutely false." General Peter Pace, vice chair of Joint Chiefs of Staff said, "We were not asked for a recommendation or for advice" (Andrews 2007). Central Command in Florida was also surprised by the decision (Ricks 2006, 163). Paul Pillar, national intelligence officer for the Near East and South Asia, said that the intelligence community had not been consulted about the decision (Ferguson 2008, 219). Bremer's response to the above issues was, "It is not my responsibility to do inter-agency coordination" (Gordon 2008).

President Bush himself was vague on whether he had made the decision to reverse the March 12 NSC consensus. When asked in 2006 by his biographer, Roger Draper, about the decision, Bush replied, "Well, the policy was to keep the army intact. Didn't happen" (Draper 2007, 211, 433). According to Edmund Andrews, Bush said, "Yeah, I can't remember, I'm sure I said, 'This is the policy, what happened?'" (Andrews 2007).

Because the official records of communications and meetings at the time of the decision are still secret, there is no way to know for certain how the decision was finally made. But what is known is that the decision was made against the judgment of military planners and without consultation with Secretary of State Colin Powell; chair of the Joint Chiefs of Staff, General Richard Myers; vice chair of the Joint Chiefs, Peter Pace; Lieutenant General David D. McKiernan, CIA director George Tenet; or the intelligence community director for the Middle East Paul Pillar.

Conclusion

This analysis ends on the ironic note that Dick Cheney was right when he said that if you have a process without integrity, "[t]hat's when you really got into big trouble." When he became vice president, he systematically broke the rules that he had articulated so cogently. In addition to short-circuiting the Military Commissions Order examined earlier in this article, he kept the president out of the loop on threats by Justice Department officials to resign over the Terrorism Surveillance Program (Gellman 2008, 292–98), he undermined Environmental Protection Agency director Christine Whitman when she tried to implement Bush's campaign promise (Gellman 2008, 88–90), and he reversed a presidential decision on a capital gains tax cut (Gellman 2008, 271–74). In none of these cases did the president receive the benefit of the advice of those whom he should have talked to about the policy issues.

The pattern that emerges from an examination of the four decisions analyzed in this article is one of secrecy, top-down control, tightly held information, disregard for the judgments of career professionals and the exclusion from deliberation of qualified executive branch experts who might have disagreed with those who initially framed the decisions. Secretary of State Colin Powell, particularly, was marginalized by the White House staff and the vice president. Powell arguably had more relevant experience than any of the other NSC principals: combat experience in Vietnam (two tours), chairmanship of the Joint Chiefs of Staff under presidents George H. W. Bush and Bill Clinton, national security advisor to President Ronald Reagan, and Secretary of State for President George W. Bush.

It is also clear in these cases of decision making that National Security Advisor Condoleezza Rice did not play the role of honest broker, nor did she effectively coordinate among the National Security Council principals. It must be admitted that she was at a disadvantage, with a vice president who dominated the national security process, a secretary of defense who disdained her, and a president who wanted to use her as a personal confidant rather than as broker among the NSC principals. Nevertheless, someone should have ensured that President Bush received the frank advice of those at the top levels of his administration who might have had different perspectives than Vice President Cheney.

Another pattern from these examples is the exclusion of career professionals, military and civilian, from rendering their advice to top-level decision makers and whose advice was most often ignored when they did manage to express their judgments. Career military lawyers were excluded from the military commissions order until the last minute, and their hasty advice was rejected. Lawyers in the State and Defense departments objected to the decision to suspend the Geneva Conventions, but they had no effect. The decision to disband the Iraqi army was made contrary to the consensus of military judgment that President Bush had confirmed months before his decision was reversed. On the decision to go to war in Iraq, many army generals had reservations (in addition to their concerns about the number of troops needed), but they considered the decision to be the commander in chief's and did not forcefully express their views. Retired Major General William L. Nash, commenting on the end of the Bush presidency, said that "[o]pen and serious debate versus ideological certitude will be a great relief to the military leaders. . . . The joke was that when you leave a meeting, everybody is supposed to drink the Kool-Aid. In the Bush administration, you had to drink the Kool-Aid before you got to go to the meeting" (DeYoung 2008).

These problems were exacerbated by the failure of the president to bring together his major staffers and departmental secretaries and deliberate about the wisdom of his decisions. The Military Commissions Order was tightly held and secret from most of the relevant experts in the administration. The decision to disband the Iraqi army was made casually, with no consultation with military leaders or Powell. Bush did call an NSC meeting on the Geneva Conventions, though one was held after he had already made up his mind. The decision to go to war in Iraq was never considered in a formal meeting of the National Security Council principals. There is some evidence that the national security policy process was more inclusive in President Bush's second term.

Arguably, the four decisions examined in this article were unwise. The Military Commissions Order designed a flawed legal process that was invalidated by the Supreme Court. The suspension of the Geneva Conventions led to the abuse and torture of detainees. The decision to disband the Iraqi army made it impossible for the United States to provide internal security in Iraq during the occupation. And the decision to go to war in Iraq led to the opprobrium of other nations of the world, the increased power of Iran, the increased recruitment of Muslim radicals who want to harm the United States, the neglect of the war against al-Qaeda in Afghanistan, the degradation of the readiness of the U.S. Army, and expenditures approaching $1 trillion.

As stated in the introduction, broader consultation would not necessarily have led to different decisions by President Bush, but listening to dissent from his own political appointees and the considered judgment of career professionals might have exposed him to alternative judgments about the consequences of his decisions.

AUTHOR'S NOTE: I would like to thank John Burke, Mary Anne Borelli, Louis Fisher, Michael Genovese, Fred Greenstein, Nancy Kassop, Dick Pious, Andrew Rudalevige, Bob Spitzer, and Jeffrey Weinberg for their comments on earlier versions of this article.

Endnotes

1. Daniel Benjamin served on the NSC staff from 1994 to 1999.
2. Janis analyzed the Bay of Pigs invasion in 1961 and the escalation of the Vietnam War in 1965 to illustrate the syndrome. He examined the Cuban missile crisis and the Marshall Plan as instances when groupthink was avoided.
3. Scott McClellan said in his book, "Bush showed Cheney great deference, especially when he designated him to take on a specific task, such as . . . the controversial warrantless wiretapping program instituted after 9/11. Bush also relied on Cheney's ability to shape what Bush considered vital national security policies on matters such as al Qaeda detainees" (2008, 85).
4. Although Bush decided that a U.S. invasion was necessary, the Taliban was defeated when there were fewer than 500 U.S. personnel in the country. U.S. airpower and the Northern Alliance won the initial victory.
5. *Hamdan v. Rumsfeld* (2006), No. 05-184, slip opinion.

6. In explaining why he did not seek counsel from his father, Bush said, "He is the wrong father to appeal to in terms of strength. There is a higher father" (Woodward 2008, 432). It was well known that Bush White House staffers and neocons thought that George H. W Bush had made a crucial mistake when he decided not to drive to Baghdad in the 1991 Gulf War.

References

Andrews, Edmund. 2007. "Envoy's Letter Counters Bush on Dismantling of Iraq Army." *The New York Times*, September 4.

Barnes, Fred. 2008. "How Bush Decided on the Surge." *Weekly Standard*, February 4.

Benjamin, Daniel. 2008. "The Decider Who Can't Make Up His Mind." *The Washington Post*, July 6.

Bose, Meena. 1998. *Shaping and Signaling Presidential Policy: The National Security Decision Making of Eisenhower and Kennedy*. College Station: Texas A&M University Press.

Bremer, Paul L. 2006. *My Year in Iraq: The Struggle to Build a Future of Hope*. New York: Simon & Schuster. Brinkley, Alan. 2008. "Black Sites." *The New York Times Book Review*, August 3.

Burke, John. 2005a. "The Neutral/Honest Broker Role in Foreign-Policy Decision Making: A Reassessment." *Presidential Studies Quarterly* 35 (June): 229–58.

———. 2005b. "Condoleezza Rice as NSC Adviser: A Case Study of the Honest Broker Role." *Presidential Studies Quarterly* 35 (September): 554–75.

———. Forthcoming. *Honest Broker? The National Security Adviser and Presidential Decision Making*. College Station: Texas A&M University Press.

Burke, John P., Fred Greenstein, Larry Berman, and Richard Immerman. 1989. *How Presidents Test Reality: Decisions on Vietnam, 1954 and 1965*. New York: Russell Sage Foundation.

Bush, George. 2001. "Detention, Treatment, and Trial of Certain Non-Citizens in the War Against Terrorism." News release, November 13.

———. 2002a. State of the Union Address. Weekly Compilation of Presidential Documents, *Administration of George W Bush, 2002* (January 29), pp. 133–39.

———. 2002b. Memorandum for the Vice President, et al., Re: Humane Treatment of al Qaeda and Taliban Detainees, February 7. In *The Torture Papers: The Road to Abu Ghraib*, eds. Karen J. Greenberg and Joshua L. Dratel. New York: Cambridge University Press, 134. Bybee, Jay S.

———. 2002. Memorandum for Alberto R. Gonzales, Counsel to the President, and William J. Haynes II, General Counsel of the Department of Defense from Assistant Attorney General Jay S. Bybee, Re: Application of Treaties and Laws to al Qaeda and Taliban Detainees, January 22. In *The Torture Papers: The Road to Abu Ghraib*, eds. Karen J. Greenberg and Joshua L. Dratel. New York: Cambridge University Press, 81–121.

Cohen, Roger. 2007. "The MacArthur Lunch." *The New York Times*, August 27.

Daalder, Ivo H. and I. M. Destler. 2009. *In the Shadow of the Oval Office*. New York: Simon & Schuster. Destler, I. M. 1972. "Comment: Multiple Advocacy, Some 'Limits and Costs.'" *American Political Science Review* 66 (3): 786–90.

———. 1981. "National Security II: The Rise of the Assistant (1961–1981)." In *The Illusion of Presidential Government*, eds. Hugh Heclo and Lester M. Salamon. Boulder, CO: Westview Press, 266–70.

DeYoung, Karen. 2006. *Soldier: The Live of Colin Powell*. New York: Alfred A. Knopf.

———. 2008. "Joint Chiefs Chairman 'Very Positive' After Meeting with Obama." *The Washington Post*, November 30.

DiIulio, John. 2002. "To: Ron Suskind, Subject: Your Next Essay on the Bush Administration." Esquire, October 24.

Draper, Robert. 2007. *Dead Certain: The Presidency of George W. Bush*. New York: Free Press.

Drumheller, Tyler. 2006. *On the Brink: An Insider's Account of How the White House Compromised American Intelligence*. New York: Carroll & Graf.

Eisenhower, Dwight D. 1965. *The White House Years: Waging Peace, 1956–1961*. New York: Doubleday.

Fallows, James. 2004. "Blind into Baghdad." *Atlantic Monthly*, January/February, pp. 52–74.

Feith, Douglas J. 2008. *War and Decision: Inside the Pentagon at the Dawn of the War on Terrorism*. New York: Harper.

Ferguson, Charles H. 2008. *No End in Sight: Iraq's Descent into Chaos*. New York: Public Affairs.

Fisher, Louis. 2005. *Military Tribunals and Presidential Power: American Revolution to the War on Terror*. Lawrence: University Press of Kansas.

Gellman, Barton. 2008. *Angler: The Cheney Vice Presidency*. New York: Penguin.

Gellman, Barton, and Jo Becker. 2007a. "A Different Understanding with the President." *Washington Post*, June 24, p. 1.

George, Alexander L. 1972. The Case for Multiple Advocacy in Making Foreign Policy. *American Political Science Review* 66 (3): 751-85.

———. 1980. *Presidential Decisionmaking in Foreign Policy: The Effective Use of Information and Advice*. Boulder, CO: Westview Press.

Golden, Tim. 2004. "After Terror, a Secret Rewriting of Military Law." *The New York Times*, October 24. Goldsmith, Jack L. 2007. *The Terror Presidency: Law and Judgment Inside the Bush Administration*. New York: W. W. Norton.

Gonzales, Alberto R. 2002. Memorandum for the President. From Alberto R. Gonzales, Re: Decision RE application of the Geneva Convention on Prisoners of War to the Conflict with al Qaeda and the Taliban," January 25. In *The Torture Papers: The Road to Abu Ghraib*, eds. Karen J. Greenberg and Joshua L. Dratel. New York: Cambridge University Press, 118.

Gordon, Michael. 2008. "Fateful Choice on Iraq Army Bypassed Debate." *The New York Times*, March 17.

Gordon, Michael, and Bernard E. Trainor. 2006. *Cobra II: The Inside Story of the Invasion and Occupation of Iraq*. New York: Pantheon.

Janis, Irving L. 1982. *Groupthink: Psychological Studies of Policy Decisions and Fiascoes*. 2nd ed. Boston: Houghton Mifflin.

Kernell, Samuel, and Samuel Popkin, eds. 1986. *Chief of Staff: Twenty-Five Years of Managing the Presidency*. Berkeley: University of California Press.

Kumar, Martha Joynt, and Terry Sullivan, eds. 2003. *The White House World: Transitions, Organization, and Office Operations*. College Station: Texas A&M University Press.

Lemann, Nicholas. 2003. "How It Came to War." *The New Yorker*, March 31.

Mayer, Jane. 2008. *Dark Side: The Inside Story of How the War on Terror Was Turned into a War on American Ideals*. New York: Doubleday.

McClellan, Scott. 2008. *What Happened: Inside the Bush White House and Washington's Culture of Deception*. New York: Public Affairs.

Mulcahy, Kevin V., and Cecil V. Crabb. 1991. "Presidential Management of National Security Policy Making, 1947–1987." In *The Managerial Presidency*, ed. James P. Pfiffner. Pacific Grove, CA: Brooks/Cole, 250–64.

Pfiffner, James P. 2008. "Decision Making, Intelligence, and the Iraq War." In *Intelligence and National Security Policymaking on Iraq: British and American Perspectives*, eds. James P. Pfiffner and Mark Phythian. College Station: Texas A&M University Press.

——. 2010. *Torture as Public Policy*. Boulder, CO: Paradigm Publishers.

Pillar, Paul. 2007. "The Right Stuff." *The National Interest*, September/October, 53.

Porter, Roger. 1980. *Presidential Decision Making*. New York: Cambridge University Press.

Powell, Colin. 2002. Memorandum to: Counsel to the President and Assistant to the President for National Security Affairs, January 26, Re: Draft Decision Memorandum for the President on the Applicability of the Geneva Convention to the Conflict in Afghanistan. In *The Torture Papers: The Road to Abu Ghraib*, eds. Karen J. Greenberg and Joshua L. Dratel. New York: Cambridge University Press, 122.

Ragavan, Chitra. 2006. "Cheney's Guy." *U.S. News and World Report*, May 29.

Ricks, Thomas. 2006. *Fiasco: The American Military Adventure in Iraq*. New York: Penguin.

Rumsfeld, Donald. 1989. "Rumsfeld's Rules." In *The Presidency in Transition*, eds. James P. Pfiffner and R. Gordon Hoxie. New York: Center for the Study of the Presidency.

——. 2002. Department of Defense, Military Commission Order No. 1, March 21. http://www.defenselink.mil/news/Mar2002/d200203211ord.pdf [accessed February 22, 2009]. Sanchez, Ricardo. S. 2003. Memorandum for Commander, U.S. Central Command; Subject: CJTF-7 Interrogation and Counter-Resistance Policy, September 14. http://www.scvhistory.com/scvhistory/signal/iraq/reports/sanchez-memo-091403.pdf [accessed February 22, 2009].

——. 2008. *Wiser in Battle: A Soldier's Story*. New York: Harper.

Sands, Philippe. 2008. *Torture Team: Rumsfeld's Memo and the Betrayal of American Values*. New York: Palgrave Macmillan.

Shane, Scott, and Mark Mazzetti. 2007. "Ex-CIA Chief, in Book, Assails Cheney on Iraq." *The New York Times*, April 27.

Suskind, Ron. 2003. "Why Are These Men Laughing?" *Esquire*, January 1.

——. 2004. *The Price of Loyalty: George W. Bush, the White House, and the Education of Paul O'Neill*. New York: Simon & Schuster.

——.2008. *The Way of the World*. New York: Harper.

Tenet, George. 2007. *At the Center of the Storm: My Years at the CIA*. New York: HarperCollins.

Walcott, Charles E., and Karen M. Hult. 1995. *Governing the White House: From Hoover Through LBJ*. Lawrence: University Press of Kansas.

Weber, Max. 1946. "Bureaucracy." In *From Max Weber: Essays in Sociology*, eds. H. H. Gerth and C. Wright Mills. New York: Oxford University Press. Woodward, Bob. 2002. *Bush at War*. New York: Simon & Schuster.

2004. *Plan of Attack*. New York: Simon & Schuster. 2008. *The War Within*. New York: Simon & Schuster.

Yoo, John. 2002. Memorandum for William J. Haynes II, General Counsel, DOD; from John Yoo, Re: Application of Treaties and Laws to al Qaeda and Taliban Detainees, January 9. In *The Torture Papers: The Road to Abu Ghraib*, eds. Karen J. Greenberg and Joshua L. Dratel. New York: Cambridge University Press, 38–79.

SECTION

8

COMMANDER-IN-CHIEF AND NATIONAL SECURITY

• • • • • • • • • • • • ▬▬▬▬▬▬▬▬▬▬▬▬▬▬▬▬▬▬▬▬

Responsibility for guarding the national security and the war powers were divided by the framers of the Constitution between Congress (which declares war) and the president (who is commander-in-chief of the armed forces). The other functions of making and conducting foreign policy are also divided between the two branches of government. Despite the intention of the framers to give Congress an important—and sometimes dominant—role in foreign policy, the military realities of the 20th century have conspired to make the conduct of foreign policy a realm dominated by the president. This section deals with the processes and politics of national security policy making and how the two branches cooperate and compete in their efforts to control the foreign relations of the United States.

The section begins with an analysis by Louis Fisher, a scholar at the Library of Congress, of how the Framers of the Constitution divided the war powers of the government. Fisher argues that modern presidents have made claims to executive authority in foreign affairs that are not fully justified by the Constitution. Fisher argues that since Truman, presidents have claimed more authority than is granted to them in the Constitution when they assert the right to take the country to war without formal congressional action. President Truman did this when he sent U.S. troops to Korea; President Johnson exceeded his authority in Vietnam; and President George W. Bush conducted the war in Iraq in ways that undermined the Constitution. Fisher concludes that there is an important constitutional role for Congress in war powers that presidents ignore at their own peril.

In the next selection, James M. Lindsay traces the ebb and flow of control of foreign policy between the president and Congress throughout the history of the United States. He argues that how aggressively Congress asserts its own prerogatives depends importantly on whether the country seems to be under threat or whether it feels secure. For instance, after 9/11, Congress gave President Bush much of what he wanted in authorizations to take the country to war and to deal domestically with the threat of terrorism. But the farther foreign policy issues are from immediate security concerns (e.g., trade policy), the less deference Congress is likely to grant power to the president.

The modern tradition of constraining the power of political executives has deep roots in Anglo-American governmental traditions, reaching back to Magna Carta. The Framers of the Constitution were influenced by their English constitutional heritage with respect to individual rights and drew heavily upon British precedents. But with respect to governmental structure, they rejected British precedent and created a separation of powers system based on a written Constitution. The principles upon which they designed the Constitution included explicit limits on the powers of government and a separation of powers structure intended to prevent the accumulation of power in any one branch of government. The selection by James Pfiffner examines several actions by President George W. Bush and argues that he has made exceptional claims to presidential authority. Four instances of President Bush's claims to presidential power are examined: his suspension of the Geneva Agreements in 2002, his denial of the writ of habeas corpus for detainees in the war on terror, his order that the National Security Agency monitor messages to or from domestic parties in the United States without a warrant, and his use of signing statements.

Jules Lobel, in the final selection, examines the claims of President Bush to extraordinary authority under the commander-in-chief clause of the Constitution. Because the United States was engaged in the War on Terror, the Bush administration argued that the inherent powers of the president include the authority to act in the nation's defense and that Congress cannot constrain the president's detention of enemy combatants, its interrogation tactics, its decision to place U.S. citizens under surveillance without warrants, and that U.S. courts have no jurisdiction to rule on the actions of the executive. Lobel challenges the reasoning of the Bush administration and argues that federal courts have always had jurisdiction to judge the extent of executive power under the Constitution; he reviews recent decisions of the Supreme Court that undercut the Bush administration's arguments for unilateral authority in national security matters.

Louis Fisher

Presidential Power in National Security

Respect for the Constitution and joint action with Congress provide the strongest possible signal to both enemies and allies. By following those principles, other countries understand that U.S. policy has a broad base of support and is not the result of temporary, unilateral presidential actions that divide the country and are likely to be reversed. National security is strengthened when presidents act in concert with the other branches and remain faithful to constitutional principles.

In periods of emergency and threats to national security (perceived or real), the rule of law has often taken a back seat to presidential initiatives and abuses. Although this pattern is a conspicuous part of American history, it is not necessary to repeat the same mistakes every time. Faced with genuine emergencies, there are legitimate methods of executive action that are consistent with constitutional values. There are good precedents from the past and a number of bad ones.

In response to the 9/11 terrorist attacks, the United States largely decided to adopt the bad ones. The responsibility for this damage to the Constitution lies primarily with the executive branch, but illegal and unconstitutional actions cannot occur and persist without an acquiescent Congress and a compliant judiciary. The Constitution's design, relying on checks and balances and the system of separation of powers, was repeatedly ignored after 9/11. There are several reasons for these constitutional violations. Understanding them is an essential first step in returning to, and safeguarding, the rule of law and constitutional government.

Making Emergency Actions Legitimate

The Constitution can be protected in times of crisis. If an emergency occurs and there is no opportunity for executive officers to seek legislative authority, the executive may take action—sometimes in the absence of law and sometimes against it—for the public good. This is called the "Lockean prerogative." John Locke advised that in the event of executive abuse, the primary remedy was an "appeal to Heaven."

Source: *Presidential Studies Quarterly*, Vol. 39, no. 2 (June 2009).

A more secular and constitutional safeguard emerged under the American system. Unilateral presidential measures at a time of extraordinary crisis have to be followed promptly by congressional action—by the entire Congress and not some subgroup within it.[1] To preserve the constitutional order, the executive prerogative is subject to two conditions. The president must (1) acknowledge that the emergency actions are not legal or constitutional; and (2) for that very reason come to the legislative branch and explain the actions taken and the reasons for the actions and ask the legislative branch to pass a bill making the illegal actions legal.

Those steps were followed by President Abraham Lincoln after the Civil War began. He took actions we are all familiar with, including withdrawing funds from the treasury without an appropriation, calling up the troops, placing a blockade on the South, and suspending the writ of habeas corpus. In ordering those actions, Lincoln never claimed to be acting legally or constitutionally, and he never argued that Article II somehow allowed him to do what he did.

Instead, Lincoln admitted to exceeding the constitutional boundaries of his office and therefore needed the sanction of Congress. He told Congress that his actions, "whether strictly legal or not, were ventured upon under what appeared to be a popular demand and a public necessity, trusting then, as now, that Congress would readily ratify them." He explained that he used not only his Article II powers but also the Article I powers of Congress, concluding that his actions were not "beyond the constitutional competency of Congress." He recognized that the superior lawmaking body was Congress, not the president. When an executive acts in this manner, he invites two possible consequences: either support from the legislative branch or impeachment and removal from office. Congress, acting with the explicit understanding that Lincoln's actions were illegal, passed legislation retroactively approving and making valid all of his acts, proclamations, and orders.[2]

The Illusory Claim of "Inherent" Powers

President Lincoln acted at a time of the gravest emergency the United States has ever faced. What happened after 9/11 did not follow his model. Although President George W. Bush initially came to Congress to seek the Authorization for the Use of Military Force, the USA PATRIOT Act, and the Iraq Resolution of 2002, increasingly the executive branch acted unilaterally and in secret by relying on powers and authorities considered "inherent" in the presidency.

On several occasions, the Supreme Court has described the federal government as one of enumerated powers. In 1995, it stated, "We start with first principles. The Constitution creates a Federal Government of enumerated powers."[3] It repeated that claim two years later.[4] In fact, it is incorrect to call the federal government one of enumerated powers. If that were true, the Court would have no power of judicial review, the president would have no power to remove department heads, and Congress would have no power to investigate. Those powers (and other powers routinely used) are not expressly stated in the Constitution.

The Framers created a federal government of enumerated and implied powers. Express powers are clearly stated in the text of the Constitution; implied powers are those that can be reasonably drawn from express powers. "Inherent" is sometimes used as synonymous with "implied," but it is radically different. Inherent powers are not drawn from express powers. Inherent power has been defined in this manner: "An authority possessed without it being derived from another. . . . Powers over and beyond those explicitly granted in the Constitution or reasonably to be implied from express powers" (Black 1979, 703).

The purpose of the U.S. Constitution is to specify and confine governmental powers in order to protect individual rights and liberties. Express and implied powers serve that principle. The Constitution is undermined by claims of open-ended authorities that cannot be located, defined, or circumscribed. What "inheres" in the president? The standard collegiate dictionary explains that "inherent" describes the "essential character of something: belonging by nature or habit."[5] How does one determine what is essential or part of nature? Those words are so nebulous that they invite political abuse, offer convenient justifications for illegal and unconstitutional actions, and endanger individual liberties (Fisher 2007a).

Whenever the executive branch justifies its actions on the basis of "inherent" powers, the rule of law is in jeopardy. To preserve a constitutional system, executive officers must identify express or implied powers for their actions. They must do so reasonably and with appropriate respect for the duties of other branches and the rights and liberties of individuals.

It is sometimes argued that if the president functions on the basis of "inherent" powers drawn from Article II, Congress is powerless to pass legislation to limit his actions. Statutory powers, it is said, are necessarily subordinate to constitutional powers. There are several weaknesses with this argument. First, when the president says that he is acting under "inherent" powers drawn from Article II, that is nothing more than a *claim* or an *assertion*. Congress is not prevented from acting legislatively because of executive claims and assertions. Neither are the courts. Second, if the president wants to claim that powers exist under Article II, the door is fully open for Congress to pass legislation pursuant to Article I. Constitutional authority is not justified by presidential *ipse dixits*. The same can be said of congressional and judicial *ipse dixits*. When one branch claims a power, the other two branches should not acquiesce. Doing so eliminates the system of checks and balances that the framers provided.

Misunderstanding *Curtiss-Wright*

Of all the misconceived and poorly reasoned judicial decisions that have expanded presidential power in the field of national security, thereby weakening the rule of law and endangering individual rights, the *Curtiss-Wright* case of 1936 stands in a class by itself. It is frequently cited by courts and the executive branch for the existence of "inherent" presidential power. In language that is plainly dicta and had no relevance to the issue before the Supreme Court, Justice George Sutherland wrote,

It is important to bear in mind that we are here dealing not alone with an authority vested in the president by an exertion of legislative power, but with such an
authority plus the very delicate, plenary and exclusive power of the president as the
sole organ of the federal government in the field of international relations—a power
which does not require as a basis for its exercise an act of Congress, but which, of
course, like every other governmental power, must be exercised in subordination to
the applicable provisions of the Constitution.[6]

Justice Sutherland's distortion of the "sole organ" doctrine will be examined in the
next section. It is sufficient to point out that the case before the Court had absolutely
nothing to do with presidential power. It concerned only the power of Congress. The
constitutional dispute was whether Congress, by joint resolution, could delegate to
the president *its* power, authorizing President Franklin D. Roosevelt to declare an
arms embargo in a region in South America.[7] In imposing the embargo, President
Roosevelt relied solely on this statutory—not inherent—authority. He acted "under
and by virtue of the authority conferred in me by the said joint resolution of Congress."[8] President Roosevelt made no assertion of inherent, independent, exclusive,
plenary, or extra-constitutional authority.

Litigation on his proclamation focused on legislative power because, during the
previous year, the Supreme Court twice had struck down the delegation by Congress
of *domestic* power to the president.[9] Therefore, the issue in *Curtiss-Wright* was
whether Congress could delegate legislative power more broadly in international affairs than it could in domestic affairs. A district court held that the joint resolution
impermissibly delegated legislative authority but said nothing about any reservoir of
inherent or independent presidential power.[10] That decision was taken directly to
the Supreme Court, where none of the briefs on either side discussed the availability of inherent or independent presidential power. As to the issue of jurisdiction, the
Justice Department advised that the question for the Court went to "the very power
of Congress to delegate to the Executive authority to investigate and make findings
in order to implement a legislative purpose."[11] The joint resolution passed by Congress, said the Justice Department, contained adequate standards to guide the president and did not fall prey to the "unfettered discretion" found by the Court in the
two 1935 delegation decisions.[12]

The brief for the private company, Curtiss-Wright, also focused solely on the issue of delegated power and did not explore the availability of independent or inherent powers for the president.[13] A separate brief, prepared for other private parties,
concentrated on the delegation of legislative power and did not attempt to locate
any freestanding or freewheeling presidential authority.[14] Given President Roosevelt's stated dependence on statutory authority and the lack of anything in the
briefs about inherent presidential power, there was no need for the Supreme Court
to discuss independent sources for executive authority.

Anything along those lines would be dicta. The extraneous matter added by Justice Sutherland in his *Curtiss-Wright* opinion has been subjected to highly critical
studies by scholars. One article regards Sutherland's position on the existence of inherent presidential power to be "(1) contrary to American history, (2) violative of
our political theory, (3) unconstitutional, and (4) unnecessary, undemocratic, and

dangerous" (Patterson 1944, 297). Other scholarly works find similar deficiencies with Sutherland's dicta (these works are summarized in Fisher 2007b; for a more detailed treatment of the sole-organ doctrine, see Fisher 2006b).

Federal courts repeatedly cite *Curtiss-Wright* to sustain delegations of legislative power to the president in the field of international affairs and, at times, to support the existence of inherent and independent presidential power for the president in foreign policy. Although some justices of the Supreme Court have described the president's foreign relations power as "exclusive," the Court itself has not denied to Congress its constitutional authority to enter the field and reverse or modify presidential decisions in the area of national security and foreign affairs (see Fisher 2006b, 23–28).

The False "Sole Organ" Doctrine

Another defective argument for inherent presidential power is Justice Sutherland's reference in *Curtiss-Wright* to a speech given by Representative John Marshall on March 7, 1800: "The President is the sole organ of the nation in its external relations, and its sole representatives with foreign nations."[15] When one reads Marshall's entire speech and understands it in the context of a House effort to either impeach or censure President John Adams, nothing said by Marshall gives any support to independent, exclusive, plenary, inherent, or extra-constitutional power for the president. Marshall's only objective was to defend the authority of President Adams to carry out an extradition treaty. In that sense, the president was not the sole organ in formulating the treaty or making national policy. He was the sole organ in *implementing* it. Marshall was stating what should have been obvious. Under the express language of Article II, it is the president's duty to "take Care that the Laws be faithfully executed." Under Article VI, all treaties made "shall be the supreme Law of the Land."

Far from being an argument for inherent or plenary power, Marshall was relying on the express constitutional duty of the president to carry out the law. He emphasized that President Adams was not attempting to make foreign policy single-handedly. He was carrying out a policy made jointly by the president and the Senate (for treaties). On other occasions, the president might be charged with carrying out a policy made by statute. In that sense, the president was the sole organ in implementing national policy as decided by the two branches.

Even in carrying out a treaty, Marshall said, the president could be restrained by a subsequent statute. Congress "may prescribe the mode" of carrying out a treaty.[16] For example, legislation in 1848 provided that in all cases of treaties of extradition between the United States and another country, federal and state judges were authorized to determine whether the evidence was sufficient to sustain the charge against the individual to be extradited.[17]

In his capacity as chief justice of the Supreme Court, Marshall held firm to his position that the making of foreign policy is a joint exercise by the executive and legislative branches, through treaties and statutes, and not a unilateral or exclusive authority of the president. With the war power, he looked solely to Congress—not to the president—for constitutional authority to take the country to war. He had no difficulty in identifying the branch that possessed the war power: "The whole powers of war being, by the Constitution of the United States, vested in Congress, the acts of that body can alone be resorted to as our guides in this enquiry."[18] When a presidential proclamation issued in time of war conflicted with a statute enacted by Congress, Marshall ruled that the statute prevails.[19]

Despite this clear meaning of Marshall's use of "sole organ," the Justice Department has repeatedly cited *Curtiss-Wright* as authority for inherent presidential power, as it did on January 19, 2006, in offering a legal defense for the National Security Agency surveillance program. The department associated the sole-organ doctrine with inherent power, pointing to "the President's well-recognized inherent constitutional authority as commander in chief and sole organ for the Nation in foreign affairs."[20] Later in this analysis, the department stated, "the President's role as sole organ for the Nation in foreign affairs has long been recognized as carrying with it preeminent authority in the field of national security and foreign intelligence."[21] Only by relying on the misconceptions of the dicta by Justice Sutherland in *Curtiss-Wright* could language like that be used. Nothing in Marshall's speech offers any support for inherent or preeminent authority of the president.

Usurping the War Power

Beginning with President Harry S. Truman's war against North Korea in 1950, presidents over the last half century have claimed the constitutional authority to take the country to war without seeking either a declaration of war or statutory authorization from Congress. Nothing is more destructive to the rule of law than allowing presidents to claim that the commander-in-chief clause empowers them to initiate war. With that single step, all other rights, freedoms, and procedural safeguards are diminished and sometimes extinguished.

The British model gave the king the absolute power to make war. The Framers repudiated that form of government, because their study of history convinced them that executives go to war not for the national interest but to satisfy personal desires of fame. The resulting military adventures were disastrous to their countries, both in lives lost and treasures squandered. John Jay warned in *Federalist* No. 4 that "absolute monarchs will often make war when their nations are to *get* nothing by it, but for purposes and objects merely personal, such as a thirst for military glory, revenge for personal affronts, ambition, or private compacts to aggrandize or support their particular families or partisans. These and a variety of other motives, which affect only the mind of the sovereign, often lead him to engage in wars not sanctified by justice or the voice and interests of his people."

Congress, and only Congress, is the branch of government authorized to decide whether to initiate war. That constitutional principle was bedrock to the Framers. They broke cleanly and crisply with the British model that allowed kings to control everything abroad, including wars. The Framers created a Constitution dedicated to popular control through elected representatives. They dreaded placing the war power in the hands of a single person. They distrusted human nature, especially executives who leaned toward war. Contrary to the July 2008 Baker-Christopher war powers report, the Constitution is not "ambiguous" about placing the war power with Congress (see Fisher 2008c, 44–45; 2009; for testimony and other articles on the war power and War Powers Resolution, see http://www.loc.gov/law/help/usconlaw/constitutional_law.php).

At the Philadelphia Convention, only one delegate (Pierce Butler of South Carolina) was prepared to give the president the power to make war. He argued that the president "will have all the requisite qualities, and will not make war but when the Nation will support it." Roger Sherman, a delegate from Connecticut, objected: "The Executive shd. be able to repel but not to commence war." Elbridge Gerry of Massachusetts said that he "never expected to hear in a republic a motion to empower the Executive alone to declare war." George Mason of Virginia spoke "agst giving the power of war to the Executive, because not (safely) to be trusted with it . . . He was for clogging rather than facilitating war" (Farrand 1937, 2:318–19).

The debates at the Philadelphia Convention and the state ratification conventions underscore the principle that the president had certain defensive powers to repel sudden attacks, but anything of an offensive nature (taking the country from a state of peace to a state of war) was reserved to Congress. That understanding prevailed from 1789 to 1950, when President Truman went to war against North Korea without ever coming to Congress for authority.

The president is commander-in-chief, but that title was never intended to give the president sole power to initiate war and determine its scope. Such an interpretation would nullify the express powers given to Congress under Article I and undercut the Framers' determination to place the power of war with the elected representatives of Congress. Eight clauses in Article I specifically define the military powers of Congress. Part of the purpose of the commander-in-chief clause is to preserve civilian supremacy. As explained by Attorney General Edward Bates, whatever soldier leads U.S. armies in battle, "he is subject to the orders of the *civil magistrate*, and he and his army are always 'subordinate to the civil power.'"[22] Military commitments are not in the hands of admirals and generals but are exercised by civilian leaders, including members of Congress. Lawmakers need to authorize military commitments and can, at any time, limit and terminate them.

Seeking "Authority" from the United Nations

When President Truman went to war against North Korea, he claimed as "authority" two resolutions adopted by the United Nations (UN) Security Council. Nothing in the legislative history of the UN Charter justifies that interpretation. It is impossible to argue under the Constitution that the president and the Senate, through the treaty process, may create a procedure that allows the president to circumvent Congress (including the House of Representatives) and obtain "authority" from an international or regional body.

During Senate action on the UN Charter, it was never contemplated that the president could use the Security Council as a substitute for Congress. All parties working on the charter recalled what had happened with the Versailles Treaty and the failure of the United States to join the League of Nations. President Woodrow Wilson opposed a series of Senate amendments to the treaty, including language requiring that Congress "shall by act of joint resolution" provide approval for any military action by the League (Fisher 2004, 82).

The need for advance approval by Congress for any military commitment was recognized by those who drafted the UN Charter (Fisher 2004, 84–87). In the midst of Senate debate on the charter, President Truman cabled from Potsdam his pledge to seek advance approval from Congress for any agreement he entered into with the UN for military operations: "When any such agreement or agreements are negotiated it will be my purpose to ask the Congress for appropriate legislation to approve them" (Fisher 2004, 91). Approval meant action by both Houses, and in advance. The Senate supported the charter with that understanding.

Each nation had to decide, consistent with its "constitutional processes," how to implement the provision in the charter regarding the use of military force. To do that, Congress passed the United Nations Participation Act of 1945. Without the slightest ambiguity, Section 6 of that statute required that the use of the agreements "shall be subject to the approval of the Congress by appropriate Act or joint resolution."[23] Yet five years later, without ever coming to Congress for authorization, Truman went to war against North Korea by relying on UN resolutions (Fisher 1995, 21; 2004, 97–104).

Truman's action became a precedent for other presidents seeking "authority" from the UN for military initiatives, including President George H. W. Bush in 1990 (for Iraq) and President Bill Clinton in 1994 and 1995 (for Haiti and Bosnia). The unconstitutionality of using the UN Charter to bypass congressional control applies to other treaties, such as mutual security pacts. It was a violation of the Constitution for President Clinton, after failing to obtain Security Council support for the war in Kosovo, to use NATO for "authority." No plausible argument can be made to require the president to seek the "approval" of each of the NATO countries but not from Congress (Fisher 1997, 1237).

Invoking the State Secrets Privilege

Especially in recent years, the executive branch has invoked the "state secrets privilege" to prevent litigants from challenging actions that appear to be illegal and unconstitutional. These civil cases include the extraordinary rendition lawsuits of Maher Arar and Khaled El-Masri and the National Security Agency surveillance cases brought against the administration and telecoms. The rule of law is threatened if judges accept the standards of "deference" or "utmost deference" when evaluating executive claims. Assertions of "national security" documents are only that: assertions. When judges fail to assert their independence in these cases, it is possible for an administration to violate statutes, treaties, and the Constitution without any effective challenge in court.

Congress has full authority to act legislatively to redress this problem. The House and the Senate have in the past year held hearings on this issue, and on August 1, 2008, the Senate Judiciary Committee reported its bill.[24] The Justice Department relies on the Supreme Court's decision in *United States* v. *Reynolds* (1953), the first time the Court recognized the state secrets privilege. The history of that litigation makes plain that the executive branch misled the courts about the presence of "state secrets" in the document sought by the plaintiffs. When the document, a U.S. Air Force accident report, was declassified and made public, it was evident that the report contained no state secrets (Fisher 2006a).

Secret Law

Increasingly, the executive branch operates on the basis of secret executive orders, memoranda, directives, and legal memos. On March 31, 2008, the Bush administration declassified and released a Justice Department legal memo prepared five years earlier on military interrogation of alien unlawful combatants outside the United States. Other legal memos remain secret. A society cannot remain faithful to the rule of law when governed by secret law, especially policies that promote broad and unchecked presidential power. If legal memos contain sensitive information, items can be redacted and the balance of the document made public. No plausible case can be made for withholding legal reasoning. Secret policy means that the rule of law is not statute or treaty, enacted in public, but confidential executive policies unknown to citizens or even to members of Congress. The public and executive agencies cannot comply with secret law. Lawmakers are unable to review and amend legal interpretations never released by the executive branch.[25]

Abuse of Signing Statements

A form of secret law appeared in a signing statement by President Bush on December 30, 2005. Congress, responding to criticism of abusive interrogations of detainees, passed legislation prohibiting cruel, inhuman, or degrading treatment or punishment of persons held in U.S. custody.[26] In signing the bill, President Bush stated that the provision would be interpreted "in a manner consistent with the constitutional authority of the president to supervise the unitary executive branch and as Commander in Chief."[27] References to the unitary executive theory and the commander-in-chief clause are far too general to understand either the nature of the objection or the scope of the claimed presidential authority. Other signing statements are generally impossible to comprehend and analyze because they are couched in such abstract references as the appointments clause, the presentment clause, the recommendations clause, and other shortcut citations.[28] Constitutional concerns deepen when presidents raise objections at the time they sign a bill and proceed to adopt policies—as with the interrogation of detainees—unknown to the country or to Congress.

Signing statements encourage the belief that the law is not what Congress places in a bill but what presidents say about the language. In 1971, President Richard M. Nixon signed a bill that included a provision calling for the withdrawal of U.S. troops from Southeast Asia. The signing statement expressed the view that the provision "does not represent the policies of the Administration."[29] A year later, a federal district court instructed President Nixon that the law was what he signed, not what he said about it.[30] When he signed the bill, it established U.S. policy "to the exclusion of any different executive or administration policy, and had binding force and effect on every officer of the Government, no matter what their private judgments on that policy, and illegalized the pursuit of an inconsistent executive or administration policy."[31] No executive statement, including that of the president, "denying efficacy to the legislation could have either validity or effect."[32]

"Authorizing" What Is Illegal

To provide assurance to the public and other branches, administrations will often announce that what it has done is fully authorized. That pattern was illustrated when the Bush administration, having violated the FISA (Foreign Intelligence Surveillance Act) statute by not seeking approval from the FISA Court, publicly stated that its Terrorist Surveillance Program was "authorized," regularly "reauthorized," and was "legal" and "lawful." Those words implied that the administration was acting in compliance with the rule of law, or "consistent" with the law, when it was in fact operating squarely against it and doing so in secret (Fisher 2008b, 291–98, 300–302). Justice Robert Jackson reminded us what is meant by the rule of law: "With all its defects, delays and inconveniences, men have discovered no technique for long preserving free government except that the Executive be under the law, and that the law be made by parliamentary deliberation."[33]

Overreaching Executive Privilege

In the past, the executive branch recognized that the president should not invoke executive privilege to defeat the rule of law. In particular, it was improper to block congressional access to information when "wrongdoing" had been committed by executive officials. The Supreme Court has noted that the power of Congress to conduct investigations "comprehends probes into departments of the Federal Government to expose corruption, inefficiency, or waste."[34] Attorney General William Rogers told a Senate committee in 1958 that the withholding of documents from Congress "can never be justified as a means of covering mistakes, avoiding embarrassment, or for political, personal, or pecuniary reasons."[35] In 1982, Attorney General William French Smith said that he would not try "to shield [from Congress] documents which contain evidence of criminal or unethical conduct by agency officials from proper review."[36] During a news conference in 1983, President Ronald Reagan remarked, "We will never invoke executive privilege to cover up wrongdoing."[37] In a memo of September 28, 1994, White House Counsel Lloyd Cutler stated that executive privilege would not be asserted with regard to communications "relating to investigations of personal wrongdoing by government officials," either in judicial proceedings or in congressional investigations and hearings.[38]

Those statements promote a basic principle. A privilege exerted by the executive branch should not be used to conceal corruption, criminal or unethical conduct, or wrongdoing by executive officials. A privilege should not be used to shield government officials who violate the law. Yet in the last two years, when Congress attempted to investigate several activities within the Justice Department, including the firings of U.S. attorneys, the administration decided that a privilege would protect top White House officials, both past and present. That interpretation provided those individuals with total immunity against any congressional investigation. Legislative efforts to exercise the power of contempt against those officials would be ineffective. Under this policy, the U.S. attorney, who is required under law to take a contempt citation to a grand jury to investigate possible wrongdoing, is prohibited from discharging that statutory duty. Through this policy, the investigative power of Congress to probe agency corruption is neutralized. Existing checks would come only from the executive department investigating itself.

On July 31, 2008, District Judge John D. Bates rejected a number of Justice Department arguments that were used to block the House contempt votes. Most importantly, he rejected the claim of absolute immunity from compelled congressional process for senior presidential aides. He found clear precedent and persuasive policy reasons to conclude that "the Executive cannot be the judge of its own privilege."[39]

This case did not concern matters of national security, an area where the executive branch frequently claims special and exclusive privileges to keep documents from Congress and the judiciary. The Justice Department relies heavily on the Supreme Court's 1988 decision in *Egan*.[40] The Court acknowledged the president's responsibilities to protect documents bearing on national security. Yet, as noted by District Judge Vaughn R. Walker in a recent ruling, the Court in *Egan* specifically said that presidential power is broad "unless Congress specifically has provided otherwise."[41] To Judge Walker, the Court's decision in *Egan* "recognizes that the authority to protect national security information is neither exclusive nor absolute in the executive branch."[42]

Watch What You Inherit

Individuals elected to the presidency need to be wary of plans that have been developed by executive agencies during the previous administration and are placed before them, in the early weeks and months, urging quick action. An example is the 1952–53 covert operation to remove Prime Minister Mohammad Mosadegh of Iran. The British and the American Central Intelligence Agency proposed to President Truman that he authorize the action, but Truman refused. When President Dwight D. Eisenhower entered the White House, he supported the plan and Mosadegh was subsequently removed and the Shah placed in power (Kinzer 2003). This U.S.

intervention undermined the reputation of the United States as a country that supported democratic government and the rule of law. Toward the end of Eisenhower's
eight years in government, another covert plan was readied and presented to the
incoming president, John F. Kennedy. The plan was the "Bay of Pigs." Invasion

Reviving Structural Checks

The Framers did not depend solely on the presidency or federal courts to protect individual rights and liberties. They distrusted human nature and chose to place their
faith in a system of checks and balances and separated powers. The rule of law finds
protection when political power is not concentrated in a single branch and when all
three branches exercise the powers assigned them, including the duty to resist encroachments of another branch. The rule of law is always at risk when Congress and
the judiciary defer to claims and assertions by executive authorities. That is the lesson of the last two centuries and particularly of the past seven years.

James Madison looked to a political system in which ambition would counteract ambition. With Congress (and the judiciary), there is often a lack of ambition to
assert institutional powers and duties. That invites executive initiatives at the expense of individual rights and constitutional values. Just as the Vietnam War helped
spell defeat for the Democrats in 1968, so did the Korean War put an end to 20 years
of Democratic control of the White House. "Korea, not crooks or Communists, was
the major concern of the voters," wrote Stephen Ambrose (1983, 1:569). The Iraq
War is widely seen as a major contribution to Republican losses in the 2006 and 2008
elections.

Although Eisenhower initially believed that Truman's decision to intervene in
Korea was "wise and necessary" (Eisenhower 1963, 82), he came to realize that it was
a serious mistake, politically and constitutionally, for a president to commit the nation to war without congressional support and approval. To Eisenhower, national
commitments would be stronger if entered into jointly by both branches. Therefore,
it was his practice to ask Congress for specific authority to deal with national security crises. He stressed the important of *collective* action by the two branches: "I deem
it necessary to seek the cooperation of the Congress. Only with that cooperation can
we give the reassurance needed to deter aggression."[43]

In 1954, when Eisenhower was under pressure to intervene in Indochina, he refused to act unilaterally. He told reporters at a press conference, "There is going to
be no involvement of America in war unless it is a result of the constitutional
process that is placed upon Congress to declare it. Now, let us have that clear; and
that is the answer."[44] He told Secretary of State John Foster Dulles that in "the absence of some kind of arrangement getting support of Congress," it "would be completely unconstitutional & indefensible" to give any assistance to the French in
Indochina.[45]

Also in 1954, Eisenhower concluded that he lacked the authority to become
involved militarily in the Formosa Straits. In a memorandum to Dulles, he

observed that "It is doubtful that the issue can be exploited without congressional approval."[46] One issue was whether Eisenhower could order an attack on airfields in China. He said that "to do that you would have to get congressional authorization, since it would be war. If congressional authorization were not obtained there would be logical grounds for impeachment. Whatever we do must be in a Constitutional manner."[47] Sherman Adams, Eisenhower's chief of staff, later recalled that Eisenhower was determined "not to resort to any kind of military action without the approval of Congress" (1961, 109).

In his memoirs, Eisenhower explained the choice between invoking executive prerogatives and seeking congressional support. On New Year's Day 1957, he met with Secretary of State Dulles and congressional leaders of both parties. House majority leader John McCormack (D-MA) asked Eisenhower whether he, as commander in chief, already possessed sufficient authority to carry out military actions in the Middle East without congressional authority. Eisenhower replied that "greater effect could be had from a consensus of Executive and Legislative opinion, and I spoke earnestly of the desire of the Middle East countries to have reassurance now that the United States would stand ready to help. . . . Near the end of this meeting I reminded the legislators that the Constitution assumes that our two branches of government should get along together" (1965, 179).

During a press conference in 1957, President Eisenhower was asked whether he, as commander in chief, could send troops wherever he wanted without seeking the approval of Congress. Instead of identifying independent or inherent powers, he pointed to the practical importance of inter-branch collaboration.[48] Eisenhower understood that lawyers and policy advisors in the executive branch could always cite various precedents and authorities to justify unilateral presidential action. It was his judgment that a commitment by the United States would have much greater impact, on allies and enemies alike, if they represented the collective judgment of both branches.

Endnotes

1. After 9/11, the Bush administration met only with the "Gang of Eight" to reveal what became known as the "Terrorist Surveillance Program." The Gang of Eight consists of four party leaders in the House and the Senate and the chair and ranking member of the two intelligence committees. The administration did not seek congressional approval until after the program had been disclosed by *The New York Times* in December 2005.
2. 12 Stat. 326 (1861). See also Fisher (2004, 47–49).
3. *United States v. Lopez,* 514 U.S. 549, 552 (1995).
4. *Boeme v. Flores,* 521 U.S. 507, 516 (1997).
5. *Merriam Webster's Collegiate Dictionary,* 10th edition (1993), 601.
6. *United States v. Curtiss-Wright Corp.,* 299 U.S. 304, 320 (1936).
7. 48 Stat. 811, ch. 365 (1934).
8. 48 Scat. 1745 (1934).
9. *Panama Refining Co. v. Ryan,* 293 U.S. 388 (1935); *Schechter Carp. v. United States,* 295 U.S. 495 (1935).

10. *United States v. Curtiss-Wright Export Corp.,* 14 F. Supp. 230 (S.D. N.Y. 1936).
11. U.S. Justice Department, Statement as to Jurisdiction, *United States v. Curtiss-Wright,* No. 98, Supreme Court, October Term, 1936, at 7.
12. Id. at 15.
13. Brief for Appellees, *United States v. Curtiss-Wright,* No. 98, Supreme Court, October Term 1936, at 3.
14. Brief for Appellees Allard, *United States v. Curtiss-Wright,* No. 98, Supreme Court, October Term, 1936.
15. 299 U.S. at 320.
16. 10 *Annals of Cong.* 614 (1800).
17. 9 Stat. 320 (1846), upheld in *In Re Kaine,* 55 U.S. 103, 111–14 (1852).
18. *Talbotv. Seeman,* 5 U.S. 1, 28 (1801).
19. *Little v. Barrem, 2* Cr. (6 U.S.) 170, 179 (1804).
20. Office of Legal Counsel, U.S. Department of Justice, "Legal Authorities Supporting the Activities of the National Security Agency Described by the President,' January 19, 2006, at 1.
21. Id. at 30.
22. 10 Op. Atty Gen. 74, 79 (1861).
23. 59 Star. 621, sec. 6 (1945).
24. S. Rept. No. 11–442, 110th Cong., 2nd sess. (2008).
25. The issue of secret legal memos was explored at a hearing on April 30, 2008, before the Senate Judiciary Committee. See also Fisher (2008d).
26. Detainee Treatment Act of 2005, Pub. L. No. 109–148, 119 Stat. 2680, 2739 (2005), codified at 42 U.S.C.A. 2000dd (West. Supp. 2007).
27. 41 *Weekly Comp. Pres. Doc.* 1919 (2005); see also Bumiller (2006).
28. "Presidential Signing Statements," Findings of the Subcommittee on Oversight and Investigations, House Armed Services Committee, August 18, 2008, available at http://www.fas.org/sgp/congress/2008/signing.pdf.
29. *Public Papers of the Presidents,* 1971, at 1114.
30. *DaCosta v. Nixon,* 55 F.R.D. 145 (E.D.N.Y. 1972).
31. Id. at 146.
32. Id. See also Fisher (2007c, 183).
33. *Youngstown Co. v. Sawyer,* 343 U.S. 579, 655 (1952).
34. *Watkins v. United States,* 354 U.S. 178, 187 (1957).
35. "Freedom of Information and Secrecy in Government," hearing before the Subcommittee on Constitutional Rights of the Senate Committee on the Judiciary, 85th Cong., 2nd sess. 5 (1958).
36. Letter of November 30, 1982, to Congressman John Dingell, reprinted in H. Rept. No. 698, 97th Cong., 2nd sess. 41 (1982).
37. *Public Papers of the Presidents,* 1983, I, at 239-
38. Memorandum for all Executive Department and Agency General Counsels from Lloyd N. Cutler, Special Counsel to the President, "Congressional Requests to Departments and Agencies for Documents Protected by Executive Privilege," September 28, 1994, at 1.
39. Committee on the Judiciary, *U.S. House of Representatives v. Harriet Miers,* Civil Action No. 08–0409 (JDB), (D.D.C. July 31, 2008), at 91.
40. *Department of the Navy v. Egan,* 484 U.S. 518 (1988).
41. *In re: National Security Agency Telecommunications Records Litigation,* MDL Docket No. 06–1791 VRW (D. Cal. July 2, 2008), at 22.
42. Id. For additional analysis of *Egan* and why Congress has access to sensitive and classified documents, see Fisher (2008a, 219). For example, *Egan* was a matter of statutory construction, not Constitutional interpretation.
43. *Public Papers of the Presidents,* 1957, at 11.
44. *Public Papers of the Presidents,* 1954, at 306.
45. Foreign Relations of the United States (FRUS), 1952–54, vol. 13, part 1, at 1242.
46. Id., vol. 14, part 1, at 611.
47. Id. at 618.
48. *Public Papers of the Presidents,* 1957, at 177–78.

References

Adams, Sherman. 1961. *Firsthand Report: The Story of the Eisenhower Administration*. New York: Harper.

Ambrose, Stephen E. 1983. *Eisenhower: Soldier, General of the Army*. 2 vols. New York: Simon & Schuster.

Black, Henry Campbell. 1979. *Black's Law Dictionary: Definitions of the Terms and Phrases of American and English Jurisprudence, Ancient and Modern*. 5th ed. St. Paul, MN: West.

Bumiller, Elizabeth. 2006. "For President, Final Say on a Bill Sometimes Comes After the Signing."
The New York Times, January 16, p. A1 1.

Eisenhower, Dwight D. 1963. *Mandate for Change*. New York: Doubleday.

———. 1965. *The White House Years: Waging Peace, 1956–1961*. New York: Doubleday.

Farrand, Max, ed. 1937. *Records of the Federal Convention of 1787*. 4 vols. New Haven, CT: Yale University Press.

Fisher, Louis. 1995. "The Korean War: On What Legal Basis Did Truman Act?" *American Journal of International Law* 89 (January): 21–39.

———. 1997. "Sidestepping Congress: Presidents Acting Under the UN and NATO." *Case Western Reserve Law Review* Al: 1237–79.

———. 2004. *Presidential War Power*. 2nd ed. Lawrence: University Press of Kansas.

———. 2006a. *In the Name of National Security: Unchecked Presidential Power and the Reynolds Case*. Lawrence: University Press of Kansas.

———. 2006b. "The Sole Organ Doctrine." Studies on Presidential Power in Foreign Relations no. 1, Law Library of Congress. http://www.loc.gov/law/help/usconlaw/pdf/SoleOrgan-Aug06.pdf [accessed February 21, 2009].

———. 2007a. "Invoking Inherent Powers: A Primer." *Presidential Studies Quarterly* 37 (March): 1–22.

———. 2007b. "Presidential Inherent Power: The 'Sole Organ' Doctrine." *Presidential Studies Quarterly* 37 (March): 139–52.

———. 2007c. "Signing Statements: Constitutional and Practical Limits." *William & Mary Bill of Rights Journal* 16: 183–210.

———. 2008a. "Congressional Access to National Security Information." *Harvard Journal on Legislation* 45: 221–35.

———. 2008b. *The Constitution and 9/11: Recurring Threats to America's Freedoms*. Lawrence: University Press of Kansas.

———. 2008c. "When the Shooting Starts: Not Even an Elite Commission Can Take Away Congress' Exclusive Power to Authorize War." *Legal Times*, July 28.

———. 2008d. "Why Classify Legal Memos?" *National Law Journal*, July 14.

———. 2009- "The Baker-Christopher War Powers Commission." *Presidential Studies Quarterly* 39 (March): 128–40.

Kinzer, Stephen. 2003. *All the Shah's Men: An American Coup and the Roots of Middle East Terror*. Hoboken, NJ: Wiley.

Patterson, C. Perry. 1944. "In re the *United States v. the Curtiss-Wright Corporation*." *Texas Law Review* 22: 286–308.

James M. Lindsay

Deference and Defiance: The Shifting Rhythms of Executive-Legislative Relations in Foreign Policy

The presidencies of Bill Clinton and George W. Bush contrast in many ways, perhaps no more so than in their divergent experiences in dealing with Congress on foreign policy. Clinton confronted a Congress that frequently sought to defy his initiatives and at times seemed to take glee in doing so. His list of defeats on Capitol Hill is long. Congress forced him to withdraw U.S. troops from Somalia in 1994. It slashed his foreign aid requests. It refused to grant him fast-track trade negotiating authority. It forced him to accept national missile defense and regime change in Iraq as goals of U.S. foreign policy even though he and many of his advisers doubted the wisdom and practicality of both. It blocked his efforts to pay U.S. back dues to the United Nations. The Senate rejected the Comprehensive Test Ban Treaty. Even when Congress backed Clinton on foreign policy, as with the dispatch of U.S. peace keepers to Bosnia and the Senate's approval of the Chemical Weapons Convention and NATO enlargement, the victories seemed to require inordinate administration effort.

Bush's experience was far different. Congress was eager to defer to his leadership on many foreign policy issues. It overwhelmingly authorized him to wage not one but two wars. It acceded to his decisions to leave the 1972 Anti-Ballistic Missile (ABM) Treaty and move to develop an expansive new national missile defense. It gave him most everything he requested for defense and foreign affairs spending. It embraced his request to begin the largest reorganization of the federal government in more than century. It gave him the trade-promotion (formerly fast-track) authority it had denied Clinton. Perhaps most significant, he had all Republicans and many Democrats rushing to tell voters that they supported his national security policies.

September 11 explains Congress's shift from defiance of Clinton to deference to Bush. The attacks on the World Trade Center and the Pentagon altered the American political landscape in the United States. Members of Congress who previously took pride in standing up to the White House suddenly saw the better part of good policy and good politics in a willingness to rally around the president.

Source: Presidential Studies Quarterly Vol. 33, No. 3 (September 2003).

The change that September 11 caused in executive-legislative relations was extreme but not unprecedented. The pendulum of power on foreign policy has shifted back and forth between Congress and the president many times over the course of American history. The reason for this ebb and flow does not lie in the Constitution. Its formal allocation of foreign policy powers, which gives important authorities to both Congress and the president, has not changed since it was drafted. Rather, the answer lies in politics. How aggressively Congress exercises its foreign policy powers turns on the critical questions of whether the country sees itself as threatened or secure and whether the president's policies are succeeding or failing. Simply put, times of peace and presidential missteps favor congressional defiance. Times of war and presidential success favor congressional deference.

The Constitution and Foreign Policy

Ask most Americans who makes foreign policy in the United States and their immediate answer is the president. Up to a point, they are right. Even a cursory reading of the Constitution makes clear that Congress possesses extensive foreign policy powers. Article 1, Section 8 assigns Congress the power to "provide for the common Defence," "To regulate Commerce with foreign Nations," "To define and punish Piracies and Felonies committed on the high Seas," "To declare War," "To raise and support Armies," "To provide and maintain a Navy," and "To make Rules for the Government and Regulation of the land and naval Forces." Article 2, Section 2 specifies that the Senate must give its advice and consent to all treaties and ambassadorial appointments. Congress' more general powers to appropriate all government funds and to confirm cabinet officials provide additional means to influence foreign policy.

The lesson in this is that when it comes to foreign affairs, Congress and the president *both* can claim ample constitutional authority. The two branches are, in Richard Neustadt's (1990, 29) oft-repeated formulation, "separated institutions *sharing* power." The question of which branch should prevail as a matter of principle when their powers conflict has been disputed ever since Alexander Hamilton and James Madison squared off two centuries ago in their famed Pacificus-Helvidius debate. Hamilton argued that the president was free to exercise his powers as he saw fit even if those actions might "affect the exercise of the power of the . . . legislature. . . . : The legislature is still free to perform its duties, according to its own sense of them; though the executive, in the exercise of its constitutional powers, may establish an antecedent state of things, which ought to weigh in the legislative decision" (Smith 1989, 52). Madison denied that there was such a thing as concurrent authority and insisted that the president could not exercise his authority in ways that would "abridge or affect" the enumerated powers of the legislature (Smith 1989, 56).

At the start of the 21st century, Hamilton's and Madison's intellectual descendants continue to spar, and they will undoubtedly continue to do so for years to come. Their battles often unleash the same passion they showed two hundred years ago. Yet, these battles are also largely academic, interesting intellectual exercises but seldom applicable to real world policy debates. The fact that the Constitution grants

Congress extensive foreign policy powers means that most executive-legislative disputes do not raise constitutional issues. They instead raise political issues and involve the exercise of political power. That is the insight behind Edward Corwin's oft-repeated observation that the Constitution is "an invitation to struggle for the privilege of directing American foreign policy" (Corwin 1957, 171).

To say that Congress can put its mark on foreign policy, however, is not the same as saying that it will try to do so. To understand why congressional activism on foreign policy varies over time, it is necessary to leave the realm of law and enter the realm of politics.

Politics and Foreign Policy

The first explanation for Congress's fluctuating say in foreign policy lies in an observation that Alexis de Tocqueville made more than 150 years ago. Surprised to find that the pre-Civil War Congress played a major role in foreign policy, he speculated that congressional activism stemmed from the country's isolation from external threat. "If the Union's existence were constantly menaced, and if its great interests were continually interwoven with those of other powerful nations, one would see the prestige of the executive growing, because of what was expected from it and of what it did" (de Tocqueville 1969, 126).

Why might threat perceptions affect how Congress behaves? When Americans believe they face few external threats—or think that international engagement could itself produce a threat—they see less merit in deferring to the White House on foreign policy and more merit to congressional activism. Debate and disagreement are not likely to pose significant costs; after all, the country is secure. When Americans believe the country faces an external threat, however, they quickly convert to the belief that the country needs strong presidential leadership. Congressional dissent that was previously acceptable suddenly looks to be unhelpful meddling at best and unpatriotic at worst. Members of Congress are no different than their constituents. They feel the same shifting sentiments toward the wisdom of deferring to the president. They are also profoundly aware that being on the wrong side of that shift could hurt them come the next election.

Throughout American history, power over foreign policy has flowed back and forth between the two ends of Pennsylvania Avenue according to this basic dynamic. In the second half of the 19th century, the United States was as secure from foreign attack as at any time in American history. This was also a time when Congress so dominated foreign policy that it has been called the era of "congressional government," "congressional supremacy," and "government-by-Congress." When the United States entered World War I, the pendulum of power swung to the White House. Woodrow Wilson experienced few congressional challenges during his war presidency. But once the war ended, Congress—and the Senate in particular—reasserted itself. Congressional activism persisted into the 1930s and even intensified. Convinced that America would be safe only as long as it kept out of Europe's political affairs, Congress's isolationist majority bitterly resisted any step President

Franklin Roosevelt tried to take that could involve the United States in the war brewing across the Atlantic.

Japan's bombing of Pearl Harbor punctured the isolationists' arguments and greatly expanded FDR's freedom to conduct foreign policy. He made virtually all of his major wartime decisions without reference to or input from Capitol Hill. When World War II ended, Congress began to reassert itself. Senior members of the House Foreign Affairs and Senate Foreign Relations Committees helped draft the United Nations Charter, the peace treaties for the Axis satellite states, and mutual security pacts such as the NATO Treaty.

But growing concerns about the Soviet Union slowed the shift of power away from the White House. As Americans became convinced in the late 1940s that hostile communist states threatened the United States and the rest of the free world, they increasingly came to agree on two basic ideas: The United States needed to resist communist expansion, and achieving this goal demanded strong presidential leadership. Most members of Congress shared these two basic beliefs (and helped promote them); those who disagreed risked punishment at the polls. The process became self-reinforcing. As more lawmakers stepped to the sidelines on defense and foreign policy over the course of the 1950s, others saw it as increasingly futile, not to mention dangerous politically, to continue to speak out. By 1960, the "imperial presidency," the flip side of a deferential Congress, was in full bloom (Schlesinger 1973). As one senator complained in 1965, members of Congress were responding to even the most far-reaching presidential decisions on foreign affairs by "stumbling over each other to see who can say 'yea' the quickest and loudest" (Sundquist 1981, 125).

The era of congressional deference to the imperial presidency came to a crashing halt with the souring of public opinion on the Vietnam War. Many Americans became convinced that communist revolutions in the third world posed no direct threat to core U.S. security interests, just as détente persuaded many that Leonid Brezhnev's Soviet Union posed less of a threat to core U.S. security interests. With the public more willing to question administration policies, so too were members of Congress. Many more had substantive disagreements with the White House over what constituted America's vital interests and how best to protect and advance them. Moreover, lawmakers had less to fear politically by the early 1970s in challenging the White House than they had only a few years earlier. Indeed, many calculated that challenging the president's foreign policies could actually help them at the ballot box by enabling them to stake out positions that their constituents favored. The result was a predictable surge in congressional activism.

Members of Congress did not always succeed in putting their stamp on foreign policy in the 1970s and 1980s. Knee-jerk support of the president was gone, but elements of congressional deference persisted among senior lawmakers (who had come of age during the era of congressional deference) and moderates (who worried that defeating the president could harm the country's credibility). Presidents from Richard Nixon through the elder George Bush often prevailed on major issues, because they could persuade these groups to join them with a simple argument: The administration's policy might have shortcomings, but rejecting the president's request would damage his standing abroad, perhaps embolden Moscow to act more aggressively, and ultimately harm American interests. Yet the mere fact that the post-Vietnam presidents had to make this argument showed how much had changed from the days of the imperial presidency. Presidents Ford, Carter, and Reagan did not get the acquiescence from Capitol Hill that Presidents Eisenhower and Kennedy did.

Although perception of the external threat facing the country provides the primary impetus to the shifting pendulum of power along Pennsylvania Avenue, it is not the only one. A second, and interrelated, factor is how well the president's foreign policy initiatives work. Presidents such as Ronald Reagan who spend their political capital wisely and can show successes for their efforts can take power back from a Congress accustomed to flexing its muscles. In contrast, presidents who commit major foreign policy blunders, as Reagan did with Iran-Contra and Clinton did in Somalia, invite congressional challenges to their power. In that respect, John F. Kennedy's (1962, 316–17) observation that "victory has 100 fathers and defeat is an orphan" is an iron law of the politics of foreign policy. In the extreme cases in which presidential decisions turn into historic debacles, as happened first with Lyndon Johnson and then with Richard Nixon in Vietnam, the result can be to change the very way Americans think about threats to their security and prosperity.

Defiance Reborn

The end of the Cold War accelerated and exacerbated the trend toward greater congressional defiance that Vietnam triggered. With the Soviet Union relegated to the ash heap of history, most Americans looked abroad and saw no threat of similar magnitude on the horizon. When asked to name the most important problem facing the United States, polls in the 1990s rarely found that more than 5 percent of Americans named a foreign policy issue. That was a steep drop from the upward of 50 percent who named a foreign policy issue during the height of the Cold War. Moreover, many Americans had trouble identifying any foreign policy issue that worried them. One 1998 poll asked people to name "two or three of the biggest foreign-policy problems facing the United States today." The most common response by far, at 21 percent, was "don't know" (Reilly 1999, 111).

These public attitudes meant that members of Congress who challenged the White House on foreign policy ran almost no electoral risks. With the public not caring enough to punish them for any excesses, lawmakers went busily about challenging Bill Clinton's foreign policy. In April 1999, for instance, during the Kosovo war, the House refused to vote to support the bombing. Not to be outdone, the Senate six months later voted down the test ban treaty even though President Clinton and 62 senators had asked that it be withdrawn from consideration. These episodes were major departures from past practice. When members of Congress had squared off against the White House in the latter half of the Cold War on issues such as Vietnam, the MX missile, and aid to the Nicaraguan contras, they had vocal public support. On Kosovo and the test ban, however, few Americans were urging Congress to challenge Clinton. To the extent that they had opinions—and many did not—most Americans sided with the president.

Just as important, the once powerful argument that members of Congress should defer to the White House on key issues lest they harm broader American interests fell on deaf ears. In 1997, the Clinton administration sought to convince Congress to give it "fast-track" negotiating authority for international trade agreements. (With fast-track authority, Congress agrees to approve or reject any trade agreement the president negotiates without amendment. This simplifies trade negotiations because other countries do not have to worry that Congress will rewrite any trade deal.) When it became clear that he lacked the votes needed to prevail, President Clinton escalated the stakes by arguing that fast track was needed because "more than ever, our economic security is also the foundation of our national strategy" (Broder 1997, A1). The decision to recast a trade issue as a national security issue—a tried and true Cold War strategy—changed few minds, however. Recognizing defeat, Clinton asked congressional leaders to withdraw the bill from consideration, marking the first time in decades that a president had failed to persuade Congress to support a major trade initiative.

Besides encouraging members of Congress to flex their foreign policy muscles, the public's diminished interest in foreign affairs after the collapse of the Soviet Union also encouraged them to cater to groups with narrow but intense preferences on foreign policy. It did so for two reasons. First, with most people focused on domestic concerns, interest groups constituted a major source of political profit or loss for politicians who did focus on foreign policy issues. Groups that had something to gain by influencing government policy became squeaky wheels, and they got the grease. Second, with the broad public looking elsewhere, the cost to members of Congress of tending to narrow interests dropped. Voters could not punish behavior they did not see.

The result of both these trends was that foreign policy in the 1990s increasingly became—to paraphrase the famed German military strategist Clausewitz—the continuation of domestic politics by other means. Lawmakers were more interested in how ethnic, business, and single-issue groups might help them win reelection and less whether the programs they championed added up to a coherent foreign policy. As former Representative Lee H. Hamilton (D-IN) put it: "Too many people place constituent interests above national interests. They don't see much difference between lobbying for highway funds and slanting foreign policy toward a particular interest group" (Mufson 2000, A1). U.S. Ambassador Chas W. Freeman, Jr., put the same point somewhat differently, arguing that the 1990s represented "the franchising of foreign policy" to interest groups (Mufson 2000, A1).

Of course, interest group influence on U.S. foreign policy was nothing new. In 1773, a group of Bostonians banded together as the Sons of Liberty and protested the tax policies of the British crown by throwing the Boston Tea Party. In the 1950s, the "China Lobby" pressed for greater support for Nationalist China. In the 1970s, human rights groups pushed for human rights legislation, and in the 1980s, steel companies and automobile manufacturers demanded protection against lower-cost foreign imports. Interest groups are so much a part of American politics that the United States is in practice "the interest group society" (Berry 1989).

What changed in the 1990s was that the countervailing push from broader interests weakened and the grip that interest groups had on their policy issues became firmer. During the Cold War, the consensus that surrounded containment helped keep narrow interests in check. Demands for particular policies had to be and usually were balanced against broader strategic considerations. At the same time, with the mass public more worried about foreign affairs, members of Congress were more cautious about indulging interest groups, especially when the executive branch objected. That reluctance eroded with the disappearance of the Soviet Union. Deference to presidential wishes decreased, because fewer lawmakers saw reason to forego rewards from interest groups simply because congressional activism made an administration's job harder.

A case in point was the House of Representative's effort in 2000 to pass a non-binding resolution labeling the massacres of Armenians that occurred in the Ottoman Empire from 1915 to 1923 as "genocide." Representative James Rogan (R-CA) sponsored the resolution. He made no claim to be a foreign policy expert—none of his committee assignments dealt with foreign policy, and he had traveled outside the United States only once in his life—but he was caught in a tight reelection race. And his congressional district happened to have the highest concentration of Armenian-Americans of any district in the United States. The resolution offered an easy way to build good will with constituents by promoting a cause they held dear. The Armenian Assembly of America, which routinely grades how members of Congress vote on issues affecting Armenia, had long lobbied for the resolution.

In another time, Rogan's resolution would have languished in committee. Party leaders would have allowed him to introduce the bill—enabling him to gain political credit with his constituents for "fighting the good fight"—but kept the bill from advancing—thereby protecting the country's broader interests. But in 2000, House Republican leaders, eager to maintain their slim majority in the face of potential Democratic inroads in the upcoming elections, embraced the bill. Speaker of the House J. Dennis Hastert (R-IL) promised Rogan that he would bring the resolution to a vote on the House floor. He personally placed the measure on the House legislative calendar. The House International Relations Committee subsequently approved it by a large margin.

As Rogan, Hastert, and other House members pushed the genocide resolution forward, they gave little thought to the consequences their symbolic gesture would have on broader U.S. interests. The result was escalating tensions with Turkey, a major American ally that, among other things, allowed U.S. and British fighter planes to use Incirlik Air Base to patrol the skies over northern Iraq. Turkey's president expressed "grave reservations" about the resolution, repeating his country's longstanding insistence that there had been no genocide (Mufson 2000, A1). Suddenly, U.S. defense companies faced the possibility that they might lose sales to Turkey and the Pentagon the possibility that it would lose the right to fly out of Incirlik. After a barrage of phone calls from Bill Clinton, other administration officials, and senior military officers warning that the resolution would significantly harm U.S. foreign policy, Hastert agreed to put off a vote on Rogan's bill.

The Deferential Congress Returns

Congress' defiance of Bill Clinton in the first post-Cold War decade rested on the public's belief that what happened outside America's borders mattered little in their lives. September 11 punctured that illusion and ended America's decade-long "holiday from history" (Krauthammer 2001, 156). Foreign policy suddenly became a top priority with the public. Not surprisingly, the pendulum of power swung sharply back toward the White House.

"Rally Round the Flag"

Bush speechwriter David Frum (2003, 272) was probably not far off the mark when he wrote that "on September 10, 2001, George Bush was not on his way to a very successful presidency." The economy had slumped, corporate accounting scandals led the evening news, and the administration's unilateralist actions abroad on issues ranging from the Kyoto Treaty on global warming to the International Criminal Court had angered friends and allies abroad. Polls taken in early September 2001 showed that Bush's public approval rating stood at only 51 percent. With the exception of Gerald Ford, who saw his popularity plummet in the wake of his decision to pardon Richard Nixon, no president had enjoyed such low ratings during his first eight months in office (Smith 2002, 44).

The impact of September 11 on American public opinion was dramatic. President Bush's approval ratings in the Gallup Poll soared to 90 percent—a figure seen only once before when his father waged the Gulf War. Although the elder Bush's approval ratings quickly returned to their pre-war levels, the younger Bush's remained high for months. On the one-year anniversary of the terrorist attacks, his approval rating stood at 70 percent (Jones 2003). Gallup found that two out of every three Americans named terrorism, national security, or war as the most important problem facing the United States. Foreign policy had reached this level of political salience only twice since the advent of scientific polling—during the early stages of both the Korean and Vietnam wars (Gallup Organization 2001). Equally important, Americans did not react to the attacks by seeking to withdraw from the world. Quite the opposite. In November 2001, 81 percent of those polled agreed that it would be "best for the future of the country if we can take an active part in world affairs" (Program on International Policy Attitudes, 2001). This marked the highest percentage favoring active engagement in the more than the half century that the question had been asked (Lindsay 2003, 43, 53).

The public rallied around Congress as well as the president—public approval of the way Congress was carrying out its job doubled from 42 percent in early September to 84 percent in early October (Smith 2002, 45). Nonetheless, the political benefits of the rally flowed to the White House and not Capitol Hill. The main reason was that the country was not split on what the government should do—as was the case, for example, during the later years of Vietnam—but remarkably unified. Bush was further helped by the fact that Democrats were in an especially weak political position to oppose any decision he might make about how to respond to the attacks. Polls had shown since the early 1970s that the American public had decidedly more confidence in the ability of Republicans to handle foreign affairs than Democrats. That left any Democrats disposed to criticize administration policy leery of being accused of being unpatriotic and skeptical that the American public was ready to listen to any criticism.

Republicans recognized the Democrats' vulnerability on this point and exploited it. The most telling incident came in February 2002. Senate Majority Leader Tom Daschle (D-SD) told reporters that he believed the war on terrorism "has been successful" but that he worried that the administration's efforts to expand the war lacked "a clear direction" (Purdum 2002, A1). The Republican rebuttal was swift and unyielding. Senate Minority Leader Trent Lott (R-MS) complained: "How dare Senator Daschle criticize President Bush while we are fighting our war on terrorism, especially when we have troops in the field? He should not be trying to divide our country while we are united." House Majority Whip Tom DeLay (R-TX) issued a one-word press release calling Daschle's comments "disgusting." Representative Tom Davis (R-VA), chairman of the National Republican Congressional Campaign Committee, accused Daschle of "giving aid and comfort to our enemies," which happens to be the legal definition of treason (Dewar 2002, A6). Few of Daschle's Democratic colleagues came to his defense.

Early Actions

The shift in political power from Capitol Hill to the White House was evident immediately. On September 14, 2001, after little debate about the consequences of what they were about to do, all but one member of Congress voted to give the president authority to retaliate against those responsible. The resolution was stunning in the breadth of authority it granted. It stated that the president could "use all necessary and appropriate force against those nations, organizations, or persons he determines planned, authorized, committed, or aided the terrorist attacks that occurred on September 11, 2001, or harbored such organizations or persons." In short, Congress effectively declared war and left it up to President Bush to decide who the enemy was.

The new congressional deference manifested itself quickly on other issues as well. In 1997, the Clinton administration had struck a deal with Senators Jesse Helms (R-NC) and Joseph Biden (D-DE), the chair and ranking member of the Senate Foreign Relations Committee, to pay most (but not all) of the back dues the United States owed to the United Nations. Efforts to appropriate all the funds needed to carry out the so-called Helms-Biden law, however, bogged down in the House. Many House Republicans were deeply skeptical of the value of the United Nations, and some representatives used the bill in an attempt to force changes in the Clinton administration's policy on the International Criminal Court and assistance to family planning organizations.

The Bush administration had taken up the cause of Helms-Biden when it assumed office. As of early September 2001, however, it had little to show for its efforts. Once the attacks on the World Trade Center and the Pentagon occurred and it became essential to build a multinational coalition to prosecute the war on terrorism, the White House found Congress much more receptive to its arguments. House leaders quickly agreed to work for passage of a stand-alone bill providing the necessary funding. They placed it on the suspension calendar, which limited debate but also required a two-thirds majority vote to pass. The bill, which the Senate had passed in February 2001, cleared on a voice vote (Pomper 2001b, 2276).

The Bush White House also tackled another previously hot issue—sanctions on Pakistan. Islamabad had triggered one set of sanctions with its May 1998 nuclear tests. U.S law required the imposition of another set of sanctions in response to General Pervez Musharraf's overthrow of Pakistan's democratically elected government in October 1999. The Clinton administration recognized that these sanctions did not necessarily serve U.S. interests. However, persuading Congress to accept that judgment was another matter entirely. In the 1990s, congressional sentiment had tilted sharply in favor of Pakistan's rival India. More than 100 lawmakers belonged to the Congressional Indian Caucus, and the Clinton administration decided not to expend its limited foreign policy capital invoking a provision in the law that allowed the president to waive the sanctions imposed in response to the nuclear tests. Immediately after the September 11 attacks, however, President Bush exercised waiver as part of his effort to ensure Pakistani support for the war on terrorism and military action against Afghanistan. In mid-October, Congress passed legislation authorizing him to waive the other sanctions that had been placed on Islamabad (Pomper 2001a, 2487).

One issue that saw congressional Democrats reverse themselves was national missile defense. Throughout the spring and summer of 2001, they had regularly criticized the administration for suggesting that it was preparing to withdraw the United States from the ABM Treaty. They argued that destroying what they called the "cornerstone of international stability" so that the Pentagon could test unproven defensive technologies was reckless at best. Many Democrats also concluded that opposing the Bush administration's missile defense plans would be politically rewarding. They believed that their decision to oppose Ronald Reagan's Strategic Defense Initiative in the 1980s had been politically profitable, and they hoped to reprise that success.

Democrats had one strong card to play in this debate—their control of the Senate. Senator Carl Levin (D-MI) used his prerogative as chair of the Senate Armed Services Committee to insert a provision in the fiscal year 2002 defense authorization bill that would have cut $1.3 billion of the $8.3 billion the administration had requested for missile defense and prohibited the Defense Department from conducting any anti-missile test that violated the ABM Treaty. The committee sustained his "chairman's mark" on a straight-line party vote. A "fierce Senate showdown" looked to be in the offing (Towell 2001, 2079). In the wake of September 11, however, Senate Democrats stripped the authorization bill of the testing provision and restored nearly all the funding the White House had requested. (A small amount was shifted to counterterrorism accounts.) In December 2001, President Bush announced that the U.S. withdrawal from the ABM Treaty. The decision passed without much comment on Capitol Hill.

Just weeks before the ABM withdrawal announcement, the White House issued the Military Order of November 13 (Bush 2001). It declared that the foreign citizens the United States detained while waging its war on terrorism could be tried before military commissions. The order offended many civil libertarians and prompted more than 300 law professors to sign a letter calling the commissions "legally deficient, unnecessary, and unwise" (Seelye 2001, B7). The order presumably implicated Congress's constitutional authority to "define and punish . . . offenses against the law

of nations" and its power to make all other laws "necessary and proper" for executing the federal government enumerated power (Tribe 2001). Still, Congress neither
rejected the president's decision nor acted to reinforce its legal basis. Even lawmakers who strongly endorsed the idea, such as former vice presidential candidate Senator Joseph Lieberman (D-CT), saw no need for congressional action. Those
lawmakers who doubted the wisdom of the military commission idea, or who worried
that it might have consequences for the civil liberties of American citizens, were either few in number or remarkably quiet. Little changed when the Justice Department
turned Jose Padilla, a suspected American-born member of al Qaeda, over to the Defense Department to be held as an enemy combatant.[1] Few members wanted to be
seen sympathizing with an alleged terrorist and criticizing a very popular president.

From Tora Bora to Baghdad

President Bush's dominance of foreign affairs continued into 2002. In February 2002,
he proposed increasing the defense budget by $48 billion. It was the largest requested
increase in real dollars in defense spending since the early years of the Reagan
buildup—and a sum roughly equal to China's total defense budget. The request
elicited few complaints from Congress, even though the bulk of the spending
increase was targeted at funding defense programs that had been on the drawing
boards for years rather than to meet new needs created by the war on terrorism. Congress did make technical adjustments that cut slightly more than $1 billion in fund-
ing. It also stripped out a provision to create a $10 billion contingency fund that the
Pentagon could have used as it saw fit; even deferential lawmakers were reluctant to
give the Defense Department that much walking around money. Nonetheless, they
signaled that they would be receptive to any specific funding requests that the Pentagon might submit. The eventual FY 2003 appropriation increased defense spending by nearly $37 billion, or a sum equal to Great Britain's entire military budget.

While President Bush was riding high in the polls in early 2003, some Democrats were deeply disappointed with what they saw as his failure to prepare the federal
government to handle counterterrorism efforts. Bush initially responded to September 11 by creating a new Office of Homeland Security in the White House. Critics
led by Senator Lieberman recommended going further and proposed establishing of
a new Cabinet department of homeland security. They argued that putting the major agencies responsible for homeland security under one roof would make it easier
to coordinate their activities and thereby improve the country's security. What was
probably not lost on many Democratic proponents of reorganization was that it enabled them to criticize the president from the right, a politically safe vantage point
for a party thought to be weak on security issues. They could argue that the White
House was not doing enough to protect Americans from the threat posed by al Qaeda
and similarly inspired terrorists.

The Bush administration resisted the idea of a new Cabinet department for
months. In March 2002, Ari Fleisher (2002), the White House spokesman, said that
"creating a cabinet department doesn't solve anything." Other administration officials argued that reorganization would make Americans less secure, because it would

divert Washington's resources and focus away from the war on terrorism. The White House also knew that many congressional Republicans were at best lukewarm toward the idea of a new Cabinet department. They believed reorganization would produce a bigger, more costly, more intrusive federal government—precisely what they had fought for years to prevent.

On June 6, President Bush surprised the country by announcing on nationwide television that he wanted to create a new Department of Homeland Security (DHS). It was doubly surprising that his reorganization plan dwarfed anything being considered on Capitol Hill. It proposed merging 22 agencies, employing nearly 170,000 workers and spending more than $35 billion annually. To top it all off, the president wanted Congress to pass the legislation authorizing the reorganization—which would be the most ambitious and complex government reshuffling since the creation of the Department of Defense in 1947—by the end of the year.

The White House insisted that the change of view reflected the merits of the argument for reorganization. Democrats argued that it reflected politics. In mid-May, the Senate Governmental Affairs Committee, which Senator Lieberman chaired, had approved a reorganization bill. The legislation had picked up a few Republican supporters. Even if the administration's allies on Capitol Hill succeeded in blocking the bill, however, the administration risked giving its critics an issue with which to attack the president. To make matters worse, at the same time that reorganization was picking up political steam, the administration was being buffeted by a string of news stories that questioned its competence in the weeks leading up to September 11. Reporters had uncovered evidence that miscommunication and squabbling between and within the CIA and FBI had contributed to the government's failure to uncover the terrorist plot. Indeed, President Bush announced his reorganization proposal the night before FBI agent Coleen Rowley was scheduled to give her much-awaited congressional testimony on how FBI headquarters had failed to pursue possible leads that might have uncovered the September 11 plot.

Whatever the motives behind the reorganization proposal, most members of Congress found it hard to oppose. Many congressional Republicans continued to dislike the idea, and Bush (2002c) had sought to defuse objection in announcing the plan by insisting that "by ending duplication and overlap, we will spend less on overhead, and more on protecting America." Even though experts dismissed the president's claim as unrealistic, most Republicans recognized that political necessity dictated that they support their party's leader. Democrats faced a different problem. After demanding the creation of a homeland security department for months they could not suddenly denounce it as a bad idea. Democrats could only applaud the president's change-of-heart and hope that voters remembered it had been a Democratic idea first. Richard Gephardt (D-MO), the leader of the House minority leader, went even further. He tried to top Bush's announcement by committing Democrats to passing a reorganization bill by the first anniversary of the September 11 attacks.

Congress ultimately failed to meet Gephardt's deadline but not because of disagreement over the substance of the reorganization. Numerous experts weighed in on the shortcomings of the administration's plan, and individual committee chairs took issue with aspects of the reorganization that affected agencies under their jurisdiction (Daalder et al. 2002; Williams and Nather 2002). Nonetheless, House and Senate leaders were determined to act quickly, and they quashed any potential revolts. By early August, each chamber had prepared legislation that reflected the basic outlines of the department the White House wanted to create.

This seemingly unstoppable legislative locomotive suddenly derailed, however, but not over the matter of which agencies would not be folded into the new organization or what authorities it would wield. Instead, the stumbling block was the question of how many of the civil service protections that they previously enjoyed would be taken from workers in the new department. Democrats saw the proposal as a domestic political issue that threatened the interests of a key Democratic constituency: organized labor. They calculated that opposing the White House's request for maximum flexibility would mobilize union supporters and benefit Democratic candidates in the November midterm elections. Republicans, by contrast, calculated that the public would see the dispute as a national security issue and punish the Democrats for being willing to narrow interests ahead of the broad public interest. The results on Election Day bore out the arguments of Republican strategists. In mid-November a lame-duck Congress passed legislation creating a new homeland security department largely along the lines of what President Bush had proposed.

As the dispute between Democrats and Republicans over civil service protections for DHS workers built up steam in late summer 2002, so too did suspicions that President Bush intended to go to war with Iraq. In his January 29, 2002 State of the Union Speech, Bush (2002b) had named Iraq, Iran, and North Korea as members of an "axis of evil, arming to threaten the peace of the world." He went on to declare that "time is not on our side. I will not wait on events, while dangers gather." He and his aides subsequently ruled out using military force to deal with the threats from Iran and North Korea. They gave no such reassurances about U.S. dealings with Iraq. Concerns that Bush (2002a) was planning to attack Iraq grew after he declared in his June 1, 2002 commencement address at West Point that Americans must "be ready for preemptive action," and his senior aides talked openly of the need for regime change in Iraq.

The administration's threats to overthrow Saddam Hussein prompted calls for members of Congress to speak to the possibility of war. The Senate Foreign Relations Committee held its first hearings on the topic at the end of July. Over the next several weeks, lawmakers from both parties began arguing that the administration could not take the country to war without congressional approval. The White House's initial response was that the 1991 Gulf War resolution, the September 11 resolution, and the president's inherent powers as commander in chief made that step unnecessary. But in early September, the White House relented and sent to Capitol Hill a draft use-of-force resolution that would have given the president nearly unbounded power. The decision to reverse course was easy to make. Administration officials recognized that Congress was virtually certain to grant its request. If Democrats decided to vote against a use-of-force resolution, Republicans could use that against them in the midterm elections.

The administration's calculations proved correct. Democratic attempts to postpone the vote until after the elections failed. Senate Majority Leader Daschle's fallback position was to substitute a restrictive resolution for the open-ended one the White House had proposed. That strategy collapsed, however, when House Minority Leader Gephardt broke ranks. He met privately with the president and agreed to support a slightly modified version of the White House proposal. Other lawmakers quickly abandoned their efforts to craft alternative resolutions. In early October, both the House and Senate voted overwhelmingly to authorize the president to go to war.

The resolution that Congress passed differed in a few ways from the one the White House initially proposed. The final resolution dropped the most egregious provision in the original, which would have authorized the president "to use all means that he determines to be appropriate" to "restore international peace and security in the region." The final resolution also contained greatly expanded language detailing the horrors of Saddam Hussein's rule, and it imposed reporting requirements on the White House. Nonetheless, the thrust of the operative paragraph remained the same: The president could take the country to war as he saw fit. In that respect, the October 2002 Iraq War resolution is unique in American history. Congress authorized the president to wage a war that he had not yet decided (at least publicly) to fight.[2]

When asked why Democrats had not done more to oppose a resolution so many of them thought unwise, Senate Majority Leader Daschle wearily replied: "The bottom line is . . . we want to move on" (Rich 2002, A21). Congress's eagerness to delegate its war power to the president drew the ire of Senator Robert Byrd (D-WV), a veteran of five decades of service on Capitol Hill. "How have we gotten to this low point in the history of Congress? Are we too feeble to resist the demand of a president who is determined to bend the collective will of Congress to his will?" (Byrd 2002, A39).

The Limits to the Deferential Congress

The return of the deferential Congress after September 11 did not carry over to all policy issues or even all foreign policy issues. As the debate over civil service protections for employees in the Department of Homeland Security showed, on some issues lawmakers conducted themselves as they had before September 11. As a general rule, the willingness of members to defy the president varied directly with the threat his policies posed to the tangible interests of their constituents.

The limits of Congress's willingness to defer to the White House were evident in domestic policy. Despite Bush's soaring poll numbers in late 2001 and early 2002, Democrats felt safe blocking his economic stimulus plan. Despite administration insistence that national security considerations made it imperative to find new energy sources in the United States, the Senate defeated a bill to open up the Arctic National Wildlife Reserve to oil exploration. Senate Democrats also used their majority status to block votes on federal judicial nominees they deemed to be too conservative. In these and other cases, "normal" politics prevailed, because the issues mattered to key constituencies and the argument that opposing the president's position would harm the war on terrorism struck most people as strained at best.

Congress's efforts to question and revise presidential initiatives could also be seen on other issues more closely linked to the war on terrorism. Immediately following September 11, the White House submitted legislation that eventually became the USA Patriot Act. The bill proposed numerous changes to the rules governing surveillance and intelligence activities. Many of the proposed changes had been discussed for years but never enacted, because the issue had never been urgent enough to overcome legislative inertia. Other proposed changes, however, went beyond anything that had been discussed before the terrorist attacks and had tremendous potential consequences for individual privacy and other civil liberties. Although Congress accommodated the White House's insistence that it move quickly on the legislation—it was on the president's desk five weeks after September 11—lawmakers made a significant change. They stipulated that its most controversial provisions would expire in 2005 unless Congress voted to renew them. The push to insert these sunset provisions came from civil libertarians in both parties who both responded to and encouraged public fears that the Patriot Act otherwise went too far in curtailing individual freedoms (Bettelheim and Palmer 2001).

The Bush White House encountered even stiffer resistance on the trade front. Despite the backdrop of September 11 and despite the fact Republicans were the majority party in the House, the House passed legislation giving the president trade-promotion authority by only a single vote. Even that victory came only after the administration promised to roll back some of the access that previous to American textile markets that previous trade legislation had given to Caribbean and Central American countries. The White House also promised that any assistance given to Pakistan for its participation in the war on terrorism would be designed "to minimize the impact on the U.S. textile and apparel industry" (Faler 2002, 45). The administration subsequently backed away from its promise to Islamabad to allow Pakistani apparel exports greater access to the U.S. market (Brainard 2001, A19).

The Senate did not vote on the trade-promotion authority bill until July. That vote took place only after Democrats forced Republicans to increase spending on Trade Adjustment Assistance programs designed to help workers who lose their jobs because of foreign competition by $12 billion. The House passed the conference report on the trade-promotion bill only after Republican leaders suppressed several revolts against its provisions. The lesson in the trade debate was clear: Lawmakers were willing to defer to the White House on issues of war and peace but not on issues that directly affected the livelihood of their constituents.

Conclusion

Congress's shifting deference to and defiance of presidential leadership in foreign affairs reflects a political dynamic that stretches back to the beginnings of the American republic. Lawmakers are willing to assert their constitutional prerogatives when they believe the United States has little to worry about abroad or the president's proposed course of action threatens to imperil American security. Conversely, when threats are clear and presidential decisions have produced success rather than failure, both politics and a sense of good policy encourage members of Congress to rally 'round the flag.

It is impossible to say how long the current era of congressional deference will last. Unlike domestic policy, in which critics have strong political incentives to criticize the White House, the political winds at the start of April 2003 blew briskly in the opposite direction. A sustained period of peace could change those calculations, but that hardly seemed to be in the offing. The country was at war with Iraq, al Qaeda's most senior leaders remained on the loose, and a confrontation over North Korea's nuclear program threatened to escalate.

The greater threat to the imperial presidency seemed to come then from the opposite direction—the threat of executive overreaching. In deciding to wage war on Iraq, President Bush took a strategic gamble of potentially historic proportions. He vowed not just to unseat a ruthless dictator and destroy his weapons of mass destruction but also to bring democracy to the Iraqi people and to the Middle East. Should the war be far bloodier and costlier than the American public is willing to tolerate, or perhaps more likely, should the military occupation needed to win the peace begin to look like the U.S. peacekeeping mission in Lebanon in 1983, the political winds could quickly reverse. In that event, President Bush would discover what President Johnson learned more than three decades ago: Although members of Congress defer to the White House when foreign policy takes off, that does not mean they will be deferential when it crashes.

Endnotes

1. The military commission order explicitly applies only to foreign citizens. Padilla's ultimate legal fate was undetermined as of March 2003.
2. The founders rejected the notion that Congress could, or should, give such contingent authority to the president (Schlesinger 1973, 26–29).

References

Berry, Jeffrey M. 1989. *The Interest Group Society*, 2d ed. Glenview, Ill.: Scott, Foreman/Little, Brown.

Bettelheim, Adriel, and Elizabeth A. Palmer. 2001. "Balancing Liberty and Security," *CQ Weekly Report*. 59:2210–13.

Brainard, Lael. 2001. "Textiles and Terrorism," *The New York Times*. December 27.

Broder, John M. 1997. "House Postpones Trade-Issue Vote," *The New York Times*. November 8.

Bush, George W. 2001. "President Issues Military Order," The White House. November 13. Available at http://www.whitehouse.gov/news/releases/2001/11/20011113–27.html.

Bush, George W. 2002a. "President Bush Delivers Graduation Speech at West Point," The White House. June 1. Available at http://www.whitehouse.gov/news/releases/2002/06/20020601–3.html.

Bush, George W. 2002b. "President Delivers State of the Union Address," The White House. January 29. Available at http://www.whitehouse.gov/news/releases/2002/01/20020129–11.html.

Bush, George W. 2002c. "Remarks by the President in Address to the Nation," The White House. June 6. Available at http://www.whitehouse.gov/news/releases/2002/06/20020606–8.html.

Byrd, Robert C. 2002. "Congress Must Resist the Rush to War," The New York Times. October 10.

Corwin, Edward S. 1957. The President: Office and Powers, 1787–1957, 4th rev. ed. New York: New York University Press.

Daalder, Ivo H., et al. 2002. "Assessing the Department of Homeland Security," Brookings Institution, Washington, DC, July 15. Available at http://www.brook.edu/dybdocroot/fp/projects/homeland/assessdhs.pdf.

De Tocqueville, Alexis. 1969. Democracy in America. New York: Anchor Books.

Dewar, Helen. "Lott Calls Daschle Divisive," The Washington Post. March 1.

Faler, Brian. 2002. "Jobs in Pakistan or North Carolina?" National Journal. 50:44–45.

Fleisher, Ari. 2002. "Press Briefing," White House. Office of the Press Secretary. March 19. Available at http://www.whitehouse.gov/news/releases/2002/03/20020319–7.html.

Frum, David. 2003. The Right Man. New York: Random House.

Gallup Organization. 2001. "Terrorism Reaches Status of Korean and Vietnam Wars as Most Important Problem," November 19.

Jones, Jeffrey M. 2003. "Latest Update Shows No Change in Support for Invasion of Iraq," Gallup Poll., March 7.

Kennedy, John F. Public Papers of the Presidents: 1961. Washington, DC: U.S. GPO.

Krauthammer, Charles. 2001. "The Hundred Days," Time. December 31.

Lindsay, James M. 2003. "Apathy, Interest, and the Politics of American Foreign Policy," The Uncertain Superpower: Domestic Dimensions of U.S. Foreign Policy after the Cold War, ed. Bernhard May and Michaela Honicke Moore. Berlin: Leske & Budrich.

Mufson, Steven. 2000. "Local Politics Is Global as Hill Turns to Armenia," The Washington Post. October 9.

Neustadt, Richard E. 1990. Presidential Power and the Modern Presidents: The Politics of Leadership from Roosevelt to Reagan. New York: Free Press.

Pomper, Miles A. 2001a. "Bill to Waive Pakistan Sanctions Clears over Protests from Appropriators and Supporters of India," CQ Weekly Report. 59:2487.

Pomper, Miles A. 2001b. "House Clears Payment of Debt to U.N. as Anti-Terrorism Effort Takes Priority," CQ Weekly. 59:2276.

Program on International Policy Attitudes. 2001. "Americans on the War on Terrorism: A Study of US Public Attitudes," November 6. Available at http://www.pipa.org/OnlineReports/Terrorism/WarOnTerr.html.

Purdum, Todd. 2002. "Democrats Starting to Fault President on the War's Future," The New York Times. March 1.

Reilly, John E. 1999. "Americans and the World: A Survey at Century's End," Foreign Policy 114:97–114.

Rich, Frank. 2002. "It's the War, Stupid," *The New York Times*. October 12.

Schlesinger, Arthur, M., Jr. 1973. *The Imperial Presidency*. Boston: Houghton-Mifflin.

Seelye, Katharine Q. "A Nation Challenged: The Military Tribunals," *The New York Times*. December 8.

Smith, Eric R.A.N. 2002. "Who Benefits? Public Opinion, Partisan Politics, and the Consequences of September 11," In *American Politics after September 11*, ed. James M. Lindsay. Cincinnati: Atomic Dog Publishing.

Smith, Jean E. 1989. *The Constitution and American Foreign Policy*. St. Paul: West Publishing.

Sundquist, James L. 1981. *The Decline and Resurgence of Congress*. Washington, DC: Brookings Institution Press.

Towell, Pat. 2001. "Armed Services Democrats' Move to Shackle Anti-Missile Program Sets up Fierce Senate Showdown," *CQ Weekly Report* 59: 2079–80.

Tribe, Laurence H. 2001. "Trial by Fury," *New Republic*. December 10.

Williams, Bob, and David Nather. 2002. "Homeland Security Debate: Balancing Swift and Sure," *CQ Weekly Report*. 60:1642–48.

James P. Pfiffner

Constraining Executive Power: George W. Bush and the Constitution

The modern tradition of constraining the power of political executives has deep roots in Anglo-American governmental traditions. The Magna Carta of 1215, the Habeas Corpus Act of 1679, the English Bill of Rights of 1689, the Common Law, and other documents and traditions of the British Constitution all provided precedents upon which the Framers of the U.S. Constitution drew. From the ratification of the U.S. Constitution to contemporary times, the experience and precedents of the presidency have also played an important role in laying the basis for the legitimate authority exercised by the president in the constitutional system. This article will examine several actions of President George W. Bush and argue that he has

Source: Presidential Studies Quarterly (March 2008).

made exceptional claims to presidential authority. Four instances of President Bush's claims to presidential power will be examined: his suspension of the Geneva Agreements in 2002, his denial of the writ of habeas corpus for detainees in the war on terror, his order that the National Security Agency monitor messages to or from domestic parties in the United States without a warrant, and his use of signing statements.

The Framers of the Constitution were influenced by their English constitutional heritage with respect to individual rights and drew heavily upon British precedents. But with respect to governmental structure, they rejected British precedent and created a separation of powers system based on a written Constitution. The principles upon which they designed the Constitution included explicit limits on the powers of government and a separation of powers structure intended to prevent the accumulation of power in any one branch of government.

The system set up by the Framers has worked reasonably well for more than two centuries of political experience (with the exception of the Civil War). In the 19th century, the Congress tended to dominate policy making, except in cases of war. But in the 20th century, the presidency accumulated sufficient power to play a dominating role in both domestic and foreign policy. One of the important constitutional confrontations between the presidency and Congress over a range of issues occurred during the "imperial" presidencies of Lyndon Johnson and Richard Nixon. In reaction to the aggrandizement of power in the presidency, Congress asserted its own constitutional authority by enacting a number of laws intended to constrain presidential power.

It is this congressional reassertion of constitutional authority in the 1970s that Vice President Cheney and President Bush intended to reverse when they came to power in 2001. The administration, particularly Vice President Cheney, who had served as chief of staff to President Ford, felt that Congress overreacted to Vietnam and Watergate and hobbled presidential power in unconstitutional ways. As he said,

> The feeling I had [during the Ford years] , and I think it's been borne out by history, that in the aftermath, especially of Vietnam and Watergate, that the balance shifted, if you will, that, in fact, the presidency was weakened, that there were congressional efforts to rein in and to place limits on presidential authority. (Walsh 2006)

A White House aide later articulated an attitude seemingly shared by many at the top levels of the Bush administration:

> The powers of the presidency have been eroded and usurped to the breaking point. We are engaged in a new kind of war that cannot be fought by old methods. It can only be directed by a strong executive who alone is not subject to the conflicting pressures that legislators or judges face. The public understands and supports that unpleasant reality, whatever the media and intellectuals say (Hoagland 2006).[1]

Those "conflicting pressures," of course, are *the whole point* of the separation of powers system. The atrocities of 9/11 gave President Bush the opportunity to achieve much of the expansion of executive power that he had sought since he became president. This article will take up four cases of extraordinary claims that President

George W. Bush has made to executive authority under the Constitution: suspending the Geneva Conventions, denying habeas corpus appeals, NSA surveillance, and signing statements.

Suspending the Geneva Conventions and Torture

George W. Bush has been the only U.S. president to defend publicly the right of United States personnel to torture detainees. Probably the president did not intend for U.S. personnel to commit the egregious acts of torture that resulted in the death of many detainees. But he did argue that U.S. personnel needed to use aggressive techniques when interrogating prisoners captured in the war on terror. Despite declarations that "we do not torture," the aggressive interrogation procedures that were used by U.S. personnel (military, CIA, and contractors) in Guantanamo, Afghanistan, and Abu Ghraib are considered by most of the world to be torture. The Bush administration, in determining the legal basis of interrogation policy, used a narrow and technical definition of "torture" set forth in an Office of Legal Counsel memorandum of August 2002 (since rescinded). President Bush vigorously argued that it was essential to the war on terror to continue to pursue "the program" of aggressive interrogation when he argued against the Detainee Treatment Act of 2005 and in favor of the Military Commissions Act of 2006.

Although other presidents had decided to withdraw from treaties, no other president decided that the Geneva Conventions did not apply to U.S. treatment of captives in wartime. Despite presidential leeway in interpreting treaties, the Supreme Court in the *Hamdan* decision held that the provisions of the Geneva Convention Common Article 3 invalidated the military commissions that President Bush had set up to try suspected terrorists held at Guantanamo. This decision prompted the Bush Administration to convince Congress to pass the Military Commissions Act of 2006.

Despite the occurrence of torture in many U.S. wars, President Bush's *policy making* with regard to enhanced interrogation practices (or torture, depending on the definition) is unprecedented in United States history. In contrast to a policy that encourages or condones torture, ad hoc torture that is against the law can be punished, and the principle that torture is forbidden can be upheld. But a policy that encourages and provides governmental sanction for coercive interrogation can easily be interpreted to justify torture, as was evident at Guantanamo and Abu Ghraib.

The Decision to Suspend the Geneva Conventions

The question of whether President Bush should declare that the Geneva Conventions did not apply to al Qaeda or the Taliban was the subject of a series of memoranda in early 2002. The memos culminated in a recommendation from counsel to the president, Alberto Gonzales, that the president should suspend the Geneva Conventions for members of al Qaeda. The January 25, 2002 memo recommended that the Geneva Convention III on Treatment of Prisoners of War (GPW) should not apply to al Qaeda and Taliban prisoners. He reasoned that the war on terror was "a new kind of war" and that the "new paradigm renders obsolete Geneva's strict limitations on questioning of enemy prisoners. . . ."[2] Gonzales argued that exempting captured al Qaeda or Taliban prisoners from treatment according to the Geneva Convention protections would preclude the prosecution of U.S. soldiers under the War Crimes Act (1997).[3]

Secretary of State Colin Powell objected to the reasoning of the Justice Department and the President's Counsel, Alberto Gonzales. In a memo of January 26, 2002, he argued that the drawbacks of deciding not to apply the Geneva Conventions outweighed the advantages because "It will reverse over a century of policy . . . and undermine the protections of the law of war for our troops, both in this specific conflict and in general; It has a high cost in terms of negative international reaction . . . ; [and] It will undermine public support among critical allies. . . ."[4] Powell also noted that applying the Convention "maintains POW status for U.S. forces . . . and generally supports the U.S. objective of ensuring its forces are accorded protection under the Convention"(2002a).

Despite Powell's memo, and in accord with the attorney general's and his counsel's recommendations, President Bush signed a memorandum on February 7, 2002 that stated: "Pursuant to my authority as Commander in Chief . . . I . . . determine that none of the provisions of Geneva apply to our conflict with al Qaeda in Afghanistan or elsewhere throughout the world because, among other reasons, al Qaeda is not a High Contracting Party to Geneva" (White House 2002). This determination denied suspected members of al Qaeda prisoner of war status and allowed the use of aggressive techniques of interrogation used by the CIA and military intelligence at Guantanamo that were later, in the fall of 2003, transferred to the prison at Abu Ghraib.

The changes in policy regarding the status of prisoners at Guantanamo upset top level military lawyers in the Judge Advocate General Corps, including lawyers in the Chairman of the Joint Chiefs of staff's office. In 2003, a group of JAG officers went to visit the New York City Bar Association's Committee on International Human Rights. They were concerned about "a real risk of disaster," a concern that later proved to be prescient (Barry, Hirsh, and Isiskoff 2004; Hersh 2004).[5]

OLC Memoranda on Torture and Presidential Power

Shortly after 9/11, the Office of Legal Counsel of the Justice Department began work on legal aspects of the treatment of prisoners captured in the war on terror. Assistant Attorney General Jay S. Bybee, head of the Office of Legal Counsel, signed a memorandum written in part by John Yoo (2006, 171). The memo dealt with how U.S. personnel could avoid punishment under Title 18 of the U.S. Code (criminal law). This law, The War Crimes Act, implemented the Convention Against Torture and Other Cruel, Inhuman and Degrading Treatment or Punishment for the United States (Klaidman, 2004).

The Geneva Conventions require that "no physical or mental torture, nor any other form of coercion, may be inflicted on prisoners of war to secure from them information of any kind whatever."[6] The Convention Against Torture, as ratified by the United States, emphasizes that "no exceptional circumstances whatsoever, whether a state of war or a threat of war, internal political instability or any other public emergency, may be invoked as a justification of torture"(Bravin 2004).[7] The U.S. Torture Victims Protection Act defines torture as an "act committed by a person acting under the color of law specifically intended to inflict severe physical or mental pain or suffering (other than pain or suffering incidental to lawful sanctions) upon another person within his custody or physical control" (18 U.S.C. Sec. 2340).

Part I of the Bybee memo interprets the above passage and construes the definition of torture narrowly; in doing so, it elevates the threshold of "severe pain" necessary to amount to torture: "We conclude that for an act to constitute torture, it must inflict pain that is . . . equivalent in intensity to the pain accompanying serious physical injury, such as organ failure, impairment of bodily function, or even death" (Bybee 1, 6). This narrow definition would allow a wide range of brutal actions that do not meet the exacting requirements specified in the memo. The memo specifically excludes from torture "cruel, inhuman, or degrading treatment or punishment," some examples of which are specified, such as wall standing, hooding, noise, sleep deprivation and deprivation of food and drink. But the memo did specify that some practices would be torture, such as severe beatings with clubs, threats of imminent death, threats of removing extremities, burning, electric shocks to genitalia, rape or sexual assault (Bybee 15, 24, 28).[8]

In Section V, the memo argued that the president's commander-in-chief authority can overcome any law. "[T]he President enjoys complete discretion in the exercise of his Commander-in-Chief authority and in conducting operations against hostile forces" (Bybee 33). Thus "Any effort to apply Section 2340A [of Title 18 U.S.C.] in a manner that interferes with the President's direction of such core war matters as the detention and interrogation of enemy combatants thus would be unconstitutional" (Bybee 31).

The administration used the commander-in-chief clause to argue that a presidential policy takes precedence over public law. Thus, the administration argued, the president is not bound by the law, despite the Article II, Section 3 provision of the Constitution that the President "shall take care that the Laws be faithfully executed." The implication was also that the commander-in-chief clause trumps the Article I, Section 8 provision that Congress has the authority to "make Rules concerning Captures on Land and Water."[9]

These memoranda, along with other policy directives by Secretary of Defense Rumsfeld and others, set the conditions for torture and abuse that occurred at Guantanamo, Abu Ghraib, and Bagram Air Force Base in Afghanistan. A number of official inquiries as well as external reports, documented incidents of gross abuse and torture, some resulting in the deaths of detainees (Pfiffner 2005).

The McCain Amendment

Senator John McCain (R-AZ) endured five years as a prisoner of war in Vietnam and suffered severe torture. Thus, his publicly expressed outrage at reports of torture perpetrated by U.S. soldiers and civilians at Guantanamo, Abu Ghraib, and in

Afghanistan carried a large measure of legitimacy. McCain introduced an amendment to the Department of Defense Appropriations Act for 2006 to ban torture by U.S. personnel, regardless of geographic location. Section 1003 of the Detainee Treatment Act of 2005 provides that "No individual in the custody or under the physical control of the United States Government, regardless of nationality or physical location, shall be subject to cruel, inhuman, or degrading treatment or punishment."[10]

Vice President Cheney led administration efforts in Congress to defeat the bill (White 2005). Cheney first tried to get the bill dropped entirely, and when that failed, to exempt the CIA from its provisions. President Bush threatened to veto the bill if it was passed. Their efforts, however, were unavailing, and the measure was passed with veto-proof majorities in both Houses, 90 to nine in the Senate, and 308 to 122 in the House. In a compromise, McCain refused to change his wording, but he did agree to add provisions that would allow civilian U.S. personnel to use the same type of legal defense that is accorded to uniformed military personnel.[11]

However, when President Bush signed the bill, he issued a signing statement that declared: "The executive branch shall construe Title X in Division A of the Act, relating to detainees, in a manner consistent with the constitutional authority of the President to supervise the unitary executive branch and as Commander in Chief and consistent with the constitutional limitations on the judicial power. . . ." (The White House 2005) This statement signaled that President Bush did not feel bound by the law that he had just signed.

Thus, President Bush, through his Office of Legal Council, claimed that he was not bound by the Geneva Conventions, that the commander-in-chief authority invalidated any laws about prisoners, and that he was not bound by the Detainee Treatment Act. These claims attempted to place President Bush outside the checks and balances of the separation of power system and the rule of law.

Military Commissions and Habeas Corpus

The Supreme Court delivered several setbacks to President Bush's claims to executive power. In *Hamdi v. Rumsfeld* (542 U.S. 507, 2004) the Court ruled that U.S. citizens had the right to challenge their imprisonment at Guantanamo in court. In *Rasul v. Bush* (542 U.S. 466, 2004), the Court held that noncitizens could challenge their detentions through *habeas corpus* petitions. And in *Hamdan v. Rumsfeld* (126 S.Ct. 2749, 2006) the Court ruled that that the military commissions set up by President Bush were unlawful, because they were not based on U.S. law and that they violated Common Article 3 of the Geneva Conventions.

The Supreme Court's Hamdan Decision

Despite the Bush administration's arguments that U.S. courts did not have jurisdiction over Guantanamo detainees, that the president's commander-in-chief authority was sufficient to detain people indefinitely, and that detainees were receiving sufficient due process rights, the Supreme Court ruled against the administration in the above mentioned cases. In *Hamdi*, the court declared that "the most elemental of liberty interests" is "the interest in being free from physical detention by one's own government ["without due process of law"] . . . . history and common sense teach us that an unchecked system of detention carries the potential to become a means for oppression and abuse of others who do not present that sort of threat. . . ." Thus "we reaffirm today the fundamental nature of a citizen's right to be free from involuntary confinement by his own government without due process of law. . . ."

This requirement of due process does not apply to "initial captures on the battle field," but "is due only when the determination is made to *continue* to hold those who have been seized." In making these judgments, the Court asserted that, despite administration arguments to the contrary, it had jurisdiction over executive branch imprisonments and that it was willing to enforce constitutional rights even during a time of war. In *Rasul v. Bush*, the Court (deciding on the basis of law, not on constitutional grounds) held that noncitizens also had the right to challenge their imprisonment through a habeas corpus petition.

On the issue of whether the United States is permitted to try non-citizen enemy combatants by the military commissions that the president had established, the Supreme Court in *Hamdan* ruled in the negative, overturning a Court of Appeals decision.[12] Justice Stevens, writing for the Court, concluded that the military commissions and procedures established by President Bush were not authorized by the Constitution or any U.S. law, and thus the president had to comply with existing U.S. laws. He explained that the "structures and procedures violate both the UCMJ and the four Geneva Conventions signed in 1949"(Hamdan 4). The Court finally concluded: "Even assuming that Hamdan is a dangerous individual who would cause great harm or death to innocent civilians given the opportunity, the Executive nevertheless must comply with the prevailing rule of law in undertaking to try him and subject him to criminal punishment" (Hamdan 7).

Perhaps the most important principle established in these Supreme court cases was Justice Sandra Day O'Conner's statement in the majority opinion in *Hamdi*: "We have long since made clear that a state of war is not a blank check for the President when it comes to the rights of the Nation's citizens."[13]

The Military Commissions Act of 2006

In order to overcome the roadblock that the Supreme Court decisions threw in the way of administration policy, President Bush sought legislation that would authorize the creation of military commissions and spell out limits on the rights of detainees. President Bush argued that the types of harsh interrogation methods that he termed "the program" were essential to the war on terror. The administration maintained that the proposed law would allow CIA interrogators more leeway than Common Article 3 of the Geneva Conventions allowed.

President Bush argued strongly for passage of the administration's proposal, saying that it would provide "intelligence professionals with the tools they need" (Smith 2006a; Smith 2006b; Babington and Weisman 2006). He maintained that

"The professionals will not step up unless there's clarity in the law. . . . I strongly recommend that this program go forward in order for us to be able to protect America"
(Bush 2006).[14] The allowed interrogation techniques were not specified in the law,
but were said to include prolonged sleep deprivation, stress positions, isolation, in-
ducing hypothermia, excessive heat, and earsplitting noises. Members of Congress,
including John McCain, also said that waterboarding[15] [MB2] was not allowed by the
Military Commissions Act, but their understanding was called into question when
Vice President Cheney seemed to refute it (Vice President's Office, 2006; Eggen,
2006b; Lewis, 2006).[16] On September 13, 2006, former Secretary of State Colin
Powell wrote a public letter to Senator McCain urging him to oppose the redefining
of treatment allowed under Common Article 3, because "the world is beginning to
doubt the moral basis of our fight against terrorism," and because "it would put our
own troops at risk" (Reid 2006).

After several weeks of contentious debate between the two political parties,
S3930 was passed by both houses of Congress. President Bush signed the Military
Commissions Act of 2006 (PL 109-366) into law on October 17, 2006. The law gave
the Bush administration most of what it wanted in dealing with detainees in ways that
were prohibited by the *Hamdan* ruling. Most directly, the law authorized the president
to establish military commissions to try alien detainees believed to be terrorists or unlawful enemy combatants. The vehement arguments made by President Bush that the
MCA was needed in order for the administration to continue to use "the program" of
"robust" interrogation techniques constitutes an admission that the administration
had used them and saw them as essential to its approach to interrogation.

Importantly, the law denied alien enemy combatants access to the courts for
writs of *habeas corpus* concerning "any aspect of the detention, transfer, treatment,
trial, or conditions of confinement of an alien who is or was detained by the United
States" (Sec. 7 (2)). Appeals that were allowed were limited to issues concerning the
constitutionality of the law itself and the administration's compliance with it, but
not the evidentiary basis for the detainee's imprisonment or his treatment while in
custody.

The law forbids the use of testimony obtained through "torture," and it specifically outlaws the more extreme forms of torture. The interrogation methods that can
be used against the accused also exclude those methods that "amount to cruel, inhuman, or degrading treatment prohibited by section 1003 of the Detainee Treatment Act of 2005" (Sec. 948r). Under the administration's interpretation, the law
prohibits only techniques that "shock the conscience," rather than the stricter prohibition in Common Article 3 which specifically forbids "outrages upon personal
dignity, in particular humiliating and degrading treatment. . . ." (Elsea 2004, p. 5;
Smith 2006a). The Military Commissions Act allocated significant new powers to
the president. It allows the president or secretary of defense to decide unilaterally
who is an enemy combatant; it allows the executive to prosecute a person using coerced testimony; and it precludes any oversight of the actions of the executive by the
judiciary (Shane and Liptak 2006).[17]

Critics complained that this language did not amount to acceptance of Common Article 3 of the Geneva conventions and would allow very harsh treatment that

could amount to torture. Techniques such as stress positions, sleep deprivation, sensory deprivation, isolation, or earsplitting noises could amount to torture, said critics, depending on the intensity and duration of their use. Statements obtained with these methods could be used against a detainee if the presiding officer decides that the "interests of justice would best be served" and that "the totality of the circumstances renders the statement reliable and possessing sufficient probative value" (Sec. 948r).

In addition, critics of the administration argued that the new law would allow U.S. forces to capture anyone declared an "enemy combatant" anywhere in the world, including those thought to have purposefully supported hostilities against U.S. co-belligerents, and hold them indefinitely. These suspects could be held without charges being filed against them and subjected to harsh interrogation techniques with no recourse to the courts for writs of *habeas corpus*. Critics also questioned whether the law could constitutionally deny the writ of *habeas corpus* to detainees, as the law purported to do (Shane and Liptak 2006; Zernike 2006; Grieve 2006; Fletcher 2006).

At the symbolic level, the Military Commissions Act sent the message to the world that the United States would continue to use harsh interrogation techniques (including waterboarding according to Vice President Cheney's statements) that most countries considered to be torture and in violation of Common Article 3 of the Geneva Conventions. At the legal level, it purported to deny *habeas corpus* for most detainees and allowed harsh interrogation methods to be used. At the constitutional level, it represents a congressional ratification of executive authority to set up unilaterally military commissions, conduct trials, and sentence detainees with limited due process rights and no judicial or congressional oversight.

With the MCA, President Bush was able to accomplish through law what he had previously asserted to be his own constitutional authority. Ratification by Congress of the president's authority to deny *habeas corpus* appeals and due process rights to detainees, however, does not necessarily make them constitutional. However, it does make it more difficult for the Supreme Court to constrain the president absent a change in the law by Congress. In seeking congressional sanction for his actions, President Bush did not abandon his claim that he, as president, had the constitutional authority to undertake them unilaterally.

Warrantless Electronic Surveillance by the National Security Agency

In December 2005, *The New York Times* revealed that the Bush administration had been secretly monitoring telephone calls and e-mails between suspected foreign terrorists and people within the domestic United States. The legal right of the executive branch to conduct electronic surveillance on foreign intelligence targets is not in dispute, but the right of the government to secretly eavesdrop or wiretap suspects within the United States without a warrant is limited by the Fourth Amendment and the law.

The Foreign Intelligence Surveillance Act

During the 1970s, it was revealed that the Nixon administration conducted a range of warrantless wiretaps in order to monitor their political adversaries (Senate Report 1978; Senate Report 1976; Schwarz and Huq 2007, 31; Bazan and Elsea 2005).[18] Congress responded to these abuses by amending Title III of the Omnibus Crime Control and Safe Streets Act of 1968, which controlled electronic surveillance by the government. The act set procedures for seeking warrants for electronic surveillance and prohibited non-warranted surveillance. Title III of the act provided an exception for certain national security surveillance undertaken under the "constitutional power of the President to take such measures as he deems necessary to protect the National against actual or potential attack. . . ., [and] to obtain foreign intelligence information deemed essential to the security of the United States. . . ." (Bazan and Elsea 2005, 17).[19]

That section of Title III was repealed by the Foreign Intelligence Surveillance Act of 1978 (FISA) (Cole, et. al. 2006).[20] It was amended to allow for the surveillance for foreign intelligence acquisition only as long as it was carried out pursuant to the Foreign Intelligence Surveillance Act of 1978. The amended act specified that: "the Foreign Intelligence Surveillance Act of 1978 shall be the *exclusive means* by which electronic surveillance, as defined in section 101 of such Act, and the interception of domestic wire, oral, and electronic communications may be conducted" (emphasis added) (Bazan and Elsea 2005).[21]

The Foreign Intelligence Surveillance Act (FISA) provides for a special court for the consideration of warrants for electronic surveillance, if probable cause is shown that the suspect is likely to be an agent of a foreign power. In requiring a warrant from the special FISA court, the law provides for three exceptions: 1) if the attorney general determines that the communication is among foreign powers or their agents and "there is no substantial likelihood that the surveillance will acquire the contents of any communication of which a United States person is a party"; 2) if the attorney general determines that there is insufficient time to obtain a warrant, but in such a case a FISA judge shall be notified within 72 hours (changed from 24 hours on December 28, 2001); and 3) surveillance can be conducted without a warrant for 15 days after Congress declares war (Bazan and Elsea 2005, pp. 25–26).

In confirming *The New York Times* report of the secret surveillance program, President Bush said that warrantless spying on domestic persons suspected of being in contact with terrorists was "a vital tool in our war against the terrorists," and that revealing the program damaged U.S. security (Sanger 2005). "It was a shameful act for someone to disclose this very important program in a time of war. The fact that we're discussing this program is helping the enemy" (Baker and Babington 2005).

It is not as if President Bush did not have the means to undertake the NSA spying within the law. He could have sought warrants by the special FISA courts set up for that very purpose. If speed was of importance, NSA could have carried out the surveillance and come back to the FISA court within 72 hours for retrospective authorization, as provided for by the law. Or if the law, as written, was too narrow to allow the kind of surveillance deemed necessary (e.g., data mining or call tagging), the president could have asked Congress to change the law (which had been amended several times since 9/11). But President Bush did none of these things; instead, he secretly ordered NSA to conduct the surveillance, and when his actions were disclosed, he asserted that he had the constitutional authority to ignore the law.

President Bush's Arguments

The administration argued that getting a FISA warrant was too cumbersome and slow and thus it had to set up a secret program for the National Security Agency to conduct the warrantless surveillance in secret. The record of the FISA court, however, does not seem to indicate that the administration had trouble obtaining warrants. From the time that the court was created in 1978 to the end of 2005, it issued 18,748 warrants and refused only five (Baker and Babington 2005). This is about as close to a rubber stamp as one could wish for. As for the problem of speed, if the need was immediate, NSA could act immediately and come back to the court for authorization within 72 hours.

The administration also argued that it had consulted with Congress about the program, since it had informed the leadership and the chair and ranking members of the Senate and House intelligence committees. President Bush said, "Not only has it been reviewed by Justice Department officials, it's been reviewed by members of the United States Congress" (Lichtblau 2006). This argument was challenged, however, by Senator Jay Rockefeller, who had been briefed on July 17, 2003. The members of Congress were sworn to secrecy and told that they could not inform their colleagues or staffers about the program. After the briefing, Rockefeller expressed his concern by writing a letter to Vice President Cheney and copying the note and putting a sealed copy in his safe as evidence that he had expressed his concern. He had no alternative route to raise concerns about what he saw as potentially illegal actions by the administration. He wrote to the vice president, "Clearly, the activities we discussed raise profound oversight issues" (Babington and Linzer 2005).

The administration also argued that the congressional Authorization to Use Military Force (AUMF) passed in a joint resolution after the September 11, 2001 attacks gave the president power by declaring that the president could:

> use all necessary and appropriate force against those nations, organization, or persons he determined planned, authorized, committed, or aided the terrorist attacks that occurred on September 11, 2001, or harbored such organizations or persons, in order to prevent any future acts of international terrorism against the United States by such nations, organizations or person (Brimmett 2006).[22]

The act, however, made no mention of foreign or domestic surveillance in its wording. The argument of the administration that the AUMF overcomes the FISA law would entail the implication that Congress intended to repeal the section of the law that declared FISA to be "the exclusive means by which electronic surveillance . . . may be conducted."

When Congress was considering the authorization for the president to use force, the administration tried to insert in the language of the resolution a provision that would have allowed the "necessary and appropriate force" could be applied "in the United States" as well as against the "nations, organizations, or persons" who were involved in the 9/11 attacks. This language was rejected by the Senate, undermining the argument that the AUMF intended to repeal FISA (Daschle 2005). In addition, because Congress explicitly provided for warrantless wiretaps for 15 days subsequent to a declaration of war, how could a resolution on the use of force, which carries less legal or constitutional weight than a declaration of war, authorize wiretaps with no limitation?[23]

Attorney General Gonzales, in explaining why the administration did not seek to amend FISA to allow for the warrantless wiretaps, replied that he was advised that such an amendment was unlikely to pass Congress (Eggen 2006a). But it is contradictory to argue that Congress likely would not grant the needed authority for warrantless wiretaps if it were asked and that at the same time, Congress had approved presidential authority for warrantless wiretaps in passing the AUMF (Cole, et. al. 2006). It was also disclosed that Justice Department lawyers drafted legislative changes to the USA Patriot Act that would have provided a legal defense for government officials who wiretapped with "lawful authorization" from the president. There would be no need for such legislation if the president clearly had inherent authority to authorize such wiretaps.[24]

In addition to Senator Rockefeller's concerns, members of the Bush administration Justice Department also had serious reservations. When the White House sought approval of continued use of the program in 2004, Acting Attorney General James B. Comey (Ashcroft's deputy), refused to grant his approval. As a result, Andrew Card, the chief of staff, and White House Counsel, Alberto Gonzales, made a special trip to the hospital to try to get Attorney General John Ashcroft (who was in the hospital recovering from major surgery) to approve the program. With a dramatic statement from his bed, Ashcroft, with Comey present, refused to overrule his deputy (Lichtblau and Risen 2006; Lichtblau 2006; Klaidman, Taylor, and Thomas 2006). Comey was then called to the White House and informed that the program would continue. Only the threat of resignations by Ashcroft, Comey, and several other high-level Justice Department officials convinced President Bush to heed the concerns of the lawyers. Only after President Bush convinced them that their concerns had been met, did they agree to the continuation of the program. What happened at the White House meeting has not been disclosed.

The question here is not whether there is a serious threat from terrorism or whether the government ought to be able to wiretap U.S. citizens without a warrant. It may or may not be good policy to allow the government to conduct such surveillance, but the constitutional process for making such decisions entails the legislative process and judicial interpretation of the law. President Bush claimed that, despite the laws enacted by Congress and duly signed by the president, he had inherent authority to ignore the law and set up a secret surveillance program that could act without warrants. The question is one of constitutional presidential authority versus the constitutional rights and duties of the other two branches. The Constitution does not give the president the authority to ignore the law. The wisdom of surveillance policy is a separate issue.

David Addington, Vice President Cheney's chief of staff and counsel, expressed his attitude toward the FISA court when he said: "We're one bomb away from getting rid of that obnoxious court" (Goldsmith 2007, 181). Jeffrey Goldsmith, director of the Office of Legal Counsel, who was involved with policy making regarding the Terrorist Surveillance Program, said: "After 9/11 they [Cheney and Addington] and other top officials in the administration dealt with FISA the way they dealt with other laws they didn't like: they blew through them in secret based on flimsy legal opinions that they guarded closely so no one could question the legal basis for the operations" (Goldsmith 2007, 181). Goldsmith pointed out that even the NSA's lawyers were not allowed to examine the legal documents that justified the Terrorist Surveillance Program (Goldsmith 2007, 182).

Signing Statements

Article I, Section 1 of the Constitution begins: "All legislative Powers herein granted shall be vested in a Congress of the United States, which shall consist of a Senate and House of Representatives." Article II of the Constitution provides that: "The executive Power shall be vested in a President of the United States of America," and that "the President shall be Commander in Chief of the Army and Navy of the United States." Despite the Article II provision that the president "shall take Care that the Laws be faithfully executed," signing statements have been used to argue that Article II provisions trump Article I of the Constitution.

The idea of presidential signing statements begins with the reasonable presumption that each coordinate branch of government should have a role in interpreting the Constitution and its own constitutional powers. As James Madison said in Federalist No. 49: "The several departments being perfectly co-ordinate by the terms of their common commission, none of them, it is evident, can pretend to an exclusive or superior right of settling the boundaries between their respective powers." Thus within the checks and balances of the Constitution, no single branch has the final say as to what the Constitution says or what public policy shall be. Each branch has a role in interpreting the Constitution, but each is subject to checks and balances from the other two branches.

Presidents since James Monroe have occasionally issued statements upon the signing of bills into law, though it was unusual for the first 150 years of the republic. Most of these signing statements were rhetorical and meant to show presidential support for the legislation or occasionally to record publicly presidential reservations about the law. Rhetorical signing statements began to increase with the Truman administration. But the more important use of signing statements has been to register questions about the constitutionality of the law in question. The use of signing statements for this purpose began to be taken seriously during the Ford and Carter presidencies, but took a significant jump during the Reagan Presidency, during which they were used in a strategic manner to signify presidential disapproval of parts of a law that he was signing (Kelley 2002).

The Reagan administration took a step toward changing the status of signing statements in 1986 when it arranged with West Publishing Company to publish signing statements in the "Legislative History" section of *The United States Congressional*

Code and Administrative News (USCCAN), which provides information about the background for the development of a law that might be relevant to its future interpretation by courts. Attorney General Edwin Meese explained that the purpose of the administration's action was so that the president's thinking when signing a bill into law "will accompany the legislative history from Congress so that all can be available to the court for future construction of what that statute really means" (Garber and Wimmer 1987).

Such a purpose seems reasonable, because it merely calls to the attention of the courts the president's perspective on the law. This benign interpretation of signing statements, however, was undercut by Meese's later statement of the intent of signing statements in 2001, in which he said that in addition to expressing the president's view of a law, that it would indicate "those provisions of the law that might not be enforced" (Kelley 2002). There is a big difference, however, between expressing an opinion on the meaning of a law and refusing to enforce the provisions of a law of which a president disapproves. Presidents Carter, Reagan, Bush, and Clinton occasionally used signing statements to indicate that they had reservations about the laws they were signing and might not enforce.

President George W. Bush, however, used signing statements to an unprecedented extent. He issued more than 1,000 constitutional challenges to provisions in 150 laws in his first six years in office (Kelley 2007; ABA 2006). He also used signing statements to assert the unilateral and unreviewable right of the executive to choose which provisions of laws to enforce and which to ignore. For instance, he used them to indicate that he did not feel bound by all of the provisions of laws regarding: reporting to Congress pursuant to the PATRIOT Act; the torture of prisoners; whistle-blower protections for the Department of Energy; the number of U.S. troops in Columbia; the use of illegally gathered intelligence; and the publication of educational data gathered by the Department of Education (Savage 2006; 2007, 228–249).

One problem with signing statements of this sort is that they can accomplish what the Framers decided not to give the president: an absolute veto. The constitutional process calls for bills to be passed by Congress and presented to the president for his signature or veto. But a signing statement, in effect, allows the president to sign the bill, and later to decide if he does not want to comply with part of the law. It also allows the president to achieve, in effect, an item veto, which the Supreme Court has declared unconstitutional. In the passage of legislation members of Congress often vote for a bill because of assurances that certain provisions have meaning. But if the executive can unilaterally decide not to enforce whatever portion of laws it believes infringe on its constitutional power, the votes of a majority of the members of Congress are effectively nullified.

The belief that he could selectively enforce the law pursuant to his signing statements may be part of the reason that President Bush did not issue any vetoes for the first five and a half years of his administration, a record unmatched since Thomas Jefferson. An example (discussed previously) of the potentially unchecked nature of signing statements occurred when President Bush strongly opposed any threatened to veto the Detainee Treatment Act, sponsored by Senator John McCain (R-AZ), forbidding torture. It was passed by both Houses of Congress by veto-proof majorities.

President Bush signed the law in a ceremony at the White House with John McCain, symbolizing the administration's intent not to use torture in order to obtain information from prisoners.

In his accompanying signing statement, however, President Bush indicated that he did not feel bound by the law and that he would enforce the law "in a manner consistent with the constitutional authority of the President. . . ." (cited previously). Thus, the president reserved for himself the right to ignore the law when he deemed it to conflict with his commander-in-chief power, but he avoided the constitutional process of having to subject his veto to a possible override by Congress. Because the administration had previously asserted that Congress could not limit the way in which the executive treated prisoners, the implication was that it would not consider itself bound by the provisions of the law. The administration also seemed to claim in the signing statement that it could avoid judicial review.

The implications of these sweeping claims to presidential authority are profound and undermine the very meaning of the rule of law. Despite the Constitution's granting lawmaking power to the Congress, the Bush administration maintained that executive authority and the commander in chief clause can overcome virtually any law that constrains the executive. President Bush was thus claiming unilateral control of the laws. If the executive claims that he or she is not subject to the law as it is written but can pick and choose which provisions to enforce, he or she is essentially claiming the unitary power to say what the law is. The "take care" clause of Article II can thus be effectively nullified.

Even though there may occur some limited circumstances in which the president is not bound by a law, expanding that limited, legitimate practice to more than 1,000 threats to not execute the law constitutes an arrogation of power by the president.[25] The Constitution does not give the president the option to decide not to faithfully execute the law. If there is a dispute about the interpretation of a law, the interaction of the three branches in the constitutional process is the appropriate way to settle the issue. The politics of passage, the choice to veto or not, and the right to challenge laws in court all are legitimate ways to deal with differences in interpretation. But the assertion by the executive that it alone has the authority to interpret the law and that it will enforce the law at its own discretion threatens the constitutional balance set up by the Constitution.

Conclusion: Thinking Constitutionally

Even if one posits that President Bush has not and would not abuse his executive power, his claim to be able to ignore the law, if allowed to stand, would constitute a dangerous precedent that future presidents might use to abuse their power. Joel Aberbach points out that "In the end, this is not a partisan issue, for someday the Democrats will have unified control, and even that somewhat-less-disciplined party might countenance a government of the type Bush and Cheney have apparently structured" (Campbell, Rockman, Rudalevige). Madison argues in Federalist No. 10, "Enlightened statesmen will not always be at the helm." Thinking constitutionally means looking ahead and realizing that future executives will likely claim the same authority as their predecessors. Claims to executive power ratchet up; they do not swing like a pendulum unless the other two branches protect their own constitutional authorities.

The rule of law is fundamental to a free society and to democracy, because neither can exist without it. As Thomas Paine argued in *Common Sense*, "in America THE LAW IS KING. For as in absolute governments the King is law . . . " (emphasis in original). James Madison put it this way in Federalist 47: "The accumulation of all powers, legislative, executive, and judiciary, in the same hands, whether of one, a few, or many, and whether hereditary, self-appointed, or elective, may justly be pronounced the very definition of tyranny." In each of the following cases of claims to constitutional authority President Bush was asserting that he alone could exercise the authority of each of the three branches:

1. **Geneva Conventions and torture:** President Bush acted as
   - *lawmaker* in suspending the treaty, which according to Article VI of the Constitution is "the supreme Law of the Land,"
   - *executive* in carrying out the policy by interrogating prisoners with harsh interrogation practices, and he acted as
   - *judge* by keeping the proceedings secret and asserting that any appeal could only be to him and that the courts had no jurisdiction to hear appeals.

2. **Military tribunals:** President Bush acted as
   - *lawmaker* in creating the commissions himself, not in accord with enacted laws,
   - *executive* in detaining suspects in prisons, and he acted as
   - *judge* in conducting the trials, imposing sentences, and serving as the final appeal.

3. **Denying habeas corpus to detainees:** President Bush acted as
   - *lawmaker* in suspending habeas corpus, which authority the Constitution gives to Congress,
   - *executive* in imprisoning detainees and not allowing them to appeal for writs of *habeas corpus* and denying them the aid of counsel (until forced to by the Supreme Court), and he acted as
   - *judge* in asserting that executive branch determinations of detainee status were final and that appeals could only be within the executive branch.

4. **NSA warrantless wiretapping:** President Bush acted as:
   - *lawmaker* by determining that he could ignore the regularly enacted law and impose his own rules in order to conduct surveillance in the United States,
   - *executive* in ordering NSA to carry out his policies, and he acted as
   - *judge* by arguing that it was his inherent right as president to do it in secret and avoid obtaining warrants from the FISA court.

5. **Signing Statements:** President Bush was
   - *undermining the separation of powers and the rule of law itself* by claiming the authority to ignore those parts of the law that he claimed impinged on his

own prerogatives and refusing to accept the legitimacy of either Congress or the courts to limit his authority.

The president should have enough power to accomplish reasonable policy goals, but not enough to override the other two branches unilaterally, acting merely on the basis of his own judgment. In these cases of extraordinary claims to executive authority, President Bush was claiming that the checks and balances in the Constitution were not binding on him. The United States Constitution created a system in which the concentration of power in one branch could be countered by actions of the other two branches. Congress and the courts still may act to undo some of President Bush's extraordinary assertions of executive authority, but his claims have severely challenged the balance of constitutional authority. The principles of constitutionalism and the rule of law underpin the foundations of the United States polity. Insofar as President Bush, in cases such as these, refused to acknowledge the constitutional limits on his executive authority, he undermined both of these fundamental principles.

Acknowledgments

I am grateful to James Dunkerley, Dean of the Institute for the Study of the Americas and Nicholas Mann, Dean of the School of Advanced Study at the University of London for their hospitality during my six-month visit with them in 2007 as S.T. Lee Professorial Fellow. Other colleagues in the U.S and the U.K. gave me helpful comments and advice as this article was being prepared, and I would like to thank Joel Aberbach, Sharrar Ali, Niels Bjerre-Poulson, Mary Boardman, Nigel Bowles, Lara M. Brown, Brian Cook, Philip Davies, John Dumbrell, George Edwards, Lou Fisher, Hugh Heclo, Jon Herbert, Matthew Holden, Don Kash, Nancy Kassop, Jeremy Mayer, Iwan Morgan, Dick Pious, Paul Quirk, Jon Roper, Richard Rose, Herman Schwartz, Bob Spitzer, and Jeffrey Weinberg.

Endnotes

1. Source: White House aide defending U.S. policies on Guantanamo Bay prisoners, secret renditions and warrantless eavesdropping in a conversation with Jim Hoagland.
2. Memorandum for the President (25 January 2002) From Alberto R. Gonzales, subject: Decision RE application of the Geneva Convention on Prisoners of War to the Conflict with al Qaeda and the Taliban." According to *Newseek*, the memo was "actually" written by David Addington, Vice President Cheney's legal aide. (Klaidman, 2004) Gonzales has been criticized in the press for saying that the "new paradigm" renders the Geneva limitations "quaint." But the context of his use of the word "quaint" is not as damning as excerpting the word makes it seem. The end of the sentence reads: ". . . renders quaint some of it provisions requiring that captured enemy be afforded such things as commissary privileges, scrip (i.e., advance of monthly pay), athletic uniforms, and scientific instruments." Whether this is a fair representation of the Geneva requirements is a separate issue.
3. The U.S. War Crimes Act (18 U.S.C. Par. 2441 (Sup. III 1997) (WCA). Section 2441 of the War Crimes Act defines "war crimes" as a "grave breach" of the Geneva Conventions, which includes "willful killing, torture or inhuman treatment, including biological experiments,

willfully causing great suffering or serious injury to body or health . . . or willfully depriving a prisoner of war of the rights of fair and regular trial prescribed in this Convention."

4. Memorandum TO: Counsel to the President and Assistant to the President for National Security Affairs, FROM: Colin L. Powell (26 January 2002) SUBJECT: Draft Decision Memorandum for the President on the Applicability of the Geneva Convention to the Conflict in Afghanistan." Many of the memoranda and oral directives included statements that detainees were to be treated "humanely" despite the more aggressive interrogation techniques to which they could be subjected. The problem was that if the detainees were in fact treated humanely, it would be more difficult to extract information from them. Thus these statements must have been considered to be pro forma, while the overall thrust of the directives was that detainees were to be subject to more aggressive interrogation techniques that were outside the Geneva Convention limits.

5. For a detailed analysis of the legal issues involved in the treatment of prisoners and the international and legal obligations of the United States regarding detainees, see: Robert K. Goldman and Brian D. Tittemore, "Unprivileged Combatants and the Hostilities in Afghanistan: Their Status and Rights Under International Humanitarian and Human Rights Law," (Washington, D.C.: American Society of International Law Task Force Paper, 2002. See also: Jennifer K. Elsea, "Lawfulness of Interrogation Techniques under the Geneva Conventions," Washington: Congressional Research Service Report to Congress (RL32567), September 8, 2004; Elsea, "U.S. Treatment of Prisoners in Iraq: Selected Legal Issues," Congressional Research Service Report for Congress (RL32395), December 2, 2004; and L.C. Green, The Contemporary Law of Armed Conflict (NY: Manchester University Press, 1993). The skeptical attitude of many in the professional military was reflected in a 2007 op-ed piece by former Generals Charles C. Krulak (former Commandant of the Marine Corps) and Joseph P. Hoar (former chief of Central Command): "As has happened with every other nation that has tried to engage in a little bit of torture—only for the toughest cases, only when nothing else works—the abuse spread like wildfire, and every captured prisoner became the key to defusing a potential ticking time bomb. Our soldiers in Iraq confront real "ticking time bomb" situations every day, in the form of improvised explosive devices, and any degree of "flexibility" about torture at the top drops down the chain of command like a stone—the rare exception fast becoming the rule." Washington Post (May 17, 2007), p. A17.

6. Article 17, paragraph 4.

7. United Nations Convention Against Torture and Other Cruel, Inhuman or Degrading Treatment or Punishment. [General Assembly Resolution 39/46, Annex, 39 U. GAOR Sup. No. 51, U.N. Doc. A.39/51 (1984). The Convention Against Torture (CAT) defines torture as "any act by which severe pain or suffering, whether physical or mental, is intentionally inflicted on a person for such purposes as obtaining from him or a third person information or a confession. . . ."

8. According to the memo, for the law to apply, the torturer must have the "specific intent to inflict severe pain" and it must be his "precise objective." (p. 3) "Thus, even if the defendant knows that severe pain will result from his actions, if causing such harm is not his objective, he lacks the requisite specific intent even though the defendant did not act in good faith." Thus one could inflict pain that amounted to torture, but not be guilty of torture if the main objective was, for instance, to extract information rather than to cause pain. This reasoning borders on sophistry. On December 30, 2004 the Bybee memo was superseded "in its entirety" by "Memorandum for James B. Comey, Deputy Attorney General from Acting Assistant Attorney General Daniel Levin Re: Legal Standards Applicable Under 18 U.S.C. par. 2340–2340A. The memo did not address the commander commander-in in-chief powers of the president because it was "unnecessary" (p. 2).

9. Article VI of the Constitution also provides that "all Treaties made, or which shall be made, under the authority of the United States, shall be the supreme Law of the Land."

10. The Detainee Treatment Act defines cruel, inhuman, or degrading treatment as "the cruel, unusual, and inhumane treatment or punishment prohibited by the Fifth, Eighth, and

Fourteenth Amendments to the Constitution, as defined in the United State Reservations, Declarations and Understandings to the United Nations Convention Against Torture and Other Forms of Cruel, Inhuman or Degrading Treatment of Punishment done at New York, December 10, 1984."

11. That is, if the U.S. person undertakes interrogation practices that "were officially authorized and determined to be lawful at the time that they were conducted, it shall be a defense that such officer, employee, member of the Armed Forces, or other agent did not know that the practices were unlawful and a person of ordinary sense and understanding would not know the practices were unlawful."

12. The commissions were established by Military Order of November 13, 2001, "Detention, Treatment, and Trial of Certain Non-Citizens in the War Against Terrorism." Available at: http://www.whitehouse.gov/news/releases/2001/11/20011113-27.html.

13. In remarks after she had retired from the Supreme Court, Justice O'Conner said about the intimidation of federal judges, "we must be ever-vigilant against those who would strongarm the judiciary into adopting their preferred policies. It takes a lot of degeneration before a country falls into dictatorship, but we should avoid these ends by avoiding these beginnings." Her remarks were reported by Nina Totenberg of National Public Radio according to Raw Story (Totenberg 2006).

14. The uniformed military, however, were not eager for the bill to pass. Major General Scott C. Black, the judge advocate general of the Army, said that "further redefinition" of the Geneva Conventions "is unnecessary and could be seen as a weakening of our treaty obligations, rather than a reinforcement of the standards of treatment." (Baker 2006).

15. Waterboarding is a technique of interrogation in which a person is bound to a flat board and his head submerged in water with a soaked cloth over his mouth (or water poured over the cloth) until the person cannot breath sufficient air and is convinced he is drowning. A Japanese officer, Yukio Asano, was sentenced to 15 years at hard labor for waterboarding an American in World War II (Pincus, 2006; Shane & Liptak, 2006).

16. Vice President Cheney was interviewed in the White House by a reporter who asked: "Would you agree that a dunk in water [of a suspected terrorist] is a no-brainer if it can save lives?" Cheney replied: "It's a no-brainer for me. . . . We don't torture. . . . But the fact is, you can have a fairly robust interrogation program without torture, and we need to be able to do *that*. And thanks to the leadership of the President now, and the action of the congress, we have that authority, and we are able to continue to [sic] Program." (emphasis added) Asked in another question about "dunking a terrorist in water," Cheney replied: "I do agree. And I think the terrorist threat, for example, with respect to our ability to interrogate high value detainees like Khalid Sheikh Mohammed, *that's* been a very important tool that we've had to be able to secure the nation." (emphasis added). The antecedent to the word "that" and "that's" in the Vice President's statements is clearly "dunking a terrorist in water," indicating that the Bush administration does not consider waterboarding to be torture (Vice President's Office 2006).

17. It does allow appeals concerning the constitutionality of the law itself and whether the administration has complied with it.

18. House Report No. 95-1283, pp. 15-21, as cited in Bazan & Elsea 2005, pp. 12-13.

19. 82 Stat. 214, 18 U.S. par 2511(3), as cited in Bazan & Elsea 2005 p. 17

20. Public Law 95-511, 92 Stat. 1783, as cited in Cole, et. al. 2006.

21. 18 U.S.C. par. 2511(2)(f), Public Law 95-511, 92 State 1783, as quoted in Bazan and Elsea 2005 p. 15.

22. Authorization for Use of Military Force, Public Law 107-40, 115 Stat. 224 (2001), passed the House and Senate on September 14, 2001 and signed by the president on September 18, 2001.

23. The NSA surveillance revelations also raised the issue of whether President Bush was truthful in reassuring questioners about government surveillance and civil liberties. In remarks in Buffalo, New York on April 20, 2004, President Bush said: "Now, by the way, any time you hear the United States government talking about wiretap, it requires—a wiretap requires a court order. Nothing has changed, by the way. When we're talking about chasing

down terrorists, we're talking about getting a court order before we do so. It's important for our fellow citizens to understand, when you think Patriot Act, constitutional guarantees are in place when it comes to doing what is necessary to protect our homeland, because we value the Constitution" (Bush 2004).

24. Justice Department spokespersons said that the drafts were not intended to affect the NSA spying and that the proposals were not presented to the Attorney General or the White House (Eggen 2006a).

25. For instance, if a law contains a one house legislative veto provision or a clearly unconstitutional infringement on the president's appointment power.

References

18 U.S.C. Sec. 2340. 1994. Available from http://uscode.house.gov/download/pls/18C113C.txt.

18 U.S.C. Sec. 2340A. 1994. *U.S. Criminal Law that Implements the U.N. Convention Against Torture*. Available from http://uscode.house.gov/download/pls/18C113C.txt.

Aberbach, Joel. 2007. "Supplying the Defects of Better Motives?" in Campbell, et al. Washington: CQ Press, 130.

American Bar Association. 2006. "Task Force on Presidential Signing Statements and the Separation of Powers Doctrine," July 2006. 14 Available from: http://www.abanet.org/op/signingstatements/aba_final_signing_statements_recommendation-report_7-24-06.pdf.

Babington, Charles, and Dafna Linzer. 2005. "Senator Sounded Alarm in '03 ," *The Washington Post*, December 20, A10.

Babington, Charlesand Jonathan Weisman, "2006. Senate Approves Detainee Bill Backed by Bush," *The Washington Post*. September 29, p. 1.

Baker, Peter. "2006. GOP Infighting on Detainees Intensifies," *The Washington Post*, September 16, p. A01.

Baker, Peter, and Charles Babington, 2005. "Bush Addresses Uproar Over Spying," *The Washington Post*, December 20, p. A01.

Barry, John, Michael Hirsh, and Michael Isiskoff, 2004. "The Roots of Torture," *Newsweek*, May 24, pp. 28–34.

Bazan, Elizabeth B., and Jennifer K. Elsea, 2005. "Presidential Authority to Conduct Warrantless Electronic Surveillance to Gather Foreign Intelligence Information," *Congressional Research Service*, January 5.

Bravin, Jess, 2004. "Pentagon Report Set Framework for Use of Torture," *Wall Street Journal*, June 7.

Brimmett, Richard F., 2006. "Authorization for Use of Military Force in Response to the 9/11 Attacks (P.L. 107–40): Legislative History," *Congressional Research Service* (Order Code RS22357), January 4.

Bush, George, 2004. "President Bush: Information Sharing, Patriot Act Vital to Homeland Security," 2004. *The White House*, April 20. Available from www.whitehous.gov/news/releases/2004/04/print/20040420-2.html.

Bush, George, 2006 Press Conference of the President. September 15. Available at http://www.whitehouse.gov/news/releases/2006/09/20060915-2.html.

Bybee, Jay S., 2002. *Memorandum for Alberto R. Gonzales, Counsel to the President re: Standards of Conduct for Interrogation under 18 U.S.C. Sec. 2340–2340A*, August 1, pp. 1–33. Available at http://www.washingtonpost.com/wp-srv/politics/documents/cheney/torture_memo_aug2002.pdf.

Campbell, Colin, Bert A. Rockman, and Andrew Rudalevige, 2007. *The George W. Bush Legacy*. Washington: CQ Press, forthcoming.

Cole, David, et. al. 2006. "On NSA Spying: A Letter to Congress," *New York Review of Books*. February 9, p. 42.

Daschle, Tom, 2005. "Power We Didn't Grant," *The Washington Post*, December 23, p. A21.

Eggen, Dan, 2006a. "2003 Draft Legislation Covered Eavesdropping," *The Washington Post*, January 28, p. A02.

Eggen, Dan, 2006b. "Cheney's Remarks Fuel Torture Debate," *The Washington Post*, October 27, p. A09.

Elsea, Jennifer K., 2004. *Lawfulness of Interrogation Techniques under the Geneva Conventions*, 2. Washington, DC. Congressional Research Service Report to Congress (RL32567). September 8, 2004.

Fletcher, Michael A., 2006. "Bush Signs Terrorism Measure," *The Washington Post*, October 18, p. A4.

Garber, Marc N. and Kurt A. Wimmer, 1987. "Presidential Signing Statements as Interpretations of Legislative Intent: An Executive Aggrandizement of Power," *Harvard Journal on Legislation* Vol. 24, p. 367.

Gonzales, Alberto R., 2002. *Memorandum for the President*, January 25. Available from http://www.msnbc.msn.com/id/4999148/site/news/.

Goldsmith, Jack, 2007. *The Terror Presidency*, New York: Norton.

Grieve, Tim, 2006. "The President's Power to Imprison People Forever," *Salon*, September 26. Available from http://www.salon.com/politics/war_room/2006/09/26/tyrannical_power/index.html.

Hamadan v. Rumsfeld, Secretary of Defense, et. al. Slip Opinion. 2005. 4, 7. Available from: http://www.supremecourtus.gov/opinions/05pdf/05-184.pdf.

Hersh, Seymour M., 2004. "The Gray Zone," *The New Yorker*, May 24, p. 42.

Hoagland, Jim, 2006. "Two Leaders' Power Failures," *The Washington Post*, March 9, p. A19.

Jefferson, Thomas, 1789. Letter to James Madison (March 15). Quoted in Schlesinger.

Kelley, Christopher S., 2002. "'Faithfully Executing' and 'Taking Care': The Unitary Executive and the Presidential Signing Statement," Paper presented at the American Political Science Association annual convention, 2002.

Kelley, Christopher S., 2007. Web page: http://www.users.muohio.edu/kelleycs//; accessed June 7, 2007.

Klaidman, Daniel, 2004. "Homesick for Texas," *Newsweek*, July 12, p. 32.

Klaidman, Daniel, Stuart Taylor, Jr., and Evan Thomas, 2006. "Palace Revolt," *Newsweek*, February 6, p. 39.

Lewis, Neil A.,"Furor over Cheney Remark on Tactics for Terror Suspects," *The New York Times*, October 28, p. A8.

Lichtblau, Eric, 2006. "Bush Defends Spy Program and Denies Misleading Public," *The New York Times,* January 2, p. 11.

Lichtblau, Eric, and James Risen, 2006. "Justice Deputy Resisted Parts of Spy Program," *The New York Times,* January 1, p. 1.

Pfiffner, James P., 2005. "Torture and Public Policy," *Public Integrity,* Vol. 7, no. 4, pp. 313–330.

Pincus, Walter, 2006. "Waterboarding Historically Controversial," *The Washington Post,* October 5, p. A17.

Powell, Colin L., 2002a. *Comments on the Memorandum of January 25, 2002.* In Greenberg, Karen J. and Dratel, Joshua L. (Eds.), *The Torture Papers: The Road to Abu Ghraib* (124–125). New York, Cambridge University Press, 2005.

Powell, Colin L., 2002. *Draft Decision Memorandum for the President on the Applicability of the Geneva Convention to the Conflict in Afghanistan,* January 26, 2,4. In Greenberg, Karen J. and Dratel, Joshua L. (Eds.), *The Torture Papers: The Road to Abu Ghraib* (122–125). New York, Cambridge University Press, 2005.

Reid, Tim, 2006b. "Republicans Defy Bush on Tougher CIA Interrogation," *Times Online,* September 15. Available from http://www.timesonline.co.uk/tol/news/world/us_and_americas/article639839.ece.

Sanger, David E., 2005. "In Address, Bush Says He Ordered Domestic Spying," *The New York Times,* December 18, p. A01.

Savage, Charlie, 2006. "Bush Challenges Hundreds of Laws," *Boston Globe,* April 30. Available from http://www.boston.com/news/nation/articles/2006/04/30/bush_challenges_hundreds_of_laws/.

Savage, Charlie, 2007. *Takeover,* New York: Little Brown.

Schlesinger, Arthur, 1973. *The Imperial Presidency,* Boston: Houghton Mifflin, p. 377.

Schwarz, Frederick A. O. and Aziz Z. Huq, *Unchecked and Unbalanced,* NY: The New Press.

Senate Report No. 94–755. 1976. "Final Report of the Select Committee to Study Governmental Operations with Respect to Intelligence Activities," *Intelligence Activities and the Rights of Americans,* Book II. (94th Congress, 2nd Session). April 24, 169.

Senate Report No. 95–511, Title I, 92 Stat. 1796. 1978. codified as amended at 50 U.S. C. par. 1801 et seq. (October 25) Available from http://uscode.house.gov/download/pls/50C36.txt.

Shane, Scott and Adam Liptak, 2006. "Shifting Power to a President," *The New York Times.* September 30, p. 1.

Smith, R. Jeffrey, 2006. "Behind the Debate: CIA Techniques of Extreme Discomfort," *The Washington Post,* September 16, p. A3.

Smith, R. Jeffrey, 2006. "Detainee Measure to Have Fewer Restrictions," *The Washington Post,* September 26, p. 1.

Totenberg, Nina, 2006. "Retired Supreme Court Justice Hits Attacks on Courts and Warns of Dictatorship," *The Raw Story,* March 10. Available from http://rawstory.com/news/2006/Retired_Supreme_Court_Justice_hits_attacks_0310.html.

Walsh, Kenneth T., 2006. "The Cheney Factor," *U.S. News & World Report,*
    January 23, p. 48.
White, Josh, 2005. "President Relents, Backs Torture Ban," *The Washington Post,*
    December 16, p. 1.
Vice President's Office, 2006. *Interview of the Vice President by Scott Hennen,*
    WDAY at Radio Day at the White House, October 24. White House Web site.
    Available at http://www.whitehouse.gov/news/releases/2006/10/print/
    20061024-7.html.
White House, 2002. *Memorandum re: Humane Treatment of al Quaeda and Taliban*
    Detainees, signed by President Bush, February 7. Available at
    http://usinfo.state.gov/xarchives/display.html?p=washfile-
    english&y=2004&m=June&x=20040623203050cpataruk0.1224024&t=livefe
    eds/wf-latest.html.
White House, 2005. "President's Statement on Signing of H.R. 2863, the
    "Department of Defense, Emergency Supplemental Appropriations to Address
    Hurricanes in the Gulf of Mexico, and Pandemic Influenza Act, 2006."
    December 30. Available at http://www.whitehouse.gov/news/releases/2005/12/
    20051230-8.html.
Yoo, John, 2006. *War by Other Means,* New York: Atlantic Monthly Press.
Zernike, Kate, 2006. "Senate Approves Broad New Rules to Try Detainees," *The*
    New York Times, September 29, p. 1.

Jules Lobel

The Commander in Chief and the Courts

The Bush administration claimed to have sweeping, inherent, and unchecked war powers to conduct its war against terror. In 2002, the Justice Department's Office of Legal Counsel argued that "Congress could no more regulate the President's ability to detain and interrogate enemy combatants than it may regulate his ability to direct troop movements on the battlefield" (U.S. Department of Justice 2002b, 35). That position was later withdrawn as "unnecessary" but was never repudiated

Source: Presidential Studies Quarterly Vol. 37, No. 1 (March 2007).

(U.S. Department of Justice 2004, 2), and the administration essentially reiterated it in the 2005 presidential signing statement stating that the executive branch would interpret the McCain Amendment's prohibition on cruel and inhumane interrogations of detainees "in a manner consistent with the constitutional authority of the President . . . as Commander in Chief and consistent with the constitutional limitations on judicial power" (Bush 2005). As a senior administration official later explained, the signing statement was intended to reserve the president's constitutional right to use harsh interrogation methods "in special situations involving national security" despite the congressional ban (Savage 2006).

Similarly, the Bush administration argued that the "President has the inherent authority to convene military commissions to try and punish captured enemy combatants even in the absence of statutory authority" (U.S. Department of Justice 2006b, 8). Although the administration did not claim that Congress had no power to regulate executive use of military commissions, it claimed that the president's inherent power "strongly counsel[ed]" against reading congressional statutes "to restrict the Commander in Chief's ability in wartime to hold enemy fighters accountable for violating the law of war" (ibid., 8–9).

The administration also claimed that the president's inherent constitutional authority as commander in chief and the nation's sole organ of foreign affairs allows him to authorize warrantless wiretapping, irrespective of the Foreign Intelligence Surveillance Act (FISA). If FISA is read to prohibit the National Security Agency's warrantless wiretapping program (which it surely does), the administration argues that it is unconstitutional (U.S. Department of Justice 2006a, 8). High-level administration advisors similarly claim that the president has the inherent authority to violate or suspend treaty provisions in wartime (U.S. Department of Justice 2002a, 16). The clearest and most sweeping statement of the president's authority came from the Department of Defense's Working Group Report on Detainee Interrogation in 2003 that "in wartime it is for the President alone to decide what methods to use to best prevail against the enemy" (U.S. Department of Defense 2003, 24).

The administration also articulated a sweeping statutory theory to support its claim of inherent authority. Boiled down to its essentials, this theory reads a declaration of war or other congressional authorization to use force as providing legislative approval for virtually all of the inherent powers that the president claims he has in the absence of such authorization. Thus, the president has claimed that the 2001 Authorization of Use of Military Force Act (AUMF), which authorizes the president to use "all necessary and appropriate force" against the people, organizations, or nations involved in the September 11 attacks, provides congressional authorization to detain American citizens or other individuals indefinitely as enemy combatants, to engage in warrantless wiretapping, and to establish military commissions to try enemy combatants. In short, according to the administration, any authorization of force triggers and provides statutory authorization for the inherent powers of the president as commander in chief to take any actions he believes necessary to fight the enemy against whom force is authorized.

Finally, the administration claimed that just as Congress cannot interfere in determining what methods and tactics the president can use in fighting its war against terror, neither can the courts. In a series of cases, the Justice Department has claimed that the courts have no jurisdiction to even hear the claims of alien enemy combatants detained in Guantanamo or elsewhere, that they can only provide the most limited facial review of citizens deemed enemy combatants and detained in the United States, that they cannot review challenges to extraordinary renditions or the National Security Agency spying program, and that any review of the military commissions established by the president be extremely deferential.

This article will evaluate the administration's claims in light of the constitutional design and theory adopted by its framers and the early leaders of the Republic. It will particularly focus on the role of the courts in matters of war and national security. The questions addressed are: (1) to what extent can Congress regulate the president's prosecution of a duly authorized war? (2) what are the president's inherent powers in conducting such warfare in the absence of congressional regulation? and (3) what is the role of the courts in deciding whether the president has overstepped his power in conducting such a war?

The Judiciary and Military Necessity in the Current Conflict with Al Qaeda

An underlying motif of the Supreme Court's recent decisions involving the administration's war on terror has been the tension between judicial review and the executive's articulation of claimed military necessity. As we have seen, the early Supreme Court generally did not defer to such claims. The modern judiciary's record has been decidedly more mixed, most infamously in *Korematsu v. United States*, in which the Court deferred to the judgment of the military authorities that the exclusion of Japanese Americans from the West Coast was a necessary war measure.[17] Moreover, in some cases, such as *Chicago & Southern Air Lines, Inc. v. Waterman Steamship Corp.*, the Court has employed broad language suggesting that executive foreign-policy decisions are political, not judicial decisions.[18] However, in the recent enemy combatant cases—*Hamdan v. Rumsfeld*, *Rasul v. Bush*, and *Hamdi v. Rumsfeld*—that Court has refused to defer to claims of broad, unreviewable executive decisions based on claimed military necessity and inherent executive power.

The Court's jurisprudence in the trilogy of recent enemy combatant cases rests critically on a distinction between military necessity on the actual battlefield in the midst of combat and claimed necessity to detain or try a detainee several years after their removal from the battlefield. In each of these cases, the Court either explicitly or implicitly found that a generalized claim of military necessity could not negate the Court's obligation to review the detainee's claims.

Most recently, in *Hamdan*, the Court struck down the administration's attempt to unilaterally establish military commissions to try alleged terrorists.[19] Justice John Paul Stevens' opinion, much of which represented the Court majority and part of which was the opinion of the plurality of four justices, rested heavily on the Court's rejection of the argument that any military or practical necessity required these commissions.

stice Stevens and the plurality framed the basic question in the case as "whether the preconditions designed to ensure that a military necessity exists to justify the use of this extraordinary tribunal have been satisfied here."[20] For the plurality, military commissions to try enemies who violate the laws of war—the type the Bush administration sought to implement—were premised on the "need to dispense swift justice, often in the form of execution, to illegal belligerents captured on the battlefield."[21] The administration, however, had failed "to satisfy the most basic precondition" for its establishment of military commissions—"military necessity."[22] Justice Stevens noted that Hamdan's tribunal was not "appointed by a commander in the field of battle, but by a retired major general stationed away from any active hostilities, . . . [and] he was not being tried for any act committed in the theatre of war."[23]

Justice Stevens, writing for the Court, returned to the theme of military necessity when discussing the statutory requirement that procedures for military commissions must be the same as those used to try American soldiers in courts-martial (which they clearly were not) unless the administration could demonstrate that the court-martial procedures would not be "practicable." The Court emphasized the military necessity that comes from battlefield exigencies, stating that the statute "did not transform the military commission from a tribunal of true exigency into a more convenient adjudicatory tool." The requirement that any deviation be necessitated by a showing of impracticability of court-martial procedures "strikes a careful balance between uniform procedure and the need to accommodate exigencies that may sometimes arise in *the theatre of war*."[24] In short, the justices both reviewed and decisively rejected the claim of military necessity upon which the lawfulness of the military commissions rested.

Similarly, Justice Anthony Kennedy, in his concurrence, emphasized the Court's finding that no exigency, practical need, or military necessity required the deviation from the normal procedures followed by court-martials. For Justice Kennedy, as with the other justices in the majority, the term " 'practicable' cannot be construed to permit deviations based on mere convenience or expedience."[25] Hamdan had been detained for four years and the government had demonstrated no exigency or evident practical need for departure from court-martial procedures.[26]

In contrast, the theme that runs throughout Justice Clarence Thomas's dissent is that the Court's decision constituted an unprecedented departure from the traditionally limited role of the courts with respect to warfare.[27] For the dissenters, the Court's determination that Hamdan's trial before a military commission that deviated from court-martial procedures and was not warranted by practical need or military necessity constituted an impermissible intrusion into the executive's power to take appropriate military measures pursuant to the congressional authorization of the use of force against those who aided the terrorist attacks that occurred on September 11, 2001. The dissenters believed that "the plurality has appointed itself the ultimate arbiter of what is quintessentially a policy and military judgment."[28] For the dissenters, the president has the power to appoint military commissions in exigent and nonexigent circumstances, and the Court should not determine whether such actions are necessary. Nor should the Court decide whether the regular court-martial procedures are "practicable," for "that determination is precisely the kind for which the 'judiciary has neither the aptitude, facilities nor responsibility.'" For Thomas, that decision is reserved to the president by Congress's authorization "to use all necessary and appropriate force against our enemies."[29] Or, as Justice Antonin Scalia's dissent argues, an order enjoining ongoing military commission proceedings "brings the Judicial Branch into direct conflict with the Executive in an area where the Executive's competence is maximal *and ours is virtually nonexistent.*"[30]

There seems absolutely no reason why the judiciary's competence to evaluate the legality of a military commission is "virtually nonexistent." One would think that the federal judiciary would have a great deal of expertise in analyzing whether deviations from basic principles of judicial procedure are necessary. For example, as Justice Kennedy asks, why should it be necessary to allow the secretary of defense or his political designee to make dispositive decisions during the middle of the trial or appoint the presiding officer at trial—powers which raise concerns about the commission's neutrality? The judiciary is certainly capable of evaluating whether a fair trial is compromised when the government can introduce into evidence statements obtained through the use of coercive interrogation methods prohibited by the Geneva Conventions and U.S. law. Nor is a court incompetent to evaluate the competing claims of fair process and necessity. Moreover, questions such as the scope and interpretation of Common Article 3 of the Geneva Conventions, the historical practice of military commissions, or whether conspiracy is a war crime all seem to be quintessential legal issues of the type courts generally grapple with. Decisions made in the heat of battle may require speed, secrecy, discretionary judgment, and immediate access to information that military commanders, and not courts, are qualified to make. But none of those attributes characterize the determination of whether military trials undertaken four years after the capture of a prisoner utilize fair, lawful, or necessary procedures. Neither Scalia nor Thomas argues that the administration's military commissions were militarily necessary or that the regular court-martial procedures were impractical, but simply claim that that decision was not for the Court to make.

Similarly, in *Hamdi v. Rumsfeld*, the Court also distinguished between judicial review of detentions on the battlefield and review over indefinite detentions of citizens once they had been removed from the theater of war.[31] The plurality opinion rejected the government's argument that any significant judicial review of a citizen detained as an enemy combatant would have a dire impact on the central functions of warmaking.

While we accord the greatest respect and consideration to the judgments of military authorities in matters relating to the actual prosecution of a war and recognize that the scope of that discretion necessarily is wide, it does not infringe on the core role of the military for the courts to exercise their own time-honored and constitutionally mandated roles of reviewing and resolving claims like those presented.[32]

Of course, the phrase "actual prosecution of the war" is somewhat vague—and the president argues that virtually everything he does to fight terrorism—electronic surveillance, indefinite detention of prisoners at Guantanamo and elsewhere, or extraordinary rendition—are matters relating to the actual prosecution of the war.

But in the context of the opinion, it is clear that the plurality distinguishes military actions taken on or near the battlefield and military decisions about individuals detained far from the actual fighting. The plurality distinguished between "initial captures on the battlefield," which the parties agreed need not receive due process, and the process required "when the determination is made to *continue* to hold those who have been seized."[33] In the latter circumstances, the Court rejected the government's assertion that the Court's role must be "heavily circumscribed."[34] The *Hamdi* plurality made clear that "what are the allowable limits of military discretion, and whether they have been overstepped in a particular case, are judicial questions."[35] In ringing words it proclaimed that "we have long since made clear that a state of war is not a blank check for the President when it comes to the rights of the Nation's citizens."[36]

The Court's decreasing deference to executive wartime determinations made away from the battlefield can also be seen in the *Hamdi*'s plurality emphasis on the narrow "context" of that case: "A United States citizen captured in a *foreign* combat zone."[37] The plurality's emphasis on Hamdi's battlefield capture came in response to the four dissenters who argued that the president has no power at all—either under the Non-Detention Act or the Constitution—to detain an American citizen as an enemy combatant and suggests that at least some justices in the plurality might have agreed with the dissenters in the case of Jose Padilla, an American citizen who was not captured on a foreign battlefield but rather detained at the Chicago airport. The administration claims that the "battlefield" in its global war against terrorism is worldwide, including the United States, but the *Hamdi* plurality defined the battlefield in that case as the armed conflict taking place in Afghanistan. While the Fourth Circuit Court of Appeals later concluded that Padilla could be detained as an enemy combatant even though he was detained in the United States because he was at one time "armed and present in a combat zone during armed conflict," the Second Circuit had reached the contrary conclusion prior to the *Hamdi* decision.[38] Apparently the government was sufficiently concerned that the Supreme Court would reverse the Fourth Circuit that they avoided Supreme Court review of Padilla's case by releasing him from detention as an enemy combatant and charging him with a crime—one having nothing to do with the enemy combatant charge—prior to the Supreme Court's taking up Padilla's appeal from the Fourth Circuit ruling.

Finally, in *Rasul v. Bush*, Justice Kennedy's concurrence again articulates the theme of the absence of direct military necessity which underlies much of the opinions in both *Hamdi* and *Hamdan*. Kennedy argued that the Court's assertion of habeas jurisdiction over the Guantanamo detainees in that case was warranted in part because the government's indefinite detention without trial or other legal proceedings of the detainees presented a "weaker case of military necessity. . . . Perhaps, where detainees are taken from a zone of hostilities, detention without proceedings or trial would be justified by military necessity for a matter of weeks; but as the period of detention stretches from months to years, the case for continued detention to meet military exigencies becomes weaker."[39] Similar, but unarticulated, reasoning undoubtedly motivated the majority to reject the government's claim that the assertion of habeas jurisdiction would impermissibly interfere with the president's ability to wage the war against terrorism.

War and Judicial Competence

Scholars such as John Yoo or Richard Posner argue for "a light judicial hand in national security matters," or for the judiciary to abstain altogether in wartime challenges to executive policies (Posner 2006, 35–37; Yoo 1996). Yoo views the *Hamdi* and *Rasul* decisions "as an unprecedented formal and functional intrusion by the federal courts into the executive's traditional powers" that will take the courts "far beyond their normal areas of expertise" (Yoo 2006, 574–75).

These scholars emphasize the judiciary's institutional deficiencies in addressing war or national security matters. Judges are generalists, unlike congressional committees or executive bureaucracies that focus on national security issues. The judiciary, unlike the Defense Department or the Senate Foreign Relations Committee, has no machinery for the systematic study of an issue. And Yoo argues that the federal judiciary is a decentralized, slow, deliberate body which erects substantial doctrinal and resource barriers on parties seeking access and whose ability to acquire and process information is more limited than the political branches (Yoo 2006, 592–600).

These critiques of judicial competence in war, national security, or foreign affairs matters ignore central and critical functions of the judiciary that are important both in wartime and times of peace. The judiciary is the one branch uniquely situated to police the legal limits imposed on executive discretion over military or national security matters. While the executive clearly has greater discretion in times of war, its power is not unbounded and still is limited by law. Determining what those legal limits are and how they apply in particular cases are often issues that involve the judiciary's expertise and experience. Issues such as whether the president has the power to detain American citizens as enemy combatants, can hold detainees indefinitely without according them fair hearings, can try detainees by means of military commissions that permit evidence obtained by torture or other coercive means to be admitted, or whether detainees can be subjected to torture or other cruel and inhumane methods of interrogation are not matters beyond the competence of judges.

Moreover, war as well as peace requires structural checks on executive overreaching, perhaps even more so because of the greater dangers of executive aggrandizement of power during wartime. Despite the arguments of those such as Yoo and Posner that either the Congress or executive branch itself can provide adequate checks, this safeguard certainly has not proven adequate during the current conflict against terrorism. Congress has been quiescent, providing virtually no check or oversight of the president's treatment, detention, or proposed military trials of enemy combatants until the Supreme Court entered the fray. Nor has Congress challenged the president's policy of extraordinary rendition, in which the executive sends suspected terrorists to countries where they will be tortured and detained indefinitely without judicial process. Indeed, even after the Supreme Court forced Congress to grapple with the defects of the administration's proposed military commissions, Congress enacted a statute that many senators believed was unconstitutional. The chairman of the Senate Judiciary Committee voted for the statute and justified his vote by stating that "the court will clean it up" (Lithwick and Schragger 2006; *Los Angeles Times* 2006).

Moreover, institutional, legal, and political checks within the executive branch have been even less effective. The Office of Legal Counsel, an institutional check within the Justice Department which is supposed to provide independent legal advice, produced secret memos written by handpicked political appointees providing advice that conformed to the bottom line their superiors desired (Pillard 2006, 1297). When the Bybee Torture Memo, which was never intended to be publicly disclosed, was leaked to the press, the resulting firestorm of criticism caused it to be withdrawn.

This problem is not limited to this administration; for decades the executive branch has sought to keep the legal advising process confidential (Pillard 2006, 1302). Moreover, the administration's discussions of legal strategy after September 11 largely excluded the military lawyers and foreign-policy officials who presumably had the expertise that Yoo or Posner believe places the executive at a comparative advantage over judges in national security matters (Golden 2004, § 1, 1; Mayer 2006). For example, when some of the military lawyers protested the administration's detainee policies, they were generally ignored by the small coterie of high-level officials who were driving the policies (Mayer 2006). The public deliberation and rational argumentation of differing opinions that characterize judicial proceedings are an institutional strength of the judiciary that has been sorely lacking in the administration's determination of legal strategy in fighting terrorism. While troop movements, battle plans, and military strategies ought to be kept secret and out of the Court's purview, legal issues and strategies, such as the definition of torture, the constitutional authority of the president to violate or suspend treaties or authorize torture, and the applicability of the Geneva Conventions in the current fight against terrorism, are matters best resolved in the course of open dialogue and debate that the judiciary, not the executive, is most institutionally attuned to.

Conclusion

The Supreme Court's assertion of judicial power to review the president's enemy combatant policies is consistent with the constitutional design to limit and provide checks on executive power, both in wartime and in peace. It is also consistent with the early judiciary's assertiveness in deciding cases challenging executive wartime decisions. But the Court's decisions nonetheless surprised many observers, perhaps because of the all too often tendency of the modern judiciary to defer to executive wartime decisions.

Commentators have offered various theories to explain the Court's muscular approach to the enemy combatant cases. Perhaps the Court has learned from the lessons of the past; maybe the Court's prior wartime precedents restraining executive power such as *Milligan* or *Youngstown Sheet & Tube* played a role in the Court's reaching the conclusions it did. Or it may be that these decisions are the result of the very slowness of the judicial process that Yoo describes—namely that the delay of three to five years between September 11, and these Court decisions meant that the Court could decide these cases when the sense of crisis had already somewhat passed. It could also be that these decisions are the product of the more general assertiveness of the late-20th-century judiciary. Such explanations have been proffered by various commentators (Waxman 2005, 1).

But perhaps these Court decisions are a reaction to the executive's claim that, in this new kind of war against terror, no law applies to the treatment of enemy combatants. The administration claims that we are at war and that neither the Constitution nor the normal human rights law applicable to peace time governs the treatment of enemy combatants. But at the same time, the administration also argues that the normal laws of war—the Geneva Conventions, the rules governing prisoners of war—do not apply because these prisoners are unlawful enemy combatants and the normal rules of war do not apply to our fight against al Qaeda. According to the administration's assertions, no law governs and whatever treatment is accorded to these prisoners is purely a matter of administration discretion. These prisoners were in what amounted to a legal black hole.

The Court pushed back against the executive's argument that these prisoners could be held totally outside of the rule of law and that there could be no review, or only extremely deferential reviews, of their detention. The administration's argument that this was a new kind of war against a nontraditional enemy ironically suggests that more robust review of the administration's detention policies is required. This new kind of war is likely to drag on for many years, decades, or generations. In this conflict, the traditional boundary lines separating war and peace, civilian and combatant, battlefield and home front have been blurred, perhaps beyond recognition, leading to both a higher chance of military error in deciding who to detain and the possibility of lifetime detention for innocent people erroneously detained. In these circumstances, the need for judicial review is greater than in past wars.

A guiding principle of the U.S. Constitution is that the government is one of limited powers. President Bush claimed virtually unlimited, unchecked power to detain and try people the government believed to be enemy combatants. It fell to the Court to tell the president that he was wrong.

Endnotes

1. *Little v. Barreme,* 6 U.S. (2 Cranch) 170 (1804).
2. *Bas v. Tingy,* 4 U.S. (Dallas) 37, 43 (1800) (emphasis added).
3. Ibid., 40 (emphasis added).
4. Ibid., 45.
5. *Talbot v. Seeman,* 5 U.S. (1 Cranch) 1 (1800).
6. Ibid., 28.
7. *United States v. Smith,* 27 F. Cas. 1192, 1230 (C.C.D.N.Y. 1806).
8. *Brown v. United States,* 12 U.S. (8 Cranch) 110, 126 (1814).
9. Ibid. (emphasis added).
10. Ibid., 129.
11. Ibid., 145.
12. Ibid., 128–29.
13. *The Apollon,* 22 U.S. (9 Wheat.) 362, 366–67 (1824).
14. *Mitchell v. Harmony,* 54 U.S. (13 How.) 115 (1851).

15. Ibid., 134–35.
16. In *Martin v. Mott*, 25 U.S. (12 Wheat.) 19 (1827), the Supreme Court did refuse to decide whether an emergency existed justifying the president's calling the militia into actual service, thus illustrating that the Court was, at times, reluctant to adjudicate executive use of emergency power. In *Martin*, however, the issue was not the executive's *independent* power: Congress had clearly authorized the president's actions. Instead, the issue was whether a soldier could refuse an executive order because he did not believe an emergency existed.
17. *Korematsu v. United States*, 323 U.S. 214 (1944).
18. *Chicago & Southern Air Lines, Inc. v. Waterman Steamship Corp.*, 333 U.S. 103 (1948).
19. *Hamdan v. Rumsfeld*, 126 S. Ct. 2749 (2006).
20. Ibid., 2777.
21. Ibid., 2782.
22. Ibid., 2785.
23. Ibid.
24. Ibid., 2793.
25. Ibid., 2801 (Kennedy, J., concurring in part).
26. Ibid., 2805, 2807–08.
27. Ibid., 2826 (Thomas, J., dissenting).
28. Ibid., 2838.
29. Ibid., 2843 (citing *Chicago & Southern Air Lines, Inc. v. Waterman Steamship Corp.*, 333 U.S. 103 [1948]).
30. Ibid., 2822 (Scalia, J., dissenting) (emphasis added).
31. *Hamdi v. Rumsfeld*, 542 U.S. 507 (2004).
32. Ibid., 535 (plurality opinion).
33. Ibid., 534 (emphasis in original).
34. Ibid., 535.
35. Ibid. (quoting *Sterling v. Constantin*, 287 U.S. 378, 401 [1932]).
36. Ibid., 536.
37. Ibid., 523.
38. *Padilla v. Hanft*, 423 F.2d 386 (4th Cir. 2005), cert. denied, 126 S. Ct. 1649 (2006); *Padilla v. Rumsfeld*, 352 F.2d 695 (2d Cir. 2003), rev'd on other grounds, 124 S. Ct. 2711 (2004).
39. *Rasul v. Bush*, 542 U.S. 466, 488 (2004) (Kennedy, J., concurring).

References

Adler, David Gray. 2006. "The Law: George Bush as Commander in Chief: Toward the Nether World of Constitutionalism," *Presidential Studies Quarterly* 36: 525–40.

Bradley, Curtis A., and Martin S. Flaherty. 2004. "Executive Power Essentialism and Foreign Affairs," *Michigan Law Review* 102: 545.

Bush, George W. 2005. "Statement on Signing of H.R. 2863, December 30. The Department of Defense, Emergency Supplemental Appropriations to Address Hurricanes in the Gulf of Mexico, and Pandemic Influenza Act, 2006," *Weekly Compilation of Presidential Documents* 41: 52.

Dennison, George M. 1974. "Martial Law: The Development of a Theory of Emergency Powers," 1776–1861. *American Journal of Legal History* 18: 52.

Editorial. 2006. "Careless Congress: Lawmakers Passed a Detainee Law of Doubtful Constitutionality Now They Expect the Courts to Clean It Up," *Los Angeles Times*, November 3, 28.

Farrand, Max, ed. 1996. *The Records of the Federalist Convention of 1787*, 4 vols., reprint. New Haven, CT: Yale University Press.

Fisher, Louis. 2006. "Lost Constitutional Moorings: Recovering the War Powers," *Indiana Law Journal* 81: 1199.

Golden, Tim. 2004. "Threats and Responses: Tough Justice; after Terror, a Secret Rewriting of Military Law," *The New York Times*, October 24, § 1, 1.

Hamilton, Alexander, James Madison, and John Jay. 1937. *The Federalist*. New York: Modern Library.

Keynes, Edward. 1982. *Undeclared War, Twilight Zone of Constitutional Power*. University Park, PA: Penn State University Press.

Jefferson, Thomas. 1810. Letter from Jefferson to Colvin, September 20. In *The Works of Thomas Jefferson*, vol. 11, edited by Paul Leicester Ford. 1905. New York: G. P. Putnam.

Lithwick, Dahlia, and Richard Schragger. 2006. "Congress Behaving Badly," *The Washington Post*, October 8, B2.

Lobel, Jules. 1989. "Emergency Power and the Decline of Liberalism," *Yale Law Journal* 98: 1385.

Locke, John. 1960. *Two Treatises of Government*, edited by P. Laslett. Cambridge, UK: Cambridge University Press.

May, Christopher. 1989. *In the Name of War: Judicial Review and the War Powers since 1918*. Cambridge, MA: Harvard University Press.

Mayer, Jane. 2006. "Annals of the Pentagon," *New Yorker*, February 27, 32.

Pillard, Cornelia. 2006. "Unitariness and Myopia: The Executive Branch, Legal Process and Torture," *Indiana Law Journal* 81: 1297.

Posner, Richard A. 2006. *Not a Suicide Pact: The Constitution in a Time of National Emergency*. New York: Oxford University Press.

Richardson, J., ed. 1897. *Compilation of the Messages and Papers of the Presidents*, vol. 1. New York: Bureau of National Literature.

Savage, Charlie. 2006. "Bush Could Bypass New Torture Ban," *Boston Globe*, January 4, A1.

Schlesinger, Arthur. 1973. *The Imperial Presidency*. Boston: Houghton Mifflin.

Sofaer, Abraham. 1976. "The Presidency, War, and Foreign Affairs: Practice under the Framers," *Law & Contemporary Problems* 40: 12.

Sofaer, Abraham. 1981. "Emergency Power and the Hero of New Orleans," *Cardozo Law Review* 2: 233.

U.S. Department of Defense. 2003. "Working Group Report on Detainee Interrogations in the Global War on Terrorism: Assessment of Legal, Historical, Policy, and Operational Considerations," April 4. Available from http://www.washingtonpost.com/wp-srv/nation/documents/040403dod.pdf.

U.S. Department of Justice. 2002a. Memorandum from John Yoo, deputy assistant attorney general and Robert J. Delahunty, special counsel, to William J. Haynes II, general counsel, Department of Defense, re: Application of treaties and laws to al Qaeda and Taliban detainees. January 9. Available from http://www.texscience.org/reform/torture/yoo-delahunty-9jan02.pdf.

U.S. Department of Justice. 2002b. Memorandum from Jay S. Bybee, assistant attorney general, Office of Legal Counsel, to Alberto R. Gonzales, counsel to the president, re: Standards of conduct for interrogation under 18 U.S.C. §§ 2340–2340A. August 1. Available from http://www.texscience.org/reform/torture/bybee-olc-torture-1aug02.pdf.

U.S. Department of Justice. 2004. Memorandum from Daniel Levin, acting assistant attorney general, Office of Legal Counsel, to James B. Comey, deputy attorney general, re: Legal standards applicable under 18 U.S.C. §§ 2340–2340A. December 30. Available from http://www.usdoj.gov/olc/dagmemo.pdf.

U.S. Department of Justice. 2006a. "Legal authorities Supporting the Activities of the National Security Agency Described by the President," January 19. Reprinted in *Indiana Law Journal* 81: 1374, 1376. Also available from http://www.usdoj.gov/opa/whitepaperonnsalegalauthorities.pdf.

U.S. Department of Justice. 2006b. *Hamdan v. Rumsfeld*. Brief for respondents.

Waxman, Seth P. 2005. *The Combatant Detention Trilogy through the Lenses of History in Terrorism, the Laws of War, and the Constitution*, edited by Peter Berkowitz. Stanford, CA: Hoover Institution Press.

Wilmerding, Lucius, Jr. 1952. "The President and the Law," *Political Science Quarterly* 67: 321.

Yoo, John C. 1996. "The Continuation of Politics by Other Means: The Original Understanding of War Powers," *California Law Review* 84: 167.

Yoo, John C. 2006. "Courts at War," *Cornell Law Review* 91: 573.

S E C T I O N

9

EVALUATING PRESIDENTS: GREATNESS AND ABUSE OF POWER

The presidency looms large in American politics, and Americans have delegated much power to their presidents. This power is not only legal and constitutional; it also is the power to affect our well-being, whether by influencing the economy or by taking the nation to war. One of the more profound presidential powers, however, is the effect that presidents have on our national psychology—whether we are complaining about how bad things are or are inspired to press on with open hearts to make progress against the very real problems that our nation (and all others) constantly face. Thus, the questions of presidential greatness and abuse of power are important issues for the United States. Presidents can call forth from Americans their best efforts and most positive instincts, or they can lead us into cynicism when they betray our trust. This section considers the issue of public attitudes toward presidents, and the various selections tell us about the importance of public trust in our presidents.

In the first selection, James P. Pfiffner puts into perspective three major scandals of the modern presidency: Watergate, Iran-Contra, and the impeachment of President Clinton. Each of these three crises called into question the judgment of the presidents involved, raised issues of impeachment, and were caused by the individual presidents themselves—not by their political "enemies." In examining the basic facts of each case, Pfiffner analyzes each president's motives and the consequences of their actions. He points out the irony that each president was hurt more by their initial denials and cover-up than if they had immediately admitted the truth about their previous behavior. But more profoundly, none of the breaches of trust of these presidents was necessary or achieved the goals that they sought. This selection serves as a reminder that the power we place in the presidency can raise powerful temptations for abuse, and that the "auxiliary precautions" of which James Madison wrote in Federalist No. 51 are still necessary.

The selection by Thomas Cronin and Michael Genovese raises explicitly the paradox that our chief executive must be powerful enough to lead the country yet must also be accountable to the people. The beginning of their title, "If Men Were Angels," comes from James Madison's classic formulation in Federalist No. 51:

> If men were angels, no government would be necessary. If angels were to govern man, neither external nor internal controls on government would be necessary. In framing a government which is to be administered by men over men, the great difficulty lies in this: you must first enable the government to control the governed; and in the next place oblige it to control itself. A dependence on the people is, no doubt, the primary control on the government; but experience has taught mankind the necessity of auxiliary precautions.

The authors observe that Americans yearn for strong leaders who will take charge and lead us where we want to go, but they also point out the "anti-government, anti-leadership, chronic-complainer syndrome" that is an inherent part of the American political tradition. They argue that one of the ways to tie the American government more closely to the American people is a strong political party system that would help overcome gridlock and make the government more responsive to the electorate. Ultimately, they argue, the American political system depends upon the quality of the citizenry. If citizens are engaged with their government, we can have both a strong presidency and democratic accountability; both are necessary for a successful polity.

In his article, "The Worst President in History?" Princeton historian Sean Wilentz argues that the Bush administration may be remembered as "a colossal historical disgrace." He compares the Bush record with past presidents who have been considered failures by historians and those who have been judged successful. The choice to pursue a preventive war in Iraq was the primary cause of the Bush Administration's problems, argues Wilentz. The increase in annual deficits and the cumulative national debt left the nation in a weak economic position, and the president's excessive claims to constitutional powers have weakened the separation of powers system.

On the other hand, Karl Rove argues in the next selection that if we take "the long view," President Bush will be remembered favorably by future generations. Rove was long-time aide to George W. Bush when he was governor of Texas, and he engineered Bush's electoral victories in 2000 and 2004. He notes that Presidents Truman and Eisenhower were both criticized when they were in office, but in later decades they were both considered to be among the more successful presidents. In Rove's judgment, President Bush will be remembered as a far-sighted leader who defended the United States in its struggle with radical Islamic terrorists. Historians will also praise Bush for his market-oriented domestic policies. These two articles by Wilentz and Rove provide sharply contrasting portraits of President Bush and his record. It will not be for many years that we will know for certain which author was more accurate.

In the final selection in the book, Andrew Rudalevige presents a historical overview of presidential power, with an emphasis on the modern presidency. He makes it clear that the issue is not a simple one and that the American people want the president to have sufficient power to be able to act to protect national security, but that they are also suspicious of executive power that might be used to infringe upon civil liberties held dear by Americans. The balance of power between Congress and the president has been a continuing theme in American politics, and during the Bush presidency the pendulum swung toward the president.

Selected Bibliography

Abshire, David, *Saving the Reagan Presidency* (College Station, TX: Texas A&M University Press, 2005).
Bailey, Thomas A., *Presidential Greatness* (New York: Appleton-Century-Crofts, 1966).
Barber, James David, *The Presidential Character,* 4th ed. (Englewood Cliffs, NJ: Prentice-Hall, 1992).
Barger, Harold M., *The Impossible Presidency* (Glenview, IL: Scott, Foresman, 1984).
Bose, Meena, and Mark Landis, *The Uses and Misuses of Presidential Ratings* (NY: Nova Science, 2003).
Brace, Paul, and Barbara Hinckley, *Follow the Leader* (New York: Basic Books, 1992).
Edwards, George C., and Philip John Davies, *New Challenges for the American Presidency* (NY: Longman, 2004).
Genovese, Michael, *The Presidential Dilemma* (New York: HarperCollins, 1995).
Lowi, Theodore, *The Personal President* (Ithaca, New York: Cornell University Press, 1985).
Mansfield, Harvey C., *Taming the Prince* (New York: Free Press, 1989).
Pfiffner, James P., *The Character Factor: How We Judge America's Presidents* (College Station: Texas A&M University Press, 2004).
Rockman, Bert A., *The Leadership Question: The Presidency in the American System* (New York: Praeger, 1984).
Rudalevige, Andrew., *The New Imperial Presidency* (Ann Arbor: University of Michigan Press, 2005).
Schlesinger, Arthur M. Jr., *The Imperial Presidency* (Boston: Houghton Mifflin, 1973).

James P. Pfiffner

Three Crises of Character in the Modern Presidency

Three major crises of confidence have shaken the modern presidency—Watergate, Iran-Contra, and President Clinton's impeachment—each of them caused not by external threats but by presidential decisions. Each of them led to serious consideration of impeachment and removal of the president from office: Nixon resigned in the face of virtually certain impeachment; Reagan saved himself by getting the truth out; and Clinton was impeached though not removed from office.[1]

These crises were rooted in the character of the presidents involved. Watergate was based in Richard Nixon's resentment of his political "enemies" and his paranoia about how they were thwarting him. He was willing to use illegal tactics in order to get back at his political enemies, and he was willing to lie to cover up the illegal actions. The diversion of funds to the Contras was allowed to happen because President Reagan either did not care or did not bother to find out what his subordinates were doing in his name. Bill Clinton was impeached, because he was willing to risk an illicit relationship and was unwilling to take responsibility for his behavior. He was willing to lie about it and encourage others to lie for him.

Each of the cases will be examined from the perspective of the president's motives, what happened in the crisis, and its consequences. The three cases will then be compared with respect to the key presidential decisions, the ironies of the outcomes, the personal culpability of each president, and finally the relative threats to the Constitution and the polity presented by the crises. The conclusion will be that each of the three presidents was guilty of serious missteps, but that President Reagan handled his crisis better by taking serious steps to get the truth out and that President Clinton's transgressions did not present as serious a threat to the Constitution as the other two crises.

Source: Essay prepared for this volume. Revised from essays in David Abshire, ed. *Triumphs and Tragedies of the Modern Presidency* (Washington: Center for the Study of the Presidency, 2000).

Watergate

What Happened

One key turning point came early in President Nixon's administration when Daniel Ellsberg, a former defense analyst, leaked to the media a lengthy internal analysis of early U.S. policy toward Vietnam. The collection of documents became known as the "Pentagon Papers" and was concerned with policymaking before Nixon became president. Nixon decided that the release of the documents was an unacceptable breach of security and ordered his aides to do something about it. In 1969, he told John Ehrlichman to establish "a little group right here in the White House. Have them get off their tails and find out what's going on and figure out how to stop it."[2] This "little group" became the "plumbers" who would figure out how to stop leaks and carry out other tasks of political intelligence and sabotage.

In order to discredit Daniel Ellsberg, Nixon operatives broke into the office of his psychiatrist in Los Angeles. Though they did not find anything useful, their intention probably was to find and release embarrassing information about Ellsberg in order to affect his trial for violating security regulations. Breaking and entering is, of course, a crime, and this attempt to deprive Ellsberg of his civil rights was included in Article II of the House Judiciary Committee impeachment charges. Nixon also encouraged breaking into the Brookings Institution to seize documents of those he thought were working on the Pentagon Papers.

The plumbers, who were funded from campaign funds and through the Committee to Reelect the President (CREEP), were to undertake a number of political intelligence operations, including the bugging of the office of Larry O'Brien at the Democratic National Headquarters in the Watergate Building. The political parties' national headquarters are not the most likely places to find valuable political intelligence, and the Nixon people probably were more interested in finding an illegitimate connection between Larry O'Brien and Howard Hughes. After the election in 1968, Nixon had received an illegal campaign contribution from Howard Hughes. But at the same time Hughes also paid Larry O'Brien on a retainer. Thus, information about the O'Brien-Hughes connection could be used to counter any Democratic disclosure or condemnation of the Nixon-Hughes connection.[3]

On the night of June 17, 1972, five of the plumbers, under the direction of Howard Hunt and Gordon Liddy, broke into the Democratic National Committee (DNC) headquarters in the Watergate building to repair a listening device they had previously set. After they were discovered and arrested, the trail led back to CREEP and the White House. The cover-up of this break-in was what eventually brought down President Nixon.

In addition to these events, the Nixon White House and reelection campaign undertook a number of other measures that are broadly covered under the rubric of Watergate. Among these were "dirty tricks" to affect the 1972 Democratic primary elections. Because Nixon judged that Senator Edmund Muskie would be his strongest opponent, his operatives tried to undermine Muskie's campaign by disrupting campaign rallies, forging letters, and financing his opponents.[4] White House officials tried to get the Internal Revenue Service (IRS) to undertake audits on Democratic opponents and their supporters. A plan for political intelligence and operations was approved by Nixon but never implemented.[5] Nixon's counsel, John Dean, and others drew up lists of political "enemies" who were to be targets of political retaliation.

Among all of these illicit activities, what eventually brought down President Nixon was his involvement with the cover-up of the crimes. Nixon never seemed to consider seriously the possibility of denouncing the break-in and promising that the White House would not conduct any such activities in the future. Nixon's lawyer, Leonard Garment, recalled:

> The transition from bungled break-in to cover-up took place automatically, without discussion, debate, or even the whisper of gears shifting, because the president was personally involved, if not in the Watergate break-in then by authorizing prior Colson and plumber activities like the Ellsberg break-in and a crazy Colson plot to firebomb the Brookings Institution in order to recover a set of the Pentagon Papers. These were potentially more lethal than Watergate. Other factors contributed to the cover-up, but I have no doubt that the main motive was Nixon's sense of personal jeopardy. His decision was not irrational, though it turned out terribly wrong.[6]

In retrospect, Nixon argued that the actions of Watergate participants themselves were minor, but the cover-up was his big mistake.[7] But he was wrong; the illegal activities, including breaking and entering, conducted by a secret White House intelligence unit were serious abuses of power. That is why Nixon felt that the Watergate break-in had to be concealed at all costs. A thorough investigation of Watergate would have opened up the whole "can of worms" that included the other illegal abuses of power in the Nixon White House. And that, in fact, is what did happen to the Nixon administration.

The Consequences

When the Watergate burglars were arrested, they did not admit that they were working for Nixon's reelection campaign, because they had been assured by Gordon Liddy that they would be taken care of and their prison sentences would be minor if it came to that. But Judge "Maximum John" Sirica gave them long prison sentences because he suspected that their silence was protecting their superiors. This led to John Dean's discussion with the president about hush money for the jailed plumbers. Dean told the president that it might cost $1 million to keep them quiet. Nixon replied: "We could get that. On the money, if you need the money you could get that. You could get a million dollars. You could get it in cash. I know where it could be gotten."[8] John Dean testified that $500,000 did go to Liddy and his men.[9]

The Senate Watergate Committee investigated many aspects of the White House activities and found out that President Nixon had set up a taping system in the White House. The tapes were subpoenaed by the special prosecutor and the House Impeachment Committee. Nixon sent to the committee transcripts of the tapes, but they had been altered in key places. Finally, the Supreme Court ruled that Nixon could not withhold the evidence on the tapes. The turning point in the House came when the "smoking gun" tape was discovered. Until that time, many

Republican members of the committee had argued that the evidence against Nixon was not conclusive and impeachment so serious a step that only conclusive proof of a crime was sufficient to vote in favor of impeachment.

In the tape of a conversation on June 23, 1972, just five days after the Watergate break-in, H. R. Haldeman told the president that FBI investigators were tracing the money carried by the Watergate burglars and were about to discover that it had come from CREEP and White House safes. He suggested that the way to stop the FBI investigation would be to have the CIA tell the FBI that further investigations would jeopardize CIA operations, and they should drop the money trail. Haldeman suggested that "the way to handle this now is for us to have Walters [of the CIA] call Pat Gray [Director of the FBI] and just say, 'Stay the hell out of this . . . this is ah, business here we don't want you to go any further on it.'" After this suggestion, Nixon told Haldeman to tell CIA director Richard Helms, "the president believes that it is going to open the whole Bay of Pigs thing up again. And . . . that they [the CIA] should call the FBI in and [unintelligible] don't go any further into this case period!"[10]

The release of the tapes and their damning evidence provided the final impetus for the House Judiciary Committee to vote articles of impeachment. Article I charged the president with failure to fulfill his oath of office and obstruction of justice. It mentioned specifically the break-in of Ellsberg's psychiatrist's office, misuse of the CIA to obstruct the Justice Department investigation, withholding evidence, and counseling perjury, among other things. Article II charged the president with failing to faithfully execute the laws by using the IRS to harass his political opponents, by using the FBI to place unlawful wiretaps on citizens, by maintaining a secret investigative unit in the White House paid for by campaign funds, and by impeding criminal investigations, among other things. Article III charged the president with refusing to honor congressional subpoenas lawfully issued by the House Judiciary Committee and impeding the Congress from constitutionally exercising its impeachment powers.

Two other articles were debated by the committee but rejected. One of the articles would have charged that the president, through the secret bombing of Cambodia during the Vietnam War, undermined the constitutional powers of Congress. The other article would have charged the president with income tax evasion when he backdated his report of the gift of his vice presidential papers to the national archives.[11] However, before the articles could be represented to the full House for action, President Nixon resigned and left office on August 9, 1974.

Iran-Contra

What Happened

In 1984 and 1985, seven U.S. hostages were kidnapped in Lebanon by Shiite Muslims closely connected to the leaders of Iran. Iran and Iraq were at war, and Iran had a desperate need for military equipment and spare parts to fix its weapons, many of which came from the United States during the period it supported the Shah of Iran. Intermediaries proposed a deal that would include the release of the hostages in exchange for the United States supplying spare airplane parts and missiles to Iran.

President Reagan had become extremely concerned with the plight of the hostages, one of whom was a CIA station chief. His concern was reflected by National Security Council (NSC) staffers, who made arrangements to exchange U.S. arms and spare parts for Iranian intervention to have the hostages in Lebanon released. NSC staffers also argued that it was important to try to reestablish U.S. ties to moderates in Iran so that when the Ayatollah Khomeini died, the U.S. would have some influence in Iran, which the U.S. did not want to fall under Soviet influence. Israel also wanted to support Iran in its war with Iraq, which Israel considered a greater security threat. So Israel agreed to ship arms to Iran, which would then be replaced by the U.S. The U.S. also shipped TOW missiles and HAWK missiles directly to Iran.

The president's decision to trade arms for hostages can be questioned on several grounds. First, the surface rationalization for the policy was to open relations with "moderates" in Iran. But it is doubtful that there were any moderates in powerful positions in Iran at the time. It was the CIA's judgment that Khomeini was in charge and that no one else would be allowed to negotiate with the Americans, especially about weapons.[12] Second, the U.S. had a firm policy not to negotiate with terrorists. In a 1985 speech, President Reagan said that Iran was part of a ". . . confederation of terrorist states . . . a new international version of Murder Inc. America will never make concessions to terrorists."[13] The Reagan administration had launched "Operation Staunch," a diplomatic campaign to stop U.S. allies in Europe from selling arms to Iran or Iraq.[14]

In a number of meetings in the White House, Secretary of State George Shultz and Secretary of Defense Caspar Weinberger argued strenuously against trading arms for hostages (e.g., on 8/6/85, 12/7/85, and 1/7/86).[15] While Weinberger and Shultz may have been right on the merits of the arguments, the elected president clearly had the authority to set policy in the executive branch. Members of the cabinet are merely advisors to the president and implementers of policy, and the president has no obligation to take their advice. On the other hand, sending arms to Iran raised the issue of the Arms Export Control Act of 1976, which prohibited the sale of U.S. arms to nations designated as sponsors of terrorism. Iran had been so designated since 1984. George Shultz asked his legal advisor, Abraham Sofaer, to consider the legality of the arms sale, and Sofaer concluded that such sales would not be legal.[16] In the December 7, 1985 meeting with the president and top aides, Casper Weinberger argued against the sale of arms and argued that it would violate the Arms Export Control Act.[17]

In addition, the National Security Act governing covert actions specified that covert actions were to be taken only after an official "finding" by the president that such action is important to national security.[18] National Security Advisor John Poindexter testified before Congress that President Reagan had signed such a finding for the earlier approaches to Iran but that Poindexter had later destroyed it to save the president from possible embarrassment. President Reagan also signed a finding on January 17, 1986 that authorized U.S. direct arms sales to Iran. The law provides that Congress is to be notified before covert actions are undertaken, or if that is impossible, "in a timely fashion."[19] Congress did not learn of the arms-for-hostages initiatives until they were disclosed in the Lebanese newspaper, *Al-Shiraa* on November 3, 1986.

The Reagan administration's actions to gain the release of the hostages over the course of several shipments of arms turned out to be futile. Several hostages were released, but three more hostages were captured. The courting of "moderates" in Iran was not successful because, first, there were no moderates in power and, second, some of the missiles were inferior equipment for which they charged artificially high prices.

In the Contra dimension of the Iran-Contra affair, White House aides, particularly national security advisor, Admiral Poindexter, and staffer Oliver North undertook to use the "profits" received from the sale of missiles to Iran to aid the Contras in Nicaragua. The problem was that Congress had passed, and President Reagan had signed, a law prohibiting the U.S. aid to the Contras. The so-called Boland Amendment (named for its author, Representative Edward P. Boland, D-Mass., chairman of the House Intelligence Committee) stated:

> During fiscal year 1985, no funds available to the Central Intelligence Agency, the Department of Defense, or any other agency or entity of the United States involved in intelligence activities may be obligated or expended for the purpose or which would have the effect of supporting, directly or indirectly, military or paramilitary operations in Nicaragua by any nation, group, organization, movement or individual.
> [Public Law 98–473, 98 STAT 1935–37, sec. 8066]

The law had not been passed without due deliberation in Congress. From the beginning of the 1980s, the Reagan administration felt the Sandinista government of Nicaragua posed a serious threat to U.S. national security interests, and support of the Contra opposition was a high priority of the administration. Financial and operational aid was provided to the Contras by the administration, but military aid was subject to a series of limitations written into public law between 1982 and 1986. Despite the best arguments of the Reagan administration, Congress was dubious of the wisdom and efficacy of continuing to arm the Contras. Thus, the Boland Amendment was passed for FY 1985.[20]

Despite the law, the administration was committed to continuing support of the Contras. President Reagan told national security advisor Robert McFarlane to keep the Contras together, "body and soul."[21] NSC staffer Oliver North proposed the "neat idea" of using the money received from the sale of arms to Iran to support the Contras by diverting the money from the U.S. treasury where it should have gone. To carry this out, North and his associates set up secret bank accounts to handle the money.

The Consequences

The secret attempt to fund the Contras was in direct violation of public law and a serious threat to the Constitution. The president's aides decided that what they could not achieve through the public constitutional process (continuing aid to the Contras) they would accomplish through secret means. There was no doubt about what the law prohibited; there had been a high level public debate over aid to the Contras throughout the 1980s, and the administration had not been able to convince a majority of the Congress that continued military aid to the Contras in 1985 was essential to U.S. security. But White House aides decided that aid to the Contras ought to continue. There is no doubt that President Reagan strongly supported aid to the Contras and that he communicated this directly to his staff. Reagan, however, denied any knowledge of the diversion of funds to the Contras, and there is no evidence that he knew about it before it was discovered by Attorney General Edwin Meese.

Revelation of arms-for-hostages deals and the diversion of funds to the Contras threw the administration into chaos for a number of months. Opinion polls showed that most Americans believed that President Reagan was lying when he denied that he had traded arms for hostages, and public approval of the president and his administration dropped significantly. Secretary of State Shultz concluded that Poindexter and North:

> . . . had entangled themselves with a gang of operators far more cunning and clever than they. As a result, the U.S. government had violated its own policies on antiterrorism and against arms sales to Iran, was buying our own citizens' freedom in a manner that could only *encourage* the taking of others, was working through disreputable international go-betweens, was circumventing our constitutional system of governance, and was misleading the American people—all in the guise of furthering some purported regional political transformation, or to obtain in actuality a hostage release. And somehow, by dressing up this arms-for-hostages scheme and disguising its worst aspects, first McFarlane, and then Poindexter, apparently with the strong collaboration of Bill Casey, had sold it to a president all too ready to accept it, given his humanitarian urge to free American hostages.[22]

Congress held hearings on the affair, and concluded that the affair was a disaster.

> In the end, there was no improved relationship with Iran, no lessening of its commitments to terrorism, and no fewer American hostages.
>
> The Iran initiative succeeded only in replacing three American hostages with another three, arming Iran with 2,004 TOWs and more than 200 vital spare parts for HAWK missile batteries, improperly generating funds for the Contras and other covert activities (although far less than North believed), producing profits for the Hakim-Secord Enterprise that in fact belonged to the U.S. taxpayers, leading certain NSC and CIA personnel to deceive representatives of their own Government, undermining U.S. credibility in the eyes of the world, damaging relations between the Executive and the Congress, and engulfing the President in one of the worst credibility crises of an Administration in U.S. history.[23]

Although the possibility of impeachment was discussed in both the executive and the legislative branch, it was not pursued by Congress. The feeling in Congress was that the country was not ready to go through another trauma so soon after the Watergate affair. In addition, there was no evidence that President Reagan knew about the diversion of funds to the Contras before it happened, the most likely grounds for impeachment. The other aspects of the opening to Iran, despite possible illegality, were not serious enough for impeachment proceedings. In addition, President Reagan did not stonewall the investigations, as Presidents Nixon and Clinton did. He established the Tower Board to investigate the matter; he brought in Special Counsel David Abshire to ensure that there would be no cover-up; and when Howard Baker became chief of staff, there was an exhaustive internal investigation.[24] He refused to claim executive privilege and turned over documents to the independent counsel and congressional investigators. Thus, President Reagan salvaged his presidency from what might have been far worse consequences.

President Clinton's Impeachment

What Happened

Shortly after graduating from college in June 1995, Monica Lewinsky came to work in the White House as one of many interns. According to her account, she and the president began having an affair in November of that year, and she received a salaried position in the Office of Legislative Affairs. By April 1996, some White House staffers felt she was seeing the president too often and had her transferred to a public affairs job in the Pentagon. Over the next 21 months, White House logs recorded that she was cleared to enter the White House 37 times.[25] While at the Pentagon, Lewinsky made friends with a former White House secretary, Linda Tripp, who also worked in the Pentagon. Tripp had been the source for a news story about an encounter between President Clinton and Kathleen Willey in the White House, and when her credibility was questioned by the president's lawyer in the fall of 1997, she began to tape her phone conversations with Lewinsky. The tapes contained assertions by Lewinsky about her relationship with the president and her frustration, because he was not calling her.

In the meantime, the suit brought against the president by Paula Jones had been under way for several years. Jones alleged that in a 1999 encounter in a Little Rock hotel room, then-Governor Clinton had crudely propositioned her and that she had turned him down. The suit was a civil action alleging sexual harassment. In the course of building their case, Jones's lawyers were gathering evidence about other women with whom Clinton might have had relationships over the years in order to demonstrate a pattern of sexual harassment.

The president gave a deposition in the Paula Jones lawsuit on January 17, 1998. With knowledge of the Tripp-Lewinsky tapes, the lawyers for Paula Jones asked Clinton if he had had sex with Lewinsky. When asked about an affair, Clinton denied a sexual relationship, providing the grounds for charges of perjury and eventual impeachment if Starr could prove that they had in fact had a sexual relationship. Having sex with an intern is not illegal (however wrong it might be), but intentionally lying about it in a civil deposition could constitute perjury. Thus, the question by Jones's lawyers about Lewinsky set Clinton up for a possible perjury charge. Based on the tapes, Starr suspected that Clinton might have tried illegally to cover up their affair.

On January 21, 1998, the story of the tapes and Lewinsky's conversations with Tripp became public, and the media began a feeding frenzy about all aspects of the scandal. President Clinton, in a strong statement, publicly denied that he had a sexual relationship with Lewinsky. "I want you to listen to me. I'm going to say this again. I did not have sexual relations with that woman, Miss Lewinsky. I never told anybody to lie—not a single time, never. These allegations are false. And I need to go back to work for the American people."[26]

Special Counsel Kenneth Starr's investigation of Clinton continued through the spring and summer of 1998. In July, Starr came to an immunity agreement with Monica Lewinsky, assuring her that she would not be prosecuted based on her testimony about her relationship with Clinton. Lewinsky testified in detail about their relationship and provided evidence that convinced the grand jury that she and Clinton had had a sexual relationship. Based on evidence from the Lewinsky testimony, Starr sought to subpoena the president to testify before a grand jury.

The Consequences

In the face of the subpoena, President Clinton agreed to testify "voluntarily" before Kenneth Starr's grand jury on August 17, 1998, about his relationship with Monica Lewinsky. During four hours of close questioning by Starr's lawyers, President Clinton carefully answered most questions but still maintained that he had not lied in his denial of a sexual relationship with Monica Lewinsky, and the president was clearly equivocating in his answers to some questions about their relationship.

In the evening, after his deposition, however, the president made a statement in a nationally televised broadcast about his testimony. In his statement, he told the nation that he regretted his relationship with Lewinsky and its consequences. "Indeed, I did have a relationship with Miss Lewinsky that was not appropriate. In fact, it was wrong. It constituted a critical lapse in judgment and a personal failure on my part for which I am solely and completely responsible. . . . I know that my public comments and my silence about this matter gave a false impression. I misled people, including even my wife. I deeply regret that." In his statement, Clinton also criticized Kenneth Starr for his relentless pursuit of evidence: "It is time to stop the pursuit of personal destruction and the prying into private lives and get on with our national life."

Several weeks later on September 9, Kenneth Starr sent his report to Congress concerning possible impeachable offenses by President Clinton. The list of charges included allegations that the president had lied under oath in his deposition in the Paula Jones sexual harassment case and in his testimony on August 17, that he had urged Lewinsky and his secretary to lie under oath, that he tried to obstruct justice by having his secretary hide evidence, and that he had tried to get Ms. Lewinsky a job to discourage her from revealing their relationship.

On October 5, the GOP-controlled House Judiciary Committee voted 21 to 16 along party lines to recommend impeachment hearings. Three days later, on October 8, the full House voted 258 to 176 (with 31 Democrats voting in favor and no Republicans against) to open an impeachment inquiry. On December 11 and 12, the Judiciary Committee voted along party lines in favor of four articles of impeachment. A Democratic motion to censure the president was easily defeated by the Republicans, and the articles were reported out to the full House.

The formal impeachment debate opened on December 18 on the floor of the House of Representatives, with the Republicans arguing that Clinton had corrupted the rule of law by committing perjury and obstructing justice and the Democrats arguing that he should be censured but not impeached. Democrats and moderate Republicans who felt that Clinton's actions were reprehensible, but not impeachable, wanted to vote to censure Clinton. Censure language was proposed by Democrats that harshly condemned Clinton for making "false statements concerning his reprehensible conduct and that he "violated the trust of the American people, lessened their esteem for the office of the president, and dishonored" the presidency.[27] But the motions for censure were not successful.

The House of Representatives met on December 19, 1998 and adopted two articles of impeachment. Article I charged that President Clinton "willfully provided perjurious, false and misleading testimony to the grand jury" on August 17, 1998 concerning his relationship with Monica Lewinsky and his attempts to cover it up. Article III charged that President Clinton "prevented, obstructed, and impeded the administration of justice" in order to "delay, impede, cover up, and conceal the existence of evidence and testimony" in the Paula Jones case by encouraging a witness to lie, by concealing evidence, and by trying to prevent truthful testimony by finding a job for Monica Lewinsky. Each of these articles concluded that "William Jefferson Clinton has undermined the integrity of his office, has brought disrepute on the presidency, has betrayed his trust as president, and has acted in a manner subversive of the rule of law and justice, to the manifest injury of the people of the United States." The two articles charging perjury in the Paula Jones deposition of January 17 and failure to respond adequately to congressional inquiries were defeated.

The trial in the Senate opened on January 7, 1999. The House impeachment brief argued that the president had indeed committed the crimes charged in the two articles—that he lied under oath before the grand jury investigating him on August 17, 1998 (Article I) and that he attempted to obstruct justice by encouraging Lewinsky to lie about their relationship, concealing evidence, and getting Lewinsky a job. On February 12, 1999, the final votes were taken, and neither of the articles received the two-thirds majority necessary for conviction and removal from office.

Comparing Three Presidents in Crises

Each one of these presidents, when faced with potentially damaging public revelations about their behavior, acted initially to limit the political damage to themselves and their administrations; and each chose paths of behavior that would threaten their presidencies. Admitting to the truth of the alleged improper behavior would have damaged their administrations, but their failures to respond truthfully led directly to much worse damage being done.

But at a deeper level, each president could not initially admit to himself that he had done anything wrong. Richard Nixon rationalized the actions of his administration by arguing that Democratic presidents had done the same thing and that his enemies were out to destroy him. Ronald Reagan rationalized his trading of arms for hostages by arguing that the hostages were merely a side issue in a strategic opening to Iran. Bill Clinton rationalized his lies by arguing that his enemies were out to get him, other presidents had done worse, his private life was not the public's business, and that he was technically telling the truth. Each of these sets of rationalization allowed the presidents to choose the path that would end up damaging them more than an initial admission would have.

The Key Decisions

Each president made initial key decisions that reflected character flaws that got them in trouble.

When he first heard about the Watergate break-in, Richard Nixon did not hesitate; he followed his first instinct, which was to limit the political damage and cover up the incident. His decision was based in part on a rational calculation that publication of the incident would hurt him politically and might uncover other damaging evidence of illegal behavior by other White House and reelection committee aides.

Ronald Reagan's initial reaction when the McFarlane trip to Iran was made public was to deny that there was any problem. The actions of his highest aides were merely intended to bring about an opening to Iran. He knew he did not approve of trading arms for hostages, so he concluded that he could not have done so. After weeks of publicity and press reports and after strong prodding by David Abshire and George Shultz, he finally was convinced that he had to tell the truth. He saved himself from further damage from the diversion of funds to the Contras by fully cooperating with the investigations, refusing to invoke executive privilege, and turning over requested documents. He thus stemmed the damage to his presidency in a way that the other two presidents did not. While the diversion of funds was a grave constitutional issue, it was done without President Reagan's knowledge.

Bill Clinton's first instinct was to deny his sexual relationship with Monica Lewinsky, just as he had with all previous allegations of sexual impropriety. He did seem to consider the possibility of telling the truth after the allegations became public; but after a poll by Dick Morris, he concluded that confessing to lying would have hurt him too much politically; so he embarked upon the firm policy of denial that resulted in his impeachment.

Ironies

The initial irony is that each president was hurt more by the denial and cover-up than they would have been if they had immediately admitted the truth about their previous behavior. The cost would have been quite high for each, but the truth did come out in the end and caused more harm at that late stage than an early admission would have.

But the more profound irony is that none of the three breaches of trust by presidents or their aides was necessary or achieved the goals that had been hoped for.

Richard Nixon needed no illegal help to prevail in 1972. Even if the Democrats had nominated Edmund Muskie, arguably their strongest candidate (they nominated George McGovern instead), Nixon's policies were popular enough to ensure his reelection. Thus the actions that led to the cover-up were unnecessary; it was only Nixon's paranoia and the tone he set that encouraged his aides to undertake the actions that eventually brought him down.

Ronald Reagan's selling of arms to Iran did not free the hostages; those who were freed were replaced by others. The selling of inferior arms at inflated prices did not endear the United States to Iran. Iran also had its own security reasons for not wanting to be pulled into the Soviet orbit. The diversion of funds from Iran to the Contras did not make a big difference in their ability to resist the government of Nicaragua. Only a small percentage of the funds intended for the Contras actually got to them.

Bill Clinton did not need to lie in his deposition in the Paula Jones case. The judge dismissed the case several months later even though it had been revealed that Clinton had lied. Neither did he need to lie directly to the American people in his finger-pointing statement. As became evident after his lies were revealed, public support for him was strong enough to weather that storm. Clinton's highest public approval ratings came during his impeachment and trial. His treatment of Kenneth Starr as his nemesis became a self-fulfilling prophecy when Starr pursued Clinton and revealed his most private and embarrassing actions.

They Did It to Themselves

Each president felt that his political enemies and the press were the cause of his troubles, but in fact each of these presidents was the primary cause of his own problems. A character flaw was the fundamental cause of each of their self-inflicted wounds.

Richard Nixon had developed deep suspicions about his political enemies and the tactics they would use to get him. But these suspicions were often projections of the tactics he used to get his enemies. Certainly Nixon did have political enemies and they wanted to beat him politically, but that is the nature of politics. Nixon's overreaction and actions against his enemies were the very things that accomplished what his enemies never could have: his resignation from the presidency in disgrace. Nixon's epiphany came in the last moments of his presidency in his farewell remarks just before leaving Washington: ". . . always remember, others may hate you, but those who hate you don't win unless you hate them, and then you destroy yourself."[28]

Ronald Reagan felt that the press was guilty of embarrassing him and undermining his attempts to repair relations with Iran. He felt that Congress tried to obstruct his policies and was generally irresponsible. Certainly Congress had different policy preferences than Reagan and passed laws of which he did not approve. But it was not the press or Congress that initiated the doomed arms for hostages initiative, and it was not their fault that North and Poindexter felt justified in breaking the law. It was Ronald Reagan's decision to trade arms for hostages, and it was his approach to policy direction and managing his White House that allowed his subordinates to pursue their illegal actions.

Bill Clinton had long blamed his enemies for working to bring him down. He felt that the press was hostile to him, and his wife blamed a "vast right wing conspiracy" for attempting to orchestrate his downfall. Certainly, Clinton had political enemies who were doing their best to undermine him. But it was not his political enemies who initiated his affair with Monica Lewinsky or led him to lie about it. It was his own denial of his actions and refusal to take responsibility for his own behavior that caused his disaster.

Threats to the Constitution and the Polity

The central themes in each of these crises of the presidency were: the rule of law, accountability to the Constitution, and abuse of power. The major threat in Watergate was to the domestic political process, the integrity of elections, and the civil rights of citizens. The major threat in Iran-Contra was to the constitutional role of

Congress, the obligation that the president take care to faithfully execute the laws, and accountability to the Constitution. The major threat in the Clinton case was the president's respect for the judicial process and his obligation to obey the law.

The Watergate activities constituted a major threat to civil liberties and the integrity of the political and electoral process. There was a secret unit paid by White House aides that was used to intimidate political enemies and illegally gather information which was unaccountable to anyone but its political directors. President Nixon used governmental agencies, such as the Treasury, FBI, and CIA for illegitimate and illegal activities. His campaign operatives illegitimately interfered with the political and electoral process.

In addition to his own lies and illegal actions, President Nixon set the tone so that his campaign and White House aides thought that he wanted them to undertake illegal and unethical activities in support of his reelection, which they did.

The Iran-Contra case presented a major threat to the rule of law and the constitutional balance between the president and Congress. Secretary of Defense Weinberger warned the president that the arms-for-hostages deal might violate the law and was unwise policy. The president's failure to notify Congress about the covert action was more troubling. But the most serious problem was the diversion of funds to the Contras in direct violation of the law. The president's aides also destroyed evidence, produced false chronologies, and lied to Congress to hide their actions. William Casey intended to set up "The Enterprise" to generate money that could be spent at his direction entirely unaccountable to the Congress, the Constitution, or the law.

The threat to the Constitution was not merely the sidestepping of the legitimate role of Congress in making foreign policy in the violations of the Arms Export Control Act and the failure to notify Congress as required by the National Security Act. These violations of the law were serious, but probably did not rise to the level of "high crimes and misdemeanors." The diversion of funds to the Contras, however, violated the law and constituted a serious breach of the Constitution by allowing the executive to make policy unilaterally in contravention of the explicit will of Congress as expressed in public law signed by the president. If such practices were permitted, it might indeed lead to the tyranny of the executive that the Framers feared. If the president had known of and approved of the diversion of funds, it would likely have led to impeachment proceedings.

As it was, there was no evidence that President Reagan had any knowledge of the diversion of funds until it was discovered by the aides of the Attorney General. Thus, no impeachment actions were taken in Congress. President Reagan's actions in the aftermath of the public disclosures and his aides' strong urgings were clearly superior to the reactions of Presidents Nixon and Clinton to their crises. He ordered that the truth be found, and he cooperated with the investigation authorities.

On the other hand, despite the Independent Counsel's conclusion that "President Reagan's conduct fell well short of criminality which could be successfully prosecuted," he failed to carry out all of his duties as president.[29] The congressional committee that investigated the Iran-Contra affair concluded:

> . . . the ultimate responsibility for the events in the Iran-Contra Affair must rest with the President. If the President did not know what his national Security Advisors were

doing, he should have. . . . It was the president's policy—not an isolated decision by North or Poindexter—to sell arms secretly to Iran and to maintain the Contras "body and soul," The Boland Amendment notwithstanding. . . . The President created or at least tolerated an environment where those who did know of the diversion believed with certainty that they were carrying out the President's policies.[30]

What President Reagan was guilty of was setting the tone in the White House that encouraged his most senior aides to believe that they were carrying out his wishes when they undertook to violate the law by giving aid to the Contras when it was against the law. With respect to selling arms to Iran, Reagan was willing to continue even after his secretaries of state and defense argued that it might be illegal.

The major issues raised by President Clinton's impeachment were not so much his personal behavior, which was deplorable, but his lying about it under oath in legal proceedings. His lies undermined the judicial system, which depends on the truthful testimony of all, particularly government officials. His lies to the American people also undermined the trust of citizens in the president and the government more generally. President Clinton was also guilty of setting the tone in his White House where lying was acceptable, insofar as his aides and appointed officials also lied to the public in his defense, even though they probably realized privately that the president was lying. His lies and actions were corrupting.

Clinton's behavior was thus corrupting of several members of the executive branch, and he did not take care that the laws be faithfully executed. His actions were deplorable and wrong but did not constitute the same level of institutional threat to the polity that Watergate and Iran-Contra did.

Endnotes

1. An earlier version of this chapter was published in David Abshire, ed. *Triumphs and Tragedies of the Modern Presidency* (Westport, CT: Praeger, 2001).
2. In 1969, Nixon told John Ehrlichman to set up "a little group right here in the White House. Have them get off their tails and find out what's going on and figure out how to stop it." Quoted in Stanley I. Kutler, *The Wars of Watergate* (NY: Alfred A. Knopf, 1990), p. 112. On May 16, 1973, Nixon in a conversation with Alexander Haig said: "The Ellsberg thing was something that we set up. Let me tell you. I know what happened here and Al knows what happens. We set up in the White House a independent group under Bud Krogh to cover the problems of leaks involving, at the time, of the Goddamn Pentagon papers; right? . . . the plumbers' operation." Tape transcript in Stanley I. Kutler, *Abuse of Power: the New Nixon Tapes* (NY: The Free Press, 1997), p. 514.
3. Fred Emery, *Watergate* (NY: Times Books, 1994), p. 30.
4. See Stanley Kutler, *Abuse of Power* (NY: The Free Press, 1997), p. 33.
5. Of the Huston Plan, Nixon said: "Well, then to admit that we approved . . . illegal activities. That's the problem." Also, "I ordered that they use any means necessary, including illegal means, to accomplish this goal." Quoted in Kutler, *Abuse of Power*, p. xxi.
6. Leonard Garment, *Crazy Rhythm* (NY: Times Books, 1997), p. 297.
7. See Kutler, *Abuse of Power*, p. xxi.
8. The New York Times, *The White House Transcripts* (NY: Vintage Books, 1973), pp. 146–147; (March 21, 1973).
9. See Michael Genovese, *The Nixon Presidency* (NY: Greenwood Press, 1990), p. 190.

10. *The White House Transcripts*, quoted in Larry Berman, *The New American Presidency* (Boston: Houghton Mifflin, 1987), p. 189.

11. See Kutler, *The Wars of Watergate*, pp. 431–434.

12. George Shultz, *Turmoil and Triumph* (NY: Charles Scribner's and Sons, 1993), p. 824. After reviewing the CIA analysis, Shultz concluded: ". . . Khomeini was firmly in power, and Rafsanjani was carrying out the Ayatollah's resolute policy of opposition to the United States; recent events in Iran suggested that no Iranian leader other then Khomeini has the power to initiate a rapprochement with the United States or even to offer such a suggestion for debate."

13. Quoted in William S. Cohen and George J. Mitchell, *Men of Zeal* (NY: Viking, 1988), p. xx.

14. See George Shultz, *Turmoil and Triumph* (NY: Charles Scribner's Sons, 1993), pp. 237, 239, 785. Shultz was angered that he was told by White House aides that the U.S. was not selling arms to Iran and that he assured our European allies of it at the same time that the U.S. was in fact selling arms to Iran. See pp. 783–924, passim.

15. See the chronology in William S. Cohen and George J. Mitchell, *Men of Zeal* (NY: Viking, 1988), p. xix–xxxi.

16. See Shultz, *Turmoil and Triumph*, p. 811.

17. See Theodore Draper, *A Very Thin Line* (NY: Hill and Wang, 1991), pp. 225–226, 247–248. See also Bob Woodward, *Shadow* (NY: Simon and Schuster, 1999), p. 137. White House counsel Peter Wallison also reported to chief of staff Donald Regan that the shipments were likely violations of the Act. See Woodward, *Shadow*, p. 109.

18. See Schultz, *Turmoil and Triumph*, p. 804.

19. See the discussion of the law in Cohen and Mitchell, *Men of Zeal*, pp. 12–13; pp. 279–288.

20. For an analysis of the Boland Amendment and its application to the National Security Council staff, see *Report of the Congressional Committees Investigating the Iran-Contra Affair* (Washington: Government Printing Office, November 1987), pp. 41–42.

21. See Draper, *A Very Thin Line*, p. 33.

22. Shultz, *Turmoil and Triumph*, p. 811.

23. *Report of the Congressional Committees Investigating the Iran-Cantra Affair*, p. 280.

24. See David Abshire's account of his experience in the Reagan White House, *To Save a Presidency: The Curse of Iran-Contra* (NY: Oxford University Press, forthcoming). On the internal Baker investigation, see Bob Woodward, *Shadow* (NY: Simon and Schuster, 1999), p. 151. It included 13 interrogations of the president, a staff of 67 people in the White House, and examined more than 12,000 documents.

25. *Washington Post* (8 February 1998), p. A20.

26. Quoted in Jeffrey Toobin, "Circling the Wagons," *The New Yorker* (July 6, 1998), p. 29.

27. *Congressional Quarterly Weekly* (22 December 1998), p. 3324.

28. Richard Nixon, *RN: The Memoirs of Richard Nixon* (NY: Grosset and Dunlop, 1978), p. 1089.

29. Lawrence E. Walsh, *Iran-Contra: The Final Report* (NY: Random House, 1993), p. 445.

30. *Report of the Congressional Committees Investigating the Iran-Contra Affair* (November 1987), pp. 21–22.

Thomas E. Cronin and Michael A. Genovese

"If Men Were Angels . . .": Presidential Leadership and Accountability

Novelist W. Somerset Maugham once said, "There are three rules for writing a novel. Unfortunately, no one knows what they are." In the same vein, we are tempted to conclude that there are three rules to being an effective president, yet no one knows exactly what they are.

As we have discussed, the presidency changes from season to season, occupant to occupant, issue to issue. We may never unravel most of the paradoxes of the American presidency. Yet there are things the American people and presidents can do to encourage realistic and effective presidential performance.

We want to be led, yet we cherish our independence and freedom. We want a "take charge" leader in the White House, yet we demand accountable and responsive leadership. Many Americans are now less content to hold presidents to account only every four years when they go to the polls, they insist on daily accountability. Our system is built on distrust of powerful leaders and the need for their accountability.

Compared with the heady days of FDR, and later the national security state of the Cold War era, the presidency of today is a more constrained office. If FDR invented the modern presidency during the depression and World War II, the demands of the Cold War further enlarged and empowered the office. But in this post–Cold War end of the century age, the demand for a strong, centralized presidency seems less pressing.

While we may on occasion need heroic leadership, we are less in need of presidential dominance than in the past 65 years. The end of the Cold War has liberated us from the need for deference to the powerful presidency model, which proved effective on occasion yet dangerous at other times. However, as the United States enters the 21st century, we are rightly still concerned with how best to keep presidents effective and honest.

Source: Thomas E. Cronin and Michael A. Genovese, *The Paradoxes of the American Presidency* (New York: Oxford University Press, 1998).

Holding Presidents to Account

As our theme suggests, any discussion of presidential leadership and accountability must take into account the ever-present paradoxes of the presidency. Some part of us wants a larger-than-life, two-gun, charismatic Mount Rushmore leader. Harrison Ford in the film *Air Force One* (1997) vivified this yearning. Still, there is the remarkably enduring antigovernment, anti-leadership, chronic-complainer syndrome. We want strong, gutsy leadership to operate on alternate days with a "national city manager." We want presidents to have a wealth of power to solve our problems, yet not so much they can do lasting damage.

Accountability implies not only responsiveness to majority desires and answerability for actions but also taking the people and their views into account. It also implies a performance guided by integrity and character. Accountability implies as well that important decisions could be explained to the people to allow them to appraise how well a president is handling the responsibilities of the office.

To whom is accountability owed? No president, it would seem, can be more than partially accountable to the people, for each president will listen to some people and some points of view more than to others. If we have learned anything in recent years, however, it is that the doctrine of presidential infallibility has been rejected. Arbitrary rule by powerful executives has always been rejected here. But what should be done when there are sharp differences between experts or when expert opinion differs sharply from the preponderance of public opinion? How much accountability, and what kind, is desirable? Is it not possible that the quest for ultimate accountability will result in a presidency without the prerogatives and independent discretion necessary for creative leadership?

The modern presidency, in fact, may be unaccountable because it is too strong and independent in certain areas and too weak and dependent in others. One of the perplexing circumstances characterizing the modern presidency is that considerable restraints sometimes exist where restraints are least desirable and inadequate restraints are available where they are needed. Also, presidential strength is no guarantee that a president will be responsive or answerable. Indeed, significant independent strength may encourage low answerability when it suits a president's short-term personal power goals.

The Presidency and Democratic Theory

How do you grant yet control power? Can leaders be empowered yet also democratized?

These are classic questions our framers faced and they have been central to debates in democratic political theory. Leadership implies power; accountability implies limits. Contradictions aside, accountability is a fundamental piece of the democratic puzzle. In essence, it denotes that public officials are answerable for their actions. But to whom? Within what limits? Through what means?

There are essentially three types of accountability: *ultimate accountability* (which the United States has via the impeachment process); *periodic accountability* (provided for by general elections and occasional landmark Supreme Court decisions); and *daily accountability* (somewhat contained in the separation of powers).[1] James Madison believed elections provided the "primary check on government" and that the separation of powers ("ambition will be made to counteract ambition") plus "auxiliary precautions" should take care of the rest.[2]

There *are* times when presidents abuse power or behave corruptly. But even in the two notable bouts with presidential abuses, Watergate and the Iran-Contra scandal, the president was stopped by the countervailing forces of a free press, an independent Congress, an independent judiciary, and a (late to be sure) aroused public.

We may hold presidents accountable, but can they be held responsible? That is, can they muster enough power to govern? One means to improve accountability and also empower leadership is to strengthen the party system in America. Our parties are, at least by European standards, relatively weak, undisciplined, and non-ideological. A stronger party system could organize and mobilize citizens and government, diminish the fragmentation of the separation of powers, and mitigate against the atomization of our citizenry. If the parties were more disciplined and programmatic, the government's ability to push through its programs would doubtless be enhanced.

A more responsible party system would also ground presidents in a more consensus-oriented style of leadership, and thereby diminish the independent, unconnected brand of leadership so often attempted by recent presidents. A more robust party system can help join the president and Congress together in a more cooperative relationship.[3]

All presidents work to be successful, but what does it mean to be a success? Great popularity? A good historical reputation? Achieving your policy goals? A high congressional box score? Getting your way?

If success is measured merely by getting one's way, then many bullies would be judged successful. But success means more than getting what one wants. In determining success, we must always ask "power for what *ends?*" because power divorced from purpose is potentially dangerous and democratically undesirable.

Presidential politics should always be concerned with central issues and values. Candidates who run for the White House and thereby seek the power to influence the lives of millions of Americans ought to do so because they have a vision of building a better and more just America. If this is not the case, those candidates who are merely seeking power for its own sake should be smoked out in the election process.

If we look on government as the enemy and politics as a dirty word, our anger turns to apathy, and power (but not responsibility) slips through our hands. We often look at politics not as a means to achieve public good, but as an evil; we see elections as the choice between the lesser of two evils; we presume that our democratic responsibilities are satisfied merely by the act of voting every so often, or we drop out of politics. Consequently, many people abandon politics altogether.

That is why politics and elections matter so much. People who give up on politics in effect abdicate the possibility of implementing their most cherished policy ideas. People who give up on politics and parties are essentially giving others power over their lives.

In a democracy, a successful president pursues and uses power, not for selfish ends, not to aggrandize his or her own status, but to help solve problems and help citizens enjoy the blessings of freedom and opportunity.

The best of democratic leaders are teachers who both understand and educate all of us about the promise and mission of America. They move the government in pursuit of the consensus generated from the values of the nation. They appeal to the best in citizens and attempt to lead the nation towards its better self.[4]

Franklin Roosevelt suggested that the presidency "is preeminently a place of moral leadership."[5] Thus, presidents may use their office as a "bully pulpit" to, when at their best, appeal to our better instincts and lead democratically. It was through politics and government that the progressive social movements of this century helped move us toward greater racial and gender equality, devised policies to expand education and opportunities to a wider segment of the population, and attempted to protect and expand the rights of citizens. These battles are far from over. As a nation we have a long way to go before we can truly grant the blessings of liberty and prosperity to all citizens, yet it is through politics—and only through politics—that we can hope to achieve these goals. And if we want our politics and our government to succeed, we must find ways for citizens to guide and encourage responsible presidential leadership.

Presidents may and have also used the powers of the presidency to promote economic stability and economic growth in America. The Roosevelts, Wilson, Kennedy, Reagan, and Clinton all strived to stimulate the economy and promoted favorable trade programs that in turn created jobs and economic security. Presidents generally know what is expected of them as promoters of economic development, yet, here again, they are likely to respond to the yearnings and lobbying of those who become actively engaged in the political process and party politics.

The ends power serves are important, but in presidential terms, virtue is not enough. A successful president must have *character* and *competence*. Character without competence (resources, skill, power) gives us noble but ineffective leaders; competence without character may lead to government by demagogues.

Presidents who lead in the democratic spirit can encourage leaders, foster citizen responsibility, and inspire others to assume leadership responsibilities in their communities. Democratic leaders establish a purposeful vision, pursue progressive goals, and question, challenge, engage, and educate citizens.

The United States needs a strong presidency and a democratically controlled presidency, and this in turn necessitates a strong civic culture.[6] Political theorist Benjamin R. Barber notes the challenge inherent in such a quest:

> At the heart of democratic theory lies a profound dilemma that has afflicted democratic practice at least since the eighteenth century. Democracy requires both effective leadership and vigorous citizenship: yet the conditions and consequences of leadership often seem to undermine civic vigor. Although it cries for both, democracy must customarily make do either with strong leadership or with strong citizens. For the most part, depending on devices of representation in large-scale societies, democracy in the West has settled for strong leaders and correspondingly weak citizens.[7]

The American presidency operates within a system of shared power, one in which the claims of many groups constantly compete. Presidential struggles with other governmental and extra-governmental centers of power stem from the larger societal conflicts over values and the allocation of wealth and opportunity. As a result, the presidency becomes a place in which few radical decisions are made; most of its domestic policies are exploratory, remedial, or experimental modifications of past practices.

Limitations on a president's freedom of action are, to be sure, often desirable. Many of the checks and balances that are still at work today were deliberately designed by the framers of the Constitution. In some measure, presidents should be the agents of their campaign commitments, their parties, and their announced programs. They should be responsive most of the time to the views of the majority of the American people. Presidential behavior should be informed by the Constitution, existing laws, and the generally understood, albeit hazier, values that define democratic procedure. The notion that party programs, spelled out in campaigns, allow the public some control over policy through the election process is a valuable brake, one that needs, if anything, to be revitalized. Other brakes that limit presidential discretion may be viewed as positive or negative, depending on an individual's political and economic views. The constraining of a president by the bureaucracy and by special interests is implicitly, if not explicitly, a kind of accountability, even if it is not exactly the kind we want as our prime constitutional safeguard against the abuse of power.

The American political system is deliberately designed to enhance the chances of special interests to veto policies that affect them. Although the various economic and professional elites may not be as cohesive and omnipotent as the power-elite school suggests, the wealthier interest groups have perpetuated decidedly favorable governmental privileges to advance their business and professional goals. Although at times of crisis, there are substantial incentives for subordinating special claims to the nation's well-being, such times are a presidential luxury. Under normal conditions, an elaborate network of influences and obligations may frustrate presidential objectives, especially in the area of domestic policy.

A president's leeway for achievement can be determined by the degree to which consensus or conflict exists among elite interest groups within a particular arena of public policy. If the policy elite of a given profession or industry share wide agreement on a particular issue, it is very difficult for a president to effect an opposing point of view. Occasional exceptions such as Medicare, automobile safety devices, and antipollution legislation are not persuasive, because the profession or industry in question seldom lost much and the costs for such programs were in most cases passed on in some way to the consumer or taxpayer. If, however, cleavage or confusion occurs over substantive or procedural matters, a president has some independent influence; although even then, the scope and type of his influence will be shaped by the character of the conflict among these elite. Thus, Johnson's efforts to create model cities as demonstrations of how social and physical planning could produce decent and livable cities soon was heavily influenced by pressures from home builders, developers, real-estate associations, big-city mayors, and other strategically positioned interests. Likewise, despite widespread public support for rapid progress on the environmental front, Carter's environmental protection recommendations soon became influenced by the views of the automobile manufacturers as well as by the unions potentially affected by stringent standards and too rapid implementation. More recently, President Clinton's efforts at health care reform met with fierce opposition from insurance companies and medical care providers who felt threatened by the proposed reforms. They were able to mobilize the public and Congress and prevented Clinton's proposals from being enacted into law. Sometimes a consensus among policy elites may be the product of presidential commitment, but the reverse is more likely to be the case.

Prior commitments to special interests inhibit planning, brake a president's capacity to focus on new problems, and help to exhaust his political credit. Despite high expectations, presidents may find themselves merely a strategically situated broker for their own party, able only in a limited way to affect existing patterns of grants or subsidies.

Every grant program generates concrete benefits to a particular group, and possessiveness characterizes nearly every group that has participated in the growth of federal aid programs since the New Deal. According to the doctrine of interest groups, the unorganized are left out of most policymaking equations. In fact, seldom does an interest group emerge that has as its aim the promotion of the public benefit, a program that would benefit everybody. At the same time, the standards to justice and respect for law deteriorate amid informal, frankly feudal negotiations among those stronger interests who can adjust the laws to their own advantage and profit.

In the end, all three branches of government and the bureaucracy listen more attentively and usually yield to the ideas from those segments of society able to represent themselves, able to shape the character of those branches, and able to supply precisely that information and argumentation needed to make the system move. So it is that the many well-heeled interests continue to enjoy a special advantage in any contest with a president who is a genuine progressive.

The founders would most certainly have been pleased to see how the system of checks and balances has thwarted executive tyranny. But they would have perhaps been less pleased with the gridlock that so often characterizes relations between the president and Congress.

"How," political scientist Bert Rockman asked in *The Leadership Question*, "can leadership be exerted yet restrained?"[8] It is a question that confounded the founders and continues to trouble us today. Political gridlock is often the reality. Is the presidency broken? Does it need to be fixed? Would-be reformers must be cautious to ensure that reform would not deform.

Is the separation-of-powers model *the* problem? Does it create deadlock and paralysis? If you are the president, there must be times when it seems so. Woodrow Wilson, writing in 1884 long before occupying the White House, saw the separation as creating a massive political escape clause for blame and responsibility. Wrote Wilson:

> Power and strict accountability for its use are the essential constituents of good government. . . . It is, therefore, manifestly a radical defect in our federal system that it parcels out power and confuses responsibility as it does. The main purpose of the Convention of 1787 seems to have been to accomplish this grievous mistake. . . . Were it possible to call together again the members of that wonderful Convention . . . they would be the first to admit that the only fruit of dividing power had been to make it irresponsible.[9]

Upon reflection, we are reminded of the positive benefit of separating, sharing, and overlapping power. If one values, as we do, deliberation, discussion, and debate; if we accept a model of democratic governing based on consensus and cooperation, then the reform agenda will be short. But some see the separation as the likely suspect in the crime of stalemate and gridlock.

Endnotes

1. Theodore C. Sorensen, *Watchmen in the Night* (Cambridge, Mass.: MIT Press, 1975).
2. James Madison, *The Federalist Papers*, No. 51. (Modern Library, 1937).
3. Sidney M. Milkis, *The President and the Parties* (New York: Oxford University Press, 1993).
4. Bruce Miroff, *Icons of Democracy* (New York: Basic Books, 1993), chap. 1.
5. James M. Burns, *Roosevelt: The Lion and the Fox* (San Diego: A Harvest/HJB Book, 1956, renewed 1984), p. 151.
6. Benjamin Barber, *Strong Democracy: Participatory Politics for a New Age* (Berkeley: University of California Press, 1984).
7. Benjamin R. Barber, "Neither Leaders Nor Followers: Citizenship under Strong Democracy," in Michael R. Beschloss and Thomas E. Cronin, eds., *Essays in Honor of James MacGregor Burns* (Englewood Cliffs, N.J.: Prentice-Hall, 1989), p. 117.
8. Bert Rockman, *The Leadership Question* (New York: Praeger, 1984), p. 221.
9. Quoted in Larry Berman, *The New American Presidency* (Boston: Little, Brown, 1987), p. 344.

Sean Wilentz

The Worst President in History?

George W. Bush's presidency appears headed for colossal historical disgrace. Barring a cataclysmic event on the order of the terrorist attacks of September 11, after which the public might rally around the White House once again, there seems to be little the administration can do to avoid being ranked on the lowest tier of U.S. presidents. And that may be the best-case scenario. Many historians are now wondering whether Bush, in fact, will be remembered as the very worst president in all of American history.

Source: By Sean Wilentz, *Rolling Stone*, April 21, 2006 © Rolling Stone LLC 2006 All Rights Reserved. Reprinted by Permission.

From time to time, after hours, I kick back with my colleagues at Princeton to argue idly about which president really was the worst of them all. For years, these perennial debates have largely focused on the same handful of chief executives whom national polls of historians, from across the ideological and political spectrum, routinely cite as the bottom of the presidential barrel. Was the lousiest James Buchanan, who, confronted with Southern secession in 1860, dithered to a degree that, as his most recent biographer has said, probably amounted to disloyalty—and who handed to his successor, Abraham Lincoln, a nation already torn asunder? Was it Lincoln's successor, Andrew Johnson, who actively sided with former Confederates and undermined Reconstruction? What about the amiably incompetent Warren G. Harding, whose administration was fabulously corrupt? Or, though he has his defenders, Herbert Hoover, who tried some reforms but remained imprisoned in his own outmoded individualist ethic and collapsed under the weight of the stock-market crash of 1929 and the Depression's onset? The younger historians always put in a word for Richard M. Nixon, the only American president forced to resign from office.

Now, though, George W. Bush is in serious contention for the title of worst ever. In early 2004, an informal survey of 415 historians conducted by the nonpartisan History News Network found that 81 percent considered the Bush administration a "failure." Among those who called Bush a success, many gave the president high marks only for his ability to mobilize public support and get Congress to go along with what one historian called the administration's "pursuit of disastrous policies." In fact, roughly one in 10 of those who called Bush a success was being facetious, rating him only as the best president since Bill Clinton—a category in which Bush is the only contestant.

The lopsided decision of historians should give everyone pause. Contrary to popular stereotypes, historians are generally a cautious bunch. We assess the past from widely divergent points of view and are deeply concerned about being viewed as fair and accurate by our colleagues. When we make historical judgments, we are acting not as voters or even pundits, but as scholars who must evaluate all the evidence, good, bad or indifferent. Separate surveys, conducted by those perceived as conservatives as well as liberals, show remarkable unanimity about who the best and worst presidents have been.

Historians do tend, as a group, to be far more liberal than the citizenry as a whole—a fact the president's admirers have seized on to dismiss the poll results as transparently biased. One pro-Bush historian said the survey revealed more about "the current crop of history professors" than about Bush or about Bush's eventual standing. But if historians were simply motivated by a strong collective liberal bias, they might be expected to call Bush the worst president since his father, or Ronald Reagan, or Nixon. Instead, more than half of those polled—and nearly three-fourths of those who gave Bush a negative rating—reached back *before* Nixon to find a president they considered as miserable as Bush. The presidents most commonly linked with Bush included Hoover, Andrew Johnson, and Buchanan. Twelve percent of the historians polled—nearly as many as those who rated Bush a success—flatly called Bush the worst president in American history. And these figures were gathered before the debacles over Hurricane Katrina, Bush's role in the Valerie Plame leak affair and the deterioration of the situation in Iraq. Were the historians polled today, that figure would certainly be higher.

Even worse for the president, the general public, having once given Bush the highest approval ratings ever recorded, now appears to be coming around to the dismal view held by most historians. To be sure, the president retains a considerable base of supporters who believe in and adore him, and who reject all criticism with a mixture of disbelief and fierce contempt—about one-third of the electorate. (When the columnist Richard Reeves publicized the historians' poll last year and suggested it might have merit, he drew thousands of abusive replies that called him an idiot and that praised Bush as, in one writer's words, "a Christian who actually acts on his deeply held beliefs.") Yet the ranks of the true believers have thinned dramatically. A majority of voters in 43 states now disapprove of Bush's handling of his job. Since the commencement of reliable polling in the 1940s, only one twice-elected president has seen his ratings fall as low as Bush's in his second term: Richard Nixon, during the months preceding his resignation in 1974. No two-term president since polling began has fallen from such a height of popularity as Bush's (in the neighborhood of 90 percent, during the patriotic upswell following the 2001 attacks) to such a low (now in the mid-30s). No president, including Harry Truman (whose ratings sometimes dipped below Nixonian levels), has experienced such a virtually unrelieved decline as Bush has since his high point. Apart from sharp but temporary upticks that followed the commencement of the Iraq war and the capture of Saddam Hussein, and a recovery during the weeks just before and after his reelection, the Bush trend has been a profile in fairly steady disillusionment.

How does any president's reputation sink so low? The reasons are best understood as the reverse of those that produce presidential greatness. In almost every survey of historians dating back to the 1940s, three presidents have emerged as supreme successes: George Washington, Abraham Lincoln, and Franklin D. Roosevelt. These were the men who guided the nation through what historians consider its greatest crises: the founding era after the ratification of the Constitution, the Civil War, the Great Depression, and the Second World War. Presented with arduous, at times seemingly impossible circumstances, they rallied the nation, governed brilliantly and left the republic more secure than when they entered office.

Calamitous presidents, faced with enormous difficulties—Buchanan, Andrew Johnson, Hoover, and now Bush—have divided the nation, governed erratically and left the nation worse off. In each case, different factors contributed to the failure: disastrous domestic policies, foreign-policy blunders and military setbacks, executive misconduct, crises of credibility and public trust. Bush, however, is one of the rarities in presidential history: He has not only stumbled badly in every one of these key areas, he has also displayed a weakness common among the greatest presidential failures—an unswerving adherence to a simplistic ideology that abjures deviation from dogma as heresy, thus preventing any pragmatic adjustment to changing realities. Repeatedly, Bush has undone himself, a failing revealed in each major area of presidential performance.

The Credibility Gap

No previous president appears to have squandered the public's trust more than Bush has. In the 1840s, President James Polk gained a reputation for deviousness over his alleged manufacturing of the war with Mexico and his supposedly covert pro-slavery views. Abraham Lincoln, then an Illinois congressman, virtually labeled Polk a liar when he called him, from the floor of the House, "a bewildered, confounded and miserably perplexed man" and denounced the war as "from beginning to end, the sheerest deception." But the swift American victory in the war, Polk's decision to stick by his pledge to serve only one term and his sudden death shortly after leaving office spared him the ignominy over slavery that befell his successors in the 1850s. With more than two years to go in Bush's second term and no swift victory in sight, Bush's reputation will probably have no such reprieve.

The problems besetting Bush are of a more modern kind than Polk's, suited to the television age—a crisis both in confidence and credibility. In 1965, Lyndon Johnson's Vietnam travails gave birth to the phrase "credibility gap," meaning the distance between a president's professions and the public's perceptions of reality. It took more than two years for Johnson's disapproval rating in the Gallup Poll to reach 52 percent in March 1968—a figure Bush long ago surpassed, but that was sufficient to persuade the proud LBJ not to seek reelection. Yet recently, just short of three years after Bush buoyantly declared "mission accomplished" in Iraq, his disapproval ratings have been running considerably higher than Johnson's, at about 60 percent. More than half the country now considers Bush dishonest and untrustworthy, and a decisive plurality consider him less trustworthy than his predecessor, Bill Clinton—a figure still attacked by conservative zealots as "Slick Willie."

Previous modern presidents, including Truman, Reagan, and Clinton, managed to reverse plummeting ratings and regain the public's trust by shifting attention away from political and policy setbacks, and by overhauling the White House's inner circles. But Bush's publicly expressed view that he has made no major mistakes, coupled with what even the conservative commentator William F. Buckley Jr. calls his "high-flown pronouncements" about failed policies, seems to foreclose the first option. Upping the ante in the Middle East and bombing Iranian nuclear sites, a strategy reportedly favored by some in the White House, could distract the public and gain Bush immediate political capital in advance of the 2006 midterm elections—but in the long term might severely worsen the already dire situation in Iraq, especially among Shiite Muslims linked to the Iranians. And given Bush's ardent attachment to loyal aides, no matter how discredited, a major personnel shake-up is improbable, short of indictments. Replacing Andrew Card with Joshua Bolten as chief of staff—a move announced by the president in March in a tone that sounded more like defiance than contrition—represents a rededication to current policies and personnel, not a serious change. (Card, an old Bush family retainer, was widely considered more moderate than most of the men around the president and had little involvement in policy-making.) The power of Vice President Dick Cheney, meanwhile, remains uncurbed. Were Cheney to announce he is stepping down due to health problems, normally a polite pretext for a political removal, one can be reasonably certain it would be because Cheney actually did have grave health problems.

Bush at War

Until the 20th century, American presidents managed foreign wars well—including those presidents who prosecuted unpopular wars. James Madison had no support from Federalist New England at the outset of the War of 1812, and the discontent grew amid mounting military setbacks in 1813. But Federalist political overreaching, combined with a reversal of America's military fortunes and the negotiation of a peace with Britain, made Madison something of a hero again and ushered in a brief so-called Era of Good Feelings in which his Jeffersonian Republican Party coalition ruled virtually unopposed. The Mexican War under Polk was even more unpopular, but its quick and victorious conclusion redounded to Polk's favor—much as the rapid American victory in the Spanish-American War helped William McKinley overcome anti-imperialist dissent.

The 20th century was crueler to wartime presidents. After winning re-election in 1916 with the slogan "He Kept Us Out of War," Woodrow Wilson oversaw American entry into the First World War. Yet while the doughboys returned home triumphant, Wilson's idealistic and politically disastrous campaign for American entry into the League of Nations presaged a resurgence of the opposition Republican Party along with a redoubling of American isolationism that lasted until Pearl Harbor.

Bush has more in common with post-1945 Democratic presidents Truman and Johnson, who both became bogged down in overseas military conflicts with no end, let alone victory, in sight. But Bush has become bogged down in a singularly crippling way. On September 10, 2001, he held among the lowest ratings of any modern president for that point in a first term. (Only Gerald Ford, his popularity reeling after his pardon of Nixon, had comparable numbers.) The attacks the following day transformed Bush's presidency, giving him an extraordinary opportunity to achieve greatness. Some of the early signs were encouraging. Bush's simple, unflinching eloquence and his quick toppling of the Taliban government in Afghanistan rallied the nation. Yet even then, Bush wasted his chance by quickly choosing partisanship over leadership.

No other president—Lincoln in the Civil War, FDR in World War II, John F. Kennedy at critical moments of the Cold War—faced with such a monumental set of military and political circumstances failed to embrace the opposing political party to help wage a truly national struggle. But Bush shut out and even demonized the Democrats. Top military advisers and even members of the president's own Cabinet who expressed any reservations or criticisms of his policies—including retired Marine Corps Gen. Anthony Zinni and former Treasury Secretary Paul O'Neill—suffered either dismissal, smear attacks from the president's supporters or investigations into their alleged breaches of national security. The wise men who counseled Bush's father, including James Baker and Brent Scowcroft, found their entreaties brusquely ignored by his son. When asked if he ever sought advice from the elder Bush, the president responded, "There is a higher Father that I appeal to."

All the while, Bush and the most powerful figures in the administration, Vice President Dick Cheney and Defense Secretary Donald Rumsfeld, were planting the seeds for the crises to come by diverting the struggle against Al Qaeda toward an all-out effort to topple their pre-existing target, Saddam Hussein. In a deliberate political decision, the administration stampeded the Congress and a traumatized citizenry into the Iraq invasion on the basis of what has now been demonstrated to be tendentious and perhaps fabricated evidence of an imminent Iraqi threat to American security, one that the White House suggested included nuclear weapons. Instead of emphasizing any political, diplomatic or humanitarian aspects of a war on Iraq—an appeal that would have sounded too "sensitive," as Cheney once sneered— the administration built a "Bush Doctrine" of unprovoked, preventive warfare, based on speculative threats and embracing principles previously abjured by every previous generation of U.S. foreign policy-makers, even at the height of the Cold War. The president did so with premises founded, in the case of Iraq, on wishful thinking. He did so while proclaiming an expansive Wilsonian rhetoric of making the world safe for democracy—yet discarding the multilateralism and systems of international law (including the Geneva Conventions) that emanated from Wilson's idealism. He did so while dismissing intelligence that an American invasion could spark a long and bloody civil war among Iraq's fierce religious and ethnic rivals, reports that have since proved true. And he did so after repeated warnings by military officials such as Gen. Eric Shinseki that pacifying postwar Iraq would require hundreds of thousands of American troops—accurate estimates that Paul Wolfowitz and other Bush policy gurus ridiculed as "wildly off the mark."

When William F. Buckley, the man whom many credit as the founder of the modern conservative movement, writes categorically, as he did in February, that "one can't doubt that the American objective in Iraq has failed," then something terrible has happened. Even as a brash young iconoclast, Buckley always took the long view. The Bush White House seems incapable of doing so, except insofar as a tiny trusted circle around the president constantly reassures him that he is a messianic liberator and profound freedom fighter, on a par with FDR and Lincoln, and that history will vindicate his every act and utterance.

Bush at Home

Bush came to office in 2001 pledging to govern as a "compassionate conservative," more moderate on domestic policy than the dominant right wing of his party. The pledge proved hollow, as Bush tacked immediately to the hard right. Previous presidents and their parties have suffered when their actions have belied their campaign promises. Lyndon Johnson is the most conspicuous recent example, having declared in his 1964 run against the hawkish Republican Barry Goldwater that "we are not about to send American boys nine or ten thousand miles away from home to do what Asian boys ought to be doing for themselves." But no president has surpassed Bush in departing so thoroughly from his original campaign persona.

The heart of Bush's domestic policy has turned out to be nothing more than a series of massively regressive tax cuts—a return, with a vengeance, to the discredited Reagan-era supply-side faith that Bush's father once ridiculed as "voodoo economics." Bush crowed in triumph in February 2004, "We cut taxes, which basically meant people had more money in their pocket." The claim is bogus for the majority of

Americans, as are claims that tax cuts have led to impressive new private investment and job growth. While wiping out the solid Clinton-era federal surplus and raising federal deficits to staggering record levels, Bush's tax policies have necessitated hikes in federal fees, state and local taxes, and co-payment charges to needy veterans and families who rely on Medicaid, along with cuts in loan programs to small businesses and college students, and in a wide range of state services. The lion's share of benefits from the tax cuts has gone to the very richest Americans, while new business investment has increased at a historically sluggish rate since the peak of the last business cycle five years ago. Private-sector job growth since 2001 has been anemic compared to the Bush administration's original forecasts and is chiefly attributable not to the tax cuts but to increased federal spending, especially on defense. Real wages for middle-income Americans have been dropping since the end of 2003: Last year, on average, nominal wages grew by only 2.4 percent, a meager gain that was completely erased by an average inflation rate of 3.4 percent.

The monster deficits, caused by increased federal spending combined with the reduction of revenue resulting from the tax cuts, have also placed Bush's administration in a historic class of its own with respect to government borrowing. According to the Treasury Department, the forty-two presidents who held office between 1789 and 2000 borrowed a combined total of $1.01 trillion from foreign governments and financial institutions. But between 2001 and 2005 alone, the Bush White House borrowed $1.05 trillion, more than all of the previous presidencies *combined*. Having inherited the largest federal surplus in American history in 2001, he has turned it into the largest deficit ever—with an even higher deficit, $423 billion, forecast for fiscal year 2006. Yet Bush—sounding much like Herbert Hoover in 1930 predicting that "prosperity is just around the corner"—insists that he will cut federal deficits in half by 2009, and that the best way to guarantee this would be to make permanent his tax cuts, which helped cause the deficit in the first place!

The rest of what remains of Bush's skimpy domestic agenda is either failed or failing—a record unmatched since the presidency of Herbert Hoover. The No Child Left Behind educational-reform act has proved so unwieldy, draconian and poorly funded that several states—including Utah, one of Bush's last remaining political strongholds—have fought to opt out of it entirely. White House proposals for immigration reform and a guest-worker program have succeeded mainly in dividing pro-business Republicans (who want more low-wage immigrant workers) from paleo-conservatives fearful that hordes of Spanish-speaking newcomers will destroy American culture. The paleos' call for tougher anti-immigrant laws—a return to the punitive spirit of exclusion that led to the notorious Immigration Act of 1924 that shut the door to immigrants from Southern and Eastern Europe—has in turn deeply alienated Hispanic voters from the Republican Party, badly undermining the GOP's hopes of using them to build a permanent national electoral majority. The recent pro-immigrant demonstrations, which drew millions of marchers nationwide, indicate how costly the Republican divide may prove.

The one noncorporate constituency to which Bush has consistently deferred is the Christian right, both in his selections for the federal bench and in his implications that he bases his policies on pre-millennialist, prophetic Christian doctrine. Previous presidents have regularly invoked the Almighty. McKinley is supposed to have fallen to his knees, seeking divine guidance about whether to take control of the Philippines in 1898, although the story may be apocryphal. But no president before Bush has allowed the press to disclose, through a close friend, his startling belief that he was ordained by God to lead the country. The White House's sectarian positions—over stem-cell research, the teaching of pseudoscientific "intelligent design," global population control, the Terri Schiavo spectacle and more—have led some to conclude that Bush has promoted the transformation of the GOP into what former Republican strategist Kevin Phillips calls "the first religious party in U.S. history."

Bush's faith-based conception of his mission, which stands above and beyond reasoned inquiry, jibes well with his administration's pro-business dogma on global warming and other urgent environmental issues. While forcing federally funded agencies to remove from their Web sites scientific information about reproductive health and the effectiveness of condoms in combating HIV/AIDS, and while peremptorily overruling staff scientists at the Food and Drug Administration on making emergency contraception available over the counter, Bush officials have censored and suppressed research findings they don't like by the Environmental Protection Agency, the Fish and Wildlife Service and the Department of Agriculture. Far from being the conservative he said he was, Bush has blazed a radical new path as the first American president in history who is outwardly hostile to science—dedicated, as a distinguished, bipartisan panel of educators and scientists (including 49 Nobel laureates) has declared, to "the distortion of scientific knowledge for partisan political ends."

The Bush White House's indifference to domestic problems and science alike culminated in the catastrophic responses to Hurricane Katrina. Scientists had long warned that global warming was intensifying hurricanes, but Bush ignored them—much as he and his administration sloughed off warnings from the director of the National Hurricane Center before Katrina hit. Reorganized under the Department of Homeland Security, the once efficient Federal Emergency Management Agency turned out, under Bush, to have become a nest of cronyism and incompetence. During the months immediately after the storm, Bush traveled to New Orleans eight times to promise massive rebuilding aid from the federal government. On March 30, however, Bush's Gulf Coast recovery coordinator admitted that it could take as long as 25 years for the city to recover.

Karl Rove has sometimes likened Bush to the imposing, no-nonsense President Andrew Jackson. Yet Jackson took measures to prevent those he called "the rich and powerful" from bending "the acts of government to their selfish purposes." Jackson also gained eternal renown by saving New Orleans from British invasion against terrible odds. Generations of Americans sang of Jackson's famous victory. In 1959, Johnny Horton's version of "The Battle of New Orleans" won the Grammy for best country and western performance. If anyone sings about George W. Bush and New Orleans, it will be a blues number.

Presidential Misconduct

Virtually every presidential administration dating back to George Washington's has faced charges of misconduct and threats of impeachment against the president or his civil officers. The alleged offenses have usually involved matters of personal misbehavior and corruption, notably the payoff scandals that plagued Cabinet officials who served presidents Harding and Ulysses S. Grant. But the charges have also included alleged usurpation of power by the president and serious criminal conduct that threatens constitutional government and the rule of law—most notoriously, the charges that led to the impeachments of Andrew Johnson and Bill Clinton, and to Richard Nixon's resignation.

Historians remain divided over the actual grievousness of many of these allegations and crimes. Scholars reasonably describe the graft and corruption around the Grant administration, for example, as gargantuan, including a kickback scandal that led to the resignation of Grant's secretary of war under the shadow of impeachment. Yet the scandals produced no indictments of Cabinet secretaries and only one of a White House aide, who was acquitted. By contrast, the most scandal-ridden administration in the modern era, apart from Nixon's, was Ronald Reagan's, now widely remembered through a haze of nostalgia as a paragon of virtue. A total of 29 Reagan officials, including White House national security adviser Robert McFarlane and deputy chief of staff Michael Deaver, were convicted on charges stemming from the Iran-Contra affair, illegal lobbying and a looting scandal inside the Department of Housing and Urban Development. Three Cabinet officers—HUD Secretary Samuel Pierce, Attorney General Edwin Meese and Secretary of Defense Caspar Weinberger—left their posts under clouds of scandal. In contrast, not a single official in the Clinton administration was even indicted over his or her White House duties, despite repeated high-profile investigations and a successful, highly partisan impeachment drive.

The full report, of course, has yet to come on the Bush administration. Because Bush, unlike Reagan or Clinton, enjoys a fiercely partisan and loyal majority in Congress, his administration has been spared scrutiny. Yet that mighty advantage has not prevented the indictment of Vice President Dick Cheney's chief of staff, I. Lewis "Scooter" Libby, on charges stemming from an alleged major security breach in the Valerie Plame matter. (The last White House official of comparable standing to be indicted while still in office was Grant's personal secretary, in 1875.) It has not headed off the unprecedented scandal involving Larry Franklin, a high-ranking Defense Department official, who has pleaded guilty to divulging classified information to a foreign power while working at the Pentagon—a crime against national security. It has not forestalled the arrest and indictment of Bush's top federal procurement official, David Safavian, and the continuing investigations into Safavian's intrigues with the disgraced Republican lobbyist Jack Abramoff, recently sentenced to nearly six years in prison—investigations in which some prominent Republicans, including former Christian Coalition executive director Ralph Reed (and current GOP aspirant for lieutenant governor of Georgia) have already been implicated, and could well produce the largest congressional corruption scandal in American history. It has not dispelled the cloud of possible indictment that hangs over others of Bush's closest advisers.

History may ultimately hold Bush in the greatest contempt for expanding the powers of the presidency beyond the limits laid down by the U.S. Constitution. There has always been a tension over the constitutional roles of the three branches of the federal government. The Framers intended as much, as part of the system of checks and balances they expected would minimize tyranny. When Andrew Jackson took drastic measures against the nation's banking system, the Whig Senate censured him for conduct "dangerous to the liberties of the people." During the Civil War, Abraham Lincoln's emergency decisions to suspend habeas corpus while Congress was out of session in 1861 and 1862 has led some Americans, to this day, to regard him as a despot. Richard Nixon's conduct of the war in Southeast Asia and his covert domestic-surveillance programs prompted Congress to pass new statutes regulating executive power.

By contrast, the Bush administration—in seeking to restore what Cheney, a Nixon administration veteran, has called "the legitimate authority of the presidency"—threatens to overturn the Framers' healthy tension in favor of presidential absolutism. Armed with legal findings by his attorney general (and personal lawyer) Alberto Gonzales, the Bush White House has declared that the president's powers as commander in chief in wartime are limitless. No previous wartime president has come close to making so grandiose a claim. More specifically, this administration has asserted that the president is perfectly free to violate federal laws on such matters as domestic surveillance and the torture of detainees. When Congress has passed legislation to limit those assertions, Bush has resorted to issuing constitutionally dubious "signing statements," which declare, by fiat, how he will interpret and execute the law in question, even when that interpretation flagrantly violates the will of Congress. Earlier presidents, including Jackson, raised hackles by offering their own view of the Constitution in order to justify vetoing congressional acts. Bush does not bother with that: He signs the legislation (eliminating any risk that Congress will overturn a veto), and then governs how he pleases—using the signing statements as if they were line-item vetoes. In those instances when Bush's violations of federal law have come to light, as over domestic surveillance, the White House has devised a novel solution: Stonewall any investigation into the violations and bid a compliant Congress simply to rewrite the laws.

Bush's alarmingly aberrant take on the Constitution is ironic. One need go back in the record less than a decade to find prominent Republicans railing against far more minor presidential legal infractions as precursors to all-out totalitarianism. "I will have no part in the creation of a constitutional double-standard to benefit the president," Senator Bill Frist declared of Bill Clinton's efforts to conceal an illicit sexual liaison. "No man is above the law, and no man is below the law—that's the principle that we all hold very dear in this country," Representative Tom DeLay asserted. "The rule of law protects you and it protects me from the midnight fire on our roof or the 3 a.m. knock on our door," warned Representative Henry Hyde, one of Clinton's chief accusers. In the face of Bush's more definitive dismissal of federal law, the silence from these quarters is deafening.

The president's defenders stoutly contend that war-time conditions fully justify Bush's actions. And as Lincoln showed during the Civil War, there may be times of military emergency when the executive believes it imperative to take immediate, highly irregular, even unconstitutional steps. "I felt that measures, otherwise unconstitutional, might become lawful," Lincoln wrote in 1864, "by becoming indispensable to the preservation of the Constitution, through the preservation of the nation." Bush seems to think that, since 9/11, he has been placed, by the grace of God, in the same kind of situation Lincoln faced. But Lincoln, under pressure of daily combat on American soil against fellow Americans, did not operate in secret, as Bush has. He did not claim, as Bush has, that his emergency actions were wholly regular and constitutional as well as necessary; Lincoln sought and received Congressional authorization for his suspension of habeas corpus in 1863. Nor did Lincoln act under the amorphous cover of a "war on terror"—a war against a tactic, not a specific nation or political entity, which could last as long as any president deems the tactic a threat to national security. Lincoln's exceptional measures were intended to survive only as long as the Confederacy was in rebellion. Bush's could be extended indefinitely, as the president sees fit, permanently endangering rights and liberties guaranteed by the Constitution to the citizenry.

Much as Bush still enjoys support from those who believe he can do no wrong, he now suffers opposition from liberals who believe he can do no right. Many of these liberals are in the awkward position of having supported Bush in the past, while offering little coherent as an alternative to Bush's policies now. Yet it is difficult to see how this will benefit Bush's reputation in history.

The president came to office calling himself "a uniter, not a divider" and promising to soften the acrimonious tone in Washington. He has had two enormous opportunities to fulfill those pledges: first, in the noisy aftermath of his controversial election in 2000, and, even more, after the attacks of September 11, when the nation pulled behind him as it has supported no other president in living memory. Yet under both sets of historically unprecedented circumstances, Bush has chosen to act in ways that have left the country less united and more divided, less conciliatory and more acrimonious—much like James Buchanan, Andrew Johnson, and Herbert Hoover before him. And, like those three predecessors, Bush has done so in the service of a rigid ideology that permits no deviation and refuses to adjust to changing realities. Buchanan failed the test of Southern secession, Johnson failed in the face of Reconstruction, and Hoover failed in the face of the Great Depression. Bush has failed to confront his own failures in both domestic and international affairs, above all in his ill-conceived responses to radical Islamic terrorism. Having confused steely resolve with what Ralph Waldo Emerson called "a foolish consistency . . . adored by little statesmen," Bush has become entangled in tragedies of his own making, compounding those visited upon the country by outside forces.

No historian can responsibly predict the future with absolute certainty. There are too many imponderables still to come in the two and a half years left in Bush's presidency to know exactly how it will look in 2009, let alone in 2059. There have been presidents—Harry Truman was one—who have left office in seeming disgrace, only to rebound in the estimates of later scholars. But so far the facts are not shaping up propitiously for George W. Bush. He still does his best to deny it. Having waved away the lessons of history in the making of his decisions, the present-minded Bush doesn't seem to be concerned about his place in history. "History. We won't know," he told the journalist Bob Woodward in 2003. "We'll all be dead."

Another president once explained that the judgments of history cannot be defied or dismissed, even by a president. "Fellow citizens, *we* cannot escape history," said Abraham Lincoln. "We of this Congress and this administration, will be remembered in spite of ourselves. No personal significance, or insignificance, can spare one or another of us. The fiery trial through which we pass, will light us down, in honor or dishonor, to the latest generation."

Karl Rove

The Long View

The Washington Post scorned President Truman as a "spoilsman" who "underesti-mated the people's intelligence." *The New York Times* columnist James Reston wrote off President Eisenhower as "a tired man in a period of turbulence." At the end of President Reagan's second term, *The New York Times* dismissed him as "simplistic" and a "lazy and inattentive man."

These harsh judgments, made in the moment, have not weathered well over time. Fortunately, while contemporary observers have a habit of getting presidents wrong, history tends to be more accurate.

So how might history view the 43rd president? I can hardly be considered an objective observer, but in this highly polarized period, who is?

However, I believe history will provide a more clear-eyed verdict on this presi-dent's leadership than the anger of current critics would suggest.

President Bush will be viewed as a far-sighted leader who confronted the key test of the 21st century.

He will be judged as a man of moral clarity who put America on wartime footing in the dangerous struggle against radical Islamic terrorism.

Source: National Review (August 31, 2007).

Following the horrors of 9/11, this president changed American foreign policy by declaring terror sponsors responsible for the deeds of those they shelter, train, and fund. America, he said, will not wait until dangers fully materialize with attacks on our homeland before confronting those threats.

The president gave the nation new tools to defeat terrorism abroad and protect our citizens at home with the Patriot Act, foreign surveillance that works in the wireless age, a transformed intelligence community, and the Department of Homeland Security.

And this president saw the wisdom of removing terrorism's cause by advocating the spread of democracy, especially in the Muslim world, where authoritarianism and repression have provided a potent growth medium for despair and anger aimed at the West. He recognized that democracy there makes us safer here.

President Bush will be seen as a compassionate leader who used America's power for good.

While the world dithered, America confronted HIV/AIDS in Africa with the President's Emergency Plan for AIDS Relief, which has supported treatment for more than 1.1 million people worldwide, over one million of them in Africa. While most of the globe ignored Sudan and Darfur or refused to act, this president labeled the violence there genocide—and pressed world leaders to take action.

A wide range of human-rights issues—from the repression in North Korea, Myanmar, and elsewhere to religious freedom to trafficking in persons—are kept on the international agenda in good part because of this president's demands for action.

And President Bush met challenges with new institutions and methods. For example, the Proliferation Security Initiative confronts the transfer of dangerous material and information. And he has reformed America's foreign aid to focus on results, accountability, transparency, and anti-corruption and pro-democracy requirements.

President Bush promotes economic growth and understands free markets provide the best path to a more hopeful tomorrow.

The president inherited an economy entering recession. It was further weakened by terrorist attacks, corporate scandals, natural disasters, and out-of-control spending with discretionary domestic spending increasing 16 percent in the last fiscal year of his predecessor. President Bush took decisive action, cutting taxes and ratcheting down this spending. The results? The net creation of 8.3 million new jobs since August 2003; higher after-tax income and greater incentives for firms to invest and expand; three years where America's economic growth led the rest of the G7 economies; and a budget on path to surplus by 2012—despite the increased spending invested in securing America's safety by standing up the new Department of Homeland Security and fighting the Global War on Terror. In the four years since taxes were last cut in 2003, the U.S. economy has grown 13 percent in real dollars. The additional growth is larger than the entire size of the Canadian economy.

This president also understands our standard of living depends on selling to the globe. The 14 nations with which we have implemented free agreements represent 7.5 percent of the world's GDP, but 43 percent of our exports. The growing number of free-trade agreements concluded and signed under this president helps explain why American exports have risen 27 percent between 2004 and 2006, creating jobs and prosperity here at home.

History will see President Bush as a reformer who focused on modernizing important institutions.

He is concerned with fundamental change that will—among other goals—strengthen the ways our children are educated and health care is provided.

In education, "No Child Left Behind" introduced accountability into our public-education system by ensuring every child's progress is measured.

Parents now know whether or not their child is learning—in their own schools, and compared to other schools. This new focus on results helped lead to more improvement in reading scores in five years than in the previous 28 combined. This reform shows that measuring leads to results.

Medicare was modernized with a prescription-drug benefit, now used by 39 million seniors. Giving seniors the drugs they need helped them avoid expensive operations and long hospital stays. The result is better health care for seniors at a lower cost to them and at a lower cost than expected to taxpayers.

The president approached other tasks—such as legal reform, higher-education assistance, transportation, and conservation and forest policy—with the same reformist spirit. And he did so on issues which are controversial within his own party, such as comprehensive immigration reform, which he has championed since he first started running for governor of Texas in 1993.

He will be seen as an innovative conservative thinker with a positive, optimistic agenda for action.

For example, his proposals to reform health care are drawn from his understanding of the values of competition and markets. A standard tax deduction for health care—similar to the deduction homeowners get for mortgage interest—would level the playing field between those who get their health insurance from employers and those who pay for it out of their own pockets and expand the number of families with coverage.

People should be able to save tax-free for out-of-pocket health costs. The Health Savings Accounts the president signed into law are the first step toward this. HSAs will help move health care toward a consumer-driven model and away from a single-payer system. More than 4.5 million American families are benefiting from HSAs today.

More competition would be created by allowing insurance to be sold across state lines or small businesses to pool risk and would lower costs and increase access.

The president has a similar focus on bold changes when it comes to opportunity and poverty. He emphasizes policies, such as welfare reform, that promote ownership and encourage personal responsibility rather than dependence on government.

His faith- and community-based initiative is encouraging social entrepreneurship to confront poverty and suffering. Billions of federal dollars can now be accessed by such groups eager to serve a neighbor in need. Already, 34 Democrat and Republican governors and more than 100 mayors of all stripes have created faith- and community-based offices to build on the federal initiative.

On energy, the environment, and climate change, he is developing a new paradigm. Emphasizing technology, increased energy-efficiency partnerships, and resource diversification, his policies are improving energy security and slowing the growth of greenhouse gases without economy-breaking mandates and regulation. The president who won criticism by rejecting the failed approach of Kyoto has implemented policies that enabled the United States to grow its economy by 3.1 percent and reduce the absolute amount of CO_2 emissions (by 1.3 percent).

In these and other areas, history will see President Bush drove policy in new directions, based on conservative principles.

He will be recognized as a strong advocate of traditional values.

He advanced a culture of life where every child is protected and welcomed.

He supported traditional marriage when it came under attack from the courts. He sought to strengthen families and encourage personal responsibility. And he understood the necessity of appointing judges who know the proper and limited role of courts and will provide impartial justice and faithful application of the Constitution.

President Bush had the political courage to confront the biggest economic challenge America faces.

The looming fiscal crises in Medicare and Social Security will result in either the impoverishment of the American people through higher taxes and lower growth or through the inability of government to deliver on its promises.

This president has worked to restrain the spending growth of entitlements, and to modernize Social Security and Medicare by injecting market forces and competition into their operation. He proposed Social Security reform that would solve the system's long-term financial shortfall while giving younger workers the choice to put some of their own money into conservative stock-market investments.

He has made it impossible for future presidents and future Congresses to ignore this challenge. The president's proposal will be the starting point for reform when it happens. When it does, Americans will be grateful President Bush made entitlement reform an issue and will be aware that valuable time was lost because of the obstructionism of his critics.

The outcome in Iraq and Afghanistan will color how history views the president.

History's concern is with final outcomes, not the missteps or advances of the moment. History will render a favorable verdict if the outcome in the Middle East is similar to what America saw after World War II.

America's persistence in Europe and Asia after that war helped Germany and Japan become democracies and allies in the struggle against Communism. If something similar happens in Iraq and Afghanistan, it will change the region and the world. For the first time, millions of citizens across the Middle East will see a working model of freedom in their region—and it will give them hope for a better future for their children by making America safer for them.

If the outcome there is like what happened in Vietnam after America abandoned our allies and the region descended into chaos, violence, and danger, history's judgment will be harsh. History will see President Bush as right, and the opponents of his policy as mistaken—as George McGovern was in his time.

Beyond his policies and actions, history will take the measure of the man.

I have known George W. Bush for nearly 34 years and have had the privilege of watching from nearby as history has placed its demands on him and our country. I know his humility and decency, his intelligence and thoughtfulness, his respect for every person he comes in contact with, his unwavering commitment to principle-based decision-making, and the quiet and compassionate hearts of the man and his graceful wife, Laura.

I have come to understand true leadership leans into the wind. It tackles big challenges with uncertain outcomes rather than taking on simple, sure tasks. It does what is right, regardless of what the latest poll or focus group says. History demands much of America and its leaders and I am confident it will judge the 43rd president as a man more than worthy of the great office the American people twice entrusted to him.

Andrew Rudalevige

A New Imperial Presidency?

"How Much Power Should They Have?" demanded the cover of *Newsweek* as 2006 began, with President George W. Bush and Vice President Dick Cheney glaring out from underneath the headline. The question was prompted by a flurry of holiday season revelations centered on aggressive claims to, and use of, unilateral presidential powers. These ranged from the detention (and treatment) of imprisoned terror suspects around the world to phone taps placed on Americans without a court warrant. "We've been able to restore the legitimate authority of the presidency," the Vice President insisted; others worried that the Constitution's checks were being unbalanced, and that the "imperial presidency" of the Vietnam/Watergate era had risen from the grave.[1]

Framing Questions

However timely, *Newsweek*'s query was of course hardly new. Indeed, little at the Constitutional Convention of 1787 provoked more debate than the shape and scope of the executive branch. Delegates had to determine how the president would be selected, how long he should serve, whether he should be able to run for office more than once,

Source: Presidential Studies Quarterly, Vol. 36, No. 3 (September 2006).

how much power he should have—even whether the president would be a "he" or a "they."[2] Some of the Framers were unconvinced of the need for an executive branch in the first place. Others thought that executive power must be strictly divided, to impede future tyranny: For them, in Virginia governor Edmund Randolph's phrase, a single executive was "the foetus of monarchy."[3] And monarchy, of course, was what the Framers wanted to avoid.

In the end, the framework of presidential power was left largely in outline form, to be worked out in practice. This began with the very first sentence of Article II: "The executive power shall be vested in a President of the United States of America." What is "the executive power"? What might it allow the president to do? About this, the document is silent.[4] Otherwise, the president was given a limited array of specified powers, many of them further truncated by a sort of Congressional asterisk—the president can finalize treaties, or appointments, only with Senate approval; the execution of the law assumes its legislative passage; no money can be spent that is not first appropriated by Congress. How these shared powers might work was itself not clarified: the expectation was, in Madison's famous phrase from the *Federalist*, that interbranch interaction would allow institutional "ambition . . . to counteract ambition."

This began immediately, when Treasury Secretary Alexander Hamilton and Congressman James Madison argued over the scope of President Washington's unilateral authority. Reduced to its essence, the dispute was—and is—relatively straightforward: Is a president limited to the specific powers affirmatively listed in the Constitution or granted in statute, or can he take whatever actions he deems in the public interest so long as those actions are not actually prohibited by the Constitution? Theodore Roosevelt's iteration of Hamilton's position put it clearly: "My belief was that it was not only [the President's] right but his duty to do anything that the needs of the Nation required unless such action was forbidden by the Constitution or by the laws." Roosevelt's successor, William Howard Taft, clarified the opposing view. "The President can exercise no power which cannot be fairly and reasonably traced to some specific grant of power or justly implied within such express grant as proper and necessary to its exercise," Taft wrote. "There is no undefined residuum of power which he can exercise because it seems to him to be in the public interest . . ."[5]

Whatever the Framers' true intent, the Hamiltonian position won out over time. The growth in the size and scope of government during and after the Great Depression, and national security apparatus built during World War II and the Cold War effectively settled the argument. H. L. Mencken noted in 1926 that, "No man would want to be President of the United States in strict accordance with the Constitution."[6] But people do want to be president, for the powers of the modern presidency go beyond anything the framers foresaw. By the time Franklin Roosevelt's "modern presidency" was institutionalized by his successors, presidents had acquired many tools to work around their constitutionally mandated weakness. They used their formal powers strategically and pro-actively; they built an executive branch in their own image, with an extensive presidential staff to oversee and control it; and they continually and creatively interpreted Constitutional vagueness in their favor to reshape the policy landscape, relying on a direct connection with the public to legitimize their actions. Arguably a new framework for American government had been created along the way.[7]

Given the demands facing the nation, few were concerned about this development. Into the 1960s, indeed, most scholars were far more worried about a Congress seemingly unwilling or unable to meet the challenges of the postwar era: the president was largely seen as a "savior."[8] Legislators' failure to prepare for World War II; their reluctance to commit to an expanded American role in the wider world after 1945; their slow deliberations in a nuclear age that required dispatch; their fragmented, seniority-dominated committee system that brought dullards to power; their tacit (and often not so tacit) defense of institutionalized racism; their short-sighted, sectional demands for local pork at the expense of wider public goods—looking at all this, many felt that leadership must be vested instead in the executive branch. If, as legal scholar Edward Corwin summed up long before Watergate, "the history of the presidency has been a history of aggrandizement," that aggrandizement was generally well-received.[9]

Yet presidents soon plunged precipitately through the circles of paradise—from "savior" to "Satan"[10]—as Vietnam and Watergate showed the dark side of presidential unilateralism. Arthur M. Schlesinger, Jr.'s iconic 1973 book, *The Imperial Presidency*, argued that recent presidents, especially Richard Nixon, had sought not presidential strength but supremacy. He focused mostly on the war powers and "the rise of presidential war" independent of congressional authorization. However, he also criticized the efforts of the Nixon administration to centralize budgeting powers and unilaterally shape policy outcomes via impoundment (the refusal to spend appropriated funds), to build up a large, politicized staff, to greatly expand the "secrecy system," and, relatedly, to broaden the notion of executive privilege. The Watergate era's indictment against the presidency began with petty campaign sabotage and quickly ratcheted up to burglary, bribery, extortion, fraud, destruction of evidence, domestic espionage, obstruction of justice, and abuse of various aspects of executive power—from efforts to inflict punitive tax audits on political opponents, to widespread impoundments (the refusal to spend money appropriated by Congress), to covert action and even secret warfare.[11]

The romantic glow of Kennedy's "Camelot" thus dispersed in the harsh glare of Vietnamese rice paddies and judiciary hearing rooms. If presidents before Nixon showed imperial ambition, it was under his administration that overreach led to the empire's fall; and in August 1974, faced with certain impeachment and removal from office, he became the first and only president to resign from office. "When the President does it, that means that it is not illegal," Nixon famously remarked.[12] But Congress, having battled Nixon the president, was now ready to turn its attention to the institution of the presidency. It was ready, in short, to *make* it illegal.

The Resurgence and Decline of Congress

Congress did so in extensive fashion. In *The Decline and Resurgence of Congress*, James L. Sundquist documents that, after a "Congress at nadir," post-Watergate legislators achieved "a collective resolve . . . to restore the balance between the executive and legislative branches. . . . A period of resurgence had begun."[13] Throughout the 1970s, legislators erected a latticework of new laws aimed at reshaping executive-legislative relationships in the substantive areas in which congressional prerogative had been slighted. Not surprisingly, the framers of this resurgence regime foresaw a much greater role for Congressional input—for both advice, and consent—than recent presidents had desired or allowed. "The President has overstepped the authority of his office in the actions he has taken," warned Representative Gillis Long (D-LA). "Our message to the President is that he is risking retaliation for his power grabs, that support for the counter-offensive is found in the whole range of congressional membership—old members and new, liberal and conservative, Democratic and Republican."[14] Congress intended to reclaim control over the nation's bottom line and forbid presidential impoundments; to have a key role in authorizing and overseeing America's military deployments and covert adventures; and to keep a close eye on executive corruption.

A partial list of enactments gives a sense of the scope of that ambition. For example, the Congressional Budget and Impoundment Control Act of 1974 prohibited unilateral presidential spending decisions and created important centralizing structures (the Budget Committees, the Congressional Budget Office [CBO]) to guide the legislative budget process. In foreign policy, the War Powers Resolution was to ensure that Congress had a say in the use of American force and the Hughes-Ryan amendment and Intelligence Oversight Act to keep it informed of covert operations. The Non-Detention Act and National Emergencies Act, as well as the Foreign Intelligence Surveillance Act (FISA) and the 1972 *Keith* decision, limited presidents' internal security powers at home. The executive branch's workings were to be made more transparent through an expanded Freedom of Information Act, various "government in the sunshine" laws, and the timely release of presidential documents; at the same time, the Supreme Court ruled in *U.S. v. Nixon* that the president's power to assert "executive privilege" was not absolute, and was reviewable by the courts. The role of money in politics was to be diminished by a new Federal Election Commission; and should all this fail, investigations of executive malfeasance would be conducted under a new independent counsel operation.

Already by 1976, journalists were keeping track of "the score since Watergate" in a running battle of "the President versus Congress"; and Congress was ahead. Indeed, President Gerald Ford would soon complain that "We have not an imperial presidency but an imperiled presidency. Under today's rules . . . the presidency does not operate effectively . . . That is harmful to our overall national interests."[15]

But it soon became clear that the resurgence regime was itself built on fragile foundations. Even in the decade following Nixon's resignation, the office of the presidency retained a solid base of authority grounded in its ability to grab the public spotlight and set the agenda; the commander-in-chief power; its potential control over policy implementation; its role in appointments; and its veto leverage. Presidents, beginning with Ronald Reagan, aggressively used executive tools—from regulatory review to signing statements—to enhance their influence over bureaucratic outputs and avoid legislative direction. They resisted probes for information and asserted executive privilege, albeit usually by less inflammatory names, over a wide range of records while shielding even historical material from public release. Through appointing personal loyalists to executive positions across the bureaucracy, sometimes by recess appointment, they sought to "implant their DNA throughout the government."[16]

The statutory side of the regime also crumbled. In some cases, efforts to specify the limits of presidential powers gave life in law to powers earlier exercised only informally; for example, the International Emergency Economic Powers Act, designed to limit presidents' powers to impose economic sanctions, led to the declaration of dozens of "national emergencies" since 1979. In other cases, Congress itself backed away from using the processes it had created to challenge the president, or failed to make them work. Most dramatically, the War Powers Resolution failed to rein in presidents' use of force, as deployments in Lebanon, Iran, Grenada, the Persian Gulf (in 1987–88), Libya, Panama, Somalia, Iraq (in 1993 and throughout the "no-fly zone" period), Haiti, Bosnia, Sudan, Afghanistan (in 1998), and Kosovo suggest. For example, though the NATO War in Kosovo utilized some 800 U.S. aircraft flying more than 20,000 air sorties at nearly 2,000 targets throughout Yugoslavia, President Clinton did not deem that troops had, in the language of the WPR, been "introduced into hostilities or into situation where imminent involvement in hostilities is clearly indicated by the circumstances."[17] By the WPR's 25th anniversary, even observers sympathetic to its intent argued it should be repealed.[18]

The Congressional Budget Act, likewise, failed to bring discipline to federal spending; after a brief blip into surplus in the late 1990s, by fiscal 2006, the federal government was more than $400 billion in the red. As importantly, the deliberative process laid out in 1974 was often honored in the breach: though 13 budget bills were required to be passed by October 1 each year, in the four fiscal years 2002 through 2005, a *total* of six such bills were passed on time. As early as 2002, outgoing CBO director Dan Crippen summed up the situation bluntly: "The Congressional budget process is dead." The beneficiary, he argued, was the president, for "without this kind of process . . . the Congress is going to be dominated by any President."[19]

To be sure, not every piece of the regime crumbled at once, or for all time. Most obviously, Clinton's impeachment and trial in 1998–99 was the first since 1868 and the first ever of an elected president. Still, while it seems strange to talk about congressional deference in that context, even this period highlighted the potential powers of the president and renewed legislative acquiescence to their use. As Clinton himself suggested after the Democrats lost Congress in 1994, "I think now we have a better balance of both using the Presidency as a bully pulpit and the President's power of the Presidency to *do* things, actually accomplish things, and . . . not permitting the presidency to be defined only by relations with the Congress"—as witnessed by the 1998 headline "Clinton Perfects the Art of Go-Alone Governing." That summer, cruise missiles were fired at the Sudan and Afghanistan at the president's order even as the House debated his fate. Clinton's success in achieving his preferred policy outcomes in this period by taking advantage of the Congressional budget process and his veto power is also notable. Even the very process of impeachment—in the face of hostile public opinion—helped to discredit it, and to encourage the expiration of the independent counsel statute in 1999.[20] If the 1970s seemed delayed affirmation of Bob Dylan's famous observation that "the times, they are a-changin'," the state of the presidency by 2001 seemed better described by the satirical observation of Dylan's fictional film alter-ego, Bob Roberts: "The times they are a-changin'—back." The "imperial" infrastructure seemed largely rebuilt.

Prerogative Unleashed: The World after September 11

Still, it is George W. Bush's presidency that provides the clearest—because most openly claimed and aggressively argued—case study of presidential unilateralism in the post-Watergate era. "I have an obligation to make sure that the Presidency remains robust. I'm not going to let Congress erode the power of the executive branch," Bush noted in 2002. The vice president—who got started in political life as a staffer in the Nixon White House—put the aim even more bluntly: "For the 35 years that I've been in this town, there's been a constant, steady erosion of the prerogatives and the powers of the president of the United States, and I don't want to be a part of that."[21]

In some areas, that attitude was translated to action even before September 11. Operating under the "theology," as one close observer put it, "that we the people have made the White House too open and too accountable," the Bush administration cracked down on Freedom of Information Act releases and increased federal executives' ability to withhold information from public view. The Presidential Record Act was amended by executive order to expand past administrations' capacity to delay or bar the opening of historical records. The administration later went to court, successfully, to defend its ability to withhold—even without formally claiming executive privilege—documents from congressional auditors or others seeking information about the energy task force headed by Vice President Cheney.[22]

The brutal attacks on New York and Washington did, however, bring a tidal wave of renewed visibility and leverage to the presidential office. President Bush's standing to lead soared, and he seized the role—and the reins. On a variety of fronts, legislators hastened to expand his authority. With just one dissenting vote in either chamber—most Senate discussion of the bill actually took place *after* the vote—Congress passed a resolution on September 14, 2001, stating that "the president has authority under the Constitution to take action to deter and prevent acts of international terrorism against the United States" and granting him the power to use "all necessary and appropriate force against those nations, organizations, or persons he determines planned, authorized, committed, or aided the terrorist attacks that occurred on September 11, 2001, or harbored such organizations or persons, in order to prevent any future acts of international terrorism against the United States by such nations, organizations, or persons."[23] In the fall of 2002, Congress passed another broad delegation of authority to use force against Iraq. On the domestic front, the USA PATRIOT Act (Public Law 107–56), passed rapidly by Congress in October 2001, was designed to enhance the executive branch's prosecutorial tools and power to conduct criminal investigations by relaxing limits on surveillance and softening the barrier between domestic law enforcement and foreign intelligence gathering. Overall, Bush received historically high levels of legislative support throughout his first term. As 2006 began, he had yet to veto a single bill, this five-year streak the longest since Thomas Jefferson's administration. When asked at a press conference about it, the president sounded bemused: "how could you veto . . . if the Congress has done what you've asked them to do?"[24]

Yet more often the president preferred to do, rather than ask. ("This administration," groused Representative David Obey [D-WI], "thinks that Article I of the

Constitution was a fundamental mistake.")[25] Its interpretation of the commander-in-chief power was perhaps broadest and most controversial. For example, in late 2001 President Bush issued a secret executive order authorizing the National Security Agency (NSA) to track communications between individuals abroad with suspected terrorist connections and Americans within the United States. On its face, this action seemed to violate FISA, which had been passed in 1978 to regulate the process by which such intelligence was gathered, after a series of surveillance abuses by the FBI, CIA, and NSA were revealed in the mid-1970s. Under the act, surveillance required a warrant from a special court. When the targets were not Americans, obtaining a warrant required only that the Justice Department establish that they were working for a foreign power; for Americans, however, there had to be probable cause that the suspect was working on behalf of a foreign power in ways that might violate criminal statutes. FISA did allow for warrantless wiretapping for 15 days after a declaration of war, and for emergency taps of up to 72 hours (increased from 24 hours after September 11) before a warrant needed to be obtained.

When the initiative was revealed in late 2005, the administration quickly dubbed it the "Terrorist Surveillance Program" and argued that the president had both inherent and statutory power to order such wiretaps. "My legal authority is derived from the Constitution, as well as the [September 2001] authorization of force by the United States Congress," President Bush told a news conference.[26] A 42-page white paper defending the NSA program, delivered to Congress by the Justice Department in January 2006, argued that "the NSA activities are supported by the President's well-recognized inherent constitutional authority as Commander in Chief and sole organ for the Nation in foreign affairs to conduct warrantless surveillance of enemy forces for intelligence purposes to detect and disrupt armed attacks on the United States." Further, far from violating the law (i.e., FISA), the president was following its letter: The September 14, 2001, congressional resolution authorizing military force should be read as direct statutory approval for the program, because wiretapping was a "fundamental incident" of warfare similar to the detention of "enemy combatants" approved by the Supreme Court in the 2004 *Hamdi* case (see following). In any case, neither FISA nor Congress generally could limit the president's "core exercise of Commander in Chief control"; any attempt to do so was simply unconstitutional.[27]

This disquisition highlighted several important touchstones for presidential power. The notion that the president is "sole organ" of the nation for foreign policy dates to the 1936 Supreme Court case *U.S. v. Curtiss-Wright*, which argued for "plenary and exclusive" presidential power in international affairs. The idea that the executive power is indivisible (that, for example, the commander-in-chief power is separable from Congress's overlapping powers to declare war and to provide for the regulation of armed forces and hostilities)[28] stems from a parallel theory of the "unitary executive." That interpretation of Article II's vesting clause implies that not only can Congress not infringe on presidential power but that only the president can set the boundaries of that power. In the white paper, for instance, the leading constitutional authority is often not the Supreme Court but the Justice Department's

Office of Legal Counsel. The brief stressed the "reasonable basis" underlying the surveillance decisions—and rather less plausibly, that this standard was equivalent to the "probable cause" required for a FISA warrant—but again, that determination was to be made entirely within the executive branch. Claiming the need for secrecy, the administration also declined to reveal to non-executive actors why it thought the FISA process was inadequate to defend national security.[29]

Following a similar unilateral logic was the administration's treatment of prisoners captured during various anti-terror operations and the Iraq war. Some were kept at so-called "black sites" run secretly by the CIA around the world. Hundreds more were imprisoned at the custom-built detention center at the U.S. naval base in Guantánamo Bay, Cuba. They were designated by the administration not as prisoners-of-war but rather as "unlawful enemy combatants," without the rights POW status confers. This decision was arrived at not by hearing (for which the Geneva Conventions did provide) but by dictate: "pursuant to my authority as Commander in Chief and Chief Executive of the United States," the president declared in February 2002, "I . . . determine that none of the provisions of Geneva apply to our conflict with al Qaeda in Afghanistan or elsewhere throughout the world . . ." He added that "our values as a Nation . . . call for us to treat detainees humanely" and "consistent with the principles of Geneva." In practice, though, in Secretary of Defense Donald Rumsfeld's translation, those detained "would be treated in 'a manner that is *reasonably* consistent' with the Conventions—"for the most part." What the other parts might mandate was not then disclosed. However, with Rumsfeld's approval, previous army regulations constraining interrogation methods were superseded. The secretary had already approved a highly secret program aimed at carrying out "instant interrogations—using force if necessary" around the world. As one intelligence official told reporter Seymour Hersh, the rules were to "grab whom you must, do what you want." That might include sexual humiliation, thought to be particularly effective in shaming Arab subjects to cooperate, and the use of attack dogs.[30] These techniques were widely transferred to other military facilities in Afghanistan and Iraq, beyond the program's original intent and often in tragically embellished form. The most notorious example was at the Abu Ghraib prison outside Baghdad in 2004, where repellant photographs came to light. Charges that detainees' human rights had been violated continued to be an issue into late 2005 as the "black sites" and the practice of "rendition"—sending prisoners to countries less encumbered by due process than the United States—came to light. The president repeatedly insisted that "we do not torture," but a list of approved techniques for interrogation included such measures as hooding, sleep deprivation, the use of painful bound positions, and "water-boarding," meant to simulate drowning. By 2005, CIA personnel had been implicated in the deaths of at least four prisoners in agency custody.[31]

The president claimed that even American citizens, arrested within the United States—could be held indefinitely without charge or lawyer if they too were labeled "enemy combatants." The determination of who qualified as an enemy combatant was, according to the president, entirely up to him, not the courts or legislature, and not even reviewable by those branches of government.[32] The president also asserted the authority to create military tribunals outside the normal judicial system for terrorism suspects and issued an executive order doing just that. Indeed, as with the NSA program, the executive powers flowing from the September 11 attacks and September 14 resolution were deemed to be practically unlimited. "Congress can no more interfere with the President's conduct of the interrogation of enemy combatants than it can dictate strategic or tactical decisions on the battlefield," the Justice Department declared.

Further, the term "torture," Justice argued, was legally limited to acts sufficient to cause, for example, "organ failure . . . or even death," and then only if inflicting such pain (and not, say, gaining information) was the "precise objective" of the interrogator. In late 2004, the administration broadened this definition somewhat (though continuing to argue that any previously approved techniques were not torture.) In any case, as a memo constructed by a working group of administration attorneys concluded, "in order to respect the President's inherent constitutional authority to manage a military campaign, 18 U.S.C. § 2340A [the prohibition against torture] as well as any other potentially applicable statute must be construed as inapplicable to interrogations undertaken pursuant to his Commander-in-Chief authority." Congress could not encroach on the exercise of that authority. Thus, when legislators overwhelmingly approved a blanket ban on torture as an amendment to a defense measure in late 2005, the president said he would prohibit torture (presumably as defined by the administration). But he also quietly noted that he would implement the provision "in a manner consistent with the constitutional authority of the President to oversee the unitary executive branch and as Commander in Chief."[33] That is, he would decide how (and, arguably, when) to apply the ban. The vehicle was itself notable: this sort of "signing statement" was used more by George W. Bush than by all his predecessors combined, fencing off not only the commander-in-chief power but requirements that Congress receive information or that appointees have certain qualifications.[34] Again, the message was that the president would determine the limits of his power and of the law itself.

John Locke, in his *Second Treatise* of 1690, defines "prerogative," as the power of the executive "to act according to discretion, for the publick good, without the prescription of the Law, and sometimes even against it." The executive needed discretion to implement the law or to set a policy course when law was lacking.[35] President Bush's efforts, building on those of his predecessors, amounted to the extensive broad practical application of this notion. The legalistic, even formulaic, nature of the language used in asserting these executive claims tended to conceal their extraordinarily broad affirmations of presidential power. But there should be no mistake: These claims effectively placed the president above the law, at least where national security is concerned. In so doing, they recast the interbranch balance of power and did so without broad deliberation or debate.

Yet even Locke's version of prerogative had some crucial natural limits. It was only legitimate as it reflected the public commonweal, and could only be temporary: executive control in the absence of legislative direction stood only until "the Legislature can be conveniently assembled to provide for it." Laws can be amended; but in a government under the law, they cannot be long ignored.

Ambition or Avoidance? The Invisible Congress

In that very American context the constraints on prerogative are even stronger. While presidents' arguments have been distinctly unitarian, the Constitution is in turn devoutly trinitarian. Presidents, naturally, cherish the *Curtiss-Wright* language; but it is far from clear that the framers intended to give the executive—or any other branch—exclusive power over much of anything. In that context, "organ" is the right word only if by it is meant an instrument whose notes are defined by the full range of pressure on its keys. One cannot have an imperial presidency without an invisible Congress.

However, despite its own clear claims to the constitutional ground presidents seek to barricade, Congress has not acted effectively to protect its own authority. As President Bush's claims regarding the September 14 resolution's relationship to the NSA program make clear, broad delegations of power can be used in ways legislators may not have anticipated.[36] Did legislators mean to allow for warrantless surveillance within the U.S., bypassing FISA's requirements? Former Senate majority leader Tom Daschle (D-SD) said not: The topic, he wrote, "never came up . . . [T]he 98 senators who voted in favor of authorization of force against al Qaeda did not believe that they were also voting for warrantless domestic surveillance." The resolution did "not authorize the President to do anything other than use force," Senator Dianne Feinstein (D-CA) added.

However, the president was right to note the breadth of the delegation of power at least implied by the resolution. And Congress did not act, at least immediately, to clarify its intent.[37]

Such inaction was particularly notable because the September 14 resolution had already been interpreted once by the Supreme Court as encompassing a delegation of power not overtly specified. The case involved Yaser Hamdi, an American citizen captured on the Afghan battlefield and designated by the president as an "enemy combatant." As a result, he was detained in a military brig for some two and a half years without charge. The courts did reject the administration's claim that Hamdi's detention could not even receive judicial consideration ("The court may not second-guess the military's enemy combatant determination," the Justice Department told the Fourth Circuit Court of Appeals). Further, the Supreme Court held that enemy combatants did require some sort of fair hearing. "A state of war is not a blank check for the President when it comes to the rights of the Nation's citizens," Justice Sandra Day O'Connor's lead opinion declared. "Whatever power the United States Constitution envisions for the Executive in its exchanges with other nations or with enemy organizations in times of conflict, it most assuredly envisions a role for all three branches when individual liberties are at stake."

This famous sound bite obscured important parts of the court's overall finding. For instance, the court did not specify what due process might entail, leaving that for the administration to determine in the absence of legislative action. And, crucially, it upheld the administration's basic claim: that the September 14 resolution (termed the "authorization to use military force," or AUMF) constituted affirmative legislative delegation to the president sufficient to name enemy combatants. While the AUMF did not discuss such a procedure, the court found that the 1971 Non-Detention Act did not apply to Hamdi's case: taking prisoners was deemed so central to armed conflict that "it is of no moment that the AUMF does not use specific language of detention." As a result, in the parallel case of another American citizen, José Padilla—arrested not on a foreign battlefield but at Chicago's O'Hare airport—a circuit court panel found that "the AUMF as interpreted by the Supreme Court in *Hamdi* authorizes the President's detention of Padilla as an enemy combatant" as well.[38] The *Hamdi* ruling was thus trumpeted in the administration's defense of the NSA program, which argued that wiretapping was similarly integral to warfare.

Did Congress mean to authorize presidents to name and detain American citizens as enemy combatants? As with the NSA, the case was far from clear—even the court was deeply divided, with O'Connor's opinion joined by only three other justices. But the courts are unlikely to rescue Congress from self-inflicted vagaries in statutory language. As Justice Lewis Powell once noted, "If the Congress chooses not to confront the President, it is not our task to do so."[39] Indeed, one dissent in *Hamdi* emphasized "the need for a clearly expressed congressional resolution of the competing claims." This was slow to emerge, however. In late 2005, the anti-torture language noted previously was passed, along with requirements that Congress be given reports on military tribunal procedures, ensuring judicial review of the tribunals' decisions by the Washington, DC, circuit court, and also limiting detainees' access to other American courts or for other claims. According to co-sponsor Carl Levin (D-MI), this was not intended to affect ongoing cases.[40] But affirmative language to that effect was not included; and the administration quickly sought to take advantage of that imprecision. The Justice Department moved to dismiss all pending cases brought by detainees, including the *Hamdan* case on the constitutionality of military tribunals awaiting Supreme Court action.

Ambition Rising? Still, that legislators had acted at all did suggest the stirrings of legislative resurgence. In fits and starts, in fact, Congress had begun to grow restive as early as 2004, when that year's election seemed to heat up the frozen ambition of the other branches of government. Bush's Democratic opponent, Senator John Kerry, fiercely criticized many of the administration's claims and policies, touting his own military service and challenging President Bush's leadership even on national security issues. The Supreme Court's 2004 decisions on the detention regime did at least serve notice of judicial concern regarding executive overreach. Further, as bad news from Iraq undercut the president's claim to a "mission accomplished," legislators began to question the administration's pre-war claims and post-invasion occupation plan. Defense department personnel testifying on behalf of additional appropriations for Iraq in 2004 were assailed for the request's lack of specificity, for the imprecision of prior spending estimates, and for the Abu Ghraib scandal. "This is a blank check," said Senator John McCain (R-AZ), and it seemed that blank checks were less fashionable than before.[41]

After a pause following President Bush's narrow reelection victory in November and inspiring Iraqi elections in late January, such criticism escalated dramatically by the fall of 2005. Abroad, continuing violence in Iraq, leading to casualties both military (U.S. troop deaths passed 2,150 in 2005, with another 15,000 wounded) and civilian (in December 2005, the president estimated the Iraqi death toll from the war at some 30,000), drove support for the war below 40 percent in many polls. Widespread negative assessments of the Iraq occupation's planning and administration did not help the public's outlook.[42] At home, the anemic response to Hurricane Katrina shook public confidence in the government's ability to react to large-scale emergencies. The president was also criticized for having appointed underqualified political loyalists to crucial management posts (Michael Brown, the Federal Emergency Management Agency director, was forced to resign after Katrina); he had to withdraw a nominee to the Supreme Court, White House counsel Harriet Miers, when she faced similar attacks. And in October 2005, the vice president's chief of staff, Lewis Libby, was indicted on perjury charges related to the leak of a CIA operative's name to the press after the operative's husband questioned the administration's rationale for the Iraq war.

The controversy surrounding torture, rendition, domestic eavesdropping, and the like added fuel to the furor on Capitol Hill. Democrats used the hearings on the nomination of Judge Samuel Alito to the Supreme Court to score the Bush administration's claims concerning executive power; even some Republicans (especially those worried about midterm elections in 2006, or themselves considering presidential bids in 2008) began to express doubts. The Patriot Act, due to expire at the end of 2005, was given only a brief extension until February 2006 when several Republican senators worried about its potential for intrusiveness and abuse joined with Senate Democrats to prevent a vote on a conference committee report that made most of the act permanent. McCain pushed anti-torture language into law; Judiciary chair Arlen Specter (R-PA) convened hearings into the legality of the NSA program. Even the reliable Fourth Circuit Court of Appeals blasted the administration's decision to charge José Padilla in the civilian courts, on charges never mentioned during his detention as an enemy combatant, in order (the court suggested) to avoid possible reversal by the Supreme Court.[43]

In some ways the galvanizing effect of events, elections, court decisions, and legislative hearings came as no surprise. Political contexts had changed; the world had changed; but the Constitution, and the hold it gave each branch on each of the others, had not changed. It remained up to Congress to use its power and to do its job. Specter suggested that if Congress was not yet showing "muscle," at least it "is showing some tendons."[44]

Still, any obituary for presidential power was at best premature. The contemporary executive retained the tools to define the terms of debate and utilize the office's structural advantages. The fact that Congress is a divided body run by collective choices gives presidents inherent advantages of (in Alexander Hamilton's terms) "decision, activity, secrecy, and dispatch." Even if they don't get the last say, presidents often get to make the first move—which itself may shape the landscape over which subsequent decisions are taken. In late 2005, President Bush sought to do just this. Seeking to re-frame opinion on Iraq, the president began an extensive schedule of speaking engagements defending his policy in Iraq, claiming steady progress and suggesting that calls for a military withdrawal from that nation were at best premature, at worst unpatriotic. A series of nominees who had faced difficulty in obtaining Senate confirmation in the post-Katrina spotlight were installed in their posts by recess appointment. The White House refused to provide an investigatory committee materials documenting its internal response to Katrina, and even prevented former FEMA director Brown from testifying about his contacts with the White House during the crisis. In January 2006, the president likewise rejected even proffered legislative support for changing FISA. There was no need to "attempt to try to pass a law on something that's already legal," because the debate might reveal information that would "help the enemy." Emphasizing the war was clearly the president's battle plan for the year to come; for "conducting war," he argued, "is a responsibility in the executive branch, not the legislative branch." He added, "I don't view it as a contest with the legislative branch."[45] And certainly, to that point, "no contest" was an apt description.

Practical Advantages, and Grave Dangers

Is there a "new imperial presidency"? That is, has the interbranch balance of power shifted back to the president to an extent comparable to the Vietnam/Watergate era? And if so, what are the consequences?

The short answer is "yes": The 1970s resurgence regime has eroded, and presidential power has expanded to fill the vacuum. There are meaningful parallels between the justificatory language of the Nixon administration and that of our most recent presidents: each stressed the notion of "inherent" presidential power, the broad sweep of the constitutional "rights" of the office. This would have endured, albeit in different forms and contexts, even had the Kerry administration replaced the Bush administration in January 2005, for the argument is not individual but institutional.

As with most interesting questions, though, the short answer is rarely the full story. The narrative here depicts a set of linear trends: the rise of presidential power to the 1960s; the overstretch of the presidency past "savior" to "Satan"; the resurgence of other political actors through the 1970s; the counter-surge of presidential initiative starting in the 1980s and accelerating into overdrive after September 11, 2001. That is certainly accurate, as generalizations go. Precedents matter, and accrete, and future presidents will rely upon what is established now as the "normal" balance of presidential-congressional power.

But despite the consistent, and often successful, efforts of presidents to expand their institutional resources past the sparse grants of Article II, they ultimately remain subject to its constraints and part of a set of potential checks and counterbalances. The modern presidency has many potent tools, and a global reach, surely unforeseen by the architects of the Constitution. Yet the framework they designed remains. Presidential power, in a real sense, is the residual left over after subtracting out the power of other actors in the system.[46]

As such, the power of the president remains conditional. And our assessment of it must also be conditional, underlain by a fundamental tension: in the American system of government strong executive leadership is at once unavoidable and unacceptable. Supreme Court Justice Robert Jackson perhaps put the dilemma best. "Comprehensive and undefined presidential powers," he wrote in 1952, "hold both practical advantages and grave dangers for the country.[47]

The advantages are clear. After all, how can one provide direction to an enormous nation, with an enormous national executive establishment, with enormous public expectations—and still hope to limit the authority necessary to meet those needs? More than four million civilian and military employees work in the federal executive branch, across fifteen Cabinet-level departments and more than one hundred agencies. The annual federal budget verges on $2.5 trillion (as much as the 1960 through 1974 budgets, combined.) A nation cannot meet crises, or even the day-to-day needs of governing, with 535 chief executives or commanders-in-chief driven by as many constituencies and spread across divided chambers. The problems of administration that arose during the Articles of Confederation period in a much smaller country, with a much smaller Congress, in what seemed a much larger world, were sufficient to drive the framers to submerge their fear of monarchy and empower a single person as president. These days, the flutter of a butterfly's wing in Wellington shifts the climate of Washington; a globalized, polarized world seems to call out for endowing leadership sufficient to match its powers to the tasks at hand.

On the other hand, presidential "leadership" is not by definition virtuous, if it does violence to Constitutional tenets. To accede to presidential hagiography—and thus executive dominance—is extraordinarily problematic for a republican form of government. The words of the anti-Federalist patriot Patrick Henry echo over the years: *If your American chief be a man of ambition, and abilities, how easy is it for him to render himself absolute?* We want men, and women, of ambition and abilities to serve as our presidents. But to pledge that their preferences should without need of persuasion become policy, that they should as a matter of course substitute command for coalition-building, is to cede something of the soul of self-governance. The dangers of unilateral authority are immense, because once those claims are asserted, they logically admit no limits.

That is not meant to be alarmist; but nor is it hypothetical. Consider the logic of the NSA white paper traced previously. Or, similarly, consider the administration's argument in the *Rumsfeld v. Padilla* enemy combatant case. The president claimed that he could, on the basis of "some evidence," remove someone from the court system and hold them without charge or trial. Deputy Solicitor General Paul Clement was subsequently asked during oral arguments before the Supreme Court to delineate the boundaries of this argument. If the September 14 resolution were insufficient authorization for such power, did the president still have the authority to deny trials to American citizens? Yes, Clement replied. Given the emergency created on September 11, "I think he would certainly today, which is to say September 12th, [2001] or April 28th, [2003]." And, in fact, "I would say the President had that authority on September 10th, [2001]." In that case, could you shoot an enemy combatant, or torture him? asked a Justice. Well, no, said Clement, "that violates our own conception of what's a war crime." Still, he was pressed, what if it were an executive command, what if torture were deemed necessary to garner intelligence? "Some systems do that to get information."

"Well," replied Clement, "our executive doesn't."

"What's constraining? That's the point. Is it just up to the good will of the executive?"

"You have to recognize that in situations where there is a war—where the Government is on a war footing—that you have to trust the executive to make the kind of quintessential military judgments that are involved in things like that."[48]

The result comes back to what Schlesinger decried in the 1970s as a "plebiscitary presidency," in which presidents claim broad discretion to act, constrained only by quadrennial referendum on their decisions—a problematic model in the world of term-limited presidents and four elections in a row in which the winner has received 51 percent of the popular vote or less. In the meantime, voters must trust that the president was acting in their interests. "Our executive doesn't," the administration claimed; but history suggests our executive could.

The point is too important to be a punch line. We must accept that executive discretion is, in fact, increasingly important. Still, within what framework ought that discretion to be exercised? Who gets to set the boundaries between the branches? Who, even, in a war with parameters and enemies as fluid as in the "global war on terror," gets to decide when it starts and ends? Much as he might prefer it, the president is not alone in his responsibilities. Nor, even if he will not admit to mistakes, is the president always right. In our separated system, legitimizing large-scale change requires bridging its divisions, by building coalitions in Congress that are persuaded that the president is right. There is a clear normative difference between a presidential assertion of power that stands because of congressional inertia and a power delegated to the president after full and free debate. Justice Antonin Scalia's dissent in *Hamdi* reminds us that "The Founders warned us about the risk, and equipped us with a Constitution designed to deal with it." Ambition must continue to counteract ambition.

The first branch's job is not to manage policy implementation on a day-to-day basis. Nor is it always to pass a new law: the resurgence regime bears witness to the inadequacy of creating a statutory framework in the absence of political will reinforcing its component parts. But Congress has a critical task nonetheless. Its job is to use debate and deliberation to distill priorities and set clear standards; to oversee and judge the decisions and actions of others by those standards; to expose both the bad and good efforts of government to public scrutiny; and to revisit its earlier debate in the light of later events. All this is Congress's job; and debate, judgment, and oversight are delegated to other actors in the system at our potential peril.

The goal of legislative deliberation is not to foster trust in government for its own sake; indeed, a healthy distrust of government is part of American history, and a valuable tool of accountability. We should, in President Reagan's words, "trust—but verify." We should work to make difficult decisions and trade-offs about the powers and goals of American government, about its very scope and direction. Indeed, given the crises that already define our new century, doing so is our highest national priority. But it will require the active involvement of *all* our ambitions. "We must recognize," said a young John F. Kennedy, campaigning in his first election in 1946, "that if we do not take an interest in our political life, we can easily lose at home what so many young men so bloodily won abroad."[49]

Endnotes

1. *Newsweek* issue of January 9, 2006; "Vice President's Remarks to the Traveling Press," Air Force Two, Office of the White House Press Secretary, December 20, 2005; Arthur M. Schlesinger, Jr., *The Imperial Presidency* (Boston: Houghton Mifflin, 1973); Andrew Rudalevige, *The New Imperial Presidency: Renewing Presidential Power after Watergate* (Ann Arbor: University of Michigan Press, 2005), from which much of what follows is drawn.

2. Whether the president should be a "she" was not, of course, discussed at the time; and in talking about the presidency I will defer to historical fact and use the masculine pronoun to describe the office's occupants. But "he" should be read as "he, someday she."

3. Randolph is quoted in Jack N. Rakove, *Original Meanings: Politics and Ideas in the Making of the Constitution* (New York: Knopf, 1996), 257. For a detailed description of the Constitutional Convention as it led to the drafting of Article II, see, among many sources, Rakove, Ch. 9; Forrest McDonald, *The American Presidency: An Intellectual History* (Lawrence: University Press of Kansas, 1994), Ch. 7.

4. See Edward S. Corwin, *The President: Office and Powers*, 5th rev. ed., with Randall W. Bland, Theodore Hinson, and Jack W. Peltason (New York: New York University Press, 1984), 3.

5. Theodore Roosevelt, *An Autobiography* (1913; reprint, New York: Da Capo Press, 1985), 372; William Howard Taft, *Our Chief Magistrate and His Powers* (1916), quoted in Christopher H. Pyle and Richard M. Pious, eds., *The President, Congress, and the Constitution: Power and Legitimacy in American Politics* (New York: Free Press, 1984), 70-71.

6. H.L. Mencken, *Notes on Democracy* (New York: Alfred A. Knopf, 1926), 185.

7. Fred I. Greenstein, "Toward a Modern Presidency," in Greenstein, ed., *Leadership in the Modern Presidency* (Cambridge, MA: Harvard University Press, 1988), 3.

8. Erwin C. Hargrove and Michael Nelson, *Presidents, Politics, and Policy* (New York: Alfred A. Knopf, 1984), 4.

9. Corwin, *President: Office and Powers*, 354.

10. Hargrove and Nelson, 4–5.

11. Schlesinger, x, 252; Michael A. Genovese, *The Watergate Crisis* (Westport, CT: Greenwood, 1999); Stanley I. Kutler, *The Wars of Watergate* (New York: Alfred A. Knopf, 1990).

12. Stephen E. Ambrose, *Nixon, Vol. III: Ruin and Recovery, 1973–1990* (New York: Touchstone, 1992), 508.

13. James L. Sundquist, *The Decline and Resurgence of Congress* (Washington, DC: Brookings Institution, 1981), Ch. 1. See also Thomas Cronin, "A Resurgent Congress and the Imperial Presidency," *Political Science Quarterly* 95 (Summer 1980): 209–37.

14. *Congressional Record*, April 18, 1973, p. 13190.

15. Dom Bonafede, Daniel Rapoport, and Joel Havemann, "The President versus Congress: The Score since Watergate," *National Journal* (May 29, 1976), 738; Ford quoted in interview with *Time* magazine (November 10, 1980), 30.

16. Mike Allen, "Bush to Change Economic Team," *Washington Post*, November 29, 2004, A1. More generally see Thomas J. Weko, *The Politicizing Presidency: The White House Personnel Office, 1948–1994* (Lawrence: University Press of Kansas, 1994).

17. Fisher, *Presidential War Powers*, 140–41; Peter Huchthausen, *America's Splendid Little Wars: A Short History of U.S. Military Engagements, 1975–2000* (New York: Viking, 2003), Ch. 4.

18. Louis Fisher and David Gray Adler, "The War Powers Resolution: Time to Say Goodbye," *Political Science Quarterly* 113 (Spring 1998), 1.

19. Dan L. Crippen, "Observations on the Current State of the Federal Budget Process," Address at the Fall Symposium of the American Association for Budget and Program Analysis, November 22, 2002.

20. *Public Papers of the Presidents*, September 25, 1995, 1475; Francine Kiefer, "Clinton Perfects the Art of Go-Alone Governing," *Christian Science Monitor* (July 24, 1998), 3; see also David Gray Adler, "Clinton in Context," in Adler and Michael A. Genovese, eds., *The Presidency and the Law: The Clinton Legacy* (Lawrence: University Press of Kansas, 2002).

21. *Weekly Compilation of Presidential Documents* (March 13, 2002), 411; Cheney quoted from NBC broadcast interview of January 27, 2003, in Tom Curry, "Executive Privilege Again at Issue," *MSNBC.com*, February 1, 2003 [http://www.msnbc.com/news/695487.asp?cp1=1], and see Kenneth T. Walsh, "The Cheney Factor," U.S. News and World Report (January 23, 2006), 42–43.

22. Thomas Blanton, director of the private National Security Archive, quoted in Dana Milbank and Mike Allen, "Release of Documents is Delayed," *Washington Post* (March 26, 2003), A15. More broadly—and for similar reaction by legislators of both parties, see Alison Mitchell, "Cheney

Rejects Broader Access to Terror Brief," *The New York Times* (May 20, 2002), A1; Alexis Simendinger, "The Power of One," *National Journal* (January 26, 2002); Kirk Victor, "Congress in Eclipse," *National Journal* (April 5, 2003), 1069–70. The PRA order is E.O. 13223. The Energy Task Force saga is described in Rudalevige, *New Imperial Presidency*, 189–91.

23. "Authorization for Use of Military Force," Public Law 107–40 (September 18, 2001).

24. "President Holds Press Conference," Office of the White House Press Secretary, December 20, 2004; more generally, see Andrew Rudalevige, "George W. Bush and Congress: New Term, New Problems—Same Results?" in Douglas Brattebo, Thomas Lansford, and Robert Maranto, eds., *The Second Term of George W. Bush: Prospects and Perils* (New York: Palgrave Macmillan, 2006).

25. Quoted in Lisa Caruso, "You've Got to Know When to Hold 'Em," *National Journal* (July 12, 2003), 2258. The sentiment was bipartisan: Sen. Chuck Hagel (R-NE) similarly complained that "[this] administration. . . . treats Congress as an appendage, a Constitutional nuisance." Quoted in David E. Rosenbaum, "In the Fulbright Mold, Without the Power," *The New York Times* (May 3, 2004), A16.

26. "Press Conference of the President," Office of the White House Press Secretary, December 19, 2005; and see Charles Lane, "White House Elaborates on Authority for Eavesdropping," *The Washington Post* (December 20, 2005), A10.

27. "Legal Authorities Supporting the Activities of the National Security Agency Described by the President," Department of Justice, January 19, 2006, 1–2, 10–11, 17, 30–31.

28. See, for example, Article I's designation of Congress's authority to regulate the "land and naval forces," "captures on land or water," the militia, and "letters of marque and reprisal" (i.e., to hire private contractors to carry out warfare.)

29. Jess Bravin, "Judge Alito's View of the Presidency: Expansive Powers," *Wall Street Journal* (January 5, 2006), A1; Dan Eggen, "White House Dismissed '02 Surveillance Proposal," *The Washington Post* (January 26, 2006), p. A4. On OLC, see "Legal authorities," 30, 34n18, 40. The white paper notes that "a full explanation . . . cannot be given in an unclassified document"; but by most accounts such an explanation was not provided during classified briefings either. See also "Press Conference of the President," Office of the White House Press Secretary (January 26, 2006).

30. See Gonzales memo of January 25, 2002, entitled "Decision re Application of the Geneva Convention on Prisoners of War to the Conflict with Al Qaeda and the Taliban"; Rumsfeld quoted in Katharine Q. Seelye, "First 'Unlawful Combatants' Seized in Afghanistan Arrive at U.S. Base in Cuba," *The New York Times* (January 12, 2002), A7 (emphasis added); Seymour Hersh, "The Gray Zone," *The New Yorker* (May 24, 2004); John Hendren, "Officials Say Rumsfeld OK'd Harsh Interrogation Methods," *Los Angeles Times* (May 21, 2004), A1; Dana Priest, "Covert CIA Program Withstands New Furor," *The Washington Post* (December 30, 2005), A1. The full text of the Gonzales memo, and many others besides, were later made public and are collected on-line in various places as well as in Karen J. Greenberg and Joshua L. Dratel, *The Torture Papers* (New York: Cambridge University Press, 2005).

31. See, e.g., Michael Fletcher, "Bush Defends CIA's Clandestine Prisons," *The Washington Post* (November 8, 2005), A15; Jane Mayer, "A Deadly Interrogation," *The New Yorker* (November 14, 2005).

32. President's Military Order of November 13, 2001; Government's Brief and Motion, August 27, 2002, *Jose Padilla v. George Bush, Donald Rumsfeld, et al.* (U.S. Dist. Court, Southern Dist. of New York—Case No. 02-4445).

33. See Jay Bybee to Alberto Gonzales, "Re: Standards of Conduct for Interrogation under 18 U.S.C. §§2340–2340A," Office of Legal Counsel, U.S. Department of Justice, August 1, 2002, 1–6, 31–39; Working Group Report on Detainee Interrogations in the Global War on Terrorism: Assessment of Legal, Historical, Policy, and Operational Considerations, U.S. Department of Defense, April 4, 2003, 21 and Section III generally; "President's Statement on Signing of H.R. 2863," office of the White House Press Secretary (December 30, 2005). More generally see James P. Pfiffner, "Torture as Public Policy," unpublished ms., George Mason University School of Public Policy, 12–14; Mayer, "A Deadly Interrogation."

34. While one can find isolated examples of the practice as early as the Jackson administration, it was Ronald Reagan who advanced it as a more systematic strategy aimed both to put the president's point of view in the "legislative history" (should the judiciary weigh in) and to better control executive branch behavior. Reagan's successors all used the tool, but none as aggressively as George W. Bush, who made more than 500 constitutional objections to legislation during his first term (by contrast, Bill Clinton made 105, over eight years.) See Phillip J. Cooper, "George W. Bush, Edgar Allan Poe, and the Use of Abuse of Presidential Signing Statements," *Presidential Studies Quarterly* 35 (September 2005): 515–32; Ron Hutcheson and James Kuhnhenn, "Bush Asserts Power over Laws," *Philadelphia Inquirer* (January 16, 2006), A1; Elizabeth Bumiller, "For President, Final Say on a Bill Sometimes Comes After the Signing," *New York Times* (January 16, 2006), A11.

35. John Locke, *Second Treatise of Government,* ed. C.B. Macpherson (Indianapolis: Hackett, 1980 [1690]), 84; see §§159–160 generally.

36. Further, presidents have become astute at adapting outdated or inexact statutes to current needs. President Roosevelt closed the banks in 1933 under the terms of a World War I law; President Clinton's 1996 designation of two million acres in Utah as conservation land, over the objections of state officials, was undertaken using a statute passed in 1906.

37. Tom Daschle, "Power We Didn't Grant," *The Washington Post* (December 23, 2005), A21; Feinstein quoted in Ron Hutcheson, "Presidential Power a Key Issue in Debate over Eavesdropping," Knight-Ridder (January 23, 2006).

38. *Hamdi v. Rumsfeld,* 124 U.S. 2633 (2004); *Padilla vs. Hanft,* 05–6396, Fourth Circuit Court of Appeals, September 9, 2005.

39. *Goldwater v. Carter,* quoted in Ronald J. Sievert, "*Campbell v. Clinton* and the Continuing Effort to Reassert Congress' Predominant Constitutional Authority to Commence, or Prevent, War," *Dickinson Law Review* 105 (Winter 2001), 167.

40. "Statement on the Department of Justice Motion to Dismiss the Hamdan Case in the Supreme Court," Office of Sen. Carl Levin, January 12, 2006.

41. Eric Schmitt, "Senators Assail Request for Aid for Afghan and Iraq Budgets," *The New York Times* (May 14, 2004), A1; Tyler Marshall, "The Conflict in Iraq: Unease Shadows Bush's Optimism," *Los Angeles Times* (September 17, 2004), A1.

42. For civilian casualty estimate, see "President Discusses War on Terror and Upcoming Iraqi Elections," in Philadelphia, Pennsylvania, Office of the White House Press Secretary, December 12, 2005; for polling data see the CNN/USA Today/Gallup Poll sequence provided at http://www.pollingreport.com/iraq.htm [accessed January 3, 2006]. For discussion of the Iraq occupation, see, inter alia, James Fallows, "Why Iraq Has No Army," *Atlantic Monthly* (December 2005); George Packer, *The Assassins' Gate* (New York: Farrar Straus Giroux, 2005); James Glanz, "Iraq Rebuilding Badly Hobbled, U.S. Report Finds," *The New York Times* (January 24, 2006), A1.

43. The Supreme Court, however, while reserving the right to visit the case's broader issues, allowed the shift.

44. Quoted in James Kuhnhenn, "Senators Taking Reins of Their Watchdog Role," *Philadelphia Inquirer* (January 29, 2006), A3.

45. Thomas B. Edsall, "Bush Appointments Avert Senate Battles," *The Washington Post* (January 5, 2006), A13; Eric Lipton, "White House Declines to Provide Storm Papers," *The New York Times* (January 25, 2006), A1; "Press Conference of the President," Office of the White House Press Secretary, January 26, 2006; Richard Wolffe and Holly Bailey, "The Bush Battle Plan: It's the War, Stupid," *Newsweek* (January 30, 2006).

46. Thanks to William Howell and Jon Pevehouse for suggesting this formulation.

47. Concurring opinion to *Youngstown Sheet and Tube Co. v. Sawyer,* 343 U.S. 579 (1952).

48. From the transcript of the oral arguments before the U.S. Supreme Court in *Rumsfeld v. Padilla,* April 28, 2004, available from the Court's Web site (http://www.supremecourtus.gov).

49. Quoted in Robert Dallek, *An Unfinished Life: John F. Kennedy, 1917–1963* (Boston: Little, Brown, 2003), 132.